THE FIRST LADY
OF HOLLYWOOD

The First Lady of Hollywood

A BIOGRAPHY OF
LOUELLA PARSONS

Samantha Barbas

UNIVERSITY OF CALIFORNIA PRESS
BERKELEY   LOS ANGELES   LONDON

University of California Press
Berkeley and Los Angeles, California
University of California Press, Ltd.
London, England

Library of Congress Cataloging-in-Publication Data

Barbas, Samantha.
    The first lady of Hollywood : a biography of Louella
Parsons / Samantha Barbas.
        p.   cm.
    Includes bibliographical references and index.
    ISBN 0–520-24213-0 (cloth : alk. paper)
    1. Parsons, Louella O. (Louella Oettinger), 1885–1973.
2. Gossip columnists—United States—Biography.   I. Title.

PN4874.P35B37   2006
070.4'4979143'092—dc22   2005008449

Manufactured in the United States of America

14   13   12   11   10   09   08   07   06   05
10   9   8   7   6   5   4   3   2   1

Printed on Ecobook 50 containing a minimum 50%
post-consumer waste, processed chlorine free. The balance
contains virgin pulp, including 25% Forest Stewardship
Council Certified for no old growth tree cutting,
processed either TCF or ECF. The sheet is acid-free and
meets the minimum requirements of ANSI/NISO
Z39.48–1992 (R 1997) (Permanence of Paper).♾

CONTENTS

ACKNOWLEDGMENTS

BIOGRAPHIES ARE NOT USUALLY EASY TO WRITE, but Louella made this job especially difficult. Because she did not make her personal papers accessible—and in some cases went out of her way to conceal information about her past—she sent me on a multistate paper chase through archives, libraries, historical societies, and countless rolls of microfilm. My deepest gratitude to the many generous librarians and archivists who assisted me: Ned Comstock of the Cinema Television Library at the University of Southern California; Rhonda Frevert of the Des Moines County, Iowa, Genealogical Society; Cheryl Gleason and Suzy Beggin of the Freeport, Illinois, Public Library; Barbara Hall and Jenny Romero of the Academy of Motion Pictures Arts and Sciences; Steve Johnson of the Harry Ransom Center at the University of Texas, Austin; David Kessler of the Bancroft Library at the University of California, Berkeley; Deb Sutton of the Lee County, Illinois, Genealogical Society; Marilyn Wurzburger of the Special Collections Department at the Hayden Library at Arizona State University; and archivists at the California Polytechnic State University at San Luis Obispo, the Chicago Historical Society, Columbia University, the Los Angeles Public Library, the University of Indiana, the University of Iowa, and the Warner Brothers Archive at the University of Southern California.

I am also indebted to the film and journalism scholars who helped me with contacts, references, and sage advice, especially Cari Beauchamp, Paul Buhle, Kathy Feeley, Val Holley, Pat McKean, Louis Pizzitola, and Rob Wagner. Walter Seltzer, Bob Thomas, and Mamie Van Doren graciously agreed to interviews. My friends, colleagues, and students at Chapman University were unfailing in their good cheer and generosity; my editor at the University of California Press, Mary Francis, was enormously insightful and encouraging. Special thanks go to my father and especially my mother, Mie Barbas, who saw me through difficult days and packed enough boxes for a lifetime.

Prologue

September 1941

IN HOLLYWOOD IT WAS A DIFFICULT TIME. Though film attendance was at an all-time high—that year eighty-five million tickets were sold each week—the major studios were under attack. The war in Europe and Asia had led to a decline in foreign markets, the House Un-American Activities Committee was investigating the alleged involvement of several prominent actors with communism, and a Senate commission accused Hollywood of warmongering by making films that promoted U.S. intervention in the overseas conflict. Moreover, the Federal Communications Commission had allowed regular commercial television broadcasting to begin on July 1, 1941, panicking those in Hollywood who saw the new medium as potentially formidable competition.[1]

Louella, too, had struggled that year. In the spring, Orson Welles's *Citizen Kane,* a scathing attack on her employer, William Randolph Hearst, had been released in theaters across the nation. Americans watched Welles's onscreen portrayal of a manipulative, megalomaniacal Hearst, and they read in national publications about Louella's conniving attempts to suppress the film. The *New York Times* and *Newsweek* described Louella as a vicious opponent of free speech who used her power to carry out her employer's tyrannical wishes. Shortly afterward, the Screen Actors' Guild launched an attack on her, publicly condemning her refusal to pay actors who appeared on her radio show and calling her an enemy of the film industry. Though Louella's worldwide readership of nearly twenty million was more than triple that of her primary rival, Hedda Hopper, pundits predicted that it would not be long until Hopper surpassed her and became the new first lady of Hollywood.

Yet all this seemed to matter little on the morning of Friday, September 12, when Louella left her home on Maple Drive in Beverly Hills for Los Angeles' Union Station. The strain of turning out a daily movie gossip column, monthly features for several fan magazines, and a weekly radio program seemed to disappear as Louella envisioned the upcoming journey to Dixon, Illinois, her hometown, over two thousand miles away. It would be no exaggeration to say that she had waited for this day all her life.

In Dixon, a town of thirty-five thousand in the heart of northern Illinois's farm country, the excitement and anticipation ran high. Mayor William Slothower had predicted that Louella Parsons Day, a celebration of the region's most famous daughter, would be "a spectacle that has never before been seen in the history of Dixon—a spectacle that few communities are privileged to witness."[2] Featuring a gala dinner, a parade through the streets of Dixon, and a radio broadcast by Louella and other Hollywood celebrities, the event had been planned for weeks by the Dixon Chamber of Commerce, the *Dixon Evening Telegraph,* the local Lions Club, and representatives from twelve local communities. Throughout the region, schools were closed for the event. Representatives of the American Legion and the Illinois Reserve Militia were scheduled to be on hand, as were several nurses, a fleet of ambulances, and Boy Scout troops from throughout the state. "Never in the history of the city has such painstaking effort and citywide cooperation been put forth in any civic undertaking, and no individual, native or otherwise, has been given such a reception as is being given to our nationally famous and much beloved Miss Parsons," crowed the *Dixon Evening Telegraph.* At least thirty thousand movie fans from northern Illinois, if not more, were expected to attend.[3]

The two-day trip from Hollywood aboard the City of Los Angeles streamliner was for Louella a working journey. With a typewriter propped up on two hatboxes, she wrote her columns and, with her publicist Virginia Lindsay, prepared her remarks for the celebration. Louella's brother, Ed Ettinger, a Hollywood publicist, accompanied her on the trip, as did a group of actors—Bob Hope, Jerry Colonna, Joe E. Brown, George Montgomery, Bebe Daniels, Ben Lyon, Ronald Reagan, and Ann Rutherford—who were scheduled to perform with Louella during the festivities. For Ronald Reagan, too, the trip to Dixon was a homecoming. A former lifeguard at Dixon's Lowell Park and a football star at Dixon High, Reagan had lived in Dixon only nine years earlier. Louella had left in 1905, though her ties to the community remained strong.

At nine in the morning on Sunday, September 14, 1941, crowds began milling around Dixon's northwestern train station. By 9:30, the assembly had filled the streets of the Dementtown section of Dixon, causing older residents to declare it the largest crowd the city had ever seen. When the train pulled in at 10:36, an estimated thirty-five thousand onlookers cheered, held signs, and readied their cameras in anticipation of Louella and "Dutch" Reagan. When Louella stepped out on the platform in the long silver fox coat she wore despite the eighty-degree heat, the throng screamed, waved, and snapped photos. Years of working in the film industry had taught her how to play for the camera; with a stiff white-gloved wave and beaming smile, she accepted a huge floral key to the city from Mayor Slothower and stepped gracefully to the microphone. What she said, though, seemed to be no phony Hollywood acceptance speech but to come truly from the heart. "This is an event, my old friends in Dixon, which I shall never forget," she told them. "I will remember this occasion as long as I live, and I know that Ronald will too.

"You remember that I always used to call our Rock River the Hudson River of the west. Then I hadn't been anywhere. Since then I have been in Switzerland, Italy—all around the world—and I still say that Dixon is the most beautiful city in the world. It's home."[4]

Very little had changed in it. As the motorcade proceeded down Galena Street, Dixon's main thoroughfare, the three-story brick buildings and square clapboard houses were as plain as they had been three decades earlier. Though the welcoming arch over the boulevard had been decorated with a "Welcome home" banner bearing pictures of Louella and Dutch, and a few new stores and movie theaters now stood by the downtown square, Dixon remained as humble, quiet, and conservative as ever. "These are not pushy, celebrity-bored crowds," Mayor Slothower had told reporters from the *Chicago Herald American,* "but ninety-nine percent native-born Americans, church-going folks, who are proud of their Dixon civic band in blue, the home guard, and the American Legion Auxiliary."[5]

At a banquet the following evening, prominent Dixonites paid tribute to Louella's rise from her rural roots. They remembered her riding her bike down a dusty road to Dixon High each day, her prize-winning oration at commencement, and the prophecy of the school principal, Benjamin Franklin Bullard, that someday she would be known as "Louella the Writer." Aspiring actresses in the community put together a dramatic sketch depicting Louella's involvement in the Kendall Club, one of Dixon's earliest social service organizations, and several longtime residents recalled that Louella, as a young reporter for the *Dixon Star,* had patrolled the streets each morning looking for a scoop. "How she used to walk down First Street going into every store along the way asking for news for the evening paper!" remembered Gwendolyn Bardwell, who had worked with Louella. After her first big story, she "walked wide eyed" around town, electrified with a thrilling sense of accomplishment. She was a "happy, ambitious scribe," claimed Mabel Shaw, the editor of the *Dixon Telegraph,* blessed with "great determination and inspiring energy." "Sometimes when fame wraps its velvet robe around a person, it changes its recipient, but not so with Louella Parsons. She loves her old friends and remembers them with graciousness," said another acquaintance. The *Telegraph* even noted that Louella had taken time out of her busy schedule to visit an "old gentleman, now blind, who used to see her on her way to school and [who] had expressed a desire to talk to her." On this day it seemed she could do no wrong.[6]

That evening, following the dedication of a Louella Parsons wing of the local hospital, a screening—the world premiere of the film *International Squadron,* starring Ronald Reagan—and the crowning of the Rock River beauty queen, Louella walked the grounds of the Charles Walgreen estate, Hazelwood, where she and the visiting celebrities were staying. Alone under the stars, she may have wondered how much her old friends had not said but had known: Louella's troubles with her first husband, John Parsons; her secret divorce; and an unhappy second marriage that she had hidden from her colleagues in Hollywood for over twenty years.

The following morning, standing on the train platform, she stared out one last time at the dusty roads, the low wooden shanties, and the deep green fields that stretched into the distance. With her brother and publicist not far behind, she lifted the hem of her fox coat, clutched her purse, and slipped gracefully into the rear car of the train. She was amazed at how simple it seemed this time; a wave, a smile, and a quick good-bye. The first time it had not been so easy.

PART I

ONE

Early Years

THOUGH DIXON WAS LOUELLA'S HOMETOWN, her story began in Freeport, Illinois, thirty miles north. Like most small communities in north-central Illinois in the 1880s, it was quiet, rural, tight-knit, and fiercely proud. Settled by miners, army volunteers in the Blackhawk war of the 1830s, and German immigrants, during the 1840s it was a regular stagecoach stop on the route to Chicago, a hundred miles east. Thanks to industrial development in the region, by the 1880s Freeport had grown into a town of fifteen thousand that was a thriving center of business and industry and one of the most important commercial centers in the area. The downtown streets were lined with general stores, clothing shops, soda fountains, and saloons. On the outskirts of town, smoke billowed into the sky from a string of factories producing leather and wooden goods—pipes, barrels, harnesses, and over six thousand pairs of shoes annually. Six days a week, men trudged off to the factories for ten hours' labor, while wives, dressed in long skirts and high collars, shopped on Stephenson Street, Freeport's main thoroughfare; cleaned their small homes; and minded their children.[1]

Visually, Freeport was snug and unassuming, a tight core of downtown streets lined with brick and wooden commercial buildings flanked by rows of small clapboard homes. In the distance lay the Pecatonica River and, beyond that, open farmland as far as the eye could see. The unpaved streets were muddy in spring, dusty in summer, and filled year-round with slow-moving horse traffic, horse dung, and debris. On windy days, complained residents, dust and dung blew into the stores and settled on open containers of flour and produce. Families here depended on wells for water, and, not knowing better, frequently dug them near stables and outside privies, leading to dozens of deaths annually. Life was hard and perilous but, at the same time, slow and comfortable, with a reassuring regularity. Days passed, seasons turned, but very little changed. Hardworking and conservative, dominated by Lutherans and Methodists, the community shunned flamboyance and ostentation, with one notable exception. During the late nineteenth and early twentieth century, Freeport residents were devoted patrons of the stage.[2]

Often described as a magnet for traveling stage companies during the late 1800s, Freeport, a major stop on the Great Western Railroad line, was known as one of the best theater towns in the state. Between 1880 and 1920, a period described by one historian as the "golden age" of the American theater, when hundreds of traveling theater companies toured the nation, there were six theaters and halls in downtown Freeport where operas, minstrel shows, and Shakespearean plays were regularly performed.[3] The Wilcoxon Opera House, the largest and most opulent in Freeport, seated eight hundred people on the main floor and in the gallery. Despite traditional associations of the theater with immorality, and despite the hostility of many religious leaders to the stage—the Methodist Episcopal Church had actually instituted a ban on theatergoing in 1877—most Freeport residents attended regularly.[4]

Like the motion pictures that followed, the theater operated according to a star system, in which actors' private lives were publicized to draw audiences and cultivate interest in performers. By 1880, theater fans could read about actors' marriages, divorces, and personal habits in major urban newspapers and in specialized trade publications like *The Theater* magazine, which catered to both professionals and fans. As one New York newspaper editorialized in 1888, commenting on the proliferation of theatrical "celebrity gossip" in the popular press, "One would think that actors and singers are the only people worth talking about in all this great, busy, active, pushing, enterprising world, and that newspapers are published for the express purpose of perpetuating the doings of actors in private life."[5]

In Freeport, theater fan culture thrived. Young male fans looking for an excuse to hang around the stage were hired by local theater owners to pass through the audience during performances and offer patrons a drink of water, free, from a pitcher and a single glass.[6] Young women dubbed "matinee girls" developed crushes on handsome male stars, the "matinee idols." Though the girls were criticized by parents and religious leaders who feared their unhealthy attachment to the stage and their frank expression of sexual desire, they persisted in their devotion, collecting tidbits of trivia about their idols and clipping photos from theatrical magazines.[7]

In 1881, twenty-three-year-old Helen Stine Oettinger was among those deeply enamored of the stage. Guided by her mother, Jeanette Wilcox Stine, she had grown up immersed in the theater and in theater fan culture. Throughout her childhood she and Jeanette had made regular trips to Chicago to see the latest plays, including *Sappho,* a controversial play celebrating female sexuality that was banned in several cities.[8] Both mother and child had dreamed of acting and were outspoken and theatrical in temperament. Helen dressed in plumed hats and garish gowns, while Jeanette had earned a reputation around town as an articulate, freethinking advocate of women's rights. Though Helen had recently married a local clothing merchant, Joshua Oettinger, and was urged by friends to give up her "childish" interest in the stage, she continued to attend the theater, dream of her favorite matinee idols, and exude her trademark flamboyance.

Helen's father, Isaac Stine, was a hardworking Jewish immigrant from Würtemberg, Germany, who had immigrated to Pennsylvania in 1847. After moving to Freeport in 1852, he purchased one of the first brick buildings in the area and opened the Star Store, a men's clothing company. By 1857, when he married Jeanette Wilcox, the daughter of a local Irish family, he was one of Freeport's most prosperous businessmen.[9] Jeanette and Isaac had five children—William, Charles, Carrie, Harriet, and Helen—and, like many German-Jewish families in the Protestant Midwest, concealed their religious background. Although most Freeport residents knew that Isaac was Jewish, the Stines regularly attended the Grace Episcopal Church.

When Isaac died in 1879, he willed the Star Store to William, his eldest son. But William wanted to pursue a law career, and after establishing his own law firm, Stine and Kern, in 1880, William transferred the ownership of the store to Helen and Harriet. The sisters became wealthy—and very desirable—young women.[10]

Enter Eli and Joshua Oettinger, two brothers of German-Jewish descent from Danville, Pennsylvania. After working in clothing stores in Chicago and Rockford, Illinois, the brothers, both in their early twenties, arrived in Freeport in 1879, where they worked at J. Levi and Company, a men's clothing house that competed with the Star Store. They heard of Helen and Harriet's acquisition of the Stine business and began courting the sisters. In September 1880 Eli married Hattie, and in January 1881 Joshua married Helen, and the ownership of the business was transferred to the Oettinger brothers.[11] Joshua and Helen moved into a small home on Clark Street, two blocks from the store, and by spring Helen was pregnant.

Helen weathered the humid summer of 1881 at home alone, while Joshua worked at the store. In early August, she went into labor. Alone in the parlor at the time, she shouted through the open window for help, and a neighbor, Luella Bixler, rushed in and delivered the child. To thank her, Helen named the baby girl Louella Rose.[12] Healthy, husky, and loud, little Louella entered the world screaming.

In the next five years, both Louella and the Oettinger Star Store flourished. In 1885, Joshua and Eli relocated the business to a larger and more centrally located building on Stephenson Street, and a third Oettinger brother, Lewis, migrated to Freeport to manage another branch of the store, called Famous Clothing, on the other side of town.[13] The prosperity enabled Joshua and Helen to move from Clark Street to a more expensive residence next to the store, and Joshua joined the Masons. "The Oettingers were respected and well thought of," recalled one Freeport resident, though they were known around town as a "Jewish family." In a town with only a few Jewish families, and possibly with an anti-Semitic climate, Joshua and Helen, eager to be accepted into the social mainstream, attended the local Episcopal church with the Stines.[14]

In May 1886, a second child, a boy named Edwin, was born to Joshua and Helen, and not long afterward, they sold their interest in the Oettinger store to Eli and moved thirty miles south, to the town of Sterling. Hoping to strike out on his own, Joshua thought that Sterling, a growing rural community without a successful clothing store, would be an ideal place for an independent venture. In 1888, he purchased a failing clothing store, and within a year he made it prosper.[15] Louella's early years were solidly middle class.

It is difficult to know whether Louella remembered that period in her life: the years in Freeport, Eddie's birth, the move to Sterling, and the family's growing fortunes. She was aware of the tensions between her mother, who was "hiding deep-rooted frustration for the theater and an innate love of drama," and her father, an "ambitious" man who was cold and reserved.[16] When Louella was almost seventy, she remembered a day in 1886 when Joshua took her to Chicago on a business trip. The big city excited and impressed her, she remembered, but it was the kindness of her father, who uncharacteristically doted on her for the entire journey, that she would cherish all her life. "In all the years and the many things that have happened to me, that memory is still fresh in my mind," she wrote.[17] Such a day, when she could bask in the undivided attention of her father, would never come again.

Sometime in the winter of 1887, Joshua's health began to fail. Though only twenty-nine, he suddenly seemed an old man—wheezing, feverish, so drained of energy that he was often unable to walk. In spite of his condition, described by one observer as "only little less than invalid," Joshua forced himself to work. With the help of a young assistant, David Lingel, Joshua opened the store each day, waited on customers, and meticulously calculated his accounts. Buoyed by "an indomitable will power," a local newspaper later claimed, "he was rarely absent from business." A "quiet, unobtrusive man, courteous in his bearing, loyal in his friendships, and honorable in his dealings," Joshua was "highly esteemed" by all.[18] Beneath the placid demeanor, however, was a man who was deeply depressed, terrified of his worsening health, and intensely afraid of death. By Louella's seventh birthday in 1888, it was clear he was suffering from tuberculosis.

On the afternoon of Saturday, May 24, 1890, Joshua was in the store, figuring the books and waiting on customers. It was not a particularly difficult day, but when he closed the store that evening he was quivering and exhausted, and he collapsed on the floor. Lingel, the store assistant, carried Joshua the short distance to the Oettinger home, where he lay in bed, half conscious, for the rest of the night. On Sunday morning came hope—for a moment, it seemed he had regained awareness—and a telegram was dispatched to Eli in Freeport alerting him to Joshua's fatal condition. When Eli arrived in Sterling that evening, it was too late. Joshua had slipped back into delirium, and by two the next afternoon, he had gone completely unconscious. At seven o'clock, Joshua Oettinger, age thirty-three, was killed by "abscesses of the lungs," reported the *Sterling Gazette*.[19] He passed away much as he had lived: quietly, without complaint, feeling little pain.

On Wednesday, May 28, Joshua's body was placed on the 1:55 train for Freeport, where it arrived two hours later. The remains were taken from the train by Joshua's Masonic brothers and carried by a horse-drawn hearse to the city cemetery. The following day, Helen returned to Sterling and announced her intention to sell the store.[20] Telegrams were sent, visits made, and by the end of the year Helen had sold the business to Joshua's stepbrother Gus, who had recently migrated from Pennsylvania. With her earnings from the sale of the business plus the two thousand dollars' worth of life insurance Joshua had carried with the Masons, Helen packed up the Sterling home and moved Louella and Eddie back to Freeport.

Those who expected to see a somber widow were shocked to see Helen in remarkably high spirits. Joshua's death seemed to embolden her, enabling her to unleash the passionate theatricality she had suppressed while living with her cold and steely husband. Immediately Helen bought a large house with a turret at the corner of North Van Buren and Monterey Streets and furnished it with velvet curtains, a piano, and oil paintings. She purchased for herself a wardrobe that would have put even the most sophisticated Chicago belle to shame: a traveling suit of thick Russian red broadcloth, a black silk dress with yellow ostrich trimming, several silk tea gowns and evening dresses, a heavy gold-colored coat, bonnets with matching gloves, and a collection of faux diamond jewelry.[21] She threw parties and teas, splurged on expensive china and silverware, and installed electric lights in the parlor.[22] Perhaps most extravagant were the trips to the theater in Chicago. With a small suitcase, her best traveling outfit, and Louella in tow, every few weeks Helen boarded the morning train headed east. She claimed that the plays were an important part of Louella's education, but her friends knew better. It was Helen, of course, who was stagestruck.

The first play Louella watched was *Cyrano de Bergerac,* with matinee idol Richard Mansfield in the starring role. Too young to understand the plot, she sat quietly in the darkened house and delighted in the bright colors onstage. At home in Freeport, Louella and Helen were regular patrons of the opera house, and when she was eight or nine, Louella put on her own plays for neighbors. After she and Helen went to a performance of *Cousin Kate* in Chicago, Louella reenacted it in the barn behind the house.[23]

If plays alerted Louella to the magic of storytelling, books turned her into a believer. Each night Helen read Louella the classics—*Black Beauty, Treasure Island, Little Women*—and before long Louella was hooked. When she learned how to read, she raided the public library. Helen urged the librarian, her good friend Harriet Lane, to monitor the girl's reading and keep her from borrowing any "trash." An attempt to borrow *Madame Bovary* was promptly thwarted, though Louella claimed that she later obtained a copy of the book from a friend. During the 1890s, dime novels were all the rage among boys, and when Eddie brought home a few tattered copies, Helen erupted into a fit—"This trash!" she shouted—and ordered Louella to burn them. Louella agreed but not before sneaking off to her room and reading as many as she could.[24]

Louella read dozens if not hundreds of books during her years in Freeport—*Last of the Mohicans, The Three Musketeers, Gulliver's Travels*—but her favorite, and the one that impressed her most deeply, was a story called *Editha's Burglar* by Frances Hodgson Burnett. Published in 1888, when Louella was seven, the book tells the tale of a London girl named Editha, a spunky, bright seven-year-old who, like Louella, was a voracious reader. In the story Editha's father is a newspaper editor, and Editha spends her days in his library, "reading papa's books and even his newspapers." "She was very fond of the newspapers," Burnett wrote, "because she found so many curious things in them."[25] Louella, seeing herself in the heroine, read the book over and over again, often staying up past her bedtime. In her first attempt at "writing," she copied the entire text into her notebook and fantasized that she had composed the novel herself.[26]

In the winter of 1891, a year and a half after Joshua's death, Helen married John Edwards, a thirty-three-year-old traveling candy salesman. Though he had come from one of the well-off pioneering families of neighboring Lee County, John, who worked for the Kranz Confectionery Company, lived alone in a rented room on North Van Buren Street, down the block from Helen. On the afternoon of December 15, 1891, in her "elaborate and elegant" parlor, Helen Stine Oettinger, in a bright red dress "cut princess style with jet trimmings," wed John Edwards, who was "faultlessly attired in the conventional black and supremely happy," reported the *Freeport Daily Journal.*[27] Later that evening, the newlyweds boarded a train to Chicago "for a brief bridal tour." Louella and Eddie stayed with their fifty-one-year-old grandmother Jeanette, a stocky, gray-haired woman who spent hours in a rocking chair reading, sucking on gumdrops, and dispensing clichéd tidbits of wisdom—"the proof of the pudding is in the eating," "don't count your chickens before they've hatched"—to her grandchildren. Underneath the matronly appearance lay a youthful spirit and a will of steel.[28]

Jeanette Wilcox was a native of Freeport and one of its finest amateur historians. Born in 1840, she was eighteen when presidential contenders Lincoln and Douglas held their famous debate in Freeport. With baby Helen in her arms, Jeanette had sat in the front row and listened as the candidates argued the pressing political matters of the day—secession, states' rights, slavery. Like most of the women there, she fell head over heels for Douglas, with his "fine manners and Southern chivalry."[29] But when Lincoln, following the debate, stopped to kiss Helen, Jeanette's allegiances changed. From that moment, she became not only an "out and out Lincolnite" but also a serious student of American politics and history. Jeanette, who had taught herself how to read, inundated Louella with tales about "the Great Emancipator, as well as other colorful information that is not in history books," Louella recalled. For a contest at the local grammar school, the River School, Louella enlisted Jeanette's help for an essay on Lincoln that won first prize. The teachers who praised Louella never knew that Jeanette had written most of the paper.[30]

When the famous humanitarian and Chicago settlement-house founder

Jane Addams visited Freeport, Jeanette took Louella to meet her. "I was so excited," Louella recalled, "I could only stare at her."[31] Addams was one of many "great women" whom Louella learned about as a child. Influenced by women's suffrage activists who lectured in Freeport during the 1870s, Jeanette was a strong supporter of women's rights. She taught Louella about the writer Louisa May Alcott, the Civil War nurse Clara Barton, and Nellie Bly, the most celebrated female journalist of the nineteenth century.[32] Bly had become famous in the 1880s as a reporter for Joseph Pulitzer's *New York World*. In 1889, as a stunt for the paper, she traveled around the world, alone, in seventy-two days, and subsequently became a national heroine. Headlines celebrated her feat, games bore her name, and songs were composed in her honor.[33] Louella was so inspired by Bly that she began writing articles and short stories that she submitted to the Freeport paper, the *Journal Standard*, which were promptly rejected.[34]

Not long into their marriage, Helen and John began to quarrel over money. Unwilling to curtail her spending despite the family's dwindling bank account, Helen continued to spend lavishly on trips, furnishings, and clothes. Eventually compromises were made. The trips to Chicago continued, but Helen was forbidden to throw the lavish parties that had made her one of Freeport's best hostesses. Clothing and laundry expenses were similarly cut back. (An acquaintance from Louella's high school days remembered that she often wore the same dress to school, one with a visibly dirty collar.)[35] Louella spent long hours in the local library after school and became a star student at Freeport High. Though she required the assistance of a tutor in math and chemistry, she excelled in the humanities, and the *Freeport Journal Standard* frequently carried news that Louella Oettinger had earned first prize in yet another essay contest.

Louella also spent hours roaming the downtown streets with her two best friends, nicknamed Twinkle and Blush. (Louella's nickname was Cherry.)[36] Circus was a large part of the summer entertainment in Freeport, and Louella fondly recalled "circus mornings." Crowds waited for the band that was carried down the street on red-and-gold wagons and the steam calliope that brought up the rear. In between were animals and cages, and women riders in spangled tights atop glossy riding horses. Parades and torchlight rallies were cherished holiday events, as was a "special parade" on certain Sunday summer mornings, when geese kept by local families were let loose downtown to feast on garbage discarded in the street.[37]

Although Louella enjoyed the simple pleasures of small-town life, by the time she was in high school she was bored. A bright, articulate, and intellectually curious teenager, she found few outlets for her budding literary ambitions and yearned for broader horizons. By the time she was in high school, she had decided to be a writer or a reporter. But no one, except her grandmother Jeanette, took her interests seriously.

Louella grew up during a transition in American women's history, when the passive, corseted, midcentury Victorian female ideal, characterized by her sexual purity and domesticity, was slowly being challenged by the more modern and independent "new woman" who sought greater opportunities outside the home. By the 1890s, over 20 percent of college students were women, and thousands of young middle-class women were pursuing such acceptably "female" occupations as clerical work, social work, and teaching.[38] But marriage and motherhood were still deemed a woman's primary goals, and working women were expected to give up their jobs upon marriage and devote their lives to domesticity. Women were also plagued by traditional assumptions about female intellectual inferiority. Despite the presence of a well-organized women's suffrage movement and several well-known women writers, Victorian-era physicians had declared women so overtaken by their sex hormones that they were incapable of pursuing professional work or serious intellectual thought.[39]

Louella dreamed of challenging the stereotypes. "I wanted to grow up as quickly as possible and to be hailed—if not as the best writer in America— at least as the youngest and the most beautiful," Louella remembered. But a full-time literary career was considered a male aspiration, and her family and the Freeport community mocked her unladylike ambitions.[40]

She expressed her anger and resentment with bragging and temper tantrums. By her own account, she lied frequently and made extraordinary and exaggerated claims about herself and her accomplishments. In general, she wrote in her autobiography, she was unbearable, caring "deeply and sincerely" about only herself. "Cold reason forces me to admit that I was not my favorite little girl—either in or out of fiction," she explained. "It is common . . . to look back on the days of childhood as the happiest. I can't truthfully say the same of myself."[41]

Sometime during Louella's first year in high school, John Edwards took what was left of his and Helen's assets and opened a small grocery on Stephenson Street. The venture soon failed, and by 1898, Louella's sophomore year in high school, John decided to move the family thirty miles south to Dixon, where he would resume his candy sales. His brother, Frank Edwards, was mayor of Dixon, and most of the Edwards clan lived in nearby Amboy. John reasoned that proximity to his well-off kin would boost not only his family's morale but also their finances. John and Helen sold the house on North Van Buren, packed their furniture and belongings into a wagon, and took Louella and Eddie out of school.[42] By the end of 1898 they were gone.

"Dixon is not a town of much apparent prosperity," the English author Anthony Trollope wrote in 1862. "It is one of those places at which great beginnings have been made, but as to which the deities presiding over new towns have not been propitious." Surrounded by prairie and cornfields, "it had a straggling, ill-conditioned, uncommercial aspect."[43]

By 1890, much had changed. Like Freeport, Dixon had gone from being a small frontier village in the 1830s to becoming, by the turn of the century, a prosperous commercial center. Founded as an army command post, Dixon grew during the 1840s and 1850s as English, German, and Irish settlers seeking livelihoods in mining and farming arrived from the East. A major stop on the Illinois Central Railroad on the banks of the Rock River, Dixon became an important transportation hub, and industry followed. In 1869 the Cumins and Noble Plow Company settled in Dixon; in 1875 the Becker and Underwood Flour Mill opened its doors; and in 1889 the town became the site of the Anglo-Swiss Condensed Milk Company, the largest condensed milk factory in the world. Thousands of workers came from nearby areas, and by 1900 the population had grown to ten thousand.[44]

Buoyed by prosperity, Dixon experienced a period of civic and cultural expansion. In 1896, a town hospital was constructed; in 1898, a public library and a new county courthouse were built; and in 1899, the town embarked on its most ambitious project, a circular auditorium seating five thousand that would be the largest building of its kind on the continent. By the turn of the century, there were seven active churches, dozens of community and charity organizations, a town band, and a library with over four thousand books.[45]

In 1899, John, Helen, Louella, and Eddie moved into an apartment on Second Street in the downtown commercial district. John took up a new job with the Bunte Confectionery Company, and thirteen-year-old Eddie started the sixth grade. Louella, at age eighteen, would have been a high school senior in Freeport, but the move to Dixon set her back. As a junior, Louella started classes at Dixon's South Side High School, affectionately dubbed "the White Brick School." As in Freeport, she excelled academically, and within a few months she had scored several academic prizes: an award for a recitation of "The Wreck of the Hesperus," a prize for a paper on James Fenimore Cooper's *The Last of the Mohicans,* and during her senior year, first prize in a contest sponsored by the Daughters of the American Revolution. For her essay, "When Is Revolution Justified," she was awarded busts of Washington, Lincoln, and Daniel Webster, which, in a well-publicized ceremony, she donated to the school.[46] Though she was still temperamental and emotional, she nonetheless acquired a tight-knit group of friends by the end of her first year in Dixon.

In 1900, Louella founded the Kendall Club, a young women's charity and social organization that attracted the daughters of several prominent Dixon families. She became known for bringing groups of her classmates to the new circular auditorium at Assembly Park during summers for the Chautauqua lectures. A series of traveling lectures and performances that lasted between three and seven days, the Chautauqua was held each summer in communities across the Midwest between the 1880s and the 1930s. Performers ranged from serious political speakers to elocutionists and Shakespearean actors, and during the series' peak in the mid-1920s, Chautauqua performers and lecturers appeared in more than ten thousand communities in forty-five states.[47]

For Louella and the Dixon community, the Chautauqua was the highlight of the summer. After an afternoon picnicking on the banks of the Rock River, Louella and her friends entered the cavernous auditorium and sought out the front row of seats. Described at the time as "the finest and most completely adapted building for Chautauqua purposes on the continent," the hall at Assembly Park was an imposing circular structure, with its 500-foot diameter and 160-foot perimeter.[48] Popular speakers such as the fiery political orator William Jennings Bryan and Theodore Roosevelt attracted thousands of visitors from throughout the region; when Roosevelt spoke in 1905, the 5,000-seat auditorium was filled. Though Louella recalled that she and her friends would often "giggle" at the lecturers, she later admitted that the oratory sparked in her an interest in public speaking.[49]

That interest found expression at Louella's high school graduation on June 4, 1901. As class speaker, Louella delivered the class prophecy and a speech titled "Great Men." It was a compelling speech, according to the *Dixon Telegraph,* on "our great men in every walk of life." Unlike many graduation orations, Louella's talk was given in a "most pleasing style."[50] At the end of the ceremony, Principal Benjamin Franklin Bullard stood on the podium and announced that Louella Oettinger would one day become a great writer.[51]

At the time of her graduation, Louella still had dreams of becoming a reporter. Yet she knew that a career in journalism was nearly impossible for a woman. Though women had worked on newspapers since the American Revolution—in both the Revolution and the Civil War, women had taken over male editorial jobs when their husbands went to battle—gender discrimination and a traditional bias against working women kept female journalists from making long-term gains in the field. By the mid–nineteenth century, there were only a handful of female editors and columnists; the most famous, Margaret Fuller, edited the *Dial* literary magazine with Ralph Waldo Emerson and wrote literary reviews for the *New York Tribune* in the 1840s. After the Civil War, when rising rates of female literacy led urban newspapers to cultivate a female audience, editors began hiring female writers to write "women's columns"—society notes, advice columns, and sections on cooking and fashion. By 1880, the U.S. census recorded 288 women in editing and reporting jobs, and by 1900 there were 2,000 female journalists, who constituted 7 percent of the profession. But with the exception of such celebrated stunt journalists as Nellie Bly and Winifred Black, who wrote sensationalistic exposés for William Randolph Hearst's *San Francisco Examiner,* very few female reporters made it beyond the "women's pages."[52] Arnold Bennett, author of an 1898 manual titled *Journalism for Women,* echoed the prevailing attitude in the profession when he wrote that women made poor reporters because they were crippled by "a failure to appreciate the importance of the maxim that business is business" and were "unreliable as a class [since] the influences of domesticity are too strong to be lightly thrown off." They suffered from "inattention to detail" and a "lack of restraint in literary style," which would only be improved with intense "moral and intellectual calisthenics."[53]

Elementary school teaching was, by contrast, a traditionally female profession, and Helen encouraged Louella to take it up as a way to contribute to the family income. In the summer of 1901, Louella accepted a contribution from Julius Benedict, a distant German relative whose estate provided funds for "those of his kin in need of an education." That fall, she enrolled in a teacher education course at the local Dixon college.[54] Founded in 1882, the Dixon Normal School and Business College, a coeducational institution with sixteen hundred students, was housed in an imposing three-story brick building on the outskirts of town. Louella lived with Helen and John in their new downtown home on First Street while she attended classes in English, history, and elementary education. Louella's college years seemed to have made little impression on her. She found her courses dull, was ambivalent about a career as a grade school teacher, and at twenty, she was being pressured by Helen to get married. Although she was pretty—described by one local resident as a "slender, winsome brunette with dark eyes and dark hair"—she had few suitors. Over the summer, she had had a brief romantic fling with twenty-nine-year-old John Parsons, but it had lasted only a few months.

John Parsons, according to Louella, was the town's "matrimonial catch."[55] John's mother, Christiana Dement, hailed from one of the oldest and most respected families in the area. Christiana's father, Colonel John Dement, had been one of the pioneer settlers of Dixon and a prominent businessman and politician who, according to one local history, was for "fifty years . . . the most powerful" man in Lee County.[56] John's father, Edwin C. Parsons, was one of the wealthiest landholders in Dixon.[57] Selfish and spoiled, John had been groomed for a future in the military. When Louella met him, he had recently graduated from a military academy in Peekskill, New York, and was on his way to South Africa with the U.S. Army. After he left in September, Louella imagined she would never see him again.

Then, the following summer, he returned unexpectedly. John had been discharged from the army after contracting dengue fever, and after several months of treatment and recuperation, came back to Dixon to take a job with his father's real estate company. Like Louella, John, at thirty, was being pressured by his parents to marry. Not long after his return to Dixon he and Louella resumed their relationship.[58] By that time, Louella, still at college, had secured a part-time writing position at a local newspaper, the *Dixon Star.*

In 1902, the *Star*'s editor, the husband of one of Louella's close friends, hired her to work on the paper during her summer vacation. As a writer for the "society page" and the first female journalist in Dixon, Louella would report the latest happenings in Dixon's social circles—weddings, engagements, formal dinners. The pay was meager, only five dollars a week, and, following the convention of the day, her column was published without a byline. "Society Doings" appeared on the third page of the paper, next to the column "The Dixon Markets" ("hogs $6.30 a pound," it reported, "cow $2.50, lard eleven cents").

For "Society Doings," Louella immersed herself in Dixon social life and the local culture of gossip, taking the first steps toward her future Hollywood career:

> The supper and dinner served by the ladies of the Lutheran church on Saturday in the church parlors was a decided success. The delicious menu promised

by the ladies was served even to the smallest detail, and those who attended the dinner speak highly of the ladies' ability in the culinary art.

The silver wedding anniversary of Mr. and Mrs. Dennis McCoy of Tenth Street and Peoria Avenue was celebrated in a very fitting manner last night at their home. The evening was spent in a social way, card playing being the chief amusement.

Mrs. Paul Lord entertained today in honor of Miss Edwina Smith. A linen shower greeted the bride-to-be.[59]

As historians, anthropologists, and sociologists have concluded, both in the United States and around the world, gossip has traditionally been used by small communities for a variety of social functions—for entertainment, to create social bonds, and to reaffirm shared social values. As sociologist James West wrote in *Plainville, USA,* a pathbreaking 1945 study of social norms and practices in rural, small-town America, gossip reinforces the community's moral codes—by repeatedly gossiping about adulterers, for example, townspeople reaffirm the value of marital fidelity. It also enables residents to escape potential condemnation for their own misdeeds. "People report, suspect, laugh at, and condemn the peccadilloes of others and walk and behave carefully to avoid being caught in any trifling missteps of their own," West wrote.[60] According to sociologist Gary Alan Fine, we use gossip as a form of emotional release, to draw attention to ourselves, and, perhaps more than anything, as an excuse to engage in small talk with others.[61]

Historically, gossip has played an important role in small-town women's cultures. According to sociologist Melanie Tebbutt, the word *gossip* was originally used in seventeenth-century England to refer to the close female friends a woman invited to attend to her at childbirth. Withdrawal to the lying-in room created a female space where they excluded men and shared intimate secrets. Only in the nineteenth century, when childbirth was medicalized, did gossip lose its connection with women's birthing rituals and come to signify idle talk. According to Tebbutt, women have used gossip both to build emotional and social bonds with one other and to gain power and status within their communities. Lacking economic and political resources, many found gossip an important form of cultural capital that they could use to gain respect, attention, or leverage with powerful men.[62]

We don't know the extent of Louella's participation in Dixon gossip, or the scope and intensity of local gossip culture. We do know, however, since

Louella implied it several times during her career, that she knew far more intimate gossip—news of romantic affairs, out-of-wedlock births, and other local "scandals"—than she was allowed to print in the *Star.* Hollywood gossip, she later claimed, was hardly different from Dixon hearsay. Just as movie celebrities embroiled themselves in extramarital affairs, the small-town "butcher might be flirting with the milkman's wife or the dry goods merchant [might] fall in love with the banker's wife," she explained in an article in *Cosmopolitan* magazine in 1934.[63]

The next summer Louella's responsibilities at the *Star,* circulation three thousand, expanded. Having proven herself as a writer and reporter, she was allowed to cover front-page news in addition to writing the society column. Evenings, she walked the streets of downtown Dixon, tattered notebook in hand, searching for news. Many years later she recalled her technique: "I took down day by day all I heard from the local storekeepers and the gossip mongers. Nine times out of ten, thanks to this gossip I knew what was going to happen the next day. In Hollywood I applied the same methods and became the best informed woman in the town."[64] Anna Geisenheimer, owner of the local corset shop, recalled that Louella used a more direct tactic: she knocked on doors and asked for news. "When the coroner of Dixon gave her copy, he was a nice man," a reporter for the rival paper, the *Dixon Telegraph,* recalled, "and when he didn't she hated him."[65]

After Louella's first front-page story for the *Star,* about a young man who shot a bartender because he wouldn't serve minors, friends recalled that she walked "wide eyed about town," thrilled by her accomplishment.[66] She later covered the trial, which was held in Dixon. The judge, a friend of the family, halted the proceedings when he saw Louella in court. "What are you doing here? This is no place for you," he said. When Louella told him that she was a reporter working for the *Star,* he replied, "You'd be better off in school." But she stayed and watched as the man was found guilty and sentenced to the penitentiary. Before he left for jail, he married his nineteen-year-old fiancée, and Louella was the only witness. Louella claimed that the story for the *Star* was later picked up by wire services and reprinted in Chicago. "I felt that I had reached the apex of my career at its very beginning," she recalled.[67]

Despite Louella's pleas, the *Star* was unwilling to hire her full-time, and reluctantly, following her graduation from college in 1903, Louella accepted a job at the Stoney Point School, a "country school" a few miles up the Rock River.[68] At the end of the 1903–4 school year, she signed on for another term, and during the following school year continued to split her time between Stoney Point and her ongoing courtship with John Parsons.

Then, in the late summer of 1905, Louella filed her resignation at Stoney Point and went with Helen to the local seamstress. They wanted a wedding gown, Helen told her, made of the finest white silk, the most expensive white lace, and hand sewn with "tiny, perfect stitches."[69] Helen had learned to be frugal over the years, but this was no time to be cheap. On October 31, Louella was going to be married.

Halloween 1905, Louella recalled, was a "bright, tangy" day. The air was cold, and the leaves descending from the maple trees were red and gold and crisp. Standing inside the library of the Parsons home on Everett Street, she could see them falling like rain and collecting in great messy piles on the lawn. In the distance there were clumps of berries clinging tightly to green bushes. She had tasted them once; they were, like that day, bittersweet.[70]

Inside the Parsons library, bittersweet berries had been strewn across the windowsills and bookcases for decoration, and a carefully arranged carpet of leaves surrounded the unlit fireplace. Dressed in her gown of white silk de chine, a pearl necklace, and with her long hair swept up atop her head, Louella descended the staircase to the strains of the Mendelssohn wedding march.[71] Though the Episcopal wedding services were private—only John's and Louella's families attended—it had been preceded by several engagement parties. Louella was feted by her friends with a bridal shower at the Kendall Club. "Much merriment" was had, reported the *Dixon Telegraph,* when the young women presented the bride-to-be with a poem too naughty to be reprinted.[72]

Though Louella reveled in the attention, the marriage soon headed for disaster. Temperamentally, John and Louella were opposites. He was haughty, cold, and arrogant, while Louella was spirited, high-strung, and emotional. As Louella later recalled, they were "an ocean apart in points of view."[73] They began fighting almost immediately. Although John was a "shrewd businessman," acquaintances remembered, he was an uncommitted and inattentive husband. "I don't think he did much of anything. He was a spoiled boy," recalled Dixon resident Sadie Mack.[74] "John was a very intelligent man, but not one to make Louella very happy," remembered another neighbor.[75]

Not long after the wedding, Louella and John made plans to move to Burlington, Iowa, a town of twenty-four thousand that was 150 miles south-east of Dixon. There John would manage the Parsons Block, a housing development owned by his father. The thought of being far away from her family and community terrified Louella. She awaited the day of departure with dread.

In December 1905, Louella and John arrived in Burlington and moved into the lower floor of a rented, two-story brick home downtown, in the North Hill neighborhood. She did not love her husband. She knew no one. It would be the darkest period of her life.

It was nothing like Dixon, and Louella knew it the moment she arrived. Perched on rock bluffs high above the Mississippi, Burlington had an austere and forbidding appearance. Early residents had quarried rock from the hillsides to build homes, churches, and schools and to pave streets and alleys. The streets were crooked, curving out of sight around hillsides and bluffs, disappearing over hilltops or at the river, or angling off around unexpected corners. While guidebooks described the layout as "quaint," to Louella this cold and labyrinthine town was hell hewed in stone.[76]

Since the 1840s, Burlington had been a ferry and steamboat port on the Mississippi. During the second half of the nineteenth century, it was also home to flourishing brewing, packing, railroad, and lumber industries and to the three pork-packing establishments that had earned the town the nickname "Porkopolis of Iowa." Although the population by the early 1900s consisted mostly of Germans, Irish, and Swedes who had migrated to Burlington to develop its industries, the social and cultural leaders of the community were Burlington's early settlers, Anglo-Saxon Protestants from New England, Virginia, and the Carolinas. Bringing their elite culture with them, they formed literary and musical societies and built opulent mansions, many of them on North Hill.[77] Described by an 1869 guidebook as the "fashionable, tiptop, bon ton, aristocratic, elegant, creme de la creme part of the city," North Hill had "aristocratic pretensions uncommon in a typical easygoing Midwestern community."[78]

Yet parts of North Hill were overrun with weeds, the North Hill park was in shambles, and in some sections the streets were ungraded and unpaved. While Burlington's elite made their homes on North Hill, so did laborers, clerks, printers, mechanics, and machinists, which led to class tensions.[79] North Third Street on North Hill was home not only to a working- and middle-class neighborhood but also to a business district with several saloons, grocers, clothing shops, and theaters. Here stood the Garrick Theater, described in ads as a "high-class vaudeville theater," and the Grand Opera House, which boasted a marble foyer, 225 upholstered opera chairs, and a "grand entrance" finished in "oiled black walnut, Queen Anne fresco and tessellated pavement, iron steps, [and] heavy push doors" and lit with a "magnificent eighteen jet chandelier."[80]

The Parsons rented a home next door to the opera house, and immediately Louella made a name for herself by creating what one neighbor described as "sanitation problems." Burlington resident Lloyd Maffitt recalled that "she didn't keep the garbage cleaned off the back porch and the neighbors raised hell. She had all the gall of a brass monkey." Eventually, this led to eviction by the city.[81]

But even before the garbage scandal, Louella had a "bad reputation," remembered Margaret Clark, who lived down the street. She was "young and she just didn't fit into the Burlington life. She made a lot of boners and they made a lot of fun of her." Dixon was a relatively easygoing community with few of Burlington's stark socioeconomic divisions. Ill equipped to handle her new social environment, Louella tried to fit in with the elite and failed miserably. One of Louella's most embarrassing social gaffes, according to Clark, was her poetry reading. "She used to come over and read poetry she'd written." Her work was "perfectly terrible, but she was awfully polite about it."[82] In response to the criticism, Louella begged John, who was well read, to teach her about art and literature, and he instructed her to "study Thomas Hardy very carefully."[83] But in spite of her self-education, her neighbors still considered her "dull and stupid" and "mousy."[84] In general, recalled resident Margaret Smith, Louella and John were social "nonentities."[85]

The criticism shattered her self-confidence as a writer. Always exceptionally dependent on the judgment of her peers, she gave up her poetry and short stories, convinced that she was as ignorant as her neighbors said. Louella later wrote of those years in the cruelest of terms: "I sometimes think of this small town, with it Midwest drab grayness, as though it were an outpost of darkest Siberia. Perhaps that sounds like a harsh indictment. I am sure it was—and is—no different from any other small town, but we remember places by the happiness or unhappiness we have felt there. I was young and homesick for my family in Dixon, and it is the memory of my misery that persists, not the reality."[86]

In early 1906, not long after the move to Burlington, Louella discovered that she was pregnant. Around the same time, she learned that John had taken up with Ruth Schaefer, a young blonde who worked at his office. On August 23, 1906, Louella's first and only child, Harriet Oettinger Parsons, was born. Abandoned by John, Louella struggled to bring up Harriet alone.[87]

Louella did have two unlikely friends in Burlington. One was Adeline Moir, a teenager who lived nearby. The other was Martin Bruhl, a pianist who performed frequently at the opera house. Louella would visit Bruhl and tell him her troubles. Bruhl was a "crazy musician" and Louella was a "crazy poetess" so they "had a good time together," recalled Bruhl's wife. Martin Bruhl described Louella as a "doll," who, he said, "would have captured the Miss America title if it had been in existence around 1905. Charisma is the word for Louella then, and her daughter Harriet was an angel. How John Parsons could have been so cruel to [leave] such a beautiful family is hard to understand." Bruhl, unlike the other neighbors, recognized her spirit and ambition. "She was allergic to mediocrity and her aim for perfection was high," he recalled.[88]

Despite Bruhl's occasional companionship, Louella spent much of her time alone or at the theater. She was a frequent patron of the opera house, and Martin Bruhl believed that it was Louella's contact with the "immortal stage stars of the day"—DeWolf Hopper, the Barrymores, David Warfield, Edwin Booth, all of whom performed at the opera house—that gave her the "background and inspiration to become the great critic of the cinema into which she developed."[89] At the Garrick Theater she watched cheap vaudeville and melodrama and, beginning in 1907, "flickers," one- or two-minute films exhibited between vaudeville acts.[90]

Developed by Thomas Edison in the 1870s, motion pictures had been first publicly exhibited at a New York vaudeville house, Koster and Bial's, in 1896. These early films, dubbed "views" or "actualities," consisted of short documentary footage of simple scenes—waves crashing on a beach, dancing chorus girls, short segments of boxing matches. The images were blurry and jerky, but viewers were nonetheless thrilled by the sight of photographic images in motion. When an onrushing train appeared on the screen, audiences leaped out of their seats. A short film of a man and woman kissing seemed so lifelike that many viewers looked behind the screen for the couple.[91]

Considered a technological novelty that could add spice to a theatrical program but that merited little interest on their own, motion pictures were initially exhibited as part of vaudeville programs. But by 1902, movies had become so popular in urban areas that special theaters were built exclusively for film exhibition. That year, a Los Angeles entrepreneur named Thomas Tally opened the nation's first nickelodeon, a motion picture theater charging a nickel admission. Most nickelodeons were simple storefronts with a sheet tacked onto the wall for a screen. Audiences sat on hard wooden benches or on the floor and sometimes spent the whole afternoon in the theater, watching the same short films over and over again. By 1905, movies had advanced from short "views" to five- or ten-minute narrative films—comedies, Westerns, adventure films, and melodramas that were crudely photographed, performed by inexperienced actors in exaggerated pantomime, and, of course, silent.

By the middle of the first decade of the twentieth century, nickelodeons flourished primarily in urban, working-class areas. In 1905, a nickelodeon boom started in Chicago; in New York alone there were over four hundred nickelodeons that exhibited films to twenty thousand patrons daily.[92] Considered vulgar by reigning cultural standards, motion pictures initially attracted few middle-class audiences, but they did appeal to thousands of immigrant workers, whose lack of English was no impediment to the wordless entertainment. The cinema's association with the immigrant working class raised the ire of religious and social elites, who saw the new medium as a corrupting "foreign" influence. Social reformers also claimed that film plots were filled with sexual innuendo and violence, and that movie theaters were the "breeding grounds of vice." In New York, Protestant reform groups attempted not only to censor films but also to shut down nickelodeons, an effort that resulted in the closure of all the city's movie theaters on Christmas Day, 1908.[93]

In the Midwest, the cinema was less likely to spark class and ethnic controversy than to arouse religious fears. In some midwestern small towns, Protestant leaders either banned film altogether or permitted only educational films shown in church-run venues. Nonetheless, according to the film historian Kathryn Fuller, the movies flourished in the rural Midwest, where by 1903, small-town theaters drew moviegoers from the surrounding countryside.[94] In 1909 the Lyric Theater, a nickelodeon, opened in Burlington and showed a complete bill of short films nightly.[95] In her autobiography, Louella claimed to have seen "movies of the funeral of King Edward VII" as well as dozens of short comedies and melodramas.[96] By the time she left Iowa, she was a movie fan—or as *Harper's* magazine described it in 1907, a "cinemaddict."[97]

Louella's only other diversion consisted of regular visits to Dixon. During summers, Louella took Harriet to Dixon to stay with John Parsons's parents, Edwin and Christiana, who gave their granddaughter expensive gifts and treated her to weekends at the nearby Lowell Park Lodge.[98] Though they knew about John's affair, they treated Louella and Harriet royally. In Dixon, Louella and Harriet also visited Helen and John Edwards, who were having marital troubles of their own.

Back in Burlington, John and Louella's marriage continued only on paper. Everyone knew of John's affair with Ruth Schaefer, and there were rumors that he planned to marry her. Finally, one day in the winter of 1910, Louella decided to leave. What triggered her departure is unclear. She may have simply snapped from the loneliness and frustration, or John may have announced his intent to marry Schaefer. Or perhaps she was prompted by the fiery destruction of the opera house next door, which had been dynamited by vandals in September.[99] She took Harriet and headed for Chicago, where she planned to look for work and start a new life. Depressed and penniless, Louella had just turned twenty-nine.

TWO

Essanay

Hog Butcher for the World,
Tool Maker, Stacker of Wheat,
Player with Railroads and the Nation's Freight Handler;
Stormy, husky, brawling,
City of the Big Shoulders:
They tell me you are wicked and I believe them, for I have seen
your painted women under the gas lamps luring the farm boys.
And they tell me you are crooked and I answer: Yes, it is true
I have seen the gunman kill and go free to kill again.
And they tell me you are brutal and my reply is: On the faces of
women and children I have seen the marks of wanton hunger.

CARL SANDBURG, "Chicago," 1916

LOUELLA WAS NO STRANGER TO THIS CITY OF BIG SHOULDERS, this gritty metropolis that, in 1910, over two million residents called home. Like Frank Cowperwood of Theodore Dreiser's 1914 novel *The Titan*, she had seen from the train window the flat brown land that ringed the city's outskirts, the Chicago River "with its mass of sputtering tugs and its black oily water," and the "little one and two story houses" that stood on the edge of town.[1] Before, on her visits from Freeport with Helen, Louella had enjoyed the bright lights of the theater district and the color of the streets downtown. Now she faced a different Chicago, one of bustling streetcars and open-air markets and filthy, rundown cold-water flats crowded with workers and their families.

Louella was not the only newcomer to seek her fortunes in Chicago. Between 1880 and 1920, nearly two and a half million immigrants arrived, having fled poverty and political persecution in southern and eastern Europe.[2]

Tens of thousands of native-born Americans also went to the city in search of employment, and many of these migrants were women. Self-supporting women—unmarried, divorced, or widowed—were the largest group of native-born Americans to move to Chicago in the early twentieth century. Between 1880 and 1930, the female labor force in Chicago increased from thirty-five thousand to four hundred thousand, or over 1,000 percent. During those years, rural towns in Iowa, Minnesota, and northern Illinois experienced a "defeminization" as daughters left the countryside for work in the city.[3]

In her autobiography, Louella described Chicago as "gutsy."[4] That word better characterized Louella. In the early twentieth century, leaving a philandering husband took strength; women were expected to tolerate affairs, considered a man's prerogative. Depressed but optimistic, Louella moved in with her aunt and uncle Hattie and Eli Oettinger, who had since moved from Freeport to a small flat on the city's North Side. She quickly found a job as a secretary in a company that manufactured stereopticons, an early form of motion picture projector, but when she found that her "chief chore seemed to be playing flunky to the boss's little blonde secretary," she moved on. Louella then secured a position at the *Chicago Tribune,* in the syndication department. Being hired by a newspaper thrilled her, but her enthusiasm was short-lived. Within a week, Louella discovered that her job was essentially clerical—she retyped the syndicated articles that came off the wire—and within two weeks, she was bored. At a salary of only nine dollars a week, considered barely subsistence wages, she was also broke.[5] She allowed herself one luxury—regular trips to the movies.

The cinema flourished in Chicago, with its large immigrant and working-class population. In 1910, there were 407 movie houses for a population of slightly over two million, twice as many movie theaters per capita as in New York.[6] Film fans often went to the movies three, four, or even five times a week, and they were lured to the theater not only by films but also by an emerging motion picture celebrity culture.

Before 1910, the actors who appeared in films were unbilled. Fearing association with the "lowbrow" cinema, they insisted on remaining anonymous. Neither they nor the heads of the fledgling New York–based film companies anticipated the level of curiosity among moviegoers, who sent hundreds of letters to the studios asking for the identities of their favorite screen players. In response to pressure from moviegoers, in 1910 Carl Laemmle, head of the IMP studio, publicized the name of his leading actress, Florence Lawrence. In a carefully planned stunt, Laemmle planted a rumor that Lawrence had been killed in a car accident, then refuted the accident with a flurry of press releases and newspaper stories that he used to publicize Lawrence's name. Laemmle set off a trend for name popularization that resulted in the development of a movie star system, much like the star system that had dominated the theater. By 1911, films were being advertised not only by "brand name"—prior to 1910, studios used their companies' reputations as a marketing tool—but also, increasingly, by the names of the stars who appeared in them.[7]

Drawing on stage tradition, film companies began publicizing personal information about their stars, both in the mainstream press and in two new motion-picture fan magazines. In February 1911, the Vitagraph studio head J. Stuart Blackton launched *Motion Picture* magazine, the nation's first publication devoted exclusively to motion pictures. Although the publication initially printed cinematic plots in short-story form, in 1912 it began printing interviews with popular film actors and question-and-answer columns that answered readers' inquiries about stars' private lives. By January 1913, the "Answer Man," the columnist who presided over the magazine's "Answers to Inquiries" section, claimed that he was receiving twenty-five hundred letters from film fans each month.[8] Beginning in 1912, another new fan publication, *Photoplay,* offered readers a similar diet of star news along with advertisements for perfumes, clothing, and cosmetics, all bearing celebrity endorsements.

Fans devoured the information and begged for more and, by 1912, began to organize into movie star fan clubs. Unlike theater fans, who had the chance of meeting their idols in person, there were few if any opportunities for film fans to see motion picture stars in the flesh. As a result, movie fans depended on tidbits of personal data about stars, rather than personal contact, to create the feeling of intimacy with their idols that was the essence of the fan-star relationship. From the fans' perspective, the more personal the information, the better. But detailed private information about stars' marriages and romantic affairs was the last thing the magazines or studios wanted to reveal. Truthful depictions of stars' often turbulent and scandalous romantic lives, they felt, would only further damage the cinema's already precarious reputation. *Motion Picture*'s Answer Man refused to respond to the hundreds of questions he received each month about actors' marriages and romantic affairs. "Questions concerning the marriages of players," the magazine warned, "will be completely ignored."[9]

By 1913, however, the magazine had changed its policy, publishing slightly more revealing articles that disclosed actors' marital status. But on the whole, the fan magazines' approach to star "gossip" was timid and innocuous. Typical pieces described actors as virtuous, hardworking, and devoted to their spouses. In an article on actress Helen Gardner's home, *Photoplay* gushed, "Here Miss Gardner and her mother, who looks no older than her daughter . . . live happily, plan pictures, design costumes, and receive their friends."[10] In their free time, actors allegedly pursued such hobbies as cooking, embroidery, gardening, reading, and socializing with friends, and the magazines took great pains to distance film actors from their allegedly debauched theatrical counterparts. In contrast to stage life, "with its night work, its daytime sleep, its irregular meals, [and] its traveling and close contact," working for a film studio was stable and dignified. A film "player is located in one neighborhood and is recognized as a permanent and respectable citizen. Evenings can be spent at home, and the normal healthiness of one's own fireside is an atmosphere conducive to refining influences," *Motion Picture* wrote in 1915.[11] These details and "slice-of-life" depictions were, of course, thoroughly false, the concoction of imaginative magazine editors, studio publicity departments, and press agents.

Though the magazines skirted carefully around actors' personal lives, they were aggressive on the subject of scenario writing. In the years around 1910, thousands of moviegoers began writing their own short "scenarios," the one- or two-page plot summaries that were the scripts of early silent films. According to one estimate, by 1913 over twenty thousand fans had submitted scenarios to studios, and thousands more were harboring half-written pieces that sat unfinished in desk drawers.[12] Thankful for the free material, the film studios encouraged the submissions and occasionally offered cash prizes for high-quality material. The fan magazines colluded with the studios, offering advice to aspiring scenarioists and frequently running scenario success stories. In 1912 *Photoplay* reported that Cordelia Ford, a housewife who wrote in her spare time, earned $250 in a screenwriting contest. Helen O'Keefe, who "scribbled" after her children had gone to bed, paid off her debts with a prize from the American Film Company; and Elaine Sterne, winner of the Thanhouser studio's screenwriting contest, earned a position with the studio as its chief scenario writer.[13]

By 1911, Louella was thoroughly immersed in movie fan culture. She bought and read the fan magazines, developed crushes on popular stars, and went to the movies almost nightly. Reviving her long-dormant interest in writing, she also tried her hand at scenarios. She wrote dozens of short scripts, which she sent to a few Chicago film studios, and received dozens of rejections. But she enjoyed the work and was intrigued by the cash prizes, so she persisted. She was determined to see her work on the screen, even if it took years. Little did she know that her encounter with the film industry would come much sooner.

Many film historians correctly cite New York as the moviemaking capital before World War I. But Chicago, between 1907 and 1915, ran a close second. The city had two assets that made it ideal for film production: a central midwestern location, perfect for shipping finished films to either coast, and over ten thousand theater actors and stagehands, frequently unemployed and eager for part-time work in the "flickers." By 1911, Chicago was home to the film industry's official trade journal, *Moving Picture World*, and two studios, Essanay and Selig.[14]

Essanay was founded by Gilbert Anderson, a cowboy actor who had starred in the famous 1903 film *The Great Train Robbery*, and George Spoor, owner of a small chain of movie theaters. Spoor had wanted to go into film production but needed an experienced hand to work with him. In 1907, Spoor and Anderson joined forces as partners and founded the studio, which they named after their initials (*S* and *A*). The studio was known for its slapstick comedies, many of which featured the studio's janitor, Ben Turpin. In one of the studio's first films, *An Awful Skate*, Turpin careened down the streets on roller skates, mowing over pedestrians. Unbeknownst to the film's viewers, the slapstick was hardly staged. Turpin could not skate, and many of the unsuspecting passersby were injured during the filming.[15]

Such disasters were common during Essanay's first years. Like most early film studios of the period, the company was a fly-by-night operation. The cavernous warehouse was packed to the gills with a collection of broken-down props—old clothes, rusted cars, headless mannequins—and its small staff, a troupe of loud and often foul-mouthed former stage actors, puttered around the studio building sets, mending costumes, performing stunts before the camera, and playing practical jokes on each other. Cameramen operated crude, hand-cranked machines, and due to poor indoor lighting, all filming had to be done outside. When the sky turned cloudy, the actors sullenly waited around the studio for the next sunny day. In 1910, Essanay set up a studio in Niles, California, to shoot its cowboy films, but its Chicago crew constantly struggled with lighting problems.[16]

Like most studios, Essanay was inundated by fan-written screenplays, which arrived at the studio at a rate of about a hundred a day. In 1911, George

Spoor decided to hire a full-time staff member to sift through the contributions and advertised in local papers for a "scenario editor." Immediately the studio was swamped with mail. Along with the usual volume of screenplays came hundreds of applications from frustrated novelists, unemployed playwrights, and former newspaper reporters, all eager to be hired for the editorial position. One of those applications was from Louella. Her resume, like most of the others, ended up in the trash.

One day over dinner Spoor's wife announced that she had met a young woman in the neighborhood who was ideal for the position. "Introduce her to me sometime," Spoor mumbled. "She's standing outside the dining room," Mrs. Spoor replied, and motioned for Louella to come to the table.[17]

Maggie Oettinger, Louella's twelve-year-old-cousin, played with a girl named Ruth Helms, who lived next door to Spoor. When Louella found out that Ruth's neighbor was the head of Essanay, she begged the girl to introduce her to Mrs. Spoor, offering her movie tickets if she would make the introduction. Though George Spoor was less impressed than his wife with Louella's possibilities as an editor, Mrs. Spoor persuaded him to hire her. In the spring of 1911, Louella quit her job at the *Tribune* and signed on with Essanay as its chief scenario editor.[18]

The job turned out to be a godsend. The generous income of twenty dollars a week enabled Louella and Harriet to move to an apartment on Magnolia Street, not far from the Argyle Street studio. Before long, Louella was saving a little each week and building a bank account; she was also reestablishing the emotional confidence she had lost in Burlington. She found her work creative and engaging, was thrilled by her position of authority, and for the first time in years, felt part of an intimate community. The sudden boost to Louella's ego allowed her to make friends, meet new men, and pour a prodigious amount of energy into her new career. She returned to Burlington that fall, and on September 29, 1911, Louella and John divorced.[19]

Louella never admitted to the public how her relationship with John Parsons really ended. For the rest of her life, she insisted that she was widowed— Parsons, she claimed, died in World War I. Indeed, after marrying Ruth Schaefer in 1917, John Parsons enlisted in the army and died in 1918 of the flu.[20] But he and Louella had divorced seven years earlier. During the early twentieth century, divorce was still considered a moral transgression, and divorced women often bore the stigma for the rest of their lives. Ashamed, Louella concealed her separation from Parsons from her friends and colleagues, and only her family and closest confidantes knew.

In late 1911, around the time of Louella's divorce, Helen and John Edwards also decided to separate. John Edwards left Dixon and returned to his hometown of Amboy, Illinois, where he lived until his death in 1931.[21] Helen sold the house in Dixon and, for the next seven years, lived with Louella and Harriet in their apartment on Magnolia Street. Essentially Louella's housekeeper, she cooked, cleaned, and cared for Harriet while Louella was at work. During Louella's four years at Essanay, that was most of the time.

Like many men and women involved in early film, Louella told friends that she was working in a "studio," creating the nation's newest "art form." In reality, the Essanay Film Company was less a studio than a factory. Like "sausages," as one director dubbed them, movies were filmed hastily and carelessly and shipped out to exhibitors as quickly as possible. The studio's five harried directors rushed around the Essanay grounds in a frantic attempt to fill their quotas, which seemed to increase every week. Because films were so short—the typical film of 1911 averaged about fifteen or twenty minutes—nickelodeon owners showed several during an evening's program. Moreover, to keep fans interested, they changed the program almost nightly. By 1911, when an estimated ten million Americans were attending movie theaters each week, the demand for films had become overwhelming.[22]

Louella's job, the first stage in the "sausage-making" process, was one of the most important. Each day she sorted through the scripts that came to the studio, found some promising ones, and sent twenty-five-dollar checks to the lucky writers whose works would be made into films. On her desk sat a row of boxes with the names of Essanay's directors, and Louella dropped the new scripts into the boxes randomly. "Directors might yell and moan over my choice of story, but when they were handed a play by me, they didn't have any other court of appeal," she recalled.[23] Often the scripts required editing, and with fellow scenario editor Edward Lowe, Louella frequently added scenes, characters, or instructions for the cameraman. She recalled that she always tried to work in a bride as a character, since "there were a lot of white dresses in the wardrobe."[24]

A humorless "bluestocking," according to one Essanay employee, Louella was consumed by her work. She perpetually scribbled in a yellow notebook, walked around the studio grounds lost in concentration, and complained bitterly when actors talked loudly outside her office.[25] Louella later claimed to have read more than twenty thousand scenarios during her years at Essanay.[26] The manuscripts arrived "on wallpaper, bits of shoe box covers, and torn envelopes" and came from a diverse range of fans—from the "blacksmith, the janitor, and the college girl and boy," Louella recalled.[27] In 1912 she purchased a script from an old woman from Waukegan, Wisconsin, only to discover that the woman had sold the same story to the rival Vitagraph studio. When Louella and George Spoor confronted the woman and asked if she had indeed sold the story to other studios, she smiled innocently. "I got it out of a magazine," she said, "and I have lots more of them if you are interested."[28] Essanay, which had already produced the film, was forced to destroy it, at a loss of several thousand dollars. For not confirming the script's originality, Louella almost lost her job.

When the day's mailbag failed to yield suitable scenarios, Louella took to the typewriter and wrote her own. Her scripts were often maudlin tearjerkers about death, betrayal, or failed romances, and some of them—she wrote over a hundred in all—depicted feminist themes. In a script called the *Broken Pledge,* three women pledge never to marry and instead remain independent; in 1915, it was turned into a film starring Gloria Swanson. Other scripts Louella wrote for specific actors, including the Essanay superstar Francis X. Bushman, who commissioned Louella to write several films that would showcase his athleticism and impressive physique.[29] In 1912, Louella wrote a script titled *Margaret's Awakening* for an aspiring six-year-old actress. The child, who appeared in the film, was billed as "Baby Parsons."

Harriet's career in the movies, cut off by her enrollment in elementary school, lasted only a year. In both *Margaret's Awakening* and a subsequent film, *The Magic Wand,* she had starring roles. In *The Magic Wand,* Harriet played a loving child who hoped to save her poor, single mother from destitution with an imaginary magic wand. The performance rated mixed reviews. One critic called Harriet "wonderfully sweet," though other reviewers were less impressed. "A delightful and very promising situation was quite ruined by its treatment in this particular picture," *Moving Picture World* wrote. "The great trouble with the picture is the child player, who never for a moment forgot the camera and was quite wooden throughout."[30] Back in Dixon they paid no attention to the critics; the town was overjoyed. "On Friday evening at the Dixon Opera House, Dixon people will have the opportunity of seeing pretty little Harriet Parsons taking a lead role in a play, *The Magic Wand,* written for the little girl by her mother," the *Dixon Evening Telegraph* announced in November 1912. "Little Harriet Parsons is said to be a clever little actress and her appearance will be of much interest to the Dixon people."[31]

Perhaps Louella's proudest accomplishment as a screenwriter was the 1912 script *Chains.* The film, about a convicted killer who marries his fiancée while awaiting execution, was based on Louella's front-page story at the *Dixon Star,* and it became one of Essanay's greatest successes. Featuring top stars Ruth Stonehouse, Francis X. Bushman, and Bryant Washburn, it was advertised as "one of the greatest, most powerful and tense dramatic studies ever offered by Essanay."[32] On the eve of his engagement to a young woman, Ruth Keene, Harry Madden becomes entangled in a barn-loft card game with some "dissolute companions." When he detects one of the players cheating, Madden quarrels with him and kills the man with his own revolver. Afterward he hides in Ruth's home but is caught and sentenced to death. Ruth's "innocent love" prompts her to marry Madden in jail. Fan magazines gave the film glowing reviews; the trade journal *Motography* hailed it as a "masterpiece of dramatic construction."[33]

Immersed in a whirlwind daily schedule of writing and editing, Louella was truly in her element. "I think," Louella told interviewers from *Photoplay* magazine, "that I have found my life vocation."[34]

In her autobiography, *The Gay Illiterate,* Louella recalled her years at Essanay as among the most joyful in her life. "Those were the days before the war," she remembered, "overbrimming with excitement. The world was my oyster, and Chicago was providing the cocktail sauce."[35]

The "Essanay gang" was eclectic, to say the least. Actor Wallace Beery, a noisy drunk, chased starlets around the lot, Francis X. Bushman came to work in a lavender limousine, and the cross-eyed Ben Turpin was so homely and clumsy that it was comic. But they were brilliant, and between 1910 and 1915, they were movie pioneers. Along with their colleagues at Biograph, Vitagraph, Selig, Fox, and Universal, the major film companies of the period, the Essanay troupe built the artistic and technological foundations of the movie industry. The studio's performers developed techniques that would become the basis of film acting, and writers and editors like Louella lay the groundwork for modern screenwriting. Essanay's directors and cameramen pioneered a repertoire of cinematic devices that are now the foundation of modern cinematography, such as the fade-in and fade-out and the double exposure. In 1912, the studio brought out a "powerful battery of searchlights" to do some evening filming on the set of a feature, *King Robert of Sicily,* and was praised by trade journals for its pioneering work with night lighting.[36]

The atmosphere at Essanay was chaotic, and minor "emergencies" happened on a near-daily basis. In 1913, several reels of finished film were stolen from the studio and found inexplicably discarded in a nearby cement mixer.[37] A Chicago policeman, not knowing that a train "holdup" in Highland Park was staged for a film, started down the track for the bandits and ruined 140 feet of film.[38] Actors frequently quit the studio when they found more promising work on the stage; when this happened, Louella was often assigned to take their parts. When the wardrobe department ran out of clothes or the prop room fell short of furniture, Louella was dispatched back to her apartment for another dress, chair, or pair of shoes.

When Francis X. Bushman, the studio's top actor, won a "most popular star" contest run by the *Ladies' World* magazine in 1912, he received over seven thousand fan letters from women ranging from teenagers to grandmothers.[39] Bushman hired three secretaries to respond to the letters, and he employed Louella as their supervisor. Her task was to ensure that "his" letters to the fans concealed the truth about Bushman's personal life—that he was married and had five children as well as a lover at the studio.[40] Louella was also told to make sure that the letters were romantic but not too passionate; just enough to keep the fans interested. Once Louella became "too fervent" with her reply, she recalled, "and some woman came in all decked out in bridal array, ready to marry him." An angry Bushman instructed her to be "less personal."[41]

During lunch hours, members of the company, many still in costume— "queerly garbed figures, some of them old and wrinkled and grey-haired, some of them young and gay and vigorous," wrote the film trade journal *Motography*—trouped down to the corner of Broadway and Winona for a working lunch at the Witt Food Emporium. "Jokes and gags are bandied about, this player is joshed and that one praised . . . and a director over in the corner is busily explaining just the sort of costumes he wants for the Colonial drama he is going to stage the first of the week," *Motography* noted in 1913.[42] After hours, many of the Essanay troupe congregated at Sternberg's saloon, on the corner of Argyle Street; others joined Louella, Francis Bushman, and actress Beverly Bayne at Bayne's apartment for long evenings of gin rummy and beer.[43] Life and work were one as Louella and her Essanay colleagues immersed themselves in each others' lives and in the movies. In the end, it was much more than a job. As editor, screenwriter, costumer, accountant, secretary, and in a few instances, even a minor actress, Louella was exposed to virtually all aspects of motion picture production. Ten years later, as a result of the strict division of labor imposed by the studio system that dominated film production between the mid-1920s and late 1940s, this kind of immersion in the artistic, financial, and technical aspects of the filmmaking process would have been impossible. Louella worked at Essanay in one of the most intimate and stimulating environments in the history of American film.

And by 1914, her work had won her a national reputation. That spring, she was mentioned in an article in *Motion Picture* magazine on women screenwriters and appeared in a piece in the *Saturday Evening Post,* which called her a "short-story writer of note."[44] Later that year she was the subject of a feature article in *Photoplay* magazine celebrating her accomplishments both as a writer and as a successful female professional.[45] Indeed, Louella was one of a handful of women who had secured important jobs in motion pictures. As a result of the loose and informal structure of the early industry, and because filmmaking was not yet taken seriously as an art or business, women were able to rise to high positions that would later be inaccessible in the male-dominated studio system. Alice Guy Blache, head of her own film studio, produced more than three hundred movies between 1910 and 1914, and Lois Weber, in 1916, became Universal Studio's highest-paid director before forming her own independent production company. Jeanie MacPherson began working as a screenwriter for director Cecil B. DeMille in 1915, Anita Loos began writing for director D. W. Griffith in 1912, and Frances Marion was America's highest-paid screenwriter from 1916 through the mid-1930s. According to some estimates, women screenwriters wrote nearly a quarter of Hollywood screenplays between 1910 and the 1930s.[46]

Louella's star was rising, and she was not modest about her success. In the summer of 1914, she returned to Dixon for a vacation and wired the *Dixon Telegraph* with instructions to announce her arrival. "Louella O. Parsons of Chicago," the *Telegraph* reported, had "made good" in the big city. As "scenario head of Essanay, every picture put out by the company is her selection and her position is one of the greatest responsibility and requires a brilliance of mind that is rare."[47]

When Louella returned from her trip, she found the studio in a panic. While she was away, someone had decided to balance the books for perhaps the first time in Essanay's history. What they found was terrifying. Though their films had been turning a profit, and the company had maintained its overseas market in spite of the European war, the studio was in trouble.[48] All fingers pointed at Spoor and Anderson, who had mismanaged the studio's finances. Actors and directors rushed around the grounds cursing "S and A," whose bad business sense and poorly planned efforts to expand the studio had brought on the crisis.

In 1913, Spoor and Anderson spent $50,000 to construct a new studio in Niles, California, where the studio's cowboy films were shot. Later that year they built a new Chicago facility down the block from the existing studio on Argyle Street.[49] These expenses would have been manageable had Anderson not decided to hire Charlie Chaplin. A rising comedic star who had worked at the Keystone film studio for $100 a week, Chaplin, in 1914, had finished his contract at Keystone and was negotiating with Carl Laemmle of the Universal Studio when Anderson offered him a weekly salary of $1,250, plus a $10,000 signing bonus. Chaplin accepted and Anderson was thrilled, but when Spoor learned about it, he was furious. Knowing that the studio could not afford Chaplin, Spoor tried unsuccessfully to break the contract. In desperation, Spoor then brought in an "efficiency man," Homer Boushey, to trim expenses around the studio. Boushey's first stop was Louella's office.

Louella hated Boushey, a dour, humorless accountant, and the feeling was mutual. After reviewing the account books in the scenario office, he declared that Louella was financially irresponsible: she had been buying too many scripts and sometimes paid up to $75 for a single manuscript. Not only were the expenses unjustified according to Boushey, but Spoor and Anderson were planning to phase out the scenario editor position and, like many film studios at the time, hire professional screenwriters. From this point on, amateurs who sent scripts received notes saying that, "in line with its policy of progress, the Essanay company has discarded the scenario from its business. The reason is that Essanay photoplays are beyond the scenario stage. The high art of production as standardized by this company cannot be sustained by mere scenarios."[50] Louella's days were numbered, and for the next few weeks she complained to her friends about the "stool pigeon" who was taking away her job.[51]

Strategically, one of those friends was Mary King, an acquaintance from the *Chicago Tribune.* An editor at the paper, as well as fiancée of its publisher, Joseph Medill Patterson, King took pity on Louella and arranged a meeting for her with James Keeley, publisher of the near-bankrupt *Chicago Herald.* King suggested to Keeley that Louella might write a movie column that would boost circulation for the floundering paper. Thrilled at the possibility of again working in journalism, in November 1914 Louella went downtown to the *Herald* office.

Keeley immediately gave her the brush-off. In light of the paper's financial troubles, he had little interest, he explained, in hiring a movie writer. A second-rate publication with a long history of money problems, the *Herald* had narrowly averted bankruptcy when Keeley, formerly an editor at the *Tribune*, purchased the paper in early 1914. Though Keeley's dream was to increase circulation by hiring well-known reporters and expanding the paper's news coverage, his financial backers—industrialist Samuel Insull and Sears, Roebuck president Julius Rosenwald—halted the plan. Instead, the *Herald*, circulation two hundred thousand, remained flimsy and undistinguished. In the words of one critic, it was as "dull as a church sermon."[52]

One of the paper's strong suits was its motion picture coverage. The daily *Herald* carried two movie columns: "Reel Facts," a short column that dispensed news and tidbits of personal information about Chicago film actors, and "In the Picture Players," a daily film review. The Sunday *Herald* also ran two features about movies, "News of the Players" and "Gossip of the Photo Theaters," as well as serialized short stories based on the plots of Essanay films. When Louella returned to the *Herald* office a second time, hoping to convince Keeley to hire her, she found that the publisher had not budged. The paper already had too many movie columns, he replied. How about a Sunday feature on screenwriting? Louella asked. Again Keeley shook his head. Louella then resorted to more desperate measures.

"I was young, and . . . . pretty," Louella recalled. So when she flirted with him, "Mr. Keeley was quite intrigued."[53] Louella's column for the *Herald*, "How to Write Photo Plays," debuted on December 20, 1914. It was the first of a weekly series on screenwriting slated to last through the spring of the following year.

Featuring a large picture of a slim and beautiful Louella with short dark hair and intense, deep-set eyes, the feature took up nearly an entire page of the Sunday magazine section. The photo of Louella was stunning; her prose, unfortunately, was not. Envisioning herself a schoolroom "scenario teacher" and her readers her pupils, she filled her column with haughty platitudes:

> DON'T say after you have been to the moving picture show: "I can write a story every bit as good as the one we just saw." Aim high and say to yourself: "I can and I will write a better story than the one I saw tonight."
>
> DON'T get discouraged over the amount of postage you have spent on worthless scripts.
>
> DON'T read over our lessons hurriedly without absorbing the contents, and expect results. Apply yourself and study hard.
>
> DON'T ask your teacher to read your work, or try to telephone her for assistance.[54]

Despite the clichéd prose, the series was a success. After a few months Louella had nearly five hundred regular readers, who sent her letters asking for advice about both their scripts and their personal matters. "Obey your mother by all means. Mothers have a way of knowing what is best for us, and if she does not want you to write any more letters to your favorite movie actor, do as she says," Louella counseled a young woman.[55]

The screenwriting column, however, was only a part-time job, and throughout the winter of 1914 Louella continued her work at Essanay, waiting for the day when the axe would finally fall. Meanwhile, the studio continued to go downhill. As film studios began producing longer, more sophisticated dramas that drew on literary material, Essanay's repertoire of cowboy films and slapsticks were going out of vogue. When Louella tried to tell Spoor that historical costume pictures, such as Adolph Zukor's famous 1912 production of *Queen Elizabeth*, were the wave of the future, he laughed and continued making his comedies and Westerns. "You're not as smart a girl as I thought you were," he told her.[56]

In mid-December, Louella, Harriet, and Helen left Chicago to spend Christmas in Dixon. After leaving Helen and Harriet in Dixon, Louella traveled alone to Burlington to visit her friend Adeline Moir. Over dinner one night Moir introduced her to a handsome and eligible bachelor named Jack McCaffrey, a forty-year-old steamboat captain who made a living piloting ships up and down the Mississippi. The son of Irish immigrants who had settled in Louisiana and eventually become prosperous plantation owners, McCaffrey had quit his studies at Northwestern University to pursue an adventurous life on the river. After several years working on boats and at odd jobs, he eventually bought a home in LeClaire, Iowa, not far from Burlington, and from his base in LeClaire continued his steamboat work. He had acquired many friends and clients in Burlington, including Adeline's father, Alexander Moir, who had once employed him.[57]

Adeline Moir remembered McCaffrey as "handsome and very intelligent." He was well educated and well spoken, and according to many acquaintances, he bore a strong resemblance to Franklin D. Roosevelt.[58] "He had a marvelous personality," recalled another neighbor. "He was one of the sweetest and one of the kindest people I have ever known."[59] He had also gained a reputation in the area for his skills as a captain, and it was rumored that he was the first to have piloted a riverboat down the Mississippi through the Gulf of Mexico and up the Atlantic coast to New York.[60] When Louella met

McCaffrey, the attraction was instant, and the spark quickly became a flame. By the time she left Burlington, she and McCaffrey were deep in the throes of a passionate romance.

Back in Chicago, Essanay's prize catch, Charlie Chaplin, did not work out as expected. When he arrived at the studio during the first week of January 1915, he was instructed by an office boy to go to the first floor, where "the head of the scenario department, Miss Louella Parsons, . . . will give you a script." "I don't use other people's scripts, I write my own," he snapped.[61] The studio eventually relented and allowed Chaplin to use his own material, but the seeds of an unhappy relationship had been sown. Chaplin left Essanay in late 1916, just as the studio was heading toward bankruptcy.

By that time, Louella was long gone. After convincing Keeley to hire her full-time, Louella quit Essanay in January 1915. In addition to the Sunday screenwriting feature, Louella would now write a daily column, "Seen on the Screen," that combined film reviews with tidbits of gossip about film stars. A precursor to her Hollywood column, it would inform Chicago's movie fans and film industry employees of the latest news from the nation's film studios.

The parting from Essanay was bittersweet. She had loved her work, grown attached to her colleagues, and gained tremendous respect for George Spoor, a "kind, generous" employer whom she would praise for decades. But she was ecstatic about her new job at the *Herald* and deeply in love with Jack McCaffrey, who less than a month after their initial meeting had proposed marriage.

On January 9, 1915, Louella and McCaffrey took a train to Crown Point, Indiana, the infamous "marriage mill" of the Midwest, where weddings were performed twenty-four hours a day, seven days a week, without a waiting period. After a brief civil wedding, they picked up Harriet from Chicago and traveled to McCaffrey's parents' plantation, Hermione, near Tallulah, Louisiana. Harriet stayed at Hermione while Louella and Jack honeymooned in New Orleans. According to Martha Sevier, McCaffrey's niece, Harriet became immediately fond of her stepfather and even wanted to change her last name to McCaffrey, but Louella forbade it.[62]

When the couple returned to Hermione, the McCaffreys offered Jack a lucrative job as a manager on the plantation. McCaffrey accepted immediately, without telling Louella, and when she found out, she exploded. "She wouldn't have any of it, she wouldn't even think about it," recalled an acquaintance, Katharine Ward. "She couldn't tolerate the country. She just couldn't put up with the small town stuff. She was just not going to have it."[63] McCaffrey agreed to return to Chicago and share the Magnolia Street apartment with Helen and Harriet.

This was a poor decision. Helen had known nothing about the elopement, and Louella had never introduced her to McCaffrey. The day after the wedding, a friend of Louella's from the *Herald,* planning to run the news in the paper, called Helen for a comment. "Did you know your daughter was married at Crown Point today?" he asked. "Married! Well I should say not!" Helen screamed over the line before hanging up. Infuriated, the reporter ran the story of his conversation with Helen in the *Herald,* and the story was reprinted in the *Dixon Telegraph* the following day.[64]

Helen then called the *Telegraph* editor and demanded a retraction of the story, which eventually appeared in early February 1915. "Some weeks ago the Chicago papers carried stories of the marriage of Miss Louella O. Parsons to Jack Murray McCaffrey. The articles were copied in the Dixon papers and from their tone led one to believe the wedding had been rather an elopement, but such was not the case," the *Telegraph* lied. "The fact that Mrs. McCaffrey was writing under the name of Louella O. Parsons in the *Chicago Herald* made it desirable to keep her marriage from becoming public and the affair look like an elopement."[65] In late January Helen sent out cards announcing the wedding, to make it appear that the event had been planned, but by then everyone in Dixon knew what had really happened.

Though Louella and McCaffrey loved each other, the marriage was destined to be turbulent. Louella "made a lot more money than he did," recalled a friend from Chicago. "And she started buying clothes and this and that for him, he just didn't like it."[66] There were also disputes about Louella's friends. Louella often dragged McCaffrey to the movies in the evening, or to Beverly Bayne's apartment to spend time with the "Essanay gang." But McCaffrey felt uncomfortable around Louella's movie star friends and thought them a bunch of pretentious snobs. He had little interest in movies and thought them "frivolous" and "boring."

As winter turned to spring and spring to summer, the truth about Jack McCaffrey became clear. Though he was good-hearted and genuinely in love with Louella, and though he grew to care deeply for Harriet and even warmed up to Helen over time, he was slow, relaxed, quiet, and unambitious. And he was uncomfortable socially and unpretentious. He would not have fit well in Hollywood. Ultimately, he was not a good match for Louella.

THREE

The Column

FOR YEARS, Louella boasted that she was the first movie gossip writer in the country. Like much of what she claimed about herself, this was exaggerated. She was not the first journalist to write about film stars. Fan magazines were flourishing by 1915, and the *Chicago Tribune* had two movie writers, Kitty Kelly and the pseudonymous "Mae Tinee," who reviewed films and occasionally commented on actors' personal lives and careers. Also, Louella's column, initially, was hardly a gossip column. In its first two months, "Seen on the Screen" read more like the business column in a film trade journal. "Alfred Hamburger announces he has taken over the Williard Theater on Fifty first Street," ran a typical item.[1]

While local theater owners, actors, and film distributors appreciated the column's focus, fans protested. They could care less about contracts and mergers; they wanted to know about the stars. In response to angry letters from readers, Louella began writing about actors' offscreen lives—what they did at home, what they ate, who they romanced, what they wore.

She was not the first writer for the mainstream press to address these topics. By 1915, *Literary Digest, Sunset,* and the *New York Times,* among other publications, ran occasional features on film actors. Nor was Louella the first to write a celebrity column in a major newspaper. Since the late nineteenth century, newspaper society columns had chronicled the exploits of stage stars, politicians, and other famous figures. But by writing a daily column exclusively devoted to motion pictures and by extending the existing celebrity journalism tradition to film stars, Louella pioneered a new journalistic format and started a new chapter in the history of American celebrity.

Celebrity journalism emerged during the second half of the nineteenth century with the growth of the mass-circulation press. By 1900 there were over a dozen daily papers in New York, and nearly as many in other major

East Coast cities, with circulations that approached a million copies per day. In an attempt to personalize the news and make stories vivid and accessible to readers, papers adopted a style of human interest journalism that, in the words of publisher S. S. McClure, conveyed "a realistic portrait of the human personalities involved."[2] Unlike news stories, which focused on the professional activities of such well-known politicians and businessmen as Thomas Edison, Theodore Roosevelt, and John D. Rockefeller, human interest pieces discussed the private lives of the rich and famous.

These "personality" pieces, with their focus on the subjects' "real selves," reflected new conceptions of selfhood that emerged in the late nineteenth century. According to celebrity historian Charles Ponce de Leon, the rise of cities and the spread of market exchange in the nineteenth century led to a realization of the artificial nature of human interaction. In the marketplace, one could be duped by an artful seller, his or her true intentions masked beneath a carefully crafted performance. The same held true in all forms of human interaction. Thus the rise of the notion of a "performing self": our public "roles" disguise true identities beneath the mask.[3]

Actors, who played with the distinction between authenticity and artifice, soon became icons in a culture that had come to see role playing as a metaphor for life. Theater actors were the most common subject of nineteenth-century personality journalism, and theater gossip columns in newspapers, such as Alan Dale's widely read column for the Hearst syndicate, promised to reveal the real lives of actors. Dale, one of the most popular theater critics in the country in the early twentieth century, had pioneered a style of celebrity journalism in which he described actors' backgrounds and personalities in interview fashion. He wrote his columns as if he were chatting with actors and foregrounded his role as an active participant in the conversations. In Dale's columns, readers learned as much about Dale's personality as about the subjects of his sketches.

Dale's revelations—about actors' home lives, marriages, and personal histories—were gossipy but hardly scandalous. In 1890, Harvard Law professor Louis Brandeis had written an influential article in the *Harvard Law Review* decrying gossip and calling for a legally enforceable right to privacy.[4] In response, the *New York Daily News* publisher Joseph Medill Patterson set down a rule that would be adopted by most major metropolitan newspapers: "no private scandal or private love affairs" were to be reported unless they came to trial in a divorce action, thus becoming part of the public record. Yet sensationalistic pieces, particularly about theater stars, often made the press.

Georgia Cayvan, one of America's popular leading ladies of the 1890s, was named by a New York paper as the other woman in an 1896 divorce case. When actress Sarah Jewett had to undergo treatment for nervous disorders, the *New York Sun* printed rumors of opium use.[5]

The theater was well-enough entrenched in American culture to withstand these attacks. But when Louella began writing for the *Herald,* the movies were young and, to many, morally questionable. In November 1907, the Chicago City Council passed a movie censorship ordinance that granted the general superintendent of police the authority to issue permits for film exhibition. Permits could be refused if the superintendent deemed the film "immoral or obscene."[6] Louella recalled that each Friday, "censorship day," the censor board went to the Essanay studio's Argyle Street headquarters and screened the studio's releases for the week.[7] Films declared objectionable had to be edited or in some cases refilmed, at great expense to the studio. The board was meticulous and efficient; in one year alone, it deleted over fifty thousand feet of film.[8] Meanwhile, a commission conducted a study to determine the effects of the cinema on Chicago's schoolchildren. When the results confirmed that motion pictures were significantly and undesirably influencing children's values and social outlook, the commission urged even more stringent censorship, of "*all* motion pictures in the city based on the negative effects on children."[9]

Far from being an isolated attack, the outcry over movies in Chicago was part of a larger battle waged across the nation. Declaring motion pictures a grave social problem, reformers urged local and state governments to regulate films. In response, Pennsylvania created the first state film censorship board, in 1911, followed by Ohio in 1913. The success of these measures led to a movement for federal censorship, and in 1914, the Reverend Wilbur Crafts, superintendent of a Protestant-led reform group called the International Reform Bureau, pressured Congressman Dudley Hughes of Georgia to introduce a bill creating a federal censorship board that would ban films that were declared "obscene, indecent, immoral, or [that] tend[ed] to corrupt the morals of children or incite[d] to crime." The bill ultimately failed, but, during its well-publicized two-year debate, censorship bills were introduced in Iowa, Maine, Nebraska, South Dakota, and Wisconsin, and by 1918 a total of twenty states were considering similar measures.[10]

Meanwhile, sociological treatises added academic fuel to the reformers' ire. Jane Addams wrote in her 1909 *Spirit of Youth and the City Streets* that the movie theater had become a "house of dreams" in which children were taught "cruel illusions" about life—romantic "absurdities which will certainly become the foundation for their working moral codes and the data from which they will judge the proprieties of life."[11] That children lacked the emotional capacity to distinguish between the screen and reality was a common theme brought up by anticinema activists. Likening movies to a drug that rendered viewers passive and impressionable, several psychologists and sociologists— most famously, Harvard University professor Hugo Munsterberg, author of the 1916 study *The Photoplay: A Psychological Study*—depicted children as helpless victims, pliable and passive surfaces upon which films could leave their tainted imprint.[12] Young women were considered particularly vulnerable to the cinema's corrupting effects, and critics feared the influence of suggestive scenes on female virtue.[13]

The reformers' attack on the cinema reflected deeper social anxieties, as film and cultural historians have amply documented. The middle-class, Anglo Saxon opponents of the cinema were part of a dying social order, a nineteenth-century Protestant society fast giving way to the industrial, secular, ethnically heterogeneous commercial culture taking root in the nation's cities. The reformers feared, quite rightly, that motion pictures, with their powerful emotional and visual appeal, were supplanting the nation's traditional sources of social and moral authority. As revealed in many of the sociological studies on film and youth, children were more deeply influenced by the cinema than by religious teachings or classroom education; mass culture had replaced the school and the church. The criticism of female cinema attendance reflected anxieties over young women's increasing sexual and economic freedom. Young working women often used the movie theater as a site, free from parental supervision, to engage in romantic and sexual encounters and to show off the fashionable clothing styles that signified their independence. Controlled largely by Jewish entrepreneurs, the movies seemed to symbolize the end of Victorianism and the fall of the Protestant elite.[14]

Despite the opposition, the motion picture industry flourished between 1910 and 1915. In an attempt to lure middle-class audiences, exhibitors had created "picture palaces," opulent movie theaters featuring plush seats, marble foyers, electric lights, and live orchestras. In 1910, Thomas Saxe's Princess Theater in Milwaukee opened a "new era in elegance," with its seating for nine hundred, a pipe organ, electric fountains in the lobby, and beveled-plate-glass-and-mahogany doors. The full-length feature film was the standard offering at these palaces. Often an hour or more in length, the new features boasted plots drawn from classical drama and literature. As a result of these developments, and combined with the aggressive marketing of the movie-star system and the rise of such popular film celebrities as Mary Pickford and Charlie Chaplin, the cinema emerged by 1915 as a truly national mass medium. That year, an estimated sixteen thousand movie theaters in America sold fifteen million admissions a week.[15]

Encouraged by the cinema's growth yet aware of the opposition, Louella adopted a narrative strategy in her column similar to that of fan magazines. To appease fans' yearnings for personal information about stars yet dignify the cinema before its opponents, Louella described film actors as virtuous upholders of middle-class values. Adopting Alan Dale's chatty style, she encouraged readers, her "dear friends," to gossip with her "over the back fence" and accompany her on visits to stars' homes, where they would see firsthand the stars in all their unscripted innocence.

In a typical column, Louella allegedly dropped in on an actress to share a meal, help her cook, or enjoy afternoon tea. In 1916, for example, Louella told her readers that she visited "Beverly Bayne at her apartment one evening. Miss Bayne went into the kitchen and cooked a dinner that would make every [restaurant] in the country try to lure her away from the studio. . . . [She was] enveloped in a dark blue kitchen apron with cheeks flushed and engaged in hard work." Later, Louella described in detail an interview she conducted over breakfast with an actress in the star's home—their conversation was intimate "after the fashion of women who are left alone to talk for a solid hour." The actress Vivian Martin, a "pretty child," "has sent me more recipes than any other film player," Louella wrote. Rivaling Myrtle Stedman's talent as a screen star was her "skill in making butterscotch pie."[16] These descriptions, of course, were fabricated, and the interviews, which were scheduled well in advance, usually took place in restaurants and hotel lobbies. Louella and Beverly Bayne were friends, and she often went to Bayne's apartment at night to drink and play cards.

Clearly, Louella's overwrought descriptions of the stars as pure and domestic were meant to defuse long-standing associations of actresses with loose sexuality. These homey chats also had another purpose—to dignify Louella. To win her readers' confidence and disarm the cinema critics, Louella portrayed herself as an amiable yet respectable middle-class mother with good sense and impeccable virtue.

To assure her readers that she was trustworthy ("just folks," as she described it) she played up her rural roots and referred frequently to her friends back in Dixon. This was a shrewd strategy in a nation that was still largely rural and that associated rural imagery with honesty and tradition. She also mentioned Harriet frequently, hoping that her maternal status would cement her propriety. Just as women's reform groups had claimed a maternal right to protect their children through film censorship, Louella argued that good mothers—herself included—used the movies as an educational tool and regulated their children's film consumption with "proper supervision."[17] "Don't let your children see any picture which comes to your theatres first. I have a little daughter, Harriet, . . . [and] I do not allow her to see any film which I have not first censored. The child's little mind is like a beautiful rose bud; if you force it open with unnatural things you will have a warped rose," she wrote in 1916.[18]

To curry favor with the reformers, she even went as far as to ally herself with a movement for educational films being spearheaded by several reform groups. When a local charity group, the Fair Hope League, instituted a Tuesday night program of instructional films for the city's underprivileged youth, she announced, "Here are the directors of a well-known charitable institution deciding that motion pictures are the best medium of presenting entertaining lessons for children. We, who have appreciated the importance of pictures as an educational factor, are delighted that other persons are beginning to give the movies credit for the good they can do."[19] This maternal relationship extended to her interviewees and her readers. She described herself as a "mother confessor" to the stars and urged readers, "Write to me and tell me your troubles. I love to hear other people's troubles."[20]

Despite the preachy tone, the column was a hit. Thanks to her time at Essanay, she had access to some of the most popular stars of the day, including Francis Bushman, Charlie Chaplin, and Mary Pickford. Having been a fan herself, she knew that fans wanted to believe that actors were as amiable and charismatic in real life as they appeared in films. With rosy, glowing details, Louella bolstered their illusions.

By mid-1915, "Seen on the Screen" had earned Louella a reputation among film fans as the city's premiere movie expert. Fans wrote to her for information about their favorite actors; some, lured by Louella's attractive photo, sent her weekly mash notes. "So you saw me on the street and think I am 'heaps' better looking than my picture. Well, that helps some," she responded to one fan. "Why didn't you get up your nerve and come speak to me? Next time don't be afraid. I won't hurt you. Honest."[21] Though she may not have warded off the threat of film censorship or changed the reformers' opinions about the movies, she seemed to have impressed several local conservative women's clubs. Intrigued by Louella's descriptions of the cinema's potential for social and educational benefit, they invited her to speak on the movies at several teas and luncheons.[22]

During her first year at the *Herald*, she scored several important interviews. One of the first was with Mary Pickford, the nation's most popular actress, in the summer of 1915. Like most cross-country travelers, Pickford changed trains in Chicago. She had arranged to briefly visit with *Photoplay* magazine editor James Quirk during the layover. Quirk, accompanied by Louella, went to the station to meet Pickford. The two were terrified by what they saw. Screaming, waving fans reached and clawed at the actress, a tiny woman practically invisible amid the crowd. Quirk and Louella rescued Pickford by routing her through the underground part of the northwestern station to Canal Street, where Quirk had a taxicab waiting.[23] That afternoon, a grateful Pickford consented to an interview with Louella, and the two women began a relationship that would continue throughout their careers.

That summer Louella also interviewed Theda Bara, the vamp made famous by her portrayal of a conniving seductress in the 1915 film *A Fool There Was*. Born Theodosia Goodman in Columbus, Ohio, Bara had been transformed by imaginative press agents into one of the sexiest and most sensational portrayers of wicked women on the screen. Press releases reported that Bara, whose name was allegedly an anagram for "Arab Death," was a temperamental Arabian princess with an insatiable sex drive; lust and heat, they said, ran in her blood. It did not take a genius to realize that all this was ballyhoo, and even the most naïve film fans had a sense that the scandalous Miss B was not all that she claimed. In 1915, press agents sensing that the public was growing wise to the ruse decided to reveal the truth before fans grew tired of the charade. After inviting several Chicago reporters to a press conference in a stifling hot room—Bara wore a fur coat and kept the windows shut, because, as an "Arabian princess," she needed heat—the publicists instructed the actress to throw off the coat, stagger to the window, and shout, "Give me air!" The group of reporters, which included Louella, ran back to their respective offices to print the news. "Her hair is like the serpent locks of Medusa, her eyes have the cruel cunning of Lucretia Borgia . . . and her hands are those of the blood-bathing Elizabeth Bathory, who slaughtered young girls that she might bathe in their life blood and so retain her beauty. Can it be that fate has reincarnated in Theda Bara the souls of these monsters of medieval times?" Louella asked her readers. "Scientists have questioned this most extraordinary of women to secure fresh evidence to support their half-proved laws of transmigration of souls, but the result has only been to prove that, though Miss Bara is the greatest delineator of evil types on the stage or screen today, she is in real life a sweet wholesome woman who detests the abnormal."[24]

By July 1915, when she launched a series of Sunday columns titled "How to Become a Movie Actress," Louella was being advertised as not only the motion picture editor of the *Herald* but also "a photoplaywright, . . . scenario editor . . . and executive since the movies were first in their infancy." Lest her readers feel intimidated by the lofty credentials, she assured them that she was no elite, highbrow critic but was every bit as passionate about the movies as the most ardent fan. She portrayed herself as one of motion pictures' most vocal public defenders, ready to roll up her sleeves and defend the movies at the drop of a hat. She made good on her word in a well-publicized feud with the *Herald*'s drama critic, Richard Henry Little. Little detested the movies, and he never hesitated to share his feelings with his readers. In an article in November 1915, he declared that movies were little more than a "passing fad": "They have certain elements that make them popular for a moment, but art alone endures, and there is no more art in the movies than there is in a bronze guinea pig." When Louella read the article, she flew into a rage. In the next day's column, she asked her readers, "Of what use is Mr. Little's scornful attitude? The movies are here to stay. Let the legitimate and its followers do their worst. Every blow directed at the motion picture is a sign of weakness on the part of the fast fading legitimate stage." She gave Little the silent treatment for over a week. Though the two made amends, she never forgave him for criticizing what she described as the world's "most wonderful art."[25] But no controversy incurred her wrath more than the "battle" over *The Birth of a Nation*.

The saga began in May 1915, when filmmaker D. W. Griffith released his three-hour epic. With a production budget of two hundred thousand dollars and a cast of thousands, it was the most elaborate and costly film ever produced. It was also violently and virulently racist. Described in advertisements as a "historical romance of the Ku Klux Klan," the film glorified the Klan's reign of terror in the South in the aftermath of the Civil War and was wildly popular among Southern audiences. President Woodrow Wilson, a former history professor who was one of the scholars Griffith consulted for the film, described *The Birth of a Nation* as "history written with lightning." One of the highest-grossing films in American history, it generated as much criticism as praise. Following protests led by the National Association for the Advancement of Colored People, the film was banned in several cities.

But not in Chicago, where the city's police board granted Griffith a permit to exhibit the film. No sooner had the license been issued than Chicago Mayor William Thompson, claiming that the permit was a mistake, banned the film on the grounds that its racist theme would incite riots, as it had in several other cities. Shortly after the injunction, Joseph McCarthy, a local booking agent for Griffith's films, filed suit against the city and began building a case against Mayor Thompson. Seeking support, McCarthy contacted one of the city's film "experts," a reporter from the *Herald* named Louella Parsons. In a secret showing of the film arranged by McCarthy, Louella and her brother, Eddie, who now lived in Chicago, viewed the three-hour film. They left awestruck. It was, Louella recalled, the "finest motion picture" they had ever seen.[26] A writer for the *Herald,* one of Louella's colleagues, thought otherwise. Supporting Thompson's decision, he deemed the film "full of morbid emotions" and urged the city to "let it stay barred."[27]

Amazed that Griffith's "screen symphony," as she dubbed it, could receive such criticism, Louella sprang into action. Approaching Keeley in his office, she demanded a retraction of the article—or at the very least, that she be allowed to print a positive review of the film. Keeley insisted that he see the film first, and upon Louella's request, exhibitor McCarthy arranged a special screening for the *Herald* editor. Impressed by what he saw, Keeley gave Louella "carte blanche to write anything I saw fit." She then started her own newspaper campaign on behalf of the film, which she described as a "colossal production" and Griffith as "the master producer of motion pictures." "It was Griffith who first lifted pictures from the mediocre and gave them the real creative power they now possess," she gushed. "He is the pioneer Belasco of pictures, and for this success, born of both hard work and talent, he deserves the highest praise."[28] In late May, when Griffith was in Chicago for the hearing, Louella interviewed him: "I want to say that it was the moment I have lived for, to personally meet this screen poet and hear from his own lips the miracle tale of his film symphonies."[29]

The court decided in favor of *The Birth of a Nation,* declaring not only that the permit had been gained lawfully but also that there was no proof the film would "engender race animosity against the Negro citizens of our community."[30] The film ran for weeks in Chicago, reaping enormous profits; Lillian Gish, the film's star, became a celebrity, and Louella and Griffith, who was in Chicago during the hearings, became friends. Never once questioning the racist content of the film, for the rest of her life Louella remained proud of her involvement in the case, referring to it as a victory for the movies and free speech.

That fall Louella triumphed again—this time in the publishing field. In late August 1915, *How to Write for the Movies,* a two-hundred-page volume based on her screenwriting series for the *Herald,* was released by the A. C. McClurg publishing house and within weeks became a local best-seller. Offering detailed advice on virtually every aspect of script construction, the book was adopted by the University of Chicago as a textbook and would go down in film history as an early classic in the screenwriting field. (One Hollywood screenwriter, Dorothy Farnum, attributed her own success to Louella's book, and, more than ten years later, it was still described by one writing manual as having a "mint of good advice.")[31] The book featured sections on plot construction, synopsis writing, and avoiding plagiarism, peppered with inspirational clichés. "Write something that tells the simple truth, and yet at the same time stimulates the finer ideals and higher instincts of humanity. Make people see life as it is, without preaching. Touch their emotions, but leave them cleared like the keen air after a refreshing rain," Louella advised.[32]

The success of *How to Write for the Movies* won her an offer to lecture at the annual Chautauqua in Dixon. On the evening of August 7, 1916, at 7:30, an audience of thousands watched as Louella introduced her talk, "Proper Films for Little Folks and Famous Film People I Have Met." "I am not a speaker," she announced shyly. "I am only a scribbler and you must not expect any William Jennings Bryan nights of oratory."[33] As the crowd laughed at Louella's reference—Bryan's speech at the Dixon Chautauqua had been one of the most memorable events in local history—Louella cleared her throat and pointed to a large movie screen.[34] There, the audience saw a short film, compliments of Louella's Essanay friends, that depicted the actors' "home life and characteristic attitudes"—in other words, shots of stars goofing around at home and at the studio.[35] When Louella told them that she knew the actors personally, the crowd was spellbound. Louella later recalled that during the talk she was "scared to death," because "the whole town was turning out for my appearance and I was trying my best to be very dignified and act very important." After Louella was interviewed by two local papers, Harriet followed the reporters outside. "Take a tip from me and don't go to hear mother," she told them. "She's terrible—I heard her rehearse."[36]

Though Louella spoke that summer in several midwestern towns and cities, including Kansas City, she maintained that her Dixon lecture was one of her greatest accomplishments as a public speaker. "Chautauqua audiences are the most critical, and I held their undivided attention for one hour and a quarter. There was no getting up and leaving, no loud whispering or laughing, and one old man who has attended every meeting told me that my lecture was the most interesting this year," she reported to the Redpath Bureau, the booking agent for the midwestern Chautauqua circuit.[37] Billed by the *Dixon Evening Telegraph* as one of the "most prominent" movie writers in America, she returned to Chicago that September exhausted but proud.[38]

The return of the big star went unnoticed. Though Louella had earned a reputation among Chicago film fans, in the *Herald* building she was little more than a girl reporter. Like most newspapers of the period, the *Herald* was virtually an all-male enterprise. Bill Forman, the sports editor, cracked lewd jokes, Jim Keeley barked out orders like a drill sergeant, and reporter Jack Lait, whom Louella called the paper's "star scribbler," chain-smoked while working late into the night.[39] The gaunt, unkempt Richard Henry Little penned his lofty criticism in the drama department on the fourth floor, and Felix Borowski, his counterpart in music, wrote similarly purple prose. Unlike drama criticism, considered to be serious and intellectual, movie writing was deemed frivolous and thus appropriate for women. A journalism handbook of the period, echoing the attitudes of most male editors, claimed that "women, because . . . [of] their quick and responsive imagination [and] their intense preoccupation with children, make good moving picture critics."[40] Chicago's two female movie columnists, Louella and her friend Frances Peck, who wrote the "Mae Tinee" movie column for the *Chicago Tribune,* received little praise from their male peers, who refused to take their work seriously. Ben Hecht, a reporter for the *Chicago Daily Journal* who later became a well-known Hollywood screenwriter, recalled that Louella had a poor reputation among the city's journalists and at one point called her "the worst reporter the town ever knew."[41]

In reality, Louella's work was far more intelligent and competent than her critics gave her credit for. Though her prose was often ponderous—in a typical column from 1915, she gushed that the actress Lillian Gish was "so delicate and pink and golden in her coloring that the word ethereal seems to fit her more nearly than any other term I have heard applied to her"—she was an excellent reporter.[42] Though she often relied on personal connections and studio press releases for information, she also did a good deal of footwork on her own. By the end of her first year, she had honed an approach to news-gathering that was resourceful, shrewd, and, given the conventions of the era, highly unladylike. She sneaked into the theaters attended by stage and screen stars, loitered for hours in the lobby of the Blackstone Hotel, a popular hang-out for actors, and eavesdropped in bathrooms. She learned to push through crowds of screaming fans to interview actors and to dash off thousand-word columns in an hour or less. In 1916, when the famed stage actress Doris Keane fainted onstage during one of her Chicago performances, Louella, who was in the audience, pushed her way backstage and "overheard the doctor say something about a visitation from the stork."[43] She dashed to the *Herald* office to print the exclusive story. As a reporting strategy, Louella frequently adopted a guise of absentmindedness: she often looked distracted and stared into the distance when she spoke. Stars, she discovered, were more likely to speak candidly when they thought she was not listening. Louella worked constantly, often twelve or fourteen hours a day, and spent late nights in the *Herald* office typing the next day's copy. She read film trade journals and fan magazines from cover to cover and scoured local publications for movie news.

Louella was not only honing her reportorial skills and her knowledge of film but also developing her talents as a critic. Each month she was invited to dozens of film premieres, and by the end of her tenure at the *Herald* she had earned a reputation as an accomplished film reviewer. Not one to mince words, Louella never hesitated to write scathing reviews, even if it meant attacking her Essanay friends. "The story itself was complicated, unconvincing, and highly improbable," she wrote of Essanay's production of *The Opal Ring.* "What a shame perfectly good energy had to be wasted."[44] Her comments were regularly reprinted in trade publications, including the nationally circulated journal *Moving Picture News;* excerpts from her reviews also appeared in the fan magazines *Motion Picture* and *Photoplay.* Though Louella would become famous for her celebrity reporting, many of her Chicago readers told her that they valued her criticism as much as her gossip.

She was also forging connections with the leaders of the burgeoning film industry. No longer the haphazard, chaotic business it had been in the Essanay days, by 1915 it had transformed into a sophisticated, well-organized, and powerful multimillion-dollar industry. According to the *New York Times,* it was the fifth most important industry in the United States, behind agriculture, transportation, oil, and steel.[45] During her years at the *Herald,* she met Carl Laemmle, head of the Universal studio; independent producer Louis B. Mayer; and theater chain owner Marcus Loew. Through them, she met Adolph Zukor, head of the Famous Players studio and future president of the Paramount Studio; Sam Katz, later an executive at Metro-Goldwyn-Mayer in Hollywood; and Samuel Goldfish, manager of the Jesse Lasky Film Company, who eventually changed his name to Samuel Goldwyn.[46] To these executives, Louella was an important ally, and her column a major source of local publicity for their productions.

Once, Louella diverged from movie reporting when Keeley gave her a "sob sister" assignment. Sob sister journalism had begun in the late nineteenth century when women reporters, most famously Winifred Black of the Hearst papers, were assigned to report in a sensationalistic, dramatic style on trials, disasters, and other emotionally charged events. The most famous examples of this journalism stemmed from the Harry Thaw–Stanford White murder trial of 1907, during which writers Dorothy Dix, Ada Patterson, and Nixola Greeley Smith gained national exposure for their stories. Though criticized for its sensationalism, sob sister writing launched many of the best female journalists of the early twentieth century.[47]

In July 1915, the *Eastland,* a ferry on Lake Michigan, capsized, killing eight hundred passengers, and Keeley sent Louella to interview the victims' families. "In the beginning I approached these small houses with reticence," she remembered. "But the eagerness of the people who were of the poorer classes to tell their stories made me forget myself. There is a curious, morbid desire to talk among people who have had trouble, and their willingness to tell me little intimate stories of their loved ones was one of the most touching things I have ever encountered."[48] She came back to the office with tears streaming down her cheeks. Years later, she still believed that the story, which appeared on the front page of the *Herald,* was one of the best she ever wrote.

Meanwhile, Louella's personal life was becoming increasingly difficult. Mc-Caffrey spent most of his time on different steamship jobs and was rarely at home. Moreover, Louella's relationship with Helen had become tense. Still angry about Louella's elopement, Helen also hated the fact that her daughter was writing about the "despised and ridiculed movies."[49] (When Louella landed her job at Essanay, Helen had told her, "When you go to church tomorrow, you needn't say that you are working in those movies. Just say you're writing for a living, and that won't be untruthful.")[50] To make matters worse, Helen was suffering from diabetes.

Louella's relationship with her own daughter, Harriet, was equally problematic. Now in elementary school, Harriet resented the time that Louella lavished on her work and took solace in books. Louella tried to soothe her with gifts and parties; on an occasion Harriet recalled many years later, Louella invited the famous cowboy actor William S. Hart to dinner, making Harriet "the most popular 10-year-old on Magnolia Street."[51] Louella even managed to get a picture of Harriet into a fan magazine. Harriet frequently went to Dixon during the summers, and Rae Shepard, a Dixon resident who was Harriet's age, remembered one time when Harriet asked her to go to the bookstore with her. "She said her mother had written her and told her [Harriet's] picture would be in a movie magazine that month. I was sure Harriet was wrong. Well, we did get the magazine—and there was Harriet's picture. She was sitting in a big chair with a book in her lap. . . . It was almost like Harriet was a celebrity," Shepard recalled.[52] These small offerings, however, were poor substitutes for time spent together, and Louella's intense commitment to her work continued to disappoint Harriet. Louella even had the gall to let work interfere with her daughter's birthday parties. On the girl's fourteenth birthday, Louella "ruined" her party, Harriet recalled, by dashing out to write the breaking story of Douglas Fairbanks and Mary Pickford's elopement.[53]

In November 1917, Keeley sent Louella to New York to cover her first film industry conference, a nationwide meeting held by the Motion Picture Theater Owners of America. Keeley had given her an expense account, which Louella managed deftly. "With shudders I blew $35 for a black dress that I considered a symphony of sophistication and gaily charged it to 'room service'!" she recalled. During the trip to New York, she visited Fort Lee, New Jersey, home of a large complex of film studios that housed the Fox, Metro, World, and Goldwyn film companies. At Fort Lee, she renewed her contacts with actresses Alice Brady, Mae Marsh, Theda Bara, and Ethel Clayton, and lunched with Lewis Selznick, head of the World Film Company, whose young son David, she recalled, was "wearing knee pants."[54] Years later, Louella would remember that conference as a turning point in her life, when she first became aware of her power and potential as a writer. "Always a ham at heart," she recalled, "I felt every eye in the place was on me as I registered 'Miss Louella Parsons, columnist, Chicago, Ill.'" At last, "I felt I had come into my own."[55]

She returned to Chicago thrilled by the "wondrous movie ball," the marble lobby of the Astor Hotel, and the "rushing, hurrying crowd."[56] But when she returned to the *Herald,* the mood was somber: the paper had been sold. Reporters made frantic phone calls, counted the dollars in their savings accounts, and cursed the name of the villain who had purchased their beloved *Herald*—William Randolph Hearst.

A flamboyant, controversial, eccentric multimillionaire, the publishing magnate William Randolph Hearst was one of the most important figures in American mass media. Born in San Francisco on April 29, 1863, to Phoebe Apperson Hearst, a former Missouri schoolteacher, and George Hearst, a miner from Missouri who fell into riches when he unearthed a silver lode, Hearst grew up surrounded by wealth, prestige, and privilege. Determined to use the family's riches for "uplifting" purposes, Phoebe Hearst regularly whisked young Willie off to Europe for grand tours of the continent's finest art and culture. At home in San Francisco, he lived in a palatial mansion, studied with private tutors, and was spoiled rotten.

After an unsuccessful stint at Harvard that resulted in his expulsion (always a practical joker, Hearst had clowned himself out of school), Hearst took over a failing newspaper in 1887 that his father had acquired, the *San Francisco Examiner.* To boost circulation, Hearst transformed the paper by using large illustrations, wild, trumped-up stories, and screaming headlines. He sensationalized the news, he explained, because "the public is even more fond of entertainment than it is of information."[57] The *Examiner* quickly became famous for its stunt journalism, and in one of the paper's most famous stunts, Hearst had a reporter jump ship in the San Francisco Bay and timed how long it took for the Coast Guard to arrive. When the rescue ferry showed up over three minutes later, long enough for a person to drown, the *Examiner* turned it into a front-page story blasting the Coast Guard for its inefficiency.[58] In another instance, Hearst reporter Annie Laurie was ordered to dress in rags and faint in the street for an exposé on the city's treatment of indigent women. By the 1890s, the Hearst press set a new standard for sensationalism and entertainment value in journalism, forcing its competitors to adopt similar practices.

In 1895, Hearst took his carnivalesque style to New York. He purchased the *New York Journal,* the paper famously accused of starting the Spanish-American War in 1898. When Hearst sent reporter Frederick Remington to Cuba to cover a possible native insurrection, Remington wrote to say that "everything is quiet. There is no war." Hearst replied, "Please remain. You furnish the pictures and I'll furnish the war."[59] The warmongering *Journal* hyped the tensions in Cuba so mercilessly that it pushed public opinion to support military intervention.

Since his days at Harvard, Hearst had harbored political aspirations. In 1903, he was elected to the House of Representatives and later ran, unsuccessfully, for mayor and governor of New York on "trust-busting" campaigns. In the spirit of the Populist and Progressive movements of the day, he argued that trusts in the milk, electricity, and railroad industries were fleecing Americans of their hard-earned wages and called for reform. Meanwhile, as he decried the exploitation of workers by money-hungry capitalists, he continued to build his wealth and a vast publishing empire. By 1920, Hearst owned twenty-two daily newspapers, six magazines, two syndication services, and a film company, in addition to ranches, mines, millions of dollars of New York real estate, and a priceless collection of European art.[60]

Hearst was not entirely to blame for the *Herald*'s ill fortunes. The newspaper's finances had always been shaky, and in 1916 Keeley committed an embarrassing blunder that only hastened the paper's demise. In an attempt to boost circulation, Keeley persuaded a professor of sociology, made famous after he had been caught in an affair with the wife of a prominent manufacturer, to write a series of articles on whatever topic he chose. The result was an embarrassing series about sex—about man's "great passions" and "basic urges"—that essentially hammered the nails in the coffin. Keeley sold the paper to Hearst at a loss, costing his backers an estimated three million dollars. Disgusted with journalism, Keeley spent the rest of his life as vice president of public relations for the Pullman Company.[61]

Most of the *Herald* employees assumed that they would lose their jobs. But in late 1917, Hearst executive Arthur Brisbane announced that Hearst planned to keep the best writers and reporters for the new publication, to be named the *Herald Examiner*. Rather than relieve the panicked reporters, the announcement threw them into a quandary. They needed their jobs, but like most Americans at the time, they despised Hearst.

In 1917 Hearst was, in the words of one biographer, "an object of national detestation."[62] America had just entered the world war, and Hearst was rabidly anti-interventionist and, by some accounts, pro-German. Throughout the country in 1917, images of Hearst had been burned in effigy, and in many cities Hearst publications were boycotted. In one of the most famous acts of anti-Hearst propaganda, the *New York Tribune,* a longtime opponent of Hearst, released a six-part series that accused Hearst of being a German sympathizer and a traitor to his country. The pamphlets were published under the title "Coiled in the Flag—Hears-s-s-t."[63]

Richard Henry Little took Louella to a window and pointed to a milk truck. "See that milkman?" Little asked. "Well go take his job—do any damned thing, but don't ever work for Hearst!"[64] But Louella was uninterested in politics or the war; she needed an income, and she was determined to keep her job. One evening she spotted Arthur Brisbane in the Blackstone Hotel, where she was waiting to interview an actor, and she asked him whether she might be able to continue "Seen on the Screen" on the new *Herald Examiner*. Brisbane, a fiercely intimidating man with a perpetually dour expression, responded without hesitation. Claiming that there was not enough "serious" interest in the movies, he barked that there was no need for Louella on a Hearst paper: not now, not next year, and most likely *never*. Louella's last installment of "Seen on the Screen" appeared on April 30, 1918.

Again Louella's life was at a crossroads. After looking in vain for a reporting job in Chicago, she began considering the possibility of moving to another city. But she was unsure. Frozen with indecision, she waited in Chicago while her bank account dwindled. *Photoplay* editor James Quirk offered her a token assignment, an article about the impact of the movies on the war effort. "Propaganda," which appeared in September 1918, praised D. W. Griffith's *Hearts of the World* as the most "effective ammunition aimed at the Prussian empire."[65] For the piece, Louella received a generous twenty-five dollars, but it was hardly enough.

Meanwhile, New York loomed as a possibility. D. W. Griffith introduced her to a press agent who offered her a job as a publicity writer at New York's Pathé film studio.[66] John Flinn, a friend who was a publicist at the Famous Players studio, mentioned that a New York newspaper, the *Morning Telegraph*, might be looking for a movie columnist. Despite the offers, she remained unconvinced, reluctant to move more than a thousand miles east, until one day at the bank she saw Mary Gish, mother of actresses Lillian and Dorothy. "How can you hesitate for a moment when New York offers so much wider opportunity for your talents?" Mrs. Gish asked. Struck by the simple truth in her words, Louella bought train tickets, went home, and announced to Helen and Harriet that they would be moving the following week.[67]

The departure was torturous. "I couldn't see through the tears that blinded my eyes as the train pulled away from the familiar landmarks," she later wrote. Louella could not bear to leave this "lush, rowdy" town where she first saw success, and in her heart, she never really did. Over thirty years later, she claimed, she was still waving good-bye.[68]

FOUR

New York

LOUELLA OFTEN WONDERED WHAT WOULD HAVE HAPPENED if she had moved to Los Angeles instead of New York. By 1918, Hollywood, which produced over three quarters of American films, was fast becoming the nation's movie capital.[1] In the new empire of sun, citrus, and celluloid, reported the newspapers and fan magazines, former mechanics and waitresses were transformed into glittering screen idols, sometimes literally overnight. While the newly minted film stars played out their real-life fantasies in their sprawling mansions, automobiles, and nightclubs, a cast of supporting characters—studio technicians, set and costume designers, publicists, and editors—made more modestly comfortable lives in the stuccoed bungalows and pastel-hued apartment buildings that lined the streets. In 1905, only five thousand residents called Hollywood home; fifteen years later, thanks to the film industry, the population had risen to over thirty-six thousand.[2]

Still, in 1918, New York was probably the better choice for the up-and-coming film columnist. The executive offices of most studios were headquartered in New York, which meant that all major decisions concerning production and distribution were issued from the East, and many of the screen's most popular actors, who had started their careers on Broadway, continued to live and act in New York. With a population of over five million and over three hundred movie theaters, the city was the nation's most lucrative venue for film exhibition.[3]

New York was also the center of the American press. After the making of women's garments, publishing and printing was the city's second largest industry, and by 1920 New York boasted over a dozen major daily newspapers, ranging from the slightly scandalous *Telegraph* to the stately *New York Times*. When Louella arrived in New York, the newspaper industry was at its peak. Between 1918 and the mid-1920s, before the advent of radio, daily newspapers were one of the most, if not *the* most, popular source of news and entertainment both in New York and across the nation. Rapid urbanization, mechanical improvements in newspaper printing, and rising literacy levels in the late nineteenth century had contributed to the tremendous growth of the newspaper medium. By 1920 over 40 percent of American city dwellers subscribed to a daily newspaper, the highest subscription rate in the history of the American press. New York alone produced 15 percent of the nation's newspapers, and in 1919 the city's publishers churned out papers at a rate of one copy for each of New York's five million residents.[4]

The atmosphere, Louella recalled, was brisk, noisy, and brimming with excitement. Honking autos jammed the streets, throngs of hurried pedestrians pushed and shoved one another on the crowded sidewalks, and throughout the city rang the constant *clang-clang-clang* of perpetual construction—bridges, streets, apartments, and skyscrapers, which during the 1920s were being built at a fast and furious pace. Not only was New York growing by leaps and bounds as a steady stream of migrants from Europe and rural America flooded into the city, it was advancing culturally, commercially, and artistically in ways unprecedented in American history. With its nightclubs and theater, its avant-garde literary and artistic scene, its thriving intellectual community and multimillion-dollar advertising and publishing industries, New York was leading the nation into a new consumer- and leisure-oriented modern age. Louella had stepped into—and indeed, would become an important contributor to—a media-driven, style-conscious culture that had elevated the power of images and image making to new and dizzying heights.

In her autobiography, Louella claimed that she arrived in New York as a poor war widow, lonely, jobless, and with a growing child to feed. She allegedly showed up on the doorstep of her brother, Eddie, who—after chastising her for moving to New York, a "tough town"—agreed to put her up while she looked for a job and a place of her own. Two weeks later, she moved into an apartment with Harriet and a housekeeper named "Jennie Mattocks," who had supposedly accompanied her from the Midwest. The happy trio would continue the life they had started in Chicago, with "Jennie" playing surrogate mother to Harriet while Louella worked.

Nothing could be further from the truth. Eddie, who had married and was by then a father, never moved to New York but stayed in Chicago. Meanwhile, Louella, Harriet, Maggie Oettinger, and "Jennie Mattocks" (the pseudonym Louella used for Helen) pooled their meager funds and squeezed into a small apartment on 116th Street. McCaffrey may have joined them briefly, but he and Louella fought because he "wasn't taking his rightful place in the family," according to one acquaintance. In Louella's eyes, McCaffrey "wasn't able to make enough money."[5] In 1918 McCaffrey found work operating an excursion boat on the Hudson River, then returned to the Midwest to take up work on the Mississippi. Not long into Louella's time in New York, he had disappeared completely from her life.

Shortly after her arrival, Louella went to the Pathé studio where, as D. W. Griffith had promised, there was a job awaiting her in the publicity department. After her success at the *Chicago Herald,* a desk job at Pathé seemed like an insult, and Louella pressed on in her search for newspaper work. Through John Flinn, she arranged an interview with editor William E. Lewis of the *Morning Telegraph,* and on a warm June morning set out for the office on West Fiftieth and Eighth Streets.

The *Telegraph* was a "theater and turf" paper known for its extensive (and somewhat flippant) coverage of sports, financial, and theatrical news. (Shortly before Louella's arrival, the *Telegraph* had announced the refusal of the English poet laureate to grant the press an interview with the headline "King's Canary Refuses to Chirp.")[6] Though Louella knew that the paper was hardly prestigious, she also knew that working on *any* New York paper meant readers and recognition on a grand scale. The city's literary and journalistic circles were made up of the nation's brightest writing talent: H. L. Mencken, Fannie Hurst, Dorothy Parker, Alexander Woollcott, Edna Ferber, and Damon Runyon wrote for New York papers in the 1920s and not only were read in New York but also were syndicated throughout the world. As historian William R. Taylor has noted, landing a job at a New York paper in the second and third decades of the twentieth century was "a little like playing the Palace."[7]

Louella may have dreamed of playing the Palace, but she ended up in a barn. Befitting its slightly raffish reputation, the *Telegraph* was headquartered in a former stable that had once housed the city's horsecar lines. As Louella approached the office, she may have smelled dirt, hay, and hooves—a distinct and distinctly unpleasant aroma that was the source of frequent complaints by the paper's staff and visitors. "The city room was always cluttered up with all sorts of people who didn't seem to have any business there," recalled Heywood Broun, who worked for the *Telegraph* from 1910 to 1912. "Very often you couldn't get to your desk because there would be a couple of chorus girls sitting there waiting for a friend who was finishing an editorial." A poker game "had been going on practically since Teddy Roosevelt charged up San Juan Hill," prostitutes and racketeers consorted with reporters, and the oaths and tall tales were as thick as the cigarette smoke that only partially masked the barnyard stench. Former gunslinger and Dodge City sheriff Bat Masterson was the paper's sports columnist, and when an enemy from Masterson's Wild West days sauntered into the office threatening to even an old score, the staff fled the building for fear of straying bullets. "I went to a car barn," Broun lamented, "instead of a school of journalism."[8]

Editor William E. Lewis, a veteran journalist who had gotten his start as a reporter in frontier mining towns in the 1880s, was friendly but gruff. Why did the *Telegraph* need a movie columnist? he asked Louella. The paper already had a daily movie page, filled with news and information culled from studio press releases. Louella then reached into her purse and pulled out a stack of letters from studio heads Carl Laemmle, Lewis Selznick, and Adolph Zukor, whom she had met in Chicago. The letters praised Louella's reportorial skills, her extensive knowledge of the industry, and the impact of her *Herald* column on Chicago film attendance. "Seen on the Screen" had been instrumental in drumming up public interest in stars and films, and its effect had been felt at the box office. "You wrote those letters yourself," Lewis said. Louella shook her head, and Lewis realized she was serious. Louella could bring important studio connections to the *Telegraph* and, with them, not only film news but also lucrative advertising.

At the end of the interview, Lewis was impressed but still not convinced. "I have to think about it. I'll give you a decision in two days," he said. But two days was too long for Louella to wait, and she called Lewis the following day. "I'm going out of town for a few days," she lied, "and I thought maybe you had some word." "You're going out of town? Where?" Lewis asked. There was a long pause. "Brooklyn," Louella replied confidently. Lewis chuckled; he knew he had a real rookie on his hands. "Before you take that long trip," he said, still laughing, "come in and talk to me." At that moment she knew she had won the job.[9]

On June 9, 1918, the *Telegraph* announced: "Louella O. Parsons, whose special moving picture stories and film criticisms are familiar to everyone in the moving picture industry," had joined the paper as a movie columnist. Louella wrote to Dixon proudly: "I really have made a very satisfactory arrangement. Am to have an office at 1493 Broadway and shall do my work away from the working end of the paper. For this they are paying me more than I made on the *Herald*, and in addition I have reserved the right to syndicate my work." The *Telegraph* boasted to readers that "Miss Parsons has a large personal acquaintance with stars, producers and directors, and is especially noted for her chatty, intimate interviews with them. . . . She will tell what is happening each day in moving picture circles. The entire industry is her field and everyone with a moving picture secret can give it to Miss Parsons for the *Morning Telegraph*."[10] With the exception of the film review sections in the *World* and the *Tribune*, Louella's column would be the only column in the city devoted exclusively to motion pictures.

The "moving picture secrets" that the *Telegraph* promised, however, were hardly the stuff of celebrity gossip. Lewis had made it clear that Louella's new column, "In and Out of Focus," would be primarily a trade column for the actors, theater owners, and studio personnel who were among the paper's regular readers. (The *Telegraph* was often dubbed the "favorite breakfast food of theatrical New York.") For "In and Out of Focus," Louella attended conventions, interviewed studio heads, and reported industry-related financial and production news. Louella did, however, run occasional celebrity "personality" pieces for the movie fans among her readers. "One does not have to have a key to the book on human nature to get a keen insight into the character of Alice Joyce," she wrote in a 1919 interview. "She breathes a veritable atmosphere of real womanhood. . . . If the eyes are the window of the soul, Alice Joyce must have a Madonna-like quality in her nature, for she has the most perfect Madonna eyes I have ever seen."[11] Of a lunch interview with actress Betty Blythe at the Gotham Hotel, she said, "Even queens must eat. Her royal highness managed eggs and bacon, toast, marmalade, prunes and tea, proving as well as being beautiful she has a hearty and healthy appetite. The queen, you see, is a mortal, even as you and I."[12] According to Louella, stars were at once ordinary and extraordinary, godlike yet mortal—a paradoxical description, common to American celebrity writing, that allowed fans to worship and at the same time identify with their idols.[13]

Moreover, Louella explained, stars were both made *and* born. Though she stressed the innate beauty and "personality" of the men and women who became cinema stars, she also used her column to expose to readers the artificial and constructed nature of movie stardom. She described the typical "rags to riches" rise of struggling young actors and actresses to fame and fortune—a process that involved luck, perseverance, and hard work, in addition to a good deal of manipulation by the studios. In her column, Louella revealed the makeovers and publicity campaigns that studios used to transform actors into stars, thus giving readers a sense of collusion in, if not knowledge about,

the star-making process. Readers felt savvy, as if they knew what went on behind the scenes. Yet Louella's accounts were hardly as revealing as she
claimed. In most cases, she never divulged the true extent of the studios' manipulation of actors' images and appearances, never let on that, in some cases,
the personality traits attributed to actors were entirely false, fabricated by film
companies to meet audiences' expectations.

With a solid knowledge of the filmmaking process, and with acquaintances and connections in every area of film production and exhibition,
Louella had, by early 1919, become a leading authority in New York on the
business and politics of the movie industry. Her column swelled with reports
of recent company mergers, the latest box office returns, and news from the
ongoing battle with the federal government over movie censorship. Louella
often used her column to support political candidates, such as future president Calvin Coolidge and New York governor Al Smith, who were sympathetic to the film industry. She also became involved in political struggles
within the New York film community and frequently endorsed candidates for
top industry positions. When state senator (and future New York mayor)
Jimmy Walker ran for the presidency of the Motion Picture Theater Owners
of America in 1922, Louella praised Walker in her column on a near-daily
basis. During her last year at the *Chicago Herald,* she had marveled at the elegant evening gown she wore to her first film industry convention. Only a
year later, her closet overflowed with black dresses, satin shoes, hats, and
evening wraps, as Louella attended two or three, sometimes even four
industry-sponsored banquets and balls each week as a representative of the
Telegraph.[14]

Her responsibilities and prestige grew rapidly. When Richard Watts, the
editor of the *Telegraph's* movie page, was called into the army in July 1919,
Louella was assigned to take over the section. As the new motion picture editor, she would assume responsibility for the headlines, layout, and all editorial content on the motion picture pages, in addition to writing her daily column. Since Louella had little experience with layout or editing, she turned
to her colleagues for help. Thankfully, W. E. Lewis had assigned to Louella
six young female assistants, whom he dubbed "the Persian Garden of Cats."
Talented writers in their own right, several of the women, including Frances
Agnew, who became a Hollywood screenwriter, went on to pursue successful literary careers.[15]

Staff writers Alfred Henry Lewis, Helen Green, and Baird Leonard sharp-
ened Louella's prose, and Bat Masterson, with his wry sense of humor and

Wild West tales, provided comic relief. Masterson also sparked in Louella an interest in prizefighting. Under his tutelage, Louella became such an expert on the sport that Masterson assigned her to cover the Jack Dempsey–Jess Willard fight in Toledo in June 1920. Just as Louella was preparing to leave for the match, W. E. Lewis objected. "She is a nice girl," Lewis said, "and I am not going to have her going to a prize fight. Ladies don't belong there." It would be six years before Louella would finally realize her dream of covering a fight. In 1926, she reported the celebrated Dempsey-Tunney match for William Randolph Hearst.[16]

But it was Theodora "Teddy" Bean, veteran newspaperwoman and Sunday editor of the *Telegraph,* who became Louella's greatest teacher, supporter, and friend during her early days in New York. Born in Minnesota and educated at Carleton College, Bean, at the turn of the century, had been one of the first women reporters in Chicago. Bean achieved fame when she secured an interview with the temperance advocate Carrie Nation, who was visiting Chicago during her famed "antisaloon" crusade. Unbeknownst to other reporters, Bean convinced Nation to spend the night at a Turkish bath, where she interviewed her for several hours. Bean had outscooped the Chicago press, and her interview with Nation was the only one to appear in local papers the following day. After her success in Chicago, Bean moved to New York, where she joined the staff of the *Telegraph* as a feature writer. An outspoken feminist, Bean gained acclaim for her coverage of the women's suffrage movement.[17]

A "handsome, imperious" woman who "abhorred sentiment," according to reporter Ishbel Ross, Bean smoked cigars, carried a walking stick, had a passion for detective stories, and could "plank steak like a chef." Every bit as hard-boiled as the male writers on the *Telegraph* staff, Bean showed Louella the ropes—how to write headlines and paste up a page, how to keep her composure, how to track down leads. Bat Masterson and his cronies may have added humor and color to Louella's life at the *Telegraph* and "the Persian Garden of Cats" may have kept the show going, but it was Teddy Bean who reminded Louella to be strong and confident when faced with male studio executives who flattered her, flirted with her, and sometimes tried to intimidate her to get the publicity they wanted.[18]

Louella first interviewed Louis B. Mayer in 1919 in New York, where he was a producer for the First National Studios. The *Morning Telegraph* had been having some "trouble" with First National, Louella recalled—a dispute over payment for First National's ads in the paper—and Mayer, in an attempt to appease the *Telegraph,* flattered Louella shamelessly. Louella, of course, knew Mayer's motives but nonetheless played along with his sweet talk; she knew a good connection when she saw one. Back at the *Telegraph,* W. E. Lewis, who was still upset with First National, threatened to run an editorial protesting the studio's plan to purchase the German film *Passion,* which Lewis denounced as "unpatriotic" in the year after the war. Louella knew the effect this would have on her relationship with Mayer and successfully pressured Lewis to withhold the editorial and drop the issue. In fact, in her review of *Passion,* Louella never mentioned that the film and the leading actress, Pola Negri, were German. Though she admitted that the film was "of foreign birth" and "unmistakably of foreign make," she hinted several times in the piece that it was French. Mayer and J. D. Williams, head of First National, were thrilled with Louella's carefully calculated deception, and Mayer, who went on to become head of the Metro-Goldwyn-Mayer studio, became an ally and friend.[19]

Irving Thalberg, who would become an influential producer for Metro-Goldwyn-Mayer in the 1920s and 1930s, was working in the New York office of Carl Laemmle's Universal Studio when Louella met him in 1919. Laemmle knew Louella from the *Herald,* and he arranged for Louella to lunch with the man, just before Thalberg's move to California to become general manager of Universal's Hollywood studio. When a very young man—he looked no more than sixteen or seventeen—walked into the restaurant and introduced himself as "Irving Thalberg," she snapped at him, thinking it was a gag. "I'm a very busy woman," Louella barked. "I've got no time for jokes." "But Miss Parsons," he replied, "I *am* Irving Thalberg." After much effort, the twenty-year-old Thalberg finally convinced Louella that he was indeed Universal's general manager. Louella also met David O. Selznick, who in the early 1920s was working as an independent producer in New York. Like most publicists and producers, Selznick sent Louella press releases and letters asking her to mention his stars in her column. "I do wish you could see your way clear to giving her [actress Marjorie Daw] a nice, illustrated write-up. And if you will remember her kindly and often in the future, you will be granting the only favor I could ask of you these radio days," he told her.[20]

Press agents often accompanied stars on their interviews with Louella, controlling their clients' responses carefully. But sometimes their plans backfired, with comic results. When Louella interviewed Clara Bow at a New York restaurant in the early 1920s, the actress came with her agent, Morrie Ryskind. "Tell Miss Parsons," prodded Ryskind, "how much you enjoy her articles." "I read you every day in the *World*," Bow said. "*Telegraph! Telegraph!*" Ryskind whispered. "Oh, I mean the *Telegram*," Bow corrected. Ryskind was ready to crawl under the table. "I don't see why I should lie," Bow replied saucily. "I never read you and I never heard of you until this morning." With Ryskind silenced, Louella continued the interview, which became the subject of a full-page article.[21]

Louella's column became noted not only for her exclusive interviews with studio executives and stars but also for its open advocacy of women's rights. In her column, Louella publicized the achievements of famous women as well as supported the careers of many female directors and writers, whose lack of "star" status and feminist politics prevented them from gaining press coverage elsewhere. "New, interesting, and vital to the feminists in the motion picture industry comes in the announcement *[sic]* made last week of the engagement of two women to direct two of the most important stars in the industry," Louella reported in August 1920. "Mary Pickford . . . is engaging Frances Marion to direct her next picture. The other woman is Mrs. Sidney Drew." The little-known film director Justine Johnson, Louella reported in 1921, was a "champion" of feminism who was "planning to make a series of productions in defense of her sex." And aspiring director Elsie Cohen, she wrote, "stands for everything that feminism means." Louella was proudest of the feminist in her family, Maggie Ettinger, who had, through Louella's connection, become a press agent for D. W. Griffith. "Miss Margaret Ettinger has been engaged by D. W. Griffith as a special representative of [the film] *Hearts of the World*," Louella boasted. "Mr. Griffith has engaged a number of women representatives and is finding their work of real value."[22]

Away from the *Telegraph*, Louella participated in several professional women's organizations, including the Woman Pays Club, a group of female artists and intellectuals that included screenwriter Anita Loos, screenwriter Frances Marion, and Hearst reporter Adela Rogers St. Johns. Guests could attend the club luncheons at the Algonquin Hotel only when invited by a member, and if the guest was male, the woman—per the group's name—paid for the meal. "It is a women's club, you see," Louella explained to her *Telegraph* readers. "Object, feminism."[23]

Louella also joined the New York Newspaper Women's Club, an organization founded in 1922 by female reporters, including Teddy Bean, who had covered the women's suffrage movement. Between 1911 and 1920, feminists had picketed, protested, and marched on Washington to win the right to vote, an effort that culminated in the passage of the Nineteenth Amendment, the women's suffrage amendment, in 1920. To cover the movement, newspapers had hired female reporters, giving them for the first time access to the newsroom in large numbers. When, following the amendment, the feminist movement began to disintegrate, many of the female reporters, without a beat to cover, were demoted to the society pages or in some cases lost their jobs. In response, several of the remaining women planned a group that would allow them not only to get together socially but also to fight for the rights of women journalists. On March 8, 1922, thirty-two women gathered together at the Hotel Vanderbilt and began the Newspaper Women's Club.[24]

Martha Coman, a graduate of Stanford who was one of the first female reporters for the *New York Herald*, was the club's first president. Teddy Bean, Emma Bugbee of the *Tribune*, and Ann Dunlap of the *American* were officers; and Louella, Jane Grant of the *New York Times*, and Esther Coster of the *Brooklyn Eagle* were elected to the board of directors. The annual dues were twenty-five dollars, which for many of the women was a week's salary. The restrictive fees were intended to keep the group serious. "Make the club exclusive rather than inclusive and then it will serve a purpose," advised Hearst reporter Helen Rowland at the group's first meeting.[25]

Indeed, the group was serious, with a feminist aim. Believing that a woman was fully capable of holding any job held by a man, the group pressured newspapers to hire more women and assisted female journalists in disputes with their employers. They also provided to potential employers a list of women who would be eligible for job interviews on short notice. In the mid-1920s, several of the members joined the Lucy Stone League, an organization devoted to the belief that women should legally keep their maiden names after marriage. The group also sponsored a tea to honor women journalists of the senior class at Columbia University and created a fund to assist unemployed newspaperwomen. The club's logo was fitting—a woman astride Pegasus with a quill pen in her hand, in place of a riding crop.

At group meetings, typically held over lunch, the women dined, networked, shared stories, and planned their annual fund-raising celebration, a gala event to honor the city's most prominent newspaperwomen. The first one took place in April 1922, and by 1924 the annual Newspaper Women's Ball had become famous for its celebrity and socialite guests. Broadway actors and New York political figures regularly attended, as did many of New York's publishing elite, including the publishers William Randolph Hearst, Adolph Ochs, Cyrus McCormick, and Joseph Medill Patterson.

In 1923, Louella became head of the club's social committee and planned the 1924 ball, held at the Hotel Astor. The following year, she coordinated the banquet and ball, held on the roof garden of the Waldorf Astoria Hotel. The club praised Louella's talent for planning, and in 1925 she was elected president of the organization. (Years later, club historians remembered her as one of the club's "more flamboyant" presidents, one who was "outspoken in broadcasting the new ground" she had covered in journalism.)[26] The Newspaper Women's Club was an important resource for Louella, professionally and personally. The network of astute, energetic women gave her both connections in the newspaper and publishing world and much-needed emotional support.[27]

By 1922, excerpts from Louella's *Telegraph* column were regularly reprinted in movie industry publications, including the trade journals *Motion Picture Herald* and *Moving Picture World,* and directors and producers began giving her cards and gifts in the hope of winning her favor. "My Dear Mrs. Parsons," Carl Laemmle wrote in a card to Louella in 1922, "I want you to know that a great many changes have been made in cutting and editing the film *Foolish Wives.* Many of these changes and eliminations were directly due to the constructive criticism printed in the *Morning Telegraph.*" Some of the gifts arrived anonymously, which worried her. "Another box of candied fruit arrived without a card during the week from the Pacific Coast," Louella wrote. "In these days of poison one cannot be too careful."[28]

In the summer of 1920, Louella rewarded herself for her hard work with a vacation to Europe. W. E. Lewis lent her the money for the trip, and her friend who accompanied her on the journey, the actress and director Olga Petrova, generously financed the steamship ticket to London. A cold, formal, and often temperamental woman originally from Britain, Petrova began to irritate Louella, and Louella, the quintessential tacky tourist (she constantly snapped photos and was "everything you have ever read about the typical American abroad," she admitted), soon annoyed her friend. After a fight, the two parted in London, and Louella traveled solo to Paris, where she arrived on the doorstep of the flamboyant former film actress Fanny Ward. Ward, whose apartment was the social center of the American expatriate community in Paris, threw a cocktail party to welcome Louella, but on the night of the party, the guest of honor never arrived: Louella spent the evening stuck in the elevator of Ward's apartment building. Louella's first European voyage, however, was not a complete disaster. On her way back through London, she met the British publisher Lord Northcliffe, who commissioned her to write an article on film for his magazine, *The Picture Goer*. And a London newspaper that interviewed Louella described her as "Queen of the American publicity writers." With suitcases full of souvenirs and an international reputation, Louella returned to New York to take up the fight against motion picture censorship.[29]

Despite the growing popularity of film, the battle over film censorship continued. By 1918, Kansas City, Chicago, Seattle, Pennsylvania, and Ohio had created official film censorship boards, and several other states were considering similar measures. In response, theater owners circulated anticensorship petitions in their communities; actors on nationwide speaking tours rallied audiences against proposed censorship legislation; and directors and studio heads published anticensorship pamphlets to be distributed at movie theaters across the country. Like the rest of the film community, Louella took up the call to arms.

"In various states a bill is about to be introduced into the legislature asking that a state censor board be appointed with power [over] the motion pictures to be shown at theaters in the state," Louella warned readers in 1919. "This bill, if passed, would be a menace to the very foundations of this government. Write to your congressman and speak freely to him and ask him not to vote for state censorship. It means having someone else decide for you what you want to see." Envisioning her column as a weapon in the anticensorship crusade, Louella lashed out against the "motion picture haters" who endorsed film regulation. Dr. Harry Bowlby, who urged the New York legislature to pass a "blue law" that would close movie theaters on Sundays, "is bitter against the film industry," Louella reported. "He feels the film men [have] no right to fight for their rights. Well the Reverend Bowlby has another thought coming. So long as the industry has any life or breath it will fight his interference. If he attempts to regulate what is obviously none of his business, he may expect retaliation and retaliation of the bitterest sort." Louella also praised directors and producers such as D. W. Griffith, who produced films so "pure and wholesome" that no censors' wrath could be incurred. At a 1921 luncheon in honor of director Charles Ray, Louella announced to the congregation of journalists and film executives that Ray's pictures were not only "invariably entertaining" but also "invariably clean."[30]

When prominent Protestant organizations in New York in 1920 convinced two state senators to sponsor a film censorship bill, industry leaders spared no expense to turn public opinion against the proposed legislation. The National Association of the Motion Picture Industry (NAMPI), the film industry's governing body, sponsored anticensorship rallies in several New York cities and even produced a short film, *The Nonsense of Censorship,* starring Douglas Fairbanks, that was exhibited in theaters throughout the nation. Their efforts were in vain. After the bill passed the state senate and assembly in February 1921 and was signed into law by Republican governor Nathan Miller in April, Louella and other industry supporters were promptly enlisted in a NAMPI campaign to force the law's repeal. That summer, NAMPI leader William A. Brady announced the creation of a "censorship committee" that would draft a bill to overturn the New York censorship law and that would plan an attack on proposed censorship legislation slated to appear on a Massachusetts referendum the following year. Louella was one of the twenty-four directors, editors, and studio representatives appointed to the committee. The prestigious group, which included D. W. Griffith, *Photoplay* editor James Quirk, and representatives from the Goldwyn, Famous Players, Selznick, Universal, First National, Fox, Metro, and International studios, began meeting regularly at the Hotel Claridge in mid-1921.[31]

After a well-publicized incident that September in which the popular film comic Fatty Arbuckle was accused of raping a young actress at a wild party in San Francisco, religious groups pushed even harder for censorship laws, and NAMPI's work grew urgent. Louella attended the meetings diligently and with her male colleagues planned anticensorship films, slogans, and campaigns to redeem Hollywood's public reputation. But there was another, even stronger motivation behind her involvement in the NAMPI campaign. In the fall of 1921, Louella fell in love.

By 1921, with McCaffrey gone, Louella actively sought romance at the many film industry conventions she attended for the *Telegraph.* During the conventions, she recalled, "[I] sat down close to the speakers' platform and [made] notes with far more of a flourish than the long, dry speeches warranted. But in the evening I went *femme fatale.*" The black dresses and evening gowns on which she splurged were more than just for keeping up professional appearances. "There is nothing immoral about a whiff of perfume or the fact that a girl can dance well, given a partner who doesn't rip off her shoe buckles," she wrote. "Sometimes an attractive hat can get you in where angels fear to tread. Why not admit it—and make it pay dividends?"[32]

"Louella was very popular with men," recalled Dorothy Manners, who became Louella's editorial assistant in the 1930s. With "lustrous" brown hair and a flawless complexion, she was "much more attractive than she was ever given credit for." Whether she had intended it or not, by late 1921 Louella had, in her own words, fallen "very deeply, very wholly, and very completely in love" with a powerful and charming married man who became, according to Manners, "the real love" of her life.[33]

Peter J. Brady was a charismatic, well-spoken former printer and photo-engraver who by the 1920s had become a powerful and well-connected New York labor leader. He was a Roman Catholic and the same age as Louella. As a child Brady moved with his parents from their native Ireland to New York. When his father died, the young Brady went to work as a newsboy and attended night school, where he took courses in photoengraving. After finishing school, he joined the photoengravers union and by 1913 had become first vice president of the Photoengravers' Union of New York and secretary of the Allied Printing Trades Council, which elected him president in 1916. Two years later, Brady was appointed by New York mayor John Hylan to serve as supervisor of the city record. As chairman of the Committee on Education of the New York division of the American Federation of Labor, Brady was also a frequent speaker on educational issues, and he testified regularly before government commissions on the need for greater funding for vocational training in public schools. By 1920 Brady was an influential and well-known figure in New York city politics.[34]

The 1920 election of Governor Nathan Miller, and his subsequent repeal of several pieces of pro-labor legislation, sent Brady and other union advocates on a tirade against the administration, which Brady described to the *New York Times* as "Governor Miller and his band of press agents." Particularly offensive to Brady and his colleagues was the Clayton-Lusk film censorship bill, which had passed into law with Miller's approval. Claiming that film censorship "had been used to delete films depicting brutal conduct by employers' hirelings and officers of the law against working people engaged in industrial disputes," Brady attacked the legislation and publicly urged its repeal. By September 1921 Brady had pledged to assist the NAMPI censorship committee in its fight against censorship, and in October he forwarded letters to the committee from several branches of the State Federation of Labor that similarly offered support. The law not only "imposed unfair tax" and unwarranted government interference on working people, Brady claimed, but also threatened their employment: by reducing film attendance, censorship would strip thousands of actors, musicians, and theater personnel of their jobs.[35]

When Louella met Brady at one of the censorship committee meetings that fall, she was entranced. Tall and handsome with chiseled features and a boyish, dimpled smile, Brady possessed a good-natured, lively wit and a talent for oratory that made him a consummate politician and riveting public speaker. A devoted activist who was described by one colleague as having "indomitable will," Brady, like Louella, was tireless and thrived on challenge.[36]

Louella's and Brady's mutual involvement in the anticensorship campaign brought them into frequent contact during the winter of 1921–22. On March 16, 1922, they were guests at a dinner dance given in honor of the film industry's new "czar," the former postmaster general, Will Hays, who recently had been hired by the studio executives to clean up Hollywood's public image in the wake of the Arbuckle scandal. Louella attended as the guest of the actress Marion Davies, while Brady dined at the head table with Hays, former mayor Hylan and Davies's lover, William Randolph Hearst. The dinner featured a six-course meal, live entertainment by Broadway performers, and the screening of a unique film. Arriving guests were filmed by a crew of cameramen, and the footage was developed and printed in time to exhibit before the end of the evening. As a "guest of honor," Brady was featured in a close-up shot near the beginning of the movie.[37]

Earlier that month, New Yorkers had seen another close-up of Brady, this one in Louella's column. On March 12, 1922, Louella published a large photograph of Brady along with a full-length article praising him for being "one of the people whose vision is broad enough to see what will happen if we are suddenly surrounded by the iron chains of state and federal film regulation" and for "making organized labor go on record as being opposed to any form of censorship." A few weeks later she invited Brady to speak on the subject of public education at the Woman Pays Club. "Mr. Brady talked for fully three quarters of an hour, and it was interesting to note that not a member left her seat during the talk," Louella wrote. "Usually many of these busy women leave the table before the speaker has finished what he has to say." She was clearly infatuated.[38]

Before long Louella's column was filled with news about Brady, whom she frequently described as an "active opponent of censorship" and a "servant of the great public." "The motion picture director's association is not willing to lie dormant when it comes to the grave issues of censorship," she wrote in the spring of 1922. "Because of this stand, Peter J. Brady was invited to address the directors at the association's rooms." Later, in April, she noted: "Peter J. Brady is the guest of honor next Tuesday at the [Theater Owners' Chamber of Commerce] luncheon." "Rita Weiman gave a party in honor of Mrs. Jesse Lasky. Among those who attended were Peter J. Brady." That spring, Louella and Brady began an affair that would last nearly seven years.[39]

As Louella's love for Brady grew, and as the couple's meetings and rendezvous continued, Louella found herself tormented. As a Catholic and a public figure, Brady knew that divorce from his wife, Rose, was out of the question. After a Washington, D.C., convention attended by both Louella and Brady (Brady was "attending the American Federation of Labor meeting, but slipped into the convention to hear Jimmy Walker's speech," according to *Motion Picture News*), Louella returned to New York and wrote a note to herself, which she inserted between the pages of her personal scrapbook. "WORRIES OF THE WEEK," she had written. "All week long I sobbed and sighed."[40]

"I wasn't happy. I couldn't be under the circumstances," she recalled. "There is no real happiness for a woman falling in love with a man who cannot get his freedom from another woman." In a world in which everything seemed to be going her way, true satisfaction was the one thing she could not have.[41]

FIVE

"The Lovely Miss Marion Davies"

Louella's work on the *Telegraph* brought her into contact with some of the most fascinating and celebrated personalities of her day. She interviewed Douglas Fairbanks, Mary Pickford, D. W. Griffith, Harold Lloyd, Gloria Swanson, and Cecil B. DeMille, discussed philosophy with Harry Houdini, and posed for a portrait by the amateur caricaturist (and renowned opera star) Enrico Caruso, whose unflattering sketch, Louella wrote, "punctured my girlish vanity."[1] She lunched at the Algonquin Hotel with novelist Fannie Hurst, danced with Rudolph Valentino, and dined with Charlie Chaplin at the home of the well-known New York entertainment lawyer Nathan Burkan. Film premieres threw her into the center of New York's cafe society, where she rubbed elbows with writers, directors, politicians, publishers, composers, and stars of society, stage, and screen. A cartoon, drawn by Ralph Barton, of the premiere of the 1923 film *Little Old New York* depicted Louella in the second row, flanked by author Rupert Hughes, artist James Montgomery Flagg, former mayor John Hylan, D. W. Griffith, and Will Hays. Behind her sat George M. Cohan, Florenz Ziegfeld, Al Jolson, Irving Berlin, Heywood Broun, Ethel Barrymore, Alexander Woollcott, and F. Scott Fitzgerald, among other literary, theatrical, and musical luminaries.[2]

Despite the affable front that Louella presented in her column and to acquaintances, she earned the reputation among her coworkers of being offputting. She was often impatient and testy, especially when she was working, and sensitive to criticism. One of Louella's assistants on the *Telegraph*, Dorothy Day, chose her words wisely when she later remarked to a Hollywood trade journal that even when Louella meant to tease she used a "pitchfork of humor."[3] Because Louella worked as a gossip columnist, her work and social life merged. Many of those who met her socially wondered whether her friendly banter was authentic, or whether they were merely being sized up for her column. Recalled Frances Marion, who met Louella in 1922, "When you greeted her, she smiled at you in an abstract manner as if mentally she were writing your obituary."[4]

In 1921, Louella met actress Bebe Daniels, who became one of her closest friends. The rare companion with whom Louella claimed she "never had the slightest hint of misunderstanding or even a temporary peeve," Daniels was twenty years younger than she.[5] Born to stage actor parents in Dallas, Daniels first appeared in the Selig company's 1908 film *A Common Enemy*. In 1915, she signed on with the Hal Roach comedy studio in Hollywood, where she made over two hundred films. In 1919, she moved to the Paramount Studio, where she became famous for her comic roles. She was also notorious for her free spirit. In 1921, she was arrested for speeding in Hollywood and sentenced to ten days in jail. Determined to enjoy her time behind bars, she had meals brought in from expensive restaurants, invited friends to visit her, and even brought in a Persian rug.[6]

Another of Louella's friends was a young actress named Hedda Hopper. A butcher's daughter from small-town Pennsylvania with theatrical aspirations, Hopper, born Elda Furry, ran away to New York as a teen and landed a spot in the chorus of the *Pied Piper*, featuring the musical comedy star DeWolf Hopper. Hopper, six foot four, twenty-seven years Furry's senior, and completely bald, had just divorced his fourth wife, and in 1913 Furry and Hopper married. The couple moved to Hollywood, where DeWolf pursued work in film. Elda scored a few film roles, including a starring part in William Farnum's 1915 film, *The Battle of Hearts*, and when she and DeWolf returned to New York the following year, she took bit parts at the studios in the New York area, as well as a major supporting role in the 1917 film *Virtuous Wives*. It was not long after *Virtuous Wives* that she decided to change her name. DeWolf's four previous wives were named Ella, Ida, Edna, and Nella, and because he couldn't always remember that she was Elda, she adopted the name Hedda on the advice of a numerologist.[7] By 1920 Hedda Hopper was making a name for herself in films, having won supporting roles in productions for the Triangle, Metro, and Goldwyn film studios. According to Frances Marion, in New York Hopper and Louella were "very good friends."[8]

But it was another actress, Marion Davies, who became Louella's closest friend in New York. Witty, generous, and well connected, Davies, sixteen years Louella's junior, would broaden Louella's horizons, provide her with much-needed companionship, and boost her career. Davies dragged Louella to "cat parties"—boisterous gatherings of actresses and women writers described by screenwriter Anita Loos as "exceedingly gay," gossipy, and "mildly flavored with gin"—and to exclusive New York social events that even Louella's *Telegraph* pass would not allow her to enter.[9] In turn, Louella listened to Davies's troubles, flattered her in her column, and threw luncheons and soirees (described by one newspaper as "jolly little parties at the Algonquin by Louella O. Parsons") in Davies's honor.[10]

Yet even their friendship at times seemed tainted. No matter how close they became, there was always a shadow hanging over their relationship, one that sometimes cast doubt on the real motivation for their alliance. The shadow, not surprisingly, was as imposing as the figure who cast it—the publisher William Randolph Hearst, who would play a major role in both women's lives for nearly three decades.

There were two important lessons that Louella learned in New York. The first became evident within a few weeks: her job at the *Telegraph* would be far more demanding, both physically and mentally, than the work she did at the *Herald.* Louella often got only four or five hours of sleep and, even when she felt tired or weak, "continued to burn the candle at both ends." "It was a vicious circle," she recalled. "Up all night getting 'color' for my column at night clubs and parties. At the office bright and early in the morning . . . when I would feel my resistance ebbing." Though Louella's colleagues at the *Telegraph* noticed her exhaustion, they did little to curb her workaholism, since her efforts brought advertisers and readers to the paper.[11]

Then there were the money problems. Despite her steady and well-paid job, Louella was almost broke. Harriet had started at the elite, private Horace Mann School, which required substantial monthly payments; and as Helen's diabetes worsened, her medical expenses increased. To make matters worse, Louella had a passion for clothes, manicures, parties, and fine handbags that further depleted her pocketbook. Though at the start of her *Morning Telegraph* career Louella had marveled at her hundred-dollar weekly salary (which by 1922 had increased to $110), she soon found it insufficient and grumbled about her financial struggles. "I have found an honest taxi driver. He should be filmed for future reference," she reported to her readers, having complained for weeks about unscrupulous drivers who fleeced her with inflated fares. By 1920 Louella had become good friends with the local pawnbroker and was borrowing regularly from both her *Telegraph* colleagues and the actors and directors she met through her column.[12]

In the fall of 1922, when Helen entered a sanitarium, Louella and Harriet moved from the apartment on 116th Street to a suite at the Algonquin Hotel.

At the end of December, Helen died. Her remains were taken to Freeport, and she was buried next to Joshua Oettinger in the city cemetery.[13]

Helen's passing marked the end of an era for Louella. Forty-one, with two marriages behind her and a sixteen-year-old daughter, Louella began seriously contemplating her financial future and career. By 1922, she was growing tired of the *Telegraph*. As a relatively well known New York film columnist, she reasoned, she could easily find a better-paying position at a more established paper. Always somewhat disreputable, the *Telegraph*, Louella recalled, had begun "to go down grade."[14] In the face of growing competition from mass-market magazines and tabloid newspapers, the *Telegraph* was losing readers. Working in a car barn was bad enough; losing her job would be unthinkable. In late 1922, in an attempt to find new work, Louella embarked on a scheme that would change her life. It began with a call to Marion Davies.

Louella first met Davies in 1919, several months after the release of Davies's first major film, *Cecilia of the Pink Roses*. Less impressed by Davies's performance than by the tremendous publicity campaign that surrounded the film—"The town is plastered with Lithos and other flamboyant advertising material of Marion Davies . . . which must have cost a fortune," reported the magazine *Town Topics* in the summer of 1918—Louella arranged an interview with Davies through the actress's press agent, Rose Shulsinger. "I expected to see a gorgeous creature in a sable coat," Louella told her readers in March 1919. "Instead I saw a slender little girl with big eyes and a rather wistful expression waiting to meet me. She had not one word about herself but began to ask me all about newspaper work and what I did and how I did it. She is like a child who had suddenly found herself in a golden palace surrounded with every luxury money can buy."[15]

The "golden palace," a reference that would have been understood by nearly everyone in New York press, film, and theatrical circles, was the whirlwind life of parties, jewels, vacations—and most recently, film stardom—that was being purchased for Davies by the fifty-four-year-old, married publishing mogul William Randolph Hearst. A bon vivant with a longtime fascination with showgirls (Hearst's wife of fifteen years, Millicent, had been a chorus line dancer), Hearst first met Davies in 1915, when she appeared in the Irving Berlin musical *Stop! Look! Listen!* Charmed by Davies's lithe figure and carefree spirit, Hearst began courting her with flowers, jewelry, and poems. The six-foot-tall, two-hundred-pound publishing giant was acting like a youth with a schoolboy crush; normally somewhat quiet and composed, Hearst, according to his longtime friend Orrin Peck, was suddenly and "desperately in love."[16]

Though smitten, Hearst was not blind. He knew that although Davies may have been affectionate toward him, she also "loved" several other men. An experienced gold digger, Davies had been encouraged by her upwardly mobile, middle-class Irish American family to take up the life of a showgirl, and at seventeen had made her first appearance on Broadway. Although Davies enjoyed her work on the stage, it was not her interest in theater or dancing that kept her performing. As Davies's domineering mother, "Mama Rose," had made clear, dancing was a way to meet wealthy older men. A prosperous liaison, preferably leading to marriage, was the ultimate goal. Davies seemed to be on the right track. By her nineteenth birthday, she had been in affairs with several wealthy financiers and socialites.

Initially, Davies saw Hearst as just another of her millionaire lovers. Though she accepted his jewels and rewarded him with flirtations, she planned to terminate their relationship whenever another suitor captured her attention. In 1917, however, much to Davies's surprise, her heart dictated a sudden change in plans. Unexpectedly, Davies had fallen in love with Hearst, and their relationship grew serious.

The deeper the relationship, the more costly Hearst's gifts. By early 1917, he had given her a chauffeured limousine, expense accounts at major department stores, private acting lessons, and large sums of cash, which he transferred directly into both Davies's and her parents' bank accounts.[17]

The one gift that Hearst wanted to give Davies but could not was a wedding ring. Though he was willing to pursue divorce, Millicent Hearst, relishing the financial and social benefits that came with being Hearst's wife, would not consider legal separation. Davies seemed not to mind her status as Hearst's lover. "Why should I run after a streetcar," she asked, "when I was already aboard?" It was perhaps to compensate for his inability to marry Davies that Hearst gave her so many extravagant presents—including, in 1917, the first installment of what would become perhaps his greatest gift of all. During that year, Hearst decided to make Davies a motion picture star.[18]

William Randolph Hearst was, by 1917, the nation's wealthiest and most powerful publisher. He also wielded considerable influence in the film industry. Hearst's involvement with movies started in 1898, when he hired cameramen to shoot live newsreel footage of the Spanish-American War. By 1915, he was not only the biggest producer and distributor of newsreels in the country but also the creator of several feature films. In 1913 he conceived the story and directed the production of the *Perils of Pauline,* a popular twenty-part fictional film series about the life of a daring adventuress, played by actress Pearl White. Four years later, along with the independent producer Ivan Abramson, Hearst established a feature film company called Graphic Film. One of Graphic's first productions, in 1918, was a saccharine melodrama titled *Cecilia of the Pink Roses,* starring Marion Davies.[19]

Cecilia, most reviewers agreed, left much to be desired. The plot was trite, the direction amateurish, and the acting clumsy. If Hearst was going to make Davies a star, he would have to do better. The obvious solution was to hire more talented directors, select better scripts, and enroll Davies in acting lessons. But Hearst being Hearst, he found a quicker solution. It was much easier to tell the world, through his papers, that Marion Davies was a brilliant actress than to actually prove it with fine acting and well-crafted films. In 1918, Hearst commissioned hundreds of newspaper and magazine ads for *Cecilia* that proclaimed Davies the most talented actress on the screen. For the film's premiere, Hearst equipped the theater with electric fans that blew the scent of hundreds of fresh roses into the audience.

Hearst launched his most spectacular publicity campaign for Davies in the fall of 1922. To promote the film *When Knighthood Was in Flower,* he embarked on what became, according to *Variety,* "the most expensive and extensive ad campaign that has ever been organized for anything theatrical." The extraordinary publicity campaign included over 650 billboards in New York, 300 subway advertising placards, special booths in department stores that sold *Knighthood* souvenir books, and a dazzling string of electric signs that all but colonized Times Square. At a film industry luncheon, humorist Will Rogers quipped that Davies's next film would be titled "When Electric Light Was in Power."[20]

Shortly after the release of *Cecilia,* Louella and Davies had begun seeing each other socially, and Davies's name frequently appeared in Louella's column. By the time of *Knighthood*'s release, they had been friends for over three years. Louella always praised Davies's acting and films, so it was hardly surprising when she began aggressively promoting the latter film. "'When Knighthood Was in Flower' has done one thing for motion pictures. It has converted many people who were heretofore inclined to look on motion pictures as a necessary evil," Louella wrote.[21]

Louella was not the only one who considered the film worthy of acclaim. The "greatest triumph" of the film, reported the *New York Review*, "is that of Marion Davies. She agreeably astonished her first night audience with a carefully-wrought and easily-expressed characterization. It looks as if Miss Davies will have to be reckoned with for herself alone hereafter."[22] *Knighthood*, declared *Variety*, was a "fine big and splendid mark on the not-so-long road-way of filmdom to date."[23] What made Louella's praise unusual, however, was how frequently—and for how long—she mentioned the film in her column. *Knighthood* was "brilliant," Louella wrote, "rich in educational and artistic value." It was on par with the finest works of DeMille or Griffith—"one of the best films ever made."[24] To help publicize the film, Louella invited Davies to luncheons at the Woman Pays Club, the Newspaper Women's Club, and the Professional Women's League. Marion Davies, she exaggerated, "is conceded to be one of the world's biggest and most popular stars." She "is the girl whom the critics all admitted has arrived, and whom the Prince of Wales calls a great artist." During the winter of 1922–23, Louella praised both Marion and *Knighthood* so lavishly that even her colleagues at the *Telegraph* grew suspicious. By early 1923, it had become clear that Louella was trying to catch Hearst's attention, with the intention of winning a position on his staff.

In 1923, Hearst owned nine daily newspapers, eleven evening papers, and fifteen Sunday papers, including two of New York's best-read papers, the *Journal* and the *American*. (Over three hundred thousand copies of the *American* were issued each day, and nearly one-fifth of New York read the Sunday *American*.) With a combined circulation of nearly seven million, the Hearst papers were read by one out of four American families. In addition to his newspaper holdings, nine magazines, including *Cosmopolitan* and *Good Housekeeping*, and his growing film company, Hearst also ran the International News Service and King Features, two national syndication services.[25] Hearst employees were well paid—Hearst had hired screenwriter Frances Marion at a weekly salary of two thousand dollars and cartoonist Rube Goldberg for more than twice as much—and had an international audience of millions.[26] A job on a Hearst paper would mean readers and exposure on an unprecedented scale.

Louella enlisted Davies's help in her ploy and begged her to tell Hearst of her interest in joining his staff. Davies promised that she would, but when several weeks went by without word from Davies or Hearst, Louella began to worry. Then, unexpectedly, in early 1923, she received a call.

It was the night of a gala dinner dance at the Hotel Astor sponsored by the

Motion Picture Theater Owners' Chamber of Commerce. Louella was in her suite at the Algonquin, dressing, when the phone rang. Davies was on the line, and she wanted to know if she could join Louella at the ball that evening. Louella agreed. An hour later, when Davies arrived at the hotel, the front desk rang and Harriet answered the phone. She heard Davies's voice and a high-pitched male voice in the background. "Your friend is here," Harriet shouted at Louella, "and there's a young man with her." When Louella finally descended to the lobby, she found that the "young man" was Hearst.[27]

At the ball, Louella told Hearst of her dissatisfaction with the *Telegraph* and her interest in working on his papers. When Hearst smiled and said nothing, Louella assumed she had blown her big chance. She was astonished when, a week later, Hearst invited her to dinner at his home on Riverside Drive. Over dinner, Hearst told Louella that he was interested in hiring her to work on the *American* and that he had the agreement ready. Sitting on the table before Louella was a three-year contract at a salary of $150 a week. She picked up the pen, then stopped. A woman of her experience, she told Hearst, was worth at least $200 a week, possibly $250. Hearst laughed. It was $150 or nothing, he said, and pushed the contract across the table. "I'll think about it," Louella replied, and walked out of the room.[28]

The following day Louella called the lawyer Nathan Burkan, a friend of Peter Brady's, and asked him to draft a contract for $250 a week. When Louella gave the new contract to Hearst a few weeks later, he refused to sign it, insisting that the salary was too high.[29]

For most of the summer of 1923 Louella kept the contract, hoping that Hearst would give in. Meanwhile, her column featured perhaps the most glowing praise of Hearst that any non-Hearst paper in America had ever published. *Little Old New York,* released by the Cosmopolitan studio in mid-1923, "has done a great deal to add to the glories of Marion Davies as well as to pin new laurels on William Randolph Hearst as film producer," Louella wrote. "*Little Old New York* . . . is a true blood sister of *When Knighthood Was in Flower.*" In her review of another Cosmopolitan production, *Unseeing Eyes,* set in the Canadian Rockies, Louella praised Hearst's use of on-location footage and complex aerial shots. "William Randolph Hearst is a wise enough showman not to attempt to foist any imitation on the public," she explained to her readers.[30]

Hearst, on vacation at his California estate, San Simeon, mulled over Louella's proposition. Though he still considered her demand excessive, in the end, prodded by Davies, he finally gave in. On November 19, Joe Willicombe, Hearst's secretary, called Louella with the announcement that Hearst had agreed to sign the contract.

On December 9, 1923, the *New York American* carried the news:

> The motion picture world paid tribute to Louella O. Parsons, on the occasion of her becoming the motion picture editor of the New York *American* yesterday. . . . Representatives of film producing companies and exhibiting interests and newspapers congratulated her and commended the New York *American* for expanding its screen space in recognition of the increasing importance of motion pictures to the public. Sidney S. Cohen, president of the Motion Picture Theater Owners' Chamber of Commerce of America, sounded the keynote when he declared that Miss Parsons in her new office was virtually the ambassador of the public to the makers of motion pictures as well as the bearers of news from the stars of the screen to the *American*'s readers. He predicted that Miss Parsons would establish a community of interest between the producers and artists and patrons of films which would vastly encourage the development of the finest pictures possible.[31]

The group that assembled at the congratulatory luncheon at the Hotel Astor was a testament to Louella's "instinctive" ability, in the words of fan magazine writer Ruth Waterbury, to cultivate powerful political contacts. In speeches addressed to the more than 250 guests, Carl Laemmle, Jimmy Walker, and Nathan Burkan, who were appointed "associate chairmen" of the luncheon, praised Louella's hard work and dedication. Louella's assistant, Dorothy Day, announced that "Louella Parsons is a real person with ideals and ideas which are the outgrowth of a good mind and a good heart," and publicist John Flinn presented her with a "genuine gold mounted alligator skin traveling bag" on behalf of her "Persian Garden of Cats." Someone read a telegram from Will Hays "felicitating Miss Parsons on the extension of her field of endeavor," and Louella gave a brief speech. S. Jay Kaufman, a writer for the *Evening Telegram,* later claimed in his column that "the luncheon at the Astor proved . . . that there isn't a better liked person hereabouts than Louella Parsons."[32]

Outside, Hearst newspaper delivery trucks decorated with pictures of Louella roared down the streets, and half-page ads championing Louella appeared in Hearst's *American* and *Journal* as well as several other New York newspapers. "Miss Parsons has been writing about the reel and the screen ever since motion pictures came into vogue," boasted one ad. "She is the personal friend of every film star, past and present, and has access to more important motion picture news than any other one writer." Other ads featured testimonials from actor Buster Keaton, Will Hays, and several studio executives that praised the columnist "who is conceded to be one of the best informed authorities on the affairs of the screen and [whose] advice has been sought and her criticism heeded by the stars, directors and producers of the screen."[33] The *Morning Telegraph* presented her with a letter signed by each member of the staff. Louella had "added luster to our paper and won the admiration of every member of this organization," the *Telegraph* claimed.[34]

The praise moved Louella more than she expected. "There was a blur over my eyes and a lump in my throat I couldn't swallow," she recalled. "For the first time in my life—I couldn't say a word."[35]

In other corners of the film and publishing world, the response was less cheerful. For those directors and actors whom Louella favored, her new alliance meant positive publicity on an unparalleled scale. For those whose standing was less secure, the combination of Louella and Hearst was potentially dangerous. With the attention of a far greater audience than she had commanded at the *Telegraph* and access to Hearst's formidable news-gathering resources, Louella now had a powerful influence over the film industry.

Speaking for many of his colleagues, a reporter for a Chicago film industry trade journal reported the news with trepidation. In a statement that needed little explanation, in January 1924 he warned his readers that, at last, as many of them had feared, "Louella Parsons has gone with Hearst."[36]

In her autobiography, Louella told the story of her alliance with Hearst differently. In Louella's version it was not her praise but her criticism of Hearst that won his attention and her job on the *American*. Upset that Hearst had publicized the $1.5 million cost of *When Knighthood Was in Flower* more than Marion Davies's talent, Louella claimed that she wrote an editorial "blasting Mr. Hearst for bragging about spending so much money on the picture. Addressing my remarks personally to Mr. Hearst, I wrote: 'Why don't you give Marion Davies a chance? She is a good actress, a beauty, and a comedy starring bet. Why talk about how much was spent on the lovely costumes and the production cost?'" Though Louella hoped that the comments would upset Hearst, she claimed that they pleased him. Impressed by her audacity, Hearst hired her.[37]

And then there is a third version of the Hearst-Louella story. An old Hollywood fable that has even been depicted in novels and films has Louella witnessing a murder that took place on a yacht off the Southern California coast. The victim was a producer named Thomas Ince, the murder weapon a pistol (in some versions, a hatpin), and the assailant Hearst, the yacht's owner.

Ince and Hearst had been negotiating a film-producing deal that, according to rumor, turned deadly. In the spring of 1924, Hearst made an agreement with the Hollywood-based Metro-Goldwyn-Mayer studio, arranging for Hearst's Cosmopolitan films to be distributed through MGM. Following the deal, Hearst moved his film production headquarters from New York to a facility in Hollywood owned by the independent director and producer Thomas Ince. In June 1924, after purchasing a home for Davies in Beverly Hills, Hearst, Davies, and director George Hill began work on Davies's first film under the new arrangement with MGM, a comedy called *Zander the Great.* Hearst had begun to split his time between Hollywood, San Simeon, and New York, often going for long periods without seeing Davies. During one of these absences, Davies began an affair with Charlie Chaplin, who was working at his nearby studio on his latest film, *The Gold Rush.*[38]

News of the affair spread quickly not only in Hollywood but also across the nation. In November 1924 Grace Kingsley, a movie columnist for the *New York Daily News,* reported that Chaplin had been paying "ardent attention" to Davies, and other fan magazines and film publications also had the two romantically linked. Hearst had dispatched spies to follow Davies in Los Angeles and knew about the affair long before Grace Kingsley's readers, but he seemed unperturbed. Intent on his goal of stardom for Davies, in the fall of 1924 Hearst began discussing with Thomas Ince the possibility of a film-producing partnership. A prolific and highly acclaimed director, Ince had earned a reputation, in the words of the *New York Times,* as a "maker of stars" and "doctor of sick films."[39]

After several weeks of negotiation, the two were near a deal in which Ince would produce *The Enchanted Isle,* based on a story that had been printed in Hearst's *Cosmopolitan* magazine. If the film were successful, Ince would join Hearst in a permanent producing alliance. In his typical manner of concluding business deals, Hearst invited Ince for a weekend cruise to San Diego on his yacht. Ince, a boating enthusiast, would be turning forty-four that weekend, and Hearst had planned a birthday dinner for the first night on the ship. On November 15, 1924, Hearst, Davies, Hearst's secretary Joe Willicombe, novelist Elinor Glyn, actresses Seena Owen and Vera Burnett,

Davies's sisters Ethel and Reine, Hearst's studio manager Dr. Daniel Goodman, and Thomas Ince boarded the *Oneida*, a 215-foot yacht with five guest staterooms, a facility for screening films, and an engine room that was two stories high.[40]

The cruise started out festive but turned ominous. Several hours after the birthday dinner, guests heard moaning from Ince's cabin and alerted Goodman. Goodman diagnosed it as a severe heart attack and immediately put Ince on a motorboat and took him to San Diego, where he boarded a train back to Los Angeles. During the train ride, however, Ince's condition worsened and, when the train stopped at Del Mar, Ince was taken to a local hotel. Someone telephoned his wife, Nell Ince, who drove to Del Mar, picked up her husband, and brought him back to their home in Beverly Hills. The following morning, November 19, over two days after he had left the *Oneida*, Ince died.[41]

The official cause of death was reported as "heart failure as the result of an attack of acute indigestion."[42] But it was not long before rumors spread. Because the Hearst papers had not mentioned the yachting party in their reports of the death, and some editions even reported that Ince had died at San Simeon, many in Hollywood grew suspicious. Why the conflicting accounts? Why was Ince cremated, and why was Hearst absent from Ince's funeral on November 21? Why did the passengers who had been on board the *Oneida* refuse to speak to the press? The only reason, they concluded, was foul play—Hearst had killed Ince on the ship and had used his newspapers to cover up the crime.

Hearst's motives were simple—jealousy. In one version of the rumor that became popular, Hearst shot Ince in a jealous rage after finding him making love to Davies. In another version, Hearst walked in on Davies and Chaplin, attempted to shoot Chaplin, and accidentally shot Ince—an impossibility, since Chaplin was not on the ship that evening. In the most ridiculous version, Hearst discovered Ince playfully embracing Davies and, in jest, pulled a hatpin from Davies's hat and aimed at Ince's arm. When Ince turned to face Hearst, the hatpin entered his heart, causing a fatal heart attack.[43] Panicked, Hearst went to the one guest on board the *Oneida* who could assist him with the cover-up: Louella.

Though there is no other evidence to corroborate the claim, Vera Burnett insisted that both Louella and Chaplin were on board the *Oneida* that night, having picked up Davies from the *Zander* set earlier in the day. When Louella heard the gunshots she allegedly ran to the scene of the crime, saw Hearst, and immediately began plotting a cover-up that involved huge payoffs to Nell Ince and the coroners of both San Diego and Los Angeles Counties. To thank Louella, Hearst promised her a position on his papers—an explanation that does not hold, since by November 1924 Louella was already working for Hearst. Moreover, Louella did not leave New York that month and was never on the ship. In another version of the story that circulated in Hollywood, Hearst enlarged Louella's responsibilities on the *American* and increased her salary to ensure that she complied with the scheme.[44]

A more plausible explanation for the Hearst papers' silence concerns the real cause of Ince's death—bootleg alcohol. At dinner that night, Davies recalled in her memoirs, the guests drank a toast to Ince "in water," since Hearst, who never touched liquor, forbade the consumption of alcohol in his presence. But others, including Ince, said that there had been a good deal of alcohol on board. As Nell Ince wrote in a letter to Hearst reporter Adela Rogers St. Johns in 1965, her husband had been under a doctor's care for angina pectoris and severe ulcers and had told her that on the *Oneida* he had "eaten quite a few salted almonds before dinner and had some champagne before dinner, both forbidden articles on his diet." Ince also told Dr. T. A. Parker, whom he saw in Del Mar, that he had consumed "considerable liquor" aboard the ship and suggested to a nurse, Jessie Howard, that it had possibly been tainted. The Hearst papers had an obvious reason for their understated coverage of Ince's death. Not only was alcohol illegal under Prohibition, but at the time the U.S. Department of Justice was investigating allegations that Hearst was involved in a bootlegging operation in Southern California.[45]

Though the story was immediately and widely circulated by Hollywood rumormongers—a testament to the anti-Louella animus that existed already by 1924—wiser heads realized that the story was false. Even the *Los Angeles Times,* Hearst's rival paper, could not find any evidence against Hearst. *Times* reporter A. M. Rochlen told Adela Rogers St. Johns that he had covered "every moment" from the time that Ince left the yacht through the examinations by "doctors, nurses, undertakers, police and coroners." He told Harry Chandler, owner of the *Times,* that there was "nothing to it."[46]

Given Louella's loyalty to Hearst, it is conceivable that she might have complied with such a cover-up. But Hearst did not murder Thomas Ince, and there was nothing to hide. Louella did not use her knowledge of "where the skeletons were buried" to win her position with Hearst.[47] Shrewdly, she had already gotten what she wanted from Hearst long before he boarded the ship.

PART II

SIX

On the Way to Hollywood

If louella worked in a car barn at the *Telegraph,* at the *American* she worked in hell. Housed in the former Rheinlander Sugar House, a gloomy building used by the British as a prison during the Revolutionary War, the offices of the *American* were, in the words of editor Gene Fowler, near-"purgatorial." In the composing room on the eighth floor, "molten lead from the linotype pots seeped through crevices in the floor, turned into pellets of hot hail . . . then fell upon the desk [of the night city editor] below."[1] Editors and reporters rushed around the dim, smoky halls, racing to meet their deadlines, and in the newsroom, harried editors worked in odd, makeshift cubicles constructed from discarded pieces of plywood. Every time two editors got in a fight, they threw a piece of wood between them.

The *American,* like the *Telegraph,* was staffed by prominent New York journalists—the novelist Nat Ferber, the celebrated sports writer Damon Runyon, and the society columnist Maury Paul, who wrote under the pseudonym Cholly Knickerbocker. One of the sharpest minds at the *American* was the paper's publisher, Hearst, who could often be seen lurking around the office checking up on employees, pasting up pages, and correcting copy. Standing six foot two and weighing 210 pounds, Hearst was intense and capricious. When reviewing the morning papers, he spread them out on the floor and turned the pages with his toes. When something pleased him, he was known to spontaneously break out into a tap dance.[2]

Some employees found him frightening. Others thought he was insane. But very few disliked him. As the longtime Hearst reporter Adela Rogers St. Johns put it, "the Chief" invoked in many of his employees a combination of reverence, affection, gratitude, and astonishment that St. Johns described as "AWE."[3] Generous and polite, Hearst "was quick to give praise for a job well done, never got angry, never raised his voice, and always prefaced his requests with 'please' and 'if you don't mind,'" according to one biographer.[4]

Hearst was particularly admired by his female staff for his support of women journalists. It was Hearst who launched the career of the first "sob sister," Winifred Black, and according to the 1920s reporter and journalism historian Ishbel Ross, Hearst "more than any other publisher . . . helped put newspaper women on the map." Hearst employed dozens of women writers, who became "the most spectacular, most highly paid newspaper women in the country." Hearst's support of female journalists has been attributed by biographers and historians to his close relationship with his mother, Phoebe, who was a devoted feminist. Though many of his women writers never even met him, Hearst monitored their progress closely and encouraged male editors to give them important assignments. Unlike most publishers at the time, Ross claimed, Hearst believed that women reporters were "essential to every paper."[5]

For her *American* column, "The Screen and Its Players," Louella cut down on the lengthy descriptions of production deals and contracts that had filled her "In and Out of Focus" column in the *Telegraph* and devoted more space to actors' offscreen lives. The *American*'s largely working- and middle-class audience "would rather know how Gloria Swanson keeps her lovely complexion than the troubles Samuel Goldwyn has in buying a current stage success," Louella explained in 1926.[6]

The new column, with its "personality" focus, reflected major changes in American culture and celebrity journalism. In the 1890s the Hearst press, with its emphasis on entertainment value, had pioneered a new brand of "story journalism" that, by the 1920s, appeared in virtually all American newspapers. These newspapers ranged from two urban tabloids that had begun publication in the early 1920s—the *New York Daily News* and the *New York Daily Mirror*—to the *New York Times*.[7] Although this new story journalism sometimes chronicled the escapades of politicians and society figures, its subjects were most often stage and screen entertainers.

Since the nineteenth century, theater stars' offstage lives had been publicized by the popular press. But the actors had not been the sole focus of this press attention: prominent businessmen, political leaders, and inventors— "idols of production," to use sociologist Leo Lowenthal's term—were praised for their professional achievements. By the 1920s, however, these idols of production had been largely replaced by "idols of consumption": actors, singers, socialites, and other artistic and literary figures who became famous for their lifestyles.[8] The growth of a national consumer culture in the early twentieth century, the decline of traditional religious moralities among the urban middle class, and the proliferation of visual mass media such as illustrated magazines and the movies had created a new, modern, secular culture that placed high value on style and appearance. Personality and "salesmanship" became desirable personal qualities, and a well-groomed appearance was touted as the key, in a mass urban society, to standing out in the crowd. With their wealth and charisma, and their ability to command fame and fortune on the basis of their looks, actors—particularly movie stars—became icons and role models for the new era. The Edisons, Rockefellers, and Roosevelts no longer represented the pinnacle of status and achievement: the Chaplins and Swansons and Fairbanks surpassed them, if not in pedigree, then certainly in popularity.[9]

Indeed, by the time Louella transferred to the *American,* movie stars had won greater fame and public adoration than perhaps any other celebrity figures in American history. In 1921, when Douglas Fairbanks and Mary Pickford honeymooned, they were literally mobbed by thousands of fans who tore at their hair and clothes. Top stars such as Clara Bow and Rudolph Valentino earned thousands of fan letters each week, major corporations used actors' endorsements for their products, and virtually every well-known actor had a national fan club.[10] Not surprisingly, in this movie-crazed climate, the fan magazines flourished, and by 1920 the major fan publications—*Photoplay, Motion Picture, Motion Picture Classic, Picture Play, Photoplay Journal,* and *Shadowland*—had a combined circulation of over a million. Additionally, most major metropolitan papers had film review columns, which were often written by women. In addition to Louella, in New York the journalist Harriet Underhill wrote for the *Herald Tribune,* along with Willela Waldorf for the *Post,* Regina Cannon for the *Graphic,* Rose Pelwick for the *Journal,* and Mildred Spain for the *Daily News.* Grace Kingsley wrote for the *Los Angeles Times,* Florence Lawrence for the *Los Angeles Examiner,* and Virginia Dale for the *Chicago Examiner.*[11] Writing for the fan magazines were editors Adele Whitely Fletcher and Elsie Seeligman and writers Adela Rogers St. Johns, Ruth Waterbury, Hazel Simpson Naylor, and Gladys Hall.[12]

In part, the female domination of movie writing was a product of the still widely held, sexist assumption that women were better reviewers of the "emotional and frivolous" cinema than men. It also reflected the fact that the majority of film audiences and film fans were female. Having entered the workplace by the thousands during the 1920s—by the end of the decade, nearly one quarter of the workforce was female—women had more disposable income than in the past, and increasingly they consumed luxury products such as fashionable clothing, cosmetics, and commercial entertainment. A *Photoplay* article from 1924 suggested that the American film audience was 75 percent female; according to the film trade journal *Moving Picture World,* "It has become an established fact that women fans constitute the major percentage of patronage."[13] In the hope of attracting these women as readers, fan magazines and newspapers hired women writers and constructed their articles as "woman to woman" chats between the female reader, the female journalist, and a celebrity actress.

Not only were women earning more in the 1920s, but they were experiencing greater sexual freedom. Both the working woman and the "flapper"—the caricature used to describe the fashionable young women of the decade who drank, smoked, and experimented sexually—sparked cultural controversy, as critics worried about the effects on society, public morals, and the family. In comparison to other mainstream cultural discourses during the 1920s, as film historian Gaylyn Studlar has written, the fan magazines took a relatively progressive, though somewhat contradictory, stance on women's changing economic and sexual roles.[14] They sometimes condemned working women and flappers, but they often encouraged them. Moving back and forth between old and new moralities, the fan magazines upheld traditional virtues of marriage and motherhood while at the same time hinting at the pleasures of liberation.

Louella adopted a similarly cautious approach in her column. Typically, she described actresses as successful career women and championed their professional achievements. Yet at the same time, she reaffirmed the importance of marriage and conservative attitudes toward female sexuality. In an interview with Mary Pickford in 1925, for example, she wrote that Pickford was the "best businesswoman in the industry" but that the actress was "more proud of her household accomplishments than anything else." A woman of virtue, as Louella described her, Pickford was happily married to actor Douglas Fairbanks and disdained "modern girls" who cared "for nothing but cocktails, cigarettes and jazz."[15] In a brilliant merger of progress and tradition, in a piece on producer and screenwriter Marion Fairfax, Louella wrote that Fairfax had found the secret to a happy marriage—a career. "Women in business make better wives because they have no time for imaginary ills and needless troubles," she explained. "So you see, girls, if you want to keep your husbands interested . . . you must follow Miss Fairfax's advice and find an interest outside your domestic difficulties."[16] It was Louella's ability to speak to the interests of female fans, and to play to both the independent women and traditionalists in her readership, that earned her a wide base of devoted readers.

Louella's own public image similarly combined tradition and progress. Though she still portrayed herself in her column as maternal and morally conservative, she was now, in tune with the changing cultural climate, also a savvy, independent working woman who participated actively in the social life of the stars. That virtue went hand in hand with a celebrity lifestyle may have seemed contradictory, but this was the point. In Louella's telling, the stars—who never drank illegally, who were unfailingly monogamous, and who were unwilling "to stay up late at night and risk not looking fresh in the morning"—were as upstanding and ethical as she.[17] This false image of propriety became Louella's trademark, and maintaining it, one of the most important projects of her career.

By 1925, Louella had become a local celebrity in her own right. By the end of her first year at the *American,* she was receiving over eight hundred fan letters a week. When Louella was hospitalized in 1924, she received dozens of letters from fans concerned about her health, and readers inundated her with requests for autographs, photos, and personal advice. Like Walter Winchell, who had written a popular Broadway gossip column in the tabloid the *New York Graphic* since 1924, Louella was famous by virtue of her association with the famous.[18]

Hearst was thrilled by Louella's success. Not only was she boosting the *American's* circulation, but she had become a kind of informal press agent for Hearst and Davies. Nearly every column began with praise for Davies or Hearst's Cosmopolitan productions. "Cosmopolitan has never had any dealings with the censor board for the reason that it has never made any censorable pictures," she announced in September 1924. "William Randolph Hearst was complimented by [Will] Hays as the one producer who never depends on suggestive or salacious titles to win favor for his pictures."[19] The praise was so lavish and frequent that some readers found it comical. "I have nothing against Hearst papers," joked a reporter at one film trade journal, "but I wish he would issue an order to Louella Parsons that [she] could tell the truth without losing [her] job. I would like to see him do it before the next Marion Davies picture is released." "W. R. Hearst got his money's worth when he hired Louella O. Parsons as the picture reviewer of the New York *American,*" quipped *Variety.* In each column, she "[goes] hook, line and sinker for Hearst and the Cosmopolitan pictures which her boss turns out."[20]

In 1925, Hearst signed another deal with MGM that gave the studio the authority not only to distribute but also to produce his Cosmopolitan films. With his fortunes now tied to MGM, he took an active concern in the studio's finances. That year, Mae Murray, one of MGM's stars who had just appeared in the movie the *Merry Widow*, signed a production deal with Germany's Ufa studio, despite the fact that she was still under contract to MGM. Murray's decision to bolt the studio was appalling to both Hearst and MGM head Louis B. Mayer, who would lose thousands by her defection. They hoped to convince the star to break her deal with Ufa, even though Murray, who had a European lover pressuring her to come to the Continent, was set on leaving MGM. Hearst, Mayer, and movie czar Will Hays devised a scheme to win the star back, a plan that involved Louella.

Louella and Murray were longtime friends who had known each other since Louella's *Chicago Herald* days. So Murray thought nothing of it when she received an invitation from Louella to a dinner party at Hearst's mansion. When she arrived at the party, Hearst opened the door and escorted her to the dining room. Seated around the table were two dozen men dressed in business suits—bankers and lawyers—and Louella. There was an eerie silence for several minutes after Murray sat down; at last, when the meal was served, Hearst turned to Murray and said, "Louella tells me you're leaving for Europe." "Yes, I have a wonderful contract with Ufa," Murray replied, and she proceeded to describe her agreement with the German studio. Hearst listened, then shook his head. "We'd have to boycott those films over here," he said. "Did it ever occur to you that going over there is not very patriotic, Miss Murray?" Hays chimed in. "That you'd be working against your country's business interests, enhancing another country's rival industry?" Hearst told Murray that he, Mayer, and Hays would prevent Murray's German films from being released in America and that she would be destroying her career. As Murray sat awkwardly, trapped in an impossible situation, Louella was poised at the end of the table, notebook and pencil in hand, ready to take down Murray's decision for the next edition of the paper. With no way out, Murray agreed to back out of the German deal and went to Europe to cancel her agreement with Ufa.[21]

A hardworking employee with important connections and the ability to attract thousands of readers, Louella was becoming one of the Hearst empire's most valuable assets. Although she and Hearst had had a minor spat in

1924 when he rewrote one of her film reviews after his dispute with Cecil DeMille over the rights to a script—Hearst had turned Louella's glowing review of *The Ten Commandments* into an attack, and she became furious—the two of them built a close relationship of trust and mutual respect.[22] Their relationship was so close that, in the summer of 1925, Hearst commissioned Louella to become his personal spy.

It began that May when Davies, who had by then moved to Beverly Hills to work full-time in films, visited New York for the premiere of her film *Zander the Great*. When Davies announced that she would be returning to California at the end of the month, Hearst urged Louella to join her. Though Louella initially protested—she didn't need to make the trip, she explained, and she'd rather stay in New York with Peter Brady—Hearst informed her that this was no vacation but a *mission*. Hearst knew that Davies had been involved with several Hollywood actors, including Charlie Chaplin, and he wanted Louella to monitor Davies's liaisons. This meant, of course, that Louella would be spying on her friend. Either she would have to betray Davies or she would have to refuse her boss's demands. It didn't take long for her to decide which allegiance was more important. With only a moment's hesitation, Louella agreed to Hearst's plan.

On May 15, a group of "more than 100 movie stars and friends and a representative group of twenty-five US World War veterans," beneficiaries of a large charitable donation from Davies, gathered at Grand Central Station to bid farewell to Davies and Louella.[23] After a week on the Lake Shore Limited, Louella stepped off the train to find a brilliant "glitter of gold."[24] Amazed that the sun could be so bright, she looked more closely and discovered that the light came from fifteen large golden keys—the "keys" to the Hollywood studios—which were presented to her by a crew of studio representatives. The studios spared no expense to welcome Louella, and she was rushed into a series of meetings, luncheons, parties, and tours. "Before I had even washed the grime off my face, I was taken for a drive through its streets," she recalled. "I felt as if I were in a dream."[25] Directors, actors, and writers turned out to celebrate her arrival, and she was honored at several dinners and parties, including affairs hosted by director Mack Sennett, Gloria Swanson, novelist Elinor Glyn, and Rudolph Valentino.[26] Louella was even invited to appear as an extra in the film *The Lights of New York,* in which she wore an elaborate period costume, a frilly dress from the 1870s. "There never was a dress with so many ruffles and bustles and flounces. It was yellow and white and black and would have made a bean pole look fat. You can imagine how I looked in my 130 pounds," she told her readers.[27]

Davies hosted some of the liveliest social events in Hollywood that summer, with plenty of music, dancing, and bootleg alcohol. Charlie Chaplin recalled that Davies often hired a bus to carry groups of actors down to the beach, where they ate, caught grunion, and made love late into the night.[28] As promised, Louella reported each of Davies's parties and romantic liaisons to Hearst, although the publisher seemed far more willing to accept her transgressions than Louella had predicted. One night in June 1925, when Hearst arrived in Hollywood to see the premiere of Chaplin's film *The Gold Rush*, Louella informed him, in front of Davies, that Davies "didn't deserve" a diamond bracelet he had given her that evening. "She's been a bad girl," Louella told him. "Don't pay any attention to Louella," Davies snapped back. "She hasn't got any brains." Hearst quietly registered Louella's remark, then patted Davies's hand and insisted that she accept the gift. "Anything that Marion does," he told Louella, "is all right with me."[29] By the premiere, all tensions had been forgotten, as Davies and Louella showed off their lavish new outfits—Louella wore a white georgette gown embroidered with rhinestones and crystals and a "Spanish shawl," reported the *Los Angeles Herald*—and later attended a party at the home of Samuel Goldwyn that had been supplied by "all of the reliable bootleggers in town."[30]

Shortly afterward, Louella was dispatched by the *American* managing editor Gene Fowler to Santa Barbara to report on a devastating 6.3 earthquake that virtually leveled the city's commercial district. Her "splendid work and splendid story," Fowler wrote to her, was "commended by important Californians."[31] This was unusual for Fowler, whose comments about Louella were usually critical. In New York, Fowler had tried to edit Louella's column, but Louella had protested. When she confronted Fowler and asked him why he "butchered" her work, Fowler replied, "Because you are totally and incurably illiterate." Louella then complained to Hearst, who ordered Fowler to keep his hands off of the column. For the next two and a half decades, Louella would pride herself on the fact that her column was never edited.[32]

Louella's "mission" that summer was not the last time she would spy on Davies for Hearst. Nor was it the last time that she would set foot in the land of "glittering gold." In less than six months, Louella would be back in the West, though the circumstances that led to her return were not what she would have predicted. Louella went back to New York in August, not knowing that in less than a year she would be on her way to California to die.

Back at home, Louella showed no indication of slowing down. In 1925, New York was in the midst of its "nightclub era"—the wild, raucous Prohibition days of flappers, bootleg gin, and speakeasies—and Louella's position as a prominent Hearst columnist took her into the highest echelons of the city's fashionable cafe society. She attended the openings of several elite New York nightclubs, partied with members of "society, stage, and the literary fraternity" at the Club Moritz, and dined at the Ritz Hotel with Davies, Charlie Chaplin, and James Quirk. She drank at some of the city's most notorious speakeasies, danced the tango with Rudolph Valentino, and spent her evenings in the arms of the "love of her life," Peter Brady.[33]

During 1925, Louella's relationship with Brady was at its peak. Both were rising stars—Brady had recently been appointed president of the Federation Bank of New York—and they used their mutual involvement in the world of film, journalism, and New York politics to continue their alliance. Louella and Brady were invited to speak at a series of film industry conventions around the Northeast, and they used the out-of-town engagements for their romantic rendezvous. Louella was also invited to make radio appearances, and in her half-hour broadcasts on station WOR, she recalled stories from her years at Essanay and "chatted intimately about screen celebrities." Her early attempts on the radio were marred by stage fright ("The first time I talked over the radio I was so depressed by the microphone that I was unable to collect my thoughts," she remembered).[34] By the end of the year, however, she had become a confident public speaker and was invited to make a "regular circuit" of the New York stations.[35]

Louella was flying high and, according to many observers, was a little out of control. She was described as being curt and testy at the Algonquin Hotel, where she lived. She resented the literati who patronized the hotel—in particular, the members of the famed Algonquin Round Table, whom she dismissed in her column as "intellectual snobs."[36] "It was harder to get a seat at the Algonquin Round Table than to be invited to dinner at Buckingham Palace," she wrote. "I . . . used to see the freeze-out that was given the brave souls who occasionally tried to force their way to that table only to be snubbed."[37] She had a tendency to be loud and overbearing, particularly when she was nursing a hangover and could have used a restraining hand.

Harriet, now in college at Wellesley, kept an eye on her mother during holiday breaks. "Happy New Year to Louella O. Parsons," wrote Baird Leonard in the January 1925 issue of *Life* magazine, "because her daughter is her mother."[38]

Louella's crash was inevitable and, if anything, came too late, several weeks or even months after her friends had predicted it. It happened on a cold winter day, gray with clouds and drizzling rain. That morning she had gone to work and in the afternoon had attended a luncheon; that night, she lay in the Fifth Avenue Hospital, wondering what she had done that "God in his anger should will me to die."[39]

There had been warnings, but Louella had ignored them. For much of 1924 she had been plagued by chronic exhaustion and in May 1925, had ended up in the hospital after catching a cold that developed into tonsillitis. During that visit she may also have had a hysterectomy.[40] Though Louella remained tired and weak for several months, her job and her social life kept her in perpetual motion.

It was finally in the following winter when she sensed that all was not well. On the morning of November 7, she woke up feverish but knew it was impossible to call in sick; she had a column to turn out, several appointments, and a lunch meeting at noon. "I remember very little about the luncheon," she recalled. "The idea of food made me sick, and I knew I should go home and go to bed. But that was nonsense." After the meeting she took a taxi back to the *American* office and, at her desk, began coughing uncontrollably and hemorrhaging. Panicked, she called Teddy Bean, who took her to a doctor and then to the Fifth Avenue Hospital. At the hospital, a doctor told her to rest. But it was election day—Jimmy Walker was running for mayor and was sure to win—and Louella was determined to attend the parties that evening. Against the doctor's wishes, she left the hospital after only a few hours and headed to a party at Hearst's home.[41] There she collapsed. After running upstairs to answer a phone call from Davies, Louella hemorrhaged again, fell on the floor, and was rushed to her suite at the Algonquin by Samuel Goldwyn and his wife. "Now I knew I was done. I couldn't even pretend to fight any longer," she recalled.[42] It was tuberculosis, the same disease that had killed Joshua Oettinger.

The following morning, Hearst called Louella and discharged her for a year on full salary, insisting that she recuperate. Confident that the dry, warm air in the Southern California desert would cure Louella's tuberculosis, Hearst summoned Harriet from Wellesley, purchased train tickets, and shipped mother and daughter to the small, rural California desert town of Colton.

This was not the first time Hearst had come to the aid of an ill-fated employee. When a valuable Hearst writer lost thousands of dollars gambling, Hearst rescued him from his debts. When cartoonist Jimmy Swinnerton came down with tuberculosis, Hearst sent him to recover in Arizona. Employees who stole from Hearst were never punished for their deeds, and many took "advances" that they never bothered to repay.[43] Sentimental and loyal to his workers, Hearst had a capacity for "sudden kindness," in the words of one biographer.[44]

To Hearst, sending Louella to Colton was simply an act of generosity that he extended to his best employees. But to Louella, Hearst had become the benevolent father figure she never had as a child. From that moment on, she vowed that she would spend the rest of her life repaying him for having saved her life. "Such loyalty, such kindness, seemed more than I could bear," Louella remembered. "Where are there words to express further the greatness and understanding of this man who is so often vilified by the people who do not know him?" "He was the best friend I ever had," she wrote more than twenty years later. "The proof of that lies in the fact that I am still here."[45]

In New York, news of Louella's illness and departure circulated quickly in press and film circles. *Variety* incorrectly reported that she had gone to California to write news; *Zits' Weekly* called it a "vacation." Another paper claimed that she had a "nervous breakdown." Only the *New York Star* had it right. "Louella O. Parsons is dangerously ill," it declared, "and her complete recovery is doubtful."[46] Even Louella was skeptical. As she sat on the westbound train, coughing and hemorrhaging, she wondered whether she would ever see New York again.

She had envisioned a sanitarium surrounded by green lawns, fountains, and palm trees, like those she had seen in Hollywood. When the train finally pulled into what looked like a deserted ghost town, her heart sank. She had been told by Hearst that Colton was a wonderful place to recuperate, but she was skeptical about the possibility of recovery. "Oh—I thought—what a hell of a place for me to die!"[47]

Though it was only fifty miles east of Los Angeles in the San Bernardino Valley, the sleepy town of Colton seemed as far away from Hollywood as New York. Founded in the 1870s as a railway stop on the Southern Pacific line, by the turn of the century it was home to several citrus ranches, a cement company, and the Globe Flour Mill, one of the largest milling establishments in the state.[48] In 1925, it had one movie theater, two telephones—both of them on one line—and a population of six thousand.[49] It was the last place Louella wanted to be.

Years later, on a radio broadcast with Louella, Harriet recalled those weeks in Colton as "our worst time." "You and I felt just like a stranded vaudeville team as the train disappeared and left us standing forlornly on the deserted platform," she remembered. A sophomore at Wellesley who was a member of the literary journal, theater club, and basketball and crew teams, Harriet traded her active college schedule for long days of confinement in a dusty, barren hotel room at her ailing mother's side. Despite the somber mood, "we had some wonderful laughs and fine talks," Harriet recalled, and near the end of her stay, she rented a car and took Louella on short jaunts around the desert.[50]

By late December, Louella was recovering. Rest and a healthy diet had improved her condition, and though she still ran a fever and had lost considerable weight, by Christmas the hemorrhages had ceased. Her strength regained, she called Hearst and asked to be moved to Palm Springs, a nearby desert town that was gaining a reputation as an international hot spot. Hearst consented, and in late December Louella moved to the Desert Inn, a famed Palm Springs hotel where artists, affluent vacationers, and members of the Hollywood film community sought sunshine and solace. "Every day some director, scenario writer, film editor, or star walks past my cottage," she wrote. With its "orange trees and flowering plants," backed by a "range of majestic mountains, positively breathtaking in their color and beauty," Palm Springs, Louella predicted, is "destined to be the greatest winter resort in the world."[51]

Energized by her new residence and improving health, Louella swung back into action. Through letters and telegrams she directed the preparations for the annual Newspaper Women's Ball and, by early 1926, began writing features and columns for syndication through the Universal News Service, one of Hearst's two major news syndication services.[52] As a New York celebrity, she was also the subject of several articles and photo layouts in the *American*, which chronicled the saga of her recovery in the desert. These texts and pictures, carefully crafted by the Hearst press, reinforced the merger of traditional and modern values that was the essence of her public image. In one article, Louella described rural Colton and New York as sharing similar tastes in movies. Defusing the potent cultural conflicts that had flared between rural and urban Americans in the 1920s, Louella wrote that, despite their different lifestyles, small-town and city dwellers both appreciated "clean and artful" films. In one photograph, displayed prominently in the *American*, Louella sat at an outdoor table with her typewriter against a backdrop of sagebrush and desert hills. Neither a flapper nor a prude, she appeared fashionably yet demurely dressed in a long skirt and blouse and gazed off into the mountains, deep in thought.[53]

In February 1926, novelist John Galsworthy retreated to the Desert Inn to work on his novel *The Silver Spoon*, and Louella, along with Darryl Zanuck, a writer for Warner Brothers who was working on a film in Palm Springs, interviewed Galsworthy for the Hearst papers. Later, Zanuck, whom Louella claimed became as close as a "blood relative" that winter, brought a film to Palm Springs to cheer her up. "What an audience we had: Indians, hotel guests, bell boys, and ranchers. It was the first picture I had seen in months, and Darryl announced that the premiere was given especially for me. It was a wonderful morale builder."[54] Zanuck kept Louella informed of the latest gossip in the California film colony, and in February 1926 Louella made two trips to visit Davies in Beverly Hills.

In March, feeling fully recovered, Louella called Hearst and told him that she was ready to come back to New York. The only telephone in Palm Springs was in the lobby of the Desert Inn, and in order to be heard over the poor connection, Louella had to shout. When Hearst said no, Louella shouted back, insisting that she was well enough to return. Hearst then proposed a plan that he claimed would make her the most powerful woman in Hollywood and potentially the most influential movie writer in the world.[55]

According to Hearst's plan, Louella would move permanently to Los Angeles and become motion picture editor of the Universal News Service. As editor, she would turn out daily columns and film reviews that would appear not only in the *Los Angeles Examiner*, the Hearst morning paper where she was to be headquartered, but also in all twenty of the Hearst papers and those that subscribed to the Universal News Service.[56] Florence Lawrence, the current film writer on the *Los Angeles Examiner*, would move to Hearst's *Chicago Examiner*, and Eileen Creelman, a New York writer who subbed for Louella when she was in Palm Springs, would take over Louella's berth on the *American*. With worldwide exposure and a salary of $350 a week, it was an offer she couldn't pass up.[57]

She didn't. Without a moment's hesitation, Louella agreed to sign a three-year contract, and for years she referred to that day in Palm Springs as the luckiest in her life. "Well, at last, boys," she said to directors Winfield Sheehan and Raoul Walsh, who were with her in the lobby, "the Hollywood writer is going to Hollywood!"[58]

The move made sense for both Louella and Hearst. By 1926, Hearst was locked into his production deal with MGM and had completed the construction of San Simeon, his palatial estate north of Santa Barbara, where he would take up residence the following year. With both Hearst and his movie enterprise in California, it was logical that Louella would follow. In addition, Hearst, like Louella, knew how difficult it was to report on Hollywood while living in New York. While in New York, Louella had been limited to the secondhand gossip telegrammed and telephoned to her by Marion Davies and Hedda Hopper and to interviews with actors and directors vacationing in New York. By moving to Hollywood, Louella would have access to breaking celebrity news and could serve as Hearst's representative to the studios— in particular, to MGM. No producer or studio boss would double-cross Hearst on a production deal, or push Davies around, if Louella threatened him with poor press in the Hearst papers.

Besides, Louella had little to keep her in New York. Harriet was away at Wellesley and planned to move to Hollywood to work as a screenwriter when she graduated in 1927. Louella's relationship with Peter Brady, strained by her prolonged stay in the desert, was becoming untenable. By late 1926 the two were fighting over Brady's reluctance to leave his marriage and their incompatible schedules, and Louella often found herself furious at his arrogance and insensitivity.[59] Maggie Oettinger (who had changed the spelling of her last name to Ettinger) had moved to Hollywood, having taken a job in the publicity department at MGM in 1924, and most of Louella's film friends were stationed in the West.

In March 1926 Louella returned to New York, packed up her suite at the Algonquin, and celebrated her new position with a round of parties. She was feted by the Professional Women's League and the Woman Pays Club, which encouraged her to establish a branch of the organization in Southern California. At a well-publicized gala affair at the Newspaper Women's Club, Louella passed the presidency of that organization to Teddy Bean. In film and journalism circles, the announcement of Louella's move was met with trepidation. With firsthand access to Hollywood news and extensive national readership, Louella would have a powerful effect on public opinion. "The appearance, every day, of her news stories and comment [from] Los Angeles," noted one writer for a Los Angeles paper, would have an effect that was potentially "beyond reckoning."[60] Meanwhile, Hollywood waited for Louella's imminent arrival.

SEVEN

Hollywood

THEY WERE THE "DAYS OF PROHIBITION, the old Montmartre Café, the Cocoanut Grove, the Charleston, and the Black Bottom," Louella recalled. "Bands were playing 'Yes, Sir, That's My Baby.' The girls were wearing knee-length evening gowns and big bows on high-heeled slippers. Clara Bow was the biggest box office star."[1] The environment in Hollywood in the mid-1920s was wild and heady, colored by the raucous pleasures of Prohibition nightlife and the newfound wealth of the movie elite. The Montmartre Café, on Sunset Boulevard, boasted crystal chandeliers and carpets from Europe and twenty-four hundred pounds of solid silver service. The premiere Hollywood nightclub in the 1920s, the Cocoanut Grove, was decorated with stuffed monkeys dangling from fake palm trees.[2] Hollywood movie theaters were literal temples of entertainment: Sid Grauman's Egyptian Theater, constructed in 1923, was an archaeologically exact replica of an Egyptian temple, complete with hieroglyphics, statuary, and sarcophagi, and the United Artists theater, designed as a Spanish cathedral, featured an elaborate mural emblazoned with larger-than-life portraits of actors Constance Talmadge, Rudolph Valentino, Douglas Fairbanks, and Charlie Chaplin.[3]

Given the city's future reputation, its founders were unlikely. In 1903, a band of Christian Prohibitionists from Kansas, seeking their fortunes in the West, established Hollywood as a small farming village and fashioned it after the conservative Midwest they had left. An ordinance passed that year banned factories and high-rise buildings; dancing, drinking, and public merrymaking were similarly prohibited. The village would be a quiet, devout Protestant utopia, as clean and bright as the California sunshine.

The Edenic visions were short lived. In 1909, William Selig of the Chicago-based Selig Film Company, in search of winter sunshine, took a troupe of actors to Southern California to shoot a film. Word of Selig's discovery traveled quickly, and by 1911 several filmmakers, including D. W. Griffith, had taken crews to the Los Angeles area. By 1912, huge barnlike studios had cropped up on deserted lots, and cheap apartment buildings and hotels were hastily erected to house the flood of newcomers seeking careers in the movies. As the population rose, from seven hundred in 1903 to seventy-five hundred in 1913, so did the founders' tempers.[4] In an attempt to chase the actors away, restaurants, apartment houses, and theaters posted signs reading "No Movies Allowed."

But the "Hollywood gold rush" continued. Spurred by the rapid growth of the Los Angeles area—between 1900 and 1920 over a million and a half migrants settled in the area to capitalize on an oil and real estate boom—Hollywood soon became a bustling factory town. By 1920, the film industry had become the largest industry in the Los Angeles area, with tens of thousands of workers and a payroll of over twenty-five million dollars.[5]

Even the apartment buildings in Hollywood were swanky. The Garden of Allah, on Sunset Boulevard, consisted of a main house and twenty-five villas built around a huge pool. The Garden Court Apartments on Hollywood Boulevard, built in Italian Renaissance style, boasted thick Oriental carpets in every room; and the Champs Elysee, owned by Thomas Ince's widow, Nell, had been built in a French Normandy style and featured crystal chandeliers.[6]

Nell Ince also owned the Villa Carlotta on Franklin Avenue, an elegant Spanish-style building that in the fall of 1926 became Louella's new home. After a brief stay with Maggie Ettinger and her young son, Gordon, Louella moved into a ground-floor apartment at the noisy Carlotta—"I might just as well be awakened by the telephone as by a rehearsing opera singer who starts warbling with the birds," she recalled—and was promptly burgled. "I didn't know whether . . . it was just a common garden variety burglar," she later wrote, "or some of the movie people looking for me with a gun."[7] Given the film industry's relationship with the Hearst press—a testy relationship dating back to 1921—she was only partially joking.

In September 1921, comedian Roscoe "Fatty" Arbuckle, second in national popularity only to Charlie Chaplin, had rented several rooms in the St. Francis Hotel in San Francisco for a weekend party. A minor actress, twenty-seven-year-old Virginia Rappe, attended the event and during the party became violently ill; two days later she died in a hospital of peritonitis. Though the peritonitis most likely stemmed from a sexually transmitted disease or a botched abortion, at the party she had screamed out: "Roscoe killed me."

Party guests interpreted her cry as an accusation of rape, and some claimed that the force of Arbuckle's weight—more than 250 pounds—had caused Rappe's bladder to rupture. Arbuckle was subsequently charged with murder, and the newspapers had a field day.

"ARBUCKLE DRAGGED RAPPE GIRL TO ROOM" read headlines in one local newspaper. "Composographs" showed pictures of prison bars superimposed on Arbuckle and juxtaposed images of Arbuckle, Rappe, and a bottle of whiskey. Lurid stories in San Francisco and Los Angeles newspapers suggested gruesome possibilities; among them, that Arbuckle had raped the actress using a jagged piece of ice or a Coke bottle. Angry moviegoers turned against Arbuckle by boycotting his films, and the Paramount Studio terminated his contract. Though Arbuckle was eventually acquitted, his career was destroyed.

Arbuckle was not the only casualty. Coming at a time when Hollywood was still under intense scrutiny by social reformers, the press circus only stirred up further antimovie sentiment. Following the Arbuckle case, the unsolved murder of director William Desmond Taylor in 1922, and the death of actor Wallace Reid from a drug overdose in 1923, film censorship bills were introduced in twenty states. Movie "czar" Will Hays, hired in the aftermath of the scandals, pressured the producers to adopt a code of self-censorship in 1924. This was expanded in 1927 into the "Don'ts and Be Carefuls," an elaborate code prohibiting the depiction of profanity, nudity, drug use, white slavery, miscegenation, and "sex perversion," among other sins. Morals clauses requiring actors to follow a strict code of behavior were written into studio contracts, and unmarried stars who were seeing each other were pressured to marry. Producers hired detectives to investigate their employees, and they fired employees seen as potential "moral liabilities."[8]

The studios had a right to be afraid of Louella. The paper that had led the campaign against Arbuckle was the *San Francisco Examiner,* published by Hearst.

Employed at the *Morning Telegraph* at the time, Louella never mentioned the Arbuckle scandal in her column, and she did not discuss the case until after his April 1922 acquittal.[9] With her falsified accounts of actors' squeaky-clean lifestyles, she had been one of the industry's greatest boosters and defenders. But Hearst was known to be unpredictable and ruthless, particularly when it came to boosting circulation in Los Angeles, where his *Evening Herald* and *Examiner* battled to maintain their lead over the *Los Angeles Times.*

Founded in 1903 as a union-friendly alternative to the *Times,* the *Examiner* was known for its photojournalism and sensational crime stories.[10] The *Examiner* staff, according to the Los Angeles newspaper historian Rob Wagner, was a "mixed bag of responsible, ethical newsmen and women and fascists, Communists, crooks, thugs, and opportunists." Many of the paper's top journalists were seasoned professionals who had come from New York and Chicago, while others had neither experience nor talent but had "conned an acceptable $25 a week living through hack reporting and a willingness to make deals and play fast and loose with facts."[11] The *Examiner* building had been designed by Julia Morgan, the famed architect who also designed Hearst's San Simeon residence. The imposing mission-style building, which featured white adobe-like walls, rounded clay roof tiles, wide arches, and wrought iron balconies, took up an entire block downtown. Louella's office was across the street from the main *Examiner* building, in the Los Angeles Railroad Building. There, she worked with her two editorial assistants, "legmen" Jimmy DeTarr and Jerry Hoffman.

DeTarr, a distant cousin, had been her legman for five years and had come over with her from New York.[12] Hoffman, who graduated to having his own *Examiner* column in the early 1930s, had been an editor at the trade journal *Motion Picture News* in the mid-1920s, when Louella hired him on a part-time basis. When the editor of the *News* demanded that Hoffman stop working for Louella, Hoffman resigned from the paper and stayed with Louella. Though a tough and critical boss, she was, Hoffman claimed, "the most generous person in the world."[13] Louella also worked closely with city editor Ray Van Ettisch, who had joined the *Examiner* in the early 1920s. Though he was known for his calm demeanor, Van Ettisch sometimes found himself pressed into bouts of temper when Louella demanded the right to cover a front-page news story and hounded him to let her steal the assignment from another reporter.[14]

Written in the same vein as her column for the *New York American,* Louella's *Examiner* column, "Flickerings from Filmland," was aimed at a readership of both industry insiders and fans. The column featured production news, reports on social events in the movie colony, and tidbits of star trivia, alongside Louella's daily film review. In her debut column on April 12, 1926, she reported:

The Ambassador Hotel in Los Angeles looks like the Astor Hotel in New York during the early days when the "fillum" men gathered to plan their campaigns over strong coffee and much scribbled table covers. They are all here—Adolph Zukor, Carl Laemmle, Winfield Sheehan, Richard Rowland, William Fox, P. A. Powers, Sam Katz, S. L. Rothapfel, and scores of lesser lights.

I am told that the exotic Pola Negri has changed her mind about Valentino. No longer is he her ideal and the one handsome sheik of her life. In short, Pola and Rudy have come to a parting of the ways. Who is next? Well I haven't heard yet but judging from Pola's past record it's a handsome lad, possibly a movie editor.[15]

The only source of daily movie news in the Los Angeles area, "Flickerings from Filmland" was read religiously both by movie fans and film industry personnel. The only other movie-related column was a daily film review by Edwin Schallert in the *Times*. "Like most people of that era, one of the first things I turned to was Louella Parsons' column," remembered silent film actress Pola Negri.[16] By the summer of 1926, the column had become so detailed and lengthy that the *Examiner* began cutting its theater section to accommodate it. Angry theater managers protested. Claiming that Louella gave studios free publicity through her column, they demanded that Louella's column be trimmed in the name of "better representation": "The theater men, who do at least patronize the *Examiner*'s advertising columns, should be given a preference in publicity."[17] Their protest was in vain, and the column continued unaltered. Thanks to Louella, the *Examiner* was experiencing a circulation boom. "[Louella] had faults, but she sold papers," recalled one colleague, "and that's why Hearst hired her and kept her on." In 1927, Louella filed exclusive reports on Pola Negri's wedding to the Russian prince Serge Mdivani, on actress Vilma Banky's marriage to actor Rod LaRocque, and on the divorce of Jack Pickford, Mary Pickford's brother. Each of these exclusive stories sold an estimated five thousand additional copies of the *Examiner*, and the Negri story prompted an additional ten thousand papers to fly from the newsstands.[18]

Between 1927 and 1929, Louella was not only cementing her position as one of the city's best-read columnists but also establishing a repertoire of news-gathering tactics and a working relationship with the studios. During the 1920s, a series of corporate mergers led to the creation of five vertically integrated film companies—Paramount, Warner Brothers, Fox, RKO, and Loews, the parent company of the MGM studio—that dominated film production, distribution, and exhibition until the late 1940s. Annually, the "Big '

Five" each produced forty to eighty movies, which were created in their massive Hollywood production facilities. For example, by the early 1930s the MGM lot spanned 117 acres and had twenty-three sound stages, a park, a miniature jungle, and the world's largest film laboratory. Movies created by the Big Five were exhibited nationwide in the theater chains they owned.[19] Though these companies owned only 15 percent of America's movie theaters, they took in almost 70 percent of box office income, since their holdings included the most profitable urban theaters in the nation. Three other film companies, Columbia, Universal, and United Artists, which owned no theaters, were also involved in production and distribution, and these "Little Three," along with the Big Five, collectively known as the majors, were the key players in the Hollywood studio system.[20]

Internally, the studios were organized into departments, each with a leader under the direct command of the studio head. One of the most important departments was the publicity department, which was responsible for disseminating to the press any information about the studio's contracted stars. Much if not most of the information was fabricated. "Studio biographies" presented phony accounts of actors' lives that portrayed them as moral, upstanding, home-loving individuals who retained their humility and work ethic despite their wealth and glamour. Special care was taken to ensure continuity between the actors' on- and offscreen personae. Those actors who portrayed "athletic types" on screen, for example, were described as being sportsmen in real life, and innocent ingenues were said to be similarly sweet and lovable offscreen. When the producers, often in response to audience input, altered the actors' type, the publicity also changed. In a famous example, when Bette Davis was hired by the Warner Brothers studio in the early 1930s, she was typed as a flirtatious blonde bombshell, and press releases described her as a "love expert" and "temptress." When the studio began casting her as a serious, temperamental vamp, the press releases were revised to depict her as a "manwrecker" exuding "fatal attraction."[21] Of all the studios, MGM was known for having the best-organized and most sophisticated publicity department, with over a hundred employees under the direction of Howard Strickling, known as the "dean of studio publicists."[22]

Publicists wrote the feature stories and press releases, copy editors reviewed them, and "planters" placed them wherever they thought they could get the best exposure—either in fan magazines, trade papers, or newspapers. Given the prominence and circulation of Louella's column, scoring an item in "Flickerings in Filmland" was a major coup. To keep in Louella's good graces, the

publicists used a technique, dubbed the trade technique, in which they promised Louella exclusive news in exchange for positive press in the column.[23]

Officially, Louella met the publicists weekly at a luncheon at the Montmartre Café.[24] Informally, she consulted them at parties, nightclubs, and her
unofficial office at the Brown Derby restaurant on Vine Street in Hollywood.
By 1928, she had become a near-permanent fixture at the Derby, and propri-
etor Bob Cobb gave Louella her own private booth. Cobb also created a special dessert for her. Louella, who loved sweets, was always on a diet. After one
of her weekly staff gatherings at the Derby, she told Cobb that she refused to
come back unless he put a nonfattening dessert on the menu. Reasoning that
a dessert with grapefruit would satisfy her, he invented the Derby's famous
Classic Grapefruit Cake. It was hardly low-calorie, but it was enough to satisfy Louella, who remained a regular customer for the rest of her life.[25]

Though she often used information given to her directly from the publicists, she prided herself on the fact that she did much of her own reporting.
This, in her mind, separated her from other movie writers and reviewers, who
relied almost exclusively on studio press material. Louella depended on her
personal connections with studio executives, producers, and actors and a co-
terie of local informants. At the Hollywood Hotel, a popular celebrity hang-
out, she paid bellboys and chambermaids for news. At the Montmartre Café,
she eavesdropped on lunching celebrities, and at Jim's Beauty Shop on Highland Avenue, she pressured manicurists and hairdressers for the latest "dirt"
on their high-profile clientele.[26] "She was a freeloader," remembered one employee of a local beauty parlor, recalling that, although Louella promised to
pay for news, she was often short on cash.[27]

Knowing the power she wielded over public opinion, young actors tried
to befriend her. Not long after Louella's arrival in Hollywood, she was approached by Bess Peters, the mother of the aspiring teenage actress Jane Peters. The elder Peters asked Louella to put in a good word for her daughter
with Winfield Sheehan, the production chief of Fox Films. Since Sheehan
owed Louella a favor, he signed Jane Peters to a yearlong contract. Shortly afterward, Peters changed her name to Carole Lombard and embarked on a
successful screen career.[28]

In film and press circles, Louella became notorious for her obsessive devotion to her work. As one fan magazine profile on Louella noted in 1926,
she wrote, interviewed, and researched between twelve and sixteen hours a
day. The magazine writer, who had planned to meet Louella one morning at
the *Examiner* office, "had to wait until late afternoon before [Louella] came

in." "[Louella] had luncheon with one of the most brightly scintillating of the movie stars and had been to several studios getting the latest facts and gossip for her next day's article. Just before dinner time she returned to her office—with the real work of writing her articles still ahead. Every day she does this," the author continued. "And not only that, but in order to make her criticisms and discussions of the movies judicious, she must have read all other recent discussions and criticisms of the movies as well as getting the opinions of the producers or actors themselves."[29]

But the hard work was paying off. According to *Editor and Publisher,* by the fall of 1926, Louella's syndicated column had over six million readers, both in Los Angeles and across the country.[30] Dubbed by one fan publication as the "official source of information" on film to readers worldwide, Louella was receiving over a thousand fan letters a week.[31] That November, she affixed her name to another three-year contract with Hearst and began one of the most fulfilling and challenging periods of her career.

Though Louella's main focus was her daily column, Hearst occasionally commissioned her to write front-page news stories and other nonmovie features. In September 1926, Louella went to Philadelphia to report on the celebrated Dempsey-Tunney boxing match.[32] For Louella, a boxing fan since her days at the *New York Morning Telegraph,* the assignment was a dream come true. With Harriet, who was returning to Wellesley after summer vacation, and fellow Hearst reporter Gene Fowler, Louella took the train east.

Because Dempsey and Tunney had both appeared in films and because "over half the movie colony" was rumored to be attending the fight, Hearst had instructed Louella to write the story with a "Hollywood" angle. But the story that resulted was less about the star-studded match than about Louella's experience covering the fight as the sole female reporter. "The night of the fight, I started to take a seat in the press box," she recalled. "This started a near riot. There were 258 male reporters, and a shout was raised that the press box was no place for a lone woman." When Tex Rickard, Dempsey's manager, called for a vote, the reporters finally decided that Louella could stay. "I couldn't help thinking what my grandmother would have said if she could have seen her favorite grand-daughter with pencil poised, sitting with all the sports writers, getting the thrill of a lifetime at being allowed to report a fight. The only woman, if you please, sitting in the seats of the high and the mighty."[33]

After Philadelphia, she went to nearby Somerville, New Jersey, where she reported on the Hall-Mills trial, one of the most sensational murder trials of the decade. Like the other journalists in the courtroom—more than 120 reporters were assigned to the case—Louella wrote melodramatically about the "drama of life" that had the entire town of Somerville as enraptured as a "motion picture audience." The Hearst papers advertised that "Miss Parsons, probably the most widely read authority on motion pictures in the country, has pictured the settings and criticized the actors of this real life drama as though it were passing before her on the silver screen." Likening the players in the trial to screen stars, Louella wrote that Mrs. Hall, on trial for the murder of her husband, had been dealt an "unsympathetic role" that she played "with realism few actresses on the screen could duplicate."[34]

In between assignments she stopped by the *American* office in New York, where she found flowers sent from D. W. Griffith. In response, she wrote Griffith, "I do want to see you and have a talk with you, and thank you in person for your friendship, which I always know I have whether I am sick or well. There are so few people one can call friend, and I have always been so proud that I could place you in that category.[35] But the point of her visit to New York was to see Peter Brady, and Louella divided her time between writing her column, which she dispatched from the *American* office, and rendezvous with her lover.

In the summer of 1927, Brady, who had been appointed chairman of Mayor Jimmy Walker's committee on aviation, traveled west and arranged for Louella to join him aboard a giant army airplane known as a Fokker, at Clover Field in Los Angeles, from which they would fly to Crissy Field in San Francisco. Using the flight as a publicity stunt, Louella brought along her typewriter, donned a pair of mechanics' overalls and a twenty-five-pound parachute, and wrote her column while flying up the California coast. Articles in the Hearst papers portrayed her as a modern Nellie Bly and lauded her for her courage and adventurousness. "She is the only newspaper woman to have written a story while flying 7000 feet in the air. She is the first civilian woman to make a flight in a government plane," reported the *San Francisco Examiner.*[36]

The landing was smooth, but she returned to find Hollywood in an uproar. In the fall of 1927, the studios were being revolutionized by sound.

It was the single greatest transformation in motion picture history. As a business, an art form, and a medium of popular entertainment, the American cinema—virtually every aspect of it—was affected by the arrival of sound technology in the mid-1920s. Though sound wreaked havoc on the studios, they had seen it coming. At the turn of the century, Thomas Edison had experimented with linking film to the phonograph, and by 1920 several inventors had created systems that were nearly feasible. Finally, in 1925, the Bell Telephone Company's research laboratory, Western Electric, developed and marketed a sound-on-disc process called the Vitaphone. Though the Vitaphone was primitive—the recording quality was poor, and voices came out distant and garbled—it was the first system that worked. Films, silent for thirty years, could now *talk*.

Rather than prompting cheers of elation throughout Hollywood, however, the Vitaphone elicited only a lukewarm response. Talking pictures might be intriguing in theory, but in practice, applying sound technology would be time-consuming, arduous, and expensive.

In order to produce and exhibit sound films, studios would have to not only purchase entirely new equipment but also wire all their theaters for sound, a process that averaged twenty thousand dollars per theater. Moreover, there was no guarantee that audiences would take to the "talkies." Film attendance was at an all-time high, and many fans, when interviewed by magazines, expressed reluctance to hear their screen idols talk. When a theater in Glendale, California, announced to the audience that it might soon be showing sound films, the audience burst into boos and catcalls. Many actors were bombarded by fan letters begging them not to let their voices be recorded.[37]

Thus, it was hardly a surprise when the major film studios, in 1925, exhibited little interest in the Vitaphone system. A year later, however, Warner Brothers, a "minor" Hollywood studio bent on expanding its operations and making it to the big time, decided to make the risky investment and signed a contract with Western Electric. During the 1926–27 season, Warner Brothers released nine films with recorded musical sound tracks, to mixed reviews. Though these films had synchronized sound, they did not talk, which disappointed many audiences. It was not until the fall of 1927, when Warner Brothers released *The Jazz Singer,* a musical containing several scenes of recorded dialogue, that the talkie era really began. When the film scored high at the box office and won rave reviews, Warners announced that all its films in the 1928–29 season would be "Vitaphoned." Grudgingly, the rest of the Hollywood studios jumped on the sound bandwagon.

Though nearly all the major studios were reluctant to invest in sound, the most reluctant was MGM. One of the most profitable and prestigious studios of the 1920s, MGM had done well with its silent productions, and studio executives Louis B. Mayer and Irving Thalberg saw little reason to change. Even more than Mayer and Thalberg, Hearst was opposed to sound. The high cost of wiring the theaters, he predicted, would put hundreds of independent movie houses out of business, thus cutting down on venues for his newsreels. "His pet screen hobby has always been his newsreels, and any condition within the industry that might threaten the distribution of this particular product would undoubtedly find Mr. Hearst ready to put up a tremendous fight to protect it," explained *Variety*.[38] To make matters worse, Davies had an incurable stutter, and the talkies would almost certainly destroy her career. Hearst ordered Louella to whip up antitalkie sentiment in her column, which she did throughout late 1927 and 1928. "I have no fear that scraping, screeching, rasping sound film will disturb our peaceful motion picture theaters. The industry is too wise to spend fortunes for machines, new equipment, and sound stages to project noise that the customers do not want to hear," she wrote.[39] "Who wants to have the art of pantomime utterly destroyed by a mechanical device that promotes conversation where it is unnecessary?" she asked in 1928.[40] "I do not believe any of the producers will be foolish enough to destroy the silence of the screen by attempting to make a series of one hundred percent talking pictures. It would be the height of folly."[41]

Despite the criticism, MGM and the rest of the studios had begun to incorporate recorded dialogue into their films by late 1928. Envisioning sound as a kind of "spice" that could be added to films for extra flavor, most film executives imagined a partial transition, in which films contained both silent and sound scenes. But public pressure for an "all talking" cinema was increasing daily. Studio financiers shuddered at the thought of the expense, while actors entered a state of terror. They had made their fortunes by their faces and gestures; none of them, save the few stage actors who had come to Hollywood, knew how to act. Joan Crawford described those tense times in a single word: panic![42] Actors frantically enlisted in voice lessons, while speech and acting coaches flocked to Hollywood to capitalize on the revolution.

After actors spent months training in diction and elocution, the moment of truth arrived: the dreaded "talkie screen test." Each morning, recalled silent-film actor Buddy Rogers, the studios "would take a star to find out if they had a voice. One morning they took Harold Lloyd in. At four the boy came out and said, 'Harold Lloyd has a voice.' The next day, Wally Beery. We waited . . . and about 3:30 in the afternoon, the door opened. The cry rang out: 'Wally Beery has a voice.'"[43] The tests were nerve-wracking but important, since multimillion-dollar careers hung in the balance. Many if not most of the stars survived. Blessed with good voices and speech coaches, and in some cases prior dramatic experience, they made the transition to the talkies with little or no damage to their careers. Even Davies passed. She had been so terrified of making her talkie screen test that she considered quitting film altogether, but Hearst brought speech and elocution coaches from Broadway to help her. On the morning of the test, Davies fortified herself with a glass of sherry, then proceeded to pass the test with flying colors. Impressed, Irving Thalberg extended her contract.[44]

But those who fell from grace fell hard. The fates of two of America's most popular silent stars, Clara Bow and John Gilbert, became tragic testaments to the fragility of stars' careers during the talkie transition. Though they passed the studio talkie tests and were put into sound films, these two failed the ultimate test—the showdown with the fans. Clara Bow's Brooklyn accent, audiences and reviewers declared, was "hard and metallic," and she quickly fell out of favor. ("All her s.a. [sex appeal] and all of her 'it,'" *Photoplay* magazine joked, "couldn't make her talkies a hit.")[45] After his talkie debut in the 1929 film *His Glorious Night,* John Gilbert became an object of national humiliation. Shocked to discover that the handsome, romantic Gilbert had a boyish, high-register voice, audiences jeered. (The morning after the premiere, *Variety* announced: "AUDIENCES LAUGHING AT GILBERT.") Some viewers were so appalled that they threw fruits and vegetables at the screen.[46]

Nerves were strained and egos fragile. A single bad review, a negative comment in a fan magazine, the rumor of a failed talkie screen test—criticism that could have been weathered in the past was now potentially fatal. And Louella, in the midst of this, became more important than ever. During the late 1920s, she devoted her column to the latest "talkie news"—who had passed their test, who had not, who was rumored to be studying with a voice coach, whose careers seemed destined for failure. Stars, directors, and producers depended on her column to gauge their own and their competitors' fortunes in the face of the upheaval.

Pola Negri read the results of her test at RKO in Louella's column, hours before she heard back from the studio. Louella often printed the outcomes, Negri recalled, "even before the people concerned were informed of it."[47] Louella also used her position to boost the imperiled careers of her friends.

Fearing that Bebe Daniels's dismissal from Paramount in 1929 would end her stardom, Louella attacked the studio in her column and announced confidently that the "gossip . . . that Bebe Daniels was finished in pictures" was a myth.[48] Louella so aggressively boosted Daniels and Davies that she was accused by *Variety* of promoting "Hollywood phoneys" and having "syndicated a story about how well the old screen stars were holding their own." "This is boloney," the publication claimed. "Louella is merely trying to stem the tide for her friends."[49]

Afraid that she would run damning accounts of actors' voices or tests, the major studio heads agreed to grant Louella first dibs on all news coming out of the studios. Because Louella's column for the *Examiner* was prepared two days in advance, the studios granted her a "48 hour exclusive," a promise that they would give Louella news at least forty-eight hours before they released it to other outlets. She now had a direct pipeline to breaking news that was virtually guaranteed. And thus began the exclusive arrangement that would ensure Louella's access to Hollywood gossip for over a decade.

Though her career was blossoming, Louella's love life was another story. She was still involved with Peter Brady, but their long-distance relationship was disintegrating. It was difficult for them to find time to talk, let alone meet, and Brady regularly fired off angry telegrams to Louella complaining about their incompatible schedules and Louella's inability to get to New York. Though she still loved him, she knew that it was time to move on. In 1927, twelve years after her ill-fated elopement with Jack McCaffrey, Louella went to the Los Angeles County Courthouse and filed for divorce from McCaffrey on grounds of desertion.[50] Now legally unattached, she began actively looking for a more permanent relationship, one potentially culminating in marriage.

In spite of her desire to find another man, she could not resist the opportunity, in the summer of 1928, to see Brady again. Knowing that Brady was one of the New York delegates to the 1928 Democratic National Convention in Houston, Louella convinced Hearst to send her to Houston to report on the convention from the "woman's angle." In June, she proposed, she would travel to Boston to see Harriet's graduation from Wellesley, then to New York to meet Brady, who would accompany her to the convention. Though by late May the itinerary had been set, a backlog of work forced her to postpone the trip for over a week. The change in plans caused Brady to change his schedule, and he sent a snide message to Louella. If she had been able to leave her "fascinating" Hollywood on time, the disruption would have been avoided.[51]

Finally, in early June 1928, Maggie Ettinger took Louella to the train station for her departure. Late as usual, Louella was running down the platform to catch her train when Maggie shouted at her. "Louella, I want you to meet someone," she yelled, pointing to a husky man behind her. "He'll be going East on the same train with you." When Louella finally got on the train, she turned and saw "the most Irish face" she'd ever seen.

Harry Watson Martin, racetrack addict and incurable practical joker, was a well-established urologist with a successful private practice in Hollywood. Born in 1890 in Redfield, South Dakota, he received his medical degree at the University of Illinois and served in the Army Medical Corps in World War I. In 1919 he moved to Hollywood, where he established a reputation as a specialist in abortions and sexually transmitted diseases, and as one who served clients from the local brothels. In 1924, he married actress Sylvia Bremer, and in 1927 they divorced. A loud and blustering but lovable Irishman with a penchant for alcohol, not long after his arrival in Hollywood, Harry dove into a shallow pool at the local Bimini Bathhouse and broke his neck. Still drunk, he held his neck in place while he walked to the nearest hospital for surgery. Notorious for his exaggerated tales, he claimed to have been a good friend of Al Capone's and to have knocked out Jack Dempsey.[52]

"His color was high, and he had startlingly blue eyes that disappeared almost completely when he smiled," Louella recalled. "He had a husky quality about his voice that I have always found particularly attractive in a man. Nice, I thought."[53] During the three-day train journey, Harry entertained Louella with jokes and stories and plenty of "subtle flattery." Louella could not help but be intrigued, but her obligation to Brady prevented her from going further. Then, as the train approached the Midwest, Louella received an angry telegram from Brady telling her that her delay prevented him from meeting her in Chicago as he had planned. If Louella wanted to see him, the telegram read, she would have to go to New York, where he *might* be able to meet her train. Furious at Brady's remarks but still eager to see him, Louella agreed to go to New York and bought tickets in Chicago. But the only train she could take departed in two days, leaving Louella in Chicago with Harry, who was there attending a medical convention. By the end of a romantic weekend, both Louella and Harry were smitten, and a confrontation with Brady seemed imminent. When Harry called Louella a week later in New

York, Brady, who was in the room, exploded. "If you see or talk to him again, I'm through," he threatened. "I'll never forgive you."[54]

Louella briefly escaped the tensions when she went to Boston in the middle of the month for Harriet's graduation. "Of all the things in the world I think this is my biggest thrill," she told her readers. During her four years at Wellesley, Harriet had been a star pupil—gifted in the classroom and an important contributor to the campus literary magazine and drama society. An avid playwright, songwriter, and director, Harriet had composed the class march and, in her senior year, directed the school play.[55] She planned to parlay her literary interests into a screenwriting career after graduation and a trip to Europe. Conveniently, Louella had secured her a coveted screenwriting position at MGM.

Upon her return to New York, Louella, Brady, and a group of Tammany Hall bigwigs boarded a private railroad car, "the Convention Special," bound for Houston. During the three-day journey south, Louella "queened it," she recalled, joking and flirting with the delegates and reveling in the flattery and attention.[56] When the entourage arrived in Houston, they were greeted by crowds and sweltering heat. Each day the temperature reached ninety-five degrees and some days even higher. "Thirty thousand perspiring Democrats are an active part of a mad scene here that makes the Christians in *Ben Hur* look like a Sunday school picnic and the battle scenes in *What Price Glory* and the *Big Parade* resemble a peace conference," she wrote in one of her first syndicated dispatches from the convention.[57] Swept up in the frenzy, she almost forgot that she and Brady were barely on speaking terms.

Per Hearst's instructions, Louella limited her reporting to the "woman's point of view." As a result, her articles mentioned nothing of the tumultuous events of the convention. Al Smith would receive the nomination, though the New York governor, an Irish-American Catholic who opposed Prohibition, raised controversy even among his own party's ranks. Barred from more substantive commentary, Louella focused on fashion—the dress styles and colors worn by the delegates' and candidates' wives. "The new color for the Democratic party . . . seems to be Catherine Blue, named in honor of Mrs. Al Smith," she wrote. But Brady and Jimmy Walker urged her to endorse Smith in one of her columns, and Louella relented. The article never made it into print. Smith's archenemy for years, Hearst promptly yanked the article from the papers.

She returned to Hollywood in July, accompanied by Brady and Walker, who were on vacation. Though thoughts of seeing Harry were on her mind,

Louella suppressed them while she escorted Brady and Walker on a whirl-wind tour of the Hollywood nightlife. One afternoon, at a special luncheon at the Montmartre Café given in honor of New York mayor Walker, Louella, seated between her two guests, looked up and saw Harry. "My heart gave one little glad leap," she recalled. "I knew then—if I had not suspected it in my heart before, that I loved Harry."[58]

From that moment, Louella committed herself to the pursuit of Harry Martin. It was a quest that consumed her almost as much as her work. "It is all right for a woman to go along with her career, thinking it can take the place in her life of a home and husband, for a little while," she wrote in her autobiography. "But the years have a way of sneaking by. Even the gayest path can be a lonesome road—if a woman is alone."[59]

In reality, Louella was hardly alone. Though she complained frequently of feel-ings of isolation, during virtually all her waking hours she was surrounded by colleagues and friends. She spent a good deal of time with Maggie Ettinger, who had since left the MGM publicity department to become one of the most successful independent publicists in Hollywood. Louella often went to Mag-gie's for late-night dinners, where they "gossiped endlessly, talked half the nights away, and generally had the time of [their] lives."[60] She also participated in the wild—and often illegal—entertainment that Prohibition had spawned. With the rest of the film colony, she spent her evenings at the Cocoanut Grove, where banquets, parties, and Charleston contests were held almost nightly and liquor flowed freely.[61] She became familiar with the nightlife on Washington Boulevard in Culver City, where gamblers, prostitutes, and mem-bers of the movie crowd frequented such notorious speakeasies as the Doo Doo Inn, the Kit Kat Club, Monkey Farm, Hoosegow, Club Royale, Harlow's Cafe, and the Sneak Inn.

A more respectable venue for nighttime pleasure was Marion Davies's beach house in Santa Monica. A colonial-style mansion surrounded by four smaller buildings, the Beach House featured a 110-foot heated swimming pool in Italian marble and over a hundred bedrooms that were occupied by Davies's family, guests, and thirty-two full-time servants. Louella, along with the rest of "Marion's crowd"—Charlie Chaplin, John Barrymore, Jesse Lasky, Louis B. Mayer, Sam and Frances Goldwyn, Norma Shearer and Irving Thal-berg, Mildred and Harold Lloyd, and Harry Crocker, among others—ap-peared regularly at the nightly dinner parties and weekend swimming parties that Davies held throughout the 1920s. Louella ("Loll," as Mary Pickford called her) was also a guest at Pickfair, the palatial Beverly Hills mansion that Pickford and her husband, Douglas Fairbanks, called home. Louella dined there regularly with Charlie Chaplin, John Barrymore, and Elinor Glyn, the famed British author.[62] She also showed up regularly at Hedda Hopper's Sunday afternoon parties. "Hedda Hopper's house seems to be the Mecca on Sunday afternoon for all filmland," she wrote in 1926. "I stopped there Sunday, and although Hedda said she had issued no invitations and it was no formal tea, half of the film colony wandered in during the course of the afternoon."[63]

Louella missed the camaraderie and support she had found in the Newspaper Women's Club and the Woman Pays Club in New York, and she continued to advocate higher status and better pay for women in journalism. Though women had risen in the ranks of the profession by the late 1920s, and they were working as managing editors, city editors, and even sports editors in many cities, they were still often caricatured as "flapperesque sob sisters" or "giggling girls," a stereotype that Louella worked to debunk. (One woman reporter on an Ohio newspaper complained that the "copy editor makes a sob sister out of women." If female reporters did not write according to the sob sister style, copy readers amended their stories to fit the mold.)[64] In a 1926 interview, Louella told *Editor and Publisher* magazine that, contrary to stereotype, the "modern newspaper woman is not only mentally alert but is smartly dressed. The idea of the dowdy-looking female with bedraggled hair and ill-fitting clothes as typical of every female reporter went out with the bicycle."[65]

In the spring of 1928, Louella organized a group of female newspaper reporters and fan magazine writers who covered Hollywood; the group met in her apartment to "swap shop talk." The informal gatherings soon became regular weekly meetings, and by 1929 the group, named the Hollywood Women's Press Club, was meeting each Wednesday at noon at the Vine Street Brown Derby. Unlike the New York Newspaper Women's Club, which worked to increase the status and visibility of female journalists, the Hollywood club was organized "to manage and conduct social meetings" and "to promote pleasure and recreation," according to its founding statement.[66]

The Wednesday lunches brimmed with companionship and enthusiasm. Bob Cobb at the Derby "gave us a rate of $1.25 a person. We could order anything we liked from squab to Cherries Jubilee," recalled Dorothy Manners, one of the group's early members. We came "to eat—and dish—and it was a lot of fun."[67] "The women of the club do no infighting," recalled another member. "That does not mean that everyone agrees with everyone else. We have had one or two brannigans that rocked us, but we have more mutual respect and interests than to indulge in open, picayune criticism of each other."[68]

Dorothy Manners, Gladys Hall, and Katherine Albert, three of the group's founding members, were well-known feature writers for the fan magazines *Motion Picture* and *Motion Picture Classic.* Ruth Biery, the West Coast editor of *Photoplay* magazine; Maude Latham, a society columnist; and Regina Carewe, a movie writer for the Hearst papers, were also part of the initial group. Together they shared gossip, vented their frustrations, and "the taboos of secrecy were thrown out the window!" recalled one member. When the group formally incorporated its bylaws in 1930 and began collecting dues, the women elected Louella president. She remained head of the organization until 1935, when she resigned, and she eventually resumed membership in 1954. The group became an important personal and professional network for Louella, and she handpicked several of her future employees from the club's membership. Member and fan magazine writer Ruth Waterbury would write Louella's radio scripts in the 1940s, and Manners became Louella's primary editorial assistant in 1934.

The club grew larger and more influential than Louella had ever imagined. By 1940, it boasted more than two dozen of the brightest and best-known women journalists and publicists in Hollywood. That year the group established its famous "Golden Apple" and "Sour Apple" awards, given annually to the stars who were most and least cooperative with the press. In honor of its founder, the group established the annual "Louella Parsons Award" in 1967. The award was bestowed yearly on "the person representing the best image of the entertainment industry to the world."[69]

On January 5, 1930, the *Los Angeles Examiner* announced, "Quietly and simply, Louella Parsons, motion picture editor at Universal Service, yesterday at dusk became the bride of Dr. Harry Watson Martin, distinguished Hollywood physician. In the presence of some three score intimate friends and relatives, the famous chronicler of Hollywood's joys and tragedies and the noted physician spoke the lines that joined them in wedlock."[70] The wedding took place in the lobby of Louella's apartment at the Villa Carlotta; Louella wore an elegant beige chiffon gown with satin shoes and matching gloves, and Harriet, in matching satin attire, served as the maid of honor. Louella and Harry had been engaged only two weeks.[71]

It was "the happiest day of my life," Louella claimed, "and the beginning of the happiest era of my life."[72]

EIGHT

Feuds

ON OCTOBER 29, 1929, the stock market crashed, sending the nation into financial crisis. Over the next three years, nine thousand banks closed their doors, Americans lost over two and a half billion dollars in deposits, and breadlines formed on street corners throughout the country. Nationwide, the unemployment rate shot up to 25 percent and as high as 70 or 80 percent in some cities.[1] Though the Great Depression would eventually wreak havoc on Hollywood, the film industry successfully weathered the first year of the crisis as the result of an attendance boom created by the talkies. Not until 1931 did the studios have to reckon with falling attendance.

Though the talkies were a financial boon to the industry, they also brought problems. In addition to requiring the costly and tedious process of reequipping theaters and production facilities, sound revived the battle over film regulation. As Broadway actors descended on the movie capital to seek their fortunes in film, they brought with them their scandalous reputations. Not only was Hollywood attracting "undesirable elements," critics claimed, but the dialogue in the talkies was violent and sexually explicit. By early 1930, a national film censorship bill, the Brookhart Bill, was being debated in Congress.[2]

Will Hays and the studio executives opposed federal censorship. Hearst, however, feared that "censorship cannot be abolished and the only thing we can do is to make it as little objectionable as possible," as he stated in a telegram to Hays in 1929. Hearst supported "uniform censorship"—the creation of a federal censorship board that would pass censorship rules acceptable to all of the different states. As things stood in 1929, the six existing state censorship boards used different standards. The Ohio board might find one scene objectionable and the Pennsylvania board another, forcing the studios to issue multiple versions of the same film. Hearst believed that his plan would not only do away with the multiple-version confusion but also protect the industry from even greater troubles at the box office. "No censorship at all would result in the irresponsibles in the profession issuing a number of pictures which would outrage the public and bring about a revival of the censorship idea in a more aggravated form than it exists at present," he explained to Hays.[3]

But an effective program of federal censorship, Hearst admitted, might take years to implement. A more immediate solution, he believed, was to force the film industry to enact more stringent self-censorship. As the reformers had repeatedly (and correctly) pointed out, the 1927 code of "Don'ts and Be Carefuls" was not being enforced by the producers. In a letter to Louella, Hearst explained:

> I think it is a moral duty to keep the morals of the public from being corrupted by the rotten sex pictures. Vulgarity invaded the stage and now there is apparently no limit to the vulgarity. Everybody knows that this has been a bad thing for the stage and yet the motion picture people have not taken the lesson to heart. Soon we will have a revolt against indecency on the screen. There will be an increase of censorship[,] and probably many states which do not now have censorship will have it, with all that this means in the way of difficulties for the producer. A little wisdom preached in the motion picture columns might avoid these complications.[4]

Prodded by Hearst, Louella used her column throughout 1929 to pressure the producers to follow the industry's self-censorship code and to assure her readers that, contrary to rumors, Hollywood was not being overtaken by "fast-living Broadway types." "You might think with all the Broadway theatrical element coming to our town the nightlife might become New Yorkish. Not a chance in Hollywood," she wrote. "Popular conception visualizes Hollywood as a place of lace-lined limousines, jewel-inlaid bathtubs, and Bacchanalian banquets. These exotic ideas of what constitute the average film star's daily routine are so directly opposed to the truth that some inspired soul must have invented this fiction."[5]

Though the 1930 censorship bill failed, the attack on the movies continued. In response, Martin Quigley, publisher of the trade journal *Exhibitors' Herald;* Father Daniel A. Lord, a Jesuit priest at St. Louis University; and Hays's assistant Jason Joy drafted a more stringent code of self-censorship, the Production Code, in 1930. The code banned profanity; homosexuality, or "sex perversion"; miscegenation; and the glorification of crime and other morally "degrading" activities, including cockfighting, bullfighting, bear-baiting, and adultery. In July 1930, Hays began a publicity campaign for the code and, in the *Ladies' Home Journal,* assured audiences that the new regulations would enable Hollywood to deal responsibly with the new "moral problems" created by sound films. In reality, the code did very little. Though the producers agreed to the code, most of them continued to pepper the talkies with the violence and sexual innuendo that 1930s audiences had come to expect in films. Catholic reform organizations continued their attacks.[6]

Hearst's interest in the censorship issue was overshadowed by concerns over losses in his publishing empire. Between 1925 and 1928, the Hearst papers, particularly in the Midwest and the East, had lost readers, and throughout 1928 Hearst made personnel and layout changes in hopes of boosting circulation. Hearst was particularly concerned about the readership of his papers' movie sections and feared that film fans were being lured away by the fan magazines. By 1930, *Screenland, Screen Play, Screenbook, Screen Stories, Screen Romances, Modern Screen,* and *Movies* had joined *Photoplay, Motion Picture Classic, Motion Picture,* and *Shadowland* in the fan magazine market, and mainstream magazines—*Liberty, True Story, Home Magazine, Collier's,* and *Redbook,* among others—were also offering detailed coverage of Hollywood.[7]

Believing that the movie pages in his papers were "sloppy and almost worthless," Hearst sent Louella on a nationwide tour to revamp his papers' motion picture coverage. Bearing a letter from Hearst, Louella traveled to Hearst's editorial offices in Pittsburgh, Detroit, Rochester, Boston, Milwaukee, Omaha, Seattle, and San Francisco. "Louella Parsons gets out a wonderful moving picture page and also a wonderful motion picture department," the letter read. "She did it on the New York *American* and she is doing it now on the Los Angeles *Examiner.* Her page is readable and well made up and clean and clear pictorially. She makes a careful selection of her features[,] and her picture pages and picture department really mean something not only to the people in the industry but to the general reader. . . . I want Miss Parsons to improve not only the appearance of the pages but the contents, and not only the contents but the methods," Hearst continued. "After that it will be up to the editor to keep it right."[8]

Louella's tour resulted in major changes. Louella instructed the movie editors to cut nearly all press releases and studio-generated publicity handouts from their sections and instead fill their pages with syndicated articles by Louella, Jerry Hoffman, and *New York American* writers Bland Johaneson and Regina Carewe. Louella then changed the layout of the sections by instituting what she called a "magazine-style makeup." For eye appeal, stories would be laid out asymmetrically, with headlines in different sizes and unusual fonts. On Sundays, the motion picture and drama sections would occupy two separate pages. Louella also instituted a new column, "Movie Go Round," a compilation of Hollywood chitchat and gossip that ran alongside her usual Sunday feature article.

Though the papers for the most part adhered to the changes, throughout the 1930s Louella often complained to Hearst that the movie editors depended too heavily on studio press material. "Now about the San Francisco *Examiner!*" Louella wrote to Hearst in 1931. "One thing I find radically wrong with our Sunday page is that they use too much press matter. I suggested to [the editor] that this junk be eliminated." "Pages made up very badly. Art poor. Too many pictures. Keep all the advertising on one page. Too much press matter. Dramatic section very poor," she wrote to editor Lloyd Thompson of the *San Francisco Examiner* in 1931.[9]

The innovations rated rave reviews. *Editor and Publisher* called Louella's improvements a "radical transformation." The *Exhibitors' Herald* predicted that the revamped movie sections, "with more real news and attractively prepared pages," would bring "substantially more interest and attention" to both the Hearst papers and Hollywood.[10] At each stop on the tour, Louella was greeted by crowds of fans who bombarded her with questions about Hollywood. In San Francisco, she was honored by local theater managers and publicity directors at a banquet at the St. Francis Hotel, and in Atlanta she dined with the mayor and several local officials. The Hearst papers chronicled her cross-country adventures with photos and feature articles. "A noted columnist, Miss Louella Parsons, stepped off the transcontinental in Atlanta smartly attired in a black ensemble completed by a luxurious silver fox fur," reported the *Atlanta Constitution.* "From the crown of her modishly bobbed head to the soles of her smartly shod feet, she is modern to a degree as those who follow . . . her daily column." As comfortable with political dignitaries as her working-class and middle-class readers, Louella was "movieland's foremost ambassador," bringing Hollywood to both the elite and the masses, the *Constitution* wrote.[11]

When she returned to Hollywood in May 1929, a group of cheering fans, along with the Montmartre Café orchestra playing "Hot Time in the Old Town Tonight," greeted her at Union Station. That summer, she celebrated her birthday with an extravagant party—"Louella Parsons threw a party and two Mack trucks hauled away the gross," *Variety* reported—and prepared for her wedding to Harry Martin.[12]

The wedding was an extravagant affair. The reception, also held at the Villa Carlotta, was wild, drunken, and attended by "everyone in Hollywood," according to the *Examiner*—that is, except Hearst, who was staying at San Simeon and unable to attend. Instead, Hearst sent an expensive piece of crystal as a wedding gift. "I am so glad to hear of your . . . marriage," he wrote in the accompanying card. "Now that you are going to wear a ball and chain[,] maybe it will make you kinder to some of your movie friends who have done likewise."[13] After the reception, Louella and Harry departed for their honeymoon, a weeklong stay at Hearst's estate at San Simeon.

Unlike the haughty John Parsons, the temperamental Peter Brady, and the kind but dull Jack McCaffrey, Harry (whom Louella called "Docky") seemed the perfect match for Louella. Though feisty, witty, and bright, he was also gentle and easygoing. Other, more competitive men might have felt themselves upstaged by Louella, but Harry was content to play second fiddle, and he actively supported his wife's career. When Louella was hospitalized in 1930 for kidney problems, Harry managed her business affairs. Throughout their marriage, he negotiated contracts for Louella, did her shopping, and even became a religious mentor. Not long after the wedding, Harry introduced her to Catholicism, and the couple soon became committed and active members of the Church of the Good Shepherd in Beverly Hills. Throughout, he maintained his own successful private practice in Hollywood. At the peak of his career in the late 1930s, he saw between eighty and a hundred patients a day and employed eight assistants. A popular Hollywood doctor and an abortionist and sexually transmitted disease specialist for the studios, Harry became one of Louella's informants. In flagrant violation of medical ethics, he sneaked Louella the results of actors' medical tests often before the patients had been notified.

In return, Louella used her influence to win Harry positions in the film industry and local government. In 1931, Louella convinced the studios to hire Harry as an "official advisor" on films dealing with medical issues. That year she also secured him a seat on the California State Boxing Commission. Louella had asked MGM boss Louis B. Mayer to get in touch with his friend Louis Lurie, who was on the commission. Pressured by Mayer, Lurie urged

Governor Clement Young to make the appointment. Young had presidential aspirations, and Mayer, Lurie reminded the governor, could help with "MGM's resources, stars, and money." In 1932, Louella used similar tactics to earn Harry a place on the Los Angeles Board of Civil Service Commissioners.[14]

Louella and Harry's relationship, according to most observers, was loving and committed. In 1947, it was still being held up as the ideal Hollywood marriage. "The example of steady devotion between Doc and Louella is something a lot of young couples in this town should emulate," wrote *Variety* columnist Florabel Muir. *Time* magazine quipped that year, "A few drinks among friends and they are necking like high school kids."[15] There were occasional fights, but they were quickly forgotten. Harry's friend Jake Ehrlich, a San Francisco attorney, recalled that at least once a week during the late 1930s he would "get a phone call from Doc saying, 'I'm going to divorce that damn woman.'" But the next day, they behaved like nothing had happened. "They used to fight but it never meant much," recalled Madalynne "Fieldsie" Lang, Carole Lombard's secretary in the 1930s and one of Louella and Harry's close friends. "It all became dinner conversation."[16]

Though Harry was not an alcoholic, drinking seemed to be "in his system," recalled Lang.[17] Throughout Hollywood, "Docky's" drunken antics were infamous. When Lombard, in the mid-1930s, staged a Roman-themed costume party, Harry and Louella showed up in togas. Harry then proceeded to pass out in a drunken stupor, his naked crotch exposed to view beneath his toga. When Lombard pointed to his crotch and asked, "What is that?" an observer cracked, "Why that's Louella Parsons' column."[18] In another famous story, when a guest at a Hollywood party stooped down to revive Harry, who was drunk on the floor, Louella stopped him. "Let him sleep," Louella reportedly said. "He needs to operate in the morning."[19]

Though they both drew sizable incomes, they spent it as quickly as they earned it. Not long after their honeymoon, they put a down payment on a home at 619 North Maple Drive in Beverly Hills, south of the Beverly Hills Hotel and just above Santa Monica Boulevard. The mortgage of $20,500, plus the cost of furniture and a maid, depleted their bank accounts. An incurable gambler, Louella was a fixture at the nearby Santa Anita racetrack, where she was known to bet on eight horses at once. She was also a regular guest at Agua Caliente, a Mexican gambling resort popular with the Hollywood crowd in the 1930s, and she gained a reputation as a mean craps player. ("You've never shot craps unless you've shot craps with Louella," recalled fellow journalist Len Riblett.)[20] "Harry might have been a restraining influence in my life and helped me overcome my tendency to regard money as something in liquid form to slip between the fingers," Louella wrote in her autobiography. "He might have. But he didn't."[21]

With her high-profile Hollywood position, her spending on clothing and jewelry became more extravagant than ever. In the late 1930s, at income tax time, after a series of depressing conferences with the tax man, Louella bought a diamond necklace. When Harry expressed concern, she assured him, "They'll let me pay for it in installments, and I'll tell the tax man it's an imitation."[22] Knowing her weakness for finery, actors and producers showered her with expensive knickknacks. "Every Christmas Eve would find the greatest of the movie greats sitting on the Aubusson rug in Louella's pink and gold parlor, watching her unwrap an avalanche of gifts," recalled Anita Loos. "Two secretaries used to stand with notebooks to keep score so that Louella could remember the next day who had sent what." Loos described the "Christmas loot" as nothing short of "breathtaking": "I recall one tribute, a silver plated copy of the Eiffel Tower that doubled as a pepper grinder. I also remember an Early American spinning wheel that did duty as a floor lamp. There were bronze bookends . . . [and] replicas of the Mona Lisa used to show up in all sorts of materials—ceramics, alabaster, wood—or printed on sofa cushions."[23]

Also contributing to Louella and Harry's indebtedness were their lavish parties. Around Hollywood, the star-studded affairs became famous. "It was amazing, the people you saw at her parties, people you didn't see at other parties," recalled photographer Murray Garrett.[24] Sometimes they entertained three hundred people in an evening, and the Maple Drive home was known around Hollywood as the "Parsons Short Order House."[25] Some of the guests were friends, but most went out of obligation, fearing retribution from Louella if they failed to show up.

Louella entertained a few times a month, sometimes even weekly. On the rare quiet weekend, she and Harry went to the beach home of Bebe Daniels and her husband, Ben Lyon, in Santa Monica. Louella had been the matron of honor at the Daniels-Lyon wedding in 1930 and in her column had broken the news of their daughter's birth. Though she knew of Daniels's pregnancy months in advance, she withheld the story, since Daniels had two films to finish. In an era when stars' pregnancies were often grounds for dismissal by the studios, Louella would not jeopardize her friend's career.[26]

Louella's most cherished weekends were spent away from Hollywood, with Hearst and Davies on the California coast. Hearst called it "the ranch." A sprawling Spanish-style castle overlooking the Pacific and set on a vast plot of land the size of Rhode Island, Hearst's San Simeon, 150 miles north of Los Angeles, was the largest and most extravagant residence in the United States. It featured acres of gardens, panoramic views, and, in each of its 165 rooms, priceless European antiques from Hearst's twenty-five-million-dollar art collection. The grand assembly room in the estate's main building, Casa Grande, featured authentic wooden pews from Renaissance churches; the dining room was ornamented with Siennese battle flags, and throughout the living quarters hung sixteenth-century French tapestries, some worth tens of thousands of dollars.

"The facade looked like a combination of Rheims Cathedral and a gigantic Swiss chalet," recalled Charlie Chaplin. "Surrounding it like vanguards were five Italian villas, set in on the edge of the plateau, each housing six guests. They were furnished in Italian style with baroque ceilings from which carved seraphs and cherubs smiled down at you." Photographer Cecil Beaton, another regular guest, described it as something "right out of a fairy story. The sun poured down with theatrical brilliance on tons of white marble and white stone. There seemed to be a thousand marble statues, pedestals, urns. The flowers were unreal in their ordered profusion."[27] It was Hearst's "little hideaway," his "little hilltop at San Simeon," and for over two decades, he and Davies called it home.[28]

In public, Hearst may have been modest about his seaside residence, but it was one of the consuming passions of his life. Built on land originally purchased by his father, George, the castle was the result of a joint collaboration by Hearst and architect Julia Morgan. Though the majority of the construction was completed in the 1920s, in time for Hearst and Davies to move in in 1926, it remained a work in progress. Never quite satisfied with it, Hearst constantly added rooms and cottages, pools and gardens, more precious antiques and more elaborate facades. Hearst had an "edifice complex," pundits joked.[29]

Each weekend during the late 1920s and 1930s, Hearst dispatched telegrams to the MGM studio ordering Louis B. Mayer to send up ten or twenty actors for a weekend at the ranch. Most stars were afraid to decline the offer, lest they offend Louella, Mayer, and Hearst, so the turnout was always healthy. Weekends at San Simeon became a regular feature of Hollywood celebrity life in the 1930s.

On Friday evenings at 6:30, guests assembled at the Southern Pacific station in Los Angeles. They took the train to San Luis Obispo, the town nearest San Simeon, and were taken up to the castle by a fleet of Hearst's private cars. The somber procession of automobiles climbing slowly up the foggy hill looked like a "funeral procession," recalled Hedda Hopper, who was one of Hearst's regular weekend guests.[30] Along the road were areas for large grazing animals, including antelope, deer, bison, elk, mountain sheep, and zebras—Hearst had the world's largest private zoo and game preserve, which housed over 120 varieties of animals. In 1928 an inventory of his zoo reported twenty-seven antelope, five kinds of deer, forty-four bison, three cougars, five lions, two bobcats, a leopard, a cheetah, three kinds of bears, a chimpanzee, three Java monkeys, a tapir, sheep, goats, two llamas, two kangaroos, and a wallaby. Often the animals strayed onto the path, causing delays. Once when Louella was being driven up the hill, a moose who had settled on the road refused to budge. She and her driver waited almost an hour until it decided to leave.[31]

On Saturdays, Hearst planned a full morning of tennis matches, hikes, and ocean swims, and the participants were expected to enjoy themselves—or at least give the appearance—lest they insult the host. According to Hearst reporter Adela Rogers St. Johns, Hearst loved to picnic, and he regularly had his weekend guests join him for pheasant and caviar beneath the shady oaks on the estate. "A picnic consisted of leaving San Simeon after lunch and stopping in a pleasant valley by a running stream. Servants went ahead with chuck wagons filled to overflowing . . . with pate de fois gras, thick filet mignon, and sparkling burgundy. After sleeping on cots under army tents, guests rode all next day to one of Mr. Hearst's faraway ranches for a dinner of chicken with all the trimmings. Automobiles waited to whisk you home in the usual luxury," recalled Hopper.[32] Hearst also led his guests on grueling daylong horseback rides, humiliating ordeals in which the vigorous septuagenarian outpaced sore, tired actors half his age. Director King Vidor described them as "sadistic."[33] In the afternoons, guests swam in the pool, a sparkling grotto of white marble flanked by Roman columns, or read one of the nine thousand volumes in the castle's two libraries.

The focal point of a weekend at San Simeon was the Saturday evening dinner in the refectory, a dim, cavernous dining room that resembled the inside of a medieval cathedral. From the center of the long wooden table, which seated more than seventy guests, Hearst and Davies presided over the extravagant multicourse meal. Though the dinners were cooked in gourmet style and featured fine cheeses and meats—"pheasant, wild duck, partridge and venison," recalled Chaplin in his autobiography —guests received paper napkins and were offered ketchup and mustard, in their original bottles, as condiments. (A fanatic about germs, Hearst thought such arrangements more "sanitary" than more elegant serving options.) After dinner, guests were ushered to Hearst's private theater, where they watched Davies's old films.

Concerned by Davies's alcoholic tendencies, Hearst banned liquor from the castle, and guests who brought their own private bottles had them promptly confiscated by the servants. But Davies always had a stash of gin hidden in her bedroom, and when Hearst had gone to bed, the guests made merry. Davies "would get a bottle after dinner and snag two or three cronies and withdraw to the mirrored ladies' room for a pleasant aftermath," remembered actress Ilka Chase.[34] One night Davies and a group of female guests were imbibing in the bathroom, and "Mr. Hearst came and threw [in] our robes and our toothbrushes," Adela St. Johns recalled. Furious, "he just opened the door and said, 'if you girls are going to stay in there all night, you'll need these!'"[35]

Louella first went to San Simeon not long after her arrival in Hollywood, and by the late 1920s she was a regular weekend guest. According to the gardener, Louella "would come up here with her twenty-seven trunks even if she was going to stay three or four days. But she was up here a lot of the time."[36] "She would like attention and sometimes she would call for me to come over, and it was only to decide which necklace she should wear, amethyst or some other necklace," recalled a housekeeper.[37] Louella often used the San Simeon weekends to collect Hollywood news, and she spent much of her time working on her column, which she dispatched to the *Examiner* office by wire. "She was always there, and she was talking to Miss Davies about what gossip was going on in Hollywood; who was doing what, who was sleeping with whom and all that sort of stuff. That was always going on," remembered another member of the San Simeon staff.[38] Hearst frequently held editorial meetings at San Simeon, and on any given weekend Hearst editors and executives Arthur Brisbane, George Young, Ray Van Ettisch, and James Richardson of the *Examiner;* Bill Curley, editor of the *New York Journal American;* and Walter Howey of the *Chicago Herald Examiner* could be found discussing finances, politics, and circulation in the refectory.

Hearst also conducted his Hollywood business at San Simeon. In the early 1930s, Hearst, Davies, and actress Constance Bennett, after watching several screen tests in Hearst's private theater, made the decision to star actor Joel McCrea in an upcoming Cosmopolitan-MGM film. McCrea was also staying

Actress Marion Davies in 1919.
Courtesy Photofest.

Louella, Janet Gaynor, Marion
Davies, and Dolores Del Rio at a
Hollywood party in the 1930s.
Courtesy Photofest.

Louella and Mary Pickford doing a radio broadcast. Courtesy Photofest.

William Randolph Hearst and Hedda Hopper at a San Simeon costume party.
Courtesy Photofest.

In 1935, Harriet Parsons and Louella celebrate the first anniversary of Harriet's job with Columbia Pictures. Courtesy Photofest.

Harriet Parsons. Courtesy Photofest.

Louella, playing herself, in the film *Hollywood Hotel*. Courtesy Photofest.

Louella presides over the "Orchid Room" in the final scene of *Hollywood Hotel*. Courtesy Photofest.

Orson Welles with Dorothy Comingore in *Citizen Kane*. Courtesy Photofest.

Film mogul Louis B. Mayer and Louella. Courtesy Photofest.

In mid-September 1941, Louella traveled to Dixon, Illinois, for "Louella Parsons Day." Courtesy Photofest.

Ronald Reagan, Louella, and Ronald Cummings. Courtesy Photofest.

at San Simeon that weekend, but he was unaware of the decision until Louella told him the following morning. "Well congratulations," she said. "I gave you the [headline] in the *Examiner* this morning." Louella had been there when the decision was made, and the news was in print before McCrea had even heard it.[39] Actress Louise Brooks recalled that female visitors had to avoid being caught alone with Hearst. Though Hearst was never known to have seduced any of his guests, Davies was always suspicious. One weekend Hearst entered the library when Brooks was alone reading, and Brooks immediately shut the book and "fled from the room." "Had Marion come upon us," Brooks said, "she would not only have deported me from the Ranch but have ordered Louella Parsons to exterminate me from the column."[40]

Louella's regular attendance at San Simeon cemented her position among Hollywood's elite. Virtually every major film star of the 1920s and 1930s vacationed at San Simeon, as did major political, social, and literary figures, including Charles Lindbergh, Herbert Hoover, George Bernard Shaw, Winston Churchill, and Calvin Coolidge, among others. By the early 1930s, Louella had also become an important member of Hearst's "inner circle." According to Adela Rogers St. Johns, Louella was one of the few people whom Hearst felt he could really trust. Visitors recall that at Hearst's parties Louella sat not with the Hollywood crowd but in a seat at the table reserved exclusively for Hearst editors. St. Johns also speculated that Hearst saw Louella not only as an employee but also as a member of his "family." Because Hearst did not have a daughter, St. Johns believed he "adopted" his favorite female writers—St. Johns, Louella, and screenwriter Frances Marion—and treated them with respect and care.[41] Louella was equally devoted to Hearst. As she told reporters from the *Philadelphia Sun Telegraph,* "Loyalty to your company and your boss is essential to success. I can't imagine a girl accepting a salary from anyone and then talking behind his back." She meant it. Many in Hollywood recalled that Louella walked out of conversations in which Hearst was criticized.[42]

In the fall of 1931, after a long weekend at San Simeon, Louella returned to Beverly Hills to hear the tragic news that Peter Brady had been killed in a plane crash over Staten Island. An aviation buff since World War I, Brady had served as chairman of Mayor Jimmy Walker's committee on aviation and as deputy commissioner of docks, in charge of the city's airport. His funeral, on September 24, was reported on the front page of the *New York Times.* Honorary pallbearers included Mayor Jimmy Walker, former governor Al Smith, and Governor Franklin Roosevelt. Over fifteen hundred friends and admirers attended, blocking the street in front of the church where the funeral was held.[43]

The death of a man she had loved for nearly a decade was devastating to Louella. "It is hard for me to talk about him but I thought you might like to know how much he always admired you and how often we have talked of your stand on different important matters," Louella wrote to Hearst not long after the accident.[44] Louella went immediately to New York, though she did not arrive in time for the funeral. For the rest of her life, she hated flying, with a vengeance.

By 1931, Louella had changed her approach to gossip writing. Gone were the flowery, saccharine descriptions of the stars that had filled her 1920s column; by the early thirties her writing had become more pointed and judgmental. The change reflected, in part, the new cultural climate brought about by the depression. Stories about stars' innocent yet lavish lifestyles became less appealing in a nation confronted with the reality of survival in hard times. During the early 1930s, exhibitors' polls conducted by the trade journal *Motion Picture Herald* regularly indicated that "down to earth stars" were the most popular among audiences; the folksy comic Will Rogers, and Marie Dressler and Wally Beery, who played "two old soaks making do" in the comedy *Min and Bill*, outranked such glamorous idols as Joan Crawford and Norma Shearer.[45] Even by the late 1920s, Louella had noticed that fans were tiring of the descriptions of stars as untouchable "heroes and heroines" and clamored for "realism of the 'just folks' brand."[46] So although writers in the early depression years continued to portray Hollywood idyllically, they focused increasingly on actors' mistakes. No longer monogamous homebodies or prim, jeweled divas entertaining genteelly in their mansions, actors now loved and lost, married and divorced, and became generally more human.[47]

Though Louella had reported on actors' divorces in the 1920s, during the early 1930s divorce stories became a staple of her column. (The divorces of particularly prominent actors, such as Dolores Del Rio and Jean Harlow, sometimes made the front page of the *Examiner.*) Divorce was a hot topic in the popular media, one that touched a nerve in the body politic and exposed a "raw point of friction between the old morality and the new," according to historian J. Herbie DiFonzo. Rising divorce rates in the late 1920s had sparked concern over what was seen as a rupture in the traditional balance of power between the sexes, since divorce was commonly viewed as an expression of female sexual and economic independence.[48] Playing to the still largely conservative public on the issue, Louella lamented the frequency of divorce among stars and turned her columns into paeans to the virtues of monogamous, heterosexual romance.

According to Louella, poor decisions often led to marital breakup—Jean Harlow had married when she was only sixteen, and "you know how these childhood affairs sometimes turn out," Louella wrote—but more frequently it was stardom that had caused problems. "It is ironic that the very things that first attracted Estelle to Jack should later become the bone of contention in their domestic life," Louella wrote in a 1931 story on the divorce of actress Estelle Taylor and prizefighter Jack Dempsey. "The aura of fame and hero worship that surrounded Jack . . . were undoubtedly the qualities which appealed to Estelle . . . when she married Jack. Yet these were the very things she sought to change about him after she became Mrs. Dempsey."[49] Though Louella never denied the many pleasures of stardom, she suggested that stars paid a heavy emotional toll for their fame. Success on the screen, she explained to her readers, did not always translate into real-life happiness.

This take on stardom—at once glamorous but freighted with potential emotional perils—was common in journalistic accounts of Hollywood in the 1930s. Like most Hollywood writers, Louella followed what historian Charles Ponce de Leon has described as the master plot of celebrity journalism—the struggle of celebrities to achieve "true success," which was not the same as material success. In the typical true-success narrative, good, deserving stars worked hard, stayed true to their roots, and gained a sense of accomplishment and personal fulfillment. By contrast, those who "went Hollywood," who forgot their true identities and meshed with the false celebrity persona, paid with failed romances or careers. By lauding the virtues of personal growth and hard work, and by critiquing material wealth, the stories at once humanized stars and salved readers' economic anxieties. During the depression, more than ever, readers took a certain comfort in the unhappiness of the rich.[50]

Despite her accounts of the potential dangers of the "Hollywood game," Louella often criticized those who didn't play it. This was done less for the benefit of her readers than as a reminder to unruly stars who defied the studios, Louella, and Hearst. Throughout the 1930s Louella used her column to pursue both personal vendettas and the economic and political interests of Hearst and the studios.

Stars were among the most highly paid people in the country, yet those contracted to the major studios were locked into a kind of indentured servitude. Because their selling power depended almost exclusively on their public image, their behavior was carefully controlled by the studios, which dictated not only their dress, diet, and leisure activities but sometimes even their romantic affairs. In his researches into Hollywood in the 1930s, writer Leo Rosten discovered that the Twentieth Century Fox studio had engaged eight of its top stars, four men and four women, in a "libidinal round robin" in which they were paired off with one another successively. This practice, apparently common among the studios, was done entirely for publicity. News of the "couples'" unions and subsequent breakups was given to the gossip columnists and fan magazines.[51] Stars were required by the studios to consent to interviews with the fan magazine writers and movie columnists and to call them with news. When stars refused to comply, Louella attacked them in the column. Those who remained recalcitrant were subject to more severe attacks, which often erupted into long-term feuds. Throughout the 1930s, Louella maintained feuds with several well-known producers and actors, whom she routinely lambasted in the column. Knowing that "catfights" between women, which played on female stereotypes, made good copy, Louella publicized her disputes with actresses, while her battles with powerful Hollywood men often took place behind closed doors.

One of the most notorious feuds of the early 1930s was between Louella and Greta Garbo. Garbo had come from her native Sweden to MGM in the mid-1920s and quickly proved herself one of the studio's least cooperative actresses. Taking issue with her salary, her contract, and the trumped-up rumors about her personal and romantic life that the studio had circulated as part of its publicity campaign, Garbo had on several occasions threatened to go back to Europe. This hardly endeared her to Louella, who thought the actress "ungrateful." But Garbo's worst sin, to Louella, was her notorious reclusiveness and her hostility toward the press. Louella first encountered this on the MGM lot in the late 1920s when she went to watch Garbo on the set. On her way, she found herself lost in a "mazelike series of screens" that had been set up to block her view—Garbo refused to work when there were visitors on the set. Garbo had also turned down Louella's requests for an interview and, at one social event, literally ran away from Louella when she saw her. Each of these transgressions was reported in the column. "She certainly has never let any newspaper writer peep beneath the surface of that cold, reserved nature. Interviews are absolutely unwelcome," Louella told her readers in 1930. "I met her one time at a dinner party at the home of a friend. She was charming, delightful, and pleasant. Then when she learned to whom she was speaking, she ran and got her hat and dashed out of the house."[52] Louella's antipathy toward Garbo never diminished, and by the end of the decade she was still attacking her. "Garbo's mystery pose has about worn itself out," she wrote in 1936. "People are tired of the bad manners she has displayed, and I venture to predict that she will not be able to get away with her actions much longer."[53]

Louella was also hostile to Jeanette MacDonald, who arrived in Hollywood in the late 1920s. The feud started at a dinner party in 1929 hosted by director Ernst Lubitsch. After dinner, a former silent film star, Carmel Myers, began singing a few songs in the living room, and most of the guests went to listen. But MacDonald and a few others remained in the dining area, and Louella, seeing MacDonald's absence as a show of condescension, was appalled and subsequently criticized her in the column.[54] "After reading the interview Jeanette MacDonald gave to the New York *Herald* in Paris, I can only hope she was misquoted," Louella wrote. "She is quoted as saying, 'Now is the time for other countries to catch up with the United States in movie production. Our producers are fumbling around, unable to tell what the public wants and curbed in their expenditures due to the depression.' Too bad such a statement ever got into print."[55] Later Louella opined, "Perhaps if Miss MacDonald intends to remain on the screen, she should guard her weight as carefully as she does her voice."[56] Katharine Hepburn, known for her unwillingness to cooperate with the press, also came under fire. "Extra Extra! Katharine Hepburn has proved that she occasionally has human impulses, that she is not all snobbery and self-satisfaction. Miss Hepburn forgot to be arrogant when she had a chance to take Adalyn Doyle under her wing and give her an opportunity to develop into a motion picture actress. The Doyle girl, who had been Miss Hepburn's stand-in in many pictures, has the same gawky awkward walk that characterized Hepburn's movements. She resembles her benefactress, however, only in a general way. Adalyn Doyle is prettier than Katharine Hepburn, who by no stretch of the imagination can ever lay any claim to beauty," Louella wrote in 1933.[57]

"Verbal spankings" were administered to actresses who, according to Louella, showed too much will and sexual independence and thus threatened their careers. "There is a romance going on in our midst that is bound to end disastrously. One of our best-known young actresses is seen daily dancing, lunching, and dining with a certain well-known actor. Her reputation, since she married, has been spotless, and she has made an enviable name on the screen for herself. Let's hope she sees this article and knows whom we mean and will stop her nonsense," Louella wrote in 1930.[58] When Clara Bow made national news in the early thirties for her alleged gambling addiction, Louella chastised Bow for weeks. "We hope Clara will not do any more foolish things, because everyone who knows her likes her and feels sorry she doesn't grow up," she told her readers.[59] Myrna Loy, who was never friendly toward Louella, paid for her attitude with bad reviews in the *Examiner.* "Myrna Loy, who did the spy act in 'Renegades' is again a spy in 'Squadrons.' Miss Loy is one of the best-looking girls on the screen, and maybe one of these days her acting will match her looks. Here's hoping," Louella wrote in 1930.[60]

Another victim was Mae West, whom Louella had described in the column as "fat, fair, and I don't know how near forty."[61] In this case the antipathy stemmed from a long-standing feud between the actress and Hearst. In the 1920s West had written and produced a play called *Sex,* and Hearst, upset by what he considered to be the play's offensive content, ran a smear campaign in the *New York American.*[62] It was also rumored that Hearst disliked West because she had insulted Marion Davies at a party. Despite her popularity at the box office—in 1935, she was voted by fan magazine polls the most popular actress in America—West received mixed reviews in Louella's column.

West's screen image exuded sex and sexual innuendo, which won her fans but also the wrath of censor boards throughout the country. West was thus forced to lighten her sexual aggression with comedy and exaggerated mannerisms, a tactic she used in a 1933 screen adaptation—*She Done Him Wrong*—of her stage play *Diamond Lil.* Despite the initial opposition of Will Hays, who claimed that the film's racy themes violated the industry's self-censorship regulations, Paramount eventually altered the script to conform to the Production Code and the film went on to become a box office success. In her column, Louella praised *She Done Him Wrong* for being "healthily naughty . . . [with] no decadent suggestion of the sort that we dislike."[63] But when West ran into trouble with the New York censor boards in 1934 for her film *It Ain't No Sin,* Louella described it as a "naughty picture" and chastised Paramount for having defied the code. "Had Paramount listened to the Hays Office, New York would not have so coldly refused her screen amours," she wrote.[64]

Those who had truly offended Hearst and Louella were subject to the "general ban"—complete banishment from the Hearst papers. One of the early victims was Ann Harding, a Hollywood newcomer who, like Garbo, was no friend of the press. "Stepping off the train at Pasadena, Ann Harding shooed away the press like so many flies. Stars who take this attitude often live long enough to step off trains without any waiting newspaper delegation," Louella wrote in 1931.[65] The prophecy came true. When Harding repeatedly refused interviews, Louella complained to Hearst, who ordered Harding out of his publications. "I am going to refuse to notice her in any Hearst paper," he wrote to Louella. "She isn't any good anyhow. . . . The young lady . . . certainly needs some disciplining, and we'll do our best."[66]

Even old friends became potential targets. Gloria Swanson, who had been a bit player at Essanay, had been a friend of Louella's for years. But when Swanson attained stardom, her turbulent romantic life became fodder for the column. Throughout the late twenties, Louella had chronicled Swanson's marriage and divorce from the French marquis Henri de la Falaise de Coudray in tones some readers described as "catty." "I have been reading your story in the San Francisco *Examiner* and can't say I find it very interesting. Us readers don't appreciate such stories as what was published about Gloria[,] and I am surprised that the Hearst papers would publish such rot," complained a Swanson fan.[67] (Swanson recalled that Louella had grown increasingly unfriendly over the years and had "a horrible way of looking at you—or rather, past you—when she wanted to cut you.")[68] Thus, it was hardly surprising that in 1931, when Swanson found herself pregnant out of wedlock, she went to great lengths to keep the news from Louella.

Determined to have her baby in peace, the actress and the baby's father, Michael Farmer, traveled to Europe that fall. To keep the voyage and the birth from Louella and her informants at the Western Union station, Swanson devised a secret code to use in her correspondence with her press secretary, lawyer, banker, and accountant. Random combinations of letters stood for key words and phrases. For example:

> Absum: We are leaving for
> Abtau: Will arrive in
> Acfry: We are traveling incognito as
> Acfub: Louella Parsons prints story that
> Adaad: Parsons asks
> Adbe: Los Angeles newspaper prints story that

Swanson's daughter Michelle was born on April 5, 1932, free of the usual press ballyhoo and without a single word in Louella's column.

Yet Louella praised as much as she criticized, and she often used the column to champion both old friends and promising newcomers. When Carole Lombard arrived in Hollywood in 1929, to ensure good publicity, and to thank Louella for having provided her first break in film, she "made it a point of putting through a personal telephone call to Louella Parsons at least once a week, and flattered the columnist with occasional impromptu visits to her home," according to Lombard's biographer.[69] In return, Louella boosted Lombard in her column. Hearst's personal favorites also received top billing in the column. "Poor Sally O'Neill, who was very satisfactory and popular on the screen, has had a series of troubles that have practically eliminated her from the attention of the producers," Hearst telegrammed Louella in 1931. "I would like very much to help her get started again. Would you please talk to some people, Winnie Sheehan and others, and see if you cannot get her a good part in some production[,] and in the meanwhile give her all the publicity you can in the paper."[70]

In 1930, Louella launched a campaign against the young producer Howard Hughes. It started that spring when Hughes held a private screening for his film *Hell's Angels* without inviting Louella. Offended but determined to see the film, Louella and her secretary sneaked into the theater. The film was not yet finished, and Hughes was "so annoyed at me that he wasn't even civil," Louella recalled. When Hughes discovered her inside the theater, he ordered her out. But Louella refused to leave and, as a result, became the first movie writer in the nation to review the film.[71] Her positive review of the film not only contributed to its box office success but also helped launch its leading actress, Jean Harlow, to stardom.

A few months later, Louella and Hughes clashed again, this time over Hughes's plan to film a controversial novel called *Queer People*. Written by two brothers, Carroll and Garrett Graham, *Queer People* tells the story of a reporter nicknamed Whitey who seeks his fortune as a Hollywood screenwriter. Moving west from New York, Whitey briefly works at the *Los Angeles Examiner,* then quits to take a night job as a piano player in a bordello and pens screenplays by day. After a few failed attempts, Whitey finally succeeds with a script that becomes the talk of the town. He is subsequently hired as a screenwriter by a major Hollywood studio and, before long, has worked his way up to a producer position. Riches and fame follow accordingly. But in the classic twist, the success goes to his head, and by the end of the novel he is implicated in the murder of a young starlet at a Beverly Hills party.

Today, the anti-Hollywood plot has become almost a cliché. But in 1930,

the book's satire of unscrupulous, money-hungry Jewish studio moguls—
"Jacob Schmaltz" and "Israel Hoffberger," thinly disguised caricatures of real-
life studio heads Carl Laemmle and Irving Thalberg—and its exposé of Hollywood nightlife nearly created a scandal. According to screenwriter and
novelist Budd Schulberg, who was working as a screenwriter at the time,
"When it was published in 1930, it was the sort of thing you would not dare
bring into a motion picture studio unless you hid it in a brown wrapper and
locked it in your middle desk drawer."[72] In the fall of 1930, Louella learned
that Hughes had bought the rights to the novel and was seeking a director
for the film. "It seems all any writer needs to do is to present Hollywood in
a bad light to get a play or book purchased. A recent book which damned
everybody in the industry has been sold as a movie," she announced in her
column in late October 1930.[73] A few weeks later, she warned that "Howard
Hughes will meet with some opposition in the motion picture industry if he
attempts to film 'Queer People.'" He will be "making a grave mistake to put
on the screen a book that so openly violates all good taste in describing motion picture folk."[74] Louella then sent the columns to Will Hays in the hope
that that he would ban the film. According to *Variety*, Hays subsequently
warned Hughes "that it would be a good idea if the story would be shelved."[75]

But Hughes refused to give up, and shortly afterward he assigned the direction to Lewis Milestone, who, according to *Variety*, "did a rave over it."[76]
After Louella called a secret conference with Milestone, threatening the director with possible blacklisting by the studios if he filmed the book, Milestone backed out of the project and Hughes reassigned it to Leo McCarey.
Then Louella met with McCarey, and a few days later McCarey begged
Hughes to switch his assignment. In the end, Hughes dropped the project.

The conflict over *Queer People* was a prelude to an even larger battle the
following year, over an "anti-newspaper" film called *Five Star Final*. During
the early thirties several Hollywood studios released films that vilified newspapers and reporters. The most notorious, *Scandal Sheet* and *The Front Page*,
dramatized journalistic misbehavior, depicting reporters as crass, drunken
scoundrels who lied, cheated, and connived to get their coveted "scoops."
The antireporter animus reflected growing public skepticism about what was
described at the time as ballyhoo. As newspapers hoping to keep afloat during the depression tried to outdo each other with more sensationalistic stories, and as press agents' publicity schemes grew ever more wild and unbe-
lievable, Americans began questioning news content. By the early 1930s,
Louella was receiving letters from readers disgusted with newspapers' and

press agents' publicity stunts; as one reader told her, "These days some of the publicity stunts being pulled off are a *scream*."[77]

"Why do the directors picture newspaper reporters as glorified editions of gangsters?" Louella wrote in September 1931. "I have looked at hundreds of pictures this last year, and with very few exceptions the newspaper men are without any sense of honor, and absolutely devoid of all politeness and courtesy. . . . Next time the producers have newspaper reporters in their films, they should get a tip on how newspaper men really conduct themselves. I, for one, am getting a little weary of seeing these caricatures."[78] Warner Brothers' release of the film *Five Star Final* later that fall only added to her wrath. Based on a Broadway hit by Louis Weitzenkorn, the film depicts a vicious tabloid editor who attempts to boost circulation by reopening an unsolved murder case. The plot was based on real life: in 1926, the Hearst tabloid the *New York Daily Mirror* had revived the Hall-Mills case, an unsolved murder from 1922, and the parallel was hardly unintentional. In the film, the reporters and investigators are drunken and foul mouthed, the editors cutthroat and manipulative, and a shady society columnist named Luella Carmody seems suspiciously like her real-life namesake.[79]

"I am in no way hostile to you or your enterprises. In fact, as you know, I am extremely well disposed towards both," Hearst wrote to Warner Brothers' studio head, Jack Warner. "I do think, however, that the patience of newspaper people has been tried . . . by the constant attacks on the newspaper fraternity in films which portray reporters as drunkards and editors as unscrupulous rascals." The note ended with a threat: "If the newspapers should reverse their attitude towards moving picture producers, I do not think it would be very beneficial for the producers."[80] The same day Louella joined the attack and had "a long talk with Jack Warner and a very satisfactory one," she wrote Hearst. During the conversation, Louella had hinted to Warner that if he withheld the release of *Five Star Final*, Davies would consider signing with Warner Brothers when her contract expired at MGM. In a telegram to Hearst, Louella explained,

> It was not necessary for me to mention our star. Jack Warner asked me when she would be free at MGM. I told him she had one more picture. He asked me if she were going to renew her contract and I said I was sure she had made no arrangements with them.
> If you think it's a good idea[,] why not let me bring Mr. and Mrs. Warner up next weekend so that you can have an informal talk with him. I feel sure

the subject would come around naturally without its being evident that any of us were trying to promote anything.

"One more thing," Louella wrote in closing. Fearing that her negotiations with Warner might ruin her relationship with MGM, Louella asked Hearst, "Will you keep my part in the Jack Warner matter confidential? L. B. Mayer and Irving Thalberg are always so nice to me."[81]

In the end, Warner Brothers released the film. In a final effort to keep *Five Star Final* off the screen, Hearst commissioned his newspaper editors to call on their city officials and ask them to ban the film from theaters. In Boston, the ban was successful, though Louella and Hearst insisted to Jack Warner that Hearst "had nothing to do with the Boston situation." The campaign against *Five Star Final* had another effect: fearing similar Hearst reprisals, Warners shelved two similar antinewspaper films.[82]

Meanwhile, the studio heads conferred and decided to rescind the forty-eight-hour exclusive. They agreed that Louella was becoming too ruthless and dictatorial; moreover, the exclusive agreement with Louella alienated them from the other movie writers and correspondents stationed in Hollywood who by the early 1930s numbered more than two hundred. Though Louella was insulted by the decision, according to Jerry Hoffman, she learned to see it as a challenge. Within weeks, she had come up with a scheme that would enable her to adhere to the studios' rules but still beat every reporter in town. The key figure in the plan was Myron Selznick, the son of Lewis Selznick and one of the top agents in Hollywood. As a favor, Selznick sneaked Louella the latest information on pending deals and contracts—news so fresh that in many cases the actors involved had not yet heard it. When Louella reported that Constance Bennett, who was under contract with the Pathé studio, was secretly negotiating to make films for Warner Brothers, the executives at both studios came under fire, and in the resulting fallout, two Pathé executives were forced to resign. "The studios were going crazy. Louella was breaking stories while deals were still pending. They couldn't figure out how she was doing it," Hoffman recalled. Finally, the publicity directors formed a committee and came to Louella. They wanted to go back to the preferential arrangement.[83]

To Louella, regaining the forty-eight-hour exclusive was one of the greatest victories of her career. "And as long as I can tear out a telephone by the roots making myself heard, that rule will stay in effect," she wrote in her autobiography. Or else, "as the boys say, 'Parsons is on the warpath again!'"[84]

NINE

Radio

At last, the great depression hit hollywood, and it hit hard. In 1931, theater admissions fell from eighty million to seventy million a week and in 1932 dropped to fifty-five million. After registering profits of $14.5 million in 1929 and $7 million in 1930, Warner Brothers lost nearly $8 million in 1931; Paramount sustained a record loss of $21 million in 1932. By 1933, Paramount, Fox, and RKO had gone into receivership, and by the mid-1930s, more than 20 percent of the workforce in Hollywood had been laid off.[1] Though the motion picture industry was better off than many American businesses, the losses came as a shock. Since 1910, profits had poured into the coffers of the movie moguls unabated; in the words of Hollywood historian Thomas Doherty, up to that point "box office had been all boom and no bust."[2]

Complicating this dismal state of affairs was the threat from radio. During the early 1920s, radio had been broadcast in several major cities, but the stations' low wattage kept it essentially an urban phenomenon. In 1927, however, the formation of national networks owned by the National Broadcasting Company and Columbia Broadcasting System turned radio into a nationwide medium, and by 1928 coast-to-coast network coverage carried programs to 80 percent of American homes. Before 1922, fewer than sixty thousand American families owned radios, but by 1930 over thirteen million had a set.[3] Millions of Americans found broadcast radio a convenient and cheap alternative to the movies, and film exhibitors panicked. They lowered admission prices and used such gimmicks as raffles, "bank nights," and door prizes to lure patrons to theaters, but, by the middle of 1932, sixty-five hundred movie theaters had closed.[4]

By the early 1930s, advertising was the accepted means of support for radio stations, and most radio shows were sponsored by major corporations. The companies were represented by New York ad agencies, which wrote and produced the programs. This meant that repeated, blatant, and often annoying product endorsements were interspersed throughout the broadcasts. Rather than stop the show for a separate commercial, stations incorporated a pitch for the product into the program's content. In a classic example of this style of "integrated advertising," the singer and 1930s radio host Rudy Vallee, portraying a nightclub host on the air, strolled among the tables and just happened to overhear a young couple talking about Fleischmann's Yeast.[5] When Jack Benny was sponsored by the makers of Jello, he began his programs with the greeting "Jello everybody." The J. Walter Thompson and Lord and Thomas advertising agencies were so powerful that they had private telephone links with the NBC and CBS studios from their offices blocks away in New York.[6]

Not surprisingly, the producers drew talent from Broadway and Hollywood. Many of the most popular early radio programs were hosted by stage and screen stars, and, like many movie personalities, Louella had been approached for a possible stint on the air. In 1928, Sunkist Oranges and its ad agency, Lord and Thomas, expressed interest in having Louella host a Hollywood-based gossip show. For unknown reasons the deal never materialized. Then in early 1931, Sunkist returned to Louella, this time with a firm contract for a half-hour celebrity-interview program to be aired at 5:30 Wednesday evenings on CBS.

Sunkist's plan was cagey. Louella would use her clout in Hollywood to line up the celebrity guests, who would appear on the show without pay, as a favor to Louella. Meanwhile, Louella would be compensated with a salary of a thousand dollars a week. As the nation's first radio gossip program, the Sunkist-sponsored program lay the groundwork for two subsequent NBC gossip programs, a 1932 show called *D. W. Griffith's Hollywood,* hosted by the director, and the long-running *Walter Winchell Show,* which also originated in 1932.[7]

Louella was ready to sign the contract when King Features, the syndication branch of the Hearst empire, heard of the impending deal and reminded her of the commission she owed them. According to the contract she had signed with Hearst in 1926, Louella was required to turn over one-third of the profits she earned from magazine articles, personal appearances, and any other work not commissioned by the Hearst Corporation. Though she was aware of the policy, she thought she could get around it. "I had the whole radio deal with the citrus growers practically completed when King Features stepped in and claimed one-third commission," Louella wrote to Hearst's secretary Joe Willicombe. Insisting that she receive the entire sum, she pointed out that Walter Winchell, who had been writing for the Hearst syndicate since 1929, "talks over the radio without dividing his money." "I want to do what Mr. Hearst thinks is right. If he told me to turn over the whole amount I would think it was right. But I do object to King Features collecting when they did no work."[8] The word came back swiftly from San Simeon: play by the rules or expect legal trouble. On February 10, 1931, Louella signed a contract with Sunkist that granted King Features its obligatory one-third. "Hope it meets with the Chief's approval," Louella wrote Willicombe. "Tell him his friendship means more to me than a million dollars. Also his good opinion."[9]

The ink had barely dried when Louella picked up the phone and began lining up guests for the program. Within hours she had called Mary Pickford, Bebe Daniels, Marion Davies, and a handful of MGM stars who were, by virtue of the studio's alliance with Hearst, indebted to Louella. Her request that they perform without pay put the actors in an awkward position. Normally they could command several thousand dollars for a radio appearance, but they feared consequences if they turned down Louella. In the end, fear won out, and by the end of the week Pickford, Constance Bennett, Norma Shearer, and Wally Beery had agreed to appear on the program. Pickford, whose usual radio fee was five thousand dollars, "will go on the show for nothing," Louella telegrammed Joe Willicombe. "She is doing it for the Hearst papers." Only Gloria Swanson refused to appear. ("Louella's programs commercially sponsored," Swanson's press agent wrote in a confidential telegram to her manager. "No reason why [Gloria] should work for Sunkist Orange people free.")[10]

Sunkist and Lord and Thomas predicted great success for the program. Before the first broadcast, both Louella and Mary Pickford had received several hundred inquiries "asking what station [their] talk [would] be on." After the program, Louella reported, there were "letters of praise from all over the country and from people I hadn't heard from in years."[11] But the reviews were lukewarm. The half-hour broadcast had been advertised as an interview program, but in reality, according to *Variety*, it became little more than a "praise session" in which Louella and the actors threw "verbal bouquets at each other" and congratulated each other on their successful careers. In the episode with Mary Pickford, *Variety* noted, "both women kept the conversation active if not especially interesting. Outside of talking about the star's next feature, the women spent the rest of their time talking about the old [Essanay] days."[12] Not far into the show's thirteen-week run, Sunkist lost interest, and the possibility of renewing the contract was never discussed. The last episode aired on May 20, 1931.

For Louella, the end of the show was in many ways a blessing. Though she had enjoyed the work, the additional responsibility had been overwhelming, and she had repeatedly complained to Harry and Hearst of being "exhausted" and "drained." "Do you think if I arranged my work in advance, I could get away for a vacation?" she asked Hearst in early April 1931. "I am very, very tired and I haven't had a vacation away from writing my column for six years."[13] When Hearst agreed, Louella began planning a summer vacation, and that June she took the Matson liner to Honolulu, where she spent a month "lounging on the beach all day." Accompanying her were Harry, Bebe Daniels, and Ben Lyon. She returned to Hollywood in July "feeling well and able to do more . . . than I have ever done in my life," she told Hearst.[14] She threw herself into her work, taking on lengthy feature articles in the *Examiner*—in 1931, she did weeklong series on Clara Bow and Gloria Swanson—and pieces for *Photoplay* and *Screenland* magazines, in addition to her daily and Sunday columns.

Meanwhile, Harriet was back in town. After a short stint as a screenwriter for MGM in 1929, Harriet had accepted a position in New York as an associate editor for James Quirk's *Photoplay* magazine. Quirk, who had known Louella and Harriet in Chicago, was glad to have "Parsons Jr." back on the staff—Harriet had actually published her first article in *Photoplay* in 1919, at the age of thirteen. But the job was short lived. Six months after moving East, Harriet contracted pneumonia, and Quirk sent her back to Hollywood to recuperate with Louella and Harry.

The recovery was slow and painful, hampered by a case of septic poisoning from an infected tooth, but when Harriet finally healed in the spring of 1931, Quirk rehired her.[15] Under the new arrangement, she would continue to live with Louella and Harry in Beverly Hills while serving as *Photoplay*'s West Coast editor. She was eager to have her job back but, at the same time, disappointed. For years she had dreamed of striking out on her own, away from Louella's formidable shadow. But even Harriet had to admit that living with Louella had its advantages. Louella gave her tips for her articles, and when Louella was in Honolulu, Harriet had taken over the column. When Louella returned from the trip, she tried to parlay this into a permanent booth for Harriet on the Hearst papers. "Some time if there is a vacancy on any of the papers that my daughter can fill I'd be glad if you would consider this," she wrote Hearst. "I hesitate to mention her[,] because I thought you might think I was pushing her forward. When I was away on my vacation[,] she wrote my column[;] and I blushingly admit there are some people who thought she did a better job than I do."[16] By the end of 1931, Harriet had a regular gossip feature, "Keyhole Portraits," that appeared in the Sunday Hearst papers alongside Louella's column.

Critics attributed Harriet's success to Louella. But even the most jaded had to admit that Harriet was, in her own right, a talented writer and reporter. In 1931, Harriet scored an important feature story for *Photoplay* on the private life of Greta Garbo, who had declined Harriet a formal interview. Determined to get the story, Harriet grabbed her notebook, got in her car, and trailed Garbo for an entire day.

The adventure began at the Olvera Street Theater in downtown Los Angeles, where Harriet caught Garbo strolling with the French director Jacques Feyder. Convinced that the two were having an affair, she trailed the couple back to Garbo's beach house. Determined to catch Feyder as he emerged from his tryst, she waited outside the house all night in her car. It was only when dawn broke that she realized she had followed the wrong vehicle. Later that day, Harriet found Garbo's house, climbed the fence, and photographed her cat. She then interviewed the grocer, newsstand operator, and police in Garbo's neighborhood. The article that resulted, "24 Hours with Garbo," was the envy of every writer in Hollywood.

"I worked my tail off," Harriet recalled. "I took it all very seriously."[17] Like Louella, Harriet was fiercely devoted to her career—perhaps a little too devoted, Louella feared. Concerned that Harriet's interest in her work might hinder her chances at marriage, in 1931 Louella began seeking a potential husband for her twenty-four-year-old daughter. She found one in Eddie Woods, the son of a prominent Arizona family who had graduated with an acting degree from the University of Southern California. For several years Woods had played bit parts for the First National Studios, but in 1931 Warner Brothers borrowed him to play the leading role in a gangster film, *Public Enemy.* A relatively unknown actor, James Cagney, had been assigned a supporting part, but at the last minute producer Darryl Zanuck switched the parts and gave Cagney the starring role. According to film historian Robert Sklar, the switch was suggested by the Hays Office. Concerned that reform groups might accuse Hollywood of glorifying crime, Hays wanted screen gangsters to be played by "ethnic types," such as Irish and Italians, rather than Americans of Anglo-Saxon stock.[18] Hays believed that Cagney, who had played working-class Irish gangsters in previous films, was perfect for the role.

But the switch infuriated Louella. By the time Zanuck made his decision, Woods and Harriet were engaged, and Louella was astonished that her old friend Zanuck would betray her. *Public Enemy* made Cagney a star, and Woods's career languished. In her column, Louella criticized both Zanuck and Warner Brothers for sabotaging Woods's chances at success. "If Eddie Woods had been given the role Cagney had, would Eddie today be in Cagney's place? I happen to know the Cagney role was originally written for Eddie, but through the friendship of someone in the studio the big part was handed the other boy," she wrote.[19]

It seemed that neither stardom nor marriage was meant for Woods that year. In the summer of 1931, a few months after he and Harriet announced their engagement, Harriet called off the wedding.[20] She explained to Louella that it was a problem of incompatibility, but Louella knew the real reason. Harriet was a lesbian.

In the movie colony, Harriet's sexual preference caused few ripples. Particularly after the transition to sound, when hundreds of gay and lesbian stage actors came to work in film, Hollywood had a thriving homosexual community. According to historian William J. Mann, Louella's attitude toward gays was "schizophrenic." Many of Louella's actor friends were openly gay, and knowing that revelations of their homosexuality would almost certainly destroy their careers, she often covered up for them and portrayed them in her column as heterosexual. But Louella wasn't "above gay-bashing when the situation arose," according to Mann.[21]

For many years, Louella had been a supporter of gay actor William "Billy" Haines, who had worked with Davies at MGM and was a frequent guest at San Simeon. In the column, Louella assured fans that he was as "innocent as a high schooler," and that he had been on dates with several young actresses and was actively seeking a wife. When Haines was caught in a raid at a Hollywood speakeasy in the early 1930s, Louella suppressed the story, but not without giving him a scare. Actress Constance Talmadge had been with Haines at the club, and according to Anita Loos, Louella "badgered" Talmadge's mother, Peg, for the details. Peg Talmadge waited for "all hell to break loose," but the story never appeared.[22]

Later, however, implications in Louella's column that Haines was gay "helped to do him in," Loos recalled. His personal life was "getting out of hand, and vague hints of misdemeanor began cropping up in Lolly's col-

umn." These hints were most likely coy innuendo; most Hollywood columnists implied homosexuality with references to actors' same-sex "friendships"
or "fear of marriage." Savvy consumers of Hollywood gossip knew the codes
and were adept at reading between the lines. Haines was summoned to Louis
B. Mayer's office and given an ultimatum. "I'm going to give you a choice,"
Mayer said. "You're either to give up that boyfriend or I'll cancel your contract." According to Loos, Haines "opted for love and told L. B. to tear up
his contract."[23]

But this was atypical. In most cases Louella colluded with the studios and
concealed actors' indiscretions. When actress Clara Bow's heavy gambling
made national press in 1931, Louella explained to her readers that Bow's problems stemmed not from underlying psychological problems, as other writers
had speculated, but from "overwork at the studio." Clara was retreating to a
"ranch," Louella assured fans, "where she will ride horseback, play tennis,
and try to restore [herself]."[24]

One of Louella's more notable cover-up jobs in the early 1930s involved the
MGM producer Paul Bern, who on September 5, 1932, was found dead in his
Beverly Hills home. The death appeared to be a suicide, but the motives were
unknown. Bern had a successful career and a new house, and had recently
married the blonde "bombshell" Jean Harlow, considered by many fans to be
one of the sexiest women on the screen.

MGM's investigation uncovered disturbing rumors, among them that
Bern had been impotent and that after unsuccessfully experimenting with a
number of mail-order stimulants and prosthetics, he shot himself. MGM also
discovered that, before moving to Hollywood from New York, Bern had married a woman named Dorothy Millette. Not long into their marriage, Millette suffered a nervous breakdown and was committed to an asylum. When
Bern moved to California, he never mentioned Millette, though the two were
legally married. It was rumored that on the night of Bern's death, Millette,
recently released from the sanitarium, caught up with Bern in Hollywood.
Terrified that she would press bigamy charges, Bern killed himself.

According to the MGM screenwriter Samuel Marx, Irving Thalberg, notified of Bern's death by the gardener, arrived at Bern's home six or seven
hours before the police.[25] The lead time gave the studio ample opportunity
to begin the cover-up. MGM contacted Louella shortly after Thalberg found
the body and within hours Louella began writing her story, which appeared
in nearly four hundred papers worldwide. In Louella's account, "artistic tendencies" and "brooding depression" caused Bern's death.

Films Will Have Difficult Time Replacing Bern

Producer Cultured, Brilliant, and Charming, Declares Louella O. Parsons

The shock of hearing that Paul Bern, one of the sweetest and most loved characters in Hollywood, has taken his life, is especially tragic at this time. Just two months ago, in his office, he told me that he had never expected to find such happiness.

What prompted him then to cut short his brilliant career just at the time that he should have been the happiest? I believe it was a suicidal mania that he could not overcome. Paul, in his way, was a genius. He was cultured, he was well-read, he was charming, but he was often erratic, as people of his temperament are apt to be.[26]

When Louella assisted with the Bern cover-up, she and Harry were on the way to New York for a monthlong trip to Europe. The trip was both a vacation and fact-finding mission for Hearst, who was in the midst of negotiations with film producers in Europe. Although Hollywood had dominated world film markets since World War I, at the end of the 1920s its hold over the European market had weakened, due in large part to the rise of nationalist governments in Germany, France, and Italy, which developed their own national film industries and imposed import quotas.[27] Hoping to get his foot in the now-closing door, in 1931 Hearst had attempted to broker a deal with the European companies that would allow him to continue exporting his newsreels. He was also negotiating an agreement with Germany's major studio, Ufa, in which the theaters Hearst owned under his Cosmopolitan company would exhibit Ufa's films.[28]

In late September and October 1932, Louella conducted a detailed survey of the European studios and reported back to Hearst. "Since both Germany and France passed a law forbidding our American producers to dub foreign voices in their films and to give German or French dialogue to our favorites, the situation abroad has been serious," Louella wrote. "Little doubt in my mind that [Germany] has ambitions to control the film product of the world."[29] The situation at Britain's Gaumont Studios was no better. "England is going about building up a quota system that will sooner or later be of serious concern to America," she explained. "The legal quota of British films, that each American producer must realize, is 12 and a half percent. I should not be surprised to see that increased, as the product of England improves."[30] After stops in Budapest and Vienna, where she reported that directors were making films in "crude, small studios," she returned to Holly-wood in late October 1932.

By then, she no longer worked out of the *Examiner* office. Instead, she built two rooms onto her Maple Drive home—an inner office and an outer office, the latter a kind of "sun parlor" with red-and-green patio furniture—where she spent most mornings. Louella usually woke up at eight in the morning, ate a breakfast of grapefruit, toast, and coffee, and read the morn-ing papers. At nine, she met her staff in her office; at ten, the phones began to ring with calls from press agents, studio heads, actors, and other inform-ants. Between ten and noon she wrote, and by one in the afternoon, the col-umn had been "whipped into shape," as she described it, and a messenger from the *Examiner* came to pick it up.[31] Each Wednesday at noon, she held her staff meeting at the Brown Derby with her assistants—Dorothy Manners and the former fan magazine writer Ruth Waterbury—her legman Neil Rau, and Sara Hamilton, a former teacher from Virginia who helped Louella with the Sunday feature stories.

Louella was frenetic, obsessive, and fiercely driven. "I have no secret of work—unless it is work," she told a fan magazine reporter. "Daytime and nighttime and all the time work. My phone rings at all hours of the night. Someone calls to tell me he's been in an automobile accident. Someone else calls to say he is shopping for a divorce in the morning. I never go to a party and have a merely social time. Someone is sure to do or say something that should go to press at once—and does."[32] Echoing sentiments held by many of Louella's colleagues, Hearst reporter Mac St. Johns believed that "Parsons was the best reporter that was ever alive in the city of Hollywood. . . . From the standpoint of the . . . ability to report news and get exclusives, there was never anyone before or since to compare with Louella." She "would wander around [parties] and you would think the woman was in a complete daze and she was paying no attention to what you were saying. And the next day every-thing that was said at the party was in the column."[33] "Louella Parsons will make you squirm until she has found out what she wants to know. She [has] that kind of determination and instinct for news," recalled another col-league.[34]

Stars and publicists who showed up at Louella's house for interviews were subject to a precise and unvarying routine. "You'd go into her game room with the black and white floor. And Harriet would be there or Dorothy Man-ners taking notes. You'd have tea and Collins the butler would serve. You could hear the clackety clack of the teletype machine which was in the office upstairs. She had this enormous picture of Hearst on the wall," recalled publicist Frank Liberman. Louella would scrawl her notes in a large, almost illegible hand on big yellow tablets of paper. Sometimes Dorothy Manners conducted the interview, "but Louella would often call you to follow up. . . . With Louella you had to be direct and honest," Liberman noted.[35] Publicists who planted false rumors or gave important news to other columnists were subject to immediate punishment—blacklisting from the column, or at the very least, a painful tongue-lashing. "I was out of her column at least twice because I didn't give her news," recalled Walter Seltzer, who worked for the MGM publicity department in the 1930s.[36] At times Louella would curse so badly that she had to mention it at confession.[37]

During 1933, Louella's shrewd news-gathering tactics won her three exclusive news stories that made international headlines. The first was on Joan Crawford, one of the most popular stars of the early 1930s. Crawford, a former chorus line dancer named Lucille LeSueur who was originally from Texas, was discovered by MGM talent scouts in 1924 and was cast in several films as an "athletic type." By the late 1920s, however, in response to audience comments, the studio began giving her fashionable, sexually charged "flapper" roles. When Crawford's screen image changed, so did her real-life habits. Determined to become as glamorous offscreen as she appeared to be in movies, she lost weight, studied etiquette, and mimicked the styles and mannerisms of the upper class. She subsequently attracted the attention of several wealthy, eligible Hollywood bachelors, including Douglas Fairbanks Jr., son of actor Douglas Fairbanks and Mary Pickford's stepson.

When Crawford wed Fairbanks Jr. in 1929, fan magazines described the union as a storybook wedding. Like Cinderella, Crawford had triumphed over her hard-scrabble roots and married the "Hollywood prince." Though Louella, like the other writers, had hyped the marriage in the column, she never liked Crawford, who had often snubbed her at parties. Consequently, Crawford received relatively few mentions in the column until the spring of 1933, when Fairbanks Jr. found himself embroiled in an alienation-of-affections suit. A man named Jorgen Dietz, a stranger to both Fairbanks and Crawford, pressed charges against Fairbanks, claiming falsely that the actor had "stolen the love" of his wife. Appalled, Louella turned to her typewriter and began writing an article in defense of Fairbanks. When Louella called Crawford for a quote, Crawford surprised Louella by insisting that she hold off on the article. "If you wait I will have another story for you," Crawford said cryptically. Intrigued, Louella drove to Crawford's house in Beverly Hills.

It did not take much prodding to coax a confession. Crawford and Fairbanks were having marital problems, the actress admitted, and she had decided to initiate a divorce. A sympathetic story about the lawsuit would look awkward in light of the breakup. Thrilled with the front-page story she'd just received, Louella thanked Crawford and turned to leave. Just as she reached the door, Crawford stopped her. Embarrassed, Crawford admitted that she'd already broken the news to another writer—her friend Katherine Albert, a former MGM publicist who was a member of the Hollywood Women's Press Club and a freelancer for the fan magazine *Modern Screen*. Though upset, Louella knew she would still get the exclusive. *Modern Screen*, a monthly publication, was scheduled to appear later that week, while Louella's story would be out in two days. Louella borrowed Crawford's typewriter and in the living room wrote the story, which she called in to the *Examiner*.[38]

On March 18, 1933, movie fans read the news:

Douglas Fairbanks Jr. and Joan Crawford Reveal Separation

Both Deny Any Other Person Causing Marital Rift
Actor Asserts He'll Try to Win Back His Wife

BY LOUELLA O. PARSONS

Joan and Doug, famous film stars, at one time considered the happiest married couple in the colony, have decided to separate. No divorce is being planned and each is emphatic in the statement that no other man or woman has entered into their matrimonial difficulties.

Joan yesterday, facing an emotional crisis that equaled any dramatic role she has ever played on the screen, begged me to say that the heart balm suit filed . . . by Jorgen Dietz against Douglas Fairbanks, Jr.[,] had absolutely nothing to do with her decision to seek her matrimonial freedom.

White faced and with sad, tragic eyes, Joan said, "The last thing in the world I want is to hurt my husband. I am seeking this separation because I know we will both be happier apart."[39]

But the Crawford-Fairbanks story was a minor victory compared to Louella's exclusive in June 1933. This one involved an old friend, Mary Pickford. Louella and Pickford had known each other since 1915, when Louella interviewed Pickford for her *Chicago Herald* column. Since then they had been friends, and when Pickford married Douglas Fairbanks Sr. in 1920, Louella was one of the first reporters to break the news, which appeared in her *New York Morning Telegraph* column. At the time, Pickford and Fairbanks were the most popular film couple in the world. Pickford, nicknamed "America's sweetheart," was known for her sweet, pixie image, and she played young girls in her films, even when she was in her thirties. Fairbanks, best known for his swashbuckling roles, had become a national icon of athleticism and rugged masculinity. Their union resulted not only in several happy years at Pickfair, the couple's palatial Beverly Hills mansion, but also in a fruitful creative alliance symbolized by United Artists, the independent film studio they founded with Charlie Chaplin in 1920.

By the late 1920s, however, weakened by the strain of celebrity life and their declining careers—neither one had weathered the transition to sound— the marriage began to disintegrate. By 1930 Fairbanks had taken up with Sylvia Ashley, an English heiress, and began spending time in London. According to Gloria Swanson, an upset Pickford began drinking. In July 1933, when he was overseas, Fairbanks sent Pickford a telegram informing her that he planned to stay with Ashley and make films in England. Pickford took it as an indication that the marriage was over, and she decided to initiate divorce proceedings. In the midst of her despair she called her friend Frances Marion, an MGM screenwriter who was also a longtime acquaintance of Louella's. Marion arranged to meet Pickford for lunch at the Vendome Restaurant in Hollywood, and she brought Louella along.

Pickford claimed that Louella's appearance at the Vendome was a surprise. "I never dreamed [Frances] would invite a newspaper columnist along," Pickford wrote in her autobiography. According to Pickford, "Without beating around the bush," Louella asked about Fairbanks and Ashley, and Pickford showed her the telegram. She asked Louella to keep the telegram a secret, but when Louella announced her intention to reveal the news, the actress "learned quickly of her folly."[40] According to Marion, however, Pickford had known Louella was coming along and purposely showed her the telegram, hoping that she would print it. According to Marion's biographer, Cari Beauchamp, Marion and Pickford had "talked about the idea of Mary's going public with the separation. Her pride mandated that she announce it before it was forced on her, and she called Frances to say she was going to tell a woman she knew at the LA *Times*." Marion told Pickford that she was making a mistake, and that the story instead should go to Louella. "After all Hearst has done for you. You have asked them before to keep things out of the paper and they have done it. If you give someone else the story now it is unfair." The two women agreed that, at the Vendome lunch, Pickford would break the news to Louella.[41]

In the false version that appeared in Louella's autobiography—an attempt to portray herself as a sympathetic friend of Pickford's—she walked into the Vendome clueless. She was leaving for a weekend with Harry at Lake Arrowhead when she received a call from Pickford inviting her to lunch. She arrived late at the restaurant, and one of the other guests said, "Mary, aren't you going to tell Louella what you told us?" Louella claimed that she was devastated when Pickford blurted out the news. "I went back home but I didn't write the story," she wrote in her autobiography. "I kept thinking that if I didn't print Mary's decision to divorce Doug it might never happen, but it was Mary herself who changed my mind. She called me later that night and said, 'If you don't use the story Louella, I'll give it to someone else.'" Though she claimed that she "hated to do it," Louella ran the news in the *Examiner* that evening. "I maneuvered to hold up the story until the final edition . . . on a Saturday night. That was the zero hour when the rival typesetters would not be on the job. For hours, after my story broke Sunday morning, no other news service could catch up with us!"[42]

Then there was a fourth version of the story, a false account that appeared in several rival newspapers after the divorce announcement. According to this version, at the luncheon Louella told Pickford that she had heard a rumor that Fairbanks and Ashley were thinking of marrying. Heartbroken, Pickford broke down and announced her intention to leave Fairbanks, which Louella printed. For years, Louella vehemently denied this "bitter, well-circulated" account. "No scoop in the world is worth telling a woman something that will break her heart. I knew nothing to tell Mary until *she* told *me*," she maintained. "There was far more of the Parsons luck involved in getting that story than any other reportorial factor."[43]

Luck, in Louella's version, but according to Pickford, deceit. After the story, Louella and Pickford were barely on speaking terms. Reporters mobbed Pickford as she came out of church and thronged around the gates of Pickfair for days, and Pickford blamed the press circus on Louella. Meanwhile, Louella's exclusive not only ran in all of the Hearst papers and syndicate subscribers but also was picked up by non-Hearst publications across North and South America, Europe, and even parts of Asia. "Heartbroken and with tear-filled eyes, America's sweetheart was facing the biggest situation in her life. Pickfair, the beautiful home built with such love by Mary Pickford and Douglas Fairbanks, is to be sold, which can mean only one thing—marital unhappiness. The marriage of Mary Pickford and Douglas Fairbanks, so long regarded as the ideal motion picture union, seems destined to end in the divorce courts," Louella stated in her typically overwrought style. It was, she maintained, "the biggest story of my career."[44]

A few weeks later Louella scored another exclusive, this time involving an unlikely subject. In the summer of 1933, the famed British playwright George Bernard Shaw was a guest at San Simeon, and when Louella came up for a weekend, she approached him for an article. Shaw had successfully eluded the press during his visit to the States, and Louella dreamed of being the first reporter to score an interview. After pressure from Marion Davies, Shaw consented, on the promise that Louella would show him the story before it went to press. Louella and Shaw went off to the parlor, and Frances Marion, who was also at San Simeon that weekend, sat in and observed.

Marion was amazed when Louella began firing off a stream of ridiculous and insensitive questions. When Louella asked Shaw whether he had written *Cashel Byron's Profession* with boxer Gene Tunney in mind, Marion could hardly believe it. "Good heavens woman, I wrote *Cashel Byron's Profession* before he was born," Shaw replied. After asking him about his relationship with Ellen Terry and his opinion of actress Sarah Bernhardt, Louella went back to her room to write the story. Later that afternoon she emerged with a draft, which she showed to Marion. Poorly written and filled with mistakes— Louella described Shaw as looking like "a jolly Santa Claus with a white beard"—the article was appalling, but Marion said nothing.

When Louella showed the article to Shaw, the playwright, disgusted, pulled out a pen and made line-by-line corrections, then signed it. Only then did Marion realize Louella's ploy. By playing dumb, "with her innocent faraway expression and her voice honey sweet," Louella had not only gotten her article, which appeared in *Screenland* magazine in July 1933, but a valuable signed manuscript.[45]

Still basking in her success, that fall she received an unexpected telegram at the *Examiner* office. Ralph Wonders, a representative of CBS Radio, had lined up a sponsor for a thirteen-week gossip show that needed a host, and he immediately thought of Louella. Intrigued, Louella wired back: "Need to know type of product program is to sponsor before deciding." The account, it turned out, was with Charis, the makers of a line of women's undergarments. If she accepted the assignment, she would be required to plug the company's best-selling product, corsets. Concerned about the possible effects on her image, she wrote to Wonders that she was having second thoughts. Wonders replied swiftly: though the program would be interspersed with commercials for Charis, Louella herself was to *"make no mention of product."*[46]

Louella accepted the offer, then wired E. J. Gough, head of Hearst's King Features syndicate. "How much [should] I charge per week? What do you think would be right? Since I have to give one third of all I make to Mr. Hearst, I would appreciate your opinion. . . . Do you think $1000 would be all right?"[47] The salary was particularly important that fall. In May, with some hesitation, Louella had taken a 10 percent pay cut—one of the Hearst Corporation's belt-tightening measures in response to the depression. Though Louella had initially protested, after being chastised by *Examiner* editor George Young she agreed. ("Thanks Louella," Hearst wired her. "I am glad you did that for the general effect on our morale.")[48] With King Features' approval, Louella entered negotiations with CBS for a thousand-dollar-a-week salary, and in December 1933 Louella, King Features, and CBS signed a three-way contract for a fifteen-minute radio program to begin in February 1934.

Since the Charis show, like the Sunkist show, would be based on "free talent"—stars would appear on the show gratis in exchange for radio publicity and praise in Louella's column—it was up to Louella to line up the prospective guests. During mid-December 1933, while Louella worked to line up a slate of stars for the show, theater owners throughout the country, hearing about the upcoming program, sent angry letters to Will Hays. "Protests from exhibitors piled into the Hays Office against the proposed tieup of stars and screen personalities with Louella Parsons for a series of broadcast interviews she is scheduled to start in February," reported *Variety*. The exhibitors feared that potential moviegoers would stay home instead of going to the theater; "competition from the air," wrote *Variety*, "is terrific enough at present." Although the studios had since rescinded a 1932 ban on radio performances by stars, the theater owners hoped that the Hays Office could pressure Louella to back out of the show.[49] In response to the exhibitors, the Hays Office assured the theater owners that no actress in her right mind would "be stupid enough to fall for any attempt to get [her] on the air for a corset program." The actresses "undoubtedly would be astute enough to understand that if they [promoted] corsets, audiences would get the impression that they were corset wearers."[50] The Hays Office was wrong. By the end of December 1933, actors May Robson, Norma Shearer, Connie Bennett, Kay Francis, and Bebe Daniels had agreed to appear on the program, and Shearer allegedly turned down a radio appearance that would have netted her twenty-five hundred dollars in order to be on Louella's show. On Wednesday, February 28, 1934, the program debuted at 10:15 A.M.

The show opened with a swing tune from the Raymond Paige Orchestra, a popular 1930s dance band, followed by a short commercial for Charis. According to radio historian John Dunning, the commercial was a "humorous affair in which the word 'corset' could not be used." Listeners were instead told how to "avoid abdominal bulge," a phrase that caused titters throughout the country each time it was read.[51] Louella and the guest then began what appeared to be spontaneous chitchat—casual conversation about Hollywood fashions, the star's family and marriage, and her latest films.

In reality, the gossip was entirely scripted. Louella had written the dialogue for the first few episodes while recovering from a minor car accident in early January 1934. ("I would like to have had more time to prepare them," she complained to Ralph Wonders. "When I tell you that I have worked two nights to get this out, you will see that it is a little difficult with my newspaper work.")[52] Later in the season, Louella and writers Edgar Allan Wolf and Jock Lawrence met at the Maple Drive house each Sunday and worked on scripts over lavish lunches of Chinese, Mexican, and Armenian food that were provided by Harry. (The lunches, Louella recalled, became more celebrated in Hollywood than the broadcasts.)[53]

Although Charis was pleased with Louella's scripts, the company was less enthusiastic about her radio voice. On the Sunkist program, audiences had complained that her voice was timid and "quivery," and though she had since taken diction lessons, she still sounded whiny. "I have always been terribly self-conscious about my voice. I do not know whether the fact that I had tuberculosis has anything to do with it, but when I get scared, my voice gets high and thin," she admitted.[54] Nonetheless, she pulled off the thirteen-week series with virtually no audience complaint. Only once that spring did she commit a major faux pas, when, during one episode, she unexpectedly extended an interview with Connie Bennett. There was time left in the show, and since the interview was going well, Louella decided to continue. This meant that one of the Raymond Paige Orchestra's musical numbers would have to be cut. Outraged, Paige and the orchestra stalked to an adjacent studio and had the line switched over. They then played their number, which went out over the air while Louella and Bennett continued their interview, not knowing they were speaking into dead microphones.[55]

Despite the mistakes and the embarrassing corset connection, the program earned praise from critics and listeners and hundreds of fan letters each week. "Dear Miss Parsons, welcome back to the mike! You are . . . my favorite columnist. I'll be reading you and hearing you!" wrote a woman from Detroit.[56] "While you and Connie Bennett were chatting in Hollywood, we back in Iowa were having coffee with our lunch. Your broadcast came over very clear and we want to hear more from you. We're for you, Louella O. Parsons, and we'll be listening Wednesday," reported a woman from Tabor, Iowa.[57]

Many of the letters were from working women, Louella's traditional fan base. During the depression, women's workforce participation rose only slightly—from 24 percent of all workers to 25 percent—but their average age increased. A large percentage of working women in the 1930s were over twenty-five and married, and they sought work to contribute to the family income during the economic crisis.[58] Louella's fans sometimes complained that her show was broadcast in the morning, when many of them were at work. "This letter is being written to say I don't like your radio program. Why? Because I never hear it. Why must you put on such a program at 10:15 A.M.? It is at that time most of the women are either slaving away in someone's office, trying to sell something to a very fussy customer, or busy making beds," wrote one fan. "It has been said that heaven helps the working girl. Now Louella, won't you please help the working girl and arrange your program for some evening hour so that we, too, may enjoy it? . . . Now just to prove to you that I am not a crab, I want you to know that I enjoy your column in the *Examiner* very much," she continued. "I have it with my coffee in the morning. Instead of coffee and donuts I have coffee and Louella Parsons. The time it takes to drink a cup of coffee is just time enough to read your column." "Your daily column is one reason why I take the *Post-Intelligencer*," wrote Eva Gove of Seattle. The column "is nearly always read and nearly always about the first thing that is." In 1934, Louella was receiving over eight hundred fan letters a week.[59]

Like her column and Sunday feature articles, the shows were presented as homey "chats" between Louella and the stars, and listeners commented that the program provided an "intimate touch" that the column sometimes missed.[60] Indeed, the letters reveal the intimacy and familiarity that many fans felt with Louella. Fans besieged her with requests for information. "I just wondered if you would mind answering a few questions about my favorite actor, Robert Montgomery. Will you please tell me the name of his wife, how old he is, what his favorite hobby is," came a typical request from Chicago.

They also asked her to pass along greetings to actors.[61] As Louella had hoped, fans saw her as their liaison to the stars. The fact that Louella was a friend of Bebe Daniels, a fan wrote, "makes me feel like we are all pals. Let's hear about her in your column a lot. Do have her on the air regularly. You are lucky to know such a grand person, for I know you are grand yourself."[62]

Thrilled by the response to the series, in the spring of 1934 Charis and CBS urged Louella to consider signing another thirteen-week contract. In the meantime, Louella had received offers from other sponsors. She told the network, "I am very glad to consider any proposition you may have had for me. My relations with Columbia have been very pleasant and with Charis, too, and naturally I shall be glad to give you the preference, provided the offers are as good as the ones I have received."[63] Two weeks later Charis came back with an offer of $1,200 a week, but by that time Louella had already signed a deal with William Paley of CBS and the Campbell Soup Company for a weekly show called *Hollywood Hotel.* The hourlong broadcast, slated for Friday evenings at nine, would earn Louella a weekly salary of $2,250 and prime-time exposure. In the summer of 1934, she signed the contract and began preparing for the show, which was slated to begin that fall.

Hollywood Hotel was not the only new responsibility Louella took on that summer. In June 1934, she also began a series of articles, "Hollywood Is My Home Town," for Hearst's *Cosmopolitan* magazine. Written in her familiar "just folks" vein, the articles likened the movie capital to a small midwestern town like Freeport or Dixon, Illinois. In Hollywood, like Dixon, "I can run two streets over to Ruth Chatterton's . . . house and borrow a cup of sugar, or I can pop in on Jessica and Richard Barthelmess and beg for a bit of lunch," she wrote. "My neighbors here are hard working folk who take their work as seriously as the village plumber, the skilled architect or the busy clerk in the general store. Their home lives are as simple, as wholesome and as natural as if they were living in the thriving cities of Muncie, Indiana, or Freeport, Illinois, instead of dwelling in the exciting kingdom of filmland."[64] The series earned her several hundred fan letters, causing the *Cosmopolitan* editors to extend the series into the spring of 1935.[65]

While she was in New York visiting the *Cosmopolitan* headquarters, Louella covered the Max Baer–Primo Carnera fight in Madison Square Garden. Thanks to Harry's position as a California athletic commissioner, they had ringside seats. "The primitive emotions of our earthly Adam before Mother Eve donned the concealing fig leaf seethed in the breasts of the snarling, howling mob of 50,000 souls." The ticket holders, who "paid a big price for the privilege of seeing Max Baer knock out Primo Carnera in the Madison Square Garden Bowl," became "temporary maniacs. I was one of those maniacs," read her syndicated dispatch.[66] Exhausted from her working vacation, in late June 1934 she returned to Hollywood to renew her Hearst contract.[67]

Harriet, too, was taking great strides in her career. Since 1930, she not only had taken over Louella's column during the latter's summer vacations but also had written short Sunday feature stories for the Hearst papers, free-lanced for *Modern Screen* magazine, and headed a movie section, "Hollywood in Review," for *Woman's Day* magazine. Then, in 1934, she changed directions and signed a contract with Columbia Pictures to direct and produce *Screen Snapshots,* a series of short films depicting Hollywood stars "at work and at play." As "producer, writer, director, narrator, cutter, location manager, casting director, and idea man," as she later described it, she produced the "snapshots" almost single-handedly.[68] Harriet, who had never had any experience in film production, at first wondered why Harry Cohn of Columbia approached her for the job. Then she realized that "it was a favor to Mother, who could help get him the stars he wanted." The job made her the only woman producer in Hollywood and, with the exception of Dorothy Arzner, who directed sixteen feature films in the 1930s and 1940s, the only woman director.

Though she could always get her foot in the door through Louella's connections, Harriet felt that she had to work "twice as hard" to prove herself. "I had two strikes against me: I was the woman behind the camera at a time when there were none, and I was Louella's daughter," she recalled.[69] By the mid-1930s, that had become something of a liability.

At 9:00 P.M. on Friday, October 5, 1934, radio listeners turned on their sets and heard what sounded like a telephone operator. "Hollywood Hotel, Hollywood Hotel. Good evening," the voice said. In the background were clicks, scratches, and operators' voices; it was so realistic that many listeners thought they had tapped into a switchboard. At last they heard the strains of the Ted Fio Rito Orchestra and the announcer, Ken Niles. Tonight, Niles told them, they were to be special guests at one of the poshest celebrity hangouts in the world. For an hour, Louella Parsons would transport them to the Orchid Room, a star-studded nightclub in the Hollywood Hotel.

In reality, there was a Hollywood Hotel, an imposing Spanish-style building at the corner of Hollywood Boulevard and Highland Avenue. Built in 1903 for Southern California's first tourists, it became a mecca for actors, who often stayed there upon arriving in Hollywood. Between 1912 and 1925, "the Who's Who of the movie capital lived there," recalled one Hollywood journalist. Jack Warner, Irving Thalberg, Louis B. Mayer, Jesse Lasky, Gloria Swanson, and Pola Negri, among other film notables, would meet on the front porch every evening, and on Thursday nights the rugs in the lobby were rolled back and the guests danced to jazz records.[70] But there was no "Orchid Room." The fictional lounge had been created for the radio program, and the show was actually broadcast from a studio at radio station KHJ in Los Angeles. Yet most listeners believed the imaginary nightspot was real. After introductions by actor Dick Powell, the show's emcee, Louella "entered" the Orchid Room and began "chatting" with the episode's featured actors. To create the illusion of being in a nightclub, radio technicians tinkled forks and glasses in the background and a group of radio actors nicknamed "the gay ad libbers" chatted quietly: "Look, there's Ginger Rogers! Isn't Connie Bennett wearing a marvelous dress!"

Like the Charis show, *Hollywood Hotel* was another "free talent" program. In addition to celebrity interviews, the program featured film previews, which were readings of short scenes from upcoming releases. In the first broadcast, Claudette Colbert and William Warren read from the script of the 1934 film *Imitation of Life*. During the program's first two seasons, Gloria Swanson, William Powell, Constance Bennett, Gary Cooper, Carole Lombard, Clark Gable, Fred Astaire, Jean Arthur, Frederick March, Mae West, Bette Davis, Lionel Barrymore, Cary Grant, Jean Harlow, Irene Dunne, Barbara Stanwyck, Errol Flynn, Marlene Dietrich, Spencer Tracy, and the Marx Brothers performed. The star-studded program was broadcast on seventy-two radio stations from coast to coast.

Though the stars and studios resented Louella's use of actors' unpaid services, they profited from the free publicity. Many studios, in fact, required their stars to appear on the show, both for publicity and to keep in Louella's favor. But not all the actors were equally agreeable, and in November 1934 *Variety* reported that Louella had "asked a picture star to sing on her air program and was informed by the star that she'd love to do it for so much money. Columnist blew up and chirped that as long as she syndicated her column, the star's name would never appear in it."[71] The "picture star" was Jeanette

MacDonald, who, as a result, was banned from the column for the next few years. At a wedding reception for Ginger Rogers and Lew Ayres, Louella walked up to MacDonald amidst a crowd of guests and said, "I think you're a bitch." "Thank you Louella," MacDonald replied. "May I say that the thought is mutual?"[72]

MacDonald's blowup was just the beginning of Louella's troubles with the show. In January 1935, Louella interrupted a musical number during a broadcast to report the death of actor Lowell Sherman. "Friends, I want to tell you Lowell Sherman died just a few moments ago," she announced. *Variety* called it "the most flagrant case of bad judgment ever launched over the air," and Paul Kennedy, one of the Scripps-Howard News Service's radio critics, nominated Louella as the season's worst performer. Later that winter, despite her testy relationship with Louella, Mae West agreed to appear on the show. But she was not going to make things easy. During the dress rehearsal, West stopped the orchestra just before a song she was to sing. "Where's the spotlight?" she asked. The show's producer, Bill Bacher, told her that they never used lighting on the show. "I don't sing without a spot," she said. Bacher repeated his explanation and brushed her off. That night when the orchestra began the opening bars of her song, she went to the microphone and said, "I'm supposed to sing a song here. But I don't think I'm going to do it." Hands on her hips, West shuffled offstage.[73]

In April 1934, the J. Walter Thompson agency, which produced the program, chastised Louella for attempting to line up actors who were already under contract to other sponsors. Mary Pickford, who had mended fences with Louella since the divorce story and had agreed to appear on *Hollywood Hotel,* was yanked from the program at the last minute when she found that her existing radio contract with Royal Gelatine made it impossible for her to go on the air. Angry that she had to line up a guest at the last minute, Louella threatened her with blacklisting from the column unless she appeared on the show. But Pickford refused, insisting that her hands were tied.[74] The relationship between the two women again turned icy.

At the end of *Hollywood Hotel's* three-year run, approximately two million dollars worth of services had been extracted from actors for free. As a result, the entire program cost only between $12,500 and $15,000 a week to produce, a fraction of what it would have cost had the actors been paid. Looking back, many stars found it hard to believe that they had actually agreed to appear on the show. Recalled Myrna Loy, who read scenes from *The Thin Man* on the program, "We didn't want to—those scenes don't come across on radio—but the studio made you do it to keep in Louella's good graces. Talk about blackmail!"[75]

They got points with Louella—and Campbell's soup. At the end of the show the actors were given a free case, either tomato or chicken. At least that choice was theirs.

TEN

The Best and the Hearst

ALL HIS LIFE, HEARST HAD DREAMED OF THE PRESIDENCY. It was a fitting aspiration for a man with lofty ideals and a regal vision of himself. Though he had served in Congress as a Democratic representative from New York from 1903 to 1907, he lost his bid for the New York governorship and, in 1904, failed in his attempt to win his party's nomination for the presidency. But his fantasies lived on. For the rest of his life, Hearst had an active hand in national politics, using his film and publishing empire to influence, manipulate, and in some cases help elect America's presidents.

In the 1932 presidential election, Hearst lent his support to Franklin Roosevelt, the popular New York Democrat. Through publicity in his papers, Hearst practically delivered the election to Roosevelt on the basis of Roosevelt's isolationist foreign policy and what Hearst perceived as Roosevelt's "centrist" take on domestic policy. Unlike Republican Louis B. Mayer, Hearst was critical of the incumbent, Herbert Hoover, whose insensitivity to workers' interests, he believed, was pushing American workers toward rebellion. In her column Louella praised the charismatic New York governor who promised to boost Hollywood's sagging fortunes. "At last we have a man at the helm who talks directly to us and gives us a confidence we haven't had since 1929," Louella told her readers. "Today he is the hero of the film colony. He isn't just a public idol, sitting on a throne, he is a close friend." He is "the man who will lead us out of all this darkness into sunshine," she wrote.[1]

During Roosevelt's first year in office, Hearst offered two "presents" to the new president. The first was a "Buy American and Spend American" campaign in which, every day for two months, beginning in late December 1932, the front pages of Hearst's twenty-seven newspapers featured three or four stories urging Americans to help end the depression by boycotting foreign products, including foreign movie stars. "We are going to have the greatest drive for American stars the world has ever seen. It will be 'Buy American' in the studios as well as in the shops," Louella told her readers in January 1933.[2] The second present to Roosevelt came in the form of a film. Shortly after the election, Hearst's Cosmopolitan productions, in partnership with MGM, produced a political parable about a Roosevelt-like president who rescues America from a devastating depression. Louella gave *Gabriel over the White House* a glowing review, writing that the film "strikes a high intensity and dynamic force. Destined to become the most talked of film of the year, it is more sensational than any sex problem play and more exciting than any murder mystery."[3] Following the press buildup, the film not only was successful at the box office but also received high praise from Roosevelt, who personally sent Hearst his thanks.

Both Hearst and MGM studio's head, Louis B. Mayer, contributed to the film, but Mayer's influence was much greater. Mayer altered several scenes in the film, including one involving a presidential speech to Congress that Hearst claimed was based on his political editorials. "I think you have impaired the effectiveness of the [scene] because you have been afraid to say the things which I wrote and which I say daily in my newspapers and which you commend me for saying but still do not sufficiently approve to put in your film," Hearst wrote to Mayer in the spring of 1933. "There were a lot of alterations in the picture which were not requested by the government and which in my humble opinion were not necessary."[4] The dispute between Hearst and Mayer over *Gabriel* was a sign of the growing tensions between the publisher and MGM, differences that revolved around politics and Marion Davies's career.

In the fall of 1933, Davies appeared in *Going Hollywood,* a musical that became the most successful film during her tenure at MGM. For Davies's costar, director Arthur Freed wanted to get Bing Crosby, who was under contract at Paramount, because he "knew Marion Davies couldn't sing." Freed got Mayer to borrow Crosby from Paramount through negotiations brokered by Louella. Though it was Crosby who made the film successful, Hearst disliked Crosby, who was known around Hollywood to be a drinker and womanizer. "Hearst didn't like Bing. I had a tough time selling Hearst on letting me use Bing opposite Marion," Freed recalled.[5]

Sometime during 1933, Irving Thalberg was given the opportunity to purchase the script of a historical drama called *The Barretts of Wimpole Street.* Thalberg initially turned it down but later became convinced that the piece would be an ideal vehicle for his wife, the actress Norma Shearer. In the meantime, Hearst had bought the script for Davies, and Thalberg asked Mayer to get it back. Mayer then told Hearst that he doubted the film would be a success if Davies starred in it and that he refused to commit MGM to any share of the cost. Hearst relented, and *Barretts* was made into a hit starring Shearer. The success of the film only added insult to injury, and to spite MGM, Hearst ordered Louella to keep Norma Shearer's name out of the column for several months.[6] When MGM publicist Howard Strickling noticed that Shearer was being omitted, he called Louella to ask why. Louella lied, telling Strickling that it was "accidental" and denying that she had received orders from Hearst to exclude Shearer. Suspicious, Strickling sent Louella three news exclusives that normally would have rated top headlines. But none of them appeared in the column, confirming his suspicions of foul play.

It was the first time any MGM star had been blacklisted by Hearst. Since the mid-1920s, when Hearst had allied with MGM, the studio's stars had always received top billing in Louella's column. Screenwriter Budd Schulberg recalled that Louella had been almost slavishly devoted to MGM. "Louella might run an item in her column because she wanted to ingratiate herself with L. B. (Mayer); everybody in town knew she was doing it to please her boss W. R. Hearst.[7] (Louella's editorial assistant Dorothy Manners remembered that when she [Dorothy] was assigned to review a Cosmopolitan or MGM picture, she was supposed to have "an orgasm." "You had to say this was the greatest thing that ever was made and better than any other picture you ever saw.")[8] The press ban on Shearer was a sign of trouble, heralding the beginning of the end of the relationship between Hearst, Louella, and MGM.

Hearst made a small peace offering to Mayer in May 1934 by having Louella write a Sunday feature article titled "Mayer's Career Dazzles: MGM Head's Achievement Is Impressive." "Fantastic, fabulous Cinderella tales of the stars who have risen to fame and wealth are printed every day in our newspapers. Not one of these glamorous stories compares in interest with the career of Louis B. Mayer, who started in life without a penny and who is today one of California's famous men and an important figure in the affairs of the nation," Louella wrote.[9] She had also praised Mayer's involvement in Republican politics, remarking in October 1934 that Mayer had been "receiving calls from men in all walks of life who prophecy dire things for our California should [Upton] Sinclair be elected governor."[10] This comment was as much to boost Mayer's ego as to hammer another nail in the coffin of socialist Sinclair's California gubernatorial campaign. Sinclair, who ran on the platform "End Poverty in California," had announced his intention to raise taxes on the film industry, prompting a major attack by the studio heads. MGM produced a series of phony newsreels, exhibited throughout the state, that falsely depicted Sinclair supporters as disheveled foreigners and vagrants. By contrast, the supporters of incumbent Republican governor Frank Merriam, who was running for reelection, appeared as upstanding, middle-class, native-born citizens. The Hearst papers contributed anti-Sinclair cartoons and editorials and, in the *Los Angeles Evening Herald,* ran a photo of a pack of young hoboes on their way to enlist in the Sinclair campaign. (The photo, like much of the newsreel footage, was false, having been taken from a Warner Brothers film, *Wild Boys of the Road.*)[11]

Despite Hearst's cooperation with Mayer, during 1934 the Hearst-MGM relationship worsened. Soon after the conversation between Louella and Strickling, Hearst executive Edgar Hatrick informed Mayer that Hearst had expected Davies to play Marie Antoinette in an upcoming film, although the script had been purchased with Norma Shearer in mind. At a party, Davies mentioned it to Thalberg, who later talked to Shearer about it; Shearer allegedly said, "If Marion wants it, she can have it!" But Mayer told Davies that he couldn't visualize her as Marie Antoinette, "so I don't want to spend that much money on a production of yours." "That last part got me burned up," Davies recalled. "I called W. R. in San Francisco and he was furious. When we saw that MGM wouldn't let me make the picture, we decided to leave the lot." A few days later, Hearst made a deal with Warner Brothers, and Davies and Cosmopolitan moved from the MGM lot in Culver City to the Warner Brothers lot in Burbank. While at MGM, Davies had worked out of an enormous fourteen-room bungalow; on the day of the move, the cottage was cut into sections, and a parade of trucks carried them across town. "The passage of this strange caravan through the heart of the colony was somewhat like an historic parade—the visible token of a high-level change involving not only picture making but social prestige and politics," observed Mayer biographer Bosley Crowther. "Anyone of an analytic nature might have sensed a transition here."[12]

The day after the contract with Warner Brothers was signed, Hearst's secretary Joe Willicombe informed the *Examiner* staff that "Chief says the moving picture connection of the Hearst institution from now on is the Warner Brothers studio. Anything that you can do to help Warner Brothers would be appreciated. . . . In fact, from now on, Chief says, give the same kind of attention to Warner Brothers that we used to give to MGM."[13] Louella adjusted her column to reflect Hearst's new allies. Actors Bette Davis, James Cagney, and Edward G. Robinson would now get top billing in the column, rather than MGM's Clark Gable, Joan Crawford, Greta Garbo, and Wallace Beery.

In 1934 Hearst was also concerned with what he perceived to be a dangerous political situation within the film industry. Since late 1933, Hollywood had been the site of a powerful unionization drive spearheaded by the Screen Actors' Guild and the Screen Writers' Guild. The story of the guilds dates back to June 1933, when President Roosevelt's plan of economic recovery, the National Recovery Act, went into effect. In an attempt to foster cooperation among trade organizations and thus boost employment, the act mandated that industries were to draw up codes of "fair competition" that would be enforceable by law. This meant that antitrust laws were waived, but in return the industries had to make concessions guaranteeing labor the right of collective bargaining and establishing minimum wages and maximum hours. The Code of Fair Competition for the movie industry was written during the summer of 1933 and signed into law on November 27.

To quell public indignation about the high salaries paid Hollywood executives, Louis B. Mayer and other industry executives took temporary pay cuts. They also wrote provisions into the code that limited actors' salaries to one hundred thousand dollars a year. This enraged the actors. The executives had steady year-round jobs, but acting work could be sporadic and acting careers notoriously short. The actors responded by starting the Screen Actors' Guild that June, and by October 1933, membership was in the hundreds. Hoping to gain access to sympathetic, left-leaning writers and actors and to exert a national voice by tapping into mass culture, the Communist Party began recruiting in Hollywood in the early 1930s. By the middle of the decade, it had over two hundred members, many of whom became involved in SAG and the Screen Writers' Guild.[14] Hearst, who had sided with labor in the past, supported SAG, as did Louella. Throughout the fall of 1933, Louella devoted space in her column to interviews with SAG leaders, including a Sunday feature article on SAG president Eddie Cantor, who attacked the producers for the salary cap.[15]

Less than a year later, however, Hearst reversed his stance when the American Newspaper Guild started an organizing campaign that spread throughout the newspaper industry. During the early years of the depression, the Hearst papers had incurred heavy financial losses—advertising in the Hearst papers had dropped by 40 percent between 1929 and 1933—and Hearst feared the consequences of unionization within his own industry. The rise of the American Newspaper Guild, combined with Roosevelt's reversal of his isolationist stance, led Hearst to turn his back on Roosevelt and the New Deal. "I think the most unfortunate thing that has occurred in Mr. Roosevelt's MIS-DEAL," he wrote to Tom White, head of his newspaper division, in 1934, "has been the encouragement of newspapermen to form guilds—and to support extreme radicalism. We are not only going to have trouble with the guilds interfering with the efficient conduct of the newspapers, but we are going to have eternal difficulty in keeping radical propaganda out of the papers, because every newspaperman as soon as he joins a radical guild becomes a radical propagandist. Already I see this radical propaganda continually creeping into our papers. I am going to stop it drastically by holding the editors as well as the contributors responsible, and letting the correspondents or reporters who continually proselytize go."[16] Hearst immediately began firing guild members from his papers, causing the guild to officially denounce the publisher, at its 1934 national convention, as "a son of a bitch."[17]

Convinced that Roosevelt was an enemy of free market capitalism, Hearst launched strident editorial attacks on the president. When Roosevelt announced his plan to create a federal income tax in 1935, Hearst declared it to be "communism." "Everywhere he looked, including his own newsrooms and Hollywood, Hearst saw threats to the foundations of American democracy, capitalism, and the free press," according to Hearst biographer David Nasaw.[18] Prodded by Hearst, Louella—who in her own right was fairly apolitical—ranted in her column about the "evils of taxation" and was reported to have intimidated actors from taking part in the pro–New Deal Motion Picture Democratic Committee. Believing that radicals and communists were taking over motion pictures and the press, in 1934 Hearst began a communist witch-hunt in every city with a Hearst paper. Editors were dispatched to pose as students and expose "subversive influences" on college campuses. That December, he turned his attack on alleged communists in the movie industry, accusing several producers of making "certain pictures [that] are propaganda." In an editorial titled "Red Pictures," Hearst announced, "Let it become commonly known that certain pictures are propaganda designed to overthrow the American form of government, to haul down the American flag and run up the RED banner of Russian Soviet Communism."[19] In a November 1934 editorial, he wrote, "If motion pictures are to be used for communistic propaganda, it will not be long before the American government will have to step in either to suppress such propaganda or to take over the film companies responsible for it and see that they are conducted on a patriotic American basis."[20]

By early 1935, Hearst's tirades had spread from the editorial page to the movie screen and the radio. On January 5, 1935, Hearst had appeared on NBC in a radio address devoted entirely to denouncing Soviet communism. His newsreels similarly contained anticommunist themes and were protested by students at Princeton University, who demonstrated against theaters showing Hearst's "offensively militaristic and Fascistic propaganda."[21] That June, anti-Hearst picketers were arrested in New York for causing disturbances outside theaters, and the American Communist Party and its front groups called for a boycott of all Hearst publications.

Meanwhile, the press had a field day. There were twelve *New York Times* stories on the anti-Hearst activities in 1935, and in late February 1935 a nationwide group of educators met in Atlantic City to discuss "the Hearst problem." The keynote address was delivered by Charles Beard, former president of the American Historical Association, who declared Hearst to be "an enemy of everything that is noblest and best in our American tradition."[22]

As bundles of Hearst papers were torched on city sidewalks and images of Hearst burned in effigy, Louella feared that she, too, would come under fire. She was right. In August 1935, the leftist magazine *New Theater* published a vicious attack on Louella, accusing her of being "Hearst's Hollywood Stooge." "Louella Parsons," the article declared, "is Hollywood's sacred cow. The feeling of reverence, fear, and awe she inspires in leaders of the motion picture industry speaks for itself. That this waddling drivel-monger, this venomous, disagreeable woman can be respected by the big shots is a sad, sad commentary upon the industry. . . . Louella's chief function is to ballyhoo Marion Davies, the blond girlfriend of her boss." The article continued, "Willie's greatest sorrow is that with all his money and power he has not been able to convince the American people that his bosom friend [Marion] is an actress. Year after year the senile Sultan of San Simeon pours out his gold in more and more lavish streams trying to buy popularity for Marion. His chief aide in that attempted fraud is Louella. Thus Willie, Marion, and Louella constitute the most powerful triumvirate in Hollywood."

The article was accompanied by an unflattering photo of Louella that accentuated her weight and double chin.[23] The same photo later appeared in a mock Hearst newspaper that was issued by a New York–based communist front organization the following month. For its front-page illustration, the creators of the "Anti-Hearst Examiner" ("Hearst in War, Hearst in Peace, Hearst in Every News Release, Spreads his Filth and Desolation to Increase His Circulation," read the masthead) had pasted the grotesque image of Louella in the lap of a large caricature of Hearst.[24]

In Hollywood the article caused a sensation. According to George Lewis, a columnist for the *Los Angeles Post-Record*, "There has been excitement in town since the *New Theater* came out with its article about Louella Parsons. The magazine's hard to get." Within hours, the issues were sold out at newsstands and "people are gathering in small circles to read the story over a subscriber's shoulders," Lewis wrote. *Variety* reported that "copies of the magazine were selling at a premium among film folk, with prices running as high as five and ten dollars a copy." The real identity of the author remained a mystery, but many believed—incorrectly—that George Lewis was the author of the article. "People have telephoned threats, called [me] a Communist, and one person sent a little tomato wired like a bomb with a note that reads, 'congratulations for an effective explosion. Next month throw this!'" he wrote. *New Theater* joked in a subsequent issue, "The popular Hollywood game seems to be trying to guess the real name of the author of the article. About the only prominent member of the film colony who hasn't been mentioned is Shirley Temple."[25]

In its September 1935 issue, *New Theater* published a follow-up article, "Louella Parsons, Reel 2." In the way of an "apology" to Louella, it wrote that "it may comfort Louella . . . that this magazine, unlike most of Hollywood, bears her no personal animus. *New Theater*'s interest in Louella extends only as far as her works, for she is the most prominent representative of that vicious and degraded form of journalism the function of which is to sell the cheap and unreal movies of Hollywood and fascist Hearst. There are a few dozen Louellas writing, some more mannered, but all produce the same pap to the same end—providing the ultimate excuse for bourgeois newspapers to claim larger grants of paid advertising." In an attempt to "put the real Hollywood in print," the magazine promised to run subsequent damning "portrait[s] of filmland," including an exposé of Louis B. Mayer, to be penned by "Joel Faith."[26]

The *New Theater* article launched open season on Louella. When Louella and Dorothy Manners were in New York in the fall of 1935 to attend a tea given by the Newspaper Women's Club at which Louella was honored, Louella consented to an interview with Joseph Alsop of the *New York Herald Tribune*. In the resulting article, Alsop accused Louella of using her column to boost her friends: "The first players she mentions when bestowing laurels are Miss Marion Davies and Clark Gable," he wrote. And he mocked Louella's description of Hollywood as a "cultural center." "Nowadays Hollywood is just like Vienna before the war," Louella had allegedly told Alsop.

"I mean, all the greatest writers in the world are there, and all the greatest musicians. The conductor of the Philadelphia Symphony Orchestra is there now." According to Alsop: "Miss Parsons was asked his name. For the first time since she had emerged from her sanctum, Miss Parsons was at a loss. Finally, she turned toward the sanctum door, behind which her cortege were transacting the day's business. 'Dorothy,' she called. 'Dorothy, what was the name of that conductor of the Philadelphia Symphony Orchestra, anyway?' 'Leopold Stokowski,' replied the unseen Dorothy, after a moment's cogitative pause. 'That's it,' said Miss P. "I can't think why I forgot. I know it every bit as well as my own name.'"[27]

The *Herald Tribune* piece was followed by another attack by *New Theater* that described Louella ("St. Louella") as Hollywood's "most publicized racketeer." According to *New Theater,* Louella blackmailed stars in exchange for expensive Christmas presents, "blood sacrifices laid on her altar."[28]

The attacks were obviously motivated by the anti-Hearst movement and Louella's "free talent" shenanigans for *Hollywood Hotel.* It also reflected a growing public animus toward newspaper gossip. Once the purview of the fan magazines, urban tabloids, and "scandal sheets," such as *Town Topics* and *Broadway Brevities,* which circulated among New York café society and the Broadway crowd, gossip had now gone mainstream with the syndication of Louella's column and the proliferation of celebrity stories in the popular press. By the mid-1930s, critics decried the proliferation of celebrity gossip as a corruption of journalistic ethics and launched attacks against the "new journalism" and its most enthusiastic purveyor, Walter Winchell. Winchell, a former vaudeville actor, had started his career as a gossip writer in the early 1920s, when he began writing a daily column for the New York trade paper the *Vaudeville News.* In 1924, he transferred to the tabloid the *Evening Graphic,* and in 1929 he took a post on Hearst's *Daily Mirror.* Syndicated by Hearst's King Features, by 1934 Winchell not only had become the country's most popular columnist but also had a national radio presence as the host of an eponymous gossip show.

In contrast to Louella's prim, dowdy image, Winchell's public persona and his writing were breezy and street-smart. In Winchell's column, divorcing couples were "Renovated," expecting women were "that way," and a mistress was a "keptive." His radio show was an aural version of his column, delivered in a brash, arrogant staccato. Even more contemptible than his corruption of the English language, according to critics, were his questionable sources. Though Winchell, like Louella, claimed that he got his news from reputable informants and studio press agents, he was accused of printing libelous information that tarnished the images of public figures and potentially destroyed careers. "He outdoes the yellow sheets in prodding impudent fingers into intimacies which any gentleman would consider deserving of privacy," wrote one editor. He "throws mud upon the institution of journalism."[29]

Though "Winchellism" was described as an affront to long-standing notions of media truth and impartiality, objectivity was a relatively new journalistic standard in the early 1930s. At the turn of the century, as the newspaper historian Michael Schudson has written, there was little discussion within the profession about reporters' potential bias or subjectivity.[30] It was only two decades later, in response to the alleged subjectivization of facts in World War I reporting, that objectivity was enshrined as a coveted, albeit elusive, journalistic ideal. By the late 1920s, in defense of the new standard, critics routinely attacked papers for publishing too much "trivial personal detail, scandal, romance, and stormy love" and described "the stuff we read in the daily press" as a form of "glorified gossip."[31] To Americans in the 1930s, Winchell and Louella had become agents and symbols of the mass media's encroachment on personal privacy and gossip's potentially dangerous influence over public opinion, politics, and culture.

Because *New Theater* was an independent, Popular Front publication with limited circulation, the article most likely did little damage to Louella's public image. Coming at a time when Louella was feeling fragile, the attack probably wounded her ego more than her reputation. By the mid-1930s, Louella "was becoming big beyond what people even recognize now; she was the Barbara Walters of her day," according to Dorothy Manners. But she was drained by her overwhelming slate of commitments, and she struggled with exhaustion. "She hardly had time to devote as much attention to the column as she needed. She was doing rehearsals for radio," Manners recalled.[32] Every Sunday, Manners went down to station KHJ and took dictation from Louella while she rehearsed for *Hollywood Hotel*. On many occasions Manners ended up writing most of the column.

Louella was also feeling threatened by the emergence of several formidable rivals. By the mid-1930s, there were almost four hundred columnists, news reporters, and feature writers assigned full-time to Hollywood; only Washington and New York had larger press corps.[33] Thirty-five of these commentators, considered "powerful" by the studios, were fed a minimum of ten news items each day by each studio, six days a week.[34] In addition to the competition from the mainstream press, by 1934 Louella faced two new Hollywood trade journals, the *Hollywood Reporter* and *Daily Variety*. The *Hollywood Reporter*, founded in 1930 by former film salesman Billy Wilkerson, was the first daily movie industry newspaper to come out of Hollywood. From the start, the paper had an antagonistic relationship with the studios. Wilkerson peppered the publication with scathing film reviews and critical editorials: "There are too many $1000 and $2000 and $3000 a week executives whose ignorance retards every effort that means anything. They have to go," read one early editorial attack.[35] *Reporter* writers were subsequently barred from studio lots. The paper was so threatening that Winfield Sheehan, head of production at the Fox studio, ordered the mailroom workers at the studio to gather up the entire morning's delivery of the *Reporter* and pile them in a heap outside his office. The papers were then set on fire.[36] When Louella heard about the trouble the producers were giving the *Reporter*, she was outraged and complained to Hearst, who instructed her to "tell the whole story" in her column "without sparing anybody."[37]

The *Reporter*'s daily gossip column, "The Rambling Reporter," was considered one of the best-read gossip columns in Hollywood.[38] Because columnist Edith Gwynne, Wilkerson's wife, refused to toe the studio line, the "Rambling Reporter" "created talk and naturally circulation. It also created something else—a healthy desire to stay out of it," recalled one Hollywood insider.[39] Gwynne and Louella were friends, and because Louella had supported the paper in its battle with the studios, the *Reporter* regularly defended Louella against her critics.

But *Daily Variety*, a spin-off of the New York theatrical publication *Variety*, was hardly an ally. In the early thirties, weekly *Variety* had a Hollywood office and put out an addition to the New York edition called *Hollywood Bulletin*. In 1931, weekly *Variety* sued the *Hollywood Reporter*, charging "news lifting," and in 1933 it established *Daily Variety* to combat the *Hollywood Reporter*.[40] The paper was headed by Arthur Ungar, who had been with *Variety* in New York for several years and was known for his "raging, cursing" disputes with studio executives and publicists. Never missing an opportunity to tear down powerful Hollywood figures, *Daily Variety* printed candid exposés of underhanded studio politics with sensationalistic headlines meant to provoke outrage. In the 1930s it also featured a gossip section, "Hollywood Inside," that frequently lampooned Louella's mistakes. In 1935, for example, it noted that "Louella Parsons went overboard on her front page story of the Fox–Twentieth Century merger by including United Artists in the deal. It was news to the UA crowd that this company was now allied with Fox, and more news that United Artists members are not entirely pleased with the new amalgamation."[41]

By 1935, Louella also had several rivals in the mainstream press, including Sheilah Graham, a British former showgirl who began writing for the North American Newspaper Alliance syndicate in 1936. Graham was known for her "good looks and cultured British speech" and for being a "tough independent" who had few qualms about telling off the studios, according to one trade journal. The Associated Press and United Press had syndicated film columnists who were generally more compliant with the studio establishment. Frederick Otheman, the United Press correspondent, had a policy of running all his copy by the studio publicity offices prior to publication, and Robin Coons of the Associated Press similarly made a name for himself by "steering clear of odoriferous stories."[42]

On the Hearst papers were movie writers Erskine Johnson, Harry Crocker, who wrote a column called "Behind the Makeup" (punsters dubbed it "Makeup the Behind"), and Jimmy Starr, who had a column, "Starr Dust," in Hearst's *Los Angeles Herald Express*. Ten years earlier Hollywood gossip writing had been dominated by women, but as Hollywood and film celebrity culture gained wider public acceptance, the profession gained status and men increasingly joined the ranks. By the mid-1930s, over half of the Hollywood news writers and film reviewers in the mainstream press were men, but most of the fan magazines, with a predominantly female readership, continued to be edited and authored by women. In 1934, the major studios accused the fan magazines of printing "sensational and salacious material" and of being "one of the major factors that brought about the church attack on films." At a meeting in August that year, the publicity directors decided to create, from the field of approximately three hundred fan magazine writers, a "white list" of fifty writers "who are established and who are noted for their honest and clean writing." Only those on the list were given access to the stars and studios. The studios also exerted strict censorship over fan magazine copy; MGM once forbade a magazine to write that Norma Shearer had two children and that Robert Montgomery was a father.[43]

In 1935, Hearst hired Marion's sister Reine Davies to write a column in the *Examiner* that covered social events in Hollywood, but when Davies began releasing news about production deals and contracts, Louella complained to Hearst that Davies had no right to encroach in the "straight news field." Though Davies continued the column, Hearst ordered her to keep her hands off of production news.[44]

Hearst's response to the Reine Davies situation was typical. The Chief generally complied with Louella's demands and, with only a few exceptions, did not edit her column. In 1933, Hearst chastised Louella for promoting certain Hollywood restaurants in the column and forbade her from future "café promotion," claiming that he wanted to "keep the papers in line with what is considered good journalistic ethics." Louella complained, "I am a little upset over that café order inasmuch as I know that I am responsible for getting a good share of their advertising for the paper. I am working about ten times as hard now as I have ever worked in my life and with a [small] staff." If she could not "mention little bits of gossip that happen in some of the cafés," she feared, she would lose not only advertising for the paper, she told Hearst, but also the cooperation of the restaurateurs who were important informants. But Hearst would not back down, and Louella ceased her aggressive plugging of the Montmartre, Brown Derby, and other Hollywood eateries.[45]

But aside from Hearst, no one changed a word in Louella's column. Even the managing editors on the *Examiner* couldn't alter the copy without asking Louella's permission. This led to frequent and frequently embarrassing mistakes. In one column, Louella quoted the title of Mary Pickford's book *Why Not Try God* as *Why Believe in God*.[46] She was quickly taken to task by readers and forced to print a correction. Not long afterward, she reported that a fan recommended the book *How I Lost My Girlish Figure* by Norman Harrington. Later, she apologized: it should have read *How I Lost My Boyish Figure*. By the late 1930s, the typos and errors had become so egregious that readers began complaining. "I've read your column for years and never thought I'd find you profane in your comments," wrote a woman from Ogdensburg, New Jersey. "Was I shocked to read the following comment: Martha Eggerth has much charm but she seems to be in need of a good dressmaker. Hell, MGM will attend to that." Apparently, the word should have been "well."[47]

In 1935, Jimmy Starr found an error in the early morning edition of Louella's column. "I thought I would be a nice rival and let her know of the mistake, which would make her column a collectors' item if the typographical error wasn't corrected," Starr recalled. He called Louella at home, but Louella was out, and her maid, Sadie, said that she might be at the Cocoanut Grove. Starr called the Grove, but Louella hadn't arrived yet. Panicked, he called "a half a dozen other places where I thought she might drop in. I left messages all over town." Louella didn't return his call until the next morning, and it was too late; the error had run and the papers were selling for a dollar a copy. In announcing the purchase of a story by MGM, *The Life of Private Tussy,* she had reported it as *The Life of Private Pussy.*[48]

Because New York–based Winchell dealt rarely with Hollywood studio and production news and because they were both on the Hearst payroll, Louella and Winchell were "technically noncompetitive," in the words of Winchell biographer Neal Gabler, and Louella did not consider him a threat. According to Gabler, Louella even offered Winchell breaking stories to use on the air. When Winchell starred in the 1937 film *Wake Up and Live,* Louella devoted an entire column to an interview with him.[49] But there were occasional spats. Louella often printed news items about Winchell without his approval, and Winchell frequently complained to Hearst. In 1933 Winchell sent a telegram to Hearst complaining that Louella published a story "without checking. [It] will hurt me in the public eye and tear down my work which took many years to build up."[50] Winchell considered Louella to be little more than a hack, a self-aggrandizing small-town biddy with no real talent. In 1938 Winchell had apparently made some unflattering comments about Louella in his column and Louella complained to Hearst, who told her that she was "at perfect liberty to sue."[51] Louella never pursued the issue.

Her relationship with columnist Sidney Skolsky was more hostile. A former Broadway columnist who came to Hollywood in 1932, Skolsky, a pill-popping hypochondriac, became famous for his informal "office." He did all his work out of Schwab's Drugstore in Hollywood, where for years he was a permanent fixture. After being fired from the *New York Daily News* syndicate in 1935, he was hired to write a Hollywood gossip column, "Hollywood Is My Beat," for Hearst's King Features. "The nearest thing to a socially minded progressive" in Hollywood, as one film industry publication described him, Skolsky's left-wing politics irked Hearst and, by extension, Louella. She was also annoyed by his grating personality and the obvious competition he presented, and it was not long before they clashed.[52] In 1938, after Skolsky beat her to a news story, the conflict got physical.

In the spring of 1938, Louella had run a front-page headline that Greta Garbo would marry the Philadelphia Symphony conductor Leopold Stokowski. Where Louella got her news Skolsky had no idea; all he knew was that Louella was wrong. The following day, to spite Louella, Skolsky ran his column with the first line, "Garbo will not marry Stokowski." (Skolsky, it turned out, was right.) Upset, Louella allegedly called Hearst and accused Skolsky of being a communist. Skolsky then telephoned Hearst at San Simeon to deny the charges. "Are you sure she didn't say columnist?" he asked. "You know, she has a difficult time pronouncing words." "I know what she said," Hearst replied. "You'll work out your contract and when we're through with you, you'll be nothing."[53]

Since Skolsky disliked Hearst, he was hardly sorry to go. Since 1937 he had been fighting with him and had complained loudly of the way his column had been "cut to the bone" by the Hearst editors. In November 1937, Ray Van Ettisch, managing editor of the *Examiner,* had written to Hearst about the "trouble with Skolsky." According to Van Ettisch, Skolsky insisted on using a part of the column called "Movie Boners," "though the Chief [gave] orders to kill it." "He became abusive, said that the *Examiner* was run by a bunch of bastards, his attitude that of the worst egomaniac with whom I have ever dealt," Van Ettisch wrote to Hearst.[54] After his confrontation with Hearst over Louella's accusations, Skolsky took his column out of the *Examiner* without finishing the contract and put it in the *Hollywood Citizen News.*[55]

About three months later, Maggie Ettinger and Alva Johnson, a writer for the *New Yorker,* were sitting with Louella in Chasen's restaurant when Skolsky came in. Maggie invited Skolsky to join them, and Johnson, Maggie, and Skolsky talked for about fifteen minutes without a word from Louella. According to one of Skolsky's friends, the reporter James Bacon, Louella finally turned to Skolsky and said, "I didn't know you were such a nice man. Else I never would have told Mr. Hearst you were a communist." Skolsky "saw red" and his first impulse "was to take a poke at her." ("If it had been Barney's Beanery I might have," he later said, "But how can you hit a woman in Chasen's?") All of a sudden Louella screamed. Skolsky had bitten Louella in the arm, then stood up and left.

In a postscript to the story, a few nights later Harry approached Skolsky at Ciro's restaurant and asked him to dance with Louella as a peace gesture. "Louella's sorry about the whole thing and wants to make up," Harry said. So Skolsky, who had never been on a dance floor in his life, danced with Louella.[56] Louella was satisfied, except for the fact that Skolsky had stepped on her feet. "From then on Louella and I became . . . well let's just say a truce existed between us," Skolsky wrote in his memoirs. "Perhaps it was a fragile truce, but fortunately its strength was never tested and it survived to the end of her life."[57]

During the mid-1930s it was Jimmie Fidler who was Louella's most threatening rival. Fidler, a former Hollywood publicist, had both a radio show—a weekly NBC gossip program sponsored by the makers of Tangee lipstick—and a syndicated column with the McNaught Syndicate, "Jimmie Fidler in

Hollywood," with 187 outlets. With his Winchell-esque, rapid-fire radio delivery, Fidler was generally considered in Hollywood to be a far more lively and charismatic broadcaster than Louella. He was also considered a better gossip, one with greater "reliability and authenticity," according to one Los Angeles magazine.[58] And, according to some accounts, the studios feared him more than Louella. His film reviews both in print and on the air were merciless, and in his pointed series of "open letters" to the stars that appeared in his column he freely criticized them, referring to box office failures (and their stars) as "stinkers." Fidler claimed to have "twenty-four tipsters" on his payroll, all of whom held key positions in the major studios. "When they phone in a story—and this may sound a little melodramatic to you, but it's true— they identify themselves merely as 'Operator Seven' or 'Operative 1001,' whichever it may be," he told a San Francisco newspaper.[59]

In November 1935, Louella heard a rumor from one of her New York connections that Clark Gable was planning to divorce his wife, Rhea. Apparently Gable's lawyer had leaked the news, and when Louella found out, she called Gable in New York. According to *Variety*, Louella, secure that she had the story, waited to release it until Gable returned to Hollywood and could give her a signed statement. The *Examiner* "was all set for a sweet circulation via street sales" when Fidler got wind of the news and announced it on his Tangee broadcast.[60] When Louella's story hit newsstands the following morning, it was already "a cold potato," *Variety* reported.[61] Had Louella gotten the exclusive, the *Examiner* would have scored an additional twenty-five thousand newspaper sales, *Variety* speculated.

Louella was so embarrassed that she lied about the story in her autobiography. According to Louella, Gable had told her that he preferred she get the news from Rhea. Louella claimed to have then called Rhea and invited her to the Maple Drive house for dinner. Louella allegedly interviewed Rhea, wrote the story, and called a messenger to take it to the *Examiner*. In the meantime, she claimed, she trapped Mrs. Gable in her living room lest she release the news to another syndicate. "We played cards. We talked clothes. And I even modeled two new hats I bought. But all evening long I kept a weather eye on the clock. A messenger had called . . . for my story, and as time went by I knew it was speeding across the wires."[62] Though she maintained for years that she got the exclusive, everyone in Hollywood knew that she had been outscooped.

The gossip game was heating up, and the turf battles became more frequent and contentious. In 1937, Louella complained to her readers that "whole items" were "swiped out of the column and put on the air." "We've never before raised our voice when the first edition has been consistently raided, but you would think some of these air commentators and other writers would at least change the language and make some effort to cover up their piracy. And may I remind some of these people who have been getting their news the easiest way that this column is copyrighted."[63] Soon afterward she wrote to Hearst that she felt she wasn't getting "proper bylines" in Hearst's *New York Daily Mirror,* which often reprinted her syndicated stories. According to Louella, a story about actress Sylvia Bruce was "a Parsons exclusive [but] the *Mirror* lifted it without a byline." This was not the first time, she complained, that the *Mirror* had run a Parsons exclusive without giving her credit.[64]

She took comfort in the success of *Hollywood Hotel.* After a "wobbly start," according to *Variety,* and "several months of sorry plodding," in 1935 the show acquired Bill Bacher, one of the highest paid producers in radio. A former New Jersey dentist who had abandoned his practice to become a radio director in New York, Bacher was—according to Mary Jane Higby, a *Hollywood Hotel* radio actress—"an intense man" with a personality as vivid as his "shock of reddish brown hair." Bacher was a notorious taskmaster, and rehearsals at times devolved into shouting matches between Louella, Bacher, and the program's emcee, actor Dick Powell. Still self-conscious about broadcasting, Louella was sometimes so nervous that she rehearsed her lines in the car on the way to the radio station. When Bacher criticized any aspect of her performance, she threw a tantrum.[65]

While Louella earned over two thousand dollars per week for the show, the twelve supporting actors for the program, who read bit parts, made only eighteen dollars each broadcast and were unbilled. According to CBS policy, if they were billed, they would not be paid. When radio actress Barbara Luddy was called to play opposite film star Francis Lederer in a scene, Luddy asked how much she could receive for the part. "You're not going to be getting paid," she was told. "You're getting billing." "I'm sorry," she replied. "I don't work for nothing." Her name was then stricken from the list of credits and she received her usual eighteen dollars. There was discontent in the ranks, to say the least, and the abuses on *Hollywood Hotel* and other, similar network radio programs led to the formation of a radio actors' union, the American Federation of Radio Artists, headed by Eddie Cantor, in 1937.[66] The film stars who appeared on the program were also disappointed with their flimsy compensation. "You rehearsed all week with that radio show," recalled actress Gypsy Rose Lee. "That was not an easy show to do. You did sketches and everything. If you were doing a film, the studio asked you to do it. About ten days later you received a case of Campbell's Soup, [which was] sent to the studio."[67]

Despite the tense atmosphere behind the scenes, by the fall of 1935 *Hollywood Hotel* was in the Crosley Reports' list of top ten most popular radio programs in the nation.[68] The most common criticism of the program was that the twenty-minute film preview scenes were often dry and hard to follow. "Parsons' piece of the program was not punchy," *Variety* commented on a November 1937 episode in which Louella previewed the Fred Astaire film *Damsel.*[69] "It was devoid of . . . chronological continuity and as entertainment it offered no more body than a film trailer."[70] But the show earned fans, who sent Louella more than a thousand letters a week. It also sold films—and soup. After one show in which an upcoming MGM film was previewed, the daily revenue for the film at Radio City Music Hall jumped from seventeen thousand to thirty-seven thousand dollars. On a check made at another theater, seventy-eight out of one hundred people queried at the box office said they were attending because they had heard about the movie on the program. "A particular broth would be mentioned on [the] show and presto! Store shelves across the nation would be swept clean of the product and distributors would be clamoring for more," recalled Mary Jane Higby. At one point Louella "forced a crisis on the cream soup division: the sponsor ran out of tomatoes."[71] The show was given a generous promotion budget, which enabled several publicity stunts. In 1937, the KHJ studio was opened to an audience of fifteen hundred and, in a promotion for the featured film, *One in a Million,* which was set in Switzerland, synthetic snow dropped from the ceiling. For one broadcast in 1937, Louella invited five hundred children from local orphanages. After the program the children were entertained by cast members on the stage, where Louella had provided a huge Christmas tree loaded with gifts.[72]

Prior to 1936, most radio shows were produced in New York, where NBC and CBS had their transmitting facilities. AT&T maintained high charges for broadcasts not based in New York; in the case of *Hollywood Hotel,* it charged to transmit the signal from Los Angeles to New York, then from New York out to stations across the country. Since Louella secured the performers for *Hollywood Hotel* at no cost, the show's producers could afford the AT&T surcharge. But the cost was prohibitive for most sponsors and producers. When Eddie Cantor attempted to relocate his program sponsored by Chase and Sanborn to Hollywood, he was informed that the move would add two thousand dollars to the weekly budget. As a result, *Hollywood Hotel* was one of the few Hollywood-based shows in the early 1930s, and it is often credited as having been one of the pioneers of West Coast radio.[73] When AT&T removed the double charges following a congressional investigation in 1936, many New York–based shows moved to Hollywood and adopted formats similar to that of *Hollywood Hotel.* One of them was the Lux Radio Theater, a movie adaptation program that between 1936 and 1942 became one of the most popular shows on the air. In the late 1930s, the Warner Brothers Academy Theater and Screen Guild Theater programs also used *Hollywood Hotel*'s film preview format. According to radio historian Michele Hilmes, *Hollywood Hotel* not only strengthened the alliance between Hollywood and the broadcasting industry but also, with its aura of glamour and use of top talent, "promoted the gossip and talk format to a kind of respectability" and thus laid the groundwork for decades of talk radio programming.[74]

In April 1935, despite rumors that Louella had accepted a radio contract from the makers of Lucky Strike cigarettes, Campbell's and CBS extended Louella's contract for another two years. It was around that time that Mary Pickford began hosting her own radio show—*Parties at Pickfair,* a half-hour program on CBS sponsored by the Associated Ice Industries. Like *Hollywood Hotel,* Pickford's program used "free talent." While Louella used fear to get actors on her program, stars went on *Pickfair* out of respect for Pickford. When Louella found out about the show—on the same network, no less—she began a campaign to sabotage the competing program. One day in the spring of 1935, Pickfair's producers received calls from two stars saying that they couldn't appear on the show as they had planned. Shortly afterward, another star called to cancel his engagement. Louella, the producers discovered, was threatening actors with banishment from the Hearst press if they agreed to appear with Pickford. In the ultimate dirty trick, Louella promised Pickford that she would appear on the program, then backed out at the last minute.[75]

But Pickford persisted despite Louella's threats. The program continued, and Louella told Pickford that she would be blacklisted from the column. Louella also blacklisted the Jesse Lasky Film Company, with which Pickford was affiliated. When Pickford threatened to complain to Hearst, Louella told her not to bother—the press ban had Hearst's sanction, so appealing to him would be useless.[76] This was not the first time Louella had used threats of blacklisting to help her radio ventures. According to *Daily Variety,* Ginger Rogers had been blacklisted from the column because she had appeared on *Pickfair* but refused to go on *Hollywood Hotel.* Fred Astaire and Frederic March were also threatened with banishment from the column when they refused Louella's request to go on the show. After continued pressure from Louella, Astaire and March finally gave in and appeared on the program.[77]

Appalled, the Screen Actors' Guild and Screen Writers' Guild decided to crack down. The leaders of the two guilds started resolutions that called on members to refuse to give free services for radio broadcasts and, with the cooperation of *Daily Variety,* vocally protested Louella's tactics. In a series of articles beginning with a March 1936 front-page exposé titled "Parsons Ices Pickford," *Variety* announced: "It's a battle of Soup vs Ice, for Louella Parsons has declared war on her old pal. The causus belli is Pickford's trying to corral pic names to the cause of ice via radio without pay." Louella's announcement that Pickford would be blacklisted "sort of stunned Miss Pickford, who has been a close friend of Miss Parsons. She was helpful in establishing the chatterer socially . . . when she first came to Hollywood." Though "there was no harm in Miss Parsons competing for talent with Miss Pickford, when Miss Parsons struck below the belt and used the powerful Hearst papers as a bludgeon to frighten people[,] . . . that was rough."[78]

Embarrassed, Louella set out to make amends to Pickford and the show's producers and, three weeks after the blowup, was reported to have received a large box of roses from *Pickfair* producer Lynn Farnol.[79] During this time she also mended fences with Jeanette MacDonald. When the mother of Gene Raymond, MacDonald's fiancée, sent Louella a letter that questioned MacDonald's sexual virtue, Louella called up Helen Ferguson, MacDonald's publicist. "This letter could really wipe up Jeanette," Louella said, and, as a peace offering to MacDonald, burned the letter. Ferguson relayed the news to MacDonald, who arranged to have lunch with Louella at the Vendome. To thank Louella, MacDonald offered to go on *Hollywood Hotel.* "So far as the hatchet is concerned," MacDonald said, "it's buried long since. I'll do the show for you not in payment for what you did for me, but because you're a good, decent woman and I like you very much."[80] After MacDonald's appearance on *Hollywood Hotel,* she was given "plenty of space" in Louella's column.[81]

But the attack on longtime nemesis Mae West continued. After West and Paramount, in 1936, released *Klondike Annie*—a film that Hearst deemed immoral for its intimations of promiscuity and miscegenation—Hearst banned all advertisements for the film in his papers. "After you have had a couple of good editorials regarding the indecency of this picture, then DO NOT mention Mae West in our papers again while she is on screen," he instructed his editors.[82] Editors who violated the rule were subject to "immediate dismissal."[83] Hearst also launched his own editorial attack on West. In one piece, "The Screen Must Not Relapse to Lewdness," Hearst accused West's Broadway plays and movies of being "largely responsible for the uprising of the churches and the moral elements of the community against the filth in moving pictures." Another Hearst editorial, "Stop Lewd Films," urged audiences to boycott the film. "The public should . . . show, through non-patronage of these productions that PANDERING TO THE LEWD ELEMENTS OF THE COMMUNITY IS NOT PROFITABLE."[84] In typical fashion, Louella cooperated with Hearst by excluding all mentions of West and *Klondike Annie* from the column.

According to the film industry trade journal *Motion Picture Herald*, the Hearst campaign had less to do with his dislike of *Klondike Annie* than the fact that "Miss West had not so long before rather firmly declined an invitation to appear as a guest star on a *Hollywood Hotel* program."[85] In other words, the *Herald* suggested inaccurately, Louella had urged the press attack. "All over Hollywood people speak in fearful whispers of the power of the Hearst newspapers. They cringe at the mere thought of getting their names on the Hearst blacklist," wrote Elizabeth Yeaman of the *Hollywood Citizen News*. "Consider the case of Mae West. She refused to appear as a guest artist on Louella Parsons' weekly radio broadcast."[86] Despite the poor publicity, the film was a success. According to the *Motion Picture Herald*, the movie was taking in between twenty-five thousand and eighty-five thousand dollars above expected box office proceeds, and West retained her position as one of the nation's top ten most popular stars.[87]

Louella entered the second half of the 1930s bruised and weakened. For the first time, her power and authority had been challenged, and she began to fear the loss of her commanding position as Hollywood's most influential gossip writer. When she panicked, friends reminded her of the power she wielded as a Hearst columnist. Even though they may have resented her, the studios depended on her for publicity, so they had no choice but to flatter her, appease her, and ply her with news. She was still the undisputed "queen of Hollywood," but that would soon change.

PART III

ELEVEN

The First Lady of Hollywood

THOUGH SHE WAS INCREASINGLY HATED IN HOLLYWOOD, Louella was more popular among American newspaper readers than ever. In 1936, a Chicago-based Louella Parsons fan club formed that had branches in several cities. Moreover, that year she was voted in a New York poll to be "far and away the choice of newspaper readers as the outstanding motion picture columnist," reported the McCann-Erickson Company, which had taken the survey. "So decisive is her superiority that she has no close rivals." By 1937, she was earning over a thousand fan letters a week, a testament not only to her ability to command readers but also to the nation's immersion in celebrity culture.[1]

By 1935, the film industry had recovered the financial losses it had experienced during the early depression years, thanks to the codes established by the National Recovery Act, a slight upswing in the economy, and the studios' successful marketing of high-gloss, "prestige" pictures. Film attendance rose from sixty million in 1933 to seventy million in 1934 to eighty million by 1935; by 1936, eighty-five million movie tickets were sold each week.[2] Movies not only were one of the most, if not *the* most, popular forms of commercial entertainment but also had become a powerful socializing agent. And Hollywood actors had become public role models and trendsetters. According to sociologist Margaret Thorp, who did an in-depth study of celebrity culture in the mid-1930s, millions of Americans learned the basic rules of social etiquette from the movies—how to dress, how to date and kiss, and even how to fall in love. When Clark Gable took off his shirt in the 1934 film *It Happened One Night,* revealing that he wore no undershirt, the men's underwear industry went into a decline that cut its business by half in one year. "So seriously do the fans take advice, so conscientiously do they copy their models, that publicity men can no longer indulge in flights of fancy about baths in goat's milk and honey . . . or exquisitely imaginative reducing diets. Every beauty hint must now be checked by an expert lest the fan sicken in her enthusiastic imitation—and sue," she wrote.[3] Robert and Helen Lynd, authors of the noted sociological study *Middletown,* an investigation of contemporary midwestern, middle-class culture, claimed that adolescents "went to school" in the movie theaters, modeling themselves after movie stars and repeating movie jokes and gestures. The movies were "not only the most universal form of recreation but a major source of ideas about life and the world in general," claimed the author of a 1935 study of community life in New York City.[4]

Critics decried the "Hollywoodization" of American culture and all that it represented: the replacement of an older, nineteenth-century set of values—hard work, frugality, and Protestant ethics—with a new, modern set of virtues centered on personality, images, and conspicuous consumption. Film stars, they lamented, earned more press and public attention than politicians, writers, and business figures; Rudolph Valentino's funeral, one critic noted, received much more attention than the funeral of Harvard president Charles Eliot Norton. Articles in the popular press attacked the studios for misleading audiences with publicity "ballyhoo" and criticized fans as "moronic" and gullible, prone to hopelessly conflating the screen and real life. Not only did fans "pattern their hairstyles, their clothes, their cookery, and their behavior after those of their favorite actors . . . but [they] also base[d] their most profound thinking on the words of those same authorities," claimed Carl Cotter in *The Coast* magazine.[5] "More than any other art," wrote philosopher Mortimer Adler in 1937, the movies "[are] the social and political problem of our day."[6]

As an agent and icon of "Hollywoodization," Louella was often attacked. In 1931, she was satirized in the Moss Hart play *Once in a Lifetime,* about a group of Broadway actors who try to capitalize on the "talkie revolution" by heading to Hollywood and posing as voice experts. On the train to Hollywood, the group encounters Helen Hobart (called "Prunella Parsnips" in some versions of the play), the author of a syndicated column called "Hollywood Happenings." Plump, effusive, and bedecked with jewels, Hobart gushes, "I write the most widely syndicated column in the United States. . . . Where on earth have you been, that you haven't heard about me? . . . Moviegoers all over the country take my word as law. Of course I earn a perfectly fabulous salary—but I'm hardly allowed to buy anything—I'm simply deluged with gifts."[7] In a 1932 comedy, *The Runt Page,* Shirley Temple played a similarly overwrought and scatterbrained newspaper columnist called "Lulu Parsnips." Critics attacked Louella for her "idiotic slop." "She employs no standard higher than your shoelace, and as often as not it is a great deal nearer the heel," claimed one magazine.[8]

But what her detractors despised, fans loved. In hundreds of letters, they praised Louella's detailed accounts of celebrity life and described her as their friend and ally. In 1935, the women of the sophomore class at Northwestern University banded together and asked her to pressure producer Irving Thalberg to cast Robert Taylor as Romeo in *Romeo and Juliet*. ("Thank you for implying I have influence. I shall speak to Irving Thalberg and tell him you cannot understand why Robert Taylor would not make a perfect Romeo," she wrote back.)[9] When David Selznick announced his plans in 1936 to film *Gone with the Wind*, Louella received thousands of casting suggestions from readers for the role of Scarlett.[10]

As the fans had hoped, Louella forwarded the suggestions to Selznick, who thanked her for the input. Lest they become angry if their candidates were not chosen, Selznick asked Louella to explain to her readers, concerning his choice of leading lady for *Gone with the Wind*, "With such a wide difference of opinion even among your own readers, everybody cannot be made happy with my final choice of cast. . . . Stars are under contract to different studios[,] and however much I might like to obtain this or that player it is more often than not impossible."[11] Though Miriam Hopkins and Paulette Goddard received the highest number of fan votes, in the end Selznick decided on the British actress Vivien Leigh. When Louella announced the decision, she was "literally bombarded with letters." "The Southerners, in particular, are protesting in bitter denunciation against a British miss being chosen while there are so many fine [American] actresses. The fans of Bette Davis, Katharine Hepburn, Jean Arthur, Miriam Hopkins, and Paulette Goddard have increased [my] mail to six times its normal size."[12]

Louella's popularity and visibility increased in September 1936, when Warner Brothers announced its plans to turn the *Hollywood Hotel* radio show into a motion picture. It was a ploy, in part, to take advantage of the success of the *Hollywood Hotel* program and also to capitalize on the studio's connection with Louella and Hearst. Because of the Hearst–Warner Brothers alliance, the film was guaranteed good reviews in the Hearst papers, and Louella could pressure the show's real-life actors to appear in the film. Jack Warner also saw the film as a way to make amends with Hearst. Since moving to Warner Brothers, Davies had made three films, all flops, and Hearst had blamed the studio for mishandling her career.

After Warner Brothers put the project on hold for the winter of 1936, Louella told her readers in the spring of 1937 that Dick Powell, *Hollywood Hotel's* emcee, and Ginger Rogers were slated to play the leads. But Rogers backed out of the film, as did Bette Davis, who had also been approached for the lead, and the film was stalled over the summer. Finally in September 1937, the film went into production with Powell and sisters Lola Lane and Rosemary Lane in the starring roles. In addition to Warner Brothers actors Ted Healy, Alan Mowbray, Glenda Farrell, and Hugh Herbert, the real-life *Hollywood Hotel* players Frances Langford, Ken Niles, and Raymond Paige would appear in the film, along with bandleader Benny Goodman. "Well, you've heard everything now. Louella Parsons is going into the movies. Jack Warner and Hal Wallis have decided for me that I ought to play myself in *Hollywood Hotel*," she announced on September 15, 1937.[13] Harry, acting as her agent, negotiated the contract, which stipulated that Louella would be available for work for five weeks, four days a week, after one o'clock in the afternoon. In addition to thirty thousand dollars paid in six installments, she received a stand-in, a hairdresser, and a private dressing room on the Warner Brothers lot.[14]

This was not the first time Louella had been asked to appear in a film. In 1932, Carl Laemmle had invited her to appear in *The Cohens and Kellys in Hollywood,* though for unknown reasons Louella declined.[15] In 1928, she had appeared as an extra in a Cosmopolitan film, *The Bellamy Trial,* and had a cameo role in MGM's *Show People,* a comedy starring Marion Davies. Louella was both thrilled and terrified by her upcoming screen appearance. Though she had always been enchanted by acting, she had no formal experience. In the week before September 20, 1937, when shooting was scheduled to start, Louella called impromptu rehearsals at her home, where she read over her scenes with professional actors and voice coaches and tried to lose weight by pedaling an exercise cycle. Though the Warner Brothers costumer Orry-Kelly created an elegant wardrobe for her—a tailored black business suit and a black evening gown complemented by diamond jewelry said to be worth thirty thousand dollars—Louella was insecure about her appearance. "Heaving coal, walking a tightrope, or even meeting a wild jungle beast face to face would be child's play compared with facing the enormous, all-seeing eye of the camera," Louella told her readers. "You start getting an inferiority complex."[16]

Producer-writer Jerry Wald wrote the screenplay, the prolific composer and lyricist Johnny Mercer did the music, and behind the camera was veteran cinematographer Charles Rosher, who had over eighty film credits to his name. Despite the respected talent, *Hollywood Hotel* was unexceptional, a clichéd and smarmy rehash of the Hollywood rags-to-riches theme. In the film, Ronnie Bowers, a young saxophonist played by Powell, comes to Hollywood on a short contract with the fictional All Star Pictures. On the same day, All Star actress Mona Marshall (Lola Lane) reads in Louella's column that she has been passed up for the starring role in an upcoming film; angry, Marshall refuses to attend a film premiere scheduled for that evening. All Star then finds a stand-in for Marshall to attend the premiere, an aspiring actress named Virginia Sanders (Rosemary Lane), and Bowers is asked to accompany her. When Marshall finds out, she demands that Bowers and Sanders be fired. Bowers then takes a job as a singing waiter in a drive-in, where he is noticed by a director who hires him to dub the voice for star Alexander Duprey in an upcoming musical. When Duprey is asked by Louella to sing on the *Hollywood Hotel* broadcast he agrees, assuming that Bowers will also dub for him on the program. But when Duprey is late for the broadcast— part of a scheme engineered by Sanders on Bowers's behalf—Bowers sings on the show in his own name and goes on to film stardom.

Hardly an actress, Louella was so stiff and restrained that most of her scenes were cut from the film. In the final version, she appears five times. In one notable scene near the beginning of the film, Louella, on her way to interview Mona Marshall, meets a wisecracking press agent in the elevator. "Hey Parsons, why don't you put me in your column sometime?" he asks. "Oh you're not news," Louella says sarcastically. "Get her," the agent says to his friend. "What does she want me to do, take a bath in champagne or something?" "Soap and water will do," Louella retorts.[17] This exchange was deemed by several critics to be one of the funniest in the film.

The film's trailer described her as "the columnist who knows all filmland's secrets," and as part of its publicity campaign for the film, Warner Brothers nicknamed Louella the "First Lady of Hollywood," a moniker that stayed with her for the rest of her career. In the contract, the studio had agreed that, in publicity material, the type for "no other member of cast except [the] stars shall be over 75% as large as type used for Miss Parsons," and that she had the right to approve all the photographic stills and newspaper publicity for the film.[18]

The film premiered in late December 1937 to mixed reviews. "*Hollywood Hotel* is a cinch to cop new box office records—a knockout show," wrote the *Hollywood Reporter*. According to *Variety*, the film was "smash musical entertainment with a lively and amusing story and some popular song numbers. There's box office draw in this one for all theatres, from first runs to the smallest houses." The Hearst reviews, naturally, were sparkling. "Miss Parsons is delightful in this, her first appearance before the movie cameras. She is unaffected and at ease as she radiates the personality which has won her the confidence of Hollywood's greatest," commented one Hearst reviewer. "I enjoyed every minute of *Hollywood Hotel* so very much," wrote Mary Pickford, who, despite her lingering animosity toward Louella, had agreed to write a review for the Hearst papers. "Louella plays herself in the film—and a very pretty and charming and slender self she is, too. I know Louella was nervous about making the film . . . but none of that nervousness registers on the screen. In fact, Louella is just the same as her many friends in Hollywood know her to be—and I claim that is pretty nice."[19] "She may be the first lady of Hollywood . . . but she's just Ma to me," wrote Harriet, who also did a review for the Hearst papers.[20]

Other reviewers were more honest. "Louella Parsons gives nothing to the film—but who expected her to?" wrote one New York critic. Joked one reporter on a Vermont paper, "Louella Parsons looks like she writes. Boy, am I sick to my stomach."[21] "Louella was a brave woman to play herself in the picture. Her acting isn't bad and she photographs quite well, though she looks more like the president of a women's club than a movie columnist," wrote another.[22]

Not long after the premiere, Jack Warner wrote to Hearst expressing "how happy we are over Louella Parsons' splendid performance in our musical production *Hollywood Hotel*. Reviews this morning praise her naturalness and dignity of performance. I believe her presence in this production will bring a mutual benefit." When Hearst saw the film in January 1938, he wrote to Warner that he agreed: "Louella was excellent. Very composed like a practiced actress. I bet she will want to be in pictures all the time."[23] Though Hearst was happy with the film, he was still upset with Warner Brothers, and shortly after *Hollywood Hotel*'s release, Hearst left the studio and went on to produce films at Twentieth Century Fox.

The thirty thousand dollars from the film appearance could not have come at a better time, since Louella and Harry were having financial troubles. They took regular weekend trips to Agua Caliente, a Tijuana gambling resort that was a favored hotspot among the Hollywood elite, and Louella lost thousands on racetrack betting. She had also become something of an antiques collector, and her home was filled with expensive (and by many accounts tasteless) old knickknacks. Then in 1937, Louella and Harry took a lavish six-week vacation to Rome, London, and Paris with actress Sally Eilers and her husband, director Joe Brown. As in 1932, she surveyed the foreign film market and relayed her observations back to Hearst. By the late 1930s, the German film industry had nationalized, forcing American distributors to leave the country, and in Italy, Mussolini similarly developed a national film industry, headquartered at Rome's Cinecitta film studio. In 1937, Louella visited Cinecitta, and in one dispatch from Rome reported on Mussolini's plan to send his son Vittorio to Hollywood to learn filmmaking from director Hal Roach. (The plan fell through when, in October 1937, not long after his arrival, the young Mussolini found himself the object of a "concerted drive of the Anti-Nazi League against his presence in town," and returned to Italy in a huff, according to *Variety*.)[24]

But this European trip was more for pleasure than business. After visiting Bebe Daniels and Ben Lyon, who had moved to London to work in theater, Louella and Harry motored through northern Italy, saw friends in Budapest, and visited the papal summer home, Castel Gandolfo. During the 1930s Louella had become increasingly devoted to Catholicism and was a regular attendee at the Church of the Good Shepherd in Beverly Hills. Her religious commitment was sincere, but some who knew her past suspected that it may have been a guise to conceal her Jewish roots. According to historian Steven Carr, during the 1930s the Jewish producers and studio moguls were still the victims of early-twentieth-century stereotypes that depicted them as "Shylocks controlling mass culture" and "stubborn foreign influences unwilling to yield to an assimilated national identity."[25] Though Louella did not openly reveal her Jewish background, she nonetheless spoke out against anti-Semitism and was known to inform Jewish studio heads Louis B. Mayer, Jack Warner, and Harry Cohn when she came across actors whom she thought "didn't like Jews." Sometimes this became an excuse to attack those who had crossed her in other ways. When one actor refused to appear without pay on Louella's radio program, Louella told Harry Cohn that she thought the actor was "not only arrogant . . . but also anti-Semitic."[26]

Also draining Louella's bank account in 1937 was Marsons Farm, a twenty-four-acre plot of land in the Northridge area of the San Fernando Valley that Louella and Harry had purchased that summer. For the rest of the year, they poured tens of thousands of dollars into the construction of a colonial-style house that they planned to use as a weekend retreat. Completed in early 1938, the home was decorated with simple woolen rugs and plain wooden furniture, and in one room Louella had installed her childhood furniture from Dixon. Throughout were housewarming gifts from Hollywood friends: a crystal candy box from Peter Lorre, a set of china figurines from Sid Grauman, a poker table from Carole Lombard and Clark Gable, and antique ceramic pitchers from Bebe Daniels and Ben Lyon. One of Louella's favorite rooms in the house was the library, which she stocked with a collection of mystery novels and decorated with an oil painting that had once hung in her grandmother Jeanette's dining room. In addition to a swimming pool and a large lawn (Louella borrowed artificial sod from a studio prop department to fill in gaps in the grass), the grounds boasted a fully functioning ranch, complete with chickens, horses, dairy cows, and an orange grove. Two olive trees stood in the garden, gifts from Gable and Lombard and Myrna Loy and Arthur Hornblow.[27]

Louella and Harry began using Marsons Farm as a weekend retreat in the spring of 1938. Each Friday Louella hurried to finish her duties in town while Harry went to the Farmers' Market on Fairfax Avenue and purchased fresh fruits and vegetables for the weekend. Zeppo Marx, Barbara Stanwyck and Robert Taylor, and Clark Gable and Carole Lombard all had estates in the area, and, according to Dorothy Manners, "Carole, Clark, Stanwyck, and Taylor got very clubby."[28] Not long after the completion of the home, Louella began hosting social events at Marsons Farm. Before long her country barbecues were as celebrated as her Maple Drive affairs. (In 1939 *Photoplay* magazine named Louella as Hollywood's "best barbecue thrower.")[29] Sometimes the parties were attended by a hundred or more guests, and Louella installed bunk beds so that guests could sleep over. In an oft-repeated story that illustrates Louella's famed hospitality (and absentmindedness), Charles Gentry of the *Detroit Times* was visiting Hollywood and called up Louella to pay his respects. Louella invited him to visit her at Marsons Farm, and the following day Gentry drove to the ranch. Harry was playing cards on the porch and waved him to a chair. After an hour's wait Louella finally showed up on horseback. She turned to him and smiled. "Hello! I'm so glad you came! You must stay for dinner! I'm giving a party for Charles Gentry of the Detroit *Times!*"[30] The days at Marsons Farm, Louella claimed, were among the happiest in her life, providing a much needed respite from her increasing anxieties.[31]

The Hearst empire was crumbling. By 1937, as a result of the depression and the anti-Hearst movement, Hearst papers in Los Angeles, San Francisco, Chicago, and Boston had lost 10 percent of their circulation. And because

Hearst had not reduced his spending to compensate for the losses, the corporation faced bankruptcy.[32] Hearst was forced to sell off not only several of his newspapers but also much of his prized art collection, and to help bail him out, Davies gave him a million dollars of her own earnings from her screen career.

Though they continued to live at San Simeon, Hearst and Davies were coming upon dark days. Despite glowing reviews from Louella, Davies's Hollywood career had all but ended in 1937. Though Louella had described Davies's last film, *Ever Since Eve,* as "a real audience picture" that brought "such spontaneous applause and laughter that those who saw it promptly put it down as a sure-fire hit," it was a box office flop.[33] Depressed, Davies began drinking heavily, and Hearst struggled to come to terms with the loss of his empire. In April 1937 Davies put on a seventy-fourth birthday party for Hearst at her Santa Monica beach house. Featuring a circus theme and attended by over five hundred guests, this was one of the last great Hearst-Davies extravaganzas. From then on, there were only a handful of parties and few guests at San Simeon. By the late 1930s only Hearst and Davies's closest friends, including Louella and Harry, were invited to the ranch for weekend retreats.

On March 5, 1938, Hearst columnist Westbrook Pegler reported what Louella had feared—the weakening of the Hearst empire was diminishing her influence in Hollywood. "For many years, the actors, more especially the women stars and the producers and publicity departments have stood in awe of Louella Parsons. This prestige appears to be diminishing now, with the consolidation and elimination of some of Mr. Hearst's papers and the narrowing of his interests in other fields," he wrote. According to Pegler, Louella appeared "to have been topped" by the *Hollywood Reporter,* a "small and strictly professional trade paper with a class circulation."[34]

By late 1937, Louella's radio career was also imperiled. In November, she had announced to the show's producers that, unless she received $5,000 a week for *Hollywood Hotel,* she would leave the show. The money was not for personal expenses, she insisted, but to pay actors who appeared on the show—the Screen Actors' Guild had turned up its pressure on Louella and her "free talent" policy, and she was determined to avoid what could become an ugly standoff with the union. In mid-November, Harry and executives from the William Morris talent agency, which represented Louella, entered negotiations with the F. Wallis Armstrong agency, which produced the show, but Armstrong rejected Louella's demands. Louella then withdrew her ultimatum and continued on at her $2,250 salary; actors continued to appear on the program without pay, and SAG's wrath mounted.[35] Finally, as a result of the trouble with SAG, the producers did not renew Louella's contract, and actor William Powell took over her spot on the program. The previews and star interviews were dropped from the show, which plummeted in ratings, and it was taken off the air in December 1938.

Knowing the importance of radio to her popularity, Louella looked for another opportunity to go back on the air. In early 1939 there were rumors that she would appear regularly on the popular Kate Smith radio program, and there was also some discussion of her hosting another "free talent" film preview show, *Hollywood Previews,* which would be produced by *Hollywood Hotel* producer Bill Bacher. Due to SAG pressure, the show never materialized.[36]

In 1936, MGM producer Irving Thalberg died suddenly at age thirty-seven after a bout with pneumonia. Louella had met Thalberg in 1919, when he was a teenager working in the New York office of Carl Laemmle's Universal Studio, and they had been friends ever since. Louella saw Thalberg a few days before he died; Norma Shearer, Thalberg's wife, had just appeared on Louella's radio show, and after the show Louella delivered Shearer back to the studio in time for Shearer's departure for a Labor Day weekend trip with Thalberg. It was during the trip that he contracted pneumonia. "The last time I saw him, they [Thalberg and Shearer] were standing with their arms around each other, blowing me kisses as I drove away," Louella recalled. "When he died, I was terribly broken up. There have only been a few deaths that touched me as deeply."[37] With the rest of Hollywood, she mourned his passing, and she wrote lengthy tributes to him in the *Examiner.* That year Hearst executive Arthur Brisbane also died. Though Louella initially despised him—Brisbane had rejected Louella's appeal to transfer to Hearst's *Chicago Examiner* after the takeover of the *Chicago Record* in 1918—he became a benefactor who, according to Adela Rogers St. Johns, bailed Louella out of debt twice.[38] In 1937 Jean Harlow, who was only twenty-six, passed away from a severe kidney infection, and in honor of the actress, one of Louella's favorite young stars, Louella and Dorothy Manners wrote a series of biographical articles that appeared both in the *Examiner* and in book form, under the title *Jean Harlow's Life Story.*[39] It sold a million copies at ten cents a copy, and years later Louella was still getting fan mail asking where the book could be found.[40]

The unexpected deaths shook Louella and reminded her of her own mortality. In her midfifties, Louella was having recurring kidney problems and reported frequent feelings of weakness. In the spring of 1938, she had a physical and mental collapse, most likely from exhaustion, and spent two weeks in Cedars of Lebanon Hospital recuperating. Later that year Harry became ill with a near-fatal bout of pneumonia, and Louella stayed with him in Good Samaritan Hospital for over two weeks while Dorothy Manners wrote the column.

The studios were filled with new names and faces, and this upset Louella, who regularly complained in her column about the changing of the guard. Many of Louella's old friends and colleagues—Mary Pickford, Douglas Fairbanks, Lillian Gish, D. W. Griffith—had retired from film. "Their withdrawal from active participation in the business they gave so much to gives me a genuine pang," she told her readers in 1937. Louella admitted that she was "often intolerant of intruders—newcomers who have little love for an industry [I] have watched grow from a small despised thing to the world's third greatest business."[41] Each week she put aside a portion of her salary to help friends from the silent era who had fallen on hard times. This was partially out of generosity, but also a shrewd business decision, since the recipients of her donations often repaid her with gossip.[42] The old Hollywood was passing, and with it, Louella feared, her own commanding position.

Somewhere in the halls of the MGM studio, her enemies were indeed plotting to unseat her. The scheme involved Louella's old friend, Hedda Hopper. In 1937, Hopper was a down-and-out actress, a bit player fallen on hard times. After her contract at MGM was canceled in 1932, she tried work in real estate and theater, and even sold cosmetics, before walking into an offer that would make her Louella's most formidable rival.

Louella and Hopper had known each other for over fifteen years. In New York, Hopper and Louella had been friends, and Louella had frequently mentioned Hopper in her *Morning Telegraph* column. When Hopper moved to Hollywood following her divorce from DeWolf Hopper in 1923, she and Louella corresponded regularly. During the 1920s, Hopper appeared in several films for MGM, including *Zander the Great*, which starred Marion Davies. Never a star in her own right, Hopper had supporting roles in more than seventy-five productions, and Louella nicknamed her "Queen of the Quickies."[43]

In 1919 Hopper was interviewed by *Photoplay* magazine, which described her as "a tall, extraordinarily tall woman with a finely poised head on broad shoulders. She had a large crooked humorous mouth, which parted to show very small and excellent teeth, a patrician nose, arched eyebrows, and the most impossible eyes!" On the screen, she had played "intellectual and artistic vampires" and was "the worst cat on the screen; the woman who steps in and breaks up the home; who had no heart, no soul, no scruples—but a brain, and wit, and a deadly fascination." But "the feline queen is anything but a catty woman off," the magazine assured its readers.[44] Hopper's friends and acquaintances knew better. Hopper was indeed catty—shrewd, conniving, outspoken, and flamboyant. A regular at Hollywood parties, she was one of Hollywood's best gossips. "You can't keep any secrets from Hedda Hopper," claimed fan magazine writer Gladys Hall, who in a 1931 *Motion Picture* magazine article described her as "the lady who knows it all."[45]

Hopper's contract with MGM brought her into contact with Hearst and Davies, and she was a frequent guest at San Simeon. Known for her fashion sense—MGM loaned her to other studios when they needed a "dressy dame"—Hopper was praised by Louella for the "clothes one sees her wearing at the Embassy and the other places where the stars congregate." Secure in her "steady job" at MGM, Hopper "can afford to buy herself a becoming frock now and then," Louella wrote in her column in 1930.[46] But the fancy clothes were not for long. The stock market crash of 1929 had wiped out her bank account, and MGM, as part of its cost-cutting measures in the depression, did not renew her contract. She then spent the next five years scrambling to make ends meet. In 1932, Ida Koverman, Louis B. Mayer's secretary, encouraged her to run for one of the seven seats on the Republican Central Committee from the Fifty-seventh Assembly District, and though Louella had been a registered Democrat, she endorsed Hopper in her column. ("Even if we differ with her in politics, we can't help but hope that Hedda will be elected," Louella wrote in August 1932.)[47] After losing the race, Hopper turned to selling real estate, then, in 1934, she went to New York to appear in a Broadway production called *Divided By Three.* When the show ended, she stayed in New York and worked at a branch of the Elizabeth Arden cosmetic company for a few months, then spent several months traveling in Europe with the screenwriter Frances Marion and her children.

Shortly after Hopper's return to Hollywood in 1936, she approached Dema Harshbarger, head of the NBC Artists' Bureau, hoping to find work in radio. Hopper impressed Harshbarger with her knowledge of Hollywood gossip—in forty-five minutes, according to Harshbarger, Hopper told her "as much about Hollywood as I could have learned in two years"—and Harshbarger secured for Hopper a fifteen-minute Hollywood gossip show sponsored by the makers of Maro Oil shampoo. She appeared for twenty-six weeks at $150 a week, but "the consensus was that she was awful," *Time* magazine later wrote, and her contract was not renewed.[48] She then appeared in a radio show called *Brenthouse,* and critics mocked her stilted delivery and phony British accent. Howard Denby of the Esquire Features Syndicate saved her from an uncertain future in radio. In 1937 he went to a press agent at MGM claiming that he was looking for someone to unseat Louella. Andy Hervey of MGM's publicity department suggested Hopper. "Why don't you talk to Hedda Hopper? I don't know if she can write. All I can tell you is that whenever we want to know what's going on with our stars we call her," Hervey said.[49] Hopper then sent Denby samples of her writing, and Esquire signed her later that year.

It was not the first time Hopper had authored a Hollywood gossip column. In 1935, she had written a movie column for Eleanor "Cissy" Patterson's *Washington Herald,* a Hearst-owned paper. Patterson met Hopper at San Simeon and decided that "anyone who could talk as fast as Miss Hopper would make a good columnist." But the column lasted only four months. Hopper claimed that she backed out of the column because she wasn't being paid enough, but she later admitted that Patterson canned her because the columns "weren't very good."[50]

Her new column for Esquire appeared in thirteen papers, including the *Los Angeles Times.* When the *Times* editor saw a sample column, he complained that it was "badly written. No news value. Might be all right for a small town weekly. Has nothing to offer a great metropolitan newspaper like the *Times.*"[51] The editor was later overruled, and Hopper's first column in the *Times* appeared on February 14, 1938. "Just twenty-three years ago my son was born," she wrote. "Since then I've acted in Broadway plays. Sold Liberty Bonds in Grand Central Station. . . . I've worked with practically every star in Hollywood. Sold real estate here—made it pay, too, but not lately. Was a contributor to one of the monthly magazines. Did special articles for the Washington *Herald.* And today I begin laboring in a new field and am hoping it will bring me as much happiness as that major event which took place twenty-three years ago." "Hollywood is mad, gay, and heartbreakingly silly," she concluded, "but you can't satirize a satire. And that's Hollywood."[52]

Saccharine and poorly written, the column was the butt of jokes in Hollywood. But Hopper persisted. At the end of her second month with Esquire, Ida Koverman, who resented "people's snickering at Hedda," held a "cat party," a gathering of actresses and prominent female journalists and screenwriters that was intended to toughen the hide of the novice columnist. Koverman invited Norma Shearer, Jeanette MacDonald, Claudette Colbert, Joan Crawford, Sophie Tucker, and Harriet Parsons, among others; Louella was not on the list. "It was a night to remember. A forest fire was blazing in the hills, and the sky was lit with flame. I was burning, too," Hopper recalled in her autobiography. The guests told her, "They've laughed at you long enough. You've been too nice to people. Now start telling the truth."[53] Koverman had been encouraged to back Hopper by Louis B. Mayer, who saw her as potential leverage against Louella. Naïvely, Mayer believed that Hopper would become an ally, docile and easily controlled.[54]

But Hopper soon proved herself a freethinker unafraid of contradicting the studios. Not long after the "cat party," Hopper started to "dig up some dirt," in her words, and began running items that criticized the studios. According to Hopper, the "one that hit home in Hollywood was a little piece on the caste system in our town." "What star in Hollywood, getting five thousand a week, would sit at the same table as an actress getting a mere one hundred dollars?" she had written.[55] *Times* publisher Norman Chandler began receiving complaints about Hopper, including a threat from one producer to cancel his advertising in the paper. But readers appreciated the change in tone. Hopper's column was picked up by sixteen papers within a month of Koverman's party.[56]

By mid-1938, Hopper was doing seven columns a week, a fan magazine story each month, and a radio show. By the summer of 1939, she had become so successful that she began looking for a New York outlet for her column. In July 1939 she wrote to Hearst about the possibility of running the column in his New York tabloid, the *Mirror*. Though the *Mirror* already ran Jimmie Fidler's column, Hopper hoped that her column might run alongside Fidler's, as it did in the *Los Angeles Times*. She wrote to Hearst several times during 1939, before he responded, "[I would] like to see [the] column in the *Mirror* and will do what I can to place it there."[57]

Louella was concerned by Hopper's entrance into the gossip field, but she was not initially threatened. Louella considered Hopper a poor writer and inexperienced reporter, and, given her limited readership, she presented relatively little competition. But in 1939 there were signs that Hopper was becoming a force to be reckoned with. One indication came in March, when Louella was visibly "outscooped" in one of the season's biggest stories—the wedding of Carole Lombard and Clark Gable, who had lived together, unmarried, for several months. When early in 1939 they announced that they were thinking about finally tying the knot, Louella forced them to promise that, when the time came, they would give her the news exclusively. They agreed, though they hinted that they might put off the wedding until the summer. In early March, Louella told the Gable fans among her readers that they could "relax," since the wedding would not be for several weeks, "unless there is a sudden elopement, which I doubt."[58]

Throughout March 1939, Louella waited for the call from Gable, but it never came. Then, unbeknownst to Louella, on the morning of March 29, Gable and Lombard, accompanied by Gable's publicist, Otto Winkler, drove to Arizona and eloped. Immediately after the ceremony, Winkler called Howard Strickling at MGM, who planned a press conference for the following day at Lombard's home.[59]

They had wanted to marry in peace, without the usual press circus that surrounded celebrity weddings. Happy with their quiet elopement, the newlyweds had a peaceful drive back to Los Angeles—that is, until Lombard began to panic. Louella would be furious that they had broken their promise, she predicted, and she demanded that Gable pull over at the nearest gas station, where she tried to phone Louella. But Louella was still in San Francisco, with most of the other Hollywood columnists on a "press junket" funded by the Twentieth Century Fox studio, and Lombard called Marion Davies for advice. After chastising her for not giving Louella the news, Davies urged Lombard to send Louella a telegram, and for good measure, one to Hearst, too. "Married this afternoon," the dispatch read. "Carole and Clark."

But the note only added insult to injury. When Louella returned home the following day and found the telegram, it was already old news. The United Press and Associated Press syndicates had gotten the break, and headlines announcing the Gable-Lombard marriage appeared in publications around the world.[60] Embarrassed, Louella told her readers that "among the first to receive a telegram from the newlyweds was William Randolph Hearst," that she had "had their promise [they] would telephone me and they did." But everyone knew that she had been outscooped.[61] Gable and Lombard had betrayed her, and the snub—from her friends, no less—upset her. Feeling weaker than she had in months, she was unprepared for the blow that hit her that summer.

The article appeared in the July 15, 1939, issue of the *Saturday Evening Post*. Titled "The First Lady of Hollywood" and illustrated with several photos of Louella posing with stars and studio bigwigs, on the surface it seemed like a tribute. It was anything but. The article began by attacking Louella's writing and appearance. Calling Louella the "most consistently inaccurate reporter who ever lived," the *Post* claimed that "in her own field, where bad writing is as . . . common as breathing, Louella's stands out like an asthmatic's gasps. . . . Plump and breathless," Louella perpetually wore an "expression of blank bewilderment" and was "twenty minutes late mentally." Though everyone in Hollywood detested her, the *Post* wrote, Louella, "a damply sentimental woman," believed that she had hundreds of friends—312, to be exact, Louella had claimed.[62]

After implying that she was an alcoholic—that she "started her day with a tumbler of whisky," it claimed inaccurately—the piece went on to attack Harry and Harriet. "A beautiful quality about [Louella's] success was that it turned out to be contagious. . . . Through osmosis, other members of her family became infected with prosperity. Harriet, her daughter, developed a talent for producing shorts at $500 a week." "The same happy experience befell Louella's husband, Dr. Harry Martin," it continued. "Relatively obscure before this marriage, after it he became the sensation of the local medicocinematic world. Studios vied with one another for his services . . . and as honor followed honor he became chief of staff of the Motion Picture Relief Fund, civil-service commissioner, and chairman of the State Boxing Commission—heights to which a simple urologist has rarely soared." "A gruesome aspect of the matter," the *Post* added, "is that Louella addresses him—and in public—as 'Docky-wocky.'"[63]

Though the byline read "Thomas Wood," in reality the article was a three-way collaboration by Wood, screenwriter-producer Nunnally Johnson, and Sidney Skolsky. Wood, who had worked for Louella briefly in 1937 as a legman, interviewed Louella for an article scheduled to run in the *New Yorker* in early 1938. When Harold Ross, the editor, turned down the piece on "literary grounds"—the article, he claimed, was poorly written—Wood approached Johnson to assist him with a rewrite. Johnson disliked Louella, and he added spite to the piece. When Skolsky heard of the project, things turned ugly. In early 1939 the *Post* purchased the revamped article with Wood's solo byline (Johnson and Skolsky insisted on remaining anonymous), and the magazine was so delighted with the piece that it commissioned Wood to write a series of articles on the private lives of the studio executives. Joked the *Hollywood Reporter,* "Who was it that suggested some studio ought to buy the Satevepost article on Louella as a vehicle to star Hedda Hopper?"[64]

It was the most critical public attack to date. The *Post,* with a circulation of three million, seriously damaged Louella's public reputation. The accusations of nepotism were justified, and the intimations of alcoholism nearly believable, since Louella, under Harry's influence, had become a heavy imbiber. Perhaps even more upsetting to Louella, the article indicated a loss of control over her public image. Since the beginning of her career with Hearst, she had used her access to his multimedia empire—newspapers, magazines, radio, and film—to create her public persona as an innocent yet glamorous "friend to the stars." Wood's piece shattered the facade, and it heralded more damning things to come.

Determined to fight back, Louella called the noted Hollywood lawyer Jerry Geisler and discussed the possibility of filing suit against the *Post*. Though Geisler warned her that it would be difficult—the article technically was not libelous, since nothing in it could be proven false—Louella insisted, and by the end of the month, he and Louella had filed a suit against the *Post* for a million dollars. Geisler filed it in the wrong court, however, and the case stalled. Rather than refile and pursue a lengthy and most likely unsuccessful legal battle, Louella, who was by that fall immersed in other projects, decided to drop the case. Instead, she planned to punish Johnson, Skolsky, and particularly Wood in other ways. Wood found himself on an unofficial Hollywood blacklist and had trouble finding work for several years; Wood's spouse, the actress Lee Patrick, received only critical reviews in the *Examiner* for the rest of her career. Since it was difficult for Louella to strike back against the popular and well-entrenched Johnson, she attacked his wife, actress Dorris Bowdon. "I ran into Dorris Bowdon last night," Louella wrote in her column. "She used to be such a pretty girl before she married."[65]

She took a minor respite from her campaign of spite that September, when Harriet and the socially prominent actor-playwright King Kennedy ("He is a charming boy," Louella described him, "witty and clever") were wed in a lavish ceremony in the garden at Marsons Farm.[66] Upon Louella's request, Louis B. Mayer had postponed the premiere of the film *Elizabeth and Essex,* at the expense of ten thousand dollars to the studio, so that celebrities could drive up to Northridge for the four-hundred-person affair. Described by *Newsweek* as one of the most elegant Hollywood weddings in recent years, it was attended by "more stars . . . than there are in the Milky Way." Both Louella and Kennedy's mother were thrilled by the marriage, which was an obvious front, since both Harriet and Kennedy were homosexual.[67] Not long after the wedding, they stopped living together and were involved with other lovers. After the couple's divorce, which Louella blamed on Kennedy, he went to work as a legman—for Hedda Hopper.

By the time of Harriet's wedding, Hopper had gone from being a minor annoyance to being a serious threat. Though her column still appeared only in the Esquire syndicate, in September 1939 she announced that she would be going on the air three times a week with a gossip show underwritten by Sunkist, Louella's former sponsor. Being without a radio show herself since *Hollywood Hotel* went off the air, Louella feared, quite rightly, that the new Sunkist program would give Hopper the edge.

Hopper also had other advantages that troubled Louella. Unlike Louella, who came to California as a member of the Hearst press, Hopper, a former actress, had always been an insider. She was loud, gregarious, and naturally theatrical—qualities that endeared her to her many friends, and that Louella, less relaxed and more reserved, had always wished for herself. And though she was only four years younger than Louella, natural good looks and a meticulous beauty regime had kept the tall, blond Hopper youthful and photogenic. She was perfectly poised to become a name in her own right, and Louella worried that it would be only a matter of time before Hopper's talents propelled her into the spotlight.

Then it happened. In October 1939, Hopper outscooped Louella on one of the most important stories of the year. Jimmy Roosevelt, the president's son, who had been working as a producer at the Samuel Goldwyn studio, was planning to separate from his wife, Betsy, and marry a nurse at the Mayo Clinic, Romelle Schneider. A longtime friend of Roosevelt's, Hopper had known that he was planning a divorce and made him promise to tell her first when he was ready to break the story. For weeks Roosevelt remained silent, but on October 21, 1939, a friend of Hopper's in New York told her that she had heard "through the grapevine" that the Roosevelt divorce was imminent. At ten that evening, Hopper phoned her assistant Hy Gardner and the two met at Roosevelt's Beverly Hills home. Pushing her way past the butler, Hopper shouted at Roosevelt, who appeared on the doorstep in bare feet and a bathrobe: "My spies from New York tipped me off. Now give." After Roosevelt confessed—he was indeed about to begin divorce proceedings—Hopper sped back to the *Times* and, literally shouting "Hold the press" as she ran through the door, managed to get the story into the Sunday paper. The exclusive article, with Hopper's byline, made the front page.[68] According to Gardner, it was "the hottest exclusive of national impact in her . . . career."[69]

In her column on Monday, Louella included only a short mention of Roosevelt, a comment criticizing his work at the Goldwyn studio. Hearst, appalled that Louella would take such an obvious crack at the president's son, ordered it out of the paper. When it appeared in the first edition—an "old employee tossed in the paragraph without knowing it had been killed," according to the *Hollywood Reporter*—editor "Cardington and everyone else at the *Examiner* threw a fit."[70]

The *Hollywood Reporter* noted a few days later, "The fight that's on between Hedda Hopper and Louella Parsons is now coming out in the open, with both on a struggle to scoop the other and much of the local gentry taking sides in the effort." The opening shots had been fired, and the feud had officially begun.[71]

Slowly, the balance of power was shifting. As publicists and actors began to side with Hopper, Louella complained of a "shortage of news." When she told her troubles to producer David Selznick in July 1939, out of sympathy Selznick mentioned that they had tested the actress Alla Nazimova for a part in his upcoming film *Rebecca*. Nazimova was a possibility, Selznick had said, but the role was still uncertain. So when Louella printed that Nazimova was set for the role, Selznick was furious. "You neither secured the story nor checked it with us," he wrote back. Then, when Nazimova was ultimately passed up for the part, Louella complained to Selznick that he had misled her. "I think it is important that you straighten this [matter] out with her one way or the other," Selznick wrote to one of his publicity managers, Bill Hebert. "If you don't, the next story we give her of a casting possibility that doesn't come true she is going to get sore all over again, and if we don't give it to her, she is going to get sore if and when it comes true."[72]

Angry with Selznick, Louella began circumventing his publicity office, getting her news about Selznick and his productions from other sources. Shortly after the Nazimova incident, Selznick reported to Hebert, "I may as well tell you that despite our precautions Louella picked up word of the joint arrival of Laurence Olivier and Vivien Leigh. My suspicion is that she picked up word of their arrival from the airline publicity bureau."[73] Louella then printed that Selznick had offered seventy-five thousand dollars for the script of *King's Row,* though Selznick had made "no offer whatever and [had] no interest in acquiring the property," he wrote to Hebert. Louella was getting her news from inaccurate sources, and her tactics were not only hurting him, Selznick claimed, but ruining her own credibility.[74]

So when Louella asked Selznick, in the fall of 1939, "as a favor to a friend," to screen an unfinished version of *Gone with the Wind*, Selznick was not about to give in. Claiming that there were "soundtracks missing, colors not straightened out, scenes missing," he turned her down. Upset, Louella called him and yelled at him over the telephone. Selznick responded with a letter: "Dear Louella, I understand that you are upset with me because I won't show you GWTW. It is hard for me to believe, Louella, that you are serious about this. Won't you please try to understand also that if I ran the picture for you I would be breaking my word, given to literally dozens of newspaper people over a period of two years, that all the members of the press would see it at one time? Surely, Louella, you wouldn't want to place me in the light of being unfair to the people who have worked so hard for me, and of being a liar and a breaker of my word with all the rest of the press?"

"God knows I have tried in every conceivable way to prove to you the extent of my friendship with you," he continued. "But I would be very disappointed indeed if I believed that you really wanted me to go this far." But Louella would not relent, and she continued to snipe at Selznick. In angry letters and telegrams she called Selznick a "fair weather friend," a "backstabber," and "unfair."[75]

"You told me, Louella, as well as others, how hurt you have been by a recent article which contained what, in your own words, were inaccurate statements about you and your family," Selznick responded, referring to the *Saturday Evening Post* article. "This makes it doubly hard to understand why you turn right around and make unfair charges against someone who has been a friend of yours for so long a time. I am disappointed and hurt that[,] after knowing me since I was a little boy, you should know me so little as to believe that I would deliberately mislead you. I did not think it was necessary to explain to you, of all people, that I am not given to such tactics."[76] Ultimately, Selznick would not relent, and Louella saw the final version of *Gone with the Wind* when she was on the East Coast that fall. Her relationship with Selznick was one of many that would deteriorate in the years to come.

TWELVE

Raising Kane

IT WAS LARGELY AS A MEANS OF DAMAGE CONTROL that Louella, in the fall of 1939, began toying with the idea of doing a personal appearance tour. Personal appearance tours had saved the sagging careers of many actors and actresses. Why not that of a wounded Hollywood columnist? In October 1939 she floated the idea by friends, who quickly put her in her place. Yes, fans would turn out to see Clark Gable or Joan Crawford, but how many would pay to see Louella? Fans would pay to see her, Louella countered, if she were surrounded by a group of attractive Hollywood stars. One idea led to another, and by mid-October Louella had made the rounds at the studios and struck a tentative agreement. On the grounds that it would be good publicity, Twentieth Century Fox, MGM, and Warner Brothers agreed to let Louella take six of their up-and-coming young actors—Arlene Whelan, June Preisser, Susan Hayward, Joy Hodges, Ronald Reagan, and Jane Wyman (the latter two had recently gotten engaged)—on a two-month personal appearance tour. Starting in San Francisco, Louella and her "Hollywood Stars of 1940" would crisscross the nation with a seventy-minute music, dance, and comedy show. Whelan and Hodges would sing, Reagan and Wyman would crack jokes, and even Louella would get in on the act.

According to the deal she struck with the Leo Morrison agency, Louella would receive not only top billing but also a generous weekly salary, rumored by the *Hollywood Reporter* to be five thousand dollars. From this she would pay the actors, though how much the troupe actually received is unclear. The tour would visit only cities with Hearst papers, thus ensuring free publicity and positive reviews. The actors, of course, profited from the publicity, but their relatively meager salary and hard work—the stars carried the burden of the show and in some cities played five times a day—made Louella the winner in the deal. After only a week of rehearsals, the troupe made a rough debut in Santa Barbara on November 15, then prepared for "the big event in my life," as Louella called it—the opening performance at the Golden Gate Theater in San Francisco.[1]

She tried to be glamorous. Bedecked in a mink coat and pearls and elegantly coiffed by her private hairdresser, who traveled with her, Louella emerged onstage at the beginning of the show and asked breathlessly, "Am I late?" The orchestra struck up "Oh Susanna," and an all-woman chorus, dressed as newsboys, sang: "Oh Louella, won't you mention me? For a movie star in Hollywood, that's what I want to be." Audiences then watched a short film ("not short enough," quipped *Variety*) of Louella being sent off by her Hollywood "friends," including Deanna Durbin, Errol Flynn, Tyrone Power, Eleanor Powell, Fred Astaire, and Mickey Rooney, who thanked her for "all the nice things you've said about me" and wished her well on her tour. When the lights came back on, Louella took the stage and read prewritten "news flashes" that emerged from a phony teletype machine—"William Powell and Ginger Rogers have been seen holding hands!" she exclaimed—and concluded her portion of the show by answering questions that audience members had left in a box in the lobby. She exited gracefully as Arlene Whelan took the stage and sang a bossa nova tune, moving "with mild undulations of her torso."[2]

As predicted, the Hearst paper gushed. The show was "sparkling," declared the *San Francisco Examiner;* Louella, in particular, it noted, had great "dramatic flair." Other reviews were more honest. "Show was too long and rough," wrote one Hollywood-based reviewer. "Motherly Louella . . . displayed negligible stage personality but by being herself made more of a hit than had she attempted dramatics, which would have been disastrous." "The act may smooth out and speed up after a week or two," predicted *Variety.* "It may even reach the point where Miss Parsons will be able to speak her lines without muffing, spluttering, and/or stumbling." Quipped one cynic, "Louella Parsons, with 'honey' and 'darling' bubbling from every pore walked upon the scene. Well my dear, it was so exciting, and so gay, and so precious from then on that we just had to shut our eyes to keep from careening dizzily to the lower floor."[3]

The non-Hearst reviews may have been poor, but the turnout was not. When the troupe hit Philadelphia, after a turbulent flight in a chartered TWA plane with "Louella Parsons and her Flying Stars" written on the fuselage, they were mobbed by fans that occupied "every available inch of standing room inside the theater . . . and overflowed down Market Street as far as the eye could see," reported the *Philadelphia Record*.[4] It became so chaotic that police were called in to control the mob. "Hate to brag," Louella wrote in her column from Camden, "but we're doing five shows daily and each one is to standing room only."[5] By December, they had given 120 performances and were barraged with requests for appearances. "The LOPersonal appearances are so successful that demands are pouring in for an extension, but Warners and MGM NEED their young players who are on the jaunt," the *Hollywood Reporter* wrote on December 6.[6] After a shopping spree on Fifth Avenue, Louella spent Christmas in New York with Harry, who had flown out to see her. "We're smashing records!" she told him. "People are wonderful to us all over!"[7]

In truth, fans came to see the actors, not Louella. It was the troupe's "s.a.," their sex appeal, that drew the crowds, according to *Variety*.[8] Louella knew she was hardly the star of the show, but the positive publicity from the tour worked wonders on her morale. When the show played Chicago, she was honored at a luncheon attended by Kenneth Olson, dean of the Medill School of Journalism, and James Cane, publicity director of CBS. "I've seen my name in lights over many theaters lately, but this, in Chicago, gives me the greatest thrill of all, because I was once so poor in this town, just a nobody with hardly a penny to my name," she told the *Herald American*. In Chicago she was guest of honor at a luncheon sponsored by several hundred members of the Chicago Headline Club, an organization composed of the alumni chapter of Sigma Delta Chi, a national journalism fraternity.[9]

In Washington, the *Post* printed a glowing tribute to "LOP, the . . . initials that are as famous as FDR and ones which command as much awe and respect as the latter three. They belong to Louella O. Parsons, the First Lady of Hollywood, confidante of the stars and undisputed ace of aces among filmdom's press correspondents."[10] On the return journey, during a layover in Albuquerque, "the airport was thronged with thousands of men and women, high school boys and girls, women's club leaders, army officers, and a special delegation of Pueblo Indians," who made Louella an honorary member of their tribe. "My new Indian name is Ba Ku La, which means Princess Starmaker," she wrote in her column. Shouting through the crowd, a "cowboy" asked her when the war was going to end, if Hitler would be assassinated, and if taxes would be lowered. Louella looked at him quizzically. "Well, you know everything, don't you?" he replied.[11]

Most gratifying to Louella was a New York interview with B. R. Crisler, drama writer for the *Times*. Friends had warned Louella that she was in for a serious panning, so when she entered Crisler's office, she fired off a defense. "I'm a blackmailer, I can't write, and I'm sure you've seen those articles about me, I'm that, too. Now what else would you like to know?"[12] Crisler was so impressed with Louella's forthrightness that he described Louella as the "friendliest soul in films." According to Crisler, she had forgotten her grudge against the *Saturday Evening Post.* "She isn't bitter about it," he wrote. "She really doesn't care. It is obvious that there is not a bigger heart in Hollywood than Miss Parsons'; nor is there anywhere in the world probably a longer memory for movies, a more formidable film background." "Nobody in the world could ever really dislike her," he concluded, "except on abstract literary grounds."[13] Back at home, Billy Wilkerson at the *Hollywood Reporter* showered her with "verbal orchids." Unlike columnist Sheilah Graham, whose tasteless jokes and comments during her public appearances defamed Hollywood, according to Wilkerson, Louella "spreads news and gossip from her rostrum in the theatres that help the picture business. . . . We say that Miss Parsons rates applause from Hollywood, as she is doing a great job for it."[14]

On January 15, 1940, Louella arrived back in Hollywood "after a skyrocketing public opinion in favor of the industry in the best of all ways," wrote the *Reporter.*[15] While in New York, she had received a lucrative offer to switch to the United Press syndicate, which she considered but turned down. William Hawkins, head of United Press, and Monte Bourjaily, then in charge of the United Press syndication service, visited her at her hotel in New York, bearing an offer that would allow not only for a significantly higher salary than she was earning with Hearst but also the ability to retain all her radio rights. The offer was too good to refuse, and Louella told the executives to return the following day with a contract.

That night, however, she began having second thoughts. "I couldn't fall asleep that night," she remembered. "I kept recalling all of Mr. Hearst's kindnesses, all the things he had done for me. . . . I remembered how much trust he had placed in me and his confidence in me as a newspaperwoman." Finally she got out of bed, went to the sitting room, and sat in the darkness. Moments later, Harry joined her. He said, "Louella, you never did intend to sign that contract, did you?" "Of course," she replied. "I'm going to."

But when Hawkins and Bourjaily returned the next day, she told them that she'd changed her mind. "I know I'd never be happy working for anyone but Mr. Hearst," she said.[16] Shortly afterward, she renewed her Hearst contract at her usual salary of $850 a week. "Dear Boss, Well you will have to put up with me for another three years," she wrote Hearst. "But I hope you are just as happy as I am." Hearst responded with a diamond pin and a note:

Dear Louella—First Lady of Hollywood

You must never shake your grandfather—first gent of San Simeon
   We belong in the same boat[17]

"I'm going to keep your letter all my life," she wrote back. "That's the very nicest letter I ever received. You know very well I'd never leave you[,] because I told you once if I went to work for anybody else I'd still be working for the Hearst papers[,] because I feel that you're not only my boss but my friend."[18]

In the spring of 1940, after flying to New York to appear on the Kate Smith radio show and announcing that she would be going on another personal appearance tour in the fall, she was informed by *Motion Picture* magazine that she had been named "one of Hollywood's ten most interesting persons." Number one on the list was Orson Welles.[19]

It was with spectacular fanfare that Orson Welles, the temperamental, imperious, twenty-three-year-old stage actor and radio star, arrived in Hollywood. Famous for his radio broadcast of H. G. Wells's novel *War of the Worlds* in 1938—Welles's depiction of the Martian invasion of America was so realistic listeners thought it was true—Welles was approached by the head of the RKO studio, George Schaefer, who hoped to hire him in an attempt to avert the studio's imminent bankruptcy. Welles had gained international acclaim for his work on Broadway—*Time* had recently celebrated Welles's theatrical achievements with a cover story titled "Marvelous Boy"—and all his life he had been touted as a prodigy. At the age of five, he was performing in the Chicago Opera; as a teenager, he was a theatrical star in Ireland; and by the time he was twenty, he was known for his brilliant—and politically and socially radical—productions for the Federal Theater Project. He had produced an all-black version of *Macbeth*, set in Haiti, and *The Cradle Will Rock,* which he had described as a leftist "labor opera." Welles went on to found his own theater company, Mercury Theater, which produced a controversial version of *Julius Caesar* that was a parable about fascism.[20]

Welles was reluctant to leave New York and refused Schaefer's initial offers. It was only when Schaefer promised Welles complete control of his films, from scripts to casting to direction and production, that he finally capitulated. Taking the Mercury Theater troupe with him, Welles moved to Hollywood in the summer of 1939. He was surprised to find the reception lukewarm. Many resented Welles for having played hard to get; others, including Louella, were angry with Schaefer for having given a complete rookie—Welles had no experience in film—a contract that was the envy of everyone in Hollywood. "Personally I haven't a thing in the world against Welles. He has proved that he is a brilliant actor-producer both in the theater and on the air. But I am becoming impatient with producers who go courting prima donnas and bend the knee before every foot that kicks them," Louella told her readers in the summer of 1939.[21]

Now that Welles was in Hollywood, all eyes were on the "would-be genius," as Louella dubbed him, to see when—and if—he would perform. Welles announced that his first project would be a screen adaptation of Joseph Conrad's *Heart of Darkness,* and for the rest of the summer he locked himself away in an expensive rented home in Brentwood and, with John Houseman and Herbert Drake of the Mercury Group, worked on the script. Shooting for *Darkness* was scheduled for October, but by early fall, when Schaefer declared that the budget for the film was too high, the project was scrapped. Welles then started work on a second project, *The Smiler with the Knife,* based on a British thriller, but this project, too, was abandoned when Welles and Schaefer were unable to agree on the female lead. Meanwhile, Hollywood jeered. The young genius with the dream contract was failing; worse yet, he was playing the quintessential theater snob, running around in a beard, quoting Shakespeare, and making snide anti-Hollywood remarks to reporters. "I hope that Welles was misquoted in the interview in which he was supposed to have said 'I shall proceed to refer to the movies only in terms of contempt.' Orson, I am afraid, is a young man who talks too much," Louella wrote. Others expressed their anger less politely. When Welles, now nicknamed "Little Orson Annie," invited important studio executives to a party, nobody came. An actor cut off Welles's necktie at the Brown Derby. After Dorothy Parker, who was screenwriting in Hollywood, was introduced to Welles, she said, referring to Welles's arrogance, "It's like meeting God without dying."[22]

Welles was not the only one to come under attack that summer. Longtime MGM screenwriter Herman Mankiewicz, an alcoholic, was finally fired by Louis B. Mayer over his drunkenness and gambling. The overweight, oafish "Mank," so accident-prone that he was considered by many in Hollywood to be a walking disaster, promptly went on a binge and ended up in a car crash. Bruised, bandaged, and laid up in Cedars of Lebanon Hospital, Mankiewicz received a visit from an old friend, Orson Welles. Out of sympathy, Welles offered Mankiewicz a job writing scripts for his Mercury Theater radio show, a long-running program that Welles continued to produce while in Hollywood. Mankiewicz accepted. Later that winter, as Mankiewicz followed Welles's saga of failure at RKO, he suggested to Welles that they make a film attacking William Randolph Hearst, an idea that Mankiewicz had toyed with for decades. Mankiewicz and his wife had been frequent visitors at San Simeon and, like many Hollywood liberals, hated the publisher for his media monopoly and red-baiting crusades. Though Welles's father had known Hearst, and though the Hearst theater critic Ashton Stevens, who was eventually the model for the character Jed Leland in the film that Welles was thinking about making, had been almost "an uncle" to Welles, Welles similarly despised the publisher, whose papers had criticized his leftist theater productions. After considering the possibility of making a movie around Hearst's alleged involvement in Thomas Ince's death, Mankiewicz and Welles agreed to make a "prismatic" film about Hearst's life, told from different points of view. The film would open with the death of Hearst—or rather, Charles Foster Kane, to be played by Welles—and would depict, in flashback mode, Hearst-Kane's rise to power, his tyranny over the American publishing industry, and his attempts to launch a talentless blonde opera singer, Susan Alexander, to stardom. Susan Alexander, of course, was based on Marion Davies.

With reams of paper and several months worth of pills that were prescribed to conquer his alcoholism, in early 1940 Mankiewicz was shipped to the Campbell Ranch, a vacation retreat in the desert town of Victorville, where he would dictate the script, tentatively titled *American,* to his secretary. In April, the 350-page script was complete, and by July 1940, after significant editing by both Mankiewicz and Welles, shooting on *American,* now renamed *Citizen Kane,* was scheduled to begin. RKO, for the most part, kept the film's script and shooting plans under wraps; if news about the film were to leak out to the wrong places, *Kane* might never see the light of day.

But Hollywood is Hollywood, where scandal is the coin of the realm and news travels fast, and by the time shooting was scheduled to start, many in the film colony ("just about EVERYONE," the *Hollywood Reporter* later claimed) knew that the film dealt with Hearst.[23] That is, everyone except Louella, who had spent most of the summer out of town. In May 1940, she had asked Joe Connolly of the International News Service for a vacation: "I want to take the Doctor away because he seems very run down since his operation—and nervous. Maybe it will help my disposition too." Connolly gave his blessings: "Your stuff this year has been the best in your entire career," he wrote.[24] After a six-week trip to Hawaii, Louella and Harry returned to California and went to San Simeon, where she spent "one of the nicest two days [she] had ever spent at the ranch." "It was such fun being with you and Marion without a lot of people," she told Hearst.[25] Shortly afterward, with Adela Rogers St. Johns, she traveled to Chicago to cover the Democratic convention, where Roosevelt was to be nominated for a third term. By 1940, Louella had switched her party affiliation from Democratic to Republican and, like Hearst, was an opponent of Roosevelt; she supported the Republican presidential candidate, Wendell Willkie. "You will be interested to hear that Hollywood without exception intends to vote for Wendell Willkie," she told Hearst shortly after the convention. "Of course I suppose this community represents the money part and probably does not reflect the attitude of the entire US[,] but so many people feel that he represents America, the land which has always meant opportunity."[26]

In mid-July 1940, she returned to Hollywood to find an invitation from Welles to a cocktail party on the *Kane* set, a standard courtesy that most directors extended to columnists. But because Louis B. Mayer had scheduled another event, the preview of the latest Clark Gable film, for the same afternoon, Louella and most of the other columnists did not attend. "Orson Welles, who was upset because most of the press attended the 'Boom Town' preview the afternoon of his cocktail party, wanted to toss another 'watch him work' shindig. But RKO nixed it because after all the bearded genius can only start work on his picture once!" Louella wrote. During the next few weeks, however, as Louella began to hear rumors that the film depicted Hearst, she asked Welles if they could meet, and the two arranged to have lunch in his RKO dressing room. The conversation that transpired became the subject of a feature article in the Sunday *Examiner,* in which Louella concluded that Welles was "a brilliant youth."[27]

Indeed, Welles was brilliant, and his genius never showed more than in his talk with Louella that afternoon. Rather than open the conversation with *Kane,* Welles, knowing Louella's strong ties to rural Illinois, asked Louella whether it was true that she was from Dixon. Her eyes lit up. Welles had grown up in Grand Detour, only six miles from Dixon, and that made them virtually neighbors, he explained. Instantly Louella's image of Welles transformed. No longer a contemptible theater snob, Welles was "just folks"—a real "hometown boy," as she would later dub him in her column, who had come to Hollywood to "do good." With newfound trust in Welles, Louella at last broached the subject of *Kane*. Was it true, as she had heard, that the film was about communism? Or, as another rumor suggested, that it depicted the life of Hearst? "It deals with a dead man," he replied. "You know when a man dies there is a great difference of opinion about his character." A film about a dead man? Louella asked. "I cover a great span of life," he continued, "and the widow of the man is really the heroine." Louella was confused, but nodded and smiled. Since she was on the RKO lot, she asked, could she see the set?[28]

At that point, the troupe was filming what would become one of the most famous scenes in the film—an allusion to *When Knighthood Was in Flower*, in which Susan Kane, the character based on Davies, was performing disastrously in an opera that had been financed and publicized by Kane. "This is just a phoney opera without any real music. It's an opera that never existed," Welles explained. Again, Louella did not understand, but she left the set feeling convinced that the "hometown boy" was on the level. Welles's description of *Kane* "sounded very complicated to me," Louella told her readers, "but it must be all right because Gregg Toland is the photographer. Gregg wouldn't be a part of a movie he didn't believe in." Earlier that summer, when Hearst heard rumors that *Kane* was based on his life, he had planned to cancel RKO ads in his papers. Confidently, Louella told Hearst that he could drop the proposed ban.[29]

Meanwhile, Hollywood snickered as Louella, enchanted by Welles and immersed in plans for her upcoming personal appearance tour, overlooked press reports, including articles in *Daily Variety* and *Newsweek*, that clearly stated the film's plot and intentions. In the September issue of a magazine called *Friday*, an article titled "Wellesapoppin" previewed *Kane* and printed six film stills from the production. A caption under the photo of actress Dorothy Comingore in the role of Susan Alexander described her as a "ringer for Marion Davies." Blindly, Louella continued to praise Welles in her column. "Let's give credit where credit is due. We all said enough about Orson Welles and the $700,000 he cost RKO before he ever faced a camera. George Schaefer, head of RKO, is in town and he was given a private preview of *Citizen Kane*. His own words are 'I am prouder of this picture than any screenplay RKO has ever made.' He was so delighted after he saw it that he gave the youthful genius a carte blanche to go ahead with his next," she told her readers. That November, when Louella saw Welles in Chicago—Louella was on the last leg of her tour, and Welles was speaking on a lecture circuit—she asked once again if the film concerned Hearst. Welles insisted that it did not.[30]

Louella returned to Hollywood in December for a quiet Christmas with Harriet and Harry. The personal appearance tour had been a success, and Louella announced to friends that she was in the process of lining up a sponsor for a reprise of the *Hollywood Hotel* radio show. The day was typical, with Louella's famed holiday turkey, many drinks, and expensive gifts from the studio heads and the "312 friends" in her circle. Noticeably absent was a present from Orson Welles. Ever the showman, he saved his spectacular gift for last.

On January 3, a small announcement appeared in the *Hollywood Reporter:* "Orson Welles is showing *Citizen Kane* to a very small group of friends tonight."[31] The private screening for the editors of *Life, Look,* and *Redbook,* the three periodicals that had reached their deadlines for February publicity, was to be secret. But after receiving a tip, the *Hollywood Reporter* broke the news and tucked the sentence quietly into its "Rambling Reporter" gossip section on the second page. That same day, *Daily Variety* ran its own blurb about *Kane:* "Nationally distributed magazines and even house organs are carrying the story, in both wordage and stills in current issues, which merely report what *Daily Variety* reported several months ago." "*Citizen Kane*," it reported, "is patterned somewhat after the biog of none other than William Randolph Hearst."[32]

Though Louella missed the blurb, Hopper spotted it, and, enraged that she had not been invited to the screening, she called Welles and left a message that she would be coming, whether Welles liked it or not. Hopper and Welles had known each other since 1934, when Hopper's son appeared in one of Welles's Broadway productions, and Welles had promised Hopper, as a friend, that she would be among the first to see *Kane*. "Dearest Hedda: I owe you the biggest apology of my life and here it comes," Welles wrote in a telegram to Hopper. "The magazine people Look and Life have to meet their deadline so we must show them the picture no matter how bad or incomplete very soon. Fully realize I have broken a solemn promise that you'd be the first to see Kane. Please understand and forgive. Come tonight if you must but it stinks. Many key shots are missing or only the tests are cut in and we need music like Britain needs planes. Love, Orson." Hopper went to the preview anyway, and when the lights came on at the end of the film she was stunned.[33]

Like most of the Hollywood community, Hopper had known that the movie was about Hearst. But she had no idea that Welles's depiction would be so dark and damning. In the film, Charles Foster Kane, the son of a silver miner turned millionaire, builds a New York publishing empire through deceit, manipulation, and sensational "yellow journalism." After an unsuccessful bid for the presidency, he pours millions of dollars into the operatic career of his untalented young lover. Kane provides Susan Alexander with costly singing lessons, builds an opera house for her, and fills his papers with glowing reviews of her performances. But no amount of money or press can turn her into a star, and she and Kane live miserably in Kane's castle, "Xanadu." Kane, bitter in his old age, becomes a violent tyrant, and Alexander a hysterical alcoholic. The parallels between Hearst and Kane are obvious—the yellow journalism, the blonde mistress, the cavernous mansion on a hill. Yet in his depiction of Hearst as violent, Marion Davies as talentless, and their relationship as cold and abusive, Welles cruelly exaggerated.

At the end of the film, Hopper stood up and shouted that *Kane* was "an outrage against a great American." As she left the screening to call Oscar Lawler, Hearst's lawyer, she shouted at Welles, "You won't get away with this."[34] Though Hopper was genuinely outraged by the film's depiction of Hearst and Davies, she also saw an opportunity to curry favor with Hearst, who was still considering placing her column in the *New York Mirror.* On the phone, she described in detail Welles's depiction of Hearst and Davies, claiming them defamatory and potentially libelous, and Lawler began conferring with the other Hearst lawyers.

The following day, the magazine *Friday* hit the newsstands. Billing itself as "the magazine that dared to tell the truth," the sensationalistic publication printed exaggerations, trumped-up scandals, and, in some cases, outright lies. In its January issue, *Friday* claimed that its reporters had seen a sneak preview of *Kane.* In reality, the closest the magazine's staff had come to the film was a press release and series of film stills that had been sent to the publication by Welles's publicist, Herbert Drake. According to Welles's biographer, Frank Brady, Dan Gillmor, *Friday*'s editor, concocted a story by "taking each photo and writing a caption for it that proved to his own satisfaction that the film was about William Randolph Hearst." Hoping to stir up controversy, the article concluded with the statement that "Louella Parsons, Hollywood correspondent for the Hearst newspaper chain, has been praising Welles lavishly, giving *Citizen Kane* a terrific advance build up. When informed of these outbursts of praise, Welles said: 'This is something I cannot understand. Wait until the woman finds out that the picture's about her boss.'"[35]

Welles had never made that comment, and when he saw it in *Friday* on January 8, he panicked.[36] Immediately he dispatched a telegram to Louella, explaining that "*Friday* magazine this week carries a vicious lie. . . . *Citizen Kane* isn't about Mr. Hearst [and] my remark was somebody's cruel invention." "A good deal of nonsense has been appearing lately about KANE," Welles continued. "Since it has been learned that the picture concerns itself with a fighting publisher, who lives in a big country house, it has been assumed that KANE is about Mr. Hearst. People seem to have forgotten Bennett, Munsey, Pulitzer, and McCormick, to mention only a few you could name. Not that it matters; KANE isn't any of them. Of course, if there hadn't been great publishers I couldn't have created a fictitious one, and some similarities to these men are unavoidable. I do hope you can make this distinction clear. . . . May we have lunch sometime next week, and when may I show you CITIZEN KANE?" he concluded. "My sincerest gratitude for all the wonderful things you have done for me and my very best to you."[37]

But Welles's attempts at civility were in vain. When Louella got the telegram, she was on the way to a party in Beverly Hills, and shortly after her arrival she received a call from Hearst. He had seen the issue of *Friday,* he explained, and the matter was urgent. Could Louella go to RKO immediately and screen *Citizen Kane?* "Yes, yes, Chief," Louella was reported to have said, and though Hearst gave few details about the article, Louella knew that Welles had lied about the film. At midnight, as Hearst issued a directive to his newspapers to ban all publicity on RKO, Louella plotted revenge.[38]

The next afternoon, January 9, 1941, Louella arrived at the RKO lot with Oscar Lawler and A. Laurence Mitchell, Hearst's lawyer in Los Angeles. The trio, along with Welles and Drake, watched *Kane* quietly; since the sound track had not been added and neither Louella nor the lawyers spoke during the film, the screening proceeded in a tense and eerie silence. When the lights came on at the end of the film, Louella was trembling. ("She was purple and her wattles were wobbling like a turkey gobbler," recalled *Kane* actress Ruth Warrick.) Furious, Louella glared at Welles. She stood up, turned, and walked out the door. Quietly, the battle over *Citizen Kane* had begun.[39]

Like Hopper, Louella began by contacting San Simeon. She told Hearst's secretary Joe Willicombe that the film was all that they had suspected—and worse. Around five thirty that evening, she received instructions from Hearst to stop *Citizen Kane.*

After first contacting movie czar Will Hays, whose help she hoped to enlist in the war against *Kane,* she placed a call to RKO. Claiming that "it was a matter of life and death to RKO," Louella demanded George Schaefer's telephone number, then proceeded to call the studio boss at home. When Schaefer's secretary answered and said that he was out, Louella threatened that unless she spoke to him immediately—within five minutes, she said—RKO would have on its hands "one of the most beautiful lawsuits in history." When Schaefer returned her call later that evening, Louella demanded that he withhold the release of *Kane* pending possible legal action. Schaefer refused, and Louella exploded. "If you boys want private lives, I'll give you private lives," she told Schaefer. If *Kane* were to be exhibited, she threatened, the Hearst papers would publish exposés on the private lives of every one of the RKO board of directors. When Schaefer held fast, insisting that the film would be premiered in February, as planned, Louella slammed down the phone.[40]

Within hours, Louella had placed calls to every major Hollywood executive—Louis B. Mayer, Joseph Schenck, Nick Schenk, Y. Frank Freeman, Darryl Zanuck, and David Selznick—and demanded that they support her in stopping *Kane*'s release. If they refused, Hearst would run "immediate editorials on Hollywood's employment of refugees and immigrants instead of handing those jobs to Americans," Louella promised.[41] During the late 1930s many of the major studios had given jobs to writers, actors, producers, and directors fleeing Hitler's Germany, and the Hearst papers had often printed remarks accusing Hollywood of being "un-American." A full-blown "Americanization campaign" like the kind Louella threatened, predicted the *New York Times,* "might lead to a Congressional investigation," which could be disastrous for the movie industry.[42] Hearst later called the studio heads, and reminded them of the number of times his papers had buried or canceled a scandalous story about a star or director. The executives had little choice but to capitulate. On January 14, Louella triumphantly telegrammed Joe Willicombe that Louis B. Mayer, Joseph Schenck (of Twentieth Century Fox), and Jack Warner had refused to book *Citizen Kane* in their theaters.[43]

But the film could still be exhibited in theaters owned by RKO. Hoping to pressure RKO to abandon the film, Louella promised David Sarnoff, head of RCA, which had a controlling interest in RKO, an "unfavorable personal article" if *Kane* were to run in RKO theaters. She also told W. G. Van Schmus, manager of Radio City Music Hall in New York, where *Kane*'s preview was scheduled, that there would be a "total press blackout if he showed the movie"—that no Hearst paper would ever again accept advertising for films that played in the Music Hall. To Nelson Rockefeller, whose family had a sizable stake in RKO and owned Radio City, she threatened a damning "double-page spread on John D. Rockefeller" in Hearst's *American Weekly* if *Citizen Kane* were shown. She also threatened the entire RKO Board of Directors with "fictionized" stories of their lives that would run in Hearst papers and magazines. Rockefeller telegrammed Louella on January 14 to say that he had had "a long talk with George Schaefer on the telephone last night" and was attempting to convince the RKO head to withhold the film.[44]

But Schaefer would not budge. Determined to release the film, Schaefer and Welles started the *Kane* publicity machine by sending ads to national magazines and preparing a radio plug for the film.[45] Hopper, determined to capitalize on the mess, not only chronicled *Kane*'s saga in her column—"It's fun to watch on the sidelines," she wrote about "the biggest story that's broken in this little old town in many a day"—but also planned a six-part radio program on the life of Orson Welles, which she aired beginning in early February.[46] ("Our friend Hedda Hopper is [aiding] Orson Welles's cause," Louella wrote to Hearst. "I think she's a louse, after pretending to be a friend.")[47] Amazingly unruffled by the chain of events, Welles remained cocky and impudent as ever. At a January 27 Author's Club luncheon in Los Angeles, he announced, "When I get *Citizen Kane* off my mind, I'm going to work on an idea for a great picture based on the life of William Randolph Hearst."[48]

A week later there was another attempt in Hollywood to suppress the film. In early February, a group of producers led by Louis B. Mayer, fearing Louella's and Hearst's threats, called Schaefer and offered him eight hundred thousand dollars to buy the film and destroy it.[49] Schaefer, who was by now convinced that *Kane* would be a financial success, refused the offer, though the decision by Radio City's manager, Van Schmus, to ban the film from the Music Hall forced him to postpone the premiere. *Kane* would be shown to the public, Schaefer insisted, though he had little idea where or when.

Meanwhile, the film was receiving excellent reviews, both in Hollywood and across the nation. The *Newsweek* critic John O' Hara called it "the best picture he ever saw," and the *New York Times* declared that it "comes close to being the most sensational film ever made in Hollywood."[50] Declaring "Mr. Genius Comes Through; 'Kane' Astonishing Picture," the *Hollywood Reporter* called the film a "few steps ahead of anything that has been made in pictures before" and Welles's performance "nothing less than astonishing."[51]

Throughout February 1941, the battle over *Kane* continued, and by March it had become a farce. With a minor contract dispute serving as a pretext

(Joseph Ermolieff, a European producer, had sued RKO for breach of a producing contract entered into in July 1939), Hearst papers across the nation lambasted Schaefer and RKO for unethical business practices.[52] Undaunted by the attack, Schaefer searched for theaters that would book the film, but found that most theater owners were reluctant to show it. He continued to postpone the preview. Impatient with the delays, Welles then announced that he would sue the studio to force the release of *Kane*.[53] Shortly after Welles's ultimatum, Hearst's rival, Henry Luce, editor of *Time*, *Life*, and *Fortune* magazines, offered RKO a million dollars for the negative and prints of *Kane*. Fearing that RKO would never release the film, and believing that "the world should see it," Luce planned to exhibit the film himself.[54]

By the end of March, with the preview indefinitely stalled and lawsuits threatened by both Hearst and Welles, the fight over *Citizen Kane* was now largely in the hands of Schaefer, Welles, and Hearst's lawyers. In an attempt to expose Welles as "unpatriotic," Louella had placed calls to the local draft board demanding to know why Welles had not been called into the service. Louella also took part in an investigation of Welles's involvement in an episode of the CBS radio series *The Free Company*, which the Hearst papers accused of "tending to encourage communism."[55] Neither effort, however, dissuaded Schaefer and Welles from showing the film, and in May RKO finally released it. *Kane* appeared in a handful of RKO theaters and independent art theaters in major cities. Hardly the success they had predicted, it flopped at the box office at a loss of $150,000 to the studio. "Thought you might like to congratulate Schaeffer and Orson Welles," Louella wrote to Hearst on May 23. "*Citizen Kane* up to date has cost them $200,000 to keep theaters open—and did $96 worth of business one night at El Capitan. Is considered the greatest flop Hollywood has ever seen. I am so sorry I am crying and I thought you would be sad about it too."[56]

The commercial failure of *Kane*, it turned out, would be the least of Welles's troubles. Though *Citizen Kane* was named the best film of 1941 by the National Board of Review and was nominated for nine Academy Awards, including best picture, best actor, and best director (it won only one, best screenplay, which Welles and Mankiewicz shared), as a result of the battle over *Kane*, Welles was essentially blacklisted in Hollywood and would make only a few films during the rest of his career. Louella omitted Welles from her column until the late 1940s, when she poked fun at his failing career and romances. Louella also blacklisted Joseph Cotten and Agnes Moorehead, who had starring roles in the film. When Agnes Moorehead won the New York

Film Critics Award for the 1942 film *The Magnificent Ambersons,* Louella sniped in her column that Hollywood was "raising its eyebrows" over the choice.[57]

Both in and out of her column, Louella also lashed out against those who had supported Welles, including producer Samuel Goldwyn, whom Louella described in a letter to Hearst as having "boosted *Citizen Kane* all over the place."[58] Goldwyn's punishment was temporary banishment from the column. Louella also attacked *Daily Variety,* which had supported Welles, and, in December 1941, proudly told Hearst that Louis B. Mayer, out of loyalty to Hearst, had discontinued MGM's advertising with the "Hollywood dirt sheet."[59] That same month, when Hearst's *American Weekly* ran a somewhat unflattering story about Marlene Dietrich, Louella reminded Hearst that "Dietrich was one of few actresses who refused to go to Welles's opening because of her respect" for Hearst.[60] Hearst then asked Louella to "make apologies," and Louella responded by praising Dietrich in the column.[61]

Though Louella shot most of the arrows in the war over *Kane,* she too was wounded in the battle. Not surprisingly, the brouhaha over *Kane* hit the mainstream press. By early February, the *New York Times, Newsweek,* and *Time* had not only chronicled the story of the ongoing controversy but also exposed Louella's role in the attempt to ban the film. After seeing *Kane,* "Lolly Parsons nearly fell out of her chair," *Time* commented in its January 27 issue. "She rose like a geyser. As the lights came on, Miss Parsons and the lawyers steamed out. . . . Next, excited Lolly Parsons phoned RKO headman Schaefer [and] appealed to him to stop *Citizen Kane.*"[62] Snickered *Newsweek,* "A few obsequious and/or bulbous middle-aged ladies think the picture ought not to be shown, owing to the fact that the picture is rumored to have something to do with a certain publisher. . . . Sycophancy of that kind, like curtseying, is deliberate. The ladies merely wait for a chance to show they can do it, even if it means cracking a femur. This time I think they may have cracked off more than they can chew."[63]

According to *Variety,* the *Omaha World Herald* had stopped carrying Louella's column, explaining that "inasmuch as the Parsons . . . daily roundup [does] not carry any mention of RKO pix," it did not "represent a true coverage of the film front."[64] Louella complained to the Chief: "I do not think the *Omaha World Herald* should be allowed to throw out my column because of RKO. I have been very careful about not saying anything serious about RKO at any time[,] and I have had RKO news although I haven't gone overboard. It looks like the whole thing has been planted by Schaefer and some of his crowd. I hope we can do something about this as I hate to lose the Omaha coverage[,] because I have so many fans there and get so many letters."[65]

"'It Can't Happen Here,'" the *Hollywood Reporter* wrote: "Louella Parsons doing a radio preview of *Citizen Kane*."[66] Though the *Reporter* joked, the film community was appalled by Louella's unethical campaign against Welles. This time she had gone too far.

And then—predictably, like clockwork—in the spring of 1941, the "free talent" controversy cracked wide open. It started at the party Louella had thrown in early January for the studio publicity directors. In addition to enlisting their help for the war on *Kane,* she had announced that she was lining up a sponsor for another "free talent" radio show.[67] The publicists politely imbibed their drinks, then went back to their offices and hit the roof. The following day, *Daily Variety* accused Louella of exploiting actors to "fatten her wallet." But none of the studio brass, particularly in the midst of the Welles controversy, were willing to pick a fight, so Louella continued to pursue sponsorship with Lever Brothers, the makers of Lifebuoy and Rinso soaps. After each of the major studios had promised that their top stars would appear on the show, Louella's deal seemed nearly clinched. In late January, Louella authorized Harry to enter into formal negotiations.[68] A contract was drawn up, ready for Louella's signature, when SAG got word and took action.[69]

In early February 1941, in response to Louella, the SAG board officially adopted a rule prohibiting its members from appearing on radio programs without compensation. The policy was adopted quietly, and neither the studios nor Louella seemed to take it seriously. Thus in March, confident that SAG's resolution would not threaten her ability to line up actors for the show, Louella signed a contract with Lever Brothers for a thirteen-week "free talent" program. Like *Hollywood Hotel, Hollywood Premiere* would feature radio adaptations of scenes from upcoming movies, followed by a short interview session. One radio historian described it as "a reduced *Hollywood Hotel* without the music and song."[70]

The show's debut, scheduled for 7 P.M. on Friday, March 28, on CBS, was heralded with the "most ambitious promotional campaign ever given the opening of a radio show," according to *Radio Daily.* Three hundred fifty supermarkets in the Los Angeles area displayed cards in their soap aisles promoting the premiere, and "special mimeographed releases went to nearly 400 newspapers throughout the country." Public schools in "35 important cities" plugged the show via bulletins read by pupils and teachers. Louella had invited several of her colleagues to come watch the opening broadcast. Given the sentiment in most Hollywood circles following *Kane,* however, many of them declined. (David Selznick had told his secretary to use the excuse that he and his wife, Irene, "were planning on leaving Friday evening for the weekend.")[71] When Lever Brothers' marketing research staff that month concluded that 96 percent of radio listeners supported "advance previewing of motion pictures on the air," executives at both Lever Brothers and CBS predicted great success for the program. Some even anticipated that *Hollywood Premiere* would become more popular than *Hollywood Hotel.*[72]

Then, on March 26, the Motion Picture Relief Fund, a charity organization for unemployed actors and studio personnel, dropped a bomb. In full-page ads in *Variety, Daily Variety,* and the *Hollywood Reporter,* the fund claimed that *Hollywood Premiere* endangered a weekly radio show for the relief fund put on by SAG members, and it "protest[ed] Miss Louella Parsons' radio show." "The Motion Picture Relief Fund has asked actors to contribute their time and talent for the benefit of their own charity," fund president Jean Hersholt wrote. "A show of the type Miss Parsons has planned requires that actors waive their usual compensation and contribute their time and talent to advertise a commercial product." SAG, in sympathy with Hersholt, published an announcement the following day that promised the fund "enforcement to the limit" of its policy against free commercial radio performances and dispatched to its twelve hundred members a notice of "disciplinary action" to be taken if they violated the rule. "If you have been asked to appear on this program," the letter read, referring specifically to *Hollywood Premiere,* "the Guild asks you to refuse to appear. If a columnist can provide $10,000 worth of acting talent for a fraction of that amount, actors' salaries will come down." The letter concluded with the guild's resolution that it would "fight as long as necessary to stop the evil of the free talent shows."[73]

After a conference the following day at which Kenneth Thompson, executive secretary of SAG, and Harry, on behalf of Louella, made "peace overtures," Louella issued a public apology that appeared in film trade journals throughout the country.

Gentlemen:

Published statements that my radio program might affect the Motion Picture Relief Fund have been the cause of great unhappiness to me. For more than twenty five years I have worked consistently to further the best interest of the Motion Picture industry and its people, including the Motion Picture Relief

Fund. Before the radio contract was signed, I received full assurance from the motion picture producers that they welcomed an opportunity for this valuable exploitation of their pictures on the type of program which I originated years ago.[74]

The letter concluded with Louella's announcement that she would discontinue the "free talent" policy at the end of *Hollywood Premiere*'s initial thirteen-week run. Either Lifebuoy would have to foot the bill for talent, or she would refuse to accept another contract.[75] True to her promise, in June 1941 Louella signed on to another thirteen-week term with Lever Brothers only after it had allocated a generous talent budget for the show. Although over 120 actors had already agreed to appear during the initial run without pay, Lever Brothers nonetheless paid them fees comparable to what they would have earned on other programs.[76]

Meanwhile, the show earned high marks from fans. "Members of the Louella Parsons fan club located in Chicago are contemplating a trip to Hollywood to be guests of the famous columnist at one of her *Hollywood Premiere* broadcasts at CBS some Friday evening," *Radio Daily* reported. "A letter to the star from one of her fans states that they are now tussling with the problem of financing the trek. Miss Parsons is the only columnist in Hollywood who has a fan club. Louella receives an average of 20 letters a week from girls who aspire to become movie columnists. Some are so ambitious to break into the Hollywood writing game that they'll even work for her without salary. One went so far as to offer to become a maid in the Parsons household provided she could study her syndicated writing technique."[77] "Any time Louella Parsons wants to have her Beverly Hills house painted free, one Charles Mason of Lexington, KY, will do the job free," wrote *San Diego Radio*. "In a letter applauding Miss Parsons' *Hollywood Premiere,* he explained that he is a painter by profession and he'll be happy to work for her without charge. He'll even provide his own transportation between Lexington and Hollywood."[78] Critics praised Louella not only for her work on *Hollywood Premiere* (thanks to voice lessons, they noted, Louella's delivery had improved vastly) but also for her contributions to American radio. "Radio owes a great deal to the much maligned Louella," wrote *Radio Daily,* which credited her with single-handedly "[helping] the radio industry establish itself in Hollywood. While Louella may . . . [use] her column to make more secure her radio [program], the final result has been to help significantly the progress of the industry in the West."[79]

Despite the public acclaim, the film community was still smoldering over the *Kane* affair. In response, in August 1941, after a well-publicized conference with the *Los Angeles Times,* MGM publicity head Howard Strickling and the other publicity directors of the major studios announced that they were rescinding the forty-eight-hour exclusive. Henceforth, "no exclusive movie news will be fed to Louella Parsons by studio blurb departments," *Variety* announced; instead, news would be released to all the columnists simultaneously.[80] "Bet you didn't know how good I am. Didn't know myself until last week when the *Times* summoned all the heads of publicity in the studios and demanded that I get no more scoops. It does not worry me[,] because I get most of my scoops outside the studios," Louella wrote to Hearst.[81]

But she revealed her true feelings later that evening. The decision had been announced on Louella's birthday, August 6, and at the party that night she got outrageously drunk. In her stupor she picked up the phone and called over a dozen friends, including Hearst, to complain of what she described as horrible treatment by the studios. Embarrassed, the following day she sent a telegram to Hearst apologizing for her "telephonitis." "Maybe I was a little thin skinned[,] but so many people telephoned all day in indignation about the thing and I guess it seemed worse on my birthday than it would have on any other day," she wrote.[82]

A few weeks later, in mid-September, despite a horrible cold, Louella traveled to Dixon for "Louella Parsons Day," the weekend of festivities that was to be the culmination of her career. As the train pulled into the station, crowds holding signs cheered.[83] When Bob Hope announced her before the assembled group of thousands, she held back tears. Even more gratifying was Louella's reunion with her aunt Carrie Roe, who remarked that Helen Oettinger would have been "the happiest woman in the world if she could have lived to see this day." "The whole thing," Louella recalled, "seems to spin in my memory like a happy but dizzy dream."[84]

She used the Dixon event, with its connotations of heartland Americanism, to promote not only herself but also Hollywood, which had recently been the subject of three well-publicized congressional investigations. In 1940, Texas congressman Martin Dies, chairman of the House Committee to Investigate Un-American Activities (later known as the House Un-American Activities Committee, or HUAC), began investigations into what he claimed was communist infiltration of the film industry. In spring of 1940, Dies heard testimony from a number of former Communist Party members, including the former Party organizer John L. Leech, who claimed falsely that

Humphrey Bogart, James Cagney, Franchot Tone, Frederic March, and a dozen other actors were communists.[85] At the same time, Congress had been debating the Neely Bill, which if passed would have ended the studios' block booking, a practice that forced exhibitors to purchase a studio's entire annual output, sight unseen, in order to get its top, class A films.[86] The hearings ultimately led to an October 1940 consent decree that allowed block booking to continue, but in blocks no larger than five films.[87] Then, in September 1941, not long before Louella left for Dixon, two isolationist senators, Burton Wheeler and Gerald Nye, claimed that the major studios had produced seventeen "war mongering" feature films that had urged the United States to become involved in the conflict in Europe and Asia and to declare war on the Axis powers. Hollywood, they claimed, was a "propaganda machine."[88] In Salt Lake City on her way to Dixon, Louella, commenting on the accusations, told the *Deseret News,* "It's the first time I've ever heard of anyone being indicted for being patriotic. We follow public trends and give people what they want. The whole thing is silly."[89]

Hearst had called Louella in Dixon during the festivities, and she was touched. "I want to thank you again for telephoning me in Dixon," she wrote to Hearst when she returned to Hollywood.[90] Harry had assured Louella that the event would be good publicity, but the press coverage of Louella Parsons Day was anything but flattering. In its coverage of the event, Henry Luce's *Time* magazine printed an unattractive photo of Louella that accentuated her weight and double chin. This particularly irked her, since she had been gaining weight steadily over the past five years and was sensitive about her appearance. Earlier that year, she had complained to Hearst about an unflattering picture of her in the *Examiner.* "Honest Louella I can't see anything offensive in the picture[,] but I have told all our people to let you alone and not bother you with pictures or anything. I am sure that nothing you can criticize will be published hereafter," Hearst wrote back in response to her protests.[91] The horrible photo in *Time* was the last thing she needed. "It is not pleasant to have fun poked at your appearance in national magazines," she wrote in her autobiography. "After . . . [seeing] myself in a Luce publication[,] I feel like something out of a horror movie."[92]

Time's article was even worse. In it, the magazine accused Louella of having arranged the event solely to undermine a publicity event that Hopper was hosting the same day. On the same weekend as Louella Parsons Day, it turned out, Hopper was serving as the mistress of ceremonies at an "all star fete" sponsored by the American Legion at its national convention in Milwaukee.[93] That the two competing events had been scheduled for the same weekend was genuinely coincidental. Though both were planned over a year in advance, Hopper had sent out her invitations first, and during the summer several actors agreed to accompany her to Milwaukee. A few weeks later, when Louella sent out her own invitations for Dixon, eyebrows were raised. Torn between their friendship with Hopper and their fear of Louella, the actors were in a bind. Many—Stan Laurel, Oliver Hardy, Jane Withers, and Carole Landis, among others—went with Hopper. Others, including Bob Hope, Jerry Colonna, and Joe E. Brown, went to Dixon on Saturday, then flew to Milwaukee to appear with Hedda. Most of the actors, fearing reprisals either way, declined both invitations and stayed in Hollywood. In the end, there were "hard feelings all around," *Variety* reported, though most felt that Louella was to blame.[94]

Emotionally and physically weak, in mid-October 1941 Louella wrote personally to Hearst asking for a vacation. "I have no doubt that you are tired," Hearst wrote back. "You do too much work." A week later, with Hearst's blessings, Louella and Harry were off to the East Coast, where they planned to rest "for a week or ten days" before heading off for a monthlong rest in Bermuda. She had wanted to go to Europe, and had tried to convince Joe Connolly of the International News Service to send her to report on the war from London, but Connolly turned her down, having already assigned reporter Inez Robb.[95] Instead Louella and Harry went to Baltimore, where Harry was to receive treatment at the Johns Hopkins hospital for what Louella described as lingering complications from a bad case of pneumonia.[96] After Baltimore, Louella and Harry traveled to New York, where they spent weekends with Hearst's son Bill Hearst Jr. at his Long Island home, attended Broadway shows with Hearst executive Dick Berlin, and held parties for the film and publishing elite in her suite at the Waldorf Astoria.[97]

The festivities came to a sudden end on December 7, 1941. On her way back from a football game with Bill Hearst and Harry, she heard over the radio that Pearl Harbor had been attacked by the Japanese. The following day, while Louella was at a Broadway performance of *The Land Is Bright,* President Roosevelt broadcast his declaration of war against Japan, which was followed three days later by a declaration of war against Germany and Italy, Japan's European allies. After making hasty plans to return to Los Angeles, she telegrammed Hearst with congratulations on his editorial of December 9. "Well fellow Americans, we are in the war and we have got to win it," Hearst had written. "Before the war is over we will have burned up all the paper houses in Japan and sunk most of their scrap iron battleships and put this bunch of Oriental marauders back on the right little tight little out of sight little island where they belong." "I was very proud when I opened the [paper] this morning to find that . . . we had the greatest writer in America," Louella immediately wrote to the Chief. "Your column was terrific the first day of the war. Doctor read it aloud to me not only once but twice, and [we] quoted it to everybody we met. . . . I guess this knocks my radio show higher than a kite, for I don't see how they can sell soap when I'm told very likely there will be a shortage," she continued. If there were a dearth of war reporters, she added—or for that matter, a shortage of movie news—she would be happy to write "about the war, instead of the movies, but I imagine you have experts."[98]

In spite of the war, public interest in Louella's column and in *Hollywood Premiere* continued. *Hollywood Premiere,* she learned, had earned approximately fourteen hundred fan letters per week, six hundred letters ahead of the *Hollywood Hotel* record.[99] But Hedda Hopper's star was rising faster. In late 1940, Hopper had signed with the *Des Moines Register* syndicate, giving her nearly three million readers in fifty papers. She had also made six short films about Hollywood for Paramount, called *Hedda Hopper's Hollywood.*

The feud between the two columnists grew more vicious and more public. In December 1941, *Variety* reported a "spat" between the columnists at KNX radio, where both Hopper and Louella recorded their programs. When Hopper went down the hall from her studio to visit Paulette Goddard, who was rehearsing with Louella for *Hollywood Premiere,* Louella "refused to speak another line" until Hopper left. An article in *Pic* magazine dramatized the conflict, describing it as a "war of the words." The piece described Louella as a "roly poly matron" with more than a few skeletons in her closet. "In her wide circle of acquaintances, there are scores of persons who would like nothing better than to write a biography of the columnist, but . . . the biographers usually succumb to literary laryngitis," it remarked. "Even Hedda Hopper hasn't stepped over the hedge into Louella's private life." The sparring continued daily, *Pic* reported, with ongoing "sniping in the trade papers, on the airwaves, and in other columns," and it was only a matter of time, the magazine predicted, until one of the rivals got the upper hand.[100]

It happened that spring. In May 1942, newspapers across the country announced that Hopper had signed a three-year contract with the *Chicago Tribune–New York News* syndicate. The extraordinary contract, based on the popularity of her column at the *Los Angeles Times,* granted her an additional twenty-seven papers and tripled her readership, bringing it to 5,750,000. Though Louella, with her 409 papers and her readership of seventeen million, still had greater exposure, "her whims no longer command Hollywood," *Time* announced. Both Hollywood loyalties and public tastes, it remarked, were shifting toward the "better liked" Hopper.[101] Indeed, the ink had hardly dried on the new contract when studio publicists began knocking at Hopper's door bearing gifts and promises. "Once a week, for some time now . . . publicity departments all over town have gathered at a command lunch to pay court to Louella Parsons at what is quaintly known as the 'Parsons idea meeting,'" *Variety* announced. "Lolly has been the only columnist to rate this kind of attention. Yesterday, the heads of publicity departments, all of 'em except one who was out of town, without command attended a private luncheon with Miss Hopper, expressing their wish to 'cooperate fully' with her, now that she has risen to the ranking position as a columnist."[102]

While Louella traversed the depths of her personal hell, Hollywood celebrated. Louella's fifteen-year hold over the film industry had been broken, and on studio lots actors, directors, and executives cheered. *Variety* expressed the feelings of many when it described the shift in power as no less than the passing of a dynasty. "The Queen Is Dead," it announced triumphantly. "Long Live the Queen!"[103]

THIRTEEN

The Gay Illiterate

IN HOLLYWOOD, there were two schools of thought on the Hopper-Louella feud. The first was that it was hype—that Hopper and Louella didn't hate each other but had staged the war for publicity. This was clearly false; Hopper and Louella resented each other, and they always would. The second was that the feud *consumed* them, and that each wanted nothing more than her rival's defeat. This, too, was a myth. Certainly Louella would not have shed tears had Hopper lost her lucrative new contract, and Hopper would not have lost any sleep if papers stopped carrying Louella's column. But both women had much more on their minds than destroying one another. They hated the rivalry but tolerated it, and they went on, indefatigably, getting their scoops, writing their news, and promoting themselves with all the finesse of a circus barker.

The second myth owes its persistence, in large part, to the exaggerated press put out by the Luce publications, which shamelessly dramatized the rivalry as a "war of the words" between two neurotic women. Playing on the stereotype of aggressive females as catty, the stories rallied public antifeminist sentiment and drew readers eager to see two "career women" destroy each other in a fit of bitchy competition. The feud stories were also good ammunition in Luce's ongoing attack on Louella. Though both women came off looking foolish, it was Louella, not Hopper, who became the queen shrew in these stories. In an anxious time of international conflict, the tale of the gossip battle was a welcome diversion from Americans' war woes, and in the early 1940s it became one of the splashiest and most sensational stories to come out of Hollywood.

The Luce campaign began in the summer of 1941, when *Life* published a photo layout, "*Life* Goes to a Hollywood House Moving," on Hopper's move from her small Fairfax Avenue bungalow to the "swankier" Beverly Hills home she had recently purchased with earnings from her column and radio show. "Hedda Hopper is a gay, boisterous, impulsive woman in her fifties who knows more Hollywood gossip than any person alive," it began. Along with a "vast, devoted following," Hopper had "two qualities" that made her one of the "top gossip purveyors of her day: she has been in movies 25 years and she never forgets." In the spring of 1942, *Time* celebrated Hopper's *Chicago Tribune–New York News* contract with an article, "Hedda Makes Hay," that celebrated the "demise" of "Louella Parsons . . . [whose] whims no longer command Hollywood." According to *Time:* "Much better liked than Lolly Parsons, when she started Hedda had to put friendships and wits against the powerful inertia of Lolly's 20 year reign on Hollywood's gossip roost." But Hopper triumphed through "great personality," a thick skin that came from having been "kicked around plenty," and her intimate knowledge of Hollywood social life. "Hedda Hopper," the article assured readers, "is the real Hollywood."[1]

The Luce articles portrayed Hopper as an underdog who had triumphed through hard work and talent, and Louella as an underhanded schemer who owed her success solely to Hearst. "Until the ascendancy of Hedda Hopper, there was the unique phenomenon of a great American industry cringing and genuflecting before the redundant figure of Louella 'Lollipop' Parsons, a Hearst columnist whose power at one time was so great she could not only demand—and get—a 24 hour break on every important news story in every studio, but who could—and did—bully the biggest stars in the business into appearing without pay on her radio program, *Hollywood Hotel,*" *Time* wrote. Wrote *Life,* "the Screen Actors' Guild eventually put a stop to the latter practice, and Hedda Hopper was largely instrumental in breaking Parsons' stranglehold on the studios. Louella Parsons is not a has-been, but neither is she any longer the ringmaster of the Hollywood circus. Hedda Hopper has a whip of her own and cracks it more expertly."[2] According to *Life,* Hopper was a hardworking journalist who "starts gathering gossip as soon as she gets up . . . and doesn't stop work till midnight." Louella received her news from studio press agents who had been blackmailed into compliance and actors who "phoned [Louella] first and eloped afterwards lest she sideswipe them forever after."[3]

The articles then went after Louella's looks. Hopper, wrote *Time,* was tall and blond and statuesque (a "handsome, headlong gossip"), while Louella was short, pudgy, and crooning—"fat, fifty, and fatuous."[4] "Prettier, wittier, more kindly by instinct," Hopper was an "actress trying to be a columnist," while Louella was "a columnist trying to be an actress. . . . Louella . . . has demonstrated in her few appearances in the movies that she is a little shaky in the acting department. Hedda Hopper, on the other hand, has tasted sweet success in both fields."[5] Hopper's radio voice was "caressingly rhythmic," while Louella's suffered from "unmusical shrillness."[6]

There were, in fact, real differences between Hopper and Louella that bore little resemblance to *Time*'s and *Life*'s dark-versus-light, Manichaean descriptions. As many in Hollywood recognized, Louella was a much more skilled, thorough, and experienced reporter than Hopper. "Hedda and Louella were not comparable," remembered one studio publicist. "They worked differently, thought differently." In particular, he claimed, Hopper "had no idea what a story was." Hopper was much more willing to play "fast and loose with facts" than Louella and wrote in a blunt and critical style. "You have to watch yourself with Hedda. When Louella has a story, she knows when it is dangerous and will check it. But Hedda will plunge in and print it, and go away in complete innocence that she had done anything wrong," said one publicist.[7] It was Hopper's lack of experience in journalism, according to many of her acquaintances, that led to her deep-seated insecurity about her position in Hollywood. "To me, Parsons was honest. Hedda lived by her wits and tried to carry herself by being bright and amusing. . . . With Hedda there was this great façade," claimed one actress.[8]

Despite, or perhaps because of, her lack of confidence, Hopper was tough, flamboyant, and outspoken. She was known for her outrageous hats—some were illuminated by battery-operated lights, and one of her favorites had a miniature Eiffel Tower on it—and each year purchased approximately 150 of them, which the IRS allowed her to deduct as a business expense.[9] In Hollywood, she worked out of a cluttered office half a block from Hollywood and Vine that was filled with hat boxes, battered furniture, and scrapbooks. "The anteroom might well be that of a dentist who had fallen into a cavity and never managed to climb out," *Time* wrote. "With its bare radiators, scarred doors and desks, signed photographs and careless gadgets, the whole suite resembles an oldtime theatrical booking agency." She had an assistant, a graduate of the University of North Carolina named David "Spec" McClure, and a secretary, Treva Davidson.[10] "Every morning she'd come in and she'd usually have her arms loaded with magazines and stuff, and she'd talk with people along the street and in the elevator. She'd talk to people in traffic. She'd come in the morning and say, 'good morning slaves!' It was the first damn thing," McClure remembered.[11] Jaik Rosenstein, who worked for

Hopper as a legman in the 1940s, described her as "unpredictable and perverse and temperamental and argumentative and bigoted and biased and an incurable ham . . . [and] captious and impetuous and cold and conniving and vindictive and cruel."[12] In an oft-repeated anecdote, when one studio publicist asked why Hopper had reduced his exclusive scoop to one line low in her column, she said: "Bitchery, baby, pure bitchery!" She nicknamed herself "the Bitch of the World."[13]

Her reporting style was no-holds-barred. When Lana Turner married Bob Topping, Hopper telephoned the press agent of the Beverly Hills Hotel, where the couple was staying, and demanded the number of their bungalow. Her plan was to enter disguised as a maid in the hopes of catching the newlyweds in bed together.[14] Not surprisingly, many actors had little patience for her outrageous tactics and what they claimed to be the many inaccuracies in her column. After Hopper printed an unflattering comment about Joan Bennett in her column, Bennett sent Hopper a skunk as a Valentine gift. The card that accompanied it read: "Here's a little Valentine, that very plainly tells the reason it reminded me so much of you—it smells!"[15] In 1943 Hopper falsely accused Joseph Cotten of having romanced teen star Deanna Durbin while they made the film *Hers to Hold* together. Cotten ordered Hopper to stop the rumors, but she refused. Shortly afterward, Cotten, who saw Hopper at a party, kicked her in the behind and Ann Sheridan dumped a dish of mashed potatoes on her.[16] The next day Cotten received hundreds of telegrams and bouquets from actors impressed by his bravado.[17] A conflict with Joan Fontaine in the Brown Derby restaurant, over unflattering comments Hopper had made in her column, became so heated that Fontaine threatened to "meet Hopper in the alley."[18]

Rather than attack Hopper directly, Louella went after the actors and press agents who appeared to be favoring Hopper. During his first week as publicity director at Warner Brothers in the mid-1940s, Bill Hendricks nearly lost his job because he contacted Hopper with an exclusive, rather than Louella. Louella promptly contacted Jack Warner and urged him to fire Hendricks. Warner forced Hendricks to make peace with Louella, and through Louella's nephew Gordon Maynard, Hendricks arranged to meet Louella for breakfast. "We can get along," she allegedly said. "All you have to do is just give me all the stories."[19] Thereafter, he did. Former MGM publicist Walter Seltzer recalled that it was the "rule" of the studio publicity department to alternate giving stories to Hopper and Louella. He particularly feared Hopper, who was "hard as nails, political and opinionated." Louella was more likely to be "forgiving," he claimed.[20]

When actors or publicists "double planted"—that is, gave stories to Louella and Hopper simultaneously—there was hell to pay. Once, when Hopper was at a Beverly Hills party, actress Gene Tierney came up to her and announced, "I've been trying to get you all afternoon to tell you I'm going to have another baby." Tierney's studio, however, had given the story to Louella the previous afternoon, and when, at the party, Louella heard that Tierney had confided in Hopper, she attacked her so mercilessly that the actress collapsed into tears. "La Tierney knew exactly how blazing mad I was. When I'm mad I do not simmer or boil. I explode!" Louella recalled. Though a crowd of celebrities witnessed the tongue-lashing, no one came to Tierney's aid—they were afraid of Louella.[21]

The Hopper-Parsons feud caused problems for the studios, which tried ingeniously to appease the rivals without playing favorites. Recognizing Louella's longtime friendships with the studios and the importance of the Hearst papers, the studio continued to give Louella the majority of exclusives. By 1942, the publicity offices had worked out a formula of doling out scoops to Louella and Hopper on a sixty-forty basis. Nonetheless, Hopper had a sizable following of loyal publicists and informants, including a "special ally," as Hopper described him—Mark Hellinger, a former columnist for the *New York Daily News* who was working as a producer at Warner Brothers. "The scoops I had on the affairs of Warner Brothers nearly drove Jack Warner out of his cotton-picking mind," Hopper recalled in her autobiography.[22] During the 1940s, Warner Brothers, Columbia, and Twentieth Century Fox tended to favor Louella with news, while Hopper had the edge with Paramount and MGM. At industry-sponsored banquets and meetings, Hopper and Louella were given seats equidistant from the principal speaker, but the studios faced a conundrum when it came to advertising displays. It was typical for most film advertisements to include blurbs from critics, but where the comments appeared in the frame of the ad reflected studios' perspective on the critics' importance. Top billing was better than bottom billing, and left was better than right. Because it was impossible to give both Louella and Hopper top position, the studios agreed to print their comments in separate ads.[23]

"Hedda gave me an ultimatum—you can't be friends with both of us," recalled Joan Fontaine. "I walked a narrow tightrope, inviting Louella to one party and Hedda to the next."[24] When Louella suspected that Frances Marion was writing Hopper's column—which, in fact, she was not—Louella turned on Marion, who had once been a friend.[25] To keep in the columnists' good graces, actors, executives, and publicists showered both women with expensive gifts, but sometimes the attempts at appeasement backfired. One Christmas, Hopper received not one but two crystal decanters, one engraved with "HH" and the other "LOP." Hopper apparently refused to return Louella's gift, commenting that it would be entertaining to ask guests, "Would you like some Jack Daniels out of Louella's bottle?"[26]

If done skillfully, playing the rivals off each other made for good publicity. In 1943, Selznick's publicity director, Whitney Bolton, planted a story with Louella about Jennifer Jones's selection for an upcoming film role. He then called Hopper and told her that Teresa Wright had been chosen for the part. "Today Hedda Hopper carried a story that of course it was silly for 'another paper' to print that Jones would get the role when everybody knew Teresa Wright would get it," Bolton told Selznick. "I like this kind of a controversy[,] and since you know that Jennifer Jones will undoubtedly receive the role, it can do no harm to continue the controversy."[27] Though Selznick did not punish Bolton for his "double planting," the producer reminded him of the importance of giving Louella news on a regular basis. "I have assured you that there is no need to give Louella all the breaks [but] Louella is entitled to preference on a portion of them because of: a) her prominence as to circulation; b) the headlines which she gives us, which are not obtainable on a national basis from other columnists."[28] Selznick advised Bolton to "keep a few stories in reserve for Louella," and to tell her "that we will have one or two important stories for her if and when she really needs something for her banner and will hold them exclusively for her."[29] Later, when Louella began threatening to run inaccurate stories about the studio that she had heard from other sources' publicists, to appease Louella, Selznick issued a memorandum to his publicists ordering that Louella be given news items at the rate of "thirty or forty a week."[30]

In addition to ending Louella's forty-eight-hour exclusive, the rivalry with Hopper diminished Louella's access to news, and she began calling publicists several times daily, begging for stories. Paranoid, she attacked them when she suspected that they were withholding news. In 1942, when Universal Studio made a deal with Deanna Durbin, they contacted advertising and publicity director John Joseph and instructed him to tell Louella. It was four in the afternoon when he reached her, and according to *Daily Variety,* "She was very indignant and wailed plentifully because she hadn't been tipped off to the yarn earlier. When Joseph pleaded innocence . . . she sarcastically replied that she didn't believe him."[31] Louella's increasingly bad temper and her desperation for news were being dubbed by some studios "the Parsons Problem." By late 1942, Louella had become so hungry for exclusives that she began paying Western Union clerks at the Waldorf Hotel, where studio executives often stayed in New York, to tip her off. There were also reports that she had hired an obstetrical nurse at Doctors' Hospital in New York to call her with the names of actresses who had gone in for abortions.[32] Still the industry loyalist, she suppressed the news, which would have been scandalous, but threatened to reveal it unless the studios gave her other stories.

By 1942, the rivalry with Hopper, her increasing alienation from the film community, and the termination of the *Hollywood Premiere* radio show were taking an emotional toll on Louella. Though *Hollywood Premiere* had been successful, her radio contract with Lever Brothers was not renewed, and the show ended in late 1941. There were rumors in the summer of 1942 that she would be going back on the air with a *Hollywood Hotel*–like preview show sponsored by Pabst Brewing Company (which promised to pay for all guest talent), but the plans never materialized.[33] Louella feared that her absence from radio was hurting her popularity, especially since Hopper had been on the air with her Sunkist show almost continuously since 1939. According to *Variety*, in late 1941 Louella did an "inward burn" when the Hearst writer Jimmy Starr was being introduced over his radio program as "the best-known reporter in Hollywood."[34]

The gossip war was played out against the backdrop of the world war, which had dramatically transformed the nation's culture and economy. Because much of the wartime defense industry was based in Southern California, thousands of workers migrated to the area, increasing the population by 15 percent. Over six million women entered the workforce to fill positions created by the defense industry and to meet the labor shortage caused by male military service. As part of its project of wartime industrial expansion, the federal government pumped billions of dollars into defense, thus ending the Great Depression and creating an economic boom. The federal budget, which was nine billion dollars in 1939, rose to one hundred billion dollars in 1945, and in some parts of the country personal incomes doubled. Between 1940 and 1942, the profits of the eight largest Hollywood studios increased from twenty million dollars to fifty million. And between 1943 and 1945, the film industry earned an average of sixty million dollars each year.[35]

In January 1942, the federal government created the Office of War Information to coordinate government information activities and a branch of this office, the Bureau of Motion Pictures, to serve as a liaison with the Hollywood film industry. Guided by the bureau's *Manual for the Motion Picture Industry,* issued in July 1942, the major studios produced dozens of newsreels and films that glorified the Allies, condemned fascist ideology, and encouraged patriotism and resource conservation. Dozens of actors and directors enlisted in the Armed Services—Jimmy Stewart, Robert Montgomery, Tyrone Power, Ronald Reagan, William Holden, and Clark Gable, among others—and were lauded by Louella, who commended them in a *Photoplay* magazine article for "fighting . . . to get this hellish war over and come home to the USA. When you speak about patriotism an actor ceases to be just an actor and becomes the greatest citizen in the world—John American."[36] To entertain the thousands of servicemen who arrived in the Los Angeles area prior to their departure for the Pacific, several stars established the Hollywood Canteen, a nightclub on the corner of Cahuenga and Sunset Boulevards, where uniformed men danced with such top stars as Betty Grable, Irene Dunne, and Joan Crawford. Within six months, over six hundred stars had entertained on the club's stage.[37]

Like the rest of Hollywood, Louella threw herself into the war effort. She urged readers to buy war bonds and, like Hearst, with his rabid anti-Japanese editorials, described the "Japs" as "treacherous, mean, and unreliable." Like the Chief, she supported the internment of Japanese Americans on the West Coast—in 1942, over one hundred thousand, perceived to be a threat to national security, were incarcerated for the duration of the war—and described them as "vermin" who never should have been admitted into the United States.[38] In April 1942, the *Examiner* ran a six-part series on the Japanese American "race problem" that not only accused Japanese Americans of disloyalty but also encouraged internment and the deprivation of their civil rights. (In drumming the Hearst philosophy of "one hundred percent Americanism" into its readers, the *Examiner* "blurred the line between fascism and patriotism," the newspaper historian Rob Wagner has written.)[39] Away from the *Examiner,* Louella volunteered regularly with several wartime service organizations, including the American Women's Voluntary Services, Bundles for Bluejackets, and the Red Cross, and both she and Harriet emceed the festivities at the Hollywood Canteen, hosting "Louella Parsons Night" and "Harriet Parsons Night."[40]

While the Office of War Information guarded politics, the Production

Code Administration, under the leadership of head administrator Joseph Breen, continued to police the morality of motion picture content.[41] Illicit sex, illegitimate pregnancies, miscegenation, and other socially and politically controversial themes were still prohibited in films, though the producers continued to test the limits. In 1941, Americans witnessed the much-publicized battle between producer Howard Hughes and the Production Code Administration over the film *The Outlaw*, which featured controversial "breast shots" of actress Jane Russell, both in the film and in publicity stills. Louella attacked Hughes for degrading Hollywood's image. "I wonder where the Hays office was when the photographs of Jane Russell were released to a national picture magazine?" she asked in the column. The Catholic organization the Legion of Decency was "up in arms—and rightly so," Louella reported. "It is unfair to the little girl, who is a sweet child and who should not make her debut in a photograph as disgusting and suggestive. The time has passed when any actress needs to appear indecently clad to win success," she wrote in January 1941.[42] Breen told Hughes that he had to reshoot the controversial scenes in order to receive a seal of approval from the Production Code Administration, and when Hughes refused, the film was shelved. Hughes finally released the film, without the seal, in May 1946, and it caused controversy almost everywhere it played.[43]

In her column, Louella celebrated stars' volunteer work on behalf of the war and criticized as un-American those whom she claimed had shirked their patriotic duty. Louella often used these claims to attack old enemies. When Greta Garbo failed to appear on a patriotic radio show called *The Victory Program*, Louella wrote, "Whether Greta Garbo did or did not agree to go on the Victory Program is not as important as the chance she missed in NOT broadcasting. So much criticism has been heaped on her head these past few months by Americans all over the country who complain that she made her money here and then sent it to Sweden. Had she appeared on the broadcast with other 100 percent Americans, much criticism might have been avoided. Garbo after all owes it to the industry to make a public appearance or give some explanation for her attitude if she wants to continue her screen career."[44] Louella criticized Mae West for her failure to appear in a live performance for the merchant marines: "Too bad Mae West couldn't see her way clear to appear on the . . . program," Louella wrote in March 1942. "All she would have had to have done was to go down and let the boys see her since they asked for her. But there will be a wonderful show anyway and every other artist has expressed his willingness to do his share."[45]

The war became personal for Louella in the spring of 1942, when Harry, insisting that it was his patriotic duty, enlisted in the Army Medical Corps, as he had in World War I. With Maggie Ettinger and Louella's close friend Virginia Zanuck, the wife of producer Darryl Zanuck, Louella accompanied Harry to the Ross Letterman Hospital in San Francisco, where he began his training on May 15, 1942. Louella drove up to San Francisco each weekend to visit him until he shipped out for the South Pacific on July 27, 1942.[46]

She recounted that difficult afternoon: "I went down the pier as far as I was permitted—laughing, somehow—clinging to my Doctor as long as I could. . . . I watched my soldier, with his major's cap so jaunty over his graying hair, as far as I could see him, and when he was out of sight I could only stand there in the middle of the street. Corey, the Irish cab driver, who was an old friend and who always drove us to Mass in San Francisco, came up and touched my arm. I followed him without a word. I think I knew where he was going." The driver took her to the Old St. Mary's Church, near Chinatown. "I went into the church. I don't know how long I stayed. Somehow I pulled myself together. I knew Harry would come back, but I also knew that until he did, that breathless pain would stay turning in my heart."[47]

With Harry gone, more than ever she sought solace and support from her friends—Clark Gable, Carole Lombard's secretary Madalynne Lang, and her husband, the director Walter Lang.[48] In January 1942, Carole Lombard, on a tour selling war bonds in Las Vegas, boarded a TWA DC-3 bound for Hollywood. The plane smashed into a cliff, killing her instantly. Louella consoled Gable after Lombard's death, and he remained a close friend of Louella's until his death in 1960. Louella was also part of an informal social network of female journalists in Los Angeles that included Adela Rogers St. Johns; Florabel Muir, who covered the Hollywood beat for the *New York Daily News;* and Agness Underwood, who worked the crime beat on Hearst's *Herald Examiner.* According to St. Johns' son, Louella was well respected by the women but was often intimidated by them. She was particularly awed by St. Johns, who, in addition to having written successful screenplays and short stories for such publications as *Good Housekeeping* and the *Saturday Evening Post,* earned national fame during the depression for an exposé on the squalid living conditions of the poor. (She was subsequently billed by the Hearst papers as the "World's Greatest Girl Reporter.")[49] Louella feared that any moment St. Johns, with her superior writing and reporting abilities, could "walk in and take over the column," he recalled.[50]

Sometime during the winter of 1942, Louella lost contact with Harry, who was in New Guinea, and she feared for his life. Through the assistance of Lee Van Atta, a correspondent for the International News Service, she learned that he was in an army hospital, suffering from what was diagnosed as a tropical fever. In January 1943 he was discharged from the army and returned to San Francisco, where he was hospitalized for two weeks. Louella went to visit him in early February, and by the end of that month he had returned to Los Angeles.[51] Although by the spring of 1943 the *Hollywood Reporter* noted that he and Louella were spotted dancing at Ciro's restaurant, Harry was still seriously ill. Within months he was back in the hospital, and Louella struggled to combine her writing responsibilities with the time-consuming task of overseeing his care. In the spring of 1943, Louella and Harry decided to sell Marsons Farm.[52]

Writing an autobiography had not initially been her idea. In October 1942, Doubleday Doran offered her a contract for an autobiographical work to be titled *The Gay Illiterate,* after the nickname she had been given by Nunnally Johnson in the 1939 *Saturday Evening Post* article. Seeing it as an ideal publicity opportunity, she embarked on the project with the help of a ghostwriter, the prolific journalist and screenwriter Richard English, who had been assigned to her by Doubleday. Since *Kane,* Louella had become almost hypervigilant about restoring her "just folks" image of small-town innocence and had played up her rural roots in press interviews. "Born and reared in Illinois, Louella Parsons has been swapping recipes since she was old enough to give fudge the hairline test. At [her] ranch she can be comfortable in an old pair of slacks. She concedes to the doctor's old-fashioned prejudice that the wife should not wear slacks in public places," *Radio Life* wrote in a feature article in 1941.[53] She hoped that the autobiography would help her image-recovery project.

During the writing of the manuscript in 1943, Louella suffered a major loss to Hopper, who had gotten the exclusive on a sensational story concerning Charlie Chaplin and a young actress, Joan Barry. That spring, Barry had contacted Hopper claiming that she was carrying Charlie Chaplin's child. After winning the young woman's trust, Hopper called in a physician to have her examined and found that indeed she was pregnant.

An aspiring actress from Detroit, Barry had come to Hollywood in the late 1930s. Shortly after her arrival she met Chaplin, who signed her to play a role in an upcoming production called *Shadow and Substance,* and by 1941 she and Chaplin had begun an affair. By the end of 1942, Chaplin wanted to end the liaison, and Barry became distraught. On December 23, 1942, Barry, armed, forced herself into Chaplin's home, held Chaplin at gunpoint, and threatened suicide. Chaplin managed to disarm her and persuade her to leave. Barry then left for New York; when she returned to Los Angeles in May 1943, she tried to meet with Chaplin to tell him she was pregnant with his child. By this time, Chaplin was involved in a serious relationship with Oona O'Neill, who was the daughter of playwright Eugene O'Neill, and who was over thirty years Chaplin's junior. Barry wanted to force Chaplin to marry her, but Chaplin refused. Barry and her mother then plotted to ruin Chaplin by "going public" about the affair.[54]

Barry sought out Hopper, she explained, because in 1941 Hopper had printed a critical piece in her column about Chaplin's penchant for seducing his young leading ladies. Knowing that Chaplin was looking for an ingénue to star in *Shadow and Substance,* Hopper wrote, "This is written for just one girl in Hollywood. I don't know who you are. You haven't been discovered yet. But I can tell you there's a luscious package for you labeled Fame. A gentleman named Charlie Chaplin will be sending it over whenever he's ready. I think you should know what's in it. You'll be that lucky girl chosen by Chaplin to play the top feminine role in *Shadow and Substance.* It's your chance, the opportunity of a lifetime. You'll be living in a dreamworld of shining limousines, sables, and exploding flash bulbs. All that will be in your tinseled package. Something more, too. Something not quite so good. The tradition of the Chaplin leading ladies has taken a definite pattern. You were nobody when he discovered you. You were sitting on top of the world for a few months. Then you were nobody again."[55] On the night that she visited Hopper's office, Barry went to Chaplin's estate, threatened him again, and during the exchange that followed the police were called. Barry was arrested and given a thirty-day jail sentence. Meanwhile, Hopper plotted action.

Hopper had always disliked Chaplin, in part for his unwillingness to pander to the gossip columnists, but even more for his progressive politics. Hopper was a member of the Motion Picture Alliance for the Preservation of American Ideals, a conservative political organization established in Hollywood in 1939 in response to what was perceived by many on the right as the growing leftist domination of the film industry.[56] "In our special field of motion pictures, we resent the growing impression that this industry is made up of and dominated by Communists, radicals and crack-pots. We pledge to fight, with every means at our organized command, any effort of any group or individual to divert the loyalty of the screen from the free America that gave it birth," read the organization's founding statement.[57]

In contrast to Hopper, who had been a staunch isolationist, Chaplin had encouraged not only U.S. intervention in the war but also the opening of a second front in Western Europe to aid the Soviets in their fight against the Nazis. Chaplin's advocacy of the second front stemmed from his antifascism and his personal friendship with several Soviets he had met in Hollywood, including the director Sergei Eisenstein.[58] On June 3, 1943, when Barry and her lawyer filed a paternity suit against Chaplin, the anti-Semitic Hopper both released the story in her column and wrote a scathing attack in which she criticized the British actor for never having become a U.S. citizen and for allegedly denying that he was Jewish (which, in fact, he was not). The column concluded: "What is to become of that child and its mother, Joan Barry? Those are the questions Hollywood has a right to ask and not only hope for an answer but to demand one."[59] Later that month in her column, she again attacked Chaplin for his citizenship and for his advocacy of the second front, and she received dozens of fan letters in response. "Just a few lines to let you know that one American woman appreciates the efforts you have made in your fight for Joan Barry's civil rights," wrote one reader. "That one small girl can't be pushed around by a lot of people with authority and influence." "Dear Miss Hopper, I wish to congratulate you on your stand in the Chaplin matter. Apparently you are the only columnist who isn't afraid of him[,] because the others either avoid it altogether or handle it with gloves," wrote a woman from Chicago. "P.S. Apparently we don't think Mr. Chaplin is a genius."[60]

Hopper and Florabel Muir, a reporter who was running a local news syndicate service, the Los Angeles City News Service, then testified before a grand jury and shared information about Barry with the FBI, which was investigating the case. Though Chaplin was eventually acquitted when blood tests proved that Barry's child was not his, the scandal marred his public reputation. By conflating his morality and political stance, according to Chaplin scholar Charles Maland, Hopper convinced a significant number of Americans that "Chaplin's moral behavior was impolitic and his politics were immoral."[61]

When Chaplin and O'Neill decided to marry in mid-June 1943, Chaplin contacted Harry Crocker, a Hearst columnist who had once worked as an assistant director for Chaplin. Through Crocker, Chaplin arranged for the announcement of the marriage to come through Louella, whose byline would be "more valuable from reader standpoint than that of Crocker's," according to *Daily Variety.*[62] "It would be better to have Louella Parsons, a friend, write it up than subject ourselves to the belligerence of other newspapers," Chaplin wrote in his autobiography, referring to Hopper.[63]

On June 17, 1943, Louella reported "the latest bombshell in the affairs of Charles Chaplin in his marriage today to 18 year old Oona O'Neill, daughter of Eugene O'Neill, America's outstanding dramatist. Early this afternoon, at a place I am pledged not to divulge, the 54-year-old comedian will wed for the fourth time a girl many years his junior."[64] Chaplin also placed Crocker in charge of all the photography at the wedding, which took place in Carpinteria, California, near Santa Barbara. This was done to give "the LA Times a burnup as a result of the Hedda Hopper tipoffs on Chaplin's difficulties with Joan Barry," according to *Variety.*[65]

In December 1943, Doubleday released *The Gay Illiterate,* a thin, hardbound volume with a maroon cover that sold for two dollars. Harriet had written the dust jacket copy, describing Louella as a "lovable, maddening, impressive, absurd, sophisticated, naive, noble, unprincipled, understanding, obtuse, admiration-inspiring, laughter-invoking character."[66] The Louella Parsons of *The Gay Illiterate* was indeed a character—sweet, innocent, and bearing little resemblance to the intelligent, shrewd, and emotionally complex woman who stood behind its pages.

Contrary to the popular stereotype, Louella claimed on the first page, she was not a "Lady Ogre Columnist." "There is the Louella O. Parsons of unpopular fable. And then there is me—the woman I live and work with and who is sometimes hurt and sometimes fighting mad about the idea of the [columnist] who eats little actors alive." Instead, she was "just another one of 'us girls,'" who enjoyed "chatting" with readers "about the best-known glamour personalities in the world. Such 'chatting' has to be informal—as all the best gossip is, whether in a column or over the back fence." The real Louella, who worked constantly, "gaily split . . . infinitives and [mixed] metaphors," and who fought for "every important Hollywood story with every ounce of [her] energy," was a small-town girl from rural Illinois, raised in a family that had surrounded her with "warmth and tenderness and good care." "We were not rich. But neither were we poor. We Oettingers were like millions of Americans who sat on the front porch in the summertime with a pitcher of lemonade—and who, in the winter, held family court around the dining room table."[67]

As a child, she wrote, she was immature, temperamental, and impatient for success as a writer. After work at the *Dixon Star,* where she "covered musical events, wrote society notes, and ran errands for the city editor," she was derailed from the pursuit of literary stardom by her marriage—at age sixteen, she lied—to John Parsons, "the gayest blade" in town. She revealed frankly her marital unhappiness and her dismal days in Burlington, which she falsely claimed to have escaped by one day, "out of the blue," taking a trip with Harriet to visit an uncle in Missoula, Montana. "That marked the beginning of the end of our marriage. From there we just drifted apart, lulled into an acceptance of the situation by sheer necessity." She and John might have reconciled their differences, she claimed, but "Captain John Parsons died aboard a boat due to dock in New York on February 14, 1919." Louella never disclosed her divorce from Parsons or her second marriage and divorce from Jack McCaffrey. Instead, she presented herself as a "war widow" who showed up in Chicago poor and jobless and who struggled in her "little effort . . . towards buying shoes for Harriet."[68]

She did, however, admit her relationship with Peter Brady and her torturous experience falling "very deeply, very wholly, and very completely in love . . . with a man who was not free to marry me." Though this disclosure was risky, Louella and English, her ghostwriter, most likely saw it as a way to humanize Louella before her young female readers. At a time when she was "confused and young and not sure" of herself, she saw Brady as a kind of father figure—"I found strength in his strength and kindness, and inspiration in his fine mind and his advice." She could write credibly about actors' failed romances, she implied, because of her own "heart-torture."[69]

One by one, she countered what she described as the many rumors about her, beginning with one of the oldest—that she had gotten her position with Hearst as a gift for covering up his murder of Thomas Ince in 1924. "The most popular and widely spread [rumor] is that I am supposed to know 'something.' This fictional something varies in style from the Edgar Allan Poe school to the Bocaccio trend, according to the rumor-monger's literary preferences. Time, I am thankful to say, has dimmed some of the more absurd stories. It is heartbreaking, to say the least, after working for 25 years getting scoops and important motion picture news stories, . . . to find oneself suspected of holding such a major appointment through even the cagiest blackmail scheme." She defended Hearst—"where are the words to express. . . . the greatness and understanding of this man who is so often vilified by people who do not know him?"—and accused Thomas Wood of having written the piece in the *Saturday Evening Post* because he was "evening up a score for his old friend Sidney Skolsky." "For a short time Sidney had been syndicated by the Hearst papers, and when his contract was not renewed he told everyone he thought I had been responsible for his dismissal. . . . I like pint-sized Sidney and his Hollywood writings, and I had nothing to do with his dismissal," she lied.[70]

She went on to attack Henry Luce, "another who dearly loves to resurrect dusty old legends whenever he feels called upon to mention my name in either *Time* or *Life* magazine. . . . I have never complained to Luce or to any of his editors when they have made fun of [me]. The only time I ever felt like putting on my own brass knuckles was in connection with the Louella Parsons Day in Dixon, my old home town. Although this festivity had been planned a year in advance, *Time* insisted that I am such a meanie I staged it to take away from the glory of another columnist who was making a 'personal' at the same time in a nearby spot."[71]

The rest of the book was a saccharine and largely falsified account of her news-gathering tactics and her infamous "scoops." She portrayed herself as a paragon of journalistic integrity, hardworking (she scribbled her column "in the Santa Anita Race track, and in the ladies' room at Ciro's") and ethical ("a reporter who lets his personal views get in the way of a news story just isn't worthy of his profession," she wrote).[72] She ended the book with a celebration of Hollywood's morals, claiming that behind the fast-living "personality boys and girls" were "folks like the Don Ameches and Robert Youngs and the Bing Crosbys and the Bob Hopes and dozens and dozens more who live just as the prosperous and firmly united family groups do all over this USA." The only exceptions were the stars of "the genius breed—the artists of the Chaplin variety—and more recently, Orson Welles, the self-elected genius."[73]

Shortly before the book's release, Louella sent the manuscript to David Selznick, hoping that he would turn it into a film. Though he was pressured by his brother Myron, Louella's agent for the book, he turned her down. Rather than a film, he suggested, "you ought to go after 1) Newspaper serialization; 2) Magazine serialization; 3) Summarized publications in the *Reader's Digest* or *Ladies' Home Journal*. I think as a radio serial it could last for a couple of years and could be something tremendous with yourself or with someone impersonating you, and with all the personalities you have known, past and present."[74] Less than a week later, the Literary Guild of America placed the book on its list of recommended reading, and according to the *Hollywood Reporter,* two studios were reported to have been bidding for it.[75] On December 9, 1944, Twentieth Century Fox—the studio allied with Hearst's Cosmopolitan film production company—purchased the rights to the book for seventy-five thousand dollars. The studio planned to market the story as the struggle of "a widowed mother at the end of World War I, her effort to find a place in the world, and her eventual success, both in business and in romance," and was rumored to have been considering either Claudette Colbert or Irene Dunne for the part of Louella.[76] Hopper cynically suggested Mae West. Reporting on the book's purchase in the *Hollywood Reporter,* columnist Edith Gwynne wrote that she "ran into Doc Martin, who said, 'they'll never be able to cast Louella's book.' They'll never find anyone sexy enough to play me!" Gwynne also wondered whether the Luce publications were "readying a blast" against Louella for her comments against the publisher.[77]

Gwynne was right. By early January 1944 *The Gay Illiterate* had sold out in every bookstore in Hollywood and was one of the top-circulating books at the Los Angeles Public Library. However, Luce's *Time* magazine damned it as "the self-recorded soundtrack of a small town, intensely feminine mind which for 30 years with unabated enthusiasm and energy has been hanging over Hollywood's back fence, talking like a ruptured water main to hundreds of thousands of other small town, intensely feminine minds." The book was "a nonstop, hypnotic colloquy, starched with babbling anecdote."[78] According to the *New York Times,* Louella "persists in the "Little Me" approach . . . [and] emerges with the self-portrait of an elfin creature—half-child, half-catamount—looking wide eyed at a wondrous world. . . . As a literary work, it has a formidable clumsiness which suggests that she frequently turns pages with a bulldozer."[79] "Mrs. Parsons' gossip column has always been an unincisive, undiscerning cliche-ridden portrait of Hollywood affairs," wrote Manny Farber in the *New Republic.* "Her book doesn't confuse the record."[80] The Communist Party paper the *Daily Worker,* following Twentieth Century Fox's purchase of the book, wrote that "it is common knowledge that Louella Parsons is one of the most ignorant newspaper writers in the history of journalism. . . . With the Sultan of San Simeon behind her, she can mangle reputations as well as grammar." "Will 20th Century Fox expose the seamy side of Louella in their film?" the *Worker* asked.[81] Because there are no records of readers' responses to the book, it is difficult to know whether *The Gay Illiterate* improved Louella's public image as she had hoped. It has, however, stood the test of time; with all its falsehoods, for decades *The Gay Illiterate* has been cited by journalists and scholars as the authoritative account of Louella's life.

Since the war, Marion Davies and Hearst had been living at Hearst's Northern California residence, Wyntoon. Located on fifty thousand acres of alpinelike forest near Lake Tahoe, the estate, designed by Julia Morgan as a summer retreat from San Simeon, had been built in the style of a Bavarian village.[82] After visiting Hearst and Davies for a weekend at Wyntoon, Louella embarked on a nationwide book tour in late January 1944. To attract publicity, at each stop she sold books and war bonds.[83] In Chicago, Louella broke all records for crowds at Marshall Field's book section and "sold out all copies of the book, including the window display in Hudson's Detroit store and set a new high for crowds in the book section of the Hutzler Department Store in Baltimore." In Detroit, the owner of the local Fox theater chain bought a hundred thousand dollars' worth of bonds from Louella in exchange for a special autographed volume. In Pittsburgh, the original manuscripts of the book were given to the Carnegie Library, and at a war bond rally there, she raised over six million dollars.[84] After appearing on the Mary Margaret McBride radio show in New York, Louella was the guest of honor at a luncheon at the Waldorf Astoria, at which former New York mayor, and friend of Louella, Jimmy Walker was toastmaster. "Through all the years I have known her, my admiration for her has been growing. In her new book she splits infinitives but she never splits friends," he quipped.[85] By early February 1944, the book had sold forty thousand copies.[86]

Louella's publishing success did not cool her wrath toward Hopper. In May 1944, *Daily Variety* reported that at a Lilly Dache fashion show, when Hopper entered the room and sat next to Maggie Ettinger, Louella, who was on the other side of the room, stalked out.[87] Hopper said to Maggie, "I'm terribly sorry. I'll move," but Maggie would have none of it. "You will not. This is silly. I'll get her back," she told Hopper. She went across the room and got Louella, causing a scene. "By that time the spectators—Loretta Young, Mary Pickford, Marion Davies, Claudette Colbert, and a hundred others—were paying more attention to us than to Lilly's hats," Hopper recalled. Later, Hopper found out that the table had been reserved for Lorena Danker, whose husband, an executive for the J. Walter Thompson company, had staged the show. Louella was appalled that Hopper had not asked permission before she sat down.[88]

That summer, two weeks after selling Marsons Farm, Louella went to Chicago with actress Gracie Allen to cover the Republican convention, at which Thomas Dewey would receive the nomination. Though she had been commissioned by Hearst to report on the "woman's angle," Louella, a registered Republican, used her dispatches from the convention to attack President Roosevelt and the New Deal. In one story she quoted a woman whom she described as a "typical woman delegate at this convention," Mrs. Alberta Huffman of Rockport, Indiana, who claimed to have been "sick and tired of the New Deal and all its ways" and who "wanted to have an active part in helping to beat it." "Now we're just average people and our friends are just average people," Huffman had allegedly said. "Then along comes the New Deal and the first we know there are class lines among us. And our farmer friends are being nagged to death by taxes."[89] Both Louella and Harriet had signed on to the Dewey campaign, and in the summer of 1944, when Dewey visited Hollywood, Louella and Harriet, along with noted Hollywood conservatives Ginger Rogers, Joel McCrea, Harold Lloyd, Edward Arnold, Darryl Zanuck, and Hedda Hopper attended a welcome party for his arrival.[90] Hopper had also covered the convention for the *Chicago Tribune* syndicate.[91]

After suffering from pneumonia for several weeks, Louella went to Palm Springs in late November 1944 for a vacation. Her recovery was quick, and by early December she was back in Hollywood, attending—and hosting—several high-profile parties. In addition to her usual Christmas dinner attended by more than twenty guests, she hosted a "tremendous soiree" for Bebe Daniels and Ben Lyon, who were visiting from London. Shortly afterward she threw a party for Fred Sammis, editor of the fan publication *Modern Screen,* who had commissioned Louella to write a regular column for the magazine. Louella had set up a massive tent in her backyard, installed a patio on which she placed a hundred white tables, and planted dozens of long-stemmed American Beauty roses for the occasion. A few hundred guests showed up. "What are you going to wear to Louella's party? someone had the naivete to ask us," wrote Edith Gwynne in the *Hollywood Reporter.* "Wear? We screamed. You don't wear anything to Lolly's parties—you just put a heavy coat of grease on your beautiful body. It's easier to slither through the crowd that way!"[92]

Her extravaganza for the *Modern Screen* editor was followed by another blowout that winter to celebrate a long-awaited radio deal. After more than two years off the air, Louella finally secured a contract for a fifteen-minute gossip show, sponsored by Jergens-Woodbury. The program was slated for Wednesday nights on ABC from 6:15 to 6:30, immediately after Walter Winchell's show. Jergens had actually chosen Hopper for the spot, but when Winchell, who disliked Hopper's politics, vigorously protested, the company settled on Louella.[93] On the new show, Louella "chatted" briefly with a guest star and recommended films she deemed to have "the best performances of the month."[94] The show also featured a short segment called the "Woodbury

Soap Box," in which Louella "got on her soap box" and editorialized on various political and social issues, ranging from the serious to ridiculous. She devoted one soapbox segment to what she described as America's "national menace in the sleeping pill habit" and urged the producers to "wake up" and eliminate references to sleeping pills in films.[95] During the next three years, over one hundred different stars and Hollywood personalities appeared on the show, including Louis B. Mayer, Walt Disney, Frank Sinatra, Al Jolson, Judy Garland, Bob Hope, Olivia DeHavilland, Spencer Tracy, Ronald Reagan, Elizabeth Taylor, Joan Crawford, Clark Gable, Gregory Peck, Ginger Rogers, Humphrey Bogart, and Shirley Temple.

Louella and Winchell had always been somewhat testy with one another, but the two maintained a relatively cordial facade. That is, until Winchell broadcast one of Louella's exclusives on his show—the three-hour time difference between New York and California enabled him to raid her column, and Louella was furious. She was nonetheless grateful for her radio presence, which she believed enabled her to compete effectively with Hopper. On the air, Hopper, who did a weekly gossip show for Armour Brothers, often attacked Louella, sparking criticism from the *Hollywood Reporter,* which complained about the way Hopper "clutters up the ether with denials of Louella's yarns."[96] By 1946, Louella was outranking Hopper in the Hooper radio ratings, a national ratings system based on samplings of listeners in thirty-six cities. Louella was ranked the second most popular Hollywood gossip broadcaster after Jimmie Fidler.[97] That year director Mervyn LeRoy celebrated Louella's radio work by giving her a cameo appearance in the film *Without Reservations.* Claudette Colbert played Kit Madden, a novelist who falls in love with an American soldier, Rusty Thomas, played by John Wayne. Convinced he will be perfect for the starring role in the upcoming film adaptation of her book, she takes him to Hollywood. In a scene near the end of the film, Louella broadcasts the news of their romance on her radio show.[98]

As in *Hollywood Hotel,* Louella appeared glamorous and composed, but the groomed charisma masked anxiety over her and Harry's poor health. In May 1945 Harry returned to the hospital with what seemed to be a reoccurrence of the fever he had contracted in the South Pacific and was in and out of the hospital for much of the summer and fall of 1945. Louella, too, struggled with recurring bouts of kidney trouble and abdominal pain, but she continued to burn the candle at both ends. In October 1945 she accepted an assignment from Hearst's *Cosmopolitan* magazine to do a monthly film review article, called "Cosmopolitan Citations." For the articles, she screened as many as a dozen films a week in the private movie theater she had installed in the Maple Drive home. She woke up at 6 A.M. to write the articles, in addition to pieces for *Photoplay* and *Modern Screen* magazines. "Here it is and I won't say it doesn't come to you without the sweat of my brow. To finally complete this classic[,] I've seen enough pictures to drive a sane woman crazy and a crazy woman crazier," she wrote to *Cosmopolitan* editor Frances Whiting in March 1946.[99]

But the hard work only exacerbated her physical problems, and in April 1946 she was hospitalized for a diaphragmatic hernia, which, according to Madalynne Lang, was caused by Louella's "old fashioned" tight corsets. In May 1946 Louella had an operation, supervised by Dr. William Flick, a specialist who had arrived from Philadelphia. It would be the first of several operations during the next two decades. "She was supposed to go in for checkups all the time. She never went. She just didn't have time. So eventually she had trouble again," Lang recalled.[100] On May 15, 1946, Dorothy Manners announced that "the best news ever printed in this column is that Louella Parsons successfully came through a major operation at the Good Samaritan Hospital yesterday morning." Louella's office was flooded with "telephone calls, [an] avalanche of telegrams, [and] notes and messages inquiring about [her]. She is so deeply and sincerely touched that she wants you to know she has received every one of them. The beautiful flowers from old friends—the notes from new friends and even those messages from fans who say 'Miss Parsons wouldn't know me but I've read her column for years and feel she is a friend.'"[101] She recovered quickly, in less than a week, and she was taken home from the hospital a day ahead of schedule. While she was being carried into the house on a stretcher, she insisted on being carried through every room. "I was so homesick," she explained.[102]

Hundreds in Hollywood, including Hopper, sent flowers and good wishes. "Dear Hedda. Thank you for the lovely flowers but more for the spirit that prompted you to think of me. It's . . . good to be alive with the promise of a complete return to health in a short time," Louella wrote back.[103] In July 1946, to recuperate, Louella went to San Simeon, where Hearst had resumed residence. Due to the expanded circulation and advertising stimulated by the war, Hearst had been able buy back many of his former newspaper and magazine holdings; his postwar empire, nonetheless, was only a fraction of what it had been in the 1920s, and the atmosphere at San Simeon was subdued.[104] According to Bebe Daniels, who was there with Louella, instead of the usual seventy-five or one hundred weekend guests, there were only six. "It was a very different San Simeon from the one we had known in those gay days before the war," she recalled.[105] Louella enjoyed a quiet two weeks, then returned to Hollywood at the end of July.[106]

By the beginning of September, she was back on the radio, and critics noted a marked improvement in her delivery. "Her enforced inactivity was not passed in idleness, judging from the general improvement in her diction, delivery, and relaxed manner," noted *Daily Variety.* "Not a line was fluffed and the excited inflections were toned down. Gone, too, was the gushy treacle that formerly dripped from her gabby sessions from her guest stars."[107] *Radio TV News* noted "a new quality in her voice which until now was lacking." "The show was sensationally good. Very warm, very human. It sounded as if for the first time a Parsons broadcast was actually rehearsed and that she had read her material before presenting it."[108] Only Frank Colby of the *Los Angeles Times* attacked her, accusing her of adopting the "phony broad a" (in "such pronunciations as 'ahsk, lahst, ahfter, cahn't, dahnce, bahth'") "in the silly belief that it will make [her] . . . cultured." Colby awarded her the distinction of having the "most slovenly speech pattern" on the radio. Jergens-Woodbury was nonetheless pleased with her performance, and the following year she started a new five-year radio deal with a substantial salary boost, and Jergens was discussing the possibility of giving Louella her own television show.[109]

In the fall of 1946, Sid Grauman, owner of the famed Grauman's Chinese Theater on Hollywood Boulevard, asked Louella to enshrine her footprints in cement in the theater's forecourt. Grauman had been collecting stars' footprints since 1927, and although over seventy-five actors had been thus immortalized by 1945, Louella was the first—and only—film columnist to receive an invitation. She called it the "highest honor" that Grauman, a longtime friend, had ever paid her. "We are very proud of Miss Parsons in Hollywood. She is the first among many Hollywood columnists," Grauman announced to the assembled crowd.

In the small, green-tinted square, Louella left her handprints and two high-heeled footprints. She signed it and dated it September 30, 1946, and at the top, in large capital letters, scrawled her daily column closure: "That's all today. See you tomorrow."[110]

FOURTEEN

War and Peace

It was, in retrospect, Hollywood's last hurrah. Boosted by millions of returning servicemen and a prosperous postwar economy, motion picture attendance in 1946 reached an all-time high. That year, ninety-five million film admissions were sold each week, and the film industry's revenues soared to $1.7 billion, up from $1.45 billion in 1945. "Maybe we are sitting around in this country waiting to buy new toasters, vacuum cleaners and cars, but we're not sitting at home my friends," Louella wrote in an article in *Cosmopolitan* in May 1946. "We're sitting in movie theaters and the producers are picking up the change."[1] Though the national economic upswing continued—between 1945 and 1950, consumer spending rose by 60 percent—by 1949, Hollywood was no longer reaping the benefits.[2] Plagued by internal labor struggles, restricted foreign markets, and battles with the federal government, in 1947 the film industry began a period of rapid and steady decline.[3] By the beginning of 1948, an 8 percent drop in domestic theater attendance and a 75 percent tax on American film earnings in Britain led the major studios to begin a series of layoffs; MGM cut its staff by a quarter, and Columbia, a third. The Screen Actors' Guild reported record levels of unemployment, and movie executives were "wearing sackcloth," according to *Newsweek*.[4]

And the troubles were just beginning. In 1948, in the culmination of the film industry's long antitrust battle with the government, the Supreme Court issued its *Paramount* decision—which declared that the Big Five and Little Three studios held a monopoly over film production, distribution, and exhibition—and forced them to divest. The studios were given five years to sell off their theater chains and were required to end the practice of block booking: films would now be sold to exhibitors on an individual basis, and the studios were prohibited from setting minimum admission prices as a condition for film rental. The decision was a blessing for independent producers and theater owners, but it spelled financial disaster for the major studios, for which exhibition had been the primary source of profit. According to *Variety* in 1948, over 70 percent of the major studios' annual profits, roughly $100 million, came from their affiliated theater chains.[5] The earnings of Paramount, the first studio to comply with the decision, plummeted from $20 million in 1949 to $6 million in 1950.[6]

Added to this was the new competition from television. Television technology had been developed in the 1920s and 1930s by the major radio corporations, and by the late 1930s the CBS and NBC networks were transmitting crude black-and-white programming to a handful of wealthy families who could afford TV sets. But Hollywood's influence thwarted large-scale TV broadcasting. In 1939, pressured by the movie industry, the Federal Communications Commission prevented the development of television as a major industry, and it was not until 1946 that the ban was finally lifted. Spurred by technological developments, the strong postwar economy, a soaring birthrate, the rapid development of the suburbs, and the subsequent demand for in-home entertainment, NBC, CBS, and ABC introduced regular prime-time television programming in several major metropolitan areas by the late 1940s. By 1949 a million television sets had been sold, and approximately one thousand sets were installed every twenty-four hours.[7]

Americans were weary from wartime dislocation and eager to return to a comfortable life in the suburbs; the national mood in postwar America was conservative and family-oriented. Former soldiers now donned gray flannel suits to work in the nation's growing corporate economy, and female war workers returned home, becoming housewives—and mothers—at an unprecedented rate. Between 1948 and 1952, a record twenty-two million children were born in the United States—the "baby boom"—and women were exhorted to pursue early marriage and domesticity.[8] Politically, too, the nation veered sharply toward the right. By 1947 the postwar rise to power of the Soviet Union and the triumph of Soviet-backed communist governments in eastern Europe had created a Red scare, and Americans feared not only the spread of communism overseas but also communist activity at home. It was an intolerant, claustrophobic cultural environment, and it became an ideal breeding ground for one of the most shameless acts of political repression in American history.

In 1947, the House Un-American Activities Committee, which in 1940 had unsuccessfully investigated accusations of communism in the film industry, returned to Hollywood with a vengeance. Established as a permanent congressional committee in 1945 and revitalized by the election of Republican majorities in the House and Senate in the November 1946 election, by 1947 it had widespread popular and political support from millions who feared that West Coast liberals—in particular, radical Hollywood screenwriters—were injecting communist themes into films and using motion pictures as agents of mass "subversion." (In 1947, a Gallup Poll reported that 61 percent of Americans wanted to outlaw the Communist Party in the United States, and, the following year, that a third of the public believed that communists controlled "important elements in the economy.")[9] It was thus with great fanfare that, in the spring of 1947, the conservative, antilabor, anti–New Deal, New Jersey congressman J. Parnell Thomas, chairman of HUAC, announced that the committee would reopen its investigations into Hollywood. Like the infamous red-baiting senator Joseph McCarthy, who rose to prominence in 1950 with accusations of communist infiltration of the federal government, Thomas saw the film industry investigations as a golden opportunity for publicity and self-promotion. He also knew that the investigations would silence not only the few directors and screenwriters who had, in fact, been involved in communist-front organizations in the 1930s and 1940s but also all Hollywood liberals. As film historians Larry Ceplair and Barry Englund have written, HUAC's accusations of subversion "simply served as a pretext for silencing a cultural and humanitarian liberalism—a liberalism of the heart—which in the eyes of America's right wing, regularly 'infected' the atmosphere in which Hollywood movies were made."[10]

The film producers, who feared reprisals at the box office, moved quickly to thwart HUAC's attack. In March 1947, Eric Johnston, president of the Motion Picture Producers' Association, went to Washington to testify before HUAC, where he "admitted the presence of Communists in Hollywood" but reiterated that the industry had successfully fought off their influence. Though Johnston was initially hostile toward HUAC, in April, realizing that his plea had not dissuaded Thomas and the committee from opening their investigation, he pledged the "full cooperation" of the Producers' Association with HUAC's demands and stated that the producers would not employ "proven communists." Then, in May 1947, Thomas traveled to Los Angeles to conduct closed hearings with fourteen members of the Motion Picture Alliance for the Preservation of American Ideals, who testified to communist infiltration of the industry.[11] The witnesses' claims were sketchy at best. In addition to one witness's description of the MGM studio's pro-Soviet film *Song of Russia,* made at the height of United States–Soviet friendship in 1943, as "Communist propaganda," Thomas heard testimony from Ginger Rogers's mother, Lela, who told investigators that her daughter had refused to speak the line "Share and share alike—that's democracy," since it supported communism.[12] Throughout the summer of 1947, HUAC investigators led by a former FBI agent continued to gather information on Hollywood communists. One potential source, which they monitored closely, was Louella's column.

This was nothing new. Aware of the wide readership of Hollywood gossip columns and the columnists' vast knowledge of the day-to-day doings of the film industry, the FBI had cultivated a relationship with the major Hollywood writers—most prominently, Winchell, Hopper, and Louella—during the 1930s. Agents followed their writings carefully for information on the activities of communist front groups and possible communist influence on film content (information classified under the heading "compic"—communist pictures). In 1949, for example, Los Angeles agents reported to FBI director J. Edgar Hoover Louella's announcement of the MGM studio's production of *Big Country,* a film that was to "stress feats of the foreign born," which the agents suspected was a possible pro-Soviet reference.[13] The FBI also provided information to Hopper and Louella that it hoped could be "leaked" through their columns. In 1947, Louella was forwarded a report from the Washington, D.C., office referring to a 1922 article in the Soviet newspaper *Pravda* that praised Charlie Chaplin as a "communist friend of humanity." The item, however, never appeared in Louella's column.[14]

Hoping to convey an image of authority and authenticity to her readers, Louella often falsely cited the FBI as a news source. In 1934, Los Angeles agents noted that Louella had announced that Paramount Studio was going to produce a film, *Private Dick,* based on the life of Melvin Purvis, head of the Chicago branch of the FBI, who brought the notorious bank robber John Dillinger to justice. According to Louella, the film had been approved by the Department of Justice. The agents forwarded the column to Hoover, who claimed that the proposed production was "not authorized by this department and Purvis did not know anything about it until he saw it in the papers."[15] After the agents informed Paramount that "such a picture by Paramount or any other Moving Picture Company was distasteful to the Division and was not and would not be authorized," Louella quickly stopped plugging the film.[16] In 1936, in reporting an extortion threat made to Ginger Rogers, Louella claimed that "federal authorities declined to comment on the case." According to a Los Angeles agent, she had "made no inquiry of this division." The FBI also received information from an unidentified informant about Louella's involvement in an alleged Hollywood prostitution ring. "Louella Parsons, Hollywood Columnist, was a former Hollywood 'madam.' She is the No. 1 shakedown artist of prominent West Coast personalities. Her modus operandi is to invite starlets to her home on the pretext of writing a column about them. There, like a magnet, she draws her blackmailing gossip from her unsuspecting starlets[,] whom she wines and introduces to the right people, while tapping every source of extortion information," the informant claimed. The bureau appeared not to have investigated this false allegation.[17]

Louella was a personal acquaintance of Hoover's and, during her 1940 public appearance tour, had visited Hoover's office in Washington. Louella and Hoover also ran into each other at social events in Del Mar, north of San Diego.[18] Louella was a regular at the Del Mar racetrack, and Hoover went for checkups at the nearby Scripps Clinic. In 1947 Louella received an autographed copy of *The Story of the FBI,* a promotional brochure put out by the Bureau's Crime Records Division, sent personally by the director.[19]

In her typical support of Johnston and the Motion Picture Producers' Association, Louella used her column and radio show to prevent and contain any potential public fallout from the investigations. She admitted the presence of communists in the industry, yet assured her readers and listeners that the producers were weeding them out "in an effort to help stem this growing threat to our national safety."[20] In April 1947, she did a "Woodbury Soap Box" radio editorial asking actors to refuse to appear in any films written by writers with "subversive tendencies." She later claimed that no editorial she had done on the air had received as much attention and that she received "many telegrams signed with Hollywood names commending me for my stand. Now, if we can only keep these same writers out of the studios, the battle wouldn't be so hard to win. They keep, by subtle innuendos, adding their own un-American ideas to the screen plays they write."[21] Yet "the majority of Hollywood," she insisted to her fans, "[is] loyal and patriotic." "Men such as L. B. Mayer, Jack Warner, Y. Frank Freeman, and Ronald Reagan have proved devoted to American ideals. The communists in Hollywood are the exception. The motion picture industry should not be put under suspicion because a few have gone to the left," she explained.[22]

As part of her damage-control project, Louella also tried to clear the names of prominent Hollywood stars who had been publicly associated with communist or liberal causes. In particular, she came to the aid of the leftist actor

John Garfield, who had been accused of affiliation with the Communist Party after the famous "Simonov incident" of May 1946, in which he and Charlie Chaplin attended a party sponsored by the Soviet consul, Konstantin Simonov, aboard a Soviet ship in Long Beach Harbor. U.S. customs agents, checking for dutiable articles, were waiting as guests left the ship, and Chaplin remarked, "Oh I see we are under the power of the American Gestapo." News photographers heard the comment, which became headline news in Hearst's *New York Journal American*.[23] On September 13, 1947, Louella wrote in her column, "There's never been a story in Hollywood more fascinating than that of John Garfield, who has done so much for the underdog that he's been accused of being left-wing. I'd stake anything I own that the Communist ideologies attributed to John are as repugnant to him as they are to you and me." He was her guest on the air later that week and, less than two weeks later, the subject of a Sunday feature article. Louella suggested that the reason Garfield had been accused of communism was because Garfield "always champion[ed] the little fellow and work[ed] so hard on his behalf."[24]

While Louella worried about the effects of the HUAC investigation on Hollywood's profits and public image, Hopper rejoiced at the witch-hunt. Using the discussion of the investigations as a pretext, throughout 1947 she attacked the industry's liberal politics in her column and, in one particularly strident piece in August, asserted that "three pictures made during the war are definitely pro-Soviet." "Red propaganda," she continued, had appeared in the wartime films *Mission to Moscow, North Star,* and *Song of Russia,* which were "in open praise of Russia." "What recent pictures can you recall in which a member of Congress has been presented as an honorable, intelligent, patriotic public servant; in what picture has an industrialist been shown as a straightforward, decent human being?" she asked. "There is certainly a communist threat in the world, and Hollywood is still a part—and a very influential part—of the world, so it can hardly escape."[25]

That year Hopper also began what would become a long and close friendship with J. Edgar Hoover. On April 7, 1947, to thank Hoover for the copy of *The Story of the FBI* he had sent her, Hopper wrote in a letter to Hoover,

I loved what you said about the Commies in the motion picture industry. But I would like it even more if you could name names and print more facts. Who's keeping the truth from the American public? Isn't that one of the jobs Mr. Eric Johnston was paid to do?

I'd like to run every one of those rats out of the country, starting with Charlie Chaplin. In no other country in the world would he have been allowed to do what he's done. And now he's finished another picture, and Miss Mary Pickford is back in New York helping him sell it.

It's about time we stood up to be counted.[26]

Hopper was scheduled to appear as a guest panelist on a broadcast of "America's Town Meeting of the Air" to debate the topic "Is There Really a Threat of Communism in Hollywood?" In August 1947, a month before the broadcast, she wrote another letter to Hoover asking for "some facts to hurl back at the angry mob" that she anticipated. "Naturally, I won't be able to accuse certain stars of being registered Communists, as even those who are deny it, always have and always will. . . . Your information will be confidential. I will not use your name, unless you give permission. In that case, I'd be very proud to say, Mr. J. Edgar Hoover, who is my choice for President, tells me so and so." Hoover then sent her several of his writings on communism in film, including an address before the American Legion in 1947 and a 1947 *Newsweek* article, "How to Fight Communism." The documents accused Soviets of planting "strong Communist factions . . . in nearly every trade union" in Hollywood in the 1930s and described screenwriter John Howard Lawson as "one of the most important Marxist strategists in Southern California."[27]

On September 21, 1947, HUAC issued subpoenas to forty-three members of the film industry requiring that they appear as witnesses at hearings in Washington scheduled for October. In response, screenwriter Philip Dunne and directors William Wyler and John Huston started the Committee for the First Amendment, a group of Hollywood liberals organized to protest HUAC and support "freedom of speech and freedom of thought." The CFA, which eventually drew more than five hundred members, chartered a plane to fly fifty prominent members to Washington to attend the hearings. Among those who went were Humphrey Bogart, Lauren Bacall, John Garfield, Jane Wyatt, Sterling Hayden, Paul Henreid, and Gene Kelly.[28] In late September, perhaps not wanting to draw attention to the charges, Louella kept the discussion of the upcoming hearings out of her column and instead launched a diatribe against the notorious Memphis film censor Lloyd Binford, who demanded that all scenes depicting African Americans be eliminated from films prior to their exhibition in the city. In mid-October 1947, Binford had demanded a rewrite of the film *Hazard* to eliminate a black character, prompting Louella to remark, "When . . . is this industry going to stop this man from attempting to run our whole motion picture business?" According to historian Kathy Feeley, Louella's remarks on Binford were intended as an oblique commentary on HUAC, to "warn of censorship and the dangers that loomed when those in authority refused to stand up for their beliefs and allowed themselves to be bullied out of fear."[29]

Yet Louella squarely addressed the HUAC hearings on her radio show, where she claimed in a "Woodbury Soap Box" editorial that, thanks to HUAC, "you may be sure from now on there will be no more of these red sympathizers turning out our scripts and directing our pictures. These men and women, plus the few actors accused, will have it made clear to them that there is no place in the American picture industry for anyone not 100 percent American in his ideals and actions. A few of these people are definitely Reds. Some of them, at one time, thought it was the smart thing to do, to be on the wrong side of the fence. Now I am glad to say the majority are coming to their senses." The piece was widely praised. Burt McMurtrie of the *Tacoma Times* wrote that "Louella Parsons pulled no punches when she broadcast on Sunday night her denunciation of those who have brought disrepute on Hollywood. She was completely right in her statement that such prosecution as is taking place has nothing to do with personal beliefs but [upholding] the highest lawmaking body and the US government." Another columnist praised Louella for her "forthright editorial against those who besmirch their fellow workers and the industry that makes possible their living. All credit to her for her stand and what she means to Hollywood." Later, in December 1947, several representatives of the Soviet film industry criticized Louella for the piece.[30] In an open letter to Hollywood, they attacked HUAC as "the police terror of American reactionaries against the foremost leaders of American culture" and described Louella as the "author of the supreme slanders of delirium against the Soviet Union."[31] When Louella heard about the attack, she claimed to be "happy." "I am delighted that Hollywood has taken a stand against communism. I am also happy to be called an enemy of communism and the Soviet government, and I shall continue to fight all subversive elements as long as I have a breath of life in my body," she told reporters.[32]

The HUAC investigation began on October 20, 1947, a week before the CFA flight. The so-called friendly witnesses who named prominent communist sympathizers were called during the first week. The list of "friendlies" included actors Ronald Reagan, George Murphy, Gary Cooper, Robert Montgomery, Robert Taylor, and Adolphe Menjou and studio heads Louis

B. Mayer and Jack Warner. Nineteen of the witnesses, most of them writers, were dubbed "unfriendly," since they refused to state whether they were members of the Communist Party or to name other party members or sympathizers. All of the nineteen, sixteen of whom were screenwriters, had in fact been members of the Communist Party or other Popular Front organizations in the 1930s and had continued their involvement in pro-Soviet activities. In the end, eleven refused to testify. One of the unfriendlies, playwright Bertolt Brecht, left the country, and the remainder became known as the Hollywood Ten.[33]

Not only did the Ten refuse to testify, claiming their First Amendment rights, but they also took a defiant stance against HUAC, responding belligerently to the congressmen's inquiries. John Howard Lawson launched a wild verbal attack on the committee and was cited for contempt and subsequently removed from the stand by the police while screeching "Hitler Germany—Hitler tactics!"[34] The other nine followed with rude and disruptive behavior, leading to more contempt citations. The Ten's bad behavior ultimately had the effect of turning support away from the CFA, which now seemed to be supporting communism. Knowing that association with the CFA, and by extension, the Hollywood Ten, could mean a loss of fans and box office revenue, the studio heads forced the actors who had taken part in the Washington flight to publicly recant.[35] "Most of the cinemoguls were scared stiff by what they thought was the average moviegoer's indignation over communism in Hollywood," *Time* noted.[36]

Both Hopper and Louella subsequently attacked the CFA in their columns. Hopper called Bogart, who had been at the head of the CFA, "one of the four most dangerous men in America" and in her column quoted letters from readers who protested the CFA. "We are all movie loving folks. In fact, it is one of our main sources of entertainment. But until we are sure that Katie Hepburn . . . and all others [are not] involved in any way in . . . Communism, we cannot and will not attend a movie in which these people play or which they write," wrote a woman from Milwaukee.[37] "We hung a huge sheet of paper on our kitchen wall. Each time new names were made public anent the un-American activities investigation, we wrote those names in with red crayon. Before attending any movie, we check cast, writers, directors against those names and, unless the picture has a clean bill of health, we cancel out," commented a reader from Colorado Springs.[38]

Less strident but nonetheless critical, on her November 9, 1947, radio show, Louella claimed, "Bogart was ill advised when he went to Washington to protest the procedure of the Thomas Committee. Because actors' names make news, they must be doubly careful that their motives are clearly understood. Bogie went to Washington with good intentions, but every day I receive hundreds of letters from people who insist he is a communist because there were some other people questioned at the hearing who were under suspicion."[39] "I am really sorry Humphrey Bogart got in that Washington mess, because it is going to take a while for the fans who idolize him to forget it. Most of them feel he shouldn't have put himself in the position of sympathizing with the men and women accused of being red," she told readers of her *Modern Screen* column. "However I don't intend to go into the Communistic question. I just want to say that no motion picture star should get mixed up in the future in any of these so-called causes. John Garfield told me he has learned his lesson and is no longer on a soapbox."[40]

Eventually, Bogart bowed to pressure from the producers and released a statement to the press that he "went to Washington because [he] thought that fellow Americans were being deprived of their constitutional rights" and that "the trip was ill-advised, even foolish." He also wrote an article for *Photoplay* magazine, titled "I'm No Communist," in which he admitted he had been a "dope."[41] Louella then began mentioning him favorably in the column.

Meanwhile, the studio executives met in early November 1947 and planned a meeting with their New York offices to determine how to deal with the Hollywood Ten. Louella traveled to New York to cover the meeting, and on November 20 wrote in her column that "the boys with Communistic ideas are going to find very hard sledding from now on in Hollywood. The producers met last week and meet this week again, and any writer or director known to have a card or to be involved with the Communists in any way will sit out his contract. New contracts, of course, will not be made with these pink-tinted gents and ladies."[42] On November 24, 1947, when Congress voted to cite the Ten for contempt, the studio executives met for two days at the Waldorf Astoria Hotel and announced after the meeting that the Ten would be suspended without pay, and that thereafter "we will not knowingly employ a Communist or a member of any party or group which advocates the overthrow of the Government of the United States by force or by any illegal or unconstitutional methods."[43] In essence, the studios instituted blacklisting. Suspected communists and prominent liberals in Hollywood on the blacklist were routinely fired or passed up for employment, and most never worked in film again. The Ten were tried for contempt in the spring and summer of 1948, and all were found guilty, fined, and sentenced to prison terms.

For Hopper, a lifelong Republican with a strict Quaker upbringing, anticommunism was a deep personal faith. For Louella—who had once been a pro-labor Democrat in her days with Peter Brady, and who had only switched party affiliation, on Hearst's urging, in the late 1930s—collusion with HUAC was less a matter of personal ideology than company policy. In early 1947, capitalizing on the widespread anti-Soviet anxiety, the Hearst papers began reprinting editorials about communist infiltration of colleges that Hearst had written at the height of his 1930s communist witch-hunt. "The Hearst papers have sounded an alarm concerning the teaching of Communism approvingly in some colleges. Communism as practiced in Russia . . . is a policy of force and violence, of robbery and rapine. . . . It is impossible to teach the actuality of Communism approvingly without being disloyal to the policies and principles of our own country," read one editorial reprinted in February 1947. "When the editorial above was published twelve years ago, it was received by many with doubt and disbelief. Today, every thoughtful and patriotic American recognizes the solemn truth of every word that Mr. Hearst wrote."[44]

The Hearst papers were also the home of a cadre of vociferous right-wing columnists—most notoriously, George Sokolsky and Westbrook Pegler—who had vocally supported Joseph McCarthy and had claimed that the film industry was "reeking with communism."[45] J. B. "Doc" Matthews, a former researcher for the prewar congressional anticommunism committee headed by Martin Dies, worked as an editorial assistant to the publisher of the *New York Journal American*. He brought to the Hearst organization an unpublished listing of over one hundred thousand individuals associated with various communist fronts—names of individuals often smeared in various Hearst publications for being "red" or "pink."[46] Anticommunism, in short, was de rigueur for Hearst writers. Louella also supported the studios' policy of blacklisting, a tactic she had been using for years.

In 1947, Louella blacklisted Frank Sinatra, banishing his name from her column in response to Sinatra's troubles with the MGM studio over *It Happened in Brooklyn*, about a soldier returning to civilian life after the war. Sinatra had problems with the script and wanted the shooting schedule changed to accommodate the demands of his career as a singer. "I won't be surprised if MGM and Frank Sinatra part company. Frank's been a very difficult boy on the lot, and I have a feeling MGM won't put up with any such nonsense. . . . I have always liked Frankie, but I think right now he needs a good talking to," she wrote in a November 1946 column.[47] In response, Sinatra sent a telegram to her that read: "I'll begin in part by saying that if you care to make a bet I'll be glad to take your money that MGM and Frank Sinatra do not part company, permanently or otherwise. In the future I'll appreciate your not wasting your breath on any lectures because when I feel I need one I'll seek advice from someone . . . who tells the truth. You have my permission to print this if you so desire and clear up a great injustice." In January 1947 she announced, as one of her New Year's resolutions, "I'm going to quit picking on Frankie Sinatra, because I think he's a mixed up boy right now. I'm not going to sass him no matter how many snippy telegrams and clippings he sends me."[48]

She and Sinatra lunched in early January, apparently at Sinatra's initiation. The *Hollywood Reporter* then dubbed Sinatra Louella's "best false friend."[49] "It's all sunshine and flowers with Frankie and me. That rootin', tootin' telegram-sending feud that Sinatra and I have been carrying on for the past six months is over," she told her *Modern Screen* readers. Apparently, as part of the process of atonement, Sinatra had told Louella, "I have been so exhausted. I have been confused. I know I did many things I shouldn't have, things that I am now sorry for." "It was as near to an apology as he gave but it was good enough for me. Exhaustion—confusion. Those two devastating demons of the spirit that follow in the trail of working too hard, of taxing one's strength almost beyond human endurance. Oh I know that story by heart. It cost me five months away from my job and a serious operation last year," Louella wrote.[50]

But the problems with Sinatra resumed later that year when Sinatra beat up Lee Mortimer, a Hearst writer and *New York Mirror* film critic, in a Sunset Strip café, allegedly over an ethnic slur that the columnist had leveled at Sinatra. The altercation resulted in Sinatra's arrest, and Hearst papers put Sinatra on a "don't use list." Finally, in March 1948, Sinatra went to visit Hearst and Davies in Beverly Hills to call a truce, and it was "a very amiable meeting," according to *Variety.* Hearst subsequently rescinded the ban, and Sinatra was back in Louella's column.[51]

Ironically, it was during the time of the 1947 HUAC hearings and the Sinatra feud that Louella, who was becoming more devout in her Catholicism, began to harbor ethical qualms about reporting on marital infidelity and divorce. While in New York, Louella had visited Cardinal Spellman, her spiritual mentor, and shortly thereafter consulted him for advice concerning an accusation by a Los Angeles Catholic newspaper, *Tidings,* which had attacked her for "printing attractive things about divorced movie people."[52] Upset and finding it difficult to combine her religious beliefs with the job of reporting

Hollywood gossip, she was considering giving up the column and requested Cardinal Spellman's opinion. To her surprise, he was sympathetic toward her work and told her that she "had a job to do, and when reporting divorce fell within that job, she had to do it."[53]

Louella's spirituality intensified with Harry's serious health problems. In December 1946 she accompanied Harry to Johns Hopkins Hospital in Baltimore, where, according to the *Hollywood Reporter,* surgeons "found the cause of Doc Martin's trouble to be abdominal." In reality, Harry learned that he was suffering from leukemia.[54] Knowing it would devastate her, he kept the news from Louella until only weeks before his death. After going to New York to do a radio broadcast over a "three-way radio hookup," in which she interviewed Robert Taylor and Barbara Stanwyck, who were on a ship mid-Atlantic, and David Niven in Hollywood, Louella returned to Johns Hopkins. Then she went back to Hollywood for Christmas and traveled back to Baltimore in the spring of 1947, in time for Harry's scheduled April operation. Louella did her radio broadcast from Harry's bedside, via walkie-talkie.[55] Following the operation, Louella and Harry returned to Beverly Hills in May 1947.[56]

Shortly afterward, in the summer of 1947, *Time* ran a cover story on Hedda Hopper. On the cover of the July issue was a striking but elegantly rendered image of Hopper wearing a hat to which had been affixed a typewriter, a microphone, and a telephone, painted by the artist Boris Chaliapin. In typical Luce fashion, the article praised Hopper and attacked Louella, poking fun at her "pudgy" figure and her "little shark-toothed prose smiles." "Hedda always asks Louella to her parties. Louella never comes," the article inaccurately claimed. The article added that relations between the rivals had been "a little shaky lately" due to Hopper's recent exclusive on the birth of Bette Davis's child. In May 1946, Hopper had scored a major scoop when Davis, who was about to have a baby, refused all interviews and disappeared from Hollywood. Hopper suspected she was hiding out in her Laguna Beach cottage, drove there, found the door open, walked in, and got the exclusive story on the birth. Angry, Louella had responded in her column, "Since Bette Davis has had so many unwelcome visitors, she has had to have her gate padlocked." "But Louella's chagrin runs deeper than that," *Time* assured its readers. "Hedda keeps chipping away, and is distinctly too ubiquitous for Louella's tastes." "The monopoly on Hollywood gossip has slipped from Louella's control," it concluded.[57]

The *Time* article followed on the heels of Hopper's well-publicized trip around the country during the summer of 1947 with her legman Spec Mc-Clure to warn Americans of the "communist threat." From Omaha, Hopper reported that she talked to six hundred women of the American Legion Auxiliary who were "deeply interested in actors and actresses who had allowed their names to be used to further communistic causes. Is it true that . . . Charlie Chaplin, Melvyn Douglas, John Garfield . . . are mixed up with the commies? If it's true, they'll avoid seeing their pictures."[58] In her dispatch from Omaha, Hopper threw in a jab at Louella, claiming that "this town is still laughing over the story which got wide circulation that their beloved Bill Jeffers was marrying his stepmother."[59] Over the air on May 25, 1947, Louella had falsely reported that Jeffers, former president of the Union Pacific Railroad and wartime boss of rubber production, had surprised his best friends by marrying his stepmother. Louella had confused him with William Jeffries, a Los Angeles mayoral candidate. It was a "simple confusion of name. . . . I am deeply apologetic," Louella told the press. But the embarrassing mistake became the subject of a *Newsweek* article.[60]

After the *Time* cover story on Hopper, Louella fell into a depression and reportedly took to her bed for several days.[61] Apparently she became so despondent that she refused to answer her phones or write her column, and the studio publicists were upset. Adela Rogers St. Johns then suggested that Louella might be cheered by a dinner party to celebrate her twenty-fifth anniversary with the Hearst Corporation. St. Johns's suggestion was relayed to Hearst, who commissioned a gala event at the Ambassador Hotel's Cocoanut Grove nightclub for March 1948. The initial plan was to collect twenty-five dollars from each of the hundreds of guests. Invitations were sent out to over eight hundred stars, producers, and publicists, in addition to all the publishers and managing editors of the Hearst chain, who were required to attend. Hopper was not invited. Over one thousand requests for invitations, "including scores from very important showbiz people," had to be turned down.[62]

Not everyone in Hollywood was equally enthused. Ingrid Bergman recalled that when she received her invitation, "I threw mine in the wastepaper basket. Then I got a second one. I threw that away too." But Walter Wanger, her producer, insisted that she go. Bergman responded, "I am not going to pay 25 dollars to have the non-pleasure of sitting with a lot of people in a big hall to celebrate Louella Parsons." Wanger offered to pay, but Bergman refused; it was a matter of principle, she claimed. Fearing the consequences, Wanger sent flowers to Louella on Bergman's behalf, claiming that she was sick and could not attend.[63] In the end, when Hearst found out that the invitees had been charged for the ticket, he footed the whole bill. The total cost for the event was over fifty thousand dollars. Too ill to attend, Hearst sent his son David to award Louella a congratulatory plaque.

The star-studded program, which featured comedy, song, and dance and a five-course meal including filet mignon and "Salad Louella Parsons," was produced and directed by Hollywood film director Mervyn LeRoy, emceed by comedian George Jessel, and broadcast over the radio by NBC.[64] The front of the Ambassador Hotel and the lobby, according to the *Hollywood Reporter,* resembled "Grand Central Station on a holiday" with fans and curious onlookers turning out "en masse." Squadrons of police were on hand to keep order.[65] Testimonials ranged from the serious—Louis B. Mayer's "We all love you, Louella. No queen can wish for richer jewels than the bright crown of friendship you possess"—to the comical. The Republican governor of California, Earl Warren, one of the honored guests, joked that Louella had made the state so attractive and famous that she was indirectly responsible for California's housing shortage. "I've never gone in much for politics, but sitting at this table is a man I'm going to vote for, and I'm saying right out loud I want him to be president, and I think all of us who know him in California feel the same way. I might even make a few speeches for him," Louella responded.[66]

Following the speeches was the performance of a song, "Louella, Louella, Louella," written by the prolific composer Jimmy McHugh: "Louella, Louella, Louella, Everyone loves you; Louella, Louella, Louella, and Dr. Martin too. Press agents live for your column, Everyone's hustling you. Oh how we love you Louella and your 900 newspapers too."[67] Newsboys then rushed in hawking a mock version of the *Examiner* with the headline "LOUELLA SURROUNDED BY FILM LEADERS IN TRIBUTE TO MISS PARSONS." The paper featured testimonials from Dorothy Manners; Eric Johnston, head of the Motion Picture Producers' Association; Seymour Berkson, general manger of the International News Service; Jim Richardson, editor of the *Examiner;* and Wynn Roccamora, Louella's agent. In one article, "Devoted Wife Wins Praise," Eddie Cantor recalled that he had gone for a checkup to Cedars of Lebanon Hospital and encountered Harry, who was a patient. "Doc would keep his eye on the clock. Louella's daily visit meant so much to him." "There is something real about Louella. When she loves you, nothing you do is wrong," wrote Cantor. According to Louis B. Mayer, she was "the best known woman in the country."[68]

On behalf of his father, David Hearst presented Louella with a gold plaque engraved with the text of letter that Hearst had sent to her shortly before the event. "My Dear Louella . . . Every day you have faithfully recorded the progress of a great art and industry. To do this requires courage, accuracy, fairness, and curiosity—the best qualities of a good reporter. You deserve the confidence and affection of our millions of readers and my hearty thanks for a good job well done."[69]

Louella then approached the podium. Wearing a low-cut white dress designed by the famous Hollywood couturier Adrian, she looked tired and thin, having lost nearly twenty pounds for the event. According to *Newsweek*, when she reached the podium to give her acceptance speech she was "incoherent and tearlogged." According to *Time* magazine, she said to the crowd: "Governor Warren, ladies and gentlemen: I suppose everyone in his lifetime has visualized just such a night as tonight, but not many people in this world are lucky enough to have such a beautiful dream come true. I'm trying hard not to get too sentimental, but my heart is so full of gratitude to all my friends, to my newspaper, my co-workers, so many of whom I see sitting out there. My only regret tonight is that Mr. Hearst is not here tonight. I feel I owe so much to him. I feel that anyone who works for the Hearst organization owes a deep debt of gratitude to Mr. Hearst, and I've always felt that one of the greatest things in my life was being able to go to him with my troubles, because you may be sure if you're right, he never fails you."[70]

She went on to thank Harry ("the most understanding person"), Ray Van Ettisch, "a wonderful managing editor and never too busy for a compliment when I have a scoop," and city editor "Jim Richardson, whom I love." She concluded with reminisces from the past ("I can't help but . . . think how happy my mother would have been tonight—she, who thought no good could come out of motion pictures") and tears. "I'll try hard not to be emotional. My years with Mr. Hearst have been the happiest years of my life. This speech wasn't very good. I'm so emotional. I thank you and I love you all and I'm so happy."[71]

Though Hearst did not attend, Marion Davies was there, and she was drunk. She entered noisily, shouting greetings to Louella and the guests, then during someone's speech about Louella's long service to Hearst, quipped that she, Davies, had been in the Chief's service a long time and he'd never given her a party. This was within earshot of the *Time* reporter. Fearing that the magazine would print Davies's comment, the next morning Louella tried to contact Henry Luce by telephone but was told that he had flown to London for the weekend. Then Louella called Luce's wife, the writer and former congresswoman Clare Boothe Luce, and asked her, "woman to woman," to ask Henry Luce not to "print unkindly about Marion or print the awful pictures of Marion that were taken," because "Mr. Hearst was an old man now" and it would be wrong to hurt him. "I'm not asking Mr. Luce to be kind about me," she said.[72] Her pleas were ignored, and *Time* blasted both Louella and Davies. The article described Louella as a "gushy, 55 year old woman," and though the article did not quote Davies's remark about Hearst, wrote that she had stormed into the party, throwing Louella a "wave and rowdy greeting" and saying, "My God what a party! Why don't they always give parties like this!"[73]

Despite *Time*'s attack, the celebration was exactly what Louella needed. Her esteem boosted, she returned to her column. "I'm still on a pink cloud and so excited over my wonderful party . . . that I am in a daze," she wrote on March 6, 1948. "I started reminiscing to myself and thought of so many things. But most of all I am so thankful to have been a reporter. Sometimes when I am tired and the phone rings all hours of the day and night, I think it would be much easier to wash dishes—at least you'd get through. Then the joy of a scoop comes along—and all is forgotten."[74]

A week later, unexpectedly, she was in the news again, this time in conjunction with Harriet, who had become one of Hollywood's top female producers. Despite Harriet's insistence that Louella stay out of her career, during the early 1940s Louella had promoted Harriet aggressively, both with the studio executives and in the column. In 1940, after six years of producing short films for Columbia, Harriet had signed with the Republic studio to produce a series of twelve short films called *Meet the Stars*.[75] In April 1941 she was elevated to "full-fledged producer" at Republic, and not long after her promotion, Louella began giving the studio an extensive publicity buildup in the column.[76] "Republic is getting the best talent in the country and spending real money—so much so that I want to again go on record as saying this company has made the greatest progress of any studio in Hollywood within the last year," Louella wrote in June 1941.[77]

Republic had promised Harriet an opportunity to produce a feature film. After Harriet submitted an original script—in her words, a comedy about a group of child stars who had become "over the hill" teenagers—Harriet found that the studio had assigned her story to another producer-director. "I was so furious I quit," she recalled. "It was always the same old story. The studio head wanted to get in good with Louella but didn't trust me because I was a woman."[78] After leaving Republic, in 1942 Harriet signed with RKO, where she worked for the next twelve years. There she came across Sir Arthur Wing Pinero's play *The Enchanted Cottage,* about a disfigured man and homely woman who find themselves transformed within the walls of a magic cottage. But this, too, was taken away from her and given to the writer-producer Dudley Nichols. She then found *Mama's Bank Account,* a comedy about a Norwegian immigrant family in San Francisco in the early years of the century, which was also assigned to another producer. The stage rights were sold to Rogers and Hammerstein, who turned it into a play, *I Remember Mama,* that became a hit.

Hopper came to Harriet's defense. "What goes on at RKO with Harriet Parsons? The studio assigned her as a producer. She digs through its files and finds *The Enchanted Cottage* and arranges a deal with Sam Goldwyn to borrow Teresa Wright. Then it's snatched away and given to a big writer-producer. Then she digs up *Mama's Bank Account* and gets Katina Paxinou all set for it. Now that too has been snatched away from her. What goes on? Harriet's clever, and I think this is pretty shabby treatment even for Hollywood."[79] As a result of Hopper's comments, RKO returned *The Enchanted Cottage* to Harriet.

For her screenwriter, Harriet chose DeWitt Bodeen, described by one film historian as a "brilliant sensitive homosexual," and they became lifelong friends. Harriet had chosen Bodeen because he was homosexual; they wanted to refashion the play, in Bodeen's words, into a "modern romance" that would "rely upon the plausibility of love between a plain and unwanted spinster and a bitter crippled soldier, each of whom sought to hide away from a world that had rejected them." According to historian William J. Mann, this was to be an allegory about the homosexual experience in America—an "excellent example of homosexual expression as enacted through heterosexual guise."[80] Shortly after beginning work on *The Enchanted Cottage,* Harriet resigned from the movie staff of the International News Service to devote herself full-time to her work at RKO. She had been on the Hearst staff for thirteen years.[81]

Predictably, Louella intervened in the project by asking David Selznick to loan actress Dorothy McGuire, who was under contract to Selznick, and to assist Harriet with the production. Selznick agreed, to appease Louella, but he later feared that Louella had not appreciated his efforts. "I loaned Dorothy McGuire. I talked Miss McGuire into taking the part. I made drastic changes in the treatment and made key suggestions, including the whole idea of the composition which is the framework of the film. . . . I made editing suggestions on the finished film. In short, I really acted as executive producer of the film. . . . All of these gestures are wasted if Louella doesn't even know about it," he wrote to one of his publicists. "I want her to know the extent of what I did, some of which Harriet doesn't know about, such as the meetings I had on the makeup question and other things on which the unit came over without her. I wish . . . that you would find the occasion diplomatically to tell Harriet about it."[82]

The Enchanted Cottage, released in 1945, received not only positive critical reviews but also a tremendous buildup in Louella's column. "Do you mind if I do a little bragging about my child this morning?" Louella wrote. "She was on the Kate Smith [radio] hour Sunday and sounded swell. She has been on 3 or 4 other programs in connection with *The Enchanted Cottage.* One of my friends telephoned from New York to say that the Astor has been playing to capacity with huge crowds waiting ever since the picture opened Friday. It's breaking records right and left."[83] In a Sunday feature story on Dorothy McGuire, Louella quoted McGuire as having asked Louella about *Mama's Bank Account:* "Isn't that the play your daughter Harriet was to have produced when RKO sold it for a stage play?" "Yes," Louella responded. "She was within a month of making it into a picture when it was sold, and while Harriet was unhappy at the time, she is pleased now that *The Enchanted Cottage* was her first picture." "It was fun working with Harriet. She is so intelligent and so understanding," McGuire had allegedly said.[84]

Buoyed by the success of the film, Harriet then tried to win back the right to produce *I Remember Mama.* In her column on April 7, 1945, Louella announced, "Here's a surprise, dear daughter. You are going to New York, and you are being sent by Charles Koerner to look at *I Remember Mama* because you are going to produce it. He hasn't told you yet. I talked to your boss, and even though you said I must never discuss you or your affairs with the head of RKO, I am still a newspaper woman and I know news!"[85] *I Remember Mama,* starring Irene Dunne, went into production in 1946 and was released in the spring of 1948.

Both Louella and Hopper attended the film's premiere in March. Predictably, Louella awarded *I Remember Mama* her "Cosmopolitan Citation" for best film of the month, calling it "one of the finest films I've ever seen . . . because it is so simple, so human, so warm hearted and gentle."[86] When Louella spotted Hopper at the premiere, she feared that Hopper would pan the film, but to her surprise, Hopper's review was glowing. "I remember

Mama and you will too, when you have seen this film, with all the elements of good theater and good cinema, humor, humanity, and hominess it will be hard to forget. . . . To Harriet Parsons, who found the story and produced the picture, must go a lot of the credit," Hopper wrote in her column.[87] When Harriet, who was in New York, read Hopper's notice in the *New York Daily News,* she called Louella to ask whether she'd seen it. Louella had, and she was shocked. Harriet then asked Louella to call Hopper and arrange a "peace parley."[88] Harriet also sent a telegram to Hopper that read, "Hedda dear, your wonderful article on *Mama* and your remarks about me made me very happy. You have always been kind and helpful to me in your column and I want you to know that I am grateful."[89]

Hopper also received dozens of telegrams from Hollywood directors, actors, and agents who were amazed by her generosity toward her rival's daughter. "At the risk of having you regard me as a simpering sentimentalist, I must tell you how wonderful I thought it was to read the friendliest and warmest tribute to Louella's daughter Harriet. Honestly Hedda, it stirred great tears of joy as I read how fairly and how genuinely you revere Harriet. I hardly know the young lady in question[,] but this I do know—that it could be a very easy matter to dismiss the subject of the opposition's daughter," wrote Ginger Rogers.[90] Louella's agent, Wynn Roccamora, also wired thanks: "Dear Hedda, let me add my small voice to the many who undoubtedly will shower you with congratulations on your fine tribute to Harriet Parsons in this morning's column. I think there are too few occasions where people in the industry are truly good sports and I certainly think you have been."[91]

Spurred by Harriet's request, Louella contacted Hopper and the two agreed to meet for lunch at Romanoff's restaurant in Hollywood.[92] Hopper recalled that day in her autobiography: "I was there early at the number one table. When [Louella] came in and sat down, mouths flew open and stayed that way. Every table seemed to need a telephone to alert friends. Around the bar was a mob six deep. In answer to telephone calls, more arrived every minute. Nobody moved. No one knew what to do."[93]

The lunch quickly became news, both in Hollywood and around the country. "Hold everything!" the *Hollywood Reporter* announced on March 17. "Louella Parsons and Hedda Hopper had lunch together at Romanoff's yesterday. That's the trouble with this place—no lasting hatreds!"[94] *Collier's* magazine devoted an entire feature article to the meeting, a piece by writer Dickson Hartwell titled "The End of a Beautiful Feud." "Those few lucky I-was-there eyewitnesses to the reconciliation rushed to telephones to flabbergast their friends with the intelligence that Parsons and Hopper were lunching together unscratched and smiling for the first time in ten years," wrote Hartwell.[95] Quipped another journalist, "Surely the world is big enough for us and the Russians: Hedda Hopper and Louella Parsons had lunch together the other day!"[96]

What Hopper and Louella discussed at the meeting is unknown. In her column on May 15, Hopper wrote, "Who says Louella Parsons hasn't got a sense of humor? At Romanoff's the other day I retorted to something she said, 'One more crack like that, honey, and I'll slug you.'" "Well it's all right if you do, dear, as long as you let me have the exclusive on the story," Louella replied.[97] According to *Collier's,* the rivals had agreed to use the same news items in their columns on a given day the following week; "by Hollywood standards this [was] as fantastic as if Stalin and Truman . . . [used] identical texts in discussing the state of the world."[98] *Collier's* also claimed that Hopper and Louella had agreed to meet weekly for lunch thereafter. But the promised meetings never materialized. Both women were too insecure to permit genuine reconciliation, and the hostilities continued.

The rumors of a truce elicited mixed responses, both in Hollywood and among the columnists' fans. According to publicist Molly Merrick, many in Hollywood "encouraged [the feud] so [Hopper and Louella] wouldn't get together and compare notes" and were terrified at the possibility of their reconciliation.[99] Many fans, too, seemed to have enjoyed the feud. Within fan circles, one either "read Hopper" or "read Parsons" and had little sympathy for the opposing camp. On September 24, 1948, Hopper received a letter from one of her fans, who notified her of the "atrocious eating manner of Miss Louella Parsons at the Pomona Fairgrounds this past week. She and a lady friend proceeded to devour full size sandwiches in four huge bites per, chewing with wide open mouths. People in the public eye should possess refined manners."[100] Though Hopper never printed the news, she kept the letter in her personal files for possible future use. Other moviegoers were disgusted by the wide press coverage given such a relatively trivial event. "Dear Sir: What with the other problems we are having, high prices, Commies, Taft-Hartley, Palestine, and our coming elections, may I congratulate you on your article, "End of a Beautiful Feud," commented one cynical *Collier's* reader. "Hundreds of thousands of your readers must have breathed easier and slept better after reading that the two Hollywood characters are speaking." The editors wrote back: "We look on the Hedda-Louella peacemaking as a model for the UN to follow. Peace, no matter what after war, is wonderful."[101]

Exhausted by the whirlwind of events that spring, in May 1948 Louella embarked on a three-week European vacation with Harry; Mecca Graham, an assistant director at Warner Brothers; and Father English of the Church of the Good Shepherd. In New York, before boarding the S.S. *America,* Louella was feted at the Silver Anniversary Ball of the New York Newspaper Women's Club. Financier Bernard Baruch and actors Irene Dunne, Mary Pickford, Buddy Rogers, Lana Turner, and Marilyn Maxwell attended, and Eleanor Roosevelt, a longtime advocate of women in journalism, sent Louella a congratulatory telegram.[102] Indeed, as the tributes acknowledged, Louella had been a pioneer in the field who helped open the newsroom to women journalists. Between 1920 and 1950, twenty-three thousand women went to work as editors and reporters, and by 1950 they constituted nearly a third of the profession. As a result of the leadership of such prominent reporters as Adela Rogers St. Johns, Dorothy Thompson, Agness Underwood, and Louella and the increased opportunities for news reporting created by the depression and the war, by the end of the 1940s few professional obstacles remained. Women were film critics, war correspondents, political commentators, and front-page reporters, and they had attained prominent positions on almost every major American newspaper.[103]

After a farewell party arranged by Hearst columnist Dorothy Kilgallen—the event featured five hundred helium-filled balloons painted "Bon Voyage Lollie and Dockie" in red and white letters—Louella and Harry sailed on the *America* for a three-week tour of France, Norway, Sweden, Ireland, England, and Italy.[104] In Paris, Louella was made an honorary member of the French Société de Journalisme, a national press organization, and in London attended a party given by the Women's Press Club of London, which also made her an honorary member.[105] In Dublin, after having been interviewed by several papers, she was asked by Prime Minister John Costello to appear on a "goodwill" broadcast, telling the world "what [she thought] of the Emerald Isle."[106] Finally, in Rome, after spending several days in the hospital with a cold, Louella visited the Vatican, where she and Harry were received in private audience by Pope Pius XII.[107] She returned to California bearing greetings to Hearst from the pope, whom she claimed "spoke highly of Mr. Hearst and complimented him on his fight against communism."[108] Not long afterward, she made a sizable donation to aid Italian war orphans and received a letter of thanks from the papal secretary written at the request of the pope.[109]

That June, shortly before the European trip, Walter Winchell had announced that his sixteen-year stint with Jergens would end in December

1948. Though his program had been consistently rated one of the top fifteen nighttime network shows, Winchell had said that he was leaving Jergens because he did not approve of a Jergens commercial for its Dryad deodorant, in which he would have to talk about the "decaying odor of bacteria." In reality, according to biographer Neal Gabler, Jergens had rejected Winchell, whose controversial and strident anticommunist statements on the air had been drawing complaints from customers. Louella stayed on with her usual spot, while Winchell switched to a show sponsored by the car manufacturer Kaiser Frazier.[110]

Though Louella had earned a 12.2 Hooper radio rating prior to her departure for the Continent—her highest rating yet—she returned to radio rusty. In early August 1948, *Variety* noted that "the fact that Miss Parsons approaches her script as though she were reading it for the first time (as occurred in a few instances last Sunday when the emphasis was directed on the wrong words and even syllables) can tend to negate the value of 'hot copy.'" Despite the criticism, in November 1948 her radio option with Jergens was picked up for another year. In the new format, Louella would tape the entire show in advance, instead of only the guest interviews as in the past.[111] Additionally, as a consequence of savings resulting from the Winchell departure, Jergens allocated an extra thousand dollars a week to the show, which would be spent on higher-priced guest stars. To launch the new format, ABC commissioned a dirigible with electric letters twenty-seven feet high and two city blocks in length that said "La Parsons" to hover over several Los Angeles neighborhoods.[112] By the end of November 1948, the show's Hooper ratings had moved up to 12.8; by the end of December, they were at 16.1; and by March 1949, 19.3, making Louella's program the ninth most popular radio show in the country.[113] While some commentators speculated that the show's success was the result of the more expensive guest stars, *Daily Variety* attributed the high ratings to the tape editing, which eliminated the gaffes and diction problems that had marred earlier broadcasts.[114]

Nonetheless, Louella's radio voice was still the butt of jokes, so lampooned in Hollywood that it had become a regular feature in a local stand-up comedy routine. Arthur Blake, a twenty-nine-year-old mimic, did an unflattering satire of Louella as part of his regular act at local nightclubs, and while Louella was in Europe during the summer of 1948, he had agreed to do the number on Eddie Cantor's radio show. Shortly before the broadcast deadline, however, he was canceled out of the program. Louella's agent, Wynn Roccamora, and several Hearst attorneys had apparently pressured Cantor to cancel Blake, though Cantor later said that he had made the decision out of respect for Louella, who was overseas and would not be able to defend herself. There were rumors around town, however, that it was Louella herself who had pressured Cantor, threatening both Cantor and NBC with a lawsuit if Blake appeared.[115]

The winter of 1948–49 was marked by celebration, illness, and, as ever, the ongoing struggle for news. Harry returned to Johns Hopkins for treatment in October 1948, came back to Hollywood in November, and was back in Johns Hopkins again by the end of the year. During his hospital stay, he had a steady stream of celebrity guests, including Frank Sinatra. Ever the gambling addict, while in the hospital Harry tried to sucker in doctors, nurses, interns, and even orderlies, offering odds as high as ten to one if they would bet with him on the 1948 presidential election. When he was informed that the hospital staff was prohibited from betting with patients, he then called Hollywood and tried to coax bets out of Darryl Zanuck, Joe Schenck, and his closest friend, MGM publicist Harry Brand. When this failed, Harry, infuriated, demanded his clothes, saying that he wanted to go find a bookie. The nurses refused to give him his clothes, and he became even more outraged. How was he to lay money with bookmakers if he didn't have any pockets to carry the money in? he asked. Not surprisingly, his attempts were thwarted, and he lay in bed while Harry Truman won the election.[116]

That December, Louella reported Louis B. Mayer's marriage to Lorena Danker, widow of the wealthy advertising executive Danny Danker. It was one of the biggest stories in Hollywood that winter, made particularly sweet for Louella by the fact that Hopper had published a report claiming that the couple would not marry.[117] Angry that Mayer had given Louella the exclusive, the *Los Angeles Times, Mirror,* and *Los Angeles Daily News* subsequently refused all MGM publicity.[118] Shortly after the Mayer exclusive, Louella was ill with a cold for two weeks, but she recovered in time to greet Harry, who returned from Johns Hopkins in January 1949. That month, the couple celebrated their nineteenth wedding anniversary at a party thrown by Rosalind Russell and Frederick Brisson at the Cocoanut Grove; two months later Louella held the five hundredth business luncheon with her staff at the Brown Derby, where she and her staff celebrated her record readership—the column appeared in 950 papers worldwide—and rehashed her most famous exclusives.[119] Little did they know that the biggest scoop was yet to come.

FIFTEEN

Scandal

IN 1949 RITA HAYWORTH AND INGRID BERGMAN were two of the nation's most beloved screen stars. Hayworth was known primarily for her sex appeal on the screen, and Bergman played a nun. Though their film personae could not have been more different, they were flip sides of the same coin, both products of the sexual schizophrenia of postwar America. The war had encouraged a kind of sexual liberalism. Separated for the duration, many couples had affairs, and across the nation there was greater tolerance for premarital sexual experimentation; but peace ushered in conservatism, as couples married, settled in the suburbs, and began the baby boom. From this sprang a paradox: even while media images grew increasingly sexual and the public discussion of matters erotic became less taboo, postwar Americans were taught to fear and condemn the unchecked female libido. Women's workforce participation during the war, claimed one textbook, had led to a "greater degree of sexual laxity" and the "decay of established moralities was the inevitable result."[1] The containment of female sexuality in the marital bedroom became a middle-class obsession during the 1950s, just as the containment of communism preoccupied the makers of foreign policy. Louella's reporting on Bergman and Hayworth in 1949–50 not only reinforced the dominant sexual ethic but also led to an odd reversal of fortune that neither woman would have expected. To many Americans, the nun became a harlot and the sex goddess, a storybook princess.

In 1949, Rita Hayworth was to millions of Americans the quintessential bombshell. She had played the starring role in that year's film noir, *Gilda,* with an unforgettably lusty bravado, popping eyeballs throughout the country with her fiery red hair, skin-tight dress, long black gloves, and a smoldering torch song called "Put the Blame on Mame." In person, Hayworth was friendly and obsequious, which allowed Louella to forgive the fact that for two years she had been married to Orson Welles. ("When Rita first separated from Orson Welles I lunched with her. She was very frank and said she couldn't live up to his giant intellect. You get fed up listening to how great a person he is and you get weary of so much egotism," she wrote in a 1947 *Photoplay* article.)[2] Louella also pitied Hayworth, who, like Louella, struggled with insecurity and depression despite her overwhelming stardom.

They had known each other for years. Louella first saw Hayworth in the Mexican gambling resort Agua Caliente in 1935. Then known by her birth name, Marguerita Cansino, the teenaged Hayworth was dancing in a team with her father, Eduardo. "As dancers," Louella recalled, "they were superb. . . . I felt that they had great potential—as dancers." Marguerita, however, was overweight, and according to Louella, "dark—almost black haired . . . and painfully shy."[3] To her surprise the next day, Louella found that the producer Winfield Sheehan, who was also in Agua Caliente, had signed the young woman to a contract with the Fox studio. Marguerita was then taken to Hollywood and renamed Rita Hayworth.

Between 1935 and 1937 Hayworth made three films, to lukewarm reviews. When Sheehan was fired as production head at Fox, the lead for the film *Ramona* was given to Loretta Young instead of Hayworth, and according to Louella, "by all the logic of Hollywood, that should have been the end of Rita Hayworth's career."[4] Enter Edward Judson, a balding automobile salesman originally from Texas, who was twenty-two years Hayworth's senior. After falling in love with Hayworth, Judson became determined to make her into a star and proceeded to act as her agent. Soon afterward, they married. After refashioning Hayworth as a seductive redhead—in one of the most famous celebrity makeovers of the 1940s, her eyebrows were plucked, her hairline was raised through electrolysis, and she lost weight—Judson then "sold" his wife to Harry Cohn of Columbia, and in 1937 she signed a contract. Hayworth soon learned that there was a price to pay for her success: Judson ruled her life outside the studio. Before she got dressed each morning, he had to approve her clothes, and he similarly regulated her social and business engagements. It was during this period that Louella got to know Hayworth. Once, during an interview, Hayworth had confided to Louella that she felt "hollow inside. As if I were a puppet." She had realized that she did not love Judson and admitted to Louella that she wanted a divorce.[5]

It was not long after her divorce, in 1942, that Hayworth met Orson Welles. Charmed by Welles, she read books and went to art galleries in an attempt to impress the well-read and politically sophisticated actor-producer.

The two married and had a daughter, Rebecca, in 1944. But this relationship failed, too, and shortly after the birth of their child they filed for divorce. Hayworth then embarked on unsuccessful romances with Jimmy Stewart and Tony Martin. After making the film *Lady from Shanghai,* in which Welles was both director and costar, and then *Gilda,* which cemented her image as a bombshell, she went to Europe in the summer of 1948. It was an independent, rebellious decision that for Hayworth was an act of assertion.[6]

Louella saw Hayworth during her European trip in the summer of 1948, at a party in Cannes. According to Louella, she looked "lethargic and drooped." Shortly after her encounter with Hayworth, Louella had lunch with society columnist Elsa Maxwell, who told Louella that she was giving a big party and had asked Aly Khan to come. Heir to the throne of the Aga Khan, the spiritual leader of the Ismaili Muslims, he was at the time one of the richest men in the world. Believing that Aly Khan was "just the man to snap Rita out of whatever ails her," Maxwell also invited Hayworth to the party.[7] They fell in love, and when Hayworth returned to Hollywood in September 1948, Aly Khan followed. That month, she appeared on Louella's radio show but refused to talk about Aly Khan on the air. After declining to go back to work at the Columbia studio, claiming that they gave her only "unsuitable scripts," Hayworth went to Mexico and Aly Khan followed. In Mexico City she held a press conference denying that they were romantically involved, but everyone in Hollywood knew about the affair.

Throughout the country, Hayworth fans eagerly followed the romance, which was avidly chronicled by the press. In November 1948, Hayworth's divorce from Welles became final, and Hayworth returned to Europe to see Aly Khan. Then, from Cannes, Aly Khan announced that he was getting a divorce and that he would marry Hayworth when it was finalized. At last, in April 1949, she and Aly Khan announced their wedding plans for May of that year.

"One Spring morning in 1949, my phone rang and the international operator told me that I was being called from Cannes. A moment later Rita was on the phone with an invitation to the wedding," Louella recalled.[8] To avoid a press circus, Aly Khan and Hayworth had announced that the wedding would be off-limits to reporters, with the exception of Louella, the only journalist invited. Hayworth had called Louella during the first week of May, and by the end of the week Louella had made arrangements not only for the trip but also for four radio broadcasts she would conduct from Europe, including one with Hayworth.[9] On May 12, Louella left for Europe via New York, accompanied by her secretary, Dottie May. Dorothy Manners wrote Louella's column in her absence, and Harriet took over her radio show.

For years, Louella had been surrounded by Hollywood royalty, but this was one of her first real encounters with true society. In Cannes, Louella stopped at the shop of famed couturier Jacques Fath, who was making Hayworth's wedding dress, and bought an expensive polka-dot hat to wear at the ceremony. Then, accompanied by Bob Considine, a writer for the International News Service, she went to buy a wedding present, an embroidered handkerchief that was said to have belonged to Marie Antoinette. A few days before the wedding, Louella lunched with Hayworth and Aly Khan and went back to the Carleton Hotel, where she was staying, to write up the interview. She had assumed that the stories were exclusives, but the following day she received a wire from New York saying that her interviews had been pirated and "parts of them were appearing in other stories out of Cannes." Suspecting that there were spies in the hotel, Louella and Dottie May subsequently worked in a locked room, they telephoned rather than wired the stories to New York, and Louella kept all carbon papers used in typing the articles. None of the remaining stories were lifted.[10]

The wedding had been scheduled to take place at L'Horizon, a seaside home owned by Aly Khan. At the estate, Louella had telephones at her disposal and was sure that no other reporters would be hanging around the secluded home. But the mayor of Cannes, a self-professed communist, insisted that the wedding take place at the city hall, which meant that Louella would have to find a phone there over which to dictate the story. Realizing that the only phone in the building was in the mayor's office, Louella approached the mayor and in her broken French explained the situation. "He was the first admitted Communist I had ever talked with, but I found that he was not averse to capitalistic ideas," she remembered. After she bribed him, the mayor consented to let her use the phone, and Louella was able to wire her stories from the wedding.[11]

The reception, held at Aly Khan's home, posed further obstacles, since he had ordered that no one was to be allowed to use any of the telephones in the château. According to Louella, a guest solved the problem by scheming to tell Aly that she promised to get him and Hayworth to talk with Elsa Maxwell in London. When they were finished, Louella would ask to speak to Maxwell from another extension and, when she was through with Maxwell, would put through her own call. The plan worked, and Louella got the exclusive story, which appeared in over six hundred newspapers worldwide. "The Arabian

Nights wedding of Rita Hayworth and Prince Aly Khan glittered to its storybook climax tonight when the bridegroom knelt and publicly kissed the foot of his tired but beautiful bride from the sidewalks of New York," she wrote. Apparently, in an early version of the story, a line read "a smiling, handsome prince in *stripped* trousers," rather than *striped* trousers. The mistake was corrected in later editions.[12]

After the reception, Louella went to Paris, where she received an order from Hearst to write a series of biographical articles on Hayworth, to be titled "Cinderella Princess." Hearst wanted the series done immediately, so Louella hired two secretaries and worked all night to complete the first two articles. Over the next two days, Louella and the secretaries finished five more. The articles were so thorough that many in Hollywood thought she had written them before she left for Europe. But "Lolly wrote it solely from memory and a coupla interviews on the spot. Get it through your noodle—the gal's a mighty damned good reporter," commented the *Hollywood Reporter*.[13]

Louella had just finished the seventh article when a cable arrived from Hearst canceling the rest of the series. Apparently Aly Khan had punched and caned three Hearst photographers who had tried to take pictures of him and Hayworth as they left for their honeymoon. "Aly Khan, having got what he wanted by being amiable, now shows himself in his true colors. His true colors are the usual colors of a spoiled Oriental prince, and might be demonstrated someday to the American girl he married," Hearst wrote in an editorial titled "A Spoiled Prince."[14]

Louella's Hayworth story, which made headlines worldwide, put Louella's name in the international spotlight. Hopper had reported incorrectly before the wedding that "Louella Parsons will not get within a mile of the wedding" and that Helen Morgan, a former editor at *Life* magazine, would be the only newspaperwoman there. (Morgan, who had resigned from *Life* to serve as Hayworth's press agent, attended the wedding but did not report it.) Fans loved Louella's flowery depiction of the event as a classic "storybook" wedding, but her stories were lampooned by the press critic A. J. Liebling in a *New Yorker* article, "Right up Louella's Ali," in June 1949. In his typically fierce prose, Liebling mocked Louella's trite and childish descriptions—"Ali bounded down the steps of his luxurious chateau, wearing cowboy-style denims and a red plaid sports shirt. He looked like a young man in love," Louella had written in one dispatch from Cannes—and her naïve commentary on what she had described as an "Existentialist ball" that she attended in Cannes with Bob Considine. "We went to the Existentialist ball the night before the luncheon. It is fashionable to visit these crazy dances—that's the only word I can use to describe their wild outbreaks. They live today, without regard for religion. I thought at first I might be in the midst of a Communist uprising, but these youngsters are not interested in politics—only in having a good time. As I looked at their faces and their expressions, I thought to myself, religion is indeed needed today to put these unhappy babes in the wood back on the right track." Liebling had concluded, "It is in Miss Parsons' account of the ball that she shows her true depth, I think. She is no mere retailer of gossip but a social thinker."[15]

In theory, the Hayworth–Aly Khan affair had all the makings of a scandal. An American movie star pursuing international romance with a famed playboy prince—at a time when both Hayworth and Aly Khan were legally married, no less—had raised the ire of more than a few moviegoers who called their conduct immoral. Before the wedding, several religious groups and the General Federation of Women's Clubs had announced plans to boycott Hayworth's films. "Her traipsing around is an insult to American womanhood," argued one member of the federation.[16] Moreover, as it was later revealed when Hayworth's daughter, Princess Yasmin Aga Khan, was born in December 1949, Hayworth had been pregnant at the time of the wedding. However, Hayworth was not vilified by the press, her fans remained loyal, and, despite the initial protests, none of her films were banned from the screen. Because many audiences associated her with her screen persona as a sex goddess, the romance seemed in character, and Louella's publicity of the "storybook wedding" may have tempered accusations of impropriety. Hayworth, in other words, got off the hook, but things would not be so easy for Ingrid Bergman.

A Swedish film actress brought to America to make films with David Selznick in 1939, Bergman exuded purity, even saintliness. She refused to be glamorized, and as a result, Selznick promoted her as "fresh and pure," exuding "natural sweetness."[17] After appearing in *Casablanca* (1941), *For Whom the Bell Tolls* (1943), *Gaslight* (1944), and *The Bells of St. Mary's* (1944), in which she played a nun, Bergman did not renew her contract with Selznick and instead formed her own production company. She then appeared in the Maxwell Anderson play *Joan of Lorraine* and, later, in the 1948 film version. Fan magazines described Bergman as being in real life as humble and morally conservative as her heroines. Though she had played promiscuous women in *Notorious* (1946) and *Arch of Triumph* (1948), these roles were, as film scholar

James Damico has suggested, interpreted by fans as further manifestations of her "purity"—namely, her "pure" devotion to her art.[18]

Like the rest of the Hollywood press, Louella sang hosannas to Bergman, whom she described as natural and unaffected. In 1946, Louella had celebrated Bergman in a Sunday feature article in which she described the actress as an "amazing woman" who had matured tremendously from the "shy, frightened Swedish girl I interviewed when she arrived in this country five years ago."[19] "I've always been a fan and admirer of Ingrid Bergman. I admit it—since the day she first came to see me at Marsons Farm and picked her first orange. She's . . . such a fine person. I like the way she and [her husband] Dr. Peter Lindstrom have worked out their way of living. Each has his own work, yet each defers to the other's opinions and ideas, and each shares interest in the other's career. That's the way it should be. If we had more women like Ingrid Bergman we'd have fewer divorces in Hollywood, or in any other town," she wrote in February 1948.[20] Louella truly admired Bergman, whom she deemed "a credit to the industry." Her clean-cut image, Louella felt, was good publicity for Hollywood.

The esteem was not mutual. "I don't think there was a German equivalent to the power of Hedda Hopper or Louella Parsons," Bergman wrote in her autobiography. "They were absolutely an American fabrication. And nothing comparable in Sweden or Italy. I was very surprised at the power those women had. . . . Hopper was funnier because she was openly nasty and asked direct and nasty questions which made you just laugh," she recalled. "But Louella tried it the other way round; she would be very, very sweet and try to trick you. For instance, she said to me once, 'We have so much in common, you and I.' And I said, 'Oh really, what?' 'We're both married to a doctor,' she said. 'How do you keep your doctor?'"[21]

But Bergman's marriage to Lindstrom was unhappy, and not long after her arrival in Hollywood, she had a series of affairs. Thanks to the Selznick publicity office's skillful management, Bergman's indiscretions stayed out of the papers. By 1946, however, the marriage to Lindstrom was beginning to unravel, and there were rumors of divorce. In January 1947, to protect Bergman, Louella assured her readers that the marriage was stronger than ever; Bergman, her husband, and their daughter, Pia, had spent Christmas together, and "that should end some of the rumors that there's trouble between Ingrid and her husband," she wrote.[22] But Bergman had been having a serious affair with photographer Robert Capa, and in late 1947, Capa admitted to Lindstrom that he had been involved with Bergman. Lindstrom announced that he wanted a divorce, but when Bergman "put on a show and started to cry," he dropped the idea.[23]

In April 1948, after seeing Roberto Rossellini's neorealist film *Paisan*, Bergman wrote the director a letter of praise. "Dear Mr. Rossellini, I saw your films *Open City* and *Paisan* and enjoyed them very much. If you need a Swedish actress who speaks English very well, who has not forgotten her German, who is not very understandable in French, and who in Italian knows only *ti amo*, I am ready to come and make a film with you," she had written.[24] After Rossellini wrote back enthusiastically, Bergman and Rossellini met in Paris in the summer of 1948 and discussed making a film together. Then, early in 1949, Rossellini went to Hollywood to negotiate a deal with Bergman and Samuel Goldwyn, who had expressed interest in the project. When Goldwyn backed out, Bergman and Rossellini went to Howard Hughes, who had recently purchased the RKO studio and who agreed to back the film. The production was to be called *Stromboli* and would be filmed on the Italian island for which it was named.

During the negotiations, Rossellini, who was broke at the time, stayed at Bergman's home in Hollywood, and the two took several day trips to the coast, raising suspicion that they were becoming romantically involved. On February 26, 1949, Louella reported that "Rossellini has been living at the home of Ingrid Bergman and her husband, Dr. Peter Lindstrom. He makes no secret of his admiration for the Swedish actress whom he came all those miles to sign."[25] Rossellini then returned to Rome, and Bergman followed in March, causing further rumors that they were having an affair. On April 13, an item appeared in the "Cholly Knickerbocker" column in the *New York Journal American,* written by Igor Cassini, about a romance between Bergman and Rossellini. The next day, Louella backed Cassini's claim by commenting that "the rumor is true."[26] Shortly afterward, Joseph Breen, director of the Production Code Administration, fearing public outcry over Bergman's adulterous behavior, wrote to Bergman demanding that she deny the rumors that she and Rossellini were romantically involved. Bergman refused Breen's request. Meanwhile, in May 1949, Lindstrom went to Rome for a conference with Bergman, in which she expressed her desire for a divorce. But both Bergman and Lindstrom agreed that a divorce announcement would jeopardize not only *Stromboli* but also *Joan of Arc,* which was running in theaters at the time. Bergman then issued a vague statement saying, "I have met my husband here and have clarified our situation. I am returning to

Stromboli to continue work on the picture. On its conclusion I will leave Italy and meet my husband either in Sweden or the United States."[27]

Meanwhile, Louella tried to protect Bergman by announcing in her column that Bergman and Lindstrom did not plan to separate. On May 5, 1949, Louella reported an exclusive story that there was to be no divorce, a claim that was confirmed when Lindstrom made an official statement to the press after an all-day conference with Bergman and Rossellini. Yet Louella acknowledged that Bergman and Rossellini were romantically involved and warned Bergman of the consequences. "Don't you believe all those stories that Ingrid Bergman's infatuation for Roberto Rossellini is just publicity," she wrote on May 7. "Dr. Lindstrom would certainly not lend his name to all this scandal. I really and sincerely believe that Ingrid had no idea she was getting so involved. She really fell madly in love with the Italian director, and like all romantic Italians, he was everything Dr. Lindstrom was not. If all this had not hit the newspapers, Ingrid would probably have got Rossellini out of her system. Movie actresses know that when they choose to become actresses they are in the limelight, and this really should be a lesson to other Hollywood actresses who play with fire."[28] Louella also noted, "The feeling in Hollywood about Ingrid Bergman is one of sadness. The Swedish actress had won the respect and admiration of everyone in the film colony, and everyone regrets that she has been the center of such stormy and sensational publicity."[29]

Complicating the increasingly convoluted love triangle was Bergman's discovery in June 1949 that she was pregnant. When Hopper was in Europe that summer, she visited Bergman in Rome and asked whether the pregnancy rumors were true. "Oh my goodness, Hedda, do I look it?" Bergman asked innocently. Hopper then printed the denial in her column. In early August 1949, however, Bergman's pregnancy was announced in the Italian paper *Corriere della Sera;* the newspaper had apparently picked up the tip from one of Rossellini's friends.[30] In desperation, Bergman announced to the press that she would quit making films and that she would divorce Lindstrom.[31] But the fact that Hopper had denied the pregnancy story in her column, and that Louella refused to acknowledge the news, confirmed for most of the American public that the Italian story was untrue.

Nonetheless, public sentiment was quickly turning against Bergman. Following Bergman's retirement announcement, Louella received hundreds of letters from readers who found Bergman's conduct immoral and demanded that her films be banned. In response, she asked her readers, "How can you ban the pictures of someone who is retiring? . . . The time to talk about a ban is when and if she makes other pictures." Louella knew that Bergman's future was shaky, but out of sympathy for the actress, she assured a reporter from *Quick* magazine that "if Ingrid ever decides to continue with her career, she will be the success she has always been."[32]

In December 1949 Bergman's publicist, Joe Steele, learned from Bergman that she was indeed pregnant. Seeing nothing but the box office failure of *Stromboli* if the baby were to be born before the public release of the film, Steele figured that the movie would have to be released before March 1950, when the baby was due. Steele then went to see Howard Hughes, who was living in a bungalow at the Beverly Hills Hotel. He told Hughes the situation in confidence and convinced him to release *Stromboli* immediately, in as many as five hundred theaters. Steele left, then Hughes did something unexpected. That Sunday night, as Louella was about to go on the air with her radio show, she received a message from Hughes that he would meet her at the station after the show with important news. After the broadcast, Hughes told her that Bergman was pregnant. Louella was upset that Hughes had not given her the news before the show, but Hughes explained that he wanted to break the story in the papers, where he felt it would have greater exposure. Hughes believed that the publicity surrounding Bergman's adulterous pregnancy would increase the film's box office take. "There were few people whose word I would have taken on a story such as this. I realized that if I wrote the story and it turned out to be untrue, the repercussions could well destroy me. But I knew that my informant would never put me in such a position. I had every reason to trust him," Louella wrote in her 1961 memoirs.[33]

Columnist Sheilah Graham, who was writing for the *Hollywood Citizen Examiner,* later insisted that she had the scoop on the Bergman story. After a friend wrote Graham with the news from Rome, she called Joe Steele, who implied that the pregnancy news was true. Graham promised Steele that she would not reveal the news on her Hollywood gossip radio show that evening, "but the cat was out of the bag." Alarmed, Steele called Louella and gave her the story.[34] In her autobiography, *Hollywood Reporter* columnist Radie Harris also claimed to have heard the news first. Harris claimed that Hughes informed her of the pregnancy when she was in Rome, but that conscience prevented her from running the story. "It was a code of ethics I had decided for myself when I got my first newspaper job," she remembered. "I would rather sleep well than eat well, and the money and kudos I would collect from this headline story, hawked around the world and eventually wrapped around fish, wouldn't ease my conscience. I waited full of suspense to see who would break the story."[35]

It was Louella, who, on Monday, December 12, 1949, reported the biggest story of her career. "INGRID BERGMAN EXPECTING BABY" read the headline that appeared in over one thousand papers worldwide. "Ingrid Bergman expects a baby in three months," Louella stated. "She has been living in a secluded apartment in Rome, close to the Italian director, Roberto Rossellini, and has refused to see anyone except close friends. . . . Few women in history, or men either, have made the sacrifice the Swedish star has made for love. Mary Queen of Scots gave up her throne because of her love for the Earl of Bothwell. Lady Hamilton, beautiful English queen of society, gave up her position in the London social world to bear a child out of wedlock to Lord Nelson. . . . Great as all these sacrifices were, none of them was any greater than the one made by Ingrid Bergman, queen of motion pictures."[36]

It was the first time Louella had ever released any news that she knew would most likely be scandalous. Though during her career dozens if not hundreds of actors had gone in for abortions, had had out-of-wedlock pregnancies, and had struggled with infidelity and addiction, Louella, always concerned with the film industry's reputation, had never divulged any transgressions that might offend public morals. But in 1950 the situation, both concerning Louella's career and in Hollywood, was different.[37]

In the studio era, news of an illegitimate pregnancy would have destroyed both the star and her studio, which had millions invested in her career. But with the breakdown of the studio system—actors now worked on an individual, film-by-film basis, rather than on long-term studio contracts—a scandal would only hurt the star and possibly her director and producer, which meant, in this case, Bergman, Rossellini, and Hughes. And though the affair offended many, by 1950 the movies were well entrenched in American culture, meaning that the Bergman affair was unlikely to turn public opinion away from Hollywood or incite the wrath of censorship advocates, as it would have in the past.

Above all, it was careerism that led Louella to break the news. Not only did she face an ongoing threat from Hopper, but Louella feared, quite rightly, that the rise of television and declining film attendance would diminish her readership and popularity. During the studio era, Louella had worked closely with the studio publicity departments, which had provided her a steady stream of news. For studio-contracted stars, interviews with Louella were a virtual condition of employment. Now, with actors' careers handled by private agencies and press agents, actors had more control over their images and were less likely to kowtow to the columnists. Interviews in mass market magazines such as *Time* and *Life,* and appearances on national television broadcasts, brought greater exposure than Louella's column, and many stars no longer saw Louella's cooperation as essential to their success. Through the Bergman story, Louella reminded an increasingly recalcitrant generation of actors of her power over public opinion and her ability to shape and potentially destroy careers.

The morning of the story, Steele, furious, called Louella on the phone. Steele later reported that Louella told him, "I just feel terrible about it—just awful. But honey, you understand I couldn't do anything else. It's a big story, I just had to do it." At five that afternoon, Steele went to Louella's home to hide out from reporters who had been hounding him all day. When he again complained to Louella, she replied, "I had to, honey, I had to. I've felt awful about it ever since. Just awful. I couldn't sleep last night for thinking about it," she repeated.[38] She offered Steele a drink, then told him that the *Examiner* would pay him five thousand dollars for his own story about Bergman. Steele declined the offer, then went into Louella's guest bedroom to take a nap. At nine that evening he woke up, Louella fixed him some eggs, and he went home. Later, Louella was falsely accused by *Look* magazine of having kidnapped Steele and hidden him from other reporters.[39]

"The story created a sensation. The greatest ever, I believe, in relation to a story about a movie personality. And resulted in the greatest effort I have ever known by other newspapers and newspaper people to deny a story," Louella recalled.[40] The day after the announcement, the *Los Angeles Times* ran an article titled "Hollywood Sees Hoax in Reports of Bergman Baby," calling it "a lie, a cruel hoax, and a preposterous phony."[41] Even an article in the Hearst evening paper, the *Los Angeles Herald Express,* denied the pregnancy report. Hearst called Louella to check whether the news about Bergman was true, and when Louella assured him that it was, Hearst called the *Herald Express* editor and yelled, "How dare you deny a Louella Parsons story!" The denial was yanked in the next edition.[42] Hopper never commented on the Bergman pregnancy in her column, but years later admitted in her autobiography, "I spent the day of the announcement rubbing egg off my face because six months before I'd interviewed Bergman at the scene of the crime."[43]

Like many Americans at the time, Louella, a Catholic, viewed Bergman's act as a moral transgression, and her presentation of the pregnancy as shocking and rebellious reinforced dominant attitudes toward female sexuality.

Had Louella been more sympathetic toward Bergman, or had she been willing to fly in the face of public opinion, she might have turned the pregnancy story into a social critique—as a pretext to champion Bergman's independence or to question the sexual double standard. Though the story did not lead to a public reassessment of sexual mores, it did raise a moral issue that Louella had not expected—namely, Louella's own journalistic ethics. Immediately after the story, "storms of debate . . . raged" about "newspapers and their ethics in splashing this extremely private story into every gossip nook in the nation," noted Max Lerner of the *New York Post*.[44] Both in journalistic circles and among the general public, Louella was criticized for her encroachment on Bergman's private life. The *Los Angeles Times* claimed proudly that it "never has specialized in this type of news and unashamedly was scooped by Louella Parsons on Dec. 12 last, when she told of the impending event," and Louella received dozens of angry letters from Bergman's fans.[45] One woman notified Bergman that she had written to Louella and "told [her] a thing or two about her nasty tongue."[46] Like HUAC's witch-hunt, Louella's story heralded more ominous encroachments on personal privacy by the government and press in years to come.

In January 1950, after leaving Harry for a checkup at Johns Hopkins, Louella went to Manhattan for two weeks, then to Boca Raton, Florida, with Harry, and then back to New York, where Sherman Billingsley, owner of the famed Stork Club, honored her with a party with three hundred of the "top names in show business."[47] While in New York, Louella discussed with Anita Loos the possibility of Loos writing a script for *The Gay Illiterate,* to be made into a Broadway play starring Carol Channing.[48] Loos eventually completed the script, which was written in an exaggerated, almost breathless style that mimicked Louella's book. "There is something of cosmic necessity about the manner in which Louella pursues her story. She is a Kansas cyclone, a tidal wave. She would knock down the Empire State Building to land that scoop on the front pages. Immediately she has done so, the demons leave Louella and she settles back in satisfaction, once more to be her own feminine self again," Loos wrote in the introduction. For unknown reasons, the play was never produced.[49]

When Louella arrived in New York, Seymour Berkson, head of the International News Service, met her at the station and shouted to her, "It's a boy, Louella," referring to Bergman's baby. Berkson ordered all of the Hearst papers to print Louella's original story "and the denials of all the other papers side by side."[50]

It was after the baby's birth that the Bergman scandal really began. Throughout the country, church groups and local censors tried to ban *Stromboli,* and some even tried to ban Bergman from the screen. To them, Bergman's act was a powerful and unwelcome reminder of the will and libido that lurked behind the seemingly most chaste of appearances. The Memphis censor Lloyd Binford tried to ban all Bergman films from the city, claiming that "Miss Bergman's conduct is a disgrace, not only to her profession, but all American women." In Birmingham, the Protestant Ministers Association urged exhibitors to ban all movies in which Bergman or Rossellini were identified, while another ministers' group in Albuquerque instructed all residents to stay away from *Stromboli.*[51] On March 14, 1950, Senator Edwin Johnson of Colorado, a leader in the Swedish American community, denounced Bergman and Rossellini for more than an hour on the floor of the U.S. Senate, calling Bergman and Rossellini "free love cultists," "moral outlaws," and "a powerful influence for evil." He urged passage of a resolution barring Bergman forever from returning to the United States and presented to the Senate a bill that would have made it mandatory for all entertainment industry members to be licensed before being permitted to work. Johnson later attacked Rossellini, intimating that he was a Nazi collaborator, fascist, and drug addict, and proposed a resolution, with the director in mind, "expressing Senate disapproval of the exhibition in the United States of motion pictures produced or directed by Fascists, Nazis, or Communists."[52]

Ultimately Bergman was not banned from the country, but her American film career was essentially over. Soon after the baby's birth she divorced Lindstrom and married Rossellini. Taking up residence in Italy, she did not work in the U.S. film industry for more than seven years. In a 1953 interview with the *Los Angeles Mirror,* Louella assured reporter Herb Stinson that Bergman held no grudge against her. "Ingrid had no hard feelings about it, and since it was bound to come out, she was glad that I was the one who broke the story," she claimed.[53] In reality, Bergman hated Louella for the rest of her life. "Louella . . . said she cried over her typewriter when she had to write the news. I think they were tears of joy," Bergman recalled in her autobiography.[54]

While Bergman's career was devastated, Louella's revived. As a result of the publicity from the story, Louella experienced a sudden boost in popularity. A pocket paperback book she wrote in early 1950, on Clark Gable's recent marriage to Douglas Fairbanks's widow, Sylvia Ashley, sold four hundred thousand copies by the end of February 1950, and Dell Publishing expected sales to reach a million by late spring.[55] In December 1949, *Variety* reported

Hedda Hopper, a rival gossip columnist who wrote for the *Chicago Tribune–New York News* syndicate. Courtesy Photofest.

Lana Turner and Louella do a "Victory Broadcast" during World War II. Courtesy Photofest.

The comedy duo Abbott and Costello clowning around with Hollywood's most powerful columnist. Courtesy Photofest.

Gracie Allen and Louella at the Brown Derby in Hollywood. Courtesy Photofest.

In 1946 director Mervyn LeRoy celebrated Louella's radio work by giving her a cameo role in the film *Without Reservations*. Courtesy Photofest.

Louella and Harry Martin at the Stork Club in New York before their European trip in 1948. Courtesy Photofest.

Louella and Charlie Chaplin.
Courtesy Photofest.

Louella in her bedroom in Beverly Hills. Courtesy Photofest.

Rosalind Russell, Louella, and Jimmy McHugh. Courtesy Photofest.

Louella and Hedda Hopper in the mid-1950s. Courtesy Photofest.

Louella and Clark Gable. Courtesy Photofest.

Louella and Marilyn Monroe. Courtesy Photofest.

Louella with Jimmy Durante and Milton Berle on a book tour for *Tell It to Louella*. Courtesy Photofest.

that Louella, as a result of the Bergman story, was "gaining on Walter Winchell in the Hooper ratings": that month she had earned a 15.1 rating, compared to Winchell's 16.7.[56] Louella was reportedly more delighted with her new rating "than with any Christmas gift."[57] In March 1950, a poll of 272 prominent female journalists taken by *Pageant* magazine ranked Louella as "one of the country's most powerful and influential women." Others on the list included Eleanor Roosevelt, Irene Dunne, Clare Booth Luce, and Dorothy Thompson.[58]

The following month, she was named "Favorite Woman Commentator on radio" by *Radio TV Mirror* magazine and that fall was featured in a lengthy article in *Look* magazine.[59] The feature, by Isabella Taves, credited Louella with having written the first gossip column and lauded her for her "unremitting service" as "Hollywood's number one booster." "She does an expert Charleston at the Mocambo on Dixieland Jazz nights and leaves a good party reluctantly, no matter how late the hour. She has a work and social schedule which would wreck many women half her age," Taves wrote.[60] At the end of the year, Louella celebrated her sixth anniversary with Jergens and her twentieth anniversary on radio with a special broadcast featuring Jack Benny, Claudette Colbert, Bing Crosby, Marion Davies, Dick Powell, and Mary Pickford. She ended the show with a tribute to Hearst, who had made "it possible for me to be on the radio all these years." The *Hollywood Reporter* described the show as a "charmingly sentimental occasion."[61]

In late 1950 Harry spent a few weeks in Honolulu and, unbeknownst to Louella, was hospitalized briefly.[62] He recuperated quickly, in time to return to Beverly Hills to spend Christmas with her. But two weeks later, he was ill again, and he and Louella left for the Mayo Clinic in New York.[63] Louella returned to Hollywood in mid-January 1951, leaving Harry at the clinic, where he would stay for the next three months. Then in March 1951, Louella, suffering from exhaustion, checked herself into Cedars of Lebanon Hospital for a brief stay.[64]

During this time, Louella, overwhelmed by her responsibilities and by Harry's deteriorating health, started drinking. She had imbibed regularly in the past, typically at social events, but during the 1950s her alcohol consumption became heavy, and observers noticed that she often seemed drunk or hung over. Esther Williams recalled that in 1950, shortly after Williams's baby was born, Louella came to her house to do an interview. Williams had set up the baby in "an old-fashioned colonial cradle," which she decided "would be picturesque and make good copy." When Williams brewed a pot of tea for Louella, Louella complained. She wanted a drink, and when Williams gave her one, she "drank like a fish."[65] Actress Jayne Meadows remembered going to Louella's house for an interview in the early 1950s and meeting Montgomery Clift, who was also there for an interview. Clift had kidded Louella about drinking during the interview, saying, "You aren't going to remember any of this in the morning. Why don't you write it down?" Despite her inebriation, according to Meadows, Louella seemed to remember everything. Louella "was a crazy nut, fisting down the sherry. And, drunk as she was, she always knew when something was going on. . . . She had a mind like a steel trap," recalled another actor.[66]

In June 1951, the Warner Brothers studio paid Louella five thousand dollars to do a cameo role in *Starlift*. The film was about an air force pilot serving in Korea who falls in love with a movie actress; the story is subsequently picked up by Louella, who played herself in the film.[67] In real life, Louella had been volunteering to visit Korean War casualties returning to Travis Air Force Base in Northern California. According to Shirley Temple, who went on an overnight trip to the base with Louella, Louella was picked up by a stretch limo "preceded by two suitcases and a hatbox." Louella entered the car clutching a rosary, a Saint Christopher medal, and a full-length black mink coat. Temple and Louella then boarded a two-engined C-47 airplane from World War II. "At last, as we roared off the runway, Louella clasped her religious medals with one hand and her safety belt with the other. What a headline it would be, she shouted. Hearst motion picture editor and former child star die in each other's arms."[68]

During the filming of *Starlift*, Louella learned that Harry, who had since returned to Los Angeles from the Mayo Clinic, was in Cedars of Lebanon Hospital in a coma, and she rushed back to Beverly Hills. Shortly afterward, at 10:30 A.M. on June 24, 1951, Harry died of leukemia at the age of sixty-one.[69] Lawyer Jake Ehrlich, Harry's close friend, recalled that in his last days Harry would call him on the phone and cry like a baby; he was terrified of dying. "But so that Louella wouldn't see it, she'd come in the room and he'd declare war. He couldn't let her see him frightened," Ehrlich recalled.[70]

The Hollywood community grieved with Louella and sent condolences by the thousands. Louella received over two thousand telegrams of sympathy, including a personal message from FBI director J. Edgar Hoover.[71] ("My husband admired you greatly and was also a staunch supporter of the ideals for which you stand," Louella wrote back. "I am deeply touched that a man as busy as you are took time to write me.")[72] The *Hollywood Reporter* remembered Harry as "genial, open hearted, and generous to a fault," while the *Examiner* described him as "a hale, vigorous man with a hearty humor." "Doc Martin enjoyed the friendship of thousands of persons in and out of the film industry who knew him as a kindly, generous man and physician with a ready quip on his lips and where necessary an encouraging word," the *Examiner* wrote.[73] Over five hundred attended the funeral at the Church of the Good Shepherd. The eulogy was delivered by Father English, who had been one of Harry's close friends. "Without question the distinguishing characteristic in the life of Dr. Martin has been his devotion—devotion to his God and country, devotion to his wife, devotion to his mother and father and devotion to his friends," said English. "The passing of this good man with his grand sense of humor, his kindly greeting, his good nature, his genuine friendship has left a void as few others have done."[74] He was buried at the Holy Cross Cemetery in Culver City; pallbearers included Hollywood executives Louis B. Mayer, Darryl Zanuck, Harry Brand, Howard Strickling, and Edward Mannix. Attending Louella were Harriet, the composer Irving Berlin, and Bebe Daniels, who flew in from London. Harry had left his estate, valued "in excess of $10,000," entirely to Louella, with the exception of five thousand dollars to his brother, Carl David Martin, five hundred dollars to Lillian Nelson, his secretary, and "any jewelry I possess" to MGM publicists Howard Strickling and Harry Brand.[75]

Louella was devastated beyond belief, so distraught that she seriously considered giving up the column. After the funeral she announced that she was going on an "indefinite leave of absence" from the *Examiner,* and she and Bebe Daniels went to Joe Schenck's cottage at Lake Arrowhead, where Daniels spent an entire weekend trying to talk her out of quitting.[76] Louella and Daniels then went back to Hollywood to visit Hearst, who had been living with Davies in her Beverly Hills home since 1947. She had seen him earlier that year at a small party on New Year's Eve hosted by Davies with Anita Loos and Davies's nephew Charlie Lederer. Hearst, who was suffering from pneumonia, had shrunk to 125 pounds and was frail and feeble. Not wanting to upset Hearst, Louella said nothing about Harry's death. Hearst then said, "Tell Dr. Martin I am expecting him to be toastmaster at my next party." "I had to fight to keep from breaking down and crying," Louella recalled. To lighten the mood, Daniels reminded Hearst of a time at San Simeon when Louella had put on her riding breeches backward. "Louella was always one to do things differently," Hearst smiled. "Nobody knew whether she was coming or going," Davies quipped.[77]

Two weeks later, unexpectedly, Louella was back at work. On July 14, 1951, Dorothy Manners announced, "On Monday you will find your girl and mine, Louella Parsons, back on the column giving you the news as only Hollywood's greatest reporter can do it. From the thousands of letters which have come in asking about her, I know how happy you will be to have her back. There's nobody like her, God bless her." But grief soon got the better of Louella, and ten days later, she announced that she planned to take a "no destination" vacation.[78] She spent her birthday, on August 6, "incognito" at the St. Francis Hotel in San Francisco, then went to Lake Tahoe for a few days.[79]

Then on August 14, 1951, Hearst died at the age of eighty-eight in Beverly Hills. During Hearst's last hours, Davies was so distraught that she was put under a sedative by a physician and was still asleep when a Beverly Hills undertaker took the body to prepare it for burial in San Francisco. Louella sent a telegram to Daniels, who was in New York on her way back to London, saying, "Our dear W. R. left us in the night," and then drove quickly from Tahoe to San Francisco to attend the funeral. In San Francisco, Louella and Adela Rogers St. Johns met in the lobby of the Fairmount Hotel, then went upstairs to cry.[80] Per the wishes of Hearst's family, Davies was not invited to the funeral, held at Grace Cathedral on Nob Hill in San Francisco. Over fifteen hundred people attended, and hundreds gathered on the streets outside.[81] At the conclusion of the half-hour-long service, the bronze coffin, draped in a cloth of purple and gold, was covered with a blanket of red roses and carried to the Cypress Lawn Cemetery in Colma, a San Francisco suburb, to be buried alongside Hearst's parents. At the funeral, Louella and St. Johns sat with the Hearst family in the front pew.[82]

After the funeral Davies released the news of the secret trust agreement that Hearst had signed in November 1950, giving her control of the Hearst empire.[83] When Millicent, Hearst's wife, heard of the agreement, she pledged to fight it on the grounds of California's community property law, which theoretically made half of Hearst's holdings hers. Rather than fight and thus jeopardize the earnings she had previously acquired from Hearst, in October 1951 Davies relinquished her rights "as voting trustee for the stock of the Hearst Corporation." The following day, October 31, Davies eloped with Horace Brown, a merchant marine captain, and less than two years later they divorced. With Hearst no longer in the picture, the friendship between Davies and Louella weakened. In an indication of their deteriorating relationship, Davies gave the news of her divorce to Hopper.[84]

Hearst's death led to immediate changes in his newspapers' editorial policy. His son Bill, who assumed the chairmanship of the corporation, attempted to disperse power within the organization by doing away with the official "Hearst policy" and encouraging local editors to "play the story for what it's worth." Bill Hearst was a devoted admirer of the anticommunist Senator Joseph McCarthy, with whom he had a close working relationship. However, the majority of the executives on the Hearst papers were even stauncher anticommunists. They pushed all the Hearst writers to launch a full-blown attack on the Reds; William Randolph Hearst, by contrast, had urged political attacks only by political columnists. Hearst entertainment writers were enlisted in the cause, and by 1952 even society columnist Igor "Cholly Knickerbocker" Cassini was attacking New York's "rich parlor pinks, traitors to their class."[85]

In spring 1951, HUAC, now chaired by Georgia Senator John Wood, returned to Hollywood to resume its investigations. Since 1947, the Soviets' explosion of an atomic bomb, the fall of China to the communists, the arrest of Julius and Ethel Rosenberg on charges of atomic espionage, and Joseph McCarthy's rise to power had increased the domestic anticommunist hysteria, and public support for HUAC was high. Surprisingly, Louella made only a few mentions of the investigation in her column, compared to her more aggressive treatment of the 1947 hearings. Her reporting on HUAC in 1947—in particular, her attacks on the CFA—had been criticized by many in Hollywood. Given her increasingly precarious status in the industry, she may have been hesitant to invoke further wrath from her colleagues. She may have also been wary of broadcasting the industry's alleged ties to communist organizations, given the ongoing losses at the box office. Nonetheless, she made clear to her readers her hard-line anticommunist stance, and for this she won the praise of FBI director Hoover, who in the late 1950s named her a "Special Correspondent."[86]

In March 1951, eight screenwriters, actors, and directors with former communist affiliations received subpoenas to appear before the committee. The first to testify was Larry Parks, a young actor who had earned acclaim for his portrayal of the title role in the 1946 film, *The Jolson Story*. Parks admitted to the committee that he had been a member of the Communist Party in the early 1940s but said that he had left it in 1945 because of "lack of interest." He initially refused to name fellow party members, but when he was told that this decision was "in contempt of the Committee" and would lead him to jail, he broke down and named names. Parks's contract with Columbia was subsequently canceled. During the next several weeks, dozens of subpoenaed witnesses took the stand, where they either became informers, denied participation in communist activities, or attempted to use their acting skills to get out of the accusations. Lucille Ball, adopting her scatterbrained Lucy Ricardo persona from her television show *I Love Lucy*, swore that she was never a member of the party but had registered as a communist voter in 1936 to please her socialist grandfather. After denying guilt, John Garfield praised the committee for its work and tried to prove his patriotism by lashing out against the Communist Party. Some witnesses invoked the Fifth Amendment, while others refused to accept their subpoenas and went underground. The thirty-one prominent Hollywood artists who testified cited an average of twenty-nine names apiece, which, excluding duplications, came out to over two hundred Hollywood communists.[87]

One of Louella's major contributions to HUAC's 1951 mission was an April 22 radio show in which she promoted the anticommunist film *I Was a Communist for the FBI*. "What possessed a young man like Larry Parks to make him become a communist. . . . Why did the Communists try to influence Hollywood's thinking. I'm about to bring you the answers to these questions, through what I regard as about the most timely and dramatic combination I've ever had on my show," she announced. Appearing on the show was Frank Lovejoy, who played the lead role in the film, and Matt Cvetic, the FBI agent who in real life had infiltrated the party between 1943 and 1950. Referring to the HUAC investigations, Louella asked, "Mr. Cvetic, what about the argument that these trials only drive the Reds further underground?" "Don't fall for that one, Miss Parsons," he replied. "The Reds try to put that idea across to discourage these trials. But the truth is, the commies always work underground, and anything that brings them out into the open hurts them. That's why Hollywood must support Larry Parks . . . to encourage more people to speak out." The program concluded with Lovejoy's recitation of a speech from the film: "The political activity of the communist party in this country is actually a vast spy system founded here by the Soviet, and composed of American traitors whose only purpose is to deliver the people of the United States into the hands of Russia as a colony of slaves. The idea of communism as common ownership and control by the people has never been practiced in Russia and never will be. Their state capitalism is a fascist horror far worse than the one Hitler intended for the world."[88]

Louella later reported proudly in her column that director Edward Dmytryk, a member of the Hollywood Ten who eventually became an informer and named names for HUAC, cited the Cvetic interview on Louella's radio show when asked by Congressman Donald Jackson for his opinion of the need for legislation to abolish the Communist Party. Dmytryk quoted from Cvetic's comment about the need to "legislate the party out of existence."[89]

Los Angeles FBI agents forwarded to Hoover Louella's radio script, and Hoover was also apprised of Louella's repeated false claims that she used the FBI as a news source. On November 20, 1950, Agent R. B. Hood reported that Louella had stated on her radio program, "The FBI is fully aware of the pro-Communist picture called *Speak Your Peace* which opposes US intervention in North Korea. The picture has been quietly shown around Hollywood for a week under the auspices of the National Council of the Arts, Sciences, and Professions. This group may be interested to know that two or three FBI men attended every showing and took the names of those present just for future reference, if you know what I mean." According to Hood, "This statement of Louella Parsons is obviously completely untrue[,] and Agents have not been attending any showings and have not been taking the names of those attending such showings."[90] In September 1951, Louella reported in her column that Hood was being transferred to Washington, D.C., to work as an assistant for Hoover; Hood then reported to the director that he had "no contact with Louella Parsons in the recent past . . . and ha[d] no idea where she obtained her inaccurate information."[91]

Louella had also come to the FBI's attention in 1949 when she reported on the Actors' Lab, a leftist, pro-labor theater group in Hollywood that was under investigation by the California State Fact-Finding Committee on Un-American Activities, known as the "little Dies committee," or the Tenney Committee, after its chairman, Jack Tenney. "The FBI is keeping a very close watch on a certain little theatre group in Hollywood. It is so infested with Communists that several of the players have resigned because they do not want to be a part of a group suspected of Red activities. The membership includes some very well known names," Louella had written in her column.[92] In public hearings in 1948, Tenney described the organization as a communist front affiliated with several of the Hollywood Ten, and in the fall the *Los Angeles Examiner* claimed that evidence "proved" that the Actors' Lab was a communist front organization. Jim Henaghan of the *Hollywood Reporter* and Hopper similarly printed innuendoes in their columns that supported the Tenney Committee's accusations. Members of the group were subsequently blacklisted, and former supporters stopped attending its productions and enrolling in its acting classes. The Lab essentially shut down as a theater company in 1950.[93]

Hopper, however, with her vitriolic anticommunist tirades, did the most political damage in Hollywood. In a famous column on July 19, 1948, she had attacked MGM producer Dore Schary, who during the 1947 hearings had gone on record opposing a blacklist. At the time an executive at RKO, Schary had testified before HUAC that, since a California law explicitly prevented the denial of employment based on political affiliation, blacklisting was illegal. He stated that he opposed the firing of two former Communist Party members, Edward Dmytryk and the screenwriter Adrian Scott. "It will be ironically amusing to watch some of the scenes behind the scenes now that Dore Schary is the big noise at Metro Goldwyn Moscow. He testified on the opposite side of the fence in Washington from Robert Taylor, James K. McGuinness and L. B. Mayer, Sam Wood, George Murphy, and other men with whom he will work," crowed Hopper. She opposed Schary, she explained, because "he expressed pinko sympathies for years in Hollywood [and] stated on the stand in Washington that he would never fire Edward Dmytryk and Adrian Scott until it was proven that their work was subversive. . . . Americans don't admire a man like that."[94] In response, Schary banned Hopper from the MGM lot.

Hopper's digs at Schary seemed anemic, however, compared to her attack in 1951 on Larry Parks. When HUAC had pressed Parks for information about Hollywood subversives, Parks had replied, "I ask you again, counsel, to reconsider forcing me to name names. . . . Don't present me with the choice of either being in contempt of this Committee and going to jail or forcing me to really crawl through the mud to be an informer."[95] At a meeting of the Motion Picture Alliance for the Preservation of American Ideals, at the American Legion Hall on March 22, 1951, Hopper attacked those in Hollywood who were sympathetic to Parks, including the alliance's president, John Wayne.

In a speech in which he was to reiterate the group's stance on HUAC—"the MPA regrets anything that will bring discredit to the industry . . . but the welfare of our country comes first and any enemies of our country must be brought into the open," read its official position—Wayne praised Parks for his "courage to answer the questions and declare himself."[96] "The American public is pretty quick to forgive a person who is willing to admit a mistake," Wayne had said.[97] Hopper lashed back: "I suggest before we let the traditional theatrical charity govern our reason that we consider whether the mud of an informer is worse than the mud of Korea mixed with 55,000 boys whose luck ran out before they came to fame in Hollywood or anywhere else. Larry Parks says he felt he'd done nothing wrong. I feel sorry for him. And I'm wondering if the mothers and families of those who've died and the wounded who are still living will be happy to know their money at the box office has supported and may continue to support those who have been so late in the defense of our country?"[98] In smearing Parks's name, Hopper "permanently hurt" the actor, according to Hopper's legman Spec McClure. Parks remained on a Hollywood blacklist until he was finally pardoned in 1962 and given a role in the film *Freud*. He made only two more films before his death in 1975.[99]

Even more than in her career as a columnist, in her work as a political reactionary Hopper seemed to have found her true calling. By the early 1950s, J. Edgar Hoover, Republican Vice President Richard Nixon, and Joseph McCarthy were among her allies; she, too, was one of Hoover's "Special Correspondents," and she met regularly with the director to discuss her political concerns. In April 1952, on a trip to New York, she attempted to meet with Hoover to discuss what she characterized as an urgent matter "about our friend Walter Winchell." During the previous year, Winchell had been falsely accused of colluding with the management of the Stork Club, a New York nightclub, in its discrimination against the black singer Josephine Baker. The accusations led to a story in the tabloid *Exposé* and a damning series in the *New York Post*. Winchell then suffered a physical and mental breakdown and took five weeks off the air. Hopper believed that the "Winchell situation . . . was maneuvered by the Communists" and that "if they can destroy Winchell then they can destroy anyone." When Hopper visited the FBI headquarters in Washington in January 1953, Hoover's staff was instructed to give her a tour, as they had "had cordial contacts with her for some years."[100]

Hopper adored Hoover, whom she praised in personal letters for having "been such a fighter against communism for so long and [doing] such a marvelous job." ("If you had your way, I feel sure you'd name names, which is the only way we'll ever get rid of them. Some day they've got to stand up and be counted," she told him.)[101] She was also a fan—"one of your greatest boosters"—of Joseph McCarthy. "It's mighty tough what I've had to take in defending you," she wrote to the senator in 1953, when he had come under attack by President Eisenhower.[102] Hoover and McCarthy became the heroes of her column, which often contained less "celebrity gossip" than political diatribe. "We've had many pictures pointing up our racial problems, political corruption in government, the evil of wealth, men driven to crime because of the supposed pressure of our capitalistic system. These are but a few devices which the Commies could use to get inverse propaganda in our films," she told readers in May 1951.[103] The *Daily Worker* had labeled her and Cecil DeMille as "two of the most bigoted, sybaritic, ostentatious, and fraudulent reactionaries in all of filmdom."[104] She wore it as a badge of honor.

But her zealotry got the better of her when, in the spring of 1951, she told reporters from the *Hollywood Citizen News* that HUAC had "whitewashed" certain prominent industry figures who were communist sympathizers and had allowed them to deny guilt under oath. "Hedda Hopper has seen some people go before the committee and deny any connections or sympathies with communist-front activities though she knows from the battles she has been through that those very persons have aided the fronts in every possible way," the *Citizen News* wrote.[105] According to *Variety,* she was subpoenaed by HUAC; in her autobiography, Hopper claimed to have never received a subpoena and that "someone . . . planted the story on that unsuspecting publication."[106] Regardless, committee chairman Wood met privately with Hopper and asked her for names—to either "put up or shut up." Hopper then retracted her accusations, admitting that she "didn't know anything."[107]

For many in Hollywood, this was the last straw. In May 1951, when Hopper was serving as an emcee for the American National Theater and Academy's fourth annual celebration, she was heckled by the audience and drew "instrumental raspberries" in the form of "hoots and toots from the orchestra pit," according to *Variety. Variety* speculated that this was "presumably either because of general right-wing political sympathies . . . or her recent specific attack on the film colony in messages to the Un-American Activities Committee."[108] By 1952, she had become so bitter and vengeful that she was an embarrassment not only to her publishers but also to fellow red-baiters. The *New York Daily News,* which carried her column, was so irked by her political comments that it "warned her to stick to the job at hand and not try to settle international affairs." After she made a speech in Chicago before the Motion Picture Theater Owners of America that urged exhibitors not to run films by actors, producers, or writers with alleged subversive ties, the notoriously right-wing Hearst columnist George Sokolsky told *Variety,* "People with Miss Hopper's obsession are very dangerous people for us [anticommunists]. They hurt us all over the country by taking an almost bloodbath attitude. They give the cause of anticommunism a bad name."[109]

Throughout the 1950s, the communist witch-hunt dragged on, and Hopper continued her starring role. Several right-wing groups, including the Motion Picture Alliance and the American Business Consultants, which published *Red Channels,* a list of alleged Communist Party members in Hollywood, assisted the studio executives by creating a blacklist of those who had been suspected of involvement in communist front organizations and a "graylist" of activists who had been involved in liberal politics or causes. The three-million-member American Legion, which threatened to boycott films to which suspected communists had contributed, compiled the names of 298 alleged Hollywood subversives, which it passed along to the studio executives. In all, 212 were black- or graylisted. In her column, Hopper regularly published the names of suspected communists that she had received either from various Hollywood informants or from the Anti-Communism Voters' League, the Committee to Proclaim Liberty, and the Americanism Educational League.[110] Tips she felt too incendiary for her column she passed on to the American Legion for use in its magazine.[111]

Though Louella was concerned with what she now genuinely believed to be a looming political threat, she was content with more marginal involvement in the anticommunist battle. Her passion was reporting, not politics, and at the time, she had other, more pressing interests. She had her religion. She had her radio show, a possible television deal, and, as ever, the column. More than anything, she sought pleasure with a vengeance. In her seventies, she was determined to enjoy the last years of a life that seemed more precious and fragile each day.

SIXTEEN

The End of an Era

HEARST AND HARRY WERE GONE. So was the old Hollywood. In 1952, film admissions hit a record low of fifty-eight million a week, down nearly forty million since 1947. Over three thousand theaters had closed since 1950, the number of studio workers regularly employed had declined 15 percent since 1947, and the studios had drastically pared their lists of contract performers. Most of the former top names were freelancing, and a crop of brash newcomers—Montgomery Clift, Marlon Brando, and James Dean, among others—shattered Hollywood's image of genteel glamour with their tough swagger and edgier, more naturalistic acting style. To keep up with the competition from television, the studios introduced 3-D film, the widescreen exhibition formats Cinerama and Cinemascope, and even Smell-O-Vision, in which scents corresponding to screen images were wafted through the theater. Nothing worked. One pundit suggested that exhibitors show movies in the street, thereby driving people into the theaters. To the moguls, it wasn't funny. By 1955, film attendance had plummeted to forty-six million tickets a week, and over 65 percent of American families owned a television set.[1]

It was the end of an era for Hollywood and for Louella. Like many of the old-timers, she refused to accept the film industry's decline and persisted in a state of denial. In her column in September 1951, Louella attacked an article in *Life* magazine that claimed the movie industry was "doomed." It was "completely erroneous," Louella told her readers. "Never in our history have we had as fine a product as this year. Do you think for a moment that *Life* would dare attack the steel, the woolen, or the automobile business as it does motion pictures? Certainly not. Yet our studios put down the red carpet for this publication, which has always taken a derogatory attitude towards Hollywood. If the picture business doesn't take some stand on an article of this type, which seeks to destroy it, then they deserve the treatment they have received from *Time* and *Life* in the past."[2]

Though the studios initially had been reluctant to go into television production, by 1952, according to *Newsweek,* they had capitulated, apparently under the theory "If you can't beat 'em, swallow 'em."[3] Universal and Columbia were producing television programs, the Republic studio and independent producer David Selznick had sold their films to TV stations, and the major TV networks had opened up studios in Hollywood. In March 1951, ABC, which was beginning television production in Hollywood, approached Louella for a possible TV series, but the deal never materialized.[4] Later that fall she made a test film for a proposed half-hour television gossip show to be sponsored by Jergens-Woodbury. When Jergens passed on the show, Louella, upset, told them that she would not renew her radio contract with them.[5] On December 23, 1951, Louella did her last Jergens radio show, an episode with one of her favorite actors, Bing Crosby, who sang "Silver Bells."[6] But she was not off the air for long. In early March 1952, she signed a contract with Colgate for a Tuesday night radio gossip show to debut at 6 P.M. on April 1 on CBS. By October, the program aired on more than two hundred stations.[7]

In addition to her newspaper and radio work, she was still doing articles for Hearst's *Cosmopolitan* magazine and the fan magazine *Modern Screen.* In a 1951 piece in *Modern Screen,* Louella, still smoldering from *Citizen Kane* after nearly ten years, attacked Orson Welles. "Many years back, I had heard that Welles was making a picture about someone I love very much. He said (and I shall remember his words always), 'It couldn't be farther from the truth.' And from that day to this, I have never forgiven him. I can take darts directed at me. I have felt the sting of many of them. But I cannot bear to see anyone I love hurt," she wrote in a piece titled "The Truth about My Feuds."[8] Louella may have still been defending the Chief, but he was no longer around to defend her. She was upset to find many of her articles for Hearst's *Cosmopolitan* edited and rewritten. "It's a bit of a shock to pick up the magazine and find a rewrite," she told the editors in 1951. "That has never happened with any of my stuff on the . . . papers."[9]

Despite her age and worsening health, Louella kept up a rigorous schedule. Each morning she woke at eight and, after coffee and a walk with her cocker spaniels, Jimmy and Woodbury, worked for six hours before taking a nap. She rarely went down to the studios and instead installed a projector in her house for film screenings and conducted interviews at her well-stocked bar.[10] "You never know if Louella is interviewing the star, the press agent . . . or maybe her two cocker spaniels which are running about," recalled one publicist. "But somehow through all the gibble-gabble, she gets the core and comes up with the story."[11] The Maple Drive house was cluttered with crystal sconces, gold-leafed mirrors, and display cases filled with old silverware that Collins, Louella's butler for over twenty years, spent hours dusting. One visitor, commenting on Louella's penchant for collecting expensive antique knickknacks, claimed to have detected "the influence of Mr. Hearst." Louella had turned two upstairs bedrooms into offices equipped with five telephones, and her assistants, Dorothy Manners, Dottie May, and Neil Rau, came daily to work. She had a "perfume bar" installed in her bedroom to display the many bottles she received as gifts, and on top of her dresser she had prominently mounted two silver-framed pictures, of the Virgin Mary and Hearst.[12]

Always on the heavy side, Louella began dieting during the 1950s. As she commented in a 1956 newspaper interview, her weight had become her "big personal problem": "Fat people have less chance of living to be old than thin people. Well, I want to live to be old. Old as old can be." She worried that she was overeating for emotional reasons. "When my husband died my interests narrowed," she recalled, and "the fat piled on." She began crash dieting in the winter of 1951. She also enlisted the services of Terry Hunt, a former boxer who ran a fitness studio or "healthatorium" on La Cienega Boulevard in Beverly Hills and who had helped condition Rita Hayworth, Claudette Colbert, Ingrid Bergman, and Hedda Hopper, among more than 750 others.[13] But Louella's strenuous weight-loss efforts only exacerbated her health problems.[14] In February 1952 she had a serious bout of flu that developed into bronchial pneumonia. Then, in July, she was back in the hospital after having suffered a minor seizure.[15] Following her recuperation at San Simeon, where she spent time with Hearst's sons and a few visiting Hearst editors, she returned to Hollywood and, by mid-August, was out on the town with her new beau, Jimmy McHugh, dining and dancing on Sunset Strip.[16]

For nearly two decades, Jimmy McHugh had been one of the most successful and prolific composers in Hollywood. The son of a plumbing engineer, McHugh was born in 1894 in Boston and began his career in music as a rehearsal pianist at the Boston Opera House. After writing the popular World War I song "Hinky Dinky Parlez Vous," McHugh was hired as house composer for Harlem's Cotton Club, where he worked for nine years. At the Cotton Club he met lyricist Dorothy Fields, and together they wrote several pieces for Broadway productions, including "I Can't Give You Anything but Love" and "On the Sunny Side of the Street." When McHugh was wiped out by the Great Depression, George Gershwin gave him a piano, and McHugh then wrote the hit "I'm in the Mood for Love." After subsequently winning an offer from MGM to compose for films, McHugh went on to score more than fifty movies, working for practically every studio in Hollywood. Among McHugh's film compositions that became popular standards were "Dinner at Eight," "I'm in the Mood for Love," "I Feel a Song Coming On," and "Thank You for a Lovely Evening." For his wartime hit "Coming In on a Wing and a Prayer" and his work producing the 1945 war bond "Aquacade," which sold $28 million in war bonds in one night, President Truman awarded McHugh the Presidential Certificate of Merit.[17] McHugh, who had a son, had separated from his wife in 1949.

Louella and McHugh, who appeared on her radio show in December 1945, had been friends for years. McHugh had written the song "Louella, Louella, Louella" for her 1948 testimonial dinner. One of Harry's favorite songs—he sang it often at parties—was McHugh's "I Can't Give You Anything but Love." Louella and McHugh were not romantically involved before Harry's death, but by the summer of 1952 "Louella and Jimmy" had become an item. In July 1952, Judy Garland prodded Louella to "tell the truth. When are you and Jimmy McHugh getting married?"[18] Louella then became "all flustered and schoolgirlish." At parties, the *Hollywood Reporter* noted, "Jimmy tastes Louella's cocktails first to see that they're just right. It's LOVE!" The romance seemed so intense that Walter Winchell wrote in his column that they would wed. When Louella denied the rumor, it was crossed out of Winchell's column at the last minute.[19]

As just about everyone in Hollywood knew, the relationship was almost entirely utilitarian. Louella was lonely, and she wanted an escort. McHugh, who managed several young actors and singers, wanted publicity for his protégés and his own budding nightclub career. Mc Hugh took Louella out almost nightly and flattered her shamelessly. While a guest star on the Larry Finley radio show, he dedicated "I'm in the Mood for Love" to Louella. And he made his song "Louella, Louella" a staple of his Hollywood nightclub act.[20] When McHugh opened at Ciro's nightclub in Hollywood, Louella attended every night for several weeks, sometimes staying out until 4 or 5 A.M.[21] A fellow Catholic, McHugh gave Louella what became one of her most cherished possessions, an electrically wired statue of the Virgin Mary for her back lawn. Louella returned McHugh's favors by buying him dozens of expensive suits and, in 1953, a costly watch engraved "To Jimmy from Louella with Love."[22] Even more valuable to McHugh was her constant promotion of him in her column. In 1952, Louella mentioned him more than twenty times.[23]

Perhaps because of her age or because of McHugh's attentions, Louella seemed more relaxed in the 1950s and expressed fewer worries about her image and the feud with Hopper. Nonetheless, she continued to flex her muscles in Hollywood. When Louella arrived late to a 1951 *Photoplay* magazine awards dinner at the Beverly Hills Hotel and was given a poor seat, she became loud and demanding and was quickly moved to a better table.[24] Later that year, several Hollywood journalists witnessed Louella in action when they got together to stage a spoof of the Academy Awards called "The Mickey Awards." (The Mickeys were designed in the shape of a Mickey Finn martini glass and had a skull and crossbones painted on them.) When Y. Frank Freeman, head of Paramount, at the last minute pressured scheduled hosts George Jessel, Dean Martin, and Jerry Lewis not to emcee the show, the reporters called an emergency meeting. One of the columnists suggested getting in touch with Louella, who was one of the sponsors of the Mickeys. Louella then called Freeman and told him that if he did not allow Martin and Lewis to officiate the program, he would "never hear the end of it." Freeman quickly capitulated. To thank her, at the ceremony "a down-front chair for her was zealously guarded in the rush-hour throng by a couple of stalwart reporters," remembered *Los Angeles Daily News* columnist Ezra Goodman, who was at the event.[25] In April 1953, Louella was feted by four hundred members of the all-male theatrical organization the Masquers, which threw a party to celebrate her thirtieth anniversary with the Hearst Corporation. Jimmy McHugh sang "Louella, Louella, Louella," and Eddie Cantor described her as "an honest person" and "one who has endeared herself to millions." "You may question at times her literacy but not her integrity," Cantor said, and the crowd broke out into spontaneous applause.[26]

Though newspaper circulation increased nationally during the early 1950s, the Hearst papers were on the decline. Between 1951 and 1955, as a result of poor financial and editorial management, circulation dropped by 5 percent, and in 1954 alone Hearst's eleven newspapers lost $1.5 million in circulation revenue and $4 million in advertising accounts.[27] The losses, however, had little effect on the readership of Louella's column for the International News Service, which appeared daily in over twelve hundred papers throughout the world and had an estimated 40 million readers. In 1952, *Time,* which had, since Hearst's death, reversed its stance on Louella, referred to her in a full-length feature as "queen of the Hollywood gossip columnists." "Every producer, director, and actor reads her column in the Los Angeles *Examiner* every morning, and each knows that all the others are reading it. That makes . . . Louella a Very Important Person," *Time* wrote. *Newsweek* called her "the town's best reporter." Hopper, "Lolly's closest rival," it reported, had 32 million readers.[28]

In 1952 Hopper published *From under My Hat,* an autobiography that was serialized in the *Woman's Home Companion* and that went on to become a national best-seller. The book took several shots at Louella, who came off, predictably, as shrewish, possessive, and spiteful. "Louella and I have been offered a fistful of money to appear on radio and in pictures together. I always accept; she always declines," Hopper claimed. "Even when our mutual friend Charles Brackett wanted us to appear together in [the 1951 film] *Sunset Boulevard,* she refused. I appeared, and for months she didn't mention the picture or the name of its star in her column." Louella had, in fact, declined the role, and the parts were then rescripted as one role for Hopper. It was not because she was afraid to appear with Hopper but because she felt that the part, as a crooning, predatory press gossip, would tarnish her reputation. Louella had recently been parodied in the MGM film *Singin' in the Rain* as Dora Bailey, an addlepated silent-era columnist who swoons over the heartthrob Don Lockwood, played by Gene Kelly.[29]

By the early 1950s, Hopper and Louella had become cultural icons—symbols, albeit much criticized and lampooned, of the nation's uneasy romance with celebrity culture. In the immediate postwar period, a number of cultural critics had decried the ubiquity of "star news" and "star images" in popular culture and what they perceived, correctly, as a national fascination with media stardom that was metastasizing to incredible proportions. By 1950, Americans could choose from a pantheon of mass-mediated icons and see and read about them in a dizzying array of formats, including radio talk shows, television variety hours, newsreels, newspapers, and mass market magazines. No longer were movie stars the nation's premiere entertainment figures; they were joined by, and in some cases their popularity was surpassed by, radio personalities, television stars, and pop musicians. Social critics claimed that the fascination with entertainment celebrities masked deep feelings of malaise. The *New Republic* announced that millions of Americans, bored by the workaday world, stale marital relationships, and the unfulfilled promises of consumer culture, were attempting to satiate their spiritual yearnings and "hunger for heroes" through larger-than-life media figures. Through film and music icons, they found "escapism and substitution," wrote the *New Yorker,* but even the most fervent star crush could not provide adequate release for the legions vexed by "mass frustrated love." Readers enjoyed celebrity gossip, declared the New York psychiatrist Gregory Zilboorg, because they were emotionally immature, having "never reached a grown-up level." "Mechanical civilization keeps people busy, and when they stop working, there is a pseudo-literary pill they can take for relaxation," he told *Newsweek*. Movie magazines and gossip columns eased daily tensions but eventually became part of the "blacking out of the individual." According to Zilboorg, Louella and Hopper churned out a kind of literary Valium for a disenchanted nation that salved its emotional shortcomings through simulated intimacy with pop idols.[30]

By 1953, Hopper and Louella headed a pack of 411 Hollywood press correspondents.[31] With the exception of Washington, Hollywood was the most widely covered city in America. In third place behind Hopper and Louella was Sheilah Graham, whose column had more than twenty million readers. Graham also wrote a monthly article for *Photoplay* and edited special paperback books for Dell Publishing, such as *Sheilah Graham's Hollywood Yearbook* and *Sheilah Graham's Hollywood Romances*.[32] The three women competed with Erskine Johnson, a columnist for the Newspaper Enterprise Association with 786 daily newspapers; Aline Mosby of the United Press and Bob Thomas of the Associated Press; Harrison Carroll and Jimmy Starr, columnists for the Los Angeles *Herald Express;* and Sidney Skolsky, Florabel Muir, and Lowell Redelings, who worked for the *Hollywood Citizen News.* On television Ed Sullivan had hosted a popular CBS variety-talk show since 1948, and Wendy Barrie filled a prime-time gossip spot on ABC. ("Hedda Hopper and the other chatter girls on the West Coast would be aghast over the way Miss Barrie handles items of alleged Hollywood news," noted the *New York Times* in 1949. "With tongue away in cheek she spoofs the latest bulletins of who is going with whom and who is no longer going with whom, interpolating her own barbed remarks as she goes along. For that alone Wendy rates an Oscar of her own.")[33] At his peak in 1950, Jimmie Fidler was heard over 486 radio stations each week by forty million people, and his gossip column appeared in 360 papers.[34]

Though the *Hollywood Reporter*'s circulation was only between eight and nine thousand, the shrewd "Rambling Reporter" columnist Mike Connolly was generally acknowledged to be the most influential gossip in the film industry.[35] In contrast to Hopper, who accused the openly gay journalist of being a "drunken faggot," Louella was an ally to Connolly, a Catholic and Illinois native.[36] According to Connolly's biographer, Val Holley, Louella described Connolly as "my greatest newspaper rival but still one of my greatest friends" and often gave him stories that she could not use in her column. Since Jimmy McHugh and Connolly shared the same birthday, each year Louella, McHugh, and Connolly celebrated together. Connolly's principal rival was Army Archerd of *Daily Variety*, who became the paper's leading columnist in 1953.[37]

Louella and Sheilah Graham, who did a radio show sponsored by the makers of Rayve Crème Shampoo, became friendly after Louella's illness in 1946. In the hospital, Louella heard Graham's broadcasts for the first time, and later told her, "I like your radio show. It's very good." When Louella went to Europe in the summer of 1948 and needed substitutes for her own radio show, Graham told Louella that she was interested, and that an appearance on Louella's show might encourage Rayve Crème to put Graham's program on the air coast to coast. Realizing that this would make Graham a rival, Louella coldly refused her offer to appear on the show.[38]

But Louella always faked a cordial front. When Graham became Louella's neighbor on Maple Drive, Louella sent her a big basket of flowers. According to Graham, Louella began to like her "because meeting on a walk around the block, I would slip her a story I could not use." Louella was particularly impressed when Graham gave her a big story for her Sunday radio show that Hopper was using as the lead in her Monday column. "At the time, I was between radio shows and it was too late for me to use it myself. When you gave Louella a scoop, she was your friend for life," Graham recalled. But Louella snubbed Graham in 1950 by refusing to invite Graham's children to a kids' party she was holding at her home with actor Bill Boyd, who played the character Hopalong Cassidy in cowboy films. The party was a stunt to publicize Boyd's upcoming appearance on Louella's radio show. Even though Louella knew that Graham's two children were enamored of the actor, she feared that if she invited them, Graham would use the opportunity to interview Boyd for her column.

To get back at Louella, Graham called Boyd and asked him to stop by her home on the way to Louella's event. When he showed up, Graham called a photographer from the *Citizen News*. "My children were regarded very highly in their circle. And to hell with Louella," Graham recalled.[39]

The press competition, combined with the demise of the studios and the subsequent changes in star publicity, made news gathering more challenging for Louella, who found herself snubbed by stars who had once feared doing anything, from vacationing to divorcing, without calling her in advance. Consequently, Louella doted even more on those stars who remained loyal and compliant. One of the most cooperative was Marilyn Monroe, who was rewarded with a generous amount of space in the column. When Louella was in the hospital in October 1952, she reported that "there were more questions asked about Marilyn Monroe that any other star, male or female. Marilyn herself had been in the same hospital not long ago, and she made a great hit with all the nurses and doctors." Later that month, in a series of articles Louella did on the women of Hollywood, titled "Ten Most Exciting Women," she put Monroe at the top of the list.[40] "Marilyn is the most exciting movie personality of this generation. She possesses the star quality that has to be natural, that can't be manufactured," Louella wrote.[41]

In early 1953, when Monroe went to a party at the Beverly Hills Hotel wearing a form-fitting gold lamé gown, *Citizen News* columnist Florabel Muir reported the next day, "With one little twist of her derriere, Marilyn Monroe stole the show. . . . The assembled guests broke into wild applause, while two other screen stars, Joan Crawford and Lana Turner, got only casual attention. After Marilyn every other girl appeared dull by contrast." Offended, Crawford summoned the press and publicly denounced Monroe's "burlesque show," adding, "Kids don't like Marilyn . . . because they don't like to see sex exploited."[42] Appalled by Crawford's attack and believing that "Marilyn should have a chance to say her piece," Louella called Monroe and "asked her to let [Louella] tell the public her side of the story."[43] In the interview, to win sympathy for Monroe, Louella played up Monroe's innocent screen image and her well-known tragic childhood as an orphan. She quoted Monroe as saying, "The thing that hit me hardest about Miss Crawford's remarks . . . is that I've always admired her for being such a wonderful mother—for taking four children and giving them a fine home. Who better than I know what that means to homeless little ones?"[44]

Monroe thanked Louella by giving her exclusives and interviews for the rest of her career. Monroe's press agent recalled an incident when, at a press reception at the Beverly Hills Hotel, Hopper grabbed one of Monroe's arms, hoping to catch her for an interview, while Louella took hold of the other. Each was pulling in the opposite direction and neither was willing to let go. Eventually Monroe gave in to Louella because she "liked Louella better."[45] When Monroe and baseball star Joe DiMaggio got married in San Francisco in 1954, they gave Louella the story, which earned more space in the *Examiner* than Louella's 1933 scoop on the divorce of Mary Pickford and Douglas Fairbanks.[46]

Marilyn Monroe could do no wrong, and Marlon Brando, no right. A belligerent, tough-talking freethinker who came to Hollywood in 1950, Brando refused to pander to the columnists and he publicly scorned the celebrity lifestyle. Louella found this appalling. Following an interview in *Life* magazine in which he claimed that his wealth and fame meant little to him, Louella wrote that if Brando was as "squirrelly" as he appeared in the article, "I don't think I want to look at Brando on the screen again." In response, Brando wrote her a letter that read, "Please stop picking on me. You are becoming offensive, not only to me, but to other people." Louella wrote back, "What about you, Marlon?"[47] When Brando won the Academy Award for *On the Waterfront* in 1955, Louella went backstage and Brando rushed up to meet her. She expected an embrace. He shook her hand.[48]

When Brando, disgusted with the script, went AWOL from the set of the 1954 film *The Egyptian,* Louella chastised him in her column for days.[49] In her typical fashion, she continued to use her column to publicly attack and discipline those who defied the producers. When Mario Lanza was in the midst of a contract dispute with MGM, Louella snidely remarked that at the Del Mar racetrack, a horse named "Lucky Lanza" unseated his rider and threw him. "Is there any moral in that for Mario?" she asked.[50] When Donald O'Connor refused to do the last film in the *Francis* series, about a man and a talking mule, Louella told her readers in 1953, "Donald O'Connor is getting on the difficult side. Whether Donald thinks he is now above the mule-movies or not, the fact remains that they are money makers. I said it before and I repeat: Don is too talented and too hot at the moment to jeopardize his career by not keeping his studio commitments—as well as his appointments."[51] Judy Garland's inability to lose fifteen pounds as directed by MGM sparked bitter words. "This is the first time I have publicly spanked Judy. But I can't understand her attitude after all that has been done for her," Louella wrote.[52]

In 1954 she also turned on Rita Hayworth, who had since divorced Aly Khan and married singer Dick Haymes. When Hayworth invited Louella to her wedding to Haymes at the Sands Hotel in Las Vegas, Louella declined, saying, "I think I'd better not this time dear. You'll have better luck without me." Haymes, an Argentinian citizen living illegally in the United States, was in trouble with the Justice Department. For much of 1954 he and Hayworth, who was having contract disputes with the Columbia studio, hid out in a secluded bungalow near Lake Tahoe. "It's unfortunate that Rita Hayworth has shut herself away. I have always been very fond of Rita and I feel sorry for her now because she seems so mixed up," Louella wrote.[53] "I've had many, many letters—most of them saying she is throwing her career away. She listens only to Dick Haymes, who certainly did not manage his own affairs too wisely. . . . I have been very fond of her through the years, but I don't understand this new girl."[54]

Charlie Chaplin also came under attack, both by Louella and, far more viciously, by Hopper. Though Chaplin had never been a member of the Communist Party, he was widely criticized by conservatives for his advocacy of liberal causes and his unwillingness to adopt American citizenship. He never testified before HUAC, but in 1949 he had come to the committee's attention due to rumors that he would attend the Scientific and Cultural Conference for World Peace, an event sponsored by the National Council of the Arts, Sciences, and Professions, which the FBI had declared to be a communist front organization. "I can hardly believe that Charlie Chaplin has the nerve to plan another movie here right on the heels of admitting that he has become a member of the Communist-organized world peace congress," Louella had written at the time. "I think his conduct has reached a point where even his old friends who said, 'Oh Charlie isn't really a Communist—he's just misguided' can no longer continue to apologize for him. It is nothing short of insolence on his part to be talking about a new film in which he will play a clown who loses his burlesque queen sweetheart to his son. I can assure him that real Americans will not pay to see him on the screen—and add more dollars to the millions he has already collected in this country," she concluded.[55]

By 1950, however, thanks in large part to his own efforts, many of Chaplin's critics, including Louella, had modified or reversed their positions. Chaplin had tried to restore his public image by rereleasing his classic 1931 film *City Lights;* he also ordered his lawyers to halt a proposed showing of his film *The Circus* as a fund-raiser for the *Daily People's World,* a San Francisco leftist paper. Louella recognized Chaplin's efforts and, in January 1950, reported that when she was in New York she dined with Frances and Sam Goldwyn and Chaplin, "who was there with Oona." "Charles was more like himself than I've seen him since he and I came to a parting of the ways over his sympathy for the Russians. Now, I believe, he has that Leftist idea out of his system. I never thought he was serious about it anyway, although he did too much talking."[56] In July 1950, the *Hollywood Reporter* noted: "Looks as though LOP and Charlie Chaplin have kissed and made up. She went all the way across the room to give him a big handshake at Charlie Feldman's party the other night."[57] This was a little too much for Louella, who did not want to go on record as being Chaplin's friend. She wired back, "Just for the record I did not . . . walk across the room to speak to Charlie Chaplin at Charles Feldman's party. You were not there so how could you know? I wish you would check things with me before you use my name or better still kindly leave my name out of your column." The *Reporter* lashed back, "Dear Louella, were you in Italy when Ingrid had her baby?"[58]

Chaplin stayed out of Louella's column until the summer of 1952, when he went to Europe for a family vacation. As a British citizen, he applied to the Immigration and Naturalization Service for a reentry permit, which he received on July 16. After setting sail, he received news from the attorney general that his reentry permit had been revoked and that he would have to answer questions about his political views before he could reenter the country.[59] This was the culmination of a long campaign by Hedda Hopper, J. Edgar Hoover, and Vice President Richard Nixon, among others, to deport Chaplin. Since 1947, Hopper had been discussing the "Chaplin problem" with J. Edgar Hoover and had also mentioned it to Nixon. "I agree with you that the way the Chaplin case has been handled has been a disgrace for years. . . . You can be sure that I will keep my eye on the case," Nixon wrote to Hopper in May 1952.[60]

Hopper celebrated the deportation, claiming that there were "hundreds of people in Hollywood . . . who are dancing in the street for joy over Attorney General McGranery's statement that before Charlie Chaplin can return to the US he will have to pass the board of immigration." "I've known him for many years. I abhor what he stands for, while I admire his talents as an actor. I would like to say 'good riddance to bad company,'" she explained.[61] Louella took a different approach. Though she too criticized Chaplin, she tried to defuse the accusations that he was a communist and traitor. In the first article of a syndicated series on Chaplin in September 1952, she dismissed Chaplin's "arrogance and apparent indifference towards his adopted country" as an expression of his "innate stubbornness," rather than one of disloyalty. In his early days in America, Louella wrote, he "was charming, amusing, and gracious, and as far as I know had no part in any alleged subversive groups."[62] During World War I, when Louella accompanied Chaplin, Douglas Fairbanks, and Mary Pickford on a war bond tour, "the revolution in Russia was going on, and he never had expressed any sympathy for the overthrow of the Czarist regime."[63] Only in the last installment did she attack Chaplin for the Simonov incident and for allegedly pro-Soviet inscriptions on the back of pictures he had given to the children of the Soviet ambassador to the United

States.[64] Many of Hopper's fans, who praised her for the attack, criticized Louella's sympathy for Chaplin. "Please . . . ask [Louella Parsons] to keep her story out of the paper about Chaplin. No one cares anything about him and we are not interested in her story about the real CC. I am surprised at Louella. I always admire and love her but I don't understand how she can stand up for a guy like C," one woman wrote Hopper.[65]

While Hopper saw herself as Hollywood's self-appointed political guardian, Louella became its moral protector. She was disturbed by the edgier, more sexually explicit content of postwar films and used her column to crusade for what she described as cleaner and more "family oriented" fare. As she explained to her readers in a 1954 *Cosmopolitan* article, the divorcement of the production companies from the theaters had made it easier for the makers of risqué films to exhibit their material. All they had to do was "to go out into the open market" and lure "any theater manager who wanted to pay the price of it." The changed content was also the result of a 1952 Supreme Court decision that decided movies were covered by the First Amendment and extended to them the same protected status granted newspapers, magazines, and other organs of free speech.[66] In 1954, Louella attacked the controversial film *The Moon Is Blue,* which raised eyebrows throughout the country with its use of the words *virgin, seduce, mistress,* and *pregnant.* That same year, when she heard of the arrival of Simone Silva, an actress who had made headlines when she posed bare breasted with actor Robert Mitchum before a photographer on a topless beach in Cannes, Louella "went on her soapbox" in outrage. "My Sunday in Palm Springs was interrupted by a call saying that Simone Silva, the girl who posed with Bob Mitchum, was on her way to Hollywood. I'm not even going to mention the name of the independent producer who is bringing her here. How dare anyone bring this girl to Hollywood. Certainly there are plenty of other girls who do not need to strip from the waist up to get publicity. I want to be the first to . . . protest her coming here," she wrote that spring.[67]

She similarly criticized the 1955 film *The Man with the Golden Arm,* in which Frank Sinatra played a drug addict. The film received the endorsement of the Catholic Legion of Decency but failed to win approval from the Production Code Administration. "The opinions on *The Man with the Golden Arm* seem to be unanimous. On all sides there is a feeling that Otto Preminger overstepped his bounds of decency in making a picture that could very well bring down federal censorship. Unfortunately, a picture of this kind will make money."[68] She encouraged the producers to make more "religious" films, since "the condition of the world is frightening and people are turning more and more to prayer and spiritual help."[69] Love and religion, she believed, were the answer to political conflict. "I believe that love is the answer to almost all the problems the world faces. If everyone in the world were happily married, as I see it, there would be less hate and viciousness and misunderstanding. Happy loving people don't make wars."[70]

She paired her moral conservatism with staunch Republicanism. Scarred by HUAC, and with the liberals in retreat, much of Hollywood had gone Republican in the 1952 election, and Louella, along with the moguls, had contributed heavily to the Eisenhower campaign. In January 1953, after making a New Year's resolution "to take it a little easier (if I could only learn how)," Louella proceeded to break that resolution by traveling to Washington with Maggie Ettinger for Eisenhower's inauguration.[71] She had been invited by the wife of Colonel James Hunter Drum of Washington, D.C., to serve on her hostess committee for visiting entertainment figures at the inauguration, an invitation for which she said she felt "greatly honored."[72] "Out of my hotel window at exactly 9:25 I had a glimpse of Mamie and Ike, who drove down the ramp of the Statler Hotel on their way to the National Presbyterian Church. I thought as I watched these two fine Americans they had started their big day right—with prayer," she reported from Washington on January 20.[73] In Washington she attended a party given by Fred Gurley, president of the Santa Fe Railway, at the Mayflower Hotel, where she met Senator Joseph McCarthy, General Omar Bradley, and the Eisenhower brothers, Edgar, Arthur, Milton, and Earl. Later that week she and Maggie stopped by the FBI headquarters and met with J. Edgar Hoover.[74]

She contacted Hoover again that summer, when she forwarded him threatening letters she had been receiving from a "crackpot." "I'm not afraid for myself, but in view of the nuts running around indulging in wholesale shootings these days, I thought you ought to see them," she wrote to the director.[75] In early June, she had received a letter that read, "We arrive in Hollywood October 1st 1953 and we'll see you and Jimmy at Ciro's on Oct 3rd. I am going to sing, cook pork chops . . . and also dance. I write letters to John Wayne. He's my father to be. See you soon alive Louella." She also called Los Angeles agents and told them that John Wayne and Gary Cooper had received letters from the same source, and that "the author of the letters is probably a psychopathic individual who might have dangerous propensities." Along with the letters, she received three small packages and two letters, addressed to John Wayne and Donald O'Connor, marked "please forward."[76] FBI investigators tracked the letters to a drugstore owner in Brooklyn who had previously been confined to a mental institution, and who had written similar threatening letters to a "big league baseball player" four or five years earlier. In June 1953, U.S. Attorney Edward Skelly advised the Los Angeles office that "inasmuch as it appears that subject is suffering from a 'mental condition' . . . no action is warranted at the time." The "crackpot" never contacted Louella again.[77]

In August 1953, after going to the Del Mar racetrack for her birthday, Louella went to New York to secure a fifty-two-week deal with NBC for a half-hour television show to be sponsored by the makers of Toni home permanents and Viceroy cigarettes. The proposed program, *See Hollywood with Louella Parsons,* which would air at 10:30 on Sunday nights, would feature interviews, film clips, and "cinema chit chat." To avoid the "free talent" problems of the past, NBC had arranged with the Screen Actors' Guild to pay stars appearing on the program a minimum of one thousand dollars.[78] Though the show was originally scheduled to debut in the winter of 1953, for unknown reasons it was delayed until December 1954. While in New York, Louella guest-starred on the show *What's My Line* and appeared on the game show *Queen for a Day.*[79] After visiting Cardinal Spellman, she returned to Hollywood in early December and remodeled her house in preparation for a "Christmas blowout."[80]

Louella was now in her seventies and in poor health, but she was still one of Hollywood's top hostesses. Liz Smith, the future *New York Post* gossip columnist, who wrote for *Modern Screen* in the mid-1950s, remembered attending a Christmas party at Louella's. Louella, "charming and vague," sat proudly in a living room with "wall to wall gifts." "My loot!" she had laughed.[81] Charles Young, a cousin of Louella's from Freeport, went to Hollywood in 1954 with his wife and teenage daughter, Diane. At a party at Louella's home, they met Gregory Peck and Clark Gable, then had dinner at Chasen's, where Louella arranged for Diane to meet her idol, Eddie Fisher. "The stars all seemed to be Louella's friends," recalled Young's widow, Phyllis Young Muller. "She was like God."[82] When not partying in Hollywood, Louella went to Las Vegas, which was fast becoming the out-of-town hotspot for the Hollywood crowd. In 1954 McHugh launched a nightclub act at the Sands Hotel, and Louella visited him almost weekly. A cryptic note in her FBI file suggests that in Vegas she may have had run-ins with the Mafia: what appears to be a transcript of a taped conversation between two mob-connected figures described a couple of "Jewish fellas who were run out of Vegas" and another figure "we put . . . in Luella [sic] Parsons' suite."[83]

Louella devoted column space not only to McHugh but also to many of his protégés, including the young singer Eddie Fisher, who owed his stardom in large part to publicity in Louella's column. Mamie Van Doren, a young actress whose career McHugh was managing, was not so lucky. In the early 1950s, McHugh had arranged for Van Doren, who was relatively inexperienced as an actress, to attend Ben Bard's Theater, a Hollywood acting school. Then, inexplicably, McHugh announced that he was taking Van Doren out of the school. Apparently Louella was jealous of McHugh's attentions to the buxom blonde actress and had pressured Bard, telling him that if he didn't dismiss her from the school she would give him only bad press. Shortly afterward, Van Doren took a screen test at Paramount, which turned her down, claiming that she looked too much like Marilyn Monroe. She later found that Louella had pressured the studio to reject her.[84]

For her upcoming TV appearance, Louella went on a crash diet, against her doctor's orders. Down to 104 pounds from her usual 130 or 140, Louella was "too thin," Mike Connolly noted in the *Hollywood Reporter* in 1954. When diet guru Gayelord Hauser sent Louella a copy of his book *How to Reduce and Stay Reduced,* he wrote on the flyleaf, "To Louella, who doesn't need this."[85] In October 1954, weakness from dieting put her in Cedars of Lebanon Hospital. Her nurses unplugged the phone in her room and she was furious. After being fed a lasagna diet, she gained weight—which she lost again, and in December she was again back in the hospital. According to one rumor, it was from exhaustion; another suggested that she had suffered a heart attack.[86] (In 1956, when Louella's car was struck by a bus, she told reporters that she sought ten thousand dollars in damages because the accident "aggravated a heart condition" from which she suffered.)[87] She then called off the television show, citing exhaustion and illness.[88]

Louella's health troubles and her increasing fear of death led her to mend some fences. Though Louella was still telling reporters that Marion Davies was her "closest friend in Hollywood," she and Davies had not spoken since Hearst's death. Finally, in 1955, after her divorce from Horace Brown, Davies contacted Louella again, and Davies, "loaded with flowers," according to the *Hollywood Reporter,* came to Louella's for a visit.[89] That year, Louella gave a copy of *The Gay Illiterate* to Hopper, signed "To my favorite rival," and Hopper reciprocated by giving Louella her best hat. Hopper later gave Louella a copy of *From under My Hat* inscribed "To Louella Parsons, the Queen, from Lady in Waiting Hedda Hopper." At a party for Hopper, Louella toasted her as a "gallant lady."[90]

In the summer of 1955, Louella and Hopper accompanied a group of Hollywood actors on a trip to Istanbul sponsored by hotel magnate Conrad Hilton, to celebrate the opening of the Istanbul Hilton. Hopper had recently been the victim of an extortion threat—"Dear Miss I will come to kill you" read a message she had received in April—but the letter turned out to be not from an angry actor, as she had thought, but two young pranksters in Brooklyn.[91] Louella wrote her columns from Istanbul. "I am so fascinated by this great city, part modern, part ancient. Oddly enough, the women of Turkey seem the most completely modern of the foreign countries I've ever visited. There are few veiled women on the streets of Istanbul," she wrote in one dispatch. While there, she was interviewed by the Turkish press. ("Unfortunately I can't read a word of what they write!" she laughed.)[92] According to King Kennedy, who was also on the trip, the Istanbul journey marked a "friendly" period between Hopper and Louella. Kennedy recalled that one day when Hopper and Louella went out sightseeing, "the sun was terrific and Louella just had a little hat on. So the very next day . . . Hopper [said], 'Well dear, you know in this sun there's nothing more dangerous than not having the back of your neck protected, and that's why I always carry with me these big hats.'" Hopper then gave Louella one of her favorite red hats.[93] Though the two were far from being friends, they had achieved a tentative rapprochement.

After going to Cairo, where Louella was made an "official guest of the city," she and the entourage were off to Jerusalem and then to Rome, where she received a visit from the playwright Tennessee Williams. Williams's visit, Louella recalled, was a little embarrassing, because she had protested MGM's decision to film his play *Cat on a Hot Tin Roof,* which she had described to her readers as immoral and sexually explicit.[94] Upon her return to Hollywood in August, she proudly announced that Harriet, who had left RKO after working for twelve years as a producer, had formed her own independent production company. The only female member of the Screen Producers' Guild, Harriet was praised in a 1956 *Newsweek* magazine piece that described her as "Hollywood's lone active woman producer." (Commenting on sexism in the film industry, she told the magazine, "After all my years of experience, I still have to convince each director that I know my job.")[95] In her last film at RKO, *Susan Slept Here,* released in 1953, Harriet had given Louella a small part. One of the main characters in the story makes a call to Louella, whose voice was recorded on the sound track.[96]

In late 1955 the producers of the Chrysler-sponsored *Climax TV* series, which featured hourlong biographical sketches of famous figures portrayed by film and television actors, approached Louella with the possibility of filming a version of her life story. CBS and the *Climax* producers were less interested in Louella than in the ability she had had to coerce Hollywood stars to perform on the show for low or no pay. They also hoped that the lineup of stars they planned to use would help the show's ratings, since the episode with Louella was slated to air during ratings week in March 1956. *Climax* had pitched actress Anne Baxter for the part, but Teresa Wright, a former stage actress with over fifteen film credits, won the role.[97] Produced by Martin Manulis and directed by John Frankenheimer, the show used the largest cast ever in the history of dramatic television, with Jack Benny, Eddie Cantor, Dan Dailey, Howard Duff, Ida Lupino, Robert Mitchum, Merle Oberon, Ginger Rogers, Robert Stack, Lana Turner, and John Wayne, among more than two dozen actors, who made cameo appearances. Based on *The Gay Illiterate,* the episode followed Louella from Essanay to the *Chicago Herald* to New York to Hollywood, lingering on her relationship with Peter Brady and her later romance with Harry Martin. In one scene, Harriet, as a little girl in New York, burst out in tears because she had seen Louella's picture on the side of a Hearst news truck. "Don't you worry," Wright-Louella told Harriet. "You just tell them that it's better to have a mother on the wagon than one that's off."[98]

Louella appeared in person at the end of the program wearing a low-cut dress and a huge gold cross. "I hope you've enjoyed my life as much as I've enjoyed living it," she stiffly told the audience. Many if not most of *Climax*'s subjects were dead, which had stirred up rumors that she was, too. "It's pretty hard to play someone who's still alive," she told *Climax* host Bill Lundigan. "And believe me, I'm very much alive."[99]

Not surprisingly, given the sentiment toward Louella in Hollywood and press circles, the reviews were poor. Ray Oviatt of the *Toledo Blade* claimed that it "established a new mark for banality"; and the *Miami Herald* quipped, "That batch of movie celebrities who had walk-on parts to lend authenticity looked like character witnesses there under subpoena."[100] It should have been called "Auntie Climax," joked one reviewer.[101] Many viewers were similarly disgusted. In a letter to a Cleveland columnist who had panned the film, one reader wrote, "It was disgusting to witness the fawning. No wonder the public is completely fed up with Hollywood and the people who make pictures. Louella Parsons means nothing to the average person so why fall all over her. I for one switched to another station."[102] However saccharine, the episode earned the highest rating ever won by the show, and Louella received dozens of congratulatory telegrams from film and press notables.[103]

Louella previewed the show alone in a control booth at CBS. Later she and several friends viewed the show at Chasen's restaurant. She thought Teresa Wright was "sensational." "It was too bad," she told the *Hollywood Reporter*, that "so many of my friends were left out. But an hour's a short time for a lifetime." "They didn't tell what a bad temper I have," she added.[104] Immediately after the show, Louella went to New York, where she was feted at a party hosted by Anita Loos. Then she traveled back to Hollywood, and then on to Europe for a monthlong vacation. According to some rumors, she had sought out a European specialist for a facelift.[105]

When Louella was in London, she saw Ingrid Bergman, who was also staying at the Savoy Hotel. "I was struck by the lack of change in her appearance. She was just as lovely; still had that same aura of purity and innocence. It was I, not she, who was stiff and embarrassed. It took time for me to adjust," Louella recalled. She claimed to have detected in her conversation with Bergman that "all was not well" between Bergman and Rossellini, and she was right. A little over a year later, the couple divorced, and on the front page of the *Examiner* Louella reported Bergman's split from the director "who had swept her off her feet so that she left home, daughter, and reputation."[106] In 1957, Bergman was back in the United States, after having won the Academy Award for *Anastasia,* her first American film in over seven years. A few months later, Louella found out about remarks that Bergman had made to an American magazine that blamed Louella for the 1950 scandal. Upset, Louella refused to go to a dinner party given in honor of Bergman and "sent her regrets in a curt note."[107]

Born in an era of horse-drawn buggies, Louella now traveled around in a chauffeured Chrysler. She had grown up without electricity, indoor plumbing, or heat, and now she lived in a modern home equipped with every creature comfort. At the turn of the century, the average life expectancy had been forty-seven. In 1956, Louella turned seventy-five. She had lived through a social and technological revolution and, though reluctant at times, had adapted to the changes. But she was now telling friends that she felt out of place and was overwhelmed by her new environment. She filled the column with news about old-timers such as Joan Crawford, Clark Gable, and Bette Davis, even though some of them had not made films in years, and she loudly lamented the passing of the old studio moguls. By the mid-1950s, Louis B. Mayer, Harry Cohn, Samuel Goldwyn, David Selznick, and Darryl Zanuck had resigned from film; Mayer, once the mightiest of them all, died in 1957. In the same column in which she published her tribute to Mayer, Louella announced that San Simeon, which the Hearst family had donated to the state of California, would be opened to the public, and that *The Birth of a Nation* was playing in art theaters in Los Angeles. "Now *Birth of a Nation* is being reissued when civil rights are a burning issue before our legislatures. It will be very interesting to see if once again it creates a national commotion," she wrote in July 1957. Shortly afterward, she went to Las Vegas to witness an atomic bomb test and, amazed and horrified, "stayed up till sunrise to see the light from the blast explode over the sky with the brilliance of 100 daytime suns."[108]

Pressured by her editors, who feared that her outmoded style would lose readers, she began gearing her column toward a younger film audience. By the mid-1950s it was estimated that 60 percent of the movie audience was between twelve and twenty-four, and one quarter of the industry's revenues were coming from drive-in theaters.[109] Louella herself received an "enormous amount of mail" from teenagers.[110] "In this day and age you have to be familiar with the teenagers or you're old-fashioned," she admitted to her readers.[111] She began writing about Elvis Presley, whom she met on his arrival in Hollywood in 1956. "He arrived at my house all alone and ill at ease. He seemed frightened at meeting me. . . . Then I noticed his shoes. On each shoe was a full-color picture of Elvis! After so many years in Hollywood nothing shocks me, but never had any star I knew worn his or her picture on his shoes."[112] But Louella was offended by Presley's cocky flamboyance. "Cut out the bad taste in your act—the hip swinging, torso-tossing nonsense. . . . Remove the gag 'Pelvis' tag that has been hooked onto your name," she wrote in an "open letter" to Presley in *Modern Screen*.[113] She was a bigger fan of the young Catholic pop star Fabian, whom she described as a "friend." "No matter where he goes on his personal appearance tours, Fabian telephones to tell me any news about himself. Fabian and Frankie [Avalon] took me to church one Sunday, then to lunch at the Beverly Hills Hotel," she told her readers.[114] She adopted the new teen lingo, describing actors and films as "cool." When Pat Boone announced that he would record McHugh's song "Louella" for Dot Records, he asked Louella if she would mind if he did a rock-and-roll version. She said she'd love it.[115] Privately, she expressed her despair. At her 1957 birthday party, put on by Jimmy McHugh, she whispered to friends, "I don't know half the people here."[116]

Louella's popularity was dwindling, and there was more to blame than teenyboppers and rock-and-roll. Years of exposure to celebrity news and the recent publicity given such scandals as the Bergman pregnancy and Robert Mitchum's 1949 arrest on narcotics charges had created a more cynical, media-savvy public that was weary of Louella's sugarcoated descriptions of the stars. One indication of the new public consciousness was the wildly successful debut of *Confidential* magazine in 1952. Robert Harrison, the publisher of popular "girlie" magazines such as *Wink, Titter,* and *Eyeful,* had been fascinated by the way that Americans were enthralled by the Estes Kefauver hearings in the Senate in 1951. The scandalous, nationally televised hearings, in which over fifty witnesses exposed the crimes of the highest-ranking Mafia crime syndicate in America, had had Americans of all walks of life glued to their sets. Sensing an audience for scandal, in 1952 Harrison began bimonthly publication of *Confidential,* which filled its pages with sensationalistic exposés of celebrity misdeeds. Among the most famous included a story describing Frank Sinatra eating Wheaties between rounds of lovemaking, and Robert Mitchum allegedly appearing naked and smeared with ketchup at a Hollywood dinner party. Articles such as "They Passed for White," "The Lavender Skeletons in TV's Closet," and "Hollywood—Where Men Are Men and Women Too" lured readers titillated by the taboos of miscegenation and homosexuality.[117]

Confidential got tips from actresses, waiters, "ex-husbands or wives, or embittered lovers like the small-time movie actor who in 1955 told *Confidential* the story of the sexual eccentricities of a fast-rising young actress who jilted him," according to *Time.* Harrison was so intent on digging up dirt that he employed a squad of private detectives equipped with small noiseless cameras and wrist-attached microphones that could pick up a sigh sixty feet away. The magazine caused not merely a stir in Hollywood but a national sensation ("Everyone reads *Confidential.* But they deny it. They say the cook brought it into the house," recalled Humphrey Bogart).[118] After five years of publication, *Confidential* was selling nearly four million copies of each issue, making it one of the best-selling magazines on American newsstands.[119]

The Hollywood producers, disgusted, finally took action in September 1955 following a story titled "The Real Reason for Marilyn Monroe's Divorce." The article detailed an attempt by Monroe's husband, Joe DiMaggio, plus Frank Sinatra and a private investigator, to break into the apartment of Monroe's vocal coach, Hal Schaefer, with whom she was allegedly having an affair. The group bungled the job and ended up in the apartment of a middle-aged woman named Florence Kotz. When the story appeared in *Confidential,* the film elite was outraged. Pressured by industry moguls, in 1957 the California attorney general, Edmund Brown, indicted Harrison. During the sensational trial, a prostitute named Ronnie Quillan went on the stand to confess that she had been a paid informant for the magazine, and several New York and Los Angeles police admitted to having been on *Confidential*'s payroll. The Hearst papers hyped the trial: the *New York Mirror* called it a "super colossal bedroom extravaganza," and the *Los Angeles Examiner* put it on the front page and sold out almost every day.

In the end, the charges were dropped on Harrison's promise to change the magazine's editorial policy and publish only flattering stories about movie stars and politicians. Predictably, circulation plummeted, though the magazine continued for over a decade. In April 1959, the magazine ran a piece on Louella, "The Hatchet Woman Hollywood Fears." "Is she really the most powerful woman in Hollywood? Can she really make or break stars?" it asked. An indication of the magazine's new, toned-down style—or perhaps the extent to which Louella had already been scandalized by the press—the article was a tired rehash of familiar rumors and accusations. Louella "couldn't write," the piece claimed, and was a "sloppy, inaccurate reporter." "Meanly vindictive," she let "loyalty to her friends get in the way of her job as a reporter," took "advantage of her position to corral enormous quantities of loot from movie studios, actors, and others," and was "extremely vain." "Six nasty words in Louella's column cost me $66,000," one actor was quoted as saying. "One hour after her column was on the streets, I lost a three-month extension on my contract. And all she really said was, 'I don't fancy that man much.'"[120] When the article came out, no one, not even Louella, raised an eyebrow. In over four pages of text, the magazine said nothing new.

Confidential opened the scandal floodgates. Several imitators were launched in the mid-1950s, including the magazines *Suppressed, Hush Hush, Inside Story, Exposed, Behind the Scenes, Rave, Whisper, Lowdown, Top Secret, Private Lives,* and *On the QT.* By 1955, the combined circulation for these amounted to more than ten million. The wildly successful tabloid *National Enquirer* began in 1957 and spawned its own set of copycats—*National Exposure, National Mirror,* and *National Limelight,* among others—with a combined circulation of more than seven million.[121] *Newsweek* asked in 1955 why

Americans were so interested in the exposé publications. The country had gotten jaded. "The US public is the most communication-glutted group of people in world history. Daily bombarded by 'facts' which conflict, daily told opposite versions of the same incidents, hopelessly incapable in this complicated world of sorting out the truth, a great many Americans have undoubtedly built a thick shell of skepticism around themselves. Having seen more than his share of legitimate scandals and exposures, the reader begins to think that every story must have some kind of a 'lowdown' beneath the surface, some 'uncensored' facts known only to a 'confidential' few," the magazine concluded.[122]

For the fan magazines, which had banked their fortunes on public naïveté, this cynicism was troubling. The major fan publications, most prominently *Modern Screen* and *Photoplay*, scrambled to find a way to appease a less gullible public without compromising their candy-coated image of Hollywood. One tactic was to acknowledge the mistakes of the scandalous stars but emphasize the clean lifestyles of the majority. *Photoplay* even went as far as to produce a chart that listed the marital, parental, and home-ownership status and community involvement of over 150 celebrities. Another approach was to describe the celebrity sinners as having erred due to work-induced stress. As Louella claimed in a 1952 *Modern Screen* article, such stars were to be "pitied" rather than vilified. As a last resort, some fan magazine editors broke down and gave in to sensationalism. Turning the scandal-magazine formula on its head, they countered stories that actors were sleeping around with pieces that asked, "Is it true that everyone in Hollywood is sleeping around?"[123]

Louella, who had delved only once into the realm of scandal with the Bergman story, abhorred the trend toward sensationalism, and she continued to glorify Hollywood. In 1955, she was still cranking out such titles as "Why the Alan Ladds Are Hollywood's Happiest Couple" and "The Role Bing [Crosby] Likes Best Is Playing a Swell Dad" and paeans to "sweet, understanding" actresses like Marie Wilson, who "never wants to hurt anybody. She is completely unselfish and puts her own interests last."[124] Like much of the popular media, Louella's writings concealed under a facade of contented middle-class domesticity the social turbulence of the decade—a mounting crusade for civil rights, nuclear fears, and the discontent of suburban housewives that would erupt into the feminist movement of the following decade. The image of Hollywood and America that she presented in her column reflected her own conservative social vision, but it was not real. "I think a Hol-

lywood columnist should print the news . . . but not betray any confi-
dences," Louella told TV journalist Ed Murrow.[125] "There are far too many
sensationalists who are getting their story inspirations from the dirty words
written on back fences."[126] Though her words were sincere, she was clearly
out of touch with the times. The creator of Hollywood gossip could no
longer live in the house that she had built.

SEVENTEEN

Eclipse

Louella was almost eighty when, in 1958, Kingsbury Smith, chief of the International News Service, renewed her contract for three years. "I hope I'll live that long," she told Smith, half jokingly. Even though she now required an extra daily nap—"I get pretty tired, and rest is very good," she wrote in a note to Jack Warner—Louella was still energetic and compulsive, with near "cyclonic" energy, as Anita Loos once described it.[1] When asked by an interviewer if and when she planned to retire, she laughed. "I'll be meeting eight deadlines a week when they have me in a wheelchair," she promised.[2]

She meant it. In April 1958, she won citywide acclaim for a major story she wrote on the murder of Johnny Stompanato, Lana Turner's abusive ex-boyfriend, by Turner's daughter, Cheryl Crane. During an argument in early April, Crane had heard Stompanato, a former bodyguard for gangster Mickey Cohen, threaten Turner with violence. Crane went to the kitchen, got a knife, and plunged it into his abdomen. Because Louella knew the intimate details of the Stompanato-Turner relationship and "how to obtain information from sources on a moment's notice," according to newspaper historian Rob Wagner, the *Examiner* city desk had Louella, rather than a crime reporter, write the story, which appeared on the front page.[3]

She followed up her success with a sensational 1958 story on the divorce of Eddie Fisher and Debbie Reynolds, a breakup that the press attributed to Elizabeth Taylor, with whom Fisher was having an affair.[4] (Hopper claimed to have gotten the scoop, which the Hearst papers paraphrased without giving her credit.)[5] The divorce led to an outpouring of hostility against Taylor, and Louella received hundreds of letters from outraged fans. Though Louella tried to defend Taylor, whom she called "an old friend" and a victim of exaggerated press accounts that demonized her, Taylor despised Louella for having publicized the divorce, and blamed her for the public sentiment against her.[6] That year Louella also infuriated Joan Crawford, when, following the death of Crawford's husband, the Pepsi magnate Alfred Steele, Louella claimed in a front-page story that Crawford was "flat broke."[7] After Pepsi executives told Crawford that the story made the company look bad, Crawford denied Louella's story and forced her to print a retraction. Louella was livid but "printed the rebuttal and never forgave Crawford," according to biographer Bob Thomas.[8]

Still insecure about her appearance and performing talent, for years Louella had refused to do a live television show. But in 1958 she finally relented and appeared on Ed Murrow's TV talk show *Person to Person,* in a segment filmed at her Maple Drive home. Looking somewhat tired and confused, she told Murrow that she still "splits the infinitives" but had changed her style to "write more about the younger set." After showing off portraits of Hearst and Cardinal Spellman on her piano and making a tour of the dining room (where at Christmas dinner the same twenty-five people had paid the same compliments to each other for twenty-five years but never tired of them, she quipped), Louella went into her den. What is a typical evening at home like? Murrow asked. "I have my radio, TV, and hi-fi. I love music," Louella said. Though rock-and-roll was too "wild" for her tastes, she liked "the sweet and tender ballads." One of her favorite records, she told Murrow, was the album *Jimmy McHugh in Hi-Fi,* for which she had written the liner notes.

Inevitably, the subject shifted to Hollywood. Louella admitted that things in the film industry "are not as good as they once were [but] I have confidence we'll get out of it beautifully." Why? She put her faith in heaven. "The one thing I treasure most is my statue in the garden of the Madonna. I have a shrine out there, and I go in the morning to say my prayers; and I am happy for the day because I know God is in his heaven and all is good for the world," she said as she smiled.[9]

In June 1959, Louella, Harriet, Jimmy McHugh, and Maggie Ettinger traveled to Quincy, Illinois, where Louella received an honorary doctorate from Quincy College, the oldest Catholic college in the state.[10] Friends and relatives from Dixon and Freeport came down for the event, and Louella was awarded a twenty-four-karat gold key to the city of Freeport.[11] Louella and the entourage left Quincy for New York, where Louella was honored at a cocktail party put on by Gloria Swanson at the Sheraton Hotel and at a dinner celebrating her thirty-seventh anniversary with the Hearst Corporation.[12] At the dinner, she received a gold typewriter and a gold bracelet with links marking "all the important things in my life, such as signing my . . . first contract with Mr. Hearst. . . . I'm staying on with the Hearst organization as long as I live and I'm useful," she told reporters. "Mr. Hearst once said to me, as long as you are enthusiastic you'll be good. I won't say I'm good, but I have never lost my enthusiasm for the Hollywood beat, and I suppose I'll fight and scratch for scoops as long as there's a breath of life in me."[13] Later in New York she did an interview for the Oral History Research Office at Columbia University, which was assembling a collection of interviews from entertainment industry figures for its Popular Arts Collection.

Her words were bitter. In the old days, she reminisced, Hollywood was a "great big village. I mean, we were all friends, the parties were small, and we would meet the same people. . . . Stars were groomed to the teeth. They never appeared in public without looking every inch a star. Today I see some of the younger generation wearing slacks, being not as well groomed and tidy as the stars were in the old days." And actors were silent—literally. Docile studio employees, they knew that their job was to look good, not to think. "We didn't have the actors' studios [and] they didn't try and be intellectual as they do today. And they weren't businessmen and women," she lamented. Now "the stars are . . . the bosses, it seems to me, because they now direct, they own part of the picture, and have a lot more to say than they did in the old days."[14]

The passing of the old Hollywood made her sad, "very, very sad." "It's made me very sad because I felt—and I hate to say anything against my beloved industry—I felt they made a very grave mistake in selling their fine pictures to TV. They could have re-released them." Also, "I think there are too many downbeat pictures now. I think people like to get out of their own troubles. . . . I think the old formula, 'Make 'em laugh, make 'em cry,' is good. That's what made Charlie Chaplin so great. In all of his nonsense there was a pathos."[15]

"I think my career has been based on luck," she concluded. "I seem to have been born under a lucky star. I'm always amazed myself. I wrote a book called *The Gay Illiterate*, and occasionally, if I forget to split a participle or use an ungrammatical phrase, my readers object. They want me to talk as if I were talking over the fence to the next door neighbor, and they don't expect me to write anything profound and deep."[16]

By the late 1950s Louella could no longer hide her anger over the changes in Hollywood and her abandonment by the industry she had built. Though she was still invited to parties, she was no longer the center of attention; at many events she sat forlornly in a corner while newcomers asked the identity of the "old lady" and old-timers politely paid their respects. But she insisted on going out, even when her health gave way in the early 1960s, prompting snide comments from observers who mocked what seemed like pathetic attempts to hold on to her youth. "When she progressed slowly to a restaurant table with Jimmy [McHugh]'s hand under one of her elbows and a waiter's hand beneath the other, she looked . . . like some richly dressed little mummy," one journalist recalled.[17]

It was perhaps because of her feelings of loss and betrayal that in the end she became, like Hopper, a staunch right-wing critic of Hollywood liberals. By 1958, her column, which had dealt with politics only sparingly, was filled with strident and incendiary anticommunist propaganda. In particular, she lashed out against those members of the Hollywood Ten who had been pardoned and had resumed work in film. When director Otto Preminger publicized the fact that Dalton Trumbo, one of the Ten, had written the script for his film *Exodus,* Louella attacked Trumbo, describing him as "one character we can do without." "I am sorry to see Otto Preminger publicize him. Look now for some of the others of his ilk to come through the opened door," she warned.[18] When Jules Dassin, who had been living in Europe since the HUAC investigations, received an Academy Award nomination as best director for *Never on Sunday* in 1961, Louella reminded readers that "just for the record, according to the 1952 annual report of [HUAC], Dassin was identified as a communist by Edward Dmytryk on April 25, 1951, and by Frank Tuttle on May 24, 1951. There are authenticated stories of Dassin's work with the *People's Daily World, The Daily Worker,* the Workers' Theater, and other Communist affiliations. His movies have always received acclaim in Russia. As of May 11, 1960, the records show he has never appeared before the Un-American Activities Committee to refute the charges."[19] She now publicly pledged to support the American Legion in its effort to "expose Un-Americanism wherever and whenever found" and urged the independent producers to sign the "Waldorf Declaration against letting communists into our industry," as the major studios had done in 1947. In 1961, when she wrote that "our popular FBI head J. Edgar remains untouchable whether it's a Democratic or Republican administration, and that's as it should be," Hoover wrote personally to Louella thanking her "for the very generous comments." It was "encouraging," he added "to know that I have the unselfish and active support of such staunch friends as you."[20]

Her ongoing attacks on movie "filth," both in and out of her column, became an embarrassment to many in Hollywood. On January 24, 1960, seven hundred film industry notables attended a Screen Producers' Guild dinner for Jack Warner at the Beverly Hilton Hotel. When Jack Benny introduced Eva Marie Saint, who was going to present an award to Warner, Benny delivered an extensive introduction. Saint then said, "All I can say after that is, oh, shit." Appalled, Louella wrote an "open letter" to Saint in her column: "If you think I'm on a soap box to lecture you about that headlined 'word' you used at the Producers' Dinner, you are mistaken. I've known you ever since you came to Hollywood, and I know you to be a fine mother, wife and actress—and a very 'nice' person as well. . . . But, my dear, never be afraid to say, 'I'm sorry.' So far, you've said everything else."[21] She saw her stand against Saint as heroic, but very few in Hollywood agreed.

Louella may have turned against the new Hollywood, but she remained faithful to Harriet, who left RKO in 1955 after having produced *Never a Dull Moment* with Irene Dunne and Fred McMurray, *Clash By Night* with Barbara Stanwyck and Marilyn Monroe, and *Susan Slept Here* with Dick Powell and Debbie Reynolds. In 1956, having become "disenchanted with Hollywood," as she later told reporters, she began work as a Broadway producer.[22] Louella raved in the column about Harriet's new career. "A relative of mine, a very happy young lady by the name of Harriet Parsons"—the "young lady" was fifty-four at the time—"telephoned from New York to say that the *Rape of the Belt,* which she is producing, opens in New York at the Helen Hayes Theater. Believe me, nothing can keep me from being in New York for my daughter's big night," she wrote in 1960.[23] True to her promise, Louella attended opening night in New York and then went to Boston, where Jimmy McHugh showed her around town and she visited "Elizabeth Arden's famous salon" to have her hair coiffed by an expensive "Parisian hair specialist."[24] *The Rape of the Belt* was Harriet's first and last theater production; the show closed after nine days. In 1961, with Louella's help, Harriet acquired the screen rights to *I Married a Psychiatrist,* a novel that was appearing serially in Hearst's *Chicago American,* but the film project never materialized.[25]

It was in that year that Louella's second and last book, *Tell It to Louella,* was published. She had accepted an advance for the book in 1959, which she spent quickly, without having written a word. A ghostwriter, Dee Katcher, was then brought in to help her with the manuscript. Putnam marketed the book to younger fans ("filled with never-before-told information and profiles on such stars as Marlon Brando, Frank Sinatra, [and] Elizabeth Taylor," read the jacket copy). But it was largely a tribute to the golden era, with several chapters on the old studio moguls—Louis B. Mayer, Irving Thalberg, the Warner brothers, and Darryl Zanuck—and "the Chief," whom she described as "a great man whether you liked him or not. Whether you agreed with him or not."[26] As she had in *The Gay Illiterate,* she attacked her detractors. In particular, she went after Ezra Goodman, a Los Angeles journalist and former *Time* correspondent who had damned her in a 452-page book called the *Fifty-Year Decline and Fall of Hollywood.* Louella fumed at Goodman's (correct) accusation that the writer Richard English had helped her with *The Gay Illiterate,* and at "an old and false story that one year all my Christmas gifts were stolen from my car and that I demanded they all be replaced."[27] According to Harriet, the Christmas present story, a staple of Hollywood gossip for decades, hurt Louella deeply. (There was no truth to the tale; "Mother gave more than she took," Harriet told reporters in 1982.)[28]

In a fitting conclusion to her tribute to the studio era, Louella ended the book with an attack on the decadent "new Hollywood." She quoted extensively from a recent piece she had written for the *Examiner,* "How Hollywood Can Meet the Challenge of Communism," in which she accused the film industry of "feeding ammunition to the Soviets in far too many pictures . . . which distort our American way of life into evil, careless morals, violence—and worst of all—perversions":

> Let us turn our best writers loose on such All-American Activities as 4-H clubs and to showing our farm people and teenage farm children, many of whom are self-supporting by breeding and caring for animals.
>
> Let's forget the sagas of our switch-blade carrying teenagers and proudly hold up to the world our young people who are entering the world of science and medicine and religion. America is one of the largest church-going nations in the world—not much of the world knows it.
>
> Americans are NOT going to hell in a sports car.
>
> Are we going to continue blindly to let the world think so when we have so much power at our disposal to combat it?
>
> I think not. I've been covering Hollywood and its product for many, many years and seen it rise triumphant over all dangers. And it will again emerge triumphant when it joins its great talents to the Herculean effort our national Government is making to keep our glorious country where it rightfully belongs—leading the parade of the Free World.[29]

Louella claimed to have received more fan mail for this article than for any other piece in her career. "Three cheers for your putting into bold print, in no uncertain language, your views on what kind of pictures Hollywood should concentrate. Your article coincided with my personal opinion for many years," wrote a reader named Helen Moreau. "I want to commend you on your wonderful article. How proud I am that there is someone like you in the movie industry," wrote Joyce Lingle. "My breakfast dishes are piled high in the sink, but they will have to wait until I finish this. . . . I believe every single mother in America will say with you that we do need some more wholesome movies not only for those abroad but for ourselves and our children," agreed Mrs. Alvin Albertson of Ontario.[30]

The *Examiner*'s review of *Tell It to Louella* was exaggerated and undeservedly positive. "A dispassionate judgment on Miss Parsons' book is that it is highly readable both for its documentary accounts of the Loreleis, Don Juans, and Calibans who were projected by the magic lanterns into national idols, and for its annotation of social and economic history," wrote reviewer Clark Kennard. But other papers were more honest.[31] ("The result is a dreary outpouring of egomaniac claptrap which if taken in more than very small and infrequent doses is likely to cause any self-respecting reporter to lose his lunch," wrote the *New York Herald Tribune*.)[32] Louella admitted to *Time* magazine that it was a "terrible book," but said that she "wrote every word of it" herself.[33] Despite their criticism, many reviewers acknowledged Louella's influence on American culture—"between the lines . . . is revealed a tough, shrewd, woman who pioneered in that special brand of Hollywood journalism, the Hollywood gossip column," noted the *New York Times* reviewer—and the importance of her column for future scholars.[34] "What would the tinsel El Dorado do without her? Almost certainly it would fold up, and researchers in the ruins would find that she had been one of its major historians," commented the *Herald Tribune*.[35]

Sensing Louella's imminent retirement, a variety of Hollywood and press organizations bestowed on her a string of awards between 1957 and 1962. In 1957, Adela Rogers St. Johns called Louella "the greatest woman reporter of this era" in a talk before the UCLA Women's Press Club, and Louella—and Hopper—were named "Women of the Year" by the *Los Angeles Times*. In 1958 Louella was named by the California Association of Press Women as an "outstanding woman journalist," one who had "done more to enhance the field of journalism" than any other female reporter. In 1959, the Screen Directors' Guild awarded Louella a special citation "in recognition of her loyalty, devotion, and many valued contributions to the motion picture industry" at its annual Screen Directors' Guild dinner. In 1960 she received a coveted Golden

Globe Award from the Hollywood Foreign Press Association. (J. Edgar Hoover sent Louella his "heartiest congratulations for this honor.")[36] In April 1960, during a trip to New York, she received a gold medallion honoring her status as a charter member of the Newspaper Women's Club; since its first meeting in 1922, the organization had grown from twenty-four to two hundred members.[37]

But the woman behind the legacy was ailing. Physically, she was in almost constant pain, suffering from colds and other bronchial ailments, in addition to ongoing heart and kidney trouble. Emotionally, despite McHugh's companionship, she seemed unfulfilled and lonely and she drank unremittingly, even when she was writing. According to Margaret Bouyette Scott, who worked at the *Examiner*, Louella would call in her column while drunk. Because the policy was to leave her column unedited, Scott "would watch deskmen literally sweat" as they took the incoherent column down, knowing that it could not be changed. In the end, managing editor Ray Van Ettisch usually ended up correcting errors.[38]

In 1959, the *Examiner* began an ad campaign for Louella that described her as the "MOST WIDELY READ FILM WRITER IN THE WORLD." "Being right is an old habit with Louella Parsons and being FIRST and RIGHT have always been her cornerstones. Millions of fans throughout the world . . . who want to know the who what when and where and all manners of this and that in filmland look to Louella Parsons. In Los Angeles they look to her too because she outranks all other film columnists like a general over a GI," preached large display ads.[39] It was a shameless, last-ditch effort to shore up her flagging readership. By the end of that year, her column appeared in only a hundred papers.

The precipitous drop in circulation was a result, in large part, of the ongoing weakening of the Hearst empire. By 1958, financial troubles and declining circulation had led to a string of closures and mergers. In Chicago in 1956, Hearst's afternoon *American* was sold to the *Tribune;* in 1959, the *San Francisco Call-Bulletin* merged with the Scripps-Howard News Service; and in Pittsburgh, the *Sun Telegraph* was sold to the morning *Post Gazette*. The *Detroit Times* shut in 1960, and in 1961 the *Boston Evening American* merged with the *Boston Daily Record*.[40] In 1958, Hearst's International News Service merged with United Press. Louella's column was to be carried by Hearst-owned papers and would be available to UPI clients on a special circuit.[41] The upshot of this was the disappearance of the column from several hundred papers.

Then, in 1962, the morning paper the *Los Angeles Examiner,* Louella's home paper for over thirty-five years, finally folded. Bill Hearst Jr. decided to shut the paper, citing low circulation and continued losses. To many, this was a shocking decision, since the *Examiner* was far more successful than Hearst's other Los Angeles paper, the afternoon *Herald-Express*. (In 1962, the *Examiner* had a Sunday circulation of 700,000 and a weekday circulation of 381,037, making it the tenth-best-selling morning paper in the country.) The afternoon paper was subsequently renamed the *Herald-Examiner* and only a few of the thousand employees from the *Examiner,* including Louella, were added to the new publication.[42] The shift to afternoon publication caused a further loss in Louella's readership and authority, according to *Variety,* "since many people didn't read her column until they arrived home in the evening," making her exclusives old news.[43] By 1962, she was down to only 70 papers, while Hopper appeared in 130.[44]

By this point, it seemed to many that Hopper had won the feud. Despite her shrill political commentary and the hostility against her in Hollywood, she was enormously visible and popular in the 1950s, largely as a result of her own efforts at self-promotion. Each year between 1954 and 1958, Hopper toured overseas with Bob Hope; moreover, she had maintained a constant radio presence throughout the decade. She had also kept up her anticommunist efforts and frequently requested from Hoover information on actors whom she suspected of "subversive" tendencies. In 1960, she called Hoover in the hope that the bureau would give her "informal guidance" regarding an actress whom she believed was a member of the Communist Party. In the end, the bureau declined her request but suggested that she "get in touch with the State Department or some of her friends . . . to secure the background data she is looking for."[45]

That same year, Hopper tried to launch her own television show, *Hedda Hopper's Hollywood,* to compete with Ed Sullivan's popular television gossip-talk program, the *Ed Sullivan Show.* For the show, she had lined up a guest list with more than twenty stars, whom she was planning to pay $210 each, the minimum union pay scale for an "interview" appearance. Sullivan threatened her, then went on record accusing Hopper of "the most grievous form of payola." "Here is a columnist using plugs in a column to get performers for free," he stated.[46] Many of the stars subsequently backed out of the program. Hopper was still able to secure commitments from several top stars, who appeared on the show for a pittance. In 1963, she published *The Whole Truth and Nothing But,* an autobiography that became serialized in *McCall's* and that headed best-seller lists in the spring of 1963. According to Hopper, when Louella heard she was working on the book, she called to ask what the book would be about. "I'm just going to tell the truth," Hopper replied. "Oh dear," Louella wailed, "that's what I was afraid of."[47] Hopper devoted an entire section of the book to Louella, whom she portrayed as conniving (as evidenced by her cagey scheme to interview George Bernard Shaw), vindictive (as in her attack on Orson Welles), and jealous (depressed over Hopper's success, Louella had demanded the testimonial dinner arranged by Hearst in 1948, Hopper claimed). She correctly described the 1948 Romanoff's lunch as a *failed* attempt at reconciliation.

In 1962, Louella had an operation to get rid of a lobster claw that had gotten stuck in her throat while she was eating bouillabaisse at Los Angeles's Scandia Restaurant. Later that year she was admitted to Cedars of Lebanon Hospital suffering from shingles of the optic nerve, complicated by pneumonia.[48] For six weeks she lay heavily sedated, and the last rites of the Catholic Church were administered.[49] Hopper visited Louella in the hospital, and "the feebleness in her voice" alarmed her. "I'm so tired of this place," Louella had said, "and I'm so sick." Hopper talked to Harry Brand, the publicity director of Twentieth Century Fox, who had been a good friend to Louella and Harry. "If you want her to live, you'd better get her out of that hospital," Hopper told Brand. "Either she's in the same room that Docky had or one exactly like it. She'll never recover until she's moved." Louella was moved to the Beverly Hills Hotel the next day and she recovered quickly.[50] Gloria Swanson, who was in her seventies, sent Louella a telegram in the hospital. "I do not suppose I have ever written you before[,] but I have heard that you were not feeling well. We sort of take it for granted that we will see our friends somewhere in this tiny world as it is today. . . . I have known you all these years—I guess it goes back to Essanay, Louella—and I have always thought of you as a sweet gentle person . . . [and] you have a very warm place in my heart."[51]

Amazingly, Louella still fought retirement. It was only in 1964, after she fell and broke a hip, that she finally gave up the column. Dorothy Manners, who had written most of the column for the previous few years, took over full-time, and she and Louella shared the byline. Finally, on December 1, 1965, Manners had her first solo byline. ("NOW THERE IS ONLY HEDDA," proclaimed *Daily Variety*.) "I feel a little bit like a buck private in a general's uniform. It will be hard to replace the finest 'newspaperman' I've ever known," Manners later told reporters. In 1974, though the column appeared in eighty-nine papers, Manners admitted to *Time* magazine that many readers found her "fluffy flowered hat style"—modeled after Louella's, of course—dull. "Some of [the columns] are frankly a little flat," she conceded. "But how many people in this town make news anymore?"[52] After forty-two years with the Hearst Corporation, Manners retired in December 1977.

Throughout the entertainment and publishing worlds, critics acknowledged that Louella's retirement marked the end of an era. "The end of Queen Lolly's reign is of more than passing interest, not only because of her once formidable power, but also because it reflects the changes that have taken place in Hollywood-style journalism. No longer do producers or performers have to humble themselves before the columnists in order to gain support for their pictures or their careers. Indeed a growing number of stars—among them Brando, Sinatra, Presley, and Doris Day—usually decline to be 'interviewed' by any journalist, preferring instead to let their work speak for itself," wrote Peter Bart in the *New York Times*.[53] In a scathing 1965 attack, "The Little Queen That Hollywood Deserved" (Louella was "narrow, semi-illiterate, and often moved by blubbering sentimentality," the article claimed), *Life* similarly noted that her departure from the field marked the demise of an old, "gaudy and narcissistic Hollywood."[54] The lines of power within the entertainment industry had become at once more intricate and diffuse, and the public, more cynical. No longer could an individual columnist engineer careers, block the release of films, or dupe readers into believing fanciful illusions of stars' goodness and innocence. The era of the superstar columnists—the Hoppers and Parsons and Winchells—had all but ended, the *Times* concluded.

Shortly after her retirement, Louella moved to the Brentwood Convalescent Home on San Vicente Boulevard, where she was cared for by an attendant paid for by the Hearst Corporation.[55] In mid-1965, after falling and breaking her shoulder, she was back in the hospital; at this time she also had three cataracts removed. Harriet, who had moved to Palm Springs, returned to Beverly Hills to care for Louella and began selling real estate to support herself. In March 1966, Louella's incredible collection of antiques and furniture, which included fine crystal; silver; seventeenth-, eighteenth-, and nineteenth-century Spanish, Italian, and English cabinets; gold-leafed mirrors; rare blue-scepter-mark Royal Berlin porcelain dinnerware; and a George IV silver basket from 1827, were auctioned off in Los Angeles. At the same time, Harriet donated Louella's fifty-four scrapbooks, containing her columns and press clippings, to the Academy of Motion Picture Arts and Sciences.[56] Louella sat quietly in a sparsely furnished room ("in a complete silence," remembered Manners, "with no reaction, utterly expressionless") while her career, possessions, friends, and memories quietly slipped away.[57]

In February 1966, Hedda Hopper died at the age of seventy-five. Though she had remained fairly active during the early 1960s—in 1964, she had covered the Republican National Convention for her syndicate; in 1965, she had traveled to Europe, and she was even the voice of the Mad Hatter in a cartoon film of *Alice in Wonderland*—by the end of 1965, her health had begun to deteriorate. In January 1966 she went to Washington, D.C., on vacation and returned to Hollywood ill and exhausted.[58] She then entered Cedars of Lebanon in late January, suffering from double pneumonia. Though the pneumonia was conquered, the medication had weakened her heart and kidneys, and on February 1, she passed away. According to one rumor, when Harriet told Louella that Hopper had died, after a long, confused silence, Louella shouted, "GOOD!"[59] At the *Los Angeles Times,* Hopper was replaced by Joyce Haber, a former Los Angeles correspondent for *Time,* whose column, by 1969, ran in ninety-three newspapers. With a "bitchy style," she won as much "respect and fear" from celebrities as her predecessor, reported *Time.* She was nicknamed "Hedda Haber."[60]

Hopper may have died with a larger readership, but Louella lived on, indefatigably. Indeed, she outlasted them all. Marion Davies died of jaw cancer in 1961, and Louella's cousin Maggie Ettinger died from cancer in 1967. Jimmy McHugh passed away in 1969. Of her friends from the early years, only Bebe Daniels, Gloria Swanson, and Mary Pickford were still alive.

Finally, it was her turn. Louella died on December 9, 1972, at the age of ninety-one, of "generalized arteriosclerosis—old age," according to the spokesperson at the Brentwood Convalescent Home. Bob Hope, who attended the funeral, was shocked to find so few paying their respects.[61] Only a handful of stars showed up—Hope, Danny Thomas, George Burns, Jack Benny, Dorothy Lamour, Irene Dunne, Cesar Romero, and David Janssen—and the church was only two-thirds filled. Many of the attendees were movie fans on the lookout for celebrities. "Where are the Bette Davises, the Joan Crawfords, the Mae Wests, the Gloria Swansons?" asked actress Alice Parker angrily. "After all, Miss Parsons did so much for the movie colony. . . . I am aghast. What has happened to our movie queens?" The pallbearers were Ben Lyon, Harry Brand, Louella's butler Louis Collins, her physician Dr. Rexford Kennamer, King Kennedy, and her cousin Gordon Maynard. Harriet led the mourners.[62]

For one of only a few times in nearly fifty years of reporting on Louella, the press was fair. "Many men have held positions of influence during the history of motion pictures; not many women have done so. If a poll had been taken during the Golden Age of Hollywood, however, the one female who would have won hands down would have been gossip columnist Louella Parsons," read *Variety*'s obituary. The paper highlighted her hard work and generosity, saying that she was "as much praised—and damned—as any Hollywood personality ever to emerge, [and that] she put aside a portion of her salary every week to help a number of silent-pix players who had fallen on evil times. . . . She was responsible for many promising newcomers getting their first breaks in motion pictures." *Variety* also acknowledged the "boundless energy and passion for work" that made Louella's scoops legion. "Despite her prejudices, her inaccuracies, her tendency to ignore facts when it fitted her purpose, she got her stories—often exclusively—by a tough-minded approach that could have a terrifying impact on her subjects," wrote the *New York Times*. "In Hollywood, Miss Parsons . . . ruled as a queen."[63] She rests next to Harry in Holy Cross Cemetery in Culver City.

Louella's legacy lives on in the culture of celebrity and the public fascination with gossip that she birthed and bred. The period immediately after her death saw an unprecedented interest in gossip and the truth "behind the scenes"—a response in large part to the press coverage of the closed-door machinations behind the Vietnam War and the Watergate scandal. Press scrutiny of both events led to public awareness of the deception that underlay power. In response to "appetites whetted by . . . Watergate," *Newsweek* wrote in 1976, newspapers began running, in both gossip columns and "hard news" stories, an increasing amount of intimate information on public figures' private lives.[64] The lines between gossip and news had blurred, and the nature of fame had changed. By the late 1970s, as critic John Lahr wrote in a 1978 essay in *Harper's* magazine, visibility had become "an end in itself." Names were more important than deeds, and the multimedia publicity surrounding the famous so vast and grandiose that actual accomplishments were almost superfluous. It was a logical, albeit disturbing, outcome of a decades-long process of celebrity-making that Louella had helped initiate—in retrospect, quite innocuously—with her "Flickerings from Filmland" fifty years earlier.[65]

As for Louella, she has lived on in the public imagination largely in caricature. In 1972, George Eells published a dual biography, *Hedda and Louella*, a book that focused heavily on the feud and portrayed both women as shrewish and neurotic "gossip monsters" who used their careers to compensate for troubled and unfulfilled personal lives.[66] The book was made into a 1985 television film, "Malice in Wonderland," starring Jane Alexander as Hopper and Liz Taylor playing a shrill and high-strung Louella. "Miss Taylor clearly gets a great deal of pleasure from her nifty impersonation of the whining Lolly," noted the *New York Times*' John O'Connor, knowing undoubtedly Taylor's real-life animosity toward Louella.[67] The film prompted an article in *People* magazine in which Taylor described Louella as "dumpy, dowdy, and dedicated to nastiness. Forget anybody that stood in her way. And her voice . . . so irritating. You just wanted to smack her."[68]

In 1999, Louella's role in the suppression of *Citizen Kane* was rehashed in an HBO film, *RKO 281*. Her alleged cover-up of Hearst's murder of Thomas Ince was depicted in *The Cat's Meow*, a 2001 film by Peter Bogdanovich. To audiences today, Louella has become a loathed and mocked symbol of an earlier era of media history, a time that seems at once positively feudal—stars kowtowing in terror while Louella, Hearst, and the moguls connived to ruin careers—and charmingly naïve. There is something almost innocent about the image of Louella in a satin dressing gown in her bedroom with three ivory telephones ringing, a teletype clacking, and Dorothy Manners taking down dictation on a rickety manual typewriter. Compared to the large-scale political and corporate control of the press during and since the Vietnam era, and the transnational, multibillion-dollar, electronic-push-of-a-button varieties of media manipulation in our own day, Louella's methods, no matter how malicious in intent, seem downright quaint.

After Louella's death, Harriet tried to dispel many of the myths about her mother. Harriet and her adopted daughter, a dancer, Evelyn Farney, retired to Beverly Hills, where in 1982 Harriet began writing a memoir. She devoted an entire chapter of the book to debunking the rumors about Louella, including the Thomas Ince story. The book was never published. Harriet died in 1983 after a two-year battle with cancer, at the age of seventy-six.[69]

The title of the book, fittingly, was "I Didn't Tell Mother." Though she had a successful career, Harriet spent her life troubled by her relationship with Louella, whose formidable reputation, she felt, obscured her own achievements. Despite her many efforts, she was never able to free herself from Louella's shadow, even in the end. The *New York Times,* in its obituary, referred to her as "Harriet Parsons, Film Maker; Daughter of Louella Parsons." She rests in Holy Cross Cemetery, not far from Louella's side.

NOTES

PROLOGUE

1. Gene Brown, *Movie Time* (New York: Macmillan, 1995), 157.
2. "It Rains, but Hollywood Stars Shine at Banquet," *Dixon Evening Telegraph,* Sept. 16, 1941.
3. "Dixon Is Proud to Have You," *Dixon Evening Telegraph,* Sept. 12, 1941, LOP Scrapbook #28, Louella Parsons Collection, Academy of Motion Pictures Arts and Sciences, Beverly Hills, California (hereafter AMPAS).
4. "It Rains."
5. "Dixon Day—Louella's Home," *Chicago Herald American,* Sept. 15, 1941, LOP Scrapbook #28, AMPAS.
6. "The City's Keys Are Yours," *Dixon Evening Telegraph,* Sept. 16, 1941, 13.

ONE. EARLY YEARS

1. Mary Barrett, *History of Stephenson County* (Freeport, IL: County of Stephenson, 1972), 636.
2. Ibid., 634.
3. Benjamin McArthur, *Actors and American Culture, 1880–1920* (Philadelphia: Temple University Press, 1984), x.
4. Ibid., chap. 5.
5. Ibid., 151.
6. Barrett, *History of Stephenson County,* 566.
7. On theatrical fan culture, see McArthur, *Actors and American Culture,* chap. 6.
8. *Los Angeles Examiner* (hereafter LAE), Sept. 2, 1940.
9. *History of Stephenson County, Illinois* (Chicago: Western Historical Company, 1880), 655.
10. Ibid.
11. *Freeport City Directory* (n.p., 1884).
12. Louella Parsons, *The Gay Illiterate* (hereafter GI) (New York: Doubleday Doran, 1944), 7. Before she was eighteen, she wrote her name "Luella," since this was

what appeared on her birth certificate. It was not until high school that she changed the spelling to "Louella."

13. "The Star Clothing House," *Illustrated Freeport*, 140–41, George Eells Collection, University of Southern California (hereafter Eells Collection, USC).

14. There were a few prosperous and well-respected Jewish merchants in Freeport, including Jacob Krohn, who had served as mayor in the 1870s. On Krohn, see *Portrait and Biographical Album, Stephenson County, Illinois* (Chicago: Chapman Brothers, 1888), 279–81; "City Loses a Leader," *Freeport Daily Bulletin*, June 21, 1901, 1.

15. *Sterling City Directory* (n.p., 1890). Joshua and Helen did not record Louella's birth until 1886, when Edwin was born; for unknown reasons, Louella's and Edwin's births were reported on the same birth certificate.

16. GI, 10.

17. LAE, Aug. 7, 1949.

18. "The Late Joshua Oettinger," *Freeport Daily Democrat*, May 31, 1890, 4.

19. *Sterling Gazette*, May 30, 1890.

20. *Sterling Democrat*, May 29, 1890.

21. "The Climax of Love," *Freeport Daily Journal*, Dec. 16, 1891, 4.

22. Louella's cousin Maggie Ettinger later attributed Louella's inability to manage money to Helen's excesses. "Extravagance," Maggie claimed, "is in her blood." Isabella Taves, "Louella Parsons," *Look*, Oct. 10, 1950, 62.

23. LAE, Mar. 19, 1944; Jan. 23, 1949; Dec. 11, 1950.

24. LAE, Sept. 8, 1947; Mar. 24, 1947; July 20, 1939.

25. Frances Hodgson Burnett, *Editha's Burglar* (New York: H. M. Caldwell, 1888), 10.

26. GI, 9.

27. "The Climax of Love," 4.

28. GI, 10.

29. LAE, Nov. 6, 1938, V, 5.

30. "News about People You Know," *Freeport Journal Standard*, Feb. 18, 1959, 10.

31. LAE, Sept. 26, 1939, I, 9.

32. *History of Stephenson County, Illinois*, 554.

33. Ishbel Ross, *Ladies of the Press* (New York: Harper, 1936), 56; Brooke Kroeger, *Nellie Bly: Daredevil, Reporter, Feminist* (New York: Times Books, 1994).

34. Though Louella claimed in her autobiography that her story "The Flower Girl of New York" appeared in the *Freeport Journal Standard*, Donald Breed, whose father was editor at the time, claimed that this was "wishful thinking." Letter from Donald Breed to George Eells, Mar. 15, 1968, Eells Collection, USC.

35. Author's conversation with anonymous, Lee County Genealogical Society, June 25, 2001.

36. "Dixon Plans Louella Parsons Day Sep. 15," clipping, n.d., LOP Scrapbook #28, Louella Parsons Collection, Academy of Motion Pictures Arts and Sciences, Beverly Hills, California (hereafter AMPAS).

37. Barrett, *History of Stephenson County,* 557.

38. By 1890, more than 15 percent of the workforce was female. See Nancy Woloch, *Women and the American Experience* (New York: McGraw Hill, 1984), 220.

39. On the rise of the "new woman," see Patricia Marks, *Bicycles, Bangs, and Bloomers: The New Woman in the Popular Press* (Lexington: University of Kentucky Press, 1990); Woloch, *Women and the American Experience,* chap. 12.

40. GI, 9, 12.

41. GI, 9.

42. *Freeport City Directory* (n.p., 1898).

43. Anthony Trollope, *North America* (Philadelphia: n.p., 1862), 172–77.

44. *The Standard General and Business Directory of the City of Dixon, Illinois* (Dixon: Twentieth Century Directory Company, 1905), 15.

45. Bob Gibler, *Dixon, Illinois* (Charleston, SC: Arcadia, 1998), 88.

46. LAE, Nov. 4, 1946; Apr. 4, 1932.

47. On Chautauqua, see Charlotte Canning, "The Most American Thing in America: Producing National Identities in Chautauqua," in *Performing America: Cultural Nationalism in American Theater,* ed. J. Ellen Gainor and Jeffery D. Mason (Ann Arbor: University of Michigan Press, 1999), 91–105; Joseph Gould, *The Chautauqua Movement: An Episode in the Continuing American Revolution* (New York: State University of New York Press, 1961).

48. Gibler, *Dixon,* 67.

49. LAE, Apr. 19, 1943, II, 5.

50. "The Twentieth Century Class," *Dixon Evening Telegraph,* June 4, 1901, 7.

51. "Mrs. Goodsell Writes Sketch," *Dixon Evening Telegraph,* Sept. 11, 1941, LOP Scrapbook #28, AMPAS; "The Twentieth Century Class," 7.

52. Marion Marzolf, *Up from the Footnote: A History of Woman Journalists* (New York: Hastings House, 1977), 21.

53. E. A. Bennett, *Journalism for Women; a Practical Guide* (New York: J. Lane, 1898).

54. "Parsons Girl to Inherit Money for Education," *Dixon Evening Telegraph,* Mar. 12, 1915, 1.

55. GI, 13.

56. Frank Everett Stevens, *History of Lee County* (Chicago: S. J. Clarke, 1914), 337, 342.

57. "Obituary," *Dixon Evening Telegraph,* Mar. 13, 1913, 4; "E. C. Parsons Died This Morning," July 27, 1913, 1.

58. "Dixon Plans Louella Parsons Day."

59. "Society Doings," *Dixon Star,* May 8, 1902, 3.

60. James West, *Plainville, USA* (New York: Columbia University Press, 1945), 45.

61. Gary Alan Fine, *Rumor and Gossip: The Social Psychology of Hearsay* (New York: Elsevier, 1976), chap. 6; also see Max Gluckman, "Gossip and Scandal," *Cur-*

rent Anthropology 4, no. 3 (June 1963): 307–16; Robert Paine, "What Is Gossip About? An Alternative Hypothesis," *Man* 2, no. 2 (June 1967): 278–85.

62. Patricia Spacks, *Gossip* (New York: Knopf, 1984); Melanie Tebbutt, *Women's Talk: A Social History of Gossip in Working-Class Neighborhoods* (Brookfield, VT: Ashgate, 1995).

63. Louella O. Parsons, "Hollywood Is My Home Town," *Cosmopolitan,* Sept. 1934, 48.

64. Miscellaneous clipping from an unidentified Paris newspaper, July 1948, LOP Scrapbook #37, AMPAS.

65. *Dixon Telegraph,* Aug. 29, 1914, 1.

66. Clipping, n.d., LOP Scrapbook #28, AMPAS.

67. Louella Parsons, *Tell It to Louella* (New York: Putnam, 1961), 98.

68. "Her First Job," *Dixon Evening Telegraph,* Sept. 12, 1941, LOP Scrapbook #28, AMPAS.

69. Harriett Gustason, *Looking Back,* vol. 1 (Freeport, IL: Stephenson County Historical Society, 1994), 62.

70. GI, 15.

71. "Social Events," *Dixon Star,* Nov. 1, 1905, 3.

72. "Social Events," *Dixon Evening Telegraph,* Oct. 28, 1905, 5.

73. Clipping, n.d., Louella Parsons Clipping File, AMPAS.

74. Sadie Mack, interview by George Eells, n.d., George Eells Collection, Arizona State University (hereafter Eells Collection, ASU).

75. Adeline Churchill, interview by George Eells, June 11, 1969, Eells Collection, ASU.

76. Federal Writers' Project, *A Guide to Burlington, Iowa* (Burlington, IA: Acres-Blackmar, 1939), 7.

77. Helen Turner McKim and Helen Parsons, *Burlington on the Mississippi, 1833–1983* (Burlington, IA: Doran and Ward, 1983), 59.

78. George Eells, *Hedda and Louella* (New York: Putnam, 1972), 36.

79. Philip Jordan, *Catfish Bend, River Town, and County Seat* (Burlington, IA: Craftsman Press, 1975), 151.

80. McKim and Parsons, *Burlington on the Mississippi,* 60–61; "The Opera House," *Burlington Commercial Statistical Review* (n.p., 1882), 38.

81. Mrs. Martin Bruhl, interview by George Eells, June 8, 1969, Eells Collection, ASU.

82. Eells, *Hedda and Louella,* 37.

83. LAE, Sept. 1, 1948, II, 3.

84. Clipping, Sept. 20, 1969, Eells Collection, USC.

85. Letter to unknown from Margaret Smith, June 20, 1969, Parsons Clipping File, Burlington Public Library, Burlington, Iowa.

86. GI, 16.

87. For unknown reasons, Harriet's birth certificate was not filed until January 15, 1907.

88. Martin Bruhl, letter to George Eells, July 11, 1969; Margaret Clark, n.d., interview by George Eells, Eells Collection, ASU.

89. Martin Bruhl, letter to George Eells, July 11, 1969, Eells Collection, ASU.

90. Robert Allen, "The Movies in Vaudeville: Historical Context of the Movies as Popular Entertainment," in *The American Film Industry*, ed. Tino Balio (Madison: University of Wisconsin Press, 1985), 57–82.

91. Charles Musser, *The Emergence of Cinema: The American Screen to 1907* (New York: Scribner's, 1990), 104, 162.

92. Kathryn Fuller, *At the Picture Show: Small Town Audiences and the Creation of Movie Fan Culture* (Washington, DC: Smithsonian, 1996), 28.

93. On opposition to the cinema by religious and social reform groups, see Fuller, *At the Picture Show,* chap. 4; and Lary May, *Screening Out the Past: The Birth of Mass Culture and the Motion Picture Industry* (New York: Oxford University Press, 1980), chap. 3.

94. Fuller, *At the Picture Show,* 40.

95. Ad for the Lyric Theater from the *Burlington Gazette,* Sept. 4, 1909, 5.

96. GI, 19.

97. Barton Currie, "Nickel Madness," *Harper's Weekly,* Aug. 24, 1907, 1246–47.

98. Gustason, *Looking Back,* 108.

99. "Burlington Opera House Wrecked by Dynamite," *Burlington Hawkeye,* Sept. 3, 1910, 1.

TWO. ESSANAY

1. Theodore Dreiser, *The Titan* (1914; reprint, New York: World Publishing, 1946), 3–4.

2. Robert G. Spinney, *City of Big Shoulders: A History of Chicago* (DeKalb: Northern Illinois University Press, 2000), 123.

3. Joanne Meyerowitz, *Women Adrift: Independent Wage Earners in Chicago, 1880–1930* (Chicago: University of Chicago Press, 1988), 4–5, 9.

4. Louella Parsons, *The Gay Illiterate* (hereafter GI) (New York: Doubleday Doran, 1944), 18.

5. Ibid.

6. Eileen Bowser, *The Transformation of Cinema, 1907–1915* (Berkeley: University of California Press, 1990), 6.

7. On the origins of the star system, see Richard De Cordova, *Picture Personalities* (Chicago: University of Illinois Press, 1990), 58–59; Samantha Barbas, *Movie Crazy: Fans, Stars, and the Cult of Celebrity* (New York: Palgrave Macmillan, 2001), 19–21.

8. Kathryn Fuller, *At the Picture Show: Small Town Audiences and the Creation of Movie Fan Culture* (Washington, DC: Smithsonian, 1996), 138.

9. "Notes of the Picture Players," *Motion Picture,* June 1912, 138.

10. De Cordova, *Picture Personalities,* 105–6.

11. Quoted in ibid., 103.

12. *Moving Picture World,* Oct. 1913, quoted in Fuller, *At the Picture Show,* 126.

13. Elaine Sterne, "Writing for the Movies as a Profession," *Photoplay,* Sept. 1914, 156.

14. Charles Jahant, "The Early Chicago Film Industry," 47, Essanay Clipping File, Academy of Motion Picture Arts and Sciences, Beverly Hills, California.

15. Ibid., 47.

16. Bowser, *Transformation of Cinema,* 151.

17. GI, 25–27.

18. Eric Ergenbright, "Louella Parsons," *Dixon Telegraph,* Dec. 14, 1936, 5.

19. This information appeared on Louella and Jack McCaffrey's marriage license from Lake County, Indiana, Jan. 12, 1915.

20. "Lt. Parsons Weds," *Dixon Evening Telegraph,* Aug. 6, 1918, 3.

21. "John Edwards of Amboy Called by Maker This Morn," *Dixon Evening Telegraph,* Oct. 2, 1931.

22. See Bowser, *Transformation of Cinema,* chap. 1.

23. *Los Angeles Examiner* (hereafter LAE), Sept. 30, 1934, V, 5.

24. Louella Parsons Oral History, Popular Arts Collection, Butler Library, Columbia University (hereafter LPOH), 84.

25. LAE, May 29, 1931.

26. LAE, Jan. 7, 1930.

27. LAE, May 3, 1936, V, 7.

28. Louella O. Parsons, "The Essanay Days," *Theatre Arts,* July 1951, 33.

29. Lawrence Quirk, *The Films of Gloria Swanson* (Secaucus, NJ: Citadel Press, 1984), n.p.

30. "The Magic Wand," *Moving Picture World,* Aug. 11, 1912; Richard J. Maturi and Mary Buckingham Maturi, *Beverly Bayne, Queen of the Movies* (Jefferson, NC: McFarland, 2001), 117.

31. "Harriet Parsons Here in Moving Pictures," *Dixon Evening Telegraph,* Nov. 26, 1912, 1.

32. Ad for Essanay, *Moving Picture World,* Nov. 8, 1912, 511.

33. "Photoplays from Essanay's," *Motography,* Oct. 26, 1912.

34. Monte M. Katterjohn, "Thumbnail Biographies," *Photoplay,* Sept. 1914, 166.

35. GI, 27.

36. Bowser, *Transformation of Cinema,* 242.

37. James S. McQuade, "Chicago Letter," *Moving Picture World,* Jan. 25, 1913.

38. "It's Old Stuff, but It's Good," *Chicago Tribune,* June 2, 1915.

39. "Bushman Thanking Friends," *Motography,* June 13, 1914, 416.

40. Gloria Swanson, *Swanson on Swanson* (New York: Random House, 1980), 42.

41. LPOH, 89.

42. Neil G. Caward, "Where the Artistic Temperament Is Fed," *Motography*, Christmas 1913, 461–62.

43. Herb Graffis, "Lolly and Her Pups," *Radio News,* n.d., LOP Scrapbook #25, Louella Parsons Collection, Academy of Motion Pictures Arts and Sciences, Beverly Hills, California; LAE, Nov. 23, 1931, 1.

44. Roy L McCardell, "Writing for the Movies," *Saturday Evening Post,* May 16, 1914, 42.

45. "Thumbnail Biographies," *Photoplay,* Sept. 1914, 166.

46. Lizzie Francke, *Script Girls: Women Screenwriters in Hollywood* (London: British Film Institute, 1994), chap. 1; Anthony Slide, *Early Women Directors* (South Brunswick, NJ: A. J. Barnes, 1977), chap. 1; also see Cari Beauchamp, *Without Lying Down: Frances Marion and the Powerful Women of Early Hollywood* (New York: Scribner, 1997).

47. *Dixon Telegraph,* Aug. 29, 1914, 1.

48. "Essanay Foreign Sales Unaffected," *Motography,* Oct. 3, 1914, 454.

49. "Essanay Growing," *Motography,* Jan. 10, 1914, 30.

50. "Essanay Not Buying," *Motography,* Oct. 30, 1915, 909.

51. LPOH, 73.

52. John McPhaul, *Deadlines and Monkeyshines: The Fabled World of Chicago Journalism* (Englewood Cliffs, NJ: Prentice-Hall, 1964), 224.

53. LPOH, 73.

54. *Chicago Herald,* Dec. 20, 1914, 6.

55. *Chicago Herald,* Apr. 12, 1915.

56. LPOH, 92.

57. Jack McCaffrey obituary, *Tallulah (LA) Madison Journal,* Sept. 6, 1957.

58. Letter from Adeline Churchill to George Eells, June 24, 1969, George Eells Collection, Arizona State University (hereafter Eells Collection, ASU).

59. Katharine Ward, interview by George Eells, Sept. 1, 1969, Eells Collection, ASU.

60. Letter from Adeline Churchill to George Eells, June 24, 1969, Eells Collection, ASU.

61. Charles Chaplin, *My Autobiography* (New York: Simon and Schuster, 1964), 16.

62. Letter from Martha Sevier to George Eells, Dec. 20, 1970, Eells Collection, ASU.

63. Katharine Ward, interview by George Eells.

64. "Mrs. Parsons Married," *Dixon Evening Telegraph,* Jan. 12, 1915, 3.

65. "Elopement Story False," *Dixon Telegraph,* Feb. 2, 1915, 3.

66. "Mrs. Bailie," interview by George Eells, n.d., Eells Collection, ASU.

THREE. THE COLUMN

1. "Seen on the Screen," *Chicago Herald,* Mar. 15, 1916.

2. Charles Ponce de Leon, *Self-Exposure: Human Interest Journalism and the*

Emergence of Celebrity in America (Chapel Hill: University of North Carolina Press, 2002), 52, 44.

3. Ibid., chap. 1.

4. Neal Gabler, *Winchell: Gossip, Power, and the Culture of Celebrity* (New York: Knopf, 1994), 78.

5. Benjamin McArthur, *Actors and American Culture, 1880–1920* (Philadelphia: Temple University Press, 1984), 149.

6. Garth Jowett, "A Capacity for Evil: The 1915 Supreme Court Mutual Decision," in *Controlling Hollywood: Censorship and Regulation in the Studio Era,* ed. Matthew Bernstein (New Brunswick, NJ: Rutgers University Press, 1999), 22.

7. "Viewing the Pics," *Motography,* Aug. 22, 1914, 280.

8. Garth Jowett, *Film, the Democratic Art* (Boston: Little, Brown, 1976), 146.

9. Ibid., 146, italics in the original. For the first influential study of the psychological effects of the movies, see Hugo Munsterberg, *The Photoplay: A Psychological Study* (New York: D. Appleton, 1916).

10. Jowett, "A Capacity for Evil," 31.

11. Jane Addams, *The Spirit of Youth and the City Streets* (New York: Macmillan, 1909), 9.

12. Munsterberg, *The Photoplay.*

13. "Nickel Theaters Crime Breeders," *Chicago Tribune,* Apr. 13, 1907. On female audiences, and on opposition to women's moviegoing in the early twentieth century, see Kathy Peiss, *Cheap Amusements: Working Women and Leisure in Turn of the Century New York* (Philadelphia: Temple University Press, 1986); Nan Enstad, *Ladies of Labor, Girls of Adventure: Working Women, Popular Culture, and Labor Politics at the Turn of the Twentieth Century* (New York: Columbia University Press, 1999); Miriam Hansen, *Babel and Babylon: Spectatorship in American Silent Film* (Cambridge: Harvard University Press, 1991).

14. See Lary May, *Screening out the Past: The Birth of Mass Culture and the Motion Picture Industry* (New York: Oxford University Press, 1980); Robert Sklar, *Movie-Made America: A Cultural History of American Movies* (New York: Vintage, 1994); Francis Couvares, ed., *Movie Censorship and American Culture* (Washington, DC: Smithsonian, 1996).

15. Jowett, *Film,* 12.

16. "Seen on the Screen," Apr. 23, 1916, 4.

17. The concept of "mothering the movies" was used by the Women's Christian Temperance Union in their campaign for state and federal film censorship. See Alison Parker, "Mothering the Movies," in *Movie Censorship and American Culture,* ed. Francis Couvares (Washington, DC: Smithsonian, 1996).

18. "Seen on the Screen," Aug. 14, 1917.

19. "Seen on the Screen," Apr. 30, 1915.

20. "Seen on the Screen," Apr. 12, 1915.

21. Louella Parsons, "How to Write Photoplays," *Chicago Herald,* Mar. 14, 1915, 6.

22. Letter from LOP to Mr. Harrison, July 24, 1916, Redpath Chautauqua Collection, University of Iowa Special Collections.

23. "Seen on the Screen," June 24, 1915, 8.

24. Eve Golden, *Vamp: The Rise and Fall of Theda Bara* (Vestal, NY: Empire Publishing, 1996), 39.

25. "The Case for the Defense," n.d., LOP Scrapbook #1, Academy of Motion Picture Arts and Sciences, Beverly Hills, California (hereafter AMPAS).

26. "Seen on the Screen," Mar. 15, 1916.

27. "Let It Stay Barred," *Chicago Herald*, May 17, 1915, 6.

28. "Seen on the Screen," May 26, 1915.

29. "D. W. Griffith in Plea for His Greatest Film," *Chicago Herald*, June 1, 1915.

30. "Chicago Court's Epoch-making Decision," *Motography*, June 19, 1915, 1.

31. Louella Parsons Oral History, Popular Arts Collection, Butler Library, Columbia University, New York (hereafter LPOH), xv, 98; Ethel M. Colson Brazelton, *Writing and Editing for Women* (New York: Funk and Wagnalls, 1927), 142.

32. Louella Parsons, *How to Write for the Movies* (Chicago: McClurg, 1915), 132.

33. "Mrs. Parsons Told of Inside of Movies," *Dixon Evening Telegraph*, Aug. 8, 1916, 1.

34. "Former Dixon Woman Reaches High Position in Movie-Land," *Dixon Evening Telegraph*, Aug. 16, 1916, 1.

35. Letter from LOP to Mr. Harrison, July 24, 1916, Redpath Chautauqua Collection, University of Iowa Special Collections.

36. Clipping, n.d., LOP Scrapbook #49, AMPAS.

37. Letter from LOP to Mr. McClure, Aug. 11, 1916, Redpath Chautauqua Collection, University of Iowa Special Collections.

38. "Former Dixon Woman," 1.

39. "Seen on the Screen," Jan. 14, 1916.

40. Brazelton, *Writing and Editing for Women*, 144.

41. William McAdams, *Ben Hecht: The Man behind the Myth* (New York: Scribner's, 1990), 276.

42. "Seen on the Screen," June 11, 1915.

43. *Los Angeles Examiner* (hereafter LAE), July 2, 1942, I, 19.

44. "Seen on the Screen," May 8, 1915.

45. Richard Koszarski, *An Evening's Entertainment: The Age of the Silent Feature Picture, 1915–1928* (New York: Scribner's, 1990), 93.

46. "Seen on the Screen," July 3, 1915.

47. On sob sisters, see Joe Saltzman, "Sob Sisters: The Image of the Female Journalist in Popular Culture," Image of the Journalist in Popular Culture, www.ijpc.org/sobsessay.pdf (accessed January 21, 2005).

48. *Editor and Publisher*, Aug. 14, 1926, LOP Scrapbook #14, AMPAS.

49. LAE, July 26, 1936, V, 5.

50. *Hollywood Reporter*, Mar. 25, 1948, 2.

51. LPOH, 44.

52. Letter from Rae Shepard to George Eells, Feb. 3, 1969, George Eells Collection, University of Southern California.

53. Script for *Hollywood Premiere* radio show, Mar. 28, 1948, Louella Parsons Collection, Cinema Television Library, University of Southern California.

54. "Seen on the Screen," Nov. 13, 1917, LOP Scrapbook #2, AMPAS.

55. Louella Parsons, *The Gay Illiterate* (hereafter GI) (New York: Doubleday, Doran, 1944), 35.

56. Ibid.

57. W. A. Swanberg, *Citizen Hearst* (New York: Scribner's, 1961), 107.

58. Ibid., 66.

59. Ibid., 127.

60. Ibid., 327.

61. John McPhaul, *Deadlines and Monkeyshines: The Fabled World of Chicago Journalism* (Englewood Cliffs, NJ: Prentice-Hall, 1964), 220–21.

62. Swanberg, *Citizen Hearst,* 349.

63. David Nasaw, *The Chief: The Life of William Randolph Hearst* (Boston: Houghton Mifflin, 2000), 268.

64. GI, 39.

65. Louella Parsons, "Propaganda!" *Photoplay,* Sept. 1918, 43.

66. LAE, Mar. 15, 1936.

67. LAE, Aug. 6, 1939, V, 5.

68. GI, 41.

FOUR. NEW YORK

1. Richard Koszarski, *An Evening's Entertainment: The Age of the Silent Feature Picture, 1915–1928* (New York: Scribner's, 1990), 99, 102; Eileen Bowser, *The Transformation of Cinema, 1907–1915* (Berkeley: University of California Press, 1990), 159, 161.

2. Koszarski, *Evening's Entertainment,* 99–104.

3. Benjamin B. Hampton, *History of the American Film Industry* (New York: Dover, 1970), 214.

4. Alfred McClung Lee, *The Daily Newspaper in America* (New York: Macmillan, 1947), 69, 71, 81, 84.

5. Adeline Churchill, interview by George Eells, n.d., George Eells Collection, Arizona State University.

6. Richard O'Connor, *Heywood Broun: A Biography* (New York: Putnam, 1975), 26.

7. William R. Taylor, *In Pursuit of Gotham: Culture and Commerce in New York* (New York: Oxford University Press, 1992), 174.

8. O'Connor, *Heywood Broun,* 27–29.

9. Louella Parsons Oral History, Popular Arts Collection, Butler Library, Columbia University, 91.

10. *New York Morning Telegraph* (hereafter NYMT), June 9, 1918, LOP Scrapbook #2, Louella Parsons Collection, Academy of Motion Pictures Arts and Sciences, Beverly Hills, California (hereafter AMPAS); "Dixon Woman Now on Big NY Daily," *Dixon Evening Telegraph,* June 14, 1918.

11. NYMT, Jan. 5, 1919, LOP Scrapbook #2, AMPAS.

12. NYMT, Feb. 16, 1919; May 1, 1921, LOP Scrapbook #2, AMPAS.

13. On the paradox of film stardom—stars' ordinariness yet extraordinariness—see Richard Dyer, *Stars* (London: BFI, 1998), chap. 2; Dyer, *Heavenly Bodies: Film Stars and Society* (New York: St. Martin's, 1986); also Richard Schickel, *Intimate Strangers* (Garden City, NY: Doubleday, 1985); and John Ellis, "Stars as Cinematic Phenomenon," in *Visible Fictions: Cinema, Television, Video* (London: Routledge and Kegan Paul, 1982), 91–108.

14. Louella Parsons, *The Gay Illiterate* (hereafter GI) (New York: Doubleday Doran, 1944), 35.

15. *Denver Post,* Oct. 25, 1927, LOP Scrapbook #15, AMPAS.

16. *Los Angeles Examiner* (hereafter LAE), July 12, 1942.

17. "Theodora Bean, Writer, Is Dead," *New York Times* (hereafter NYT), Aug. 6, 1926.

18. Ishbel Ross, *Ladies of the Press* (New York: Harper, 1936), 258.

19. LAE, June 8, 1944; David Pratt, "O Lubitsch, Where Wert Thou?" *Wide Angle* 13, no. 1 (Jan. 1991): 42.

20. GI, 64; David Thomson, *Showman: The Life of David O. Selznick* (New York: Knopf, 1992), 57.

21. LAE, May 16, 1931, II, 5.

22. NYMT, Apr. 2, 1922, LOP Scrapbook #6, AMPAS; Sept. 27, 1918, LOP Scrapbook #4, AMPAS.

23. NYMT, May 3, 1921, LOP Scrapbook #5, AMPAS.

24. Ross, *Ladies of the Press,* 246.

25. Elizabeth V. Burt, ed., *Women's Press Organizations, 1881–1999* (Westport, CT: Greenwood Press, 2000), 172–73.

26. Ibid., 175.

27. NYMT, Jan. 29, 1922, LOP Scrapbook #6, AMPAS; "Women Writers Hail Celebrities at Annual Fete," clipping, n.d., LOP Scrapbook #10, AMPAS; *Variety,* Feb. 24, 1926, LOP Scrapbook #10, AMPAS; NYMT, Mar. 19, 1922, LOP Scrapbook #6, AMPAS.

28. George Eells, *Hedda and Louella* (New York: Putnam, 1972), 88; NYMT, Dec. 29, 1921, LOP Scrapbook #5, AMPAS.

29. GI, 51.

30. NYMT, Mar. 30, 1919, LOP Scrapbook #4, AMPAS; NYMT, Oct. 21, 1921, LOP Scrapbook #5, AMPAS; Sumner Smith, "Charles Ray Stands the Acid Test of Praise at Luncheon for Newspapermen," *Moving Picture World,* Dec. 17, 1921.

31. "N.A.M.P.I. Entrenches in Massachusetts for First Censorship Referendum Battle," *Moving Picture World,* Oct. 15, 1921, 753.

32. GI, 47.

33. Manners quoted in Amy Fine Collins, "Idol Gossips," *Vanity Fair* (Apr. 1997): 360; GI, 47, 60.

34. "Peter Brady Killed as Plane Hits House," NYT, Sept. 21, 1931, 1; NYT, Apr. 25, 1916, 4; "Hylan," NYT, Jan. 2, 1918, 1; "Citizens Oppose Politics in Schools," NYT, Jan. 29, 1921, 7.

35. NYT, May 8, 1922, 19; "Denies Governor's Claim to Economy," NYT, June 26, 1922, 14; "Against Film Censorship," NYT, Sept. 18, 1922, 12; "Organized Labor Is Screen's Champion, *Moving Picture World,* Oct. 29, 1921, 1021.

36. "The Late Peter J. Brady," NYT, Sept. 24, 1931, 24.

37. Program for the Fourth Annual Dinner Dance of the Motion Picture Directors' Association, Mar. 16, 1922, in Douglas Gomery, ed., *The Will Hays Papers* (Frederick, MD.: University Publications of America, 1988), microfilm, reel 4; "Hay's Debut," *Moving Picture World,* Apr. 1, 1922, 454.

38. NYMT, Mar. 12, 1922, Apr. 21, 1922, LOP Scrapbook #6, AMPAS.

39. NYMT, Mar. 29, 1922, LOP Scrapbook #6, AMPAS; Feb. 23, 1922, Sept. 15, 1923, LOP Scrapbook #7, AMPAS.

40. "Pictures and People," *Motion Picture News,* May 20, 1922, 2829; undated note in LOP Scrapbook #6, AMPAS.

41. GI, 60.

FIVE. "THE LOVELY MISS MARION DAVIES"

1. Louella Parsons, *Tell It to Louella* (New York: Putnam, 1961), 219.

2. Marion Davies, *The Times We Had* (New York: Bobbs Merrill, 1975).

3. Dorothy Day, "What One Critic Thinks and Says about Another," *FBO News,* Dec. 15, 1923, LOP Scrapbook #10, Louella Parsons Collection, Academy of Motion Pictures Arts and Sciences, Beverly Hills, California (hereafter AMPAS).

4. Frances Marion, *Off with Their Heads!* (New York: Macmillan, 1972), 82.

5. Louella Parsons, *The Gay Illiterate* (hereafter GI) (New York: Doubleday Doran, 1944), 101.

6. On Bebe Daniels, see Bebe Daniels and Ben Lyon, *Life with the Lyons* (London: Odhams, 1953).

7. Hedda Hopper, *From under My Hat* (Garden City, NY: Doubleday, 1952), 129.

8. Marion Davies, *Off with Their Heads!,* 97.

9. Anita Loos, *A Girl Like I* (New York: Viking, 1966), 208.

10. *New York City Mirror,* Apr. 28, 1925, LOP Scrapbook #10, AMPAS.

11. GI, 46.

12. *New York Morning Telegraph* (hereafter NYMT), Jan. 18, 1922, LOP Scrapbook #6, AMPAS; GI, 59.

13. "Mrs. J. Edwards, Former Freeport Woman, Expires," *Freeport Journal Standard,* Dec. 30, 1922, 6.

14. Louella Parsons Oral History, Popular Arts Collection, Butler Library, Columbia University, 64.

15. Louis Pizzitola, *Hearst over Hollywood* (New York: Columbia University Press, 2002), 126; NYMT, Mar. 9, 1919, LOP Scrapbook #4, AMPAS.

16. Fred Lawrence Guiles, *Marion Davies* (New York: Bantam, 1973), 71, 80; Pizzitola, *Hearst over Hollywood,* 166.

17. Guiles, *Marion Davies,* 67.

18. Adela Rogers St. Johns, *The Honeycomb* (Garden City, NY: Doubleday, 1969), 143; Davies, *The Times We Had,* 21.

19. Pizzitola, *Hearst over Hollywood,* 169.

20. "Knighthood in Chicago Opens Tremendously," *Variety,* Oct. 20, 1922, 44; "Knighthood Beats Robin Hood to First Chicago Opening," *Variety,* Oct. 13, 1922, 46; "Inside Stuff on Pictures," *Variety,* Oct. 20, 1922, 42; NYMT, Oct. 8, 1922, LOP Scrapbook #7, AMPAS.

21. NYMT, Sept. 14, Sept. 17, Dec. 22, 1922, Apr. 8, July 15, 1923, LOP Scrapbook #7, AMPAS.

22. Guiles, *Marion Davies,* 459; Nasaw, *The Chief,* 324.

23. "When Knighthood Was in Flower."

24. NYMT, Sept. 14, 1922, July 15, 1923, LOP Scrapbook #8, AMPAS.

25. Oswald Garrison Villard, *Some Newspapers and Newspaper-Men* (New York: Knopf, 1923), 319, 20.

26. David Nasaw, *The Chief: The Life of William Randolph Hearst* (Boston: Houghton Mifflin, 2000), 455.

27. "TOCC Gives Elaborate Annual Party," *Moving Picture World,* Dec. 16, 1922, 630.

28. GI, 73.

29. GI, 71.

30. NYMT, Feb. 27, Oct. 11, Oct. 22, 1923, LOP Scrapbook #7, AMPAS.

31. "Famous Film Critic Felicitated by Craft on Joining *New York American,*" *New York American,* Dec. 9, 1923, LOP Scrapbook #10, AMPAS.

32. George Eells, *Hedda and Louella* (New York: Putnam, 1972), 50; "Famous Film Critic Felicitated"; Dorothy Day, "What One Critic Thinks and Says about Another," *FBO News,* Dec. 15, 1923; "Luncheon to Honor Miss Parsons," NYMT, Dec. 9, 1923, LOP Scrapbook #10, AMPAS; S. Jay Kaufman, "Around the Town," *Evening Telegram,* Dec. 9, 1923, LOP Scrapbook #10, AMPAS.

33. "Famous Film Critic Felicitated"; ad in *New York American,* Feb. 10, 1924, LOP Scrapbook #10, AMPAS; GI, 73.

34. Letter from *Morning Telegraph* to Louella Parsons, n.d., George Eells Collection, University of Southern California.

35. GI, 73.

36. Clipping, Jan. 12, 1924, LOP Scrapbook #10, AMPAS.

37. GI, 68; Swanberg, *Citizen Hearst,* 345.

38. Nasaw, *The Chief,* 342.

39. Guiles, *Marion Davies,* 185; J. Boothe, "Thomas Ince, Director Extraordinary," *Motography,* May 16, 1914, 335; "Thomas Ince Dies; Producer of Films," *New York Times* (hereafter NYT), Nov. 20, 1924, 4.

40. "Ince Had Deal with Hearst," NYT, Nov. 21, 1924, 22.

41. Nasaw, *The Chief,* 344.

42. The *New York Times* reported inaccurately that he had a heart attack on a train to San Diego. "Ince's Death Natural, Prosecutor Asserts," NYT, Dec. 11, 1924, 6.

43. Amy Fine Collins, "Idol Gossips," *Vanity Fair* (Apr. 1997): 368.

44. Peter Brown, *The MGM Girls* (New York: St. Martin's Press, 1983), 140.

45. Davies, *The Times We Had,* 66; St. Johns, *The Honeycomb,* 189; "Ince's Death Natural"; Pizzitola, *Hearst over Hollywood,* 232.

46. St. Johns, *The Honeycomb,* 216.

47. Contemporary depictions of the *Oneida* story have kept the rumor alive. For recent retellings, see Patricia Hearst and Cornelia Frances Biddle, *Murder at San Simeon* (New York: Scribner's, 1996); Collins, "Idol Gossips"; and *The Cat's Meow,* a film by director Peter Bogdanovich released in 2001.

SIX. ON THE WAY TO HOLLYWOOD

1. Gene Fowler, *Skyline* (New York: Viking, 1961), 64.

2. Ibid., 95, 98.

3. Adela Rogers St. Johns, *The Honeycomb* (Garden City, NY: Doubleday, 1969), 124.

4. W. A. Swanberg, *Citizen Hearst* (New York: Scribner's, 1961), 84.

5. Ishbel Ross, *Ladies of the Press* (New York: Harper, 1936), 36.

6. "The Screen and Its Players," Apr. 16, 1925, LOP Scrapbook #12, Louella Parsons Collection, Academy of Motion Pictures Arts and Sciences, Beverly Hills, California (hereafter AMPAS).

7. Charles Ponce de Leon, *Self-Exposure: Human Interest Journalism and the Emergency of Celebrity in America* (Chapel Hill: University of North Carolina Press, 2002), 46–47. It was the tabloids, in particular, that took the story-journalism format to new and often ethically dubious heights. The *Daily News,* established in 1919, had by 1924 gained a readership of 800,000, the nation's largest at the time. To meet the competition, Hearst started the *Daily Mirror* in 1924—"ninety percent entertainment and ten percent information" was the formula Hearst set out for the new publication—and by 1926, the *Mirror* had a circulation of 370,000. George Douglas, *The Golden Age of the Newspaper* (Westport, CT: Greenwood Press, 1999), 230.

8. Leo Lowenthal, "The Triumph of Mass Idols," in *Literature, Popular Culture, and Society* (Englewood Cliffs, NJ: Prentice-Hall, 1961), 109–40.

9. Warren I. Susman, "Personality and the Making of Twentieth Century Culture," in Susman, *Culture as History: The Transformation of American Society in the Twentieth Century* (New York: Pantheon, 1984), 271–85; William Leach, *Land of Desire: Merchants, Power, and the Rise of a New American Culture* (New York: Pantheon, 1993). Also see Lary May, *Screening Out the Past: The Birth of Mass Culture and the Motion Picture Industry* (New York: Oxford, 1980); Richard Schickel, *Intimate Strangers* (Garden City, NY: Doubleday, 1985).

10. See Samantha Barbas, *Movie Crazy: Fans, Stars, and the Cult of Celebrity* (New York: Palgrave Macmillan, 2001), chap. 5.

11. *New York Times* (hereafter NYT), Sept. 20, 1925, LOP Scrapbook #12, AMPAS.

12. Gaylyn Studlar, "The Perils of Pleasure? Fan Magazine Discourse as Women's Commodified Culture in the 1920s," *Wide Angle* 13, no. 1 (Jan. 1991): 9.

13. Ibid., 7.

14. Ibid.

15. "The Screen and Its Players," July 26, 1925, LOP Scrapbook #12, AMPAS.

16. "The Screen and Its Players," Sept. 27, 1925, LOP Scrapbook #12, AMPAS.

17. "The Screen and Its Players," Sept. 10, 1925, LOP Scrapbook #12, AMPAS.

18. "The Screen and Its Players," July 9, 1925, LOP Scrapbook #12, AMPAS.

19. *San Francisco Examiner,* Sept. 14. 1924, LOP Scrapbook #12, AMPAS.

20. *Variety,* June 4, 1924, LOP Scrapbook #10, AMPAS.

21. Jane Kesner Ardmore, *The Self-Enchanted* (New York: McGraw Hill, 1959), 163–64.

22. Louella Parsons, *Tell It to Louella* (New York: Putnam, 1961), 44.

23. *New York Mirror,* May 15, 1925, LOP Scrapbook #10, AMPAS.

24. *San Francisco Examiner,* May 24, 1925, LOP Scrapbook #10, AMPAS.

25. Ibid.

26. *Los Angeles Herald,* May 20, June 10, June 21, 1925, LOP Scrapbook #10, AMPAS.

27. *Los Angeles Examiner,* July 11, 1925, LOP Scrapbook #10, AMPAS.

28. Charles Chaplin, *My Autobiography* (New York: Simon and Schuster, 1964), 312.

29. Fred Lawrence Guiles, *Marion Davies* (New York: Bantam, 1973), 172.

30. *Los Angeles Herald,* June 27, 1925, LOP Scrapbook #10, AMPAS; Louis Pizzitola, *Hearst over Hollywood* (New York: Columbia University Press, 2002), 231.

31. Telegram from Gene Fowler to LOP, June 30, 1925, LOP Scrapbook #11, AMPAS.

32. H. Allen Smith, *The Life and Legend of Gene Fowler* (New York: Morrow, 1977), 188–89.

33. *New York Moving Picture World,* n.d.; *Washington Star,* Aug. 23, 1924; *Bridgeport Times,* Apr. 6, 1925; *Variety,* Mar. 11, 1925, LOP #10; *New York American,* Mar. 21, 1925, LOP Scrapbook #9, AMPAS.

34. Clipping, Mar. 21, 1925, LOP Scrapbook #9, AMPAS.

35. *Bridgeport (CT) Times,* Apr. 6, 1925, LOP Scrapbook #10, AMPAS.

36. George Eells, *Hedda and Louella* (New York: Putnam, 1972), 117.

37. *Los Angeles Examiner,* Mar. 8, 1951, II, 7.

38. Baird Leonard, "Lines for a New Years Card," *Life,* Jan. 2, 1925, LOP Scrapbook #10, AMPAS.

39. Louella Parsons, *The Gay Illiterate* (hereafter GI) (New York: Doubleday Doran, 1944), 78.

40. A note from Davies, addressed to Louella in the Roosevelt Hospital, referred cryptically to "that other little matter you are having done in the hospital." "I think I'll try it myself," Davies wrote. Letter from Marion Davies to Louella, 1924, courtesy of Nick Langdon of the Marion Davies Fan Club.

41. GI, 78.

42. Ibid.

43. Swanberg, *Citizen Hearst,* 353; Marion Davies, *The Times We Had* (New York: Bobbs Merrill, 1975), 118.

44. Swanberg, *Citizen Hearst,* 418.

45. Parsons, *Tell It to Louella,* 93.

46. *New York Star,* Mar. 26, 1926; *New York Graphic,* Feb. 13, 1926, LOP #10, AMPAS.

47. GI, 80.

48. *History of San Bernardino and Riverside County* (Chicago: Western Historical Association, 1922), 224–26.

49. Population statistics courtesy of Carolina Barrera, city clerk of Colton, CA, correspondence with author, Sept. 30, 2002.

50. *Hollywood Premiere,* script, Mar. 28, 1948, Louella Parsons Collection, USC.

51. *Detroit Times,* Mar. 1, 1926; Mar. 7, 1926; *Los Angeles Examiner,* Feb. 28, 1926, LOP Scrapbook #15, AMPAS.

52. In 1926, Louella was appointed motion picture editor for the Universal Service, the Hearst wire service for the morning papers. But in 1937, when Universal merged with the International News Service, the Hearst evening news service, Louella became motion picture editor of the International News Service.

53. *New York American,* Feb. 24, 1926, LOP Scrapbook #10, AMPAS.

54. GI, 84.

55. Ibid.

56. On the Universal Syndicate, see Moses Koenisgberg, *King News: An Autobiography* (Philadelphia: F. S. Stokes, 1941).

57. "Louella Parsons Gets New Job on Los Angeles Paper," *Denver Post,* Apr. 4, 1926, LOP Scrapbook #13, AMPAS.

58. GI, 84.

59. "P. J. Brady Chosen Labor Bank Head," NYT, May 17, 1923, 2; GI, 105.

60. Clippings, n.d.; "Marion Feted during Eastern Trip," n.d.; "Promotion Value of Writers' Work," Apr. 15, 1926, all in LOP Scrapbook #13, AMPAS.

1. Louella Parsons, *The Gay Illiterate* (hereafter GI) (New York: Doubleday Doran, 1944), 24.

2. Kevin Starr, *Material Dreams: Southern California through the 1920s* (New York: Oxford University Press, 1990), 98.

3. Starr, *Material Dreams,* 100.

4. Bruce Torrence, *Hollywood: The First Hundred Years* (New York: New York Zoetrope, 1982), 76.

5. Ibid., 87.

6. Ibid., 108.

7. *Los Angeles Examiner* (hereafter LAE), Aug. 18, 1926; LOP, Scrapbook # 14, Louella Parsons Collection, Academy of Motion Pictures Arts and Sciences, Beverly Hills, California (hereafter AMPAS).

8. On the Arbuckle scandal and its aftermath, see Sam Stoloff, "Fatty Arbuckle and the Black Sox," in *Headline Hollywood,* ed. Adrienne McLean and David Cook (New Brunswick, NJ: Rutgers University Press, 2001); Samantha Barbas, "The Political Spectator," *Film History* 11, no. 2 (1999): 217–28; Stuart Oderman, *Roscoe "Fatty" Arbuckle* (Jefferson, NC: McFarland, 1994).

9. Kathy Feeley, "Louella Parsons and Hedda Hopper's Hollywood: The Rise of the Celebrity Gossip Industry in Twentieth-Century America, 1910–1950" (Ph.D. diss., City University of New York, 2003), 54.

10. In 1925, the *Examiner*'s circulation was 167,935, behind the *Evening Herald* and ahead of the *Times.* Rob Wagner, *Red Ink, White Lies: The Rise and Fall of Los Angeles Newspapers, 1920–1962* (Upland, CA: Dragonflyer Press, 2000), introduction.

11. Ibid.

12. "Hollywood Chatter," *Variety,* Oct. 9, 1929.

13. Jerry Hoffman, interview by George Eells, n.d., George Eells Collection, Arizona State University.

14. Wagner, *Red Ink, White Lies,* chap. 1.

15. "Heavy Guns of Film World Desert NY for LA," LAE, Apr. 12, 1926, 11.

16. Pola Negri, *Memoirs of a Star* (Garden City, NY: Doubleday, 1970), 355.

17. "LOP Riles LA Legit Managers," clipping, LOP Scrapbook #14, AMPAS.

18. Negri, *Memoirs of a Star,* 355.

19. Ronald Davis, *The Glamour Factory: Inside Hollywood's Big Studio System* (Dallas: Southern Methodist University Press, 1993), 5, 138.

20. Robert Sklar, *Movie-Made America: A Cultural History of American Movies* (New York: Vintage, 1994), 149; Richard Maltby, *Hollywood Cinema: An Introduction* (Cambridge, MA: Blackwell, 1990), 63, 65–66.

21. Cathy Klaprat, "The Star as Market Strategy: Bette Davis in Another Light," in *The American Film Industry,* ed. Tino Balio (Madison: University of Wisconsin Press, 1985), 351–76.

22. Davis, *The Glamour Factory,* 138–39.

23. "Louella Parsons Dead at 91," *Variety,* Dec. 13, 1972, Louella Parsons Clipping File, AMPAS.

24. Clipping, Sept. 23, 1927, LOP Scrapbook #14, AMPAS.

25. Sally Wright Cobb, *The Brown Derby Restaurant: A Hollywood Legend* (New York: Rizzoli, 1996), n.p.

26. O. O. McIntyre, "New York Day by Day," n.d., LOP Scrapbook #13, AMPAS.

27. Clipping, Sept. 23, 1927, LOP Scrapbook #14, AMPAS.

28. Larry Swindell, *Screwball: The Life of Carole Lombard* (New York: Morrow, 1975), 33.

29. Velva Darling, "Is Feature Writing Hard Work?" n.d., LOP Scrapbook #13, AMPAS.

30. Philip Schuyler, "Where Shadow Gods Are Manufactured," *Editor and Publisher,* Sept. 10. 1927, LOP Scrapbook #14, AMPAS. According to media historian Kathy Feeley, Parsons's rise to power was a result of the standardization and consolidation of news content in the U.S. press during this period. The total number of newspapers in the nation sharply dropped and syndicates and wire services rose. "Louella Parsons and Hedda Hopper's Hollywood," 62.

31. *Variety,* Nov. 24, 1926, LOP Scrapbook #14, AMPAS.

32. "Miss Parsons to Cover Fight at Quaker City," LOP Scrapbook #14, AMPAS; *Dixon Evening Telegraph,* Aug. 3, 1926, LOP Scrapbook #14, AMPAS.

33. LAE, Sept. 30, 1927.

34. LAE, Nov. 14, 1926.

35. Telegram from D. W. Griffith to LOP, Oct. 25, 1926, *D. W. Griffith Papers* (Frederick, MD: University Publications of America, 1982).

36. Clipping, June 3, 1927, LOP Scrapbook #14, AMPAS.

37. Donald Crafton, *The Talkies: American Cinema's Transition to Sound* (New York: Scribner's, 1997), 489.

38. "Hearst Aid to Independents in Exhibiting Field Providing Practical Plan Is Worked Out," *Variety,* July 27, 1929, 347.

39. GI, 117.

40. LAE, Apr. 22, 1928.

41. LAE, May 22, 1927.

42. Samuel Marx, *Mayer and Thalberg: The Make-Believe Saints* (New York: Random House, 1975), 105.

43. *Hollywood, the End of an Era* (London: Thames Video, 1980).

44. David Nasaw, *The Chief: The Life of William Randolph Hearst* (Boston: Houghton Mifflin, 2000), 409.

45. Crafton, *The Talkies,* 499.

46. Leatrice Joy Fountain, *Dark Star* (New York: St. Martin's Press, 1985), chap. 11.

47. Negri, *Memoirs of a Star,* 355.

48. Bebe Daniels and Ben Lyon, *Life with the Lyons* (London: Odhams, 1953), 143.

49. "Film Producing Not Now Bounded," *Variety*, Aug. 28, 1929, 2.

50. "Divorce Is Granted Mrs. Luella Parsons," *Dixon Evening Telegraph*, June 25, 1928, 1.

51. GI, 111.

52. "Dr. H. W. Martin Claimed by Death," LAE, June 25, 1951, Louella Parsons Clipping File, Academy of Motion Pictures Arts and Sciences (hereafter AMPAS).

53. GI, 103.

54. GI, 112.

55. Biography of Harriet Parsons, Harriet Parsons Clipping File, AMPAS; "Junior Stars at Wellesley," Mar. 24, 1927, LOP Scrapbook #13, AMPAS.

56. GI, 112.

57. "30,000 in Mob Scene Outdo Battle Films," LAE, June 27, 1928, 3.

58. GI, 115.

59. Ibid.

60. GI, 86.

61. Jim Heimann, *Out with the Stars: Hollywood Nightlife in the Studio Era* (New York: Abbeville Press, 1985), 35.

62. GI, 87.

63. LAE, Dec. 8, 1926.

64. Silas Bent, *Ballyhoo: The Voice of the Press* (New York: Boni, 1927), 5.

65. *Editor and Publisher*, Aug. 14, 1926, LOP Scrapbook #12, AMPAS.

66. Minutes, 4/29/36, Hollywood Women's Press Club Collection, AMPAS (hereafter HWPCC).

67. Dorothy Manners oral history, HWPCC.

68. This and the next quote come from Dorothy Manners's Founders Day luncheon speech, 1967, HWPCC.

69. *Hollywood Women's Press Club History*, n.d., HWPCC.

70. "Miss Parsons Becomes Bride of Dr. Martin," LAE, Jan. 7, 1930, LOP Scrapbook #16, AMPAS.

71. "Louella Parsons Files Bridal Notice," LAE, Dec. 20, 1929, LOP Scrapbook #13, AMPAS.

72. GI, 116.

EIGHT. FEUDS

1. Alan Brinkley, *The Unfinished Nation*, vol. 2 (New York: McGraw Hill, 1997), 680–85.

2. Donald Crafton, *The Talkies: American Cinema's Transition to Sound* (New York: Scribner's, 1997), 463.

3. WRH to Hays, Feb. 19, 1929, in *The Will Hays Papers*, ed. Douglas Gomery (Frederick, MD: University Publications of America, 1988), microfilm.

4. WRH to LOP, Mar. 24, 1931, Carton 12, William Randolph Hearst Collection,

Bancroft Library, University of California, Berkeley (hereafter Hearst Collection, UCB).

5. *Los Angeles Examiner* (hereafter LAE), Sept. 24, 1929, LOP Scrapbook #16, Louella Parsons Collection, Academy of Motion Pictures Arts and Sciences, Beverly Hills, California (hereafter AMPAS).

6. On the implementation of—and resistance to—the Production Code in 1930–31, see Gregory Black, *Hollywood Censored* (Cambridge: Cambridge University Press, 1994); Leonard Leff and Jerold Simmons, *The Dame in the Kimono: Hollywood Censorship and the Production Code* (New York: Doubleday, 1990); Francis Couvares, ed., *Movie Censorship and American Culture* (Washington, DC: Smithsonian, 1996); Frank Walsh, *Sin and Censorship: The Catholic Church and the Motion Picture Industry* (New Haven: Yale University Press, 1996).

7. Crafton, *The Talkies*, 481.

8. Letter from WRH to Hearst editors, n.d., LOP Scrapbook #13, AMPAS.

9. LOP to Lloyd Thompson, Nov. 1, 1931, Carton 12, Hearst Collection, UCB.

10. "Miss Parsons Inaugurates Radical Changes," *Editor and Publisher,* June 22, 1929, LOP Scrapbook #16, AMPAS.

11. *Atlanta Constitution,* Apr. 14, 1929, LOP Scrapbook #16, AMPAS.

12. "Hollywood Chatter," *Variety,* Aug. 21, 1929.

13. WRH to LOP, n.d., LOP Scrapbook #16, AMPAS.

14. Louis Lurie, interview by George Eells, n.d., George Eells Collection, Arizona State University (hereafter Eells Collection, ASU).

15. "Hollywood's Back Fence," *Time,* Jan. 24, 1944, 56.

16. George Eells, *Hedda and Louella* (New York: Putnam, 1972), 150.

17. Ibid.

18. Larry Swindell, *Screwball: The Life of Carole Lombard* (New York: Morrow, 1975), 168–69.

19. Bob Thomas, telephone interview by author, Feb. 3, 2004.

20. Len Riblett, interview by George Eells, n.d., Eells Collection, ASU.

21. Louella Parsons, *The Gay Illiterate* (hereafter GI) (New York: Doubleday Doran, 1944), 121.

22. Isabella Taves, "Louella Parsons," *Look,* Oct. 10, 1950, 60–61.

23. Anita Loos, *The Talmadge Girls* (New York: Viking, 1978), 68–69.

24. Charles Champlin, "Private Lives of Hollywood's Powerful Columnists," 126, Louella Parsons Clipping File, AMPAS.

25. "Hollywood's Back Fence," 54.

26. Bebe Daniels and Ben Lyon, *Life with the Lyons* (London: Odhams, 1953), 179.

27. Beaton cited in Victoria Kastner, *Hearst Castle: Biography of a Country House* (New York: H. N. Abrams, 2000), 129.

28. Ibid., 21.

29. Ken Murray, *The Golden Days of San Simeon* (Garden City, NY: Doubleday, 1971), 20.

30. Ibid., 24.

31. Ferdinand Lundberg, *Imperial Hearst* (New York: Equinox, 1936), 453.

32. Hedda Hopper, *From under My Hat* (Garden City, NY: Doubleday, 1952), 129.

33. David Nasaw, *The Chief: The Life of William Randolph Hearst* (Boston: Houghton Mifflin, 2000), 441.

34. Ilka Chase, *Past Imperfect* (Garden City, NY: Doubleday Doran, 1942), 116.

35. St. Johns quoted in Kastner, *Hearst Castle,* 130.

36. Stanley Heaton, "Gardening and Road Construction," Hearst San Simeon Oral History Project, Special Collections, California Polytechnic University, San Luis Obispo (hereafter HSSOHP), 8.

37. Ann Miller, "San Simeon during Its Time of Transition," HSSOHP, 21.

38. August Wahlberg, "Working for WR Hearst," HSSOHP, 88.

39. John Kobal, *People Will Talk* (New York: Knopf, 1985), 56.

40. Barry Paris, *Louise Brooks* (New York: Knopf, 1989), 238.

41. Adela Rogers St. Johns, *The Honeycomb* (Garden City, NY: Doubleday, 1969), 348.

42. LOP to WRH, Nov. 7, 1931, Carton 12, Hearst Collection, UCB.

43. "Peter Brady Funeral to Be Held Tomorrow," *New York Times* (hereafter NYT), Sept. 23, 1931; "Peter J. Brady Dies in Airplane Crash," NYT, Sept. 22, 1931, 1.

44. LOP to WRH, Sept. 24, 1931, Carton 12, Hearst Collection, UCB.

45. Tino Balio, *Grand Design: Hollywood as a Modern Business Enterprise* (New York: Scribner, 1993), 146.

46. *Editor and Publisher,* Aug. 14, 1926, LOP Scrapbook #12, AMPAS.

47. Louella "criticized" the stars cautiously. In Louella's column, stars made poor marriage choices and bad business deals, but they never had abortions, illegitimate pregnancies, or homosexual relationships. By limiting stars' transgressions to the morally safe if not trivial, Louella fulfilled readers' cravings for the seemingly intimate truth while drawing attention from actors' real, potentially more scandalous activities.

48. J. Herbie DiFonzo, *Beneath the Fault Line: The Popular and Legal Culture of Divorce in Twentieth-Century America* (Charlottesville: University Press of Virginia, 1997), 61.

49. LAE, Apr. 16, 1931.

50. Charles Ponce de Leon, *Self-Exposure: Human Interest Journalism and the Emergency of Celebrity in America* (Chapel Hill: University of North Carolina Press, 2002), 107–9.

51. Rosten cited in Richard Griffith, *The Talkies* (New York: Dover, 1971), 96.

52. LAE, Mar. 2, 1930.

53. LAE, May 10, 1936.

54. Edward Baron Turk, *Hollywood Diva: A Biography of Jeanette MacDonald* (Berkeley: University of California Press, 1998), 71–72.

55. LAE, Aug. 26, 1931.

56. LAE, Dec. 3, 1933.

57. LAE, Nov. 18, 1933.

58. LAE, Dec. 15, 1932.

59. LAE, July 30, 1930.

60. LAE, Dec. 15, 1930.

61. LAE, June 13, 1932

62. Jill Watts, *Mae West: An Icon in Black and White* (New York: Oxford University Press, 2001), 217–18.

63. LAE, Feb. 18, 1933.

64. LAE, July 11, 1934.

65. LAE, Jan. 27, 1933.

66. WRH to LOP, May 12, 1933, Carton 17, Hearst Collection, UCB.

67. Grace Wofford to LOP, Nov. 27, 1931, Gloria Swanson Collection, Harry Ransom Humanities Research Center, University of Texas, Austin.

68. Gloria Swanson, *Swanson on Swanson* (New York: Random House, 1980), 190.

69. Swindell, *Screwball,* 230.

70. WRH to LOP, Jan. 30, 1931, Carton 12, Hearst Collection, UCB.

71. Donald Bartlett and James Steele, *Empire: The Life, Legend, and Madness of Howard Hughes* (New York: Norton, 1979), 68.

72. Schulberg quoted in Carroll Graham and Garrett Graham, *Queer People* (New York: Vanguard Press, 1930; reprint, Carbondale: Southern Illinois University Press, 1976), 280.

73. LAE, Oct. 25. 1930.

74. LAE, Nov. 16, 1930.

75. "Outside Pressure Chills Meggers on Queer People," *Variety,* Apr. 15, 1931, 6.

76. Ibid.

77. Letter from Tabor, Iowa, Mar. 4, 1934, Louella Parsons Collection, Charis Radio Show Files, University of Southern California. For popular depictions of journalists in the 1930s, see Alex Barris, *Stop the Presses: The American Newspaperman in Films* (South Brunswick, NJ: A. S. Barnes, 1976); see also Howard Good, *The Drunken Journalist: The Biography of a Film Stereotype* (Lanham, MD: Scarecrow Press, 2000).

78. LAE, Sept. 20, 1931.

79. Louis Weitzenkorn, *Five Star Final* (New York: S. French, 1931).

80. WRH to Jack Warner, Nov. 6, 1931, Carton 12, Hearst Collection, UCB.

81. LOP to WRH, Nov. 6, 1931, Carton 12, Hearst Collection, UCB.

82. Nasaw, *The Chief,* 413.

83. Eells, *Hedda and Louella,* 232.

84. GI, 123.

NINE. RADIO

1. Tino Balio, *Grand Design: Hollywood as a Modern Business Enterprise* (New York: Scribner, 1993), 15.

2. Thomas Doherty, *Pre-Code Hollywood: Sex, Immorality, and Insurrection in American Cinema* (New York: Columbia University Press, 1999), 29.

3. Christopher Sterling and John Kittross, *Stay Tuned: A Concise History of American Broadcasting* (Belmont, CA: Wadsworth, 1978), 112; Norman Finkelstein, *Sounds in the Air: The Golden Age of Radio* (New York: Scribner's, 1993), 13.

4. Doherty, *Pre-Code Hollywood,* 28.

5. Michele Hilmes, *Only Connect: A Cultural History of Broadcasting in the United States* (Belmont, CA: Wadsworth, 2002), 83.

6. Finkelstein, *Sounds in the Air,* 32.

7. Hilmes, *Only Connect,* 66.

8. LOP to JW, n.d., Carton 12, William Randolph Hearst Collection, Bancroft Library, University of California, Berkeley (hereafter Hearst Collection, UCB).

9. LOP to JW, Feb. 10, 1931, Carton 12, Hearst Collection, UCB.

10. Warren to Lance Heath, Feb. 21, 1931, Gloria Swanson Collection, Harry Ransom Humanities Research Center, University of Texas, Austin.

11. *Los Angeles Examiner* (hereafter LAE), Feb. 24, 1931, 31.

12. "Mary Pickford-Louella Parsons," *Variety,* Feb. 25, 1931, 64.

13. LOP to WRH, Apr. 3, 1931, Carton 12, Hearst Collection, UCB.

14. LOP to WRH, Apr. 8, 1931, Carton 12, Hearst Collection, UCB.

15. LOP to MD, May 7, 1931, Carton 12, Hearst Collection, UCB.

16. LOP to WRH, Nov. 4, 1931, Carton 12, Hearst Collection, UCB.

17. Katharine Lowrie, "Fan Magazine Reporters Underrated as Journalists," n.d., Harriet Parsons Clipping File, Academy of Motion Pictures Arts and Sciences (hereafter AMPAS).

18. Donald Crafton, *The Talkies: American Cinema's Transition to Sound* (New York: Scribner's, 1997), 477; Robert Sklar, *City Boys: Cagney, Bogart, Garfield* (Princeton: Princeton University Press, 1992), 30–31.

19. LAE, May 22, 1932.

20. LAE, Mar. 5, 1931, 15.

21. William J. Mann, *Behind the Screen: How Gays and Lesbians Shaped Hollywood, 1910–1969* (New York: Viking, 1961), 154.

22. Ibid., 149.

23. William J. Mann, *Wisecracker: The Life and Times of William Haines, Hollywood's First Openly Gay Star* (New York: Viking, 1998).

24. LAE, June 4, 1931.

25. See Samuel Marx, *Deadly Illusions: Jean Harlow and the Murder of Paul Bern* (New York: Random House, 1990).

26. LAE, Sept. 7, 1932, 7.

27. Crafton, *The Talkies,* 418, 436.

28. Louis Pizzitola, *Hearst over Hollywood* (New York: Columbia University Press, 2002), 316–19.

29. LAE, Oct. 30, 32.

30. LAE, Oct. 23, 32.

31. Dorothy Manners Oral History, n.d., Hollywood Women's Press Club Collection, AMPAS; Herb Stinson, "Backstage with Louella," n.d., Louella Parsons Clipping File, AMPAS.

32. Clipping, n.d., 1934, George Eells Collection, Arizona State University (hereafter Eells Collection, ASU).

33. Mac St. Johns, interview by George Eells, n.d., Eells Collection, ASU.

34. Herb Stinson, "Louella Parsons," *Los Angeles Mirror*, May 7, 1953, Louella Parsons Clipping File, AMPAS.

35. Frank Liberman, interview by George Eells, n.d., Eells Collection, ASU.

36. Walter Seltzer, telephone interview by author, May 3, 2004.

37. "Personality," *Time*, Aug. 25, 1952, 36.

38. Bob Thomas, *Joan Crawford* (New York: Simon and Schuster, 1978), 93–94.

39. LAE, Mar. 18, 1933.

40. Mary Pickford, *Sunshine and Shadow* (Garden City, NY: Doubleday, 1955), 319–21.

41. Cari Beauchamp, *Without Lying Down: Frances Marion and the Powerful Women of Early Hollywood* (New York: Scribner, 1997), 311.

42. Louella Parsons, *The Gay Illiterate* (hereafter GI) (New York: Doubleday Doran, 1944), 127.

43. Ibid.

44. LAE, July 2, 1933, 1; GI, 126.

45. Beauchamp, *Without Lying Down*, 309–10.

46. Wonders to LOP, Nov. 9, 1933, LOP Collection, Charis Radio Show Files, Box 4, University of Southern California (hereafter Charis Files), italics in the original.

47. LOP to E. J. Gough, Nov. 13, 1933; E. J. Gough to LOP, Nov. 14, 1933, Charis Files, Box 4.

48. WRH to LOP, May 1, 1933, Carton 17, Hearst Collection, UCB.

49. On the 1932 ban, see Michele Hilmes, *Hollywood and Broadcasting: From Radio to Cable* (Urbana: University of Illinois Press, 1990).

50. "Parsons' Corsets," *Variety*, Dec. 11, 1933, 3.

51. John Dunning, *Tune in Yesterday: The Ultimate Encyclopedia of Old Time Radio* (Englewood Cliffs, NJ: Prentice-Hall, 1976), 412.

52. LOP to Wonders, Feb. 9, 1934, Charis Files, Box 4.

53. GI, 153.

54. GI, 154.

55. Dunning, *Tune in Yesterday*, 412.

56. B. Henderson to LOP, Feb. 28, 1934, Charis Files, Box 4.

57. Fan letter from Tabor, Iowa, to LOP, Mar. 2, 1934, Charis Files, Box 4.

58. Alice Kessler-Harris, *Out to Work: A History of Wage Earning Women in the United States* (New York: Oxford University Press, 1982), 258–59.

59. Anonymous to LOP, Mar. 28, 1934; Eva Gove to LOP, Mar. 4, 1934, Charis Files, Box 4.

60. Fan letter from Mildred McCloud, May 17, 1934, Charis Files, Box 4.

61. Lillian McWilliams to LOP, Apr. 27, 1934, Charis Files, Box 4.

62. Fan letter from Tabor, Iowa; B. Henderson; Virginia Hitchcock to LOP, n.d., Charis Files, Box 4.

63. LOP to RW, May 19, 1934, Charis Files, Box 4.

64. Louella O. Parsons, "Hollywood Is My Home Town," *Cosmopolitan,* Sept. 1934, 48.

65. LAE, Aug. 14, 1935, 4.

66. LAE, June 15, 1934, 15.

67. Louella Parsons, *Tell It to Louella* (New York: Putnam, 1961), 103–4.

68. "Parsons Jr.," *Hollywood Studio Magazine,* Oct. 1982, Harriet Parsons Clipping File, AMPAS.

69. Mann, *Behind the Screen,* 193.

70. Ezra Goodman, *The Fifty-Year Decline and Fall of Hollywood* (New York: Simon and Schuster, 1961), 442.

71. "Hollywood Inside," *Daily Variety,* Nov. 8, 1934, 2.

72. Edward Baron Turk, *Hollywood Diva: A Biography of Jeanette MacDonald* (Berkeley: University of California Press, 1998), 72.

73. Mary Jane Higby, *Tune in Tomorrow* (New York: Cowles, 1968), 64.

74. "It's Getting Tough for Radio Chatters to Get Free Talent," *Variety,* Apr. 6, 1935, 1.

75. James Kotsilibas-Davis, *Myrna Loy: Being and Becoming* (New York: Knopf, 1987), 123.

TEN. THE BEST AND THE HEARST

1. *Los Angeles Examiner* (hereafter LAE), Mar. 26, 1933.

2. LAE, Jan. 29, 1933.

3. LAE, Apr. 7, 1933, I, 18.

4. WRH to L. B. Mayer, Mar. 17, 1933, Carton 17, William Randolph Hearst Collection, Bancroft Library, University of California, Berkeley (hereafter Hearst Collection, UCB).

5. John Kobal, *People Will Talk* (New York: Knopf, 1985), 639.

6. Samuel Marx, *Mayer and Thalberg: The Make Believe Saints* (New York: Random House, 1975), 223.

7. Budd Schulberg, *Moving Pictures* (New York: Stein and Day, 1981), 430.

8. Dorothy Manners Oral History, Hollywood Women's Press Club Collection,

Academy of Motion Pictures Arts and Sciences, Beverly Hills, California (hereafter HWPCC).

9. LAE, May 20, 1934.

10. LAE, Oct. 14, 1934.

11. Ronald Brownstein, *The Power and the Glitter: The Hollywood-Washington Connection* (New York: Pantheon, 1990), 42.

12. Bosley Crowther, *Hollywood Rajah: The Life and Times of Louis B. Mayer* (New York: Holt, 1960), 200.

13. Joe Willicombe to George Young, Nov. 5, 1934, Carton 19, Hearst Collection, UCB.

14. Brownstein, *The Power and the Glitter,* 48–53.

15. LAE, Oct. 22, 1933.

16. WRH to Tom White, Apr. 4, 1934, Carton 19, Hearst Collection, UCB.

17. David Nasaw, *The Chief: The Life of William Randolph Hearst* (Boston: Houghton Mifflin, 2000), 485.

18. Ibid., 502.

19. W. R. Hearst, "Red Pictures," LAE, Dec. 15, 1934.

20. WRH to George Young, Nov. 5, 1934, Carton 19, Hearst Collection, UCB.

21. Louis Pizzitola, *Hearst over Hollywood* (New York: Columbia University Press, 2002), 345.

22. Nasaw, *The Chief,* 506.

23. Joel Faith, "Louella Parsons, Hearst's Hollywood Stooge," *New Theater,* Aug. 1935, Louella Parsons Clipping File, Academy of Motion Pictures Arts and Sciences, Beverly Hills, California (hereafter AMPAS).

24. Pizzitola, *Hearst over Hollywood,* 347.

25. "Louella Parsons: Reel 2," *New Theater,* Sept. 1935, Louella Parsons Clipping File, AMPAS.

26. "Louella Parsons: Reel 2."

27. Joseph Alsop, "Miss Louella Parsons Speaking," *New York Herald Tribune,* Oct. 27, 1935, LOP Scrapbook #20, AMPAS.

28. S.F. Van Buren, "They Cover Hollywood," n.d., Trade Journals Clipping File, AMPAS.

29. Quoted in Neal Gabler, *Winchell: Gossip, Power, and the Culture of Celebrity* (New York: Knopf, 1994), 134.

30. Michael Schudson, *Discovering the News: A Social History of Newspapers* (New York: Basic Books, 1978), 120.

31. Silas Bent, *Ballyhoo: The Voice of the Press* (New York: Boni, 1927), 5.

32. Dorothy Manners Oral History, n.d., HWPCC.

33. Leo Rosten, *Hollywood, the Movie Colony* (New York: Arno Press, 1970), 7.

34. Grover Jones, "Knights of the Keyhole," *Collier's,* Apr. 16, 1938, 25.

35. Wilkerson quoted in Ezra Goodman, *The Fifty-Year Decline and Fall of Hollywood* (New York: Simon and Schuster, 1961), 57.

36. Marcia Borie, "Reporting on Hollywood for 60 Years," *Hollywood Reporter,* Sept. 28, 1990, Trade Journals Clipping File, AMPAS.

37. J. Willicombe to LOP, Mar. 13, 1933, Carton 17, Hearst Collection, UCB.

38. Val Holley, *Mike Connolly and the Manly Art of Hollywood Gossip* (Jefferson, NC: McFarland, 2003), 87, 89.

39. "The Trade Paper Racket," Louella Parsons Clipping File, AMPAS.

40. Goodman, *The Fifty-Year Decline and Fall of Hollywood,* 71.

41. "Hollywood Inside," *Daily Variety* (hereafter DV), May 28, 1935, 2.

42. Alfred O'Malley, "They Cover Hollywood," n.d., Trade Journals Clipping File, AMPAS.

43. Goodman, *The Fifty-Year Decline and Fall of Hollywood,* 78.

44. "Hollywood Inside," DV, Nov. 15, 1935, 2.

45. LOP to WRH, Oct. 14, 1933, Carton 19, Hearst Collection, UCB.

46. LAE, Aug. 17, 1935, I, 13.

47. LAE, Aug. 9, 1941, I, 11.

48. Jimmy Starr, *Barefoot on Barbed Wire* (Lanham, MD: Scarecrow Press, 2001), 249.

49. Gabler, *Winchell,* 255, 277.

50. Walter Winchell to WRH, June 23, 1933, Carton 16, Hearst Collection, UCB.

51. Kathy Feeley, "Louella Parsons and Hedda Hopper's Hollywood: The Rise of the Celebrity Gossip Industry in Twentieth-Century America, 1910–1950" (Ph.D. diss., City University of New York, 2003), 134.

52. Alfred O'Malley, "They Cover Hollywood," n.d., Trade Journals Clipping File, AMPAS.

53. James Bacon, "Riotous Memories of Sidney Skolsky," *Los Angeles Herald Examiner,* May 10, 1983.

54. Ray Van Ettisch to WRH, Nov. 24, 1937, Carton 22, Hearst Collection, UCB.

55. Sidney Skolsky, *Don't Get Me Wrong—I Love Hollywood* (New York: Putnam, 1975), 42–43.

56. Bacon, "Riotous Memories."

57. Skolsky, *Don't Get Me Wrong,* 45. Louella later denied that she had anything to do with Skolsky's firing, but all evidence—in particular, Louella's animosity toward Skolsky and her involvement in Hearst's anticommunist campaign—suggests the contrary. That Hearst would fire Skolsky for his political position is also corroborated by Hearst's treatment of Winchell, who in the late 1930s began inserting his political opinions into his column. When Winchell wrote of his support of Spain's Republican government, which was in Hearst's eyes tantamount to communism, Hearst instructed his editors to "edit Winchell very carefully and leave out any dangerous or disagreeable paragraphs." They were to "leave out the whole column" if

necessary. Hearst wrote in a telegram to Louella that Winchell "has no institutional loyalty, and furthermore is a pink." Hearst telegram quoted in Feeley, "Louella Parsons and Hedda Hopper's Hollywood," 134.

58. "Fidler, the Man Nobody Throws," *The Coast,* n.d., Trade Journals Clipping File, AMPAS.

59. Jones, "Knights of the Keyhole," 26.

60. "Hollywood Inside," DV, Nov. 20, 1935, 2.

61. "Hollywood Inside," DV, Nov. 16, 1935, 2.

62. Louella Parsons, *The Gay Illiterate* (hereafter GI) (New York: Doubleday Doran, 1944), 130–31.

63. LAE, Oct. 4, 1937.

64. LOP to WRH, Oct 26, 1937, Carton 17, Hearst Collection, UCB.

65. Mary Jane Higby, *Tune in Tomorrow* (New York: Cowles, 1968), 61.

66. Ibid., 65–66.

67. Gypsy Rose Lee, interview by George Eells, n.d., George Eells Collection, Arizona State University.

68. "Agencies' Showmanship in 35," DV, Jan. 1, 1936, 157.

69. "Hollywood Inside," DV, Nov. 10, 1937, 2.

70. "Hollywood Inside," DV, Apr. 14, 1937, 2.

71. Higby, *Tune in Tomorrow,* 67.

72. "Snow Falls at Bacher Stunt Broadcast," DV, Dec. 23, 1936, 32.

73. Higby, *Tune in Tomorrow,* 23.

74. Michele Hilmes, *Hollywood and Broadcasting: From Radio to Cable* (Urbana: University of Illinois Press, 1990), 67.

75. Higby, *Tune in Tomorrow,* 67.

76. "Parsons Ices Pickford," *Variety,* Mar. 2, 1936, 1.

77. Ibid.

78. Ibid.

79. "Hollywood Inside," DV, Mar. 24, 1936, 2.

80. Edward Baron Turk, *Hollywood Diva: A Biography of Jeanette MacDonald* (Berkeley: University of California Press, 1998), 190.

81. Hollywood Inside," DV, Mar. 24, 1936, 2.

82. Quoted in Jill Watts, *Mae West: An Icon in Black and White* (New York: Oxford University Press, 2001), 217.

83. "Hollywood Inside," DV, Aug. 29, 1936, 2.

84. "Klondike Annie Brings Trouble," *Motion Picture Herald,* Mar. 7, 1936, Trade Journals Clipping File, AMPAS.

85. Ibid.

86. Elizabeth Yeaman, "Power of Hearst Press Discounted by Results in Editorial Campaign," *Hollywood Citizen,* Mar. 14, 1936, Trade Journals Clipping File, AMPAS.

87. "Klondike Annie Brings Trouble."

1. *Los Angeles Examiner* (hereafter LAE), Sept. 6, 1936.

2. Tino Balio, *Grand Design: Hollywood as a Modern Business Enterprise* (New York: Scribner's, 1993), 30.

3. Margaret Thorp, *America at the Movies* (New Haven: Yale University Press, 1939), 94.

4. Robert Lynd and Helen Lynd, *Middletown* (New York: Harcourt, Brace, 1929), 265; Caroline Ware, *Greenwich Village* (New York: Houghton Mifflin, 1935), 350.

5. Carl Cotter, "The Forty Hacks of the Fan Mags," *The Coast,* Feb. 1939, Fans Clipping File, Academy of Motion Pictures Arts and Sciences, Beverly Hills, California (hereafter AMPAS).

6. Leo Rosten, *Hollywood, the Movie Colony* (New York: Arno Press, 1970), 360. Adler is quoted on p. 368.

7. Moss Hart and George Kaufman, *Once in a Lifetime* (New York: Farrar and Rinehart, 1930), 37–40.

8. Thomas Wood, "The First Lady of Hollywood," *Saturday Evening Post,* July 15, 1939, 10.

9. LAE, Oct. 7, 1935.

10. Ibid.

11. DOS to LOP, Sept. 23, 1936, Selznick online exhibit, Harry Ransom Humanities Center, University of Texas, www.hrc.utexas.edu/exhibitions/online/gwtw/scarlett/ (accessed Jan. 25, 2005).

12. LAE, Jan. 18, 1939.

13. LAE, Sept. 15, 1937.

14. Louella Parsons's *Hollywood Hotel* contract, Sept. 17, 1937, *Hollywood Hotel* Files, Warner Brothers Collection, University of Southern California (hereafter *Hollywood Hotel* Files).

15. LOP to WRH, Jan. 26, 1932, Carton 12, William Randolph Hearst Collection, Bancroft Library, University of California, Berkeley.

16. LAE, Sept. 26, 1937.

17. *Hollywood Hotel,* dir. Busby Berkeley, Warner Brothers, 1938.

18. Charles Einfeld to R. J. Obringer, Sept. 17, 1937, *Hollywood Hotel* Files. Louella also turned her experience as an "actress" into the subject of a feature article, "I Get In and Out of the Movies," in the February 1938 issue of *Photoplay* magazine.

19. LAE, Feb. 9, 1938.

20. LAE, Jan. 9, 1938.

21. LAE, Feb. 6, 1938.

22. Clipping, n.d., LOP Scrapbook #23, AMPAS.

23. WRH to J. Warner, Jan. 22, 1938, Jack L. Warner Collection, University of Southern California.

24. "Il Duce's Phone Call to Vittorio in H'Wood Climaxed Italo-U.S. Idea," *Variety*, Oct. 13, 1937, 5.

25. Neal Gabler, *An Empire of Their Own: How the Jews Created Hollywood* (New York: Anchor, 1988); Steven Alan Carr, *Hollywood and Anti-Semitism: A Cultural History up to World War II* (New York: Cambridge University Press, 2001), 133.

26. "Actor Dale Robertson Returns to His Roots," *Senior World,* n.d., www.seniorworld.com/articles/a19971006095843.html (accessed Jan. 25, 2005).

27. "Hollywood's First Gossip," *House Beautiful,* Feb. 1943, 18.

28. Dorothy Manners Oral History, Hollywood Women's Press Club Collection, AMPAS.

29. Christopher Finch and Linda Rosenkrantz, *Gone Hollywood* (Garden City, NY: Doubleday, 1979), 240.

30. "Tales of Hoffman," *Hollywood Reporter* (hereafter HR), Mar. 4, 1948, 5.

31. Louella Parsons, *The Gay Illiterate* (hereafter GI) (New York: Doubleday Doran, 1944), 171.

32. David Nasaw, *The Chief: The Life of William Randolph Hearst* (Boston: Houghton Mifflin, 2000), 529.

33. LAE, June 18, 1937, I, 7.

34. Clipping, Mar. 15, 1938, LOP Scrapbook #21, AMPAS.

35. "Parsons Double Soup Nixed by Mine Host," *Daily Variety* (hereafter DV), Nov. 12, 1937.

36. "Parsons, Bacher Plan New Show," *Variety,* Aug. 2, 1938.

37. Louella Parsons Oral History, Popular Arts Collection, Butler Library, Columbia University, 110.

38. Adela Rogers St. Johns, *The Honeycomb* (Garden City, NY: Doubleday, 1969), 486.

39. LAE, June 9, 1937, 1.

40. GI, 136.

41. LAE, Nov. 28, 1937, V, 7.

42. "Louella Parsons Dead at 91," *Variety,* Dec. 13, 1972.

43. George Eells, *Hedda and Louella* (New York: Putnam, 1972), 107.

44. Delight Evans, "Learn about Vampires from Her," *Photoplay,* Sept. 1919, 64.

45. Gladys Hall, "The Lady Who Knows It All," *Motion Picture,* June 1931, 47.

46. LAE, July 11, 1930.

47. LAE, Aug. 26, 1932, I, 11.

48. "The Gossipist," *Time,* July 28, 1947, 60.

49. Jaik Rosenstein, *Hollywood Leg Man* (Los Angeles: Madison Press, 1950), 29.

50. Collie Small, "Gossip Is Her Business," *Saturday Evening Post,* Jan. 11, 1947, 58.

51. Hedda Hopper, *From under My Hat* (Garden City, NY: Doubleday, 1952), 220.

52. "Hedda Hopper's Hollywood" *Los Angeles Times,* Feb. 14, 1938, 9.

53. Hedda Hopper, with James Brough, *The Whole Truth and Nothing But* (New York: Doubleday, 1962), 64.

54. Cari Beauchamp, *Without Lying Down: Frances Marion and the Powerful Women of Early Hollywood* (New York: Scribner's, 1997), 337.

55. Hopper, *From under My Hat,* 226.

56. Beauchamp, *Without Lying Down,* 337.

57. WRH to HH, July 30, 1939.

58. LAE, Mar. 8, 1939, 7.

59. Lyn Tornabene, *Long Live the King* (New York: Putnam, 1976), 235.

60. Larry Swindell, *Screwball: The Life of Carole Lombard* (New York: William Morrow, 1975), 251; Warren Harris, *Gable and Lombard* (New York: Simon and Schuster, 1974), 106.

61. LAE, Mar. 30, 1939, 1.

62. Wood, "The First Lady of Hollywood," 10.

63. Ibid.

64. "Rambling Reporter," HR, July 26, 1939, 2.

65. "Rambling Reporter," HR, Nov. 25, 1939, 2; Ezra Goodman, *The Fifty Year Decline and Fall of Hollywood* (New York: Simon and Schuster, 1961), 23.

66. GI, 172.

67. "Parsons Jr.: Produced What Mom Juiced," *Hollywood Studio Magazine,* Oct. 1982, 30, Harriet Parsons Clipping File, AMPAS; Hopper, *The Whole Truth,* 67; William J. Mann, *Behind the Screen: How Gays and Lesbians Shaped Hollywood, 1910–1969* (New York: Viking, 2001), 195.

68. Hopper, *From under My Hat,* 226–29.

69. Hy Gardner, "A Friend Named Hedda Hopper," Hedda Hopper Clipping File, AMPAS.

70. "Rambling Reporter," HR, Oct. 26. 1939, 2.

71. "Rambling Reporter," HR, Nov. 2, 1939, 2.

72. DOS to Hebert, July 24, 1939, Administrative Studio Files, 1938–1943, David O. Selznick Collection, Harry Ransom Humanities Research Center, University of Texas, Austin (hereafter Selznick Collection).

73. DOS to Hebert, Aug. 24, 1939, Administrative Studio Files, Selznick Collection.

74. DOS to LOP, July 8, 1940, Administrative Studio Files, Selznick Collection.

75. DOS to LOP, Oct. 7 1939, Administrative Studio Files, Selznick Collection.

76. DOS to LOP, July 24, 1939, Administrative Studio Files, Selznick Collection.

TWELVE. RAISING KANE

1. *Los Angeles Examiner* (hereafter LAE), Nov. 15, 1939, 7.

2. Pat Kelly, "Lolly Parsons' Big H'wood Sendoff via Film Trailer but SF Reception So-So," *Variety,* Nov. 22, 1939, 45.

3. Ibid.; "LOP Holds 'Em Breathless at Golden Gate," *San Francisco Chronicle,*

n.d., LOP Scrapbook #25, Louella Parsons Collection, Academy of Motion Pictures Arts and Sciences, Beverly Hills, California (hereafter AMPAS).

4. Mildred Martin, "Overflow Crowd Flocks to See Louella O. Parsons," *Philadelphia Record,* n.d., LOP Scrapbook #25, AMPAS.

5. LAE, Nov. 27, 1939, 7.

6. "Rambling Reporter," *Hollywood Reporter* (hereafter HR), Dec. 6, 1939, 2.

7. "Rambling Reporter," HR, Dec. 1, 1939, 2.

8. "Loew's State, NY," *Variety,* Dec. 27, 1939, 37.

9. Ann Marsters, "LOP Tells Story of Start to Fame in Chicago," *Chicago Sunday Herald American,* Jan. 7, 1940, LOP Scrapbook #25, AMPAS.

10. "Chicago Honors Louella Parsons, Film Writer at College Inn Luncheon," clipping, n.d.; Andrew Kelly, "Starlets Are New York Hit in Vaudeville Tour," *Washington Post,* n.d.; "LOP to Introduce Future Stars to Washington This Week," *Washington Post,* Dec. 28, 1939, LOP Scrapbook #25, AMPAS.

11. LAE, Nov. 23, 1939, 9.

12. "Rambling Reporter," HR, Jan. 17, 1940, 2.

13. B. R. Crisler, "This Singular Cinema," *New York Times* (hereafter NYT), Dec. 24, 1939, sec. 9, p. 6, col. 1.

14. W. R. Wilkerson, "Tradeviews," HR, Nov. 21, Dec. 2, 1939, 1.

15. "Rambling Reporter," HR, Jan. 6, 1940, 2.

16. Louella Parsons, *Tell It to Louella* (New York: Putnam, 1961), (hereafter TL), 105.

17. WRH to LOP, Jan. 14, 1940, Carton 15, William Randolph Hearst Collection, Bancroft Library, University of California, Berkeley (hereafter Hearst Collection, UCB).

18. LOP to WRH, Jan. 16, 1940, Carton 15, Hearst Collection, UCB.

19. TL, 105; Clipping, n.d., LOP Scrapbook #25, AMPAS.

20. Ronald Brownstein, *The Power and the Glitter: The Hollywood-Washington Connection* (New York: Pantheon, 1990), 94.

21. LAE, July 29, 1939, 12.

22. LAE, Apr. 24, 1940, 7; Richard Meryman, *Mank* (New York: William Morrow, 1978), 244–45.

23. W. R. Wilkerson, "Tradeviews," HR, Mar. 12, 1941.

24. LOP to WRH, May 14, 1940, Carton 15, Hearst Collection, UCB.

25. LOP to WRH, July 2, 1940, Carton 15, Hearst Collection, UCB.

26. LOP to WRH, July 14, 1940, Carton 15, Hearst Collection, UCB.

27. LAE, Aug. 18, 1940, 9; LAE, Aug. 27, 1940, 12.

28. LAE, Aug. 27, 1940, 12.

29. "RKO Hears Hearst Threat over 'Kane,'" *Daily Variety* (hereafter DV), Jan. 13, 1941, 4.

30. "Miscellany," *Newsweek,* Sept. 16, 1940, 2; Louis Pizzitola, *Hearst over Hollywood* (New York: Columbia University Press, 2002), 396; LAE, Nov. 13, 1940, 9.

31. "Rambling Reporter," HR, Jan. 3, 1941, 2.

32. "Hollywood Insider," DV, Jan 3, 1941, 2.

33. Frank Brady, *Citizen Welles* (New York: Scribner's, 1989), 273.

34. Hedda Hopper, with James Brough, *The Whole Truth and Nothing But* (New York: Doubleday, 1962), 70.

35. Brady, *Citizen Welles*, 277.

36. *Friday* later printed a retraction. See "*Citizen Kane* Is Not about Louella Parsons' Boss," *Friday,* Feb. 14, 1941, 9.

37. Welles to LOP, Jan. 8, 1941, Orson Welles Collection, Lilly Library, Indiana University.

38. "Hearst Bans RKO in Newspapers," DV, Jan. 10, 1941, 1.

39. Warrick quoted in *The Battle over Citizen Kane,* videorecording directed by Thomas Lennon and Michael Epstein (Boston: PBS Video, 1996).

40. LOP to Laurence Mitchell, Feb. 5, 1941, Carton 35, Hearst Collection, UCB.

41. "Hearst-Kane Reprisal Will Slap All Majors," DV, Jan. 13, 1941, 1.

42. Douglas Churchill, "Orson Welles Scares Hollywood," NYT, Jan. 19, sec. 9, p. 5, col. 6.

43. LOP to Joe Willicombe, Jan. 14, 1941, Carton 35, Hearst Collection, UCB.

44. Nelson Rockefeller to Louella Parsons, Jan. 14, 1941, Carton 35, Hearst Collection, UCB.

45. "Schaefer Curbs Kane Preview Setup," DV, Jan. 17, 1941, 5; "RKO Announces Huge Natl Campaign for Kane," *Variety* (hereafter V), Jan. 22, 41, 1.

46. "Hedda Hopper's Hollywood," *Los Angeles Times,* Jan. 15, 1941, 12; "Welles to Demand RKO Release His Kane Pic," DV, Feb. 4, 1941, 7.

47. LOP to Joe Willicombe, Mar. 10, 1941, Carton 35, Hearst Collection, UCB.

48. Ronald Gottesman, ed., *Focus on Citizen Kane* (Englewood Cliffs, NJ: Prentice-Hall, 1971), 83.

49. Brady, *Citizen Welles,* 288.

50. John O'Hara, "Citizen Kane," *Newsweek,* Mar. 17, 1941, 60; Pauline Kael, *The Citizen Kane Book* (Boston: Little, Brown, 1971), 43.

51. "Mr. Genius Comes Through; 'Kane' Astonishing Picture," HR, Mar. 12, 1941, 3.

52. "Hearst Opens Blast on RKO-Schaefer; Citizen Kane Release Still Indef," V, Feb. 19, 1941.

53. "Welles Suing RKO on 'Citizen Kane' in Effort to Force Pic's Release," V, Mar. 12, 1941, 16.

54. "Luce Rumored on Citizen Kane Deal," HR, Mar. 12, 1941.

55. "Welles' Suspicion," V, Apr. 16, 1941, 52.

56. LOP to WRH, May 23, 1941, Carton 35, Hearst Collection, UCB.

57. Ezra Goodman, *The Fifty-Year Decline and Fall of Hollywood* (New York: Simon and Schuster, 1961), 23.

58. LOP to JW, Apr. 4, 1941, Carton 35, Hearst Collection, UCB.

59. LOP to WRH, Dec. 4, 1941, Carton 35, Hearst Collection, UCB.

60. LOP to WRH, Dec. 29, 1941, Carton 35, Hearst Collection, UCB.

61. WRH to LOP, Dec. 31, 1941, Carton 35, Hearst Collection, UCB.

62. "Citizen Welles Raises Kane," *Time,* Jan. 27, 1941, 71.

63. O'Hara, "Citizen Kane," 60.

64. "Omaha Slashes Louella," DV, Apr. 17, 1941, 2.

65. LOP to WRH, Aug. 6, 1941, Carton 35, Hearst Collection, UCB.

66. "Rambling Reporter," HR, Apr. 2, 1941, 2.

67. "Hollywood Inside," DV, Jan. 8, 1941, 2.

68. "Louella Parsons Deal Hinges on Ability to Get Pic Stars," DV, Jan. 23, 1941, 4.

69. "Hollywood Inside," DV, Feb. 10, 1941, 2.

70. "Louella Gets on Soap Box March 28," HR, Mar. 10, 1941, 7.

71. LOP to DOS, Mar. 26, 1941, Administrative Studio Files, 1938–1943, Selznick Collection, Harry Ransom Humanities Research Center, University of Texas, Austin (hereafter Selznick Collection).

72. "Hollywood Premiere," *Radio Daily,* Apr. 11, 1941.

73. "SAG CRACKDOWN ON PARSONS," DV, Mar. 27, 1941; "Storm Breaks over Body Odor Broadcast," DV, Mar. 27, 1941, 1.

74. "A Letter from Louella Parsons to SAG," DV, Mar. 28, 1941.

75. "Parsons Free Shows Kayoed," DV, Mar. 28, 1941, 1.

76. "Rambling Reporter," HR, June 2, 1941, 2.

77. "Columnist Fans," *Radio Life,* June 29, 1941.

78. *San Diego Radio,* May 11, 1941, LOP Scrapbook #26, AMPAS.

79. Joseph Weissmans, "Hollywood Dots," *Radio Daily,* June 6, 1941, LOP Scrapbook #26, AMPAS; "Parsons Mike Technique Still off the Beam," DV, Mar. 31, 1941, 4.

80. "Hollywood Inside," V, Aug. 29, 1941, 2.

81. LOP to WRH, n.d., Carton 35, Hearst Collection, UCB.

82. LOP to WRH, Aug. 7, 1941, Carton 35, Hearst Collection, UCB.

83. "Home Town Hails Louella Parsons," *News of the Day,* vol. 13, no. 202, Sept. 17, 1941, newsreel, Film and Television Archive, University of California, Los Angeles.

84. Louella Parsons, *The Gay Illiterate* (hereafter GI) (New York: Doubleday Doran, 1944), 163.

85. Thomas Schatz, *Boom and Bust: The American Cinema in the 1940s* (New York: Scribner's, 1997), 34.

86. Ibid., 13.

87. Ibid., 20.

88. Ibid., 36, 40.

89. "Deseret News Columnist Here," Sept. 13, 1941, LOP Scrapbook #26, AMPAS.

90. LOP to WRH, Sept. 18, 1941, Carton 35, Hearst Collection, UCB.
91. WRH to LOP, Aug. 6, 1941, Carton 35, Hearst Collection, UCB.
92. GI, 146.
93. "Double Dates," *Time,* Sept. 22, 1941, 55.
94. "Hedda's Legion Queening in Milwaukee Splits Billing with Lolly's Fete in Ill," V, Sept. 17, 1941, 2.
95. LOP to WRH, Dec. 4, 1941, Carton 35, Hearst Collection, UCB.
96. LOP to WRH, Oct. 22, 1941, Carton 35, Hearst Collection, UCB.
97. LOP to WRH, Oct. 19, 1941, Carton 35, Hearst Collection, UCB.
98. LOP to WRH, Dec. 9, 1941, Carton 35, Hearst Collection, UCB.
99. Weissmans, "Hollywood Dots."
100. "Parsons vs. Hopper," *Pic,* May 13, 1941, Louella Parsons Clipping File, Academy of Motion Pictures Arts and Sciences.
101. "Hedda Makes Hay," *Time,* May 25, 1942, 51.
102. "Hollywood Inside," DV, May 8, 1942, 2.
103. Ibid.

THIRTEEN. THE GAY ILLITERATE

1. "Hedda Makes Hay," *Time,* May 25, 1942, 52.
2. Ibid.; Francis Sill Wickware, "Hedda Hopper," *Life,* Nov. 20, 1944, 63.
3. Wickware, "Hedda Hopper," 63; "Hedda Makes Hay," 52.
4. "The Gossipist," *Time,* July 28, 1947, 60.
5. Collie Small, "Gossip Is Her Business," *Saturday Evening Post,* Jan. 11, 1947, 14.
6. Ibid., 15.
7. "The Gossipist," 62.
8. Letter from Alex Tiers to George Eells, n.d., George Eells Collection, Arizona State University (hereafter Eells Collection, ASU).
9. George Eells, *Hedda and Louella* (New York: Putnam, 1972), 271.
10. "The Gossipist," 62.
11. David McClure, interview by George Eells, n.d., Eells Collection, ASU.
12. Jaik Rosenstein, *Hollywood Leg Man* (Los Angeles: Madison Press, 1950), 21.
13. "The Gossipist," 62.
14. Ibid.
15. Christopher Finch and Linda Rosenkrantz, *Gone Hollywood* (Garden City, NY: Doubleday, 1979), 135.
16. Ibid.
17. Val Holley, *Mike Connolly and the Manly Art of Hollywood Gossip* (Jefferson, NC: McFarland, 2003), 116.
18. "Hollywood Inside," *Daily Variety* (hereafter DV), Mar. 5, 1942, 2.
19. Ronald Davis, *The Glamour Factory: Inside Hollywood's Big Studio System* (Dallas: Southern Methodist University Press, 1993), 149.
20. Walter Seltzer, telephone interview by author, May 1, 2004.

21. Louella Parsons, *Tell It to Louella* (New York: Putnam, 1961), 68.

22. Hedda Hopper, with James Brough, *The Whole Truth and Nothing But* (New York: Doubleday, 1962), 66.

23. "The Gossipist," 62.

24. Joan Fontaine, *No Bed of Roses* (New York: Berkley, 1979), 160.

25. Frances Marion, interview by George Eells, n.d., Eells Collection, ASU.

26. Sam Kashner and Jennifer McNair, *The Bad and the Beautiful: Hollywood in the Fifties* (New York: Norton, 2002), 277.

27. Whitney Bolton to DOS, Nov. 2, 1943, Administrative Studio Files, 1938–1943, David O. Selznick Collection, Harry Ransom Humanities Research Center, University of Texas, Austin (hereafter Selznick Collection).

28. DOS to Joe Steele, May 24, 1943, Administrative Studio Files, Selznick Collection.

29. DOS to Bolton, Sept. 10, 1941, Administrative Studio Files, Selznick Collection.

30. DOS to Steele, May 25, 1943, Administrative Studio Files, Selznick Collection.

31. "Hollywood Inside," DV, Feb. 2, 1942, 2.

32. DOS to Bolton, Apr. 25, 1942, Administrative Studio Files, Selznick Collection.

33. "Rambling Reporter," *Hollywood Reporter* (hereafter HR), Aug. 4, 1942, 2.

34. "Hollywood Inside," DV, Aug. 27, 1941, 2.

35. Clayton Koppes, "Regulating the Screen," in *Boom and Bust: American Cinema in the 1940s,* ed. Thomas Schatz (New York: Scribner, 1997), 269; John Morton Blum, *V Was for Victory* (New York: Harcourt Brace Jovanovich, 1976), 92–94.

36. *Photoplay,* 1944, Box 2, Louella Parsons Collection, Cinema Television Library, University of Southern California.

37. "Hollywood Inside," DV, July 21, 1943, 2.

38. Louella Parsons, *The Gay Illiterate* (hereafter GI) (New York: Doubleday Doran, 1944), 97.

39. Rob Wagner, *Red Ink, White Lies: The Rise and Fall of Los Angeles Newspapers, 1920–1962* (Upland, CA: Dragonflyer Press, 2000), 163–64.

40. Jim Heimann, *Out with the Stars: Hollywood Nightlife in the Studio Era* (New York: Abbeville Press, 1985), 209–12.

41. Koppes, "Regulating the Screen," 262–81.

42. *Los Angeles Examiner* (hereafter LAE), Jan. 24, 1941, I, 13.

43. Thomas Schatz, ed., *Boom and Bust: American Cinema in the 1940s* (New York: Scribner's, 1997), 36, 320.

44. LAE, Feb. 7, 1942.

45. LAE, Mar. 4, 1942.

46. "Rambling Reporter," HR, July 29, 1942, 2.

47. GI, 193.

48. Harriet Gustason, "Hollywood Trip—a la Louella," *Looking Back,* vol. 1: *1982–1985* (Freeport, IL: Stephenson County Historical Society, 1994), 61.

49. On St. Johns, see "Writer Adela Rogers St. Johns Dies at 94," *Los Angeles Times,* Aug. 11, 1988, 3.

50. Mac St. Johns, interview by George Eells, n.d., Eells Collection, ASU.

51. LAE, Dec. 28, 1942; "Dr Harry W. Martin Claimed by Death," LAE, June 25, 1951, Louella Parsons Clipping File, Academy of Motion Pictures Arts and Sciences, Beverly Hills, California (hereafter AMPAS).

52. "Rambling Reporter," HR, Feb. 3, 1943, 2.

53. Michelle Mason, "Louella Parsons Is Just a Woman at Heart," *Radio Life,* Nov. 2, 1941, LOP Scrapbook #29, AMPAS.

54. Charles Maland, *Chaplin and American Culture* (Princeton, NJ: Princeton University Press, 1989), 200.

55. Wickware, "Hedda Hopper," 63.

56. Ronald Brownstein, *The Power and the Glitter: The Hollywood-Washington Connection* (New York: Pantheon, 1990), 74, 75, 89.

57. Larry Ceplair and Steven Englund, *Inquisition in Hollywood: Politics in the Film Community, 1930–1960* (Berkeley: University of California Press, 1983), 211.

58. Maland, *Chaplin and American Culture,* 186–90.

59. Ibid., 209.

60. To Hopper from unknown, Feb. 12, 1944; from Esther Klooster, Feb. 10, 1944, Chaplin File, Hedda Hopper Collection, AMPAS.

61. Maland, *Chaplin and American Culture,* 209; Florabel Muir, *Headline Happy* (New York: Holt, 1950), chap. 8.

62. Jane Scovell, *Oona: Living in the Shadows* (New York: Warner Books, 1998), 117.

63. Charles Chaplin, *My Autobiography* (New York: Simon and Schuster, 1964), 415.

64. "Charlie Chaplin Will Wed Today," LAE, June 16, 1943, LOP Scrapbook #30, AMPAS.

65. "Hollywood Inside," DV, June 17, 1943, 2.

66. GI, book jacket.

67. Ibid., 1–3, 10.

68. Ibid., 17–19.

69. Ibid., 61.

70. Ibid., 79, 144.

71. Ibid., 145–47.

72. Ibid., 2, 124, 127.

73. Ibid., 185.

74. DOS to LOP, Nov. 29, 1943, Administrative Studio Files, Selznick Collection.

75. "Rambling Reporter," HR, Dec. 1, 1943, 2.

76. *Variety,* Dec. 9, 1943, LOP Scrapbook #30, AMPAS.

77. "Rambling Reporter," HR, Dec. 10, 1943, 2.

78. "Hollywood's Back Fence," *Time,* Jan. 24, 1944, 54.

79. Frank Nugent, "Hard Boiled Alice in Wonderland," *New York Times,* Jan. 9, 1944, sec. 7, p. 6, col. 3.

80. Manny Farber, "Mrs. Parsons, etc." *New Republic,* Jan. 10, 1944, 53.

81. David Platt, "Film Front," *Daily Worker,* Apr. 17, 1944, Louella Parsons File, U.S. Department of Justice.

82. David Nasaw, *The Chief: The Life of William Randolph Hearst* (Boston: Houghton Mifflin, 2000), 425.

83. "Rambling Reporter," HR, Feb. 3, 1944, 2.

84. Ibid.

85. "Hollywood Inside," DV, Feb. 9, 1944, 2.

86. "Hollywood Inside," DV, Feb. 7, 1944, 2.

87. DV, May 3, 1944, LOP Scrapbook #32, AMPAS.

88. Hedda Hopper, *From under My Hat* (Garden City, NY: Doubleday, 1952), 243.

89. LAE, June 26, 1944.

90. Clipping, 1944, LOP Scrapbook #32, AMPAS.

91. Brownstein, *The Power and the Glitter,* 91.

92. "Rambling Reporter," HR, Feb. 20, 1945, 2.

93. Hopper, *The Whole Truth,* 229.

94. "Rambling Reporter," HR, Jan. 17, 1946, 2.

95. Louella Parsons show radio script, July 13, 1947, Louella Parsons Collection, Cinema Television Library, University of Southern California.

96. "Rambling Reporter," HR, June 5, 1945, 2.

97. "Rambling Reporter," HR, Jan. 3, 1946, 2.

98. "Colbert Comedy Hews to Sure Fire Line," *Los Angeles Times,* June 14, 1946, A2.

99. LOP to Whiting, March 28, 1946, Louella Parsons Collection, Cinema Television Library, University of Southern California.

100. George Eells, *Hedda and Louella* (New York: Putnam, 1972), 257.

101. LAE, May 15, 1946.

102. "Just for Variety," DV, June 11, 1946, 6.

103. LOP to HH, Aug. 6, 1946, Louella Parsons File, Hedda Hopper Collection, AMPAS.

104. Nasaw, *The Chief,* 579–80; Wagner, *Red Ink, White Lies,* 194.

105. Bebe Daniels and Ben Lyon, *Life with the Lyons* (London: Odhams, 1953), 177–78.

106. "Just for Variety," DV, July 11, 1946, 4.

107. "Louella Returns," DV, Sept. 3, 1946, 8.

108. Clipping, n.d., LOP Scrapbook #37, AMPAS.

109. Clipping from *Billboard,* Apr. 3, 1948, LOP Scrapbook #31, AMPAS.

110. "LOP footprints at Grauman's," *LAE*, Oct. 5, 1946, LOP Scrapbook #37, AMPAS; Stacey Endres and Robert Cushman, *Hollywood at Your Feet: The Story of the World Famous Chinese Theater* (Los Angeles: Pomegranate Press, 1992), 201.

FOURTEEN. WAR AND PEACE

1. "Cosmopolitan Citations," *Cosmopolitan,* May 1946, Box 3, Louella Parsons Collection, Cinema Television Library, University of Southern California (hereafter LOP collection, USC).

2. Lynn Spigel, *Make Room for TV: Television and the Family Ideal in the Postwar Period* (Chicago: University of Chicago Press, 1992), 32.

3. Thomas Schatz, *Boom and Bust: American Cinema in the 1940s* (New York: Scribner's, 1997), 289–91.

4. "An Industry Gets over the Jitters," *Newsweek,* May 10, 1948, 58.

5. "Independents Day," *Time,* May 17, 1948, 91–92; Schatz, *Boom and Bust,* 329.

6. Ronald Davis, *The Glamour Factory: Inside Hollywood's Big Studio System* (Dallas: Southern Methodist University Press, 1993), 358; Ernest Borneman, "United States versus Hollywood: The Case Study of an Antitrust Suit," in *The American Film Industry,* ed. Tino Balio (Madison: University of Wisconsin Press, 1985), 449–62.

7. Charles Higham, *Hollywood at Sunset* (New York: Saturday Review Press, 1972), 73.

8. See Elaine Tyler May, *Homeward Bound: American Families in the Cold War Era* (New York: Basic Books, 1988).

9. Cited in Cynthia Baron, "As Red as a Burlesque Queen's Garters: Cold War Politics and the Actors' Lab in Hollywood," in *Headline Hollywood,* ed. Adrienne McLean and David Cook (New Brunswick, NJ: Rutgers University Press, 2001), 144.

10. Larry Ceplair and Steven Englund, *Inquisition in Hollywood: Politics in the Film Community, 1930–1960* (Berkeley: University of California Press, 1983), 254. On the HUAC hearings in Hollywood, also see Eric Bentley, *Are You Now or Have You Ever Been: The Investigation of Show Business by the Un-American Activities Committee, 1947–1958* (New York: Harper and Row, 1972); Patrick McGilligan and Paul Buhle, *Tender Comrades: A Backstory of the Hollywood Blacklist* (New York: St. Martin's Press, 1997); Stephen Vaughn, "Political Censorship during the Cold War: The Hollywood Ten," in *Movie Censorship and American Culture,* ed. Francis Couvares (Washington, DC: Smithsonian, 1996).

11. "Johnson Admits Reds in Hwood but Scoffs at Their Influence," *Variety* (hereafter V), Apr. 16, 1947, 1.

12. Otto Friedrichs, *City of Nets: A Portrait of Hollywood in the 1940s* (New York: Harper and Row, 1986), 303.

13. "Current Film Productions of Interest," 1949, Louella Parsons File, U.S. Department of Justice (hereafter LOP File, DOJ).

14. Charles Maland, *Chaplin and American Culture* (Princeton, NJ: Princeton

University Press, 1989), 288; See Irvin Molotsky, "The Chaplin Files: Can It Happen Again?" *New York Times* (hereafter NYT), Jan. 22, 1986, A20.

15. Hoover to Tolson, Oct. 26, 1934, LOP File, DOJ Files.

16. Hoover to William Stanley, Oct. 30, 1934, LOP File, DOJ Files.

17. Hanson to Hoover, Dec. 9, 1936, LOP File, DOJ Files.

18. LOP to Hoover, Jan. 4, 1940, LOP File, DOJ Files.

19. *Los Angeles Examiner* (hereafter LAE), Feb. 5, 1957.

20. LAE, May 1, 1947.

21. LAE, Apr. 10, 1947, I, 13.

22. Radio script, Louella Parsons Show, August 31, 1947, LOP collection, USC.

23. Maland, *Chaplin and American Culture,* 254.

24. LAE, Sept. 28, 1947.

25. Hedda Hopper, "Looking at Hollywood," *Los Angeles Times* (hereafter LAT), Aug. 14, 1947, 3.

26. Hopper to Hoover, Apr. 7, 1949, Hedda Hopper file, U.S. Department of Justice.

27. JEH to HH, Aug. 25, 1947, Hedda Hopper file, U.S. Department of Justice.

28. On the CFA, see Schatz, *Boom and Bust,* 311.

29. Kathy Feeley, "Louella Parsons and Hedda Hopper's Hollywood: The Rise of the Celebrity Gossip Industry in Twentieth-Century America, 1910–1950" (Ph.D. diss., City University of New York, 2003), 221. On October 27, 1947, Louella praised the producers for eliminating "the pink tinge" that had tainted a Broadway musical, *Call Me Mister,* in the upcoming film version. She was referring to a skit about the "Red Ball Express," a segregated trucking company that had delivered supplies to the front line in the war. See Jim Tuck, *McCarthyism and New York's Hearst Press: A Study of Roles in the Witch Hunt* (Lanham, MD: University Press of America, 1995), 32.

30. "Soviet Artists Blast Hollywood Red Drive," n.d., LOP Scrapbook #37, Louella Parsons Collection, Academy of Motion Pictures Arts and Sciences, Beverly Hills, California (hereafter AMPAS).

31. "Russians Suggest Hollywood Rebel," NYT, Dec. 9, 1947, 9.

32. "LOP Happy about Red Attack," n.d., LOP Scrapbook #37, AMPAS.

33. Victor Navasky, *Naming Names* (New York: Viking, 1980), 78–85.

34. Schatz, *Boom and Bust,* 311.

35. Steven Ross, "When Stars Speak Out: Movie Stars, Politics, and the Power of Audience Reception," manuscript, 18.

36. "Pink Slips," *Time,* Dec. 8, 1947, 28.

37. Hedda Hopper, "Looking at Hollywood," LAT, Oct. 23, 1947, sec. 2, p. 9.

38. Hedda Hopper, "Looking at Hollywood," LAT, Nov. 7, 1947, sec. 1, p. 10.

39. Jeffrey Meyers, *Bogart: A Life in Hollywood* (Boston: Houghton Mifflin, 1997), 210.

40. *Modern Screen,* 1947, Folder 4, LOP collection, USC.

41. Friedrichs, *City of Nets,* 327.

42. LAE, Nov. 20, 1947.

43. "Film Industry's Policy Defined," V, Nov. 26, 1947, 9.

44. LAE, Feb. 8, 1947.

45. Navasky, *Naming Names,* 154.

46. Lindsay Chaney and Michael Cieply, *The Hearsts: Family and Empire—the Later Years* (New York: Simon and Schuster, 1981), 135–36.

47. LAE, Nov. 14, 1946.

48. J. Randy Taraborelli, *Sinatra: Behind the Legend* (Secaucus, NJ: Carroll Publishing Group, 1997), 82.

49. "Rambling Reporter," *Hollywood Reporter* (hereafter HR), Jan. 29, 1947, 2.

50. "Good News," *Modern Screen,* May 1947, Box 2, Folder 3, LOP collection, USC.

51. "Just for Variety," DV, Mar. 23, 1948, 4.

52. "Rambling Reporter," HR, Sept. 17, 1948, 2.

53. Isabella Taves, "Louella Parsons," *Look,* Oct. 10, 1950, 60–61.

54. "Rambling Reporter," HR, Apr. 4, 1947, 2.

55. "Lop at Bowie to Award Cup," clipping, Apr. 10, 1947, LOP Scrapbook #37, AMPAS.

56. "Rambling Reporter," HR, Apr. 24, 1947, 2.

57. "The Gossipist," *Time,* July 28, 1947, 60.

58. Hedda Hopper, "Looking at Hollywood," LAT, Aug. 6, 1947, sec. 2, p. 8.

59. Hedda Hopper, "Looking at Hollywood," LAT, Aug. 2, 1947, sec. 2, p. 5.

60. "Telling Off Lolly," *Newsweek,* June 9, 1947, 64.

61. Dwight Whitney, Hollywood correspondent for *Time,* had gathered the material for the story, and Louella snubbed him at parties for years. When Whitney left *Time* and was temporarily unemployed, Louella attacked him in her column, going as far as to suggest that his children were suffering from malnutrition. See Ezra Goodman, *The Fifty-Year Decline and Fall of Hollywood* (New York: Simon and Schuster, 1961), 24.

62. "Hollywood Inside," DV, Mar. 2, 1948, 2.

63. Ingrid Bergman, *My Story* (New York: Delacorte Press, 1980), 139.

64. Program, Louella O. Parsons Testimonial Dinner, Box 3:27, John Stahl Collection, University of Southern California.

65. "Rambling Reporter," HR, Mar. 2, 1948, 2.

66. Louella's acceptance speech, LOP Scrapbook #42, AMPAS.

67. Clipping, n.d., LOP Scrapbook #42, AMPAS.

68. Mock "LA Examiner," n.d., LOP Scrapbook #42, AMPAS.

69. WRH to LOP, n.d., LOP Scrapbook #42, AMPAS.

70. "We Love You Louella," *Time,* Mar. 15, 1948, 98–99.

71. Acceptance speech, LOP Scrapbook #42, AMPAS.

72. Alex Tiers to George Eells, George Eells Collection, University of Southern California.

73. "We Love You Louella," 98.

74. LAE, Mar. 6, 1948.

75. "Hollywood Inside," DV, Sept. 27, 1946, 2.

76. "Hollywood Inside," DV, Apr. 23, 1941, 2.

77. LAE, June 4, 1941.

78. "Parsons Jr.," *Hollywood Studio Magazine,* Oct. 1982, Harriet Parsons Clipping File, AMPAS.

79. Hedda Hopper, "Looking at Hollywood," LAT, Mar. 12, 1948, sec. 1, p. 16.

80. William J. Mann, *Behind the Screen: How Gays and Lesbians Shaped Hollywood, 1910–1969* (New York: Viking, 2001), 194–95.

81. "Rambling Reporter," HR, Nov. 6, 1944, 2.

82. DOS to Colby, Apr. 23, 1945, Administrative Studio Files, 1938–1943, Selznick Collection, Harry Ransom Humanities Research Center, University of Texas, Austin.

83. LAE, May 2, 1945.

84. LAE, Mar. 25, 1945.

85. LAE, Apr. 7, 1945, I, 9.

86. "Cosmopolitan Citations," *Cosmopolitan,* Apr. 1948, Box 3, LOP collection, USC.

87. Hedda Hopper, "Looking at Hollywood," LAT, Mar. 12, 1948, sec. 1, p. 16

88. Hedda Hopper, *From under My Hat* (Garden City, NY: Doubleday, 1952), 75

89. Harriet Parsons to Hedda Hopper, Mar. 15, 1948, Harriet Parsons Files, Hedda Hopper Collection, AMPAS.

90. Ginger Rogers to HH, Mar. 12, 1948, Harriet Parsons Files, Hedda Hopper Collection, AMPAS.

91. Wynn Roccamora to HH, Mar. 12, 1948, Harriet Parsons Files, Hedda Hopper Collection, AMPAS.

92. In 1941, *Pic* magazine had falsely claimed that "one day Hedda suggested to Louella that they end the whole affair. The idea was to kiss and make up publicly at a charity ball. Louella liked the idea, but it never materialized." According to *Pic,* Louella had allegedly "begged out at the last minute saying that her husband, Dr Martin, didn't feel her health would permit such an experience. . . . Hollywood rumors are that [she] withdrew because she neither trusted Hedda's wit nor the apparent honesty of the plan." "Parsons vs. Hopper," *Pic,* May 13, 1941, Louella Parsons Clipping File, AMPAS.

93. Hopper, *From under My Hat,* 244–45.

94. HR, Mar. 17, 1948.

95. Dickson Hartwell, "End of a Beautiful Feud," *Collier's,* June 5, 1948, 22.

96. Irving Hoffman, "Tales of Hoffman," HR, Mar. 5, 1948.

97. "Hedda Hopper's Hollywood," LAT, May 15, 1948.

98. Hartwell, "End of a Beautiful Feud," 22.

99. Molly Merrick, interview by George Eells, n.d., George Eells Collection, Arizona State University.

100. Grace Mullen to Hedda Hopper, Sept. 24, 1948, Louella Parsons File, Hedda Hopper Collection, AMPAS.

101. Hartwell, "End of a Beautiful Feud," 22.

102. Gloria Swanson, "Gloria's Glories," May 27, 1948, LOP Scrapbook #43, AMPAS.

103. Kathleen Cairns, *Front Page Women Journalists* (Lincoln: University of Nebraska Press, 2003), xi, xii, 4.

104. Dorothy Kilgallen, "Voice of Broadway," *New York Journal American,* n.d., LOP Scrapbook #43, AMPAS.

105. *Hollywood Shopping News,* July 19, 1948, LOP Scrapbook #43, AMPAS.

106. LAE, June 22, 1948, I, 15.

107. LAE, Oct. 9, 1958.

108. *New York American,* July 29, 1948, LOP Scrapbook #43, AMPAS.

109. "Rambling Reporter," HR, Sept. 29, 1948, 2.

110. Neal Gabler, *Winchell: Gossip, Power, and the Culture of Celebrity* (New York: Knopf, 1994), 376.

111. "Rambling Reporter," HR, Nov. 17, 1948, 2.

112. "Rambling Reporter," HR, Nov. 10, 1948.

113. "Hollywood Inside," DV, Nov. 18, 1948.

114. *Advertising Age,* Jan. 10, 1949, LOP Scrapbook #44, AMPAS; "Hollywood Inside," DV, Mar. 18, 1949.

115. "Rambling Reporter," HR, June 16, 1948, 2.

116. George Dixon, "Dixon Says," Nov. 9, 1948, LOP Scrapbook #44, AMPAS.

117. Bosley Crowther, *Hollywood Rajah: The Life and Times of Louis B. Mayer* (New York: Holt, 1960), 271.

118. "Rambling Reporter," HR, Dec. 10, 1948, 2.

119. "Rambling Reporter," HR, Mar. 16, 1949, 2.

FIFTEEN. SCANDAL

1. Elaine Tyler May, *Homeward Bound: American Families in the Cold War Era* (New York: Basic Books, 1988), 69, 116.

2. *Photoplay,* 1947, Box 2, Folder 3, Louella Parsons Collection, Cinema Television Library, University of Southern California.

3. Louella Parsons, *Tell It to Louella* (New York: Putnam, 1961), (hereafter TL), 73–74.

4. Ibid., 74.

5. Ibid., 77.

6. See Barbara Leaming, *If This Was Happiness: A Biography of Rita Hayworth* (New York: Viking, 1989).

7. TL, 82.

8. TL, 84.

9. "Rambling Reporter," HR, May 9, 1949, 2.

10. TL, 85.

11. TL, 87.

12. "Rambling Reporter," HR, June 6, 1949, 2.

13. "Rambling Reporter," HR, June 8, 1949, 2.

14. A. J. Liebling, "The Wayward Press," New Yorker, June 11, 1949, 87–93.

15. Ibid.

16. "Clubwoman Asks Boycott of Rita's Films," Los Angeles Times (hereafter LAT), Friday, Jan. 14, 1949, 22.

17. Memo from David O. Selznick, ed. Rudy Behlmer, 144–45, cited in Kathy Feeley, "Louella Parsons and Hedda Hopper's Hollywood: The Rise of the Celebrity Gossip Industry in Twentieth-Century America, 1910–1950" (Ph.D. diss., City University of New York, 2003), 244.

18. James Damico, "Ingrid from Lorraine to Stromboli: Analyzing the Public's Perception of a Film Star," in Star Texts: Image and Performance in Film and Television, ed. Jeremy Butler (Detroit: Wayne State University Press, 1991), 250; also see Adrienne McLean, "The Cinderella Princess and the Instrument of Evil: Revisiting Two Postwar Hollywood Star Scandals," in Headline Hollywood, ed. Adrienne McLean and David Cook (New Brunswick, NJ: Rutgers University Press, 2001), 163–89.

19. Los Angeles Examiner (hereafter LAE), Nov. 3, 1946.

20. LAE, Feb. 24, 1948.

21. John Kobal, People Will Talk (New York: Knopf, 1985), 471.

22. LAE, Jan. 23, 1947, II, 5.

23. Laurence Leamer, As Time Goes By: The Life of Ingrid Bergman (New York: HarperCollins, 1986), 150.

24. Joseph Steele, Ingrid Bergman, an Intimate Portrait (New York: McKay, 1959), 161.

25. LAE, Feb. 26, 1949, I, 11.

26. Feeley, "Louella Parsons and Hedda Hopper's Hollywood," 252.

27. Leaming, If This Was Happiness, 190.

28. LAE, May 15, 1949, I, 13.

29. LAE, May 5, 1949, II, 5.

30. Steele, Ingrid Bergman, 259.

31. LAE, July 31, 1949.

32. TL, 58.

33. Ibid.

34. Sheilah Graham, The Rest of the Story (New York: Coward McCann, 1964), 143.

35. Radie Harris, Radie's World (New York: Putnam, 1975), 166–67.

36. "Ingrid Bergman Expecting Baby," LAE, Dec. 12, 1949, 1.

37. Media scholars James Lull and Stephen Hinerman define the modern media scandal as an event that occurs when "the intentional or reckless personal actions of specific persons . . . disgrace or offend the idealized, dominant morality of a social community." The actions or events must be "widely circulated by mass media, effectively narrativized into a story, and inspire widespread interest and discussion." The Bergman story and its subsequent fallout clearly fit this description. See James Lull and Stephen Hinerman, eds., *Media Scandals: Morality and Desire in Popular Culture* (New York: Columbia University Press, 1997).

38. Steele, *Ingrid Bergman,* 262–63.

39. TL, 61.

40. TL, 59–60.

41. "Hollywood Sees Hoax in Reports of Bergman Baby," LAT, Dec. 13, 1949, 2.

42. TL, 60.

43. Hedda Hopper, *From under My Hat* (Garden City: Doubleday, 1952), 242.

44. Max Lerner, *New York Post,* Dec. 15, 1949, LOP Scrapbook #48, Louella Parsons Collection, Academy of Motion Pictures Arts and Sciences, Beverly Hills, California (hereafter AMPAS).

45. Editorial, LAT, Dec. 15, 1949.

46. "Act of God," *Time,* Dec. 26, 1949, 51.

47. "Rambling Reporter," HR, Feb. 6, 1950, 2.

48. "Rambling Reporter," HR, Feb. 10, 1950, 2.

49. Anita Loos, *The Gay Illiterate,* manuscript, in author's possession.

50. TL, 62.

51. "Many Exhibs Defer," *Variety* (hereafter V), Feb. 8, 1950, 1.

52. Feeley, "Louella Parsons and Hedda Hopper's Hollywood," 287.

53. Herb Stinson, "Louella Parsons," *The Mirror,* May 7, 1953, Louella Parsons Clipping File, AMPAS.

54. Kobal, *People Will Talk,* 472.

55. "LOP's Big Take on Clark Gable Book," HR, Feb. 27, 1950, 4.

56. "Hollywood Inside," *Daily Variety* (hereafter DV), Dec. 25, 1949, 2.

57. DV, Dec. 21, 1949, 2.

58. LAE, Mar. 14, 1950.

59. "Rambling Reporter," HR, Apr. 11, 1950, 2.

60. Isabella Taves, "Louella Parsons," *Look,* Oct. 10, 1950, 60.

61. "Rambling Reporter," HR, Feb. 5, 1950, 2.

62. "Rambling Reporter," HR, Dec. 19, 1950, 2.

63. "Rambling Reporter," HR, Dec. 28, 1950, 2.

64. "Rambling Reporter," HR, Mar. 5, 1951, 2.

65. Ester Williams with Digby Diehl, *The Million Dollar Mermaid* (New York: Simon and Schuster, 1999), 180.

66. Kobal, *People Will Talk,* 606.

67. Note, July 11, 1951, Louella Parsons File, Warner Brothers Collection, University of Southern California; "Hollywood Inside," DV, June 19, 1951, 2; Rudy Behlmer, *Hollywood's Hollywood: The Movies about the Movies* (Secaucus, NJ: Citadel Press, 1976), 307.

68. Shirley Temple Black, *Child Star* (New York: McGraw Hill, 1988), 469.

69. "Dr. Martin Is Dead, Fox Film Official," NYT, June 25, 1951, 19.

70. Ehrlich, interview by George Eells, n.d., George Eells Collection, Arizona State University (hereafter Eells Collection, ASU).

71. Hoover to LOP, June 25, 1951, Louella Parsons File, U.S. Department of Justice (hereafter LOP File, DOJ).

72. LOP to Hoover, July 4, 1951, LOP File, DOJ.

73. "Dr. Harry Martin Claimed by Death," June 25, 1951, Louella Parsons Clipping File, AMPAS.

74. "500 at Last Rites of Harry Martin," Louella Parsons Clipping File, AMPAS.

75. "Dr. Martin Leaves Estate to Widow Louella Parsons," LAE, July 17, 1951, Louella Parsons Clipping File, AMPAS.

76. "Hollywood Inside," DV, July 3, 1951, 2.

77. Bebe Daniels and Ben Lyon, *Life with the Lyons* (London: Odhams, 1953), 178.

78. "Just for Variety," DV, July 17, 1951, 2.

79. "Just for Variety," DV, Aug. 7, 1951, 2.

80. W. A. Swanberg, *Citizen Hearst* (New York: Scribner's 1961), 520.

81. "Just for Variety," DV, Aug. 15, 1951, 2.

82. Lawrence Davies, "1500 at Cathedral for Hearst Service," NYT, Aug. 18, 1951, 11

83. David Nasaw, *The Chief: The Life of William Randolph Hearst* (Boston Houghton Mifflin, 2000), 600.

84. Fred Lawrence Guiles, *Marion Davies* (New York: Bantam, 1973), 423.

85. Lindsay Chaney and Michael Cieply, *The Hearsts: Family and Empire—the Later Years* (New York: Simon and Schuster, 1981), 136.

86. Hoover to Louella, March 25, 1960, LOP File, DOJ; Larry Ceplair and Steven Englund, *Inquisition in Hollywood: Politics in the Film Community, 1930–1960* (Berkeley: University of California Press, 1983), 376.

87. Ceplair and England, *Inquisition in Hollywood,* 372.

88. Teletype, Apr. 21, 1951, LOP File, DOJ.

89. LAE, May 6, 1951; Daniel Leab, *I Was a Communist for the FBI: The Unhappy Life and Times of Matt Cvetic* (University Park: Pennsylvania State University Press, 2000)

90. Nichols to Tolson, Nov. 20, 1950.

91. Jones to Nicholson, Sept. 15, 1951, LOP File, DOJ.

92. SAC Hood to Hoover, Jan. 27, 1949.

93. Cynthia Baron, "As Red as a Burlesque Queen's Garters: Cold War Politic and the Actors' Lab in Hollywood," in *Headline Hollywood,* ed. Adrienne McLean and David Cook (New Brunswick, NJ: Rutgers University Press, 2001), 143–60.

94. "Hedda Hopper's Hollywood," LAT, July 19, 1948.

95. Stefan Kanfer, *A Journal of the Plague Years* (New York: Atheneum, 1983), 126

96. Agenda for MPA General Membership Meeting, Mar. 22, 1951, American Legion File, Hedda Hopper Collection, AMPAS.

97. Kanfer, *A Journal of the Plague Years,* 130.

98. "Hedda Hopper's Hollywood," LAT, Mar. 26, 1951.

99. David McClure, interview by George Eells, n.d. Eells Collection, ASU.

100. Nichols to Tolson, Apr. 17, 1952, Hedda Hopper file, U.S. Department of Justice.

101. Anthony Slide, "Hedda Hopper's Hollywood," 2, Hedda Hopper Clipping File, AMPAS.

102. Hopper to McCarthy, Dec. 7, 1953, McCarthy Files, Hedda Hopper Collection, AMPAS.

103. "Hedda Hopper," LAT, May 21, 1951, 8.

104. Slide, "Hedda Hopper's Hollywood," 2.

105. "A Valiant Fighter," *Hollywood Citizen News,* Apr. 26, 1951, Hedda Hopper Clipping File, AMPAS.

106. "Hollywood Inside," DV, Apr. 25, 1951, 2; Hedda Hopper, with James Brough, *The Whole Truth and Nothing But* (New York: Doubleday, 1962), 280.

107. "Hedda Won't Testify at Commie Hearings," V, Sept. 24, 1951, Hedda Hopper Clipping File, AMPAS.

108. "Hedda Hissed at ANTA Antics," V, May 9, 1951, 2.

109. V, Nov. 8, 1953.

110. Slide, "Hedda Hopper's Hollywood," 3.

111. Letter to the editor, *American Legion Magazine,* July 1960, American Legion File, Hedda Hopper Clipping file, AMPAS.

SIXTEEN. THE END OF AN ERA

1. Lynn Spigel, *Make Room for TV: Television and the Family Ideal in the Postwar Period* (Chicago: University of Chicago Press, 1992), 32.

2. *Los Angeles Examiner* (hereafter LAE), Sept. 9, 1951.

3. Ronald Davis, *The Glamour Factory: Inside Hollywood's Big Studio System* (Dallas: Southern Methodist University Press), 372.

4. "ABC Going into TV Film Production on Coast, Lolly Parsons to Tee Off," *Variety* (hereafter V), Mar. 7, 1951, 1.

5. "Louella Parsons TV Yen Prompts Split with Jergens," V, Oct. 4, 1951, 1.

6. "Louella Parsons Concludes 21 Years in Radio, Turns to TV," LAE Dec. 23, 1951.

7. "Rambling Reporter," *Hollywood Reporter* (hereafter HR), Mar. 25, 1952, 2.

8. "The Truth about My Feuds," *Modern Screen,* May 1951, in *The Best of Modern Screen,* ed. Mark Bego (New York: St. Martin's Press, 1986), 184.

9. LOP to *Cosmopolitan* editors, Sept. 24, 1952, Box 2, Louella Parsons Collection, Cinema Television Library, University of Southern California (hereafter USC).

10. "Personality," *Time,* Aug. 25, 1952, 36.

11. Herb Stinson, "Louella Parsons," *New York Mirror,* May 7, 1953, Louella Parsons Clipping File, Academy of Motion Pictures Arts and Sciences, Beverly Hills, California (hereafter AMPAS).

12. Stinson, "Louella Parsons"; *Columbus (GA) Ledger,* Nov. 15, 1954, LOP Scrapbook #58, Louella Parsons Collection, AMPAS.

13. Ezra Goodman, "Accentuating the Curves and the Muscles," *New York Times* (hereafter NYT), Feb. 6, 1949, sec. 10, p. 5.

14. Gordon Sinclair, clipping, n.d., LOP Scrapbook #58, AMPAS.

15. "Rambling Reporter," HR, July 25, 1952, 2.

16. "Hollywood Inside," *Daily Variety* (hereafter DV), Aug. 18, 1952, 2.

17. "Jimmy McHugh, 75, Prolific Cleffer of Legit, Pix Standards, Dies on Coast," V, May 28, 1969, 60; "Hollywood's Top Tunesmith," *Toronto Star Weekly,* Oct. 14, 1944, 5; Myrtle Gebhart, "Hub's Famed Song Composer Gives Mother Credit for Success," *Boston Sunday Post,* Sept. 2, 1945, 4; George W. Clarke, "The Story behind a Song Hit," *Green Magazine,* Apr. 28, 1940, 4, McHugh Clipping File, AMPAS.

18. "Rambling Reporter," HR, July 1, 1952, 2.

19. "Rambling Reporter," HR, Nov. 6, 1952, 2.

20. "Hollywood Inside," DV, Jan. 6, 1953.

21. "Rambling Reporter," HR, Dec. 1, 1953, 2.

22. George Eells, *Hedda and Louella* (New York: Putnam, 1972), 302.

23. "Hedda Hopper," *Los Angeles Times,* Jan. 2, 1953.

24. Ezra Goodman, *The Fifty-Year Decline and Fall of Hollywood* (New York: Simon and Schuster), 22.

25. Ibid., 28.

26. Louella Parsons tribute, Louella Parsons Collection, University of Southern California.

27. Lindsay Chaney and Michael Cieply, *The Hearsts: Family and Empire—the Later Years* (New York: Simon and Schuster, 1981), 143.

28. *Newsweek,* Feb. 22, 1954, 62–63.

29. Hedda Hopper, *From under My Hat* (Garden City, NY: Doubleday, 1952), 244.

30. "The Voice and the Kids," *New Republic,* Nov. 6, 1944, 593; E. J. Kahn, "The Slaves of Sinatra," *New Yorker,* Nov. 1946; "The Curious Craze for 'Confidential' Magazines," *Newsweek,* July 11, 1955, 50–51.

31. "Hollywood Profiled," *Newsweek,* June 9, 1952, 54.

32. Sam Kashner and Jennifer McNair, *The Bad and the Beautiful: Hollywood in the Fifties* (New York: Norton, 2002), 297.

33. Jack Gould, "Programs in Review," NYT, Oct. 2, 1949, sec. 10, p. 9.

34. "Jimmie Fidler, 89, Hollywood Columnist," NYT, Aug. 12, 1988, sec. D, p. 18.

35. Goodman, *The Fifty-Year Decline and Fall of Hollywood,* 53.

36. Kashner and McNair, *The Bad and the Beautiful,* 283.

37. Val Holley, *Mike Connolly and the Manly Art of Hollywood Gossip* (Jefferson, NC: McFarland, 2003), 98.

38. Graham, *The Rest of the Story,* 149–50.

39. Ibid., 133–35.

40. LAE, Oct. 19, 1952, III, 1.

41. Louella Parsons, *Tell It to Louella* (New York: Putnam, 1961), (hereafter TL), 170.

42. Donald Spoto, *Marilyn Monroe* (New York: HarperCollins, 1993), 236.

43. TL, 185.

44. Spoto, *Marilyn Monroe,* 275.

45. Pat Newcombe, interview by George Eells, n.d., George Eells Collection, University of Southern California.

46. "Rambling Reporter," HR, Oct. 6, 1954, 2.

47. LAE, June 3, 1953.

48. TL, 94.

49. Peter Manso, *Brando: The Biography* (New York: Hyperion, 1994), 383–84.

50. LAE, Sept. 2, 1952.

51. LAE, Oct. 31, 1953, I, 11.

52. Paul O'Neil, "The Little Queen That Hollywood Deserved," *Life,* June 4, 1965.

53. LAE, Mar. 24, 1954, II, 7.

54. LAE, Apr. 9, 1955, I, 13.

55. LAE, Apr. 7, 1949, II, 5.

56. LAE, Feb. 1, 1950, I, 17.

57. "Rambling Reporter," HR, July 26, 1950, 2.

58. "Rambling Reporter," HR, July 28, 1950, 2.

59. Charles Maland, *Chaplin and American Culture* (Princeton, NJ: Princeton University Press, 1989), 280.

60. Anthony Slide, "Hedda Hopper's Hollywood," 2, Hedda Hopper Clipping File AMPAS.

61. Maland, *Chaplin and American Culture,* 280.

62. "Comedian Labeled Genius Was Law unto Himself," LAE, Sept. 23, 1952.

63. "Country That Made Chaplin Famous Is One He Refused," LAE, Sept. 24, 1952.

64. Maland, *Chaplin and American Culture,* 301–2.

65. Unknown to HH, Sept. 22, 1952; Raymond Accorsi to HH, Sept. 23, 1952; Anna Doran to HH, Sept. 21, 1952, Chaplin Files, Hedda Hopper Collection, AMPAS.

66. "The New Hollywood Battle of Censorship."

67. LAE, Apr. 20, 1954.

68. LAE, Dec. 30, 1955, II, 7.

69. LAE, July 7, 1954, III, 7.

70. "Louella Parsons, Gossip Columnist, Dies," NYT, Dec. 10, 1972, 85:1.

71. LAE, Jan. 1, 1953.

72. "Louella at Inauguration," LAE, Dec. 17, 1952, Louella Parsons File, Regional History Collection, University of Southern California.

73. LAE, Jan. 21, 1953, II, 7.

74. LOP to Hoover, Jan. 17, 1953, Louella Parsons File, U.S. Department of Justice (hereafter LOP File, DOJ).

75. LOP to Hoover, June 4, 1953, LOP File, DOJ.

76. Untitled, July 15, 1953, LOP File, DOJ.

77. Untitled, July 15, 1953, LOP File, DOJ.

78. In April the guild passed a resolution forbidding its members to make guest appearances on film TV shows unless paid for their services. "Guild's TV Terms May Be Accepted," NYT, Aug. 12, 1955, 37.

79. LAE, Nov. 4, 1953.

80. "Rambling Reporter," HR, Nov. 27, Dec. 6, Dec 17, 1953, 2.

81. Liz Smith, *Natural Blonde: A Memoir* (New York: Random House, 2000), 104.

82. Harriett Gustason, *Looking Back,* vol. 1 (Freeport, IL: Stephenson County Historical Society, 1994), 61.

83. Untitled, n.d., LOP File, DOJ.

84. Van Doren claimed that later, after she had been a minor star for a while at Universal, she received a call from a reporter for the Hollywood scandal magazine *Confidential* who claimed to have heard a rumor that she and her mother had been prostitutes. Her attorney, Jerry Geisler, called *Confidential* and found out that the source for the rumor had been Louella. Van Doren believed that Louella was influential in getting the Catholic organization the Legion of Decency to blacklist her films, and that Louella prevented her from attaining stardom. Mamie Van Doren, telephone interview by author, February 15, 2004. Also Mamie Van Doren, *Playing the Field* (New York: Putnam, 1987), chap. 6.

85. "Rambling Reporter," HR, Jan. 26, 1954, Jan. 28, 1955, 2.

86. "Rambling Reporter," HR, Oct. 28, Nov. 5, Dec. 31, 1954, 2.

87. "Louella Parsons Seeks $10,000 for Bus Crash," LAT, Oct. 12, 1956, 5.

88. "Rambling Reporter," HR, Dec. 31, 1954; "Louella Calls Off TV Show," Aug. 26, 1955, *Los Angeles Mirror News,* Louella Parsons Clipping File, AMPAS.

89. Stinson, "Rambling Reporter," HR, Sept. 22, 1954; Aug. 12, 1955.

90. "Rambling Reporter," HR, Jan. 8, 1957, 2.

91. New York office to Hoover, Apr. 23, 1955, Hedda Hopper File, DOJ.

92. LAE, June 5, 13, 20, 1955.

93. King Kennedy, interview by George Eells, n.d., Eells Collection, ASU.

94. LAE, June 22, 26, July 20, 1955.

95. "American Women at Work," *Newsweek,* Feb. 27, 1956, 77.

96. "Loquacious Louella," V, Jan. 29, 1954.

97. "Rambling Reporter," HR, Feb. 9, 1956, 2.

98. "The Hatchet Woman Hollywood Fears," *Confidential,* Apr. 1959, Louella Parsons File, Regional History Collection, University of Southern California.

99. *Climax! The Louella Parsons Story,* Mar. 8, 1956, Film and Television Archive, University of California, Los Angeles.

100. *Toledo Blade,* Mar. 10, 1956, LOP Scrapbook #58, AMPAS.

101. Jay Nelson Tuck, *New York Post,* Mar. 9, 1956, LOP Scrapbook #58, AMPAS.

102. *Cleveland News,* Mar. 23, 1956, LOP Scrapbook #58, AMPAS.

103. *Time,* Mar. 19, 1956, LOP Scrapbook #58, AMPAS.

104. "Just for Variety," DV, Mar. 12, 1956, 2.

105. Untitled document, Louella Parsons File, Hedda Hopper Collection, AMPAS.

106. LAE, Nov. 7, 1957.

107. TL, 63–64.

108. LAE, July 4, 1957.

109. Davis, *The Glamour Factory,* 375.

110. Louella Parsons Oral History, Popular Arts Collection, Butler Library, Columbia University, 105.

111. LAE, Feb. 4, 1959.

112. TL, 220.

113. "Good News," *Modern Screen,* 1955, Box 2, Folder 3, LOP Collection, USC.

114. TL, 223.

115. "Just for Variety," DV, Feb. 7, 1957, 2.

116. "Just for Variety," DV, July 12, Aug. 6, 1957, 2.

117. Kashner and McNair, *The Bad and the Beautiful,* 17.

118. Goodman, *The Fifty-Year Decline and Fall of Hollywood,* 51; "Putting the Papers to Bed," *Time,* Aug. 26, 1957, 61; Mary Desjardins, "Systematizing Scandal: *Confidential* Magazine, Stardom, and the State of California," in *Headline Hollywood,* ed. Adrienne McLean and David Cook (New Brunswick, NJ: Rutgers University Press, 2001), 206–31.

119. Jeanette Walls, *Dish: The Inside Story on the World of Gossip* (New York: HarperCollins, 2000), 14.

120. "The Hatchet Woman Hollywood Fears," 60–61.

121. Walls, *Dish,* 45.

122. "The Curious Craze for 'Confidential' Magazines," 50–51.

123. Desjardins, "Systematizing Scandal," 216; Goodman, *The Fifty-Year Decline and Fall of Hollywood,* 79.

124. LAE, Jan. 30, 1955.

125. *Person to Person,* Nov. 7, 1958, Film and Television Archive, University of California, Los Angeles.

126. TL, 48.

1. Anita Loos, manuscript, in author's possession.

2. Murray Illson, "Hollywood Her World," *New York Times* (hereafter NYT), Dec. 10, 1972, 85.

3. Rob Wagner, *Red Ink, White Lies: The Rise and Fall of Los Angeles Newspapers, 1920–1962* (Upland, CA: Dragonflyer Press, 2000), 231.

4. Ezra Goodman, *The Fifty-Year Decline and Fall of Hollywood* (New York: Simon and Schuster, 1961), 83.

5. Hedda Hopper, with James Brough, *The Whole Truth and Nothing But* (New York: Doubleday, 1962), 21.

6. *Los Angeles Examiner* (hereafter LAE), Mar. 10, 1961.

7. "Joan Crawford Admits She's Broke," LAE, June 1, 1959, 1.

8. Bob Thomas, *Joan Crawford* (New York: Simon and Schuster, 1978), 215–16.

9. *Person to Person,* Nov. 7, 1958, Film and Television Archive, University of California, Los Angeles.

10. "Quincy College Will Honor Ex-Dixonite LOP," *Dixon Evening Telegraph,* May 28, 1959, 1.

11. LAE, June 9, 1959.

12. GS to LOP, June 16, 1959, Gloria Swanson Collection, Harry Ransom Humanities Research Center, University of Texas, Austin.

13. LAE, June 13, 1959.

14. Louella Parsons Oral History, Popular Arts Collection, Butler Library, Columbia University (hereafter LPOH), 95–96.

15. LPOH, 112.

16. LPOH, 114–15.

17. Paul O'Neil, "The Little Queen That Hollywood Deserved," *Life,* June 4, 1965.

18. LAE, Jan. 27, 1960.

19. LAE, Mar. 6, 1961.

20. Hoover to LOP, Dec. 1, 1961, Louella Parsons File, U.S. Department of Justice (hereafter LOP File, DOJ).

21. Goodman, *The Fifty-Year Decline and Fall of Hollywood,* 400.

22. "Parsons Jr.: Produced What Mom Juiced," *Hollywood Studio Magazine,* Oct. 1982, Harriet Parsons Clipping File, Academy of Motion Pictures Arts and Sciences, Beverly Hills, California (hereafter AMPAS).

23. LAE, July 11, 1960.

24. LAE, Nov. 2, 1960.

25. LAE, June 6, 1961.

26. Louella Parsons, *Tell It to Louella* (New York: Putnam, 1961), 107.

27. Ibid., 72.

28. "Parsons Jr.: Produced What Mom Juiced."

29. "The Challenge of Communism," LAE, Apr. 30, 1961, Louella Parsons File, Regional History Collection, University of Southern California (hereafter USC).

30. "Reaction: Readers Agree," LAE, May 21, 1961, Louella Parsons File, Regional History Collection, USC.

31. Clark Kennard, "Tell It to Louella," LAE, Nov. 19, 1961, Louella Parsons File, Regional History Collection, USC.

32. Jim Billings, "Louella Tells about Herself," LOP Scrapbook #61, AMPAS.

33. "No. 1 Movie Fan," Time, Nov. 24, 1961, 47.

34. Murray Schumach, "Don't Ruffle This Lady," NYT, Dec. 10, 1961, 34.

35. John Hutchens, New York Herald Tribune, Dec. 1, LOP Scrapbook #61, AMPAS.

36. Hoover to LOP, Mar. 25, 1960, LOP File, DOJ.

37. LAE, Apr. 30, 1960.

38. Wagner, Red Ink, White Lies, 204.

39. LAE, Apr. 22, 1959, LOP Scrapbook #60, AMPAS.

40. Lindsay Chaney and Michael Cieply, The Hearsts: Family and Empire—the Later Years (New York: Simon and Schuster, 1981), chap. 4.

41. "Just for Variety," Variety, May 26, 1958, 2.

42. "Los Angeles Examiner to Close, Mirror There May Also Be Shut," NYT, Jan. 5, 1962, 20; Wagner, Red Ink, White Lies, 298.

43. "Louella Parsons Dead at 91," Variety, Dec. 13, 1972.

44. "Through a Keyhole Darkly," Time, Feb. 15, 1963, 52.

45. DeLoach to Mohr, May 13, 1960, Hedda Hopper File, DOJ.

46. "Moses and the Money Changers," Time, Jan. 11, 1960, 38.

47. Hopper, The Whole Truth, 60.

48. "Louella Parsons in Hospital," NYT, Apr. 14, 1962, 14.

49. George Eells, Hedda and Louella (New York: Putnam, 1972), 336.

50. Hopper, The Whole Truth, 78.

51. GS to LOP, Mar. 22, 1963, Gloria Swanson Collection, Harry Ransom Humanities Research Center, University of Texas, Austin.

52. "A Guide to Syndicated Survivors," Time, June 3, 1964, 39.

53. Peter Bart, "Dimming Days of Wine and Glory," NYT, June 13, 1965, X13.

54. O'Neil, "The Little Queen That Hollywood Deserved."

55. JW to LOP, Dec. 5, 1965, Jack Warner Collection, Box 72, Folder P, 1965, Cinema Television Library, USC.

56. Advertisement, LAT, Mar. 27, 1966, LOP Clipping File, AMPAS; "Pages from the Past," Los Angeles Herald-Examiner, Apr. 24, 1966, LOP Clipping File, AMPAS.

57. Amy Fine Collins, "Idol Gossips," Vanity Fair, Apr. 1997, 375.

58. "Hollywood," Time, Feb. 11, 1966, 52.

59. Collins, "Idol Gossips."

60. "A Guide to Syndicated Survivors," 39.

61. William Faith, *Bob Hope: A Life in Comedy* (Cambridge, MA: Da Capo Press, 2003), 351.

62. "Mass for Louella Parsons Attended by Stars on Coast," NYT, Dec. 14, 1972, 50.

63. Illson, "Hollywood Her World"; "Louella Parsons Dead at 91," *Variety,* Dec. 13, 1972."

64. "Gossipmania," *Newsweek,* May 24, 1976, 56. Also see George Eells, "Whatever Became of the Common Scolds?" *Look,* Nov. 3, 1970, 90.

65. John Lahr, "Notes on Fame," *Harper's,* Jan. 1978, 77–80.

66. Nora Ephron, "Hedda and Louella," NYT, Apr. 23, 1972, BR7.

67. John J. O'Connor, "Malice in Wonderland," NYT, May 10, 1985.

68. "Liz and the Gossips," *People,* Mar. 17, 1985, 51.

69. "Harriet Parsons, Filmmaker, Daughter of Louella Parsons," NYT, Jan. 4, 1983, D18.

BIBLIOGRAPHY

Addams, Jane. *The Spirit of Youth and the City Streets.* New York: Macmillan, 1909.

Allen, Robert. "The Movies in Vaudeville: Historical Context of the Movies as Popular Entertainment." In *The American Film Industry,* ed. Tino Balio. Madison: University of Wisconsin Press, 1985.

Ardmore, Jane Kesner. *The Self-Enchanted.* New York: McGraw Hill, 1959.

Balio, Tino. *Grand Design: Hollywood as a Modern Business Enterprise.* New York: Scribner's, 1993.

————, ed. *The American Film Industry.* Madison: University of Wisconsin Press, 1985.

Barbas, Samantha. *Movie Crazy: Fans, Stars, and the Cult of Celebrity.* New York: Palgrave Macmillan, 2001.

Barrett, Mary. *History of Stephenson County.* Freeport, IL: County of Stephenson, 1972.

Barris, Alex. *Stop the Presses: The American Newspaperman in Films.* South Brunswick, NJ: A. S. Barnes, 1976.

Bartlett, Donald, and James Steele. *Empire: The Life, Legend, and Madness of Howard Hughes.* New York: Norton, 1979.

Beauchamp, Cari. *Without Lying Down: Frances Marion and the Powerful Women of Early Hollywood.* New York: Scribner's, 1997.

Bego, Mark, ed. *The Best of Modern Screen.* New York: St. Martin's, 1986.

Behlmer, Rudy. *Hollywood's Hollywood: The Movies about the Movies.* Secaucus, NJ: Citadel Press, 1976.

Bennett, E. A. *Journalism for Women; a Practical Guide.* New York: J. Lane, 1898.

Bent, Silas. *Ballyhoo: The Voice of the Press.* New York: Boni, 1927.

Bergman, Ingrid. *My Story.* New York: Delacorte Press, 1980.

Bernstein, Matthew, ed. *Controlling Hollywood: Censorship and Regulation in the Studio Era.* New Brunswick, NJ: Rutgers University Press, 1999.

Black, Gregory. *Hollywood Censored.* Cambridge: Cambridge University Press, 1994.

Black, Shirley Temple. *Child Star.* New York: McGraw Hill, 1988.

Blum, John Morton. *V Was for Victory.* New York: Harcourt Brace Jovanovich, 1976.

Bowser, Eileen. *The Transformation of Cinema, 1907–1915.* Berkeley: University of California Press, 1990.

Brady, Frank. *Citizen Welles.* New York: Scribner's, 1989.

Braudy, Leo. *The Frenzy of Renown.* New York: Oxford University Press, 1986.

Brazelton, Ethel Colson. *Writing and Editing for Women.* New York: Funk and Wagnalls, 1927.

Brinkley, Alan. *The Unfinished Nation.* Vol. 2. New York: McGraw Hill, 1997.

Brown, Gene. *Movie Time.* New York: Macmillan, 1995.

Brown, Peter. *The MGM Girls.* New York: St. Martin's Press, 1983.

Brownstein, Ronald. *The Power and the Glitter: The Hollywood-Washington Connection.* New York: Pantheon, 1990.

Burnett, Frances Hodgson. *Editha's Burglar.* New York: H. M. Caldwell, 1888.

Burt, Elizabeth V., ed. *Women's Press Organizations, 1881–1999.* Westport, CT: Greenwood Press, 2000.

Butler, Jeremy, ed. *Star Texts: Image and Performance in Film and Television.* Detroit: Wayne State University Press, 1991.

Cairns, Kathleen. *Front Page Women Journalists.* Lincoln: University of Nebraska Press, 2003.

Carr, Steven Alan. *Hollywood and Anti-Semitism: A Cultural History up to World War II.* New York: Cambridge University Press, 2001.

Ceplair, Larry, and Steven Englund. *Inquisition in Hollywood: Politics in the Film Community, 1930–1960.* Berkeley: University of California Press, 1983.

Chaney, Lindsay, and Michael Cieply. *The Hearsts: Family and Empire—the Later Years.* New York: Simon and Schuster, 1981.

Chaplin, Charles. *My Autobiography.* New York: Simon and Schuster, 1964.

Chase, Ilka. *Past Imperfect.* Garden City, NY: Doubleday Doran, 1942.

Cobb, Sally Wright. *The Brown Derby Restaurant: A Hollywood Legend.* New York: Rizzoli, 1996.

Couvares, Francis, ed. *Movie Censorship and American Culture.* Washington, DC: Smithsonian, 1996.

Crafton, Donald. *The Talkies: American Cinema's Transition to Sound.* New York: Scribner's, 1997.

Crowther, Bosley. *Hollywood Rajah: The Life and Times of Louis B. Mayer.* New York: Holt, 1960.

Daniels, Bebe, and Ben Lyon. *Life with the Lyons.* London: Odhams, 1953.

Davies, Marion. *The Times We Had.* New York: Bobbs Merrill, 1975.

Davis, Ronald. *The Glamour Factory: Inside Hollywood's Big Studio System.* Dallas: Southern Methodist University Press, 1993.

De Cordova, Richard. *Picture Personalities: The Emergence of the Star System in America.* Chicago: University of Illinois Press, 1990.

DiFonzo, J. Herbie. *Beneath the Fault Line: The Popular and Legal Culture of Divorce in Twentieth-Century America.* Charlottesville: University Press of Virginia, 1997.

Doherty, Thomas. *Pre-Code Hollywood: Sex, Immorality, and Insurrection in American Cinema.* New York: Columbia University Press, 1999.

Douglas, George. *The Golden Age of the Newspaper*. Westport, CT: Greenwood Press, 1999.

Dreiser, Theodore. *The Titan*. 1914. Reprint, New York: World Publishing, 1946.

Dunning, John. *Tune in Yesterday: The Ultimate Encyclopedia of Old Time Radio*. Englewood Cliffs, NJ: Prentice-Hall, 1976.

Dyer, Richard. *Stars*. London: BFI, 1998.

Eells, George. *Hedda and Louella*. New York: Putnam, 1972.

Endres, Stacey, and Robert Cushman. *Hollywood at Your Feet: The Story of the World-Famous Chinese Theater*. Los Angeles: Pomegranate Press, 1992.

Faith, William. *Bob Hope: A Life in Comedy*. Cambridge, MA: Da Capo Press, 2003.

Federal Writers' Project. *A Guide to Burlington, Iowa*. Burlington, IA: Acres-Blackmar, 1939.

Feeley, Kathy. "Louella Parsons and Hedda Hopper's Hollywood: The Rise of the Celebrity Gossip Industry in Twentieth-Century America, 1910–1950." Ph.D. diss., City University of New York, 2003.

Finch, Christopher, and Linda Rosenkrantz. *Gone Hollywood*. Garden City, NY: Doubleday, 1979.

Fine, Gary Alan. *Rumor and Gossip: The Social Psychology of Hearsay*. New York: Elsevier, 1976.

Finkelstein, Norman. *Sounds in the Air: The Golden Age of Radio*. New York: Scribner's, 1993.

Fontaine, Joan. *No Bed of Roses*. New York: Berkley, 1979.

Fountain, Leatrice Joy. *Dark Star*. New York: St. Martin's Press, 1985.

Fowler, Gene. *Skyline*. New York: Viking, 1961.

Francke, Lizzie. *Script Girls: Women Screenwriters in Hollywood*. London: British Film Institute, 1994.

Friedrichs, Otto. *City of Nets: A Portrait of Hollywood in the 1940s*. New York: Harper and Row, 1986.

Fuller, Kathryn. *At the Picture Show: Small Town Audiences and the Creation of Movie Fan Culture*. Washington, DC: Smithsonian, 1996.

Gabler, Neal. *An Empire of Their Own: How the Jews Created Hollywood*. New York: Anchor, 1988.

———. *Winchell: Gossip, Power, and the Culture of Celebrity*. New York: Knopf, 1994.

Gibler, Bob. *Dixon, Illinois*. Charleston, SC: Arcadia, 1998.

Golden, Eve. *Vamp: The Rise and Fall of Theda Bara*. Vestal, NY: Empire Publishing, 1996.

Good, Howard. *The Drunken Journalist: The Biography of a Film Stereotype*. Lanham, MD: Scarecrow Press, 2000.

Goodman, Ezra. *The Fifty-Year Decline and Fall of Hollywood*. New York: Simon and Schuster, 1961.

Gottesman, Ronald, ed. *Focus on Citizen Kane*. Englewood Cliffs, NJ: Prentice-Hall, 1971.

Graham, Carroll, and Garrett Graham. *Queer People.* Carbondale: Southern Illinois University Press, 1976.

Graham, Sheilah. *The Rest of the Story.* New York: Coward McCann, 1964.

Griffith, Richard. *The Talkies.* New York: Dover, 1971.

Guiles, Fred Lawrence. *Marion Davies.* New York: Bantam, 1973.

Gustason, Harriett. *Looking Back.* Vol. 1. Freeport, IL: Stephenson County Historical Society, 1994.

Hampton, Benjamin. *History of the American Film Industry.* New York: Dover, 1970.

Harris, Radie. *Radie's World.* New York: Putnam, 1975.

Harris, Warren. *Gable and Lombard.* New York: Simon and Schuster, 1974.

Hart, Moss, and George Kaufman. *Once in a Lifetime.* New York: Farrar and Rinehart, 1930.

Heimann, Jim. *Out with the Stars: Hollywood Nightlife in the Studio Era.* New York: Abbeville Press, 1985.

Higby, Mary Jane. *Tune in Tomorrow.* New York: Cowles, 1968.

Higham, Charles. *Hollywood at Sunset.* New York: Saturday Review Press, 1972.

Hilmes, Michele. *Hollywood and Broadcasting: From Radio to Cable.* Urbana: University of Illinois Press, 1990.

———. *Only Connect: A Cultural History of Broadcasting in the United States.* Belmont, CA: Wadsworth, 2002.

History of San Bernardino and Riverside County. Chicago: Western Historical Association, 1922.

History of Stephenson County, Illinois. Chicago: Western Historical Company, 1880.

Holley, Val. *Mike Connolly and the Manly Art of Hollywood Gossip.* Jefferson, NC: McFarland, 2003.

Hopper, Hedda. *From under My Hat.* Garden City, NY: Doubleday, 1952.

Hopper, Hedda, with James Brough. *The Whole Truth and Nothing But.* New York: Doubleday, 1962.

Jordan, Philip. *Catfish Bend, River Town, and County Seat.* Burlington, IA: Craftsman Press, 1975.

Jowett, Garth. *Film, the Democratic Art.* Boston: Little, Brown, 1976.

Kael, Pauline. *The Citizen Kane Book.* Boston: Little, Brown, 1971.

Kanfer, Stefan. *A Journal of the Plague Years.* New York: Atheneum, 1983.

Kashner, Sam, and Jennifer McNair. *The Bad and the Beautiful: Hollywood in the Fifties.* New York: Norton, 2002.

Kastner, Victoria. *Hearst Castle: Biography of a Country House.* New York: H. N. Abrams, 2000.

Kessler-Harris, Alice. *Out to Work: A History of Wage Earning Women in the United States.* New York: Oxford, 1982.

Kobal, John. *People Will Talk.* New York: Knopf, 1985.

Koenisgberg, Moses. *King News: An Autobiography.* Philadelphia: F. S. Stokes, 1941.

Koszarski, Richard. *An Evening's Entertainment: The Age of the Silent Feature Picture, 1915–1928.* New York: Scribner's, 1990.

Kotsilibas-Davis, James. *Myrna Loy: Being and Becoming.* New York: Knopf, 1987.

Kroeger, Brooke. *Nellie Bly: Daredevil, Reporter, Feminist.* New York: Times Books, 1994.

Leamer, Laurence. *As Time Goes By: The Life of Ingrid Bergman.* New York: Harper-Collins, 1986.

Leaming, Barbara. *If This Was Happiness: A Biography of Rita Hayworth.* New York: Viking, 1989.

Lee, Alfred McClung. *The Daily Newspaper in America.* New York: Macmillan, 1947.

Leff, Leonard, and Jerold Simmons. *The Dame in the Kimono: Hollywood Censorship and the Production Code.* New York: Doubleday, 1990.

Loos, Anita. *A Girl Like I.* New York: Viking, 1966.

———. *The Talmadge Girls.* New York: Viking, 1978.

Lowenthal, Leo. "The Triumph of Mass Idols." In *Literature, Popular Culture, and Society.* Englewood Cliffs, NJ: Prentice Hall, 1961.

Lull, James, and Stephen Hinerman, eds. *Media Scandals: Morality and Desire in Popular Culture.* New York: Columbia University Press, 1997.

Lundberg, Ferdinand. *Imperial Hearst.* New York: Equinox, 1936.

Lynd, Robert, and Helen Lynd. *Middletown.* New York: Harcourt, Brace, 1929.

Maland, Charles. *Chaplin and American Culture.* Princeton, NJ: Princeton University Press, 1989.

Maltby, Richard. *Hollywood Cinema: An Introduction.* Cambridge, MA: Blackwell, 1990.

Mann, William J. *Behind the Screen: How Gays and Lesbians Shaped Hollywood, 1910–1969.* New York: Viking, 2001.

———. *Wisecracker: The Life and Times of William Haines, Hollywood's First Openly Gay Star.* New York: Viking, 1998.

Manso, Peter. *Brando: The Biography.* New York: Hyperion, 1994.

Marion, Frances. *Off with Their Heads!* New York: Macmillan, 1972.

Marx, Samuel. *Deadly Illusions: Jean Harlow and the Murder of Paul Bern.* New York: Random House, 1990.

———. *Mayer and Thalberg: The Make Believe Saints.* New York: Random House, 1975.

Marzolf, Marion. *Up from the Footnote: A History of Woman Journalists.* New York: Hastings House, 1977.

Maturi, Richard J., and Mary Buckingham Maturi. *Beverly Bayne, Queen of the Movies.* Jefferson, NC: McFarland, 2001.

May, Elaine Tyler. *Homeward Bound: American Families in the Cold War Era.* New York: Basic Books, 1988.

May, Lary. *Screening Out the Past: The Birth of Mass Culture and the Motion Picture Industry.* New York: Oxford University Press, 1980.

McAdams, William. *Ben Hecht: The Man behind the Myth.* New York: Scribner's, 1990.

McArthur, Benjamin. *Actors and American Culture, 1880–1920.* Philadelphia: Temple University Press, 1984.

McKim, Helen Turner, and Helen Parsons. *Burlington on the Mississippi, 1833–1983.* Burlington, IA: Doran and Ward, 1983.

McLean, Adrienne, and David Cook, ed. *Headline Hollywood.* New Brunswick, NJ: Rutgers University Press, 2001.

McPhaul, John. *Deadlines and Monkeyshines: The Fabled World of Chicago Journalism.* Englewood Cliffs, NJ: Prentice-Hall, 1964.

Meryman, Richard. *Mank.* New York: William Morrow, 1978.

Meyerowitz, Joanne. *Women Adrift: Independent Wage Earners in Chicago, 1880–1930.* Chicago: University of Chicago Press, 1988.

Meyers, Jeffrey. *Bogart: A Life in Hollywood.* Boston: Houghton Mifflin, 1997.

Muir, Florabel. *Headline Happy.* New York: Holt, 1950.

Munsterberg, Hugo. *The Photoplay: A Psychological Study.* New York: D. Appleton, 1916.

Murray, Ken. *The Golden Days of San Simeon.* Garden City, NY: Doubleday, 1971.

Musser, Charles. *The Emergence of Cinema: The American Screen to 1907.* New York: Scribner's, 1990.

Nasaw, David. *The Chief: The Life of William Randolph Hearst.* Boston: Houghton Mifflin, 2000.

Navasky, Victor. *Naming Names.* New York: Viking, 1980.

Negri, Pola. *Memoirs of a Star.* Garden City, NY: Doubleday, 1970.

O'Connor, Richard. *Heywood Broun: A Biography.* New York: Putnam, 1975.

Paris, Barry. *Louise Brooks.* New York: Knopf, 1989.

Parsons, Louella. *The Gay Illiterate.* New York: Doubleday Doran, 1944.

———. *How to Write for the Movies.* Chicago: McClurg, 1915.

———. *Tell It to Louella.* New York: Putnam, 1961.

Peiss, Kathy. *Cheap Amusements: Working Women and Leisure in Turn of the Century New York.* Philadelphia: Temple University Press, 1986.

Pickford, Mary. *Sunshine and Shadow.* Garden City, NY: Doubleday, 1955.

Pizzitola, Louis. *Hearst over Hollywood.* New York: Columbia University Press, 2002.

Ponce de Leon, Charles. *Self-Exposure: Human Interest Journalism and the Emergency of Celebrity in America.* Chapel Hill: University of North Carolina Press, 2002.

Portrait and Biographical Album, Stephenson County, Illinois. Chicago: Chapman Brothers, 1888.

Quirk, Lawrence. *The Films of Gloria Swanson.* Secaucus, NJ: Citadel Press, 1984.

Rosenstein, Jaik. *Hollywood Leg Man.* Los Angeles: Madison Press, 1950.

Ross, Ishbel. *Ladies of the Press.* New York: Harper, 1936.

Rosten, Leo. *Hollywood, the Movie Colony.* New York: Arno Press, 1970.

Sabini, John, and Maury Silver. *Moralities of Everyday Life.* New York: Oxford University Press, 1982.

Sandburg, Carl. *Chicago Poems*. New York: Henry Holt, 1916.

Schatz, Thomas. *Boom and Bust: American Cinema in the 1940s*. New York: Scribner's, 1997.

Schickel, Richard. *Intimate Strangers*. Garden City, NY: Doubleday, 1985.

Schudson, Michael. *Discovering the News: A Social History of Newspapers*. New York: Basic Books, 1978.

Schulberg, Budd. *Moving Pictures*. New York: Stein and Day, 1981.

Scovell, Jane. *Oona: Living in the Shadows*. New York: Warner Books, 1998.

Sklar, Robert. *City Boys: Cagney, Bogart, Garfield*. Princeton: Princeton University Press, 1992.

———. *Movie-made America: A Cultural History of American Movies*. New York: Vintage, 1994.

Skolsky, Sidney. *Don't Get Me Wrong—I Love Hollywood*. New York: Putnam, 1975.

Slide, Anthony. *Early Women Directors*. South Brunswick, NJ: A. J. Barnes, 1977.

Smith, H. Allen. *The Life and Legend of Gene Fowler*. New York: Morrow, 1977.

Smith, Liz. *Natural Blonde: A Memoir*. New York: Random House, 2000.

Spacks, Patricia. *Gossip*. New York: Knopf, 1984.

Spigel, Lynn. *Make Room for TV: Television and the Family Ideal in the Postwar Period*. Chicago: University of Chicago Press, 1992.

Spinney, Robert G. *City of Big Shoulders: A History of Chicago*. DeKalb: Northern Illinois University Press, 2000.

Spoto, Donald. *Marilyn Monroe*. New York: HarperCollins, 1993.

The Standard General and Business Directory of the City of Dixon, Illinois. Dixon: Twentieth Century Directory Company, 1905.

Starr, Jimmy. *Barefoot on Barbed Wire*. Lanham, MD: Scarecrow Press, 2001.

Starr, Kevin. *Material Dreams: Southern California through the 1920s*. New York: Oxford University Press, 1990.

Steele, Joseph. *Ingrid Bergman: An Intimate Portrait*. New York: McKay, 1959.

Sterling, Christopher, and John Kittross. *Stay Tuned: A Concise History of American Broadcasting*. Belmont, CA: Wadsworth, 1978.

Stevens, Frank Everett. *History of Lee County*. Chicago: S. J. Clarke, 1914.

St. Johns, Adela Rogers. *The Honeycomb*. Garden City, NY: Doubleday, 1969.

Studlar, Gaylyn. "The Perils of Pleasure? Fan Magazine Discourse as Women's Commodified Culture in the 1920s." *Wide Angle* 13, no. 1 (Jan. 1991).

Susman, Warren I. "Personality and the Making of Twentieth-Century Culture," in *Culture as History: The Transformation of American Society in the Twentieth Century*. New York: Pantheon, 1984.

Swanberg, W. A. *Citizen Hearst*. New York: Scribner's, 1961.

Swanson, Gloria. *Swanson on Swanson*. New York: Random House, 1980.

Swindell, Larry. *Screwball: The Life of Carole Lombard*. New York: Morrow, 1975.

Taraborelli, J. Randy. *Sinatra: Behind the Legend*. Secaucus, NJ: Carroll Publishing Group, 1997.

Taylor, William R. *In Pursuit of Gotham: Culture and Commerce in New York.* New York: Oxford University Press, 1992.

Tebbutt, Melanie. *Women's Talk: A Social History of Gossip in Working-Class Neighborhoods.* Brookfield, VT: Ashgate, 1995.

Thomas, Bob. *Joan Crawford.* New York: Simon and Schuster, 1978.

Thomson, David. *Showman: The Life of David O. Selznick.* New York: Knopf, 1992.

Thorp, Margaret. *America at the Movies.* New Haven: Yale University Press, 1939.

Tornabene, Lyn. *Long Live the King.* New York: Putnam, 1976.

Torrence, Bruce. *Hollywood: The First Hundred Years.* New York: New York Zoetrope, 1982.

Trollope, Anthony. *North America.* Philadelphia: n.p., 1862.

Tuck, Jim. *McCarthyism and New York's Hearst Press: A Study of Roles in the Witch Hunt.* Lanham, MD: University Press of America, 1995.

Turk, Edward Baron. *Hollywood Diva: A Biography of Jeanette MacDonald.* Berkeley: University of California Press, 1998.

Van Doren, Mamie. *Playing the Field.* New York: Putnam, 1987.

Villard, Oswald Garrison. *Some Newspapers and Newspaper-Men.* New York: Knopf, 1923.

Wagner, Rob. *Red Ink, White Lies: The Rise and Fall of Los Angeles Newspapers, 1920–1962.* Upland, CA: Dragonflyer Press, 2000.

Walls, Jeanette. *Dish: The Inside Story on the World of Gossip.* New York: HarperCollins, 2000.

Watts, Jill. *Mae West: An Icon in Black and White.* New York: Oxford University Press, 2001.

Weitzenkorn, Louis. *Five Star Final.* New York: S. French, 1931.

West, James. *Plainville, USA.* New York: Columbia University Press, 1945.

Woloch, Nancy. *Women and the American Experience.* New York: McGraw Hill, 1984.

INDEX

Compositor:	Binghamton Valley Composition
Text:	Adobe Garamond 11/14
Display:	Adobe Garamond and Perpetua Italic
Printer and Binder:	Maple-Vail Manufacturing Group